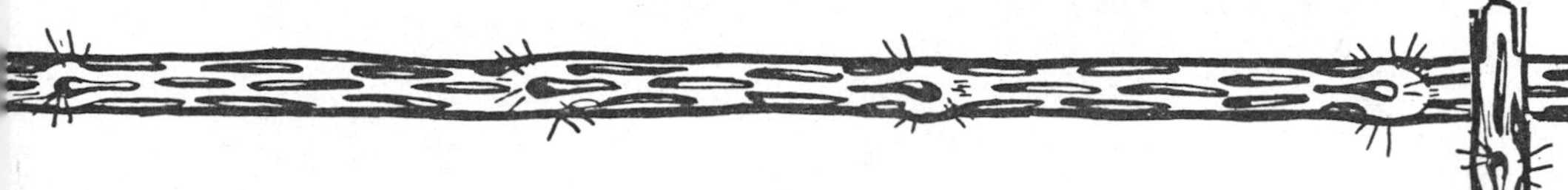

...This is no ordinary travel book...a very loving and accurate picture of what the traveler might see, if only given the chance...

High Times

...a most unusual book which in all probability will often be imitated through the years but unlikely surpassed...

The News (Mexico City)

..If you are planning on a Mexican safari, this book is more necessary than your toothbrush or dictionary...

The New Mexican

...The guide is surprisingly complete...succeeds in reducing the impact of crossing the border both for the traveler and the people and places visited... (VVVV)

The Village Voice

THE
PEOPLE'S GUIDE
TO
MEXICO
BY
Carl Franz
"WHEREVER YOU GO.... THERE YOU ARE"
SANTA FE
NEW MEXICO

Published by John Muir Publications
P.O. Box 613
Santa Fe, New Mexico 87501

Illustrated by Glen Strock and Toby Williams
Typeset by Barbara Luboff and Di Jordan
Printed in the United States of America

First Edition, December 1972
Second Printing, June 1973
Second Edition, May 1974
Third Edition, April 1975
Fourth Edition, May 1976
Seventh Printing, December 1979
Eighth Printing, April 1982
Ninth Printing, July 1983

Library of Congress Catalog Number 78-71187
ISBN 0-912528-15-X

Table of contents

Cover, Illustrations and Graphics:

GLEN STROCK

Special Thanks:

Toby Williams, for contributions marked TW and
Peter Aschwanden, for Day of the Dead cartoons

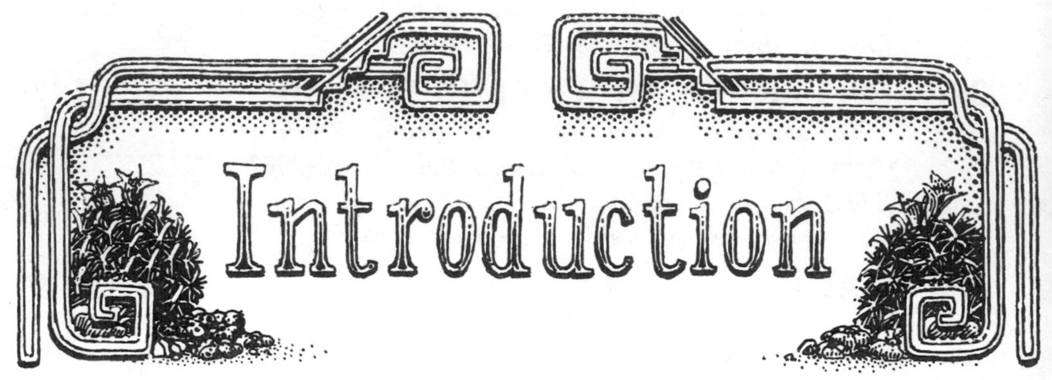

People often say to me, "Hey, I hear you're writing a book. What's it about?"

"Mexico," I respond, "It's sort of a guidebook."

This book *is* about Mexico. But it's also about living, travelling and taking things as they come in a foreign country. And it's about driving conditions and health and how to cross the border. It's about drinking the water without getting sick and how to enjoy yourself regardless of how close you are to the nearest 'recommended' tourist attraction.

It is not about which hotels to stay in or the most interesting villages to visit. The purpose of this book is to teach you how to find out those things for yourself.

Many books have been written about Mexico under the guise of 'guidebooks' that, in reality, are nothing more than compilations of hotels, restaurants and nightclubs, along with a few tips about where to buy authentic handicrafts that almost look as if they came from Mexico and not Taiwan. That type of guidebook, actually a directory, tells you that Mexico can put you up in reasonable style and comfort, in air-conditioned rooms with sterilized meals, for less than it would cost at home. These books don't guide you to Mexico—they guide you away from it.

Travelling is difficult at times; nothing much is familiar when we get to wherever we're going. For many people this is a strain. Because they don't understand everything that is happening, they try to diminish the experience, to make it unimportant and less real.

This is when you hear the panicky tourist say, "Well, how much is that in *real* money?" or "Let's get some *real* food for a change." They've just lost contact, both with Mexico and with themselves.

One of the main purposes of this book is to show the traveller how to accept, as calmly as possible, the sights and experiences of a strange place. It began, in fact, as a series of anecdotes I'd written for friends about various adventures we (Lorena, Steve, myself and others) had had in Mexico. Our friends enjoyed the stories, but their inevitable reaction was, "Fine for you but what about *me?* Can I get along?" To back up our assurances that they could indeed make it on their own, we began compiling detailed information about the country. Some of that information isn't positive or cheery, but we wanted our friends to know what they were really headed for, not just what a travel agent would like them to believe.

Guidebooks tend to stress fun and ignore problems. In this book, however, you'll get all the information. Warnings and precautions should make your trip easier and more enjoyable, rather than nerve-wracking. And when you ask others how their trip went, take 'horror' stories with a grain of salt. "Had a great time but..." is a favorite opening. These are the stories you hear most often because they are the ones people enjoy telling most. No one wants to admit that they went to Mexico and were bored stiff, though surely that must happen on occasion.

When you feel nervous while travelling, either out of ignorance of what's happening or out of fear of what you've heard might happen, you cut yourself off from experience—good or bad. You communicate in only one sense: defensively. That's why tourists often speak to 'natives' in the tones one would use to address a lamp post. When you are relaxed, you can communicate, even if it's just a quick smile or a passing greeting.

When the first edition of this book was published in 1972, I had no idea that change would come to Mexico as quickly as it has. I innocently believed that the book would require only minor revisions every few years. This present edition, the fifth, has taken more than a year to write and edit, a good measure of the extent to which Mexico has changed. It also reflects additional experience, research and observations of those who have contributed to the book.

But though Mexico has changed—new highways, resort areas, the *peso* devalued (a boon to tourists), higher inflation—it still remains one of the most 'foreign' countries in the western world. The volume of tourism is increasing and the tourists themselves are changing; many are attracted not by *fiestas* and low prices but by the country itself. With more than 6,000 miles of coastline, vast and almost unexplored areas of mountains, desert and jungle, Mexico is also drawing those interested in the outdoors and adventuring.

This book has been greatly expanded—about double its former size—and includes many new illustrations. (In order to keep the size and weight to less than that of an encyclopedia, I've written a separate book, *The People's Guide To Camping In Mexico*. See back of book.) There's much more practical advice on travelling and living in Mexico, plus information on customs, daily life and how Mexicans enjoy themselves. And since the information and advice attempts to cover such a broad range of topics, it seems only natural that it be readable and understandable by everyone who goes there.

Which brings up one of the main purposes of this book: to help travellers to be both aware and appreciative of what they see and experience and to lessen the impact, not only on them but on the places and people they travel to see. Keeping the mutual shock to a minimum will benefit all of us. So remember, please:

wherever you go...there you are!

Carl Franz
San Simón de Limón, Mexico

There's really only one way to use a book of this type effectively; *as you need it.* There are sections you may never need and never read and others that you'll use as a continual reference.

If you know nothing about Mexico or just wonder, then you might like to read it all before leaving. As you travel, specific questions will come to mind. "What's the word for motor oil?", "How do I order coffee?", "Where do I get my tourist card?" Keep the book handy; it should provide the answers.

Use the Table of Contents and Index liberally. If the order of the chapters doesn't seem logical, you're right; it isn't. But neither is Mexico.

The Spanish words and phrases in the text and Appendix were included to help you out, not to teach you the language. Anyone with a genuine interest in communicating will—or should—buy a dictionary and basic grammar book. The Spanish I've included is not necessarily logical or even according to the rules, but it represents the reality of Mexico versus the tourist agency image. I've yet to hear a Mexican say, "Would you please fill my car's gasoline tank, sir?" It's a hell of a lot easier for both you and the attendant if you say, *"Lleno, por favor,"* (Full, please) and leave it at that.

I suggest that you take extensive notes as you travel, either in the book or on paper that can be kept between the pages: maps to hot springs, a special campsite, the name of a strange fruit or a cheap hotel. When you meet others on the road, exchange this information. After you've returned home, show your book to friends interested in Mexico; they might like to copy your notes or question you on specific points of the book's content.

This book was designed to be useful for an entire trip, not just one part of it. Draw in it, use it for a hot pad, make corrections, rip out pages, glue in new ones, waterproof it, roll joints out of the Index, do anything—just use and enjoy it; that's what it's for.

ACKNOWLEDGEMENTS

Editing and Research: Lorena Havens, Linda Reybine, Lety Hall.

Encouragement, Suggestions, Criticism and more: Ken Luboff, Eve Muir, Steve Rogers, Susan Fiksdal, Tom Scott, Dr. Matt Kelly, Lic. Napoleón Negrete, Nacho and Teresa Espinosa, Mauro Lopez, Felicia and family, Martha Brewster.

Design and Layout: Glen Strock, Lorena Havens, Di Jordan

Proofreading: John Bott

Typesetting: Barbara Luboff, Di Jordan

Photo Reductions: Technigraph, Inc., Santa Fe

Many of our readers also gave valuable assistance and comments. I wish I could list them all but many are anonymous: Mike Shawcross, Woodruff Bryne, Dr. Zeidner, Maggi Moreau...keep writing, it all helps.

"While we are abroad, let us not exhibit vain tricks and trances."

Pierre Delattre
Tales of a Dalai Lama

"Boy, when you cross that Rio Grande, you in *another country*!"

Texas Border Patrolman

to Joy and Lorena

TRAVELLING IN MEXICO

Planning your trip...A typical day on the road...Travel routines and schedules...Indulge yourself!...Where to go?...What do you want to do?...Car, plane, bus or hitching?...Travelling with friends...On your own...With kids: advantages, toys, food, health, language, babysitters...

"What you guys need is to take a trip," I said, refilling Rob and Nancy's coffee cups. "It sounds as if you've both got a good case of boredom and boob tube-itis. Walk on foreign shores, hear the babble of strange tongues. Fiery local liquors, mouth-watering sauces, land of contrasts—all that sort of thing."

"Maybe you're right," Rob said. "I could sure stand a few weeks off."

"Why don't we?" Nancy added, suddenly perking up from the slump she'd been in since they'd arrived an hour earlier. It was obvious that rainy Fall weather, combined with the prospect of months of more to follow, was weighing heavily on their spirits.

"We might even have enough money to take one of those cheap flights to Europe!" Nancy added. "I've always wanted to see the..."

"Europe?" I interrupted, "Did I hear you say *Europe*?"

"Sure," Nancy said, "You know, foreign shores, England, France, Germany..."

"I know the geography," I said, shaking my head from side to side, astonished that when I first suggested a trip they'd thought...

"How much money do you have?" I asked, reaching for a pencil and a sheet of paper. Rob named a figure. I turned to Lorena, absorbed in filling empty gelatin capsules with some arcane herbal mixture, her first line of defense against autumn colds and fevers. "Did you hear that?" I laughed. "They're going to Europe where a cup of coffee costs TWENTY DOLLARS and all they've got is..."

"Twenty dollars?" Rob burst out. "You're out of your mind!"

"Have you read TIME magazine lately?" I countered. "Do you know what a bun costs in Paris? Do you? Huh? Do you?" I had him now; I would only have to play my hole card. "Do you know what a glass of beer is in Berlin? Do you? Tell me!"

He looked stricken; I could see that he was quickly estimating, based on a twenty dollar cup of coffee, what a stein of his favorite beverage would be.

"That's impossible!" he answered, visibly shaken.

"That's what you think!" I laughed. "But of course if you'd rather, there's always the Orient. By the time you both buy round trip tickets to Japan, you'll have enough left over to order a combination noodle dinner for two."

There was a long silence. A light rain tapped against the kitchen windows; Lorena pulled her shawl higher around her neck.

"What you need," I began, "is someplace cheap. Someplace where the weather is good, lots of sunbathing and stuff like that. Beaches." Their ears perked up. "A place that's reasonably close. Do you know how far away Europe is?" I didn't wait for an answer. "No, you want someplace not too far away and easy to get to. No standing in long lines. No sitting around airports waiting for a late flight."

"That just wouldn't happen to be..." Rob began.

"Mexico!" I cried. "Why didn't I think of it sooner?"

Lorena groaned; it had been agreed that we wouldn't make a trip this winter; instead, we'd stay home and catch up on long delayed projects—like jobs, saving money, building fences, fixing the roof and filling holes in the driveway. I'd agreed not to discuss Mexico, but this was obviously an urgent exception! This was my brother, in desperate need of advice! The hell with promises!

"...if you decide to drive I'll loan you a tent, but if you take the bus...you can't miss San Simón, they've got this incredible...markets you just won't believe...you drink some of the coconut milk and then add *tequila*...Spanish isn't important, just "*sí*" and "*no*" will do...this old colonial hotel with gigantic gardens..."

"Are you ready for lunch?"

I broke off my monologue, startled by Lorena's sudden interruption. Where had the last two hours gone? I looked at Rob and Nancy, their eyes had that dreamy far-away look seen on so many faces in bus stations, airport lounges and train depots.

"I think we'll just go on home," Nancy said. "We want to look over this map Carl loaned us and figure out a few details." They reached for their coats.

Rob stopped at the door. He turned to me with a questioning look. "Are you *sure*," he asked, "that we can live in Mexico for ten bucks a week?"

I caught a sharp glance from Lorena, coughed, and then said, "Weeelll...maybe that's a little low. I might have exaggerated *some*." He started to give me a familiar 'Here we go again' smile; but I quickly added, "Just remember what a beer will cost in Europe!" He gave us a wave and then closed the door behind them.

"*Hasta luego*!" I cried, going back to the kitchen table to spread out another map. It was brand new, no hot sauce stains or blurry roads from spilled *Carta Blanca*. I'd have to discuss it with Lorena, of course, but wouldn't there be enough time between finding a job and fixing the driveway to make just a quick dash south?

For some people much of the enjoyment of a trip is in planning: they haunt libraries and bookstores, send off for brochures and itineraries, draw lines and x's on maps and consult astrological charts for a propitious departure date. Others are militantly casual about long journeys; they get out of bed one morning, stick a toothbrush and a change of clothes in a flight bag and head off in a generally southerly direction. Whichever style suits you best, several factors will aid in making the right decisions about your trip. Read over and give some thought to the following pages before saying anything rash like, "We're going to hitchhike to Peru," or "I think a two week, 10,000 mile bus ride would be just what the doctor ordered."

Locate a map of Mexico in order to gloat over all the places you'll be visiting and conjure up a few armchair adventures. This helps pull you through the tedium of packing and the daily feeling of despair before leaving for work. Unfortunately, this can also lead to unforseen difficulties.

Unless you are adept at interpreting the map, you will tend to look at Mexico in terms of miles rather than actual geography. "On the second day," you say authoritatively, puffing clouds of smoke into your wife's eagerly respectful face, "we'll cross, hack! cough!" and you tap the map with the pipe stem, "this range of mountains!" On closer examination you might discover that you've just casually pointed to over four hundred miles of one-lane dirt road, jammed with trucks and interrupted by several slow ferries. Obviously, on the evening of the second day you're not going to be where you'd so confidently planned. If this upsets you, you're on your way to greater irritations when the remainder of your carefully contrived schedule goes completely to pieces.

"The schedule is Veracruz Monday and Merida on Tuesday!" you say emphatically, accelerating to an appropriately schedule-meeting, nerve-shattering speed. As the countryside blurs by, you feel the muscles knot in the back of your neck. Your friends are staring rigidly at the highway in front of the car. You are having fun?

If your time is limited, you'll be tempted to travel great distances at a marathon pace in order to see as much as possible. We've met a discouraging number of people who were so exhausted and spaced-out from driving or riding thousands of miles in a few days, that they thought only of finding a hotel room and mustering up strength for the return trip. The most lasting impression these people have of Mexico is smelly gas stations, lousy breakfasts with cold coffee, hotel lobbies and ragged kids trying to shine their shoes whenever they slumped onto a park bench.

It may be glamorous to say to friends, "Why, we visited over 20 archaeological sites, 15 cities, 9 beaches and 17 native markets...in ten days!" but if your trip is for pleasure, make it that—not an ordeal.

Personal interests and energy level are very important. Many travellers fail to take them into account, however, and instead force themselves into a type of trip that they assume they *should* be making.

A good example of this is the Church-Ruin-Runaround, usually two or three weeks of frantic cathedral gazing and temple crawling that leaves the tourist completely exhausted. I find historical monuments only slightly more interesting than bridges and tunnels.

Another trap is the I-am-a-camera routine. Victims can be seen with their Instamatics and Nikons all but grafted to their faces, madly snapping miles of over-exposures. These same slides and photos will be used at home to send friends and relatives into trances of stupefying boredom.

When we first went to Mexico, our idea of travelling was to cover as many miles as we could between dawn and collapse, usually about midnight. We travelled through the country so quickly that I often thought the place we'd been yesterday was the destination for today.

The return was equally frantic; when we finally stepped out of the car in the U.S., we were ankle deep in snow and wearing sandals. My memories of that trip are slightly surreal: beautiful sand beach, diarrhea and wondering where in the hell we were but not really caring.

Our hectic pace on that trip taught us a basic fact about travelling: it costs money. Following this brainstorm it soon became clear that the longer the stops were, the longer the trip could be. This rather obvious fact is the basis for our present travel routine. We can't afford to do a great deal of moving around, especially when travelling in a vehicle. We compute how many miles we can afford to travel and then break that up according to how much time can be spent on the trip.

Our plan, for example, might be to travel for six months with several places in mind to spend a month or more. When making long stops we either camp or rent a cheap house or room. If travelling by car, we park and try to forget that it's there. We use buses, hitchhike or walk to get supplies and see the local sights. It is really quite amazing how your expenses decrease when you stop driving.

When we've tired of one place, we repack and move on to another.

This routine is modified by stops at markets, rivers, ruins, beer joints or any other diversion that tempts us. When driving we travel three or four hundred miles only on a very hard day and a hundred miles or less when in a really low-key mood.

After we adopted this type of travel and living routine, we were not surprised to find that others had discovered it too. There is a virtual migratory circuit of people who are able to spend a great deal of time travelling on little money. (See *Travelling Cheap.*)

We left our palm hut situated on a beautiful isolated beach and moved on south, hoping to travel into Central America before the summer rains. That day and evening were typical of many we spent while travelling in our VW van.

I sat between Steve and Lorena on an improvised bench of blankets stacked on a beer case, my back supported by a bulky tent and a large bundle of clothing. By twisting my legs to the right to avoid the gear shift, by pressing them downward to avoid the tape recorder, by supporting myself with an arm behind each seat and by craning my head around the mirror—generally contorting my entire body—I was able to sit quite comfortably for as long as 15 minutes.

Then Steve would turn to me and shout over the roar of the decaying muffler and the thumping beat of the tape recorder, "Any *cerveza* left?"

There was always beer and he certainly knew it; he just couldn't seem to ask for it outright. Instead Steve used this thinly worn ploy, my cue to move from my long sought-after position of comfort and lean back for a beer. But it wasn't merely a matter of reaching into a handy open case. No, we had the beer in the icebox. I could either turn around in the seat, jostling both Steve and Lorena severely, or lie on my back and reach a twisted arm around to open the icebox door. This was no easy feat. With my hand on the handle I would slowly pull the door open and attempt to extract the beers, one by one, without causing a general landslide.

This, of course, was seldom successful. I would then have to climb over the seat, shovel the beer and ice and whatever else had fallen back into the box, close the door and climb back into the front. After I had handed out the beers and taken a few drinks, Lorena would give her line in the play:

"Steve, if you see a wide spot, I have to take a leak."

"My God!" I thought. "A Wide Spot! Some mythical pull-off designed especially for bird-bladdered tourists by the Mexican Highway Department." I gnashed my teeth quietly as we pulled to a stop, three minutes after my acrobatics with the beer. While Lorena sat in the bushes, I opened the side doors of the van and attempted to restore some sort of order to the icebox. As a precausion, I put a good stock of beer in the front seat. After that clever piece of planning, I had only to lift myself and allow one of them to reach into the case beneath me.

A few bottles later, Steve announced that he was hungry. Some people say such things casually, meaning it as a statement of condition, not necessarily to be reacted to immediately, just something to keep in the back of one's mind should a restaurant appear. But Steve is different. 'To Be Hungry' is for him a statement of absolute existence, of total irrefutable fact. This great all-consuming Hunger cannot be delayed. Like the lighting of a fuse, the time between the igniting statement and fatal destruction is not long.

His eyes began to move nervously about the front of the van. "Isn't there anything to eat up here?" came the plaintive query.

"No," I said wearily, anticipating the next line.

"Well, how about in the back?" he asked with perfect timing, knowing quite well that the back was jammed with food, all carefully and deeply packed away.

"I don't think there's anything very accessible back there," I stalled.

We drove on for a few minutes, Steve watching the road closely for any sign of a cafe, restaurant or vendor. I sat quietly, dreading the inevitable. It didn't take long.

"*I have got to have something to eat!*" Steve suddenly cried. "I don't care if it's only a lousy piece of bread!" he continued, hammering out the words on the steering wheel with his hand. "I have just got to have *something*!'"

My cue. Sighing deeply I began the tortuous climb over the seat, knowing only too well that I would probably be back there for an hour, rooting through boxes, bags and icebox, preparing a meal for that cavernous, insatiable mouth.

"Find anything?" Steve asked, glancing back greedily before my feet had hit the floor.

"Hold on, dammit!" I snapped. "I'm not an acrobat!"

He turned back to the job of driving, but I felt his eyes on the rearview mirror, watching my every movement, appraising the possible food value of everything I touched. I found a few pieces of bread and a box of dried-up miscellaneous vegetables. "What the hell?" I thought, "he'll eat it." A thick coating of gooey peanut butter, several slices of pungent onion and a slab of hard green tomato, all topped wth a generous serving of sightly rancid mayonnaise. Steve gobbled it up, licking his fingers of every smear and crumb. I waited.

"Any more?"

An avocado, badly bruised and overripe. He smacked his lips as he tossed the pit onto the floor. "What else have you got back there?"

"How about a roast beef sandwich, order of fries and a cup of coffee?" I sneered, handing him a mushy banana that we had had for days.

Steve laughed at my joke, gorging down the banana and throwing the skin into the back.

"Thanks," I said, picking the slimy peeling off my knee.

"For what?" he answered, as usual oblivious to anything not actually involving the ingestion of food. Garbage is nothing; he does not recognize its existence. It is in a class with trees and rocks and other inedible things.

"Forget it. Never mind," I muttered gloomily, wondering when this meal would end.

"How about that pineapple we got yesterday?" he called, apparently bottomless.

"Are you serious?" I yelled. "If you think I'm going to cut up an entire pineapple, you're out of your mind!"

With that question settled, he went into the second part of his routine: "Let's stop at the next restaurant then, because I'm still hungry."

I agreed, knowing that until he had eaten from a plate, with a fork, he would never be satisfied or silenced. Half an hour later we came to a cafe and screeched to a stop.

After our usual meal of beans, rice and *tortillas*, we were back on the highway, beers in hand. Steve, suddenly tired after hours of eating and drinking, warned us to keep an eye out for a camping place. I mentally moved the stage equipment and adjusted the lights for the next scene.

"How about that?" Lorena said, pointing in the twilight to a sheltered clearing in a beautiful grove of trees.

"What? Where?" Steve asked, sleepily driving on.

"There was a good spot back there," I said, knowing it was hopeless.

"I didn't see it until it was too late," Steve said, adding, "Oh, what the hell? There'll be something better up ahead."

He was occasionally correct in his predictions and we'd agree while sitting around a blazing fire that it was lucky we hadn't stopped in a worse place earlier. But other nights that better camping spot never materialized and we'd find ourselves on the highway long after dark, heads heavy with fatigue, tempers ground to a raw edge against the swaying motion of the van as we rolled endlessly around dark mountain curves. The night jealously hid all of the wide spots, side roads, fields, dumps and clearings that had been so plentiful earlier. Would we ever find a place?

"There's a road!"

Steve, reacting quickly to Lorena's shout, stopped the van and backed slowly to a vague turn-off. We bounced and bumped down a dark winding trail, peering desperately into the thick brush on each side for a parking space. We travelled on without success for half an hour when the road widened abruptly and ended in a small grassy clearing.

We stopped, then sat in dazed silence, the sound of the engine still echoing in our ears like the pounding of a distant surf. Mosquitoes hummed anxiously against the windows. Steve switched the radio on and began a careful search for gospel music, a nightly ritual while on the road. We sat quietly, listening to the reedy sound of Brother Bob's Country Choir, crackling and wavering as it floated down from some pious Southern state to this deserted Mexican back road. Lorena dug into the icebox for the last of the beer, then produced a bag of peanuts that she'd hidden since Guaymas. We nursed the cold beers for as long as possible, letting that good gospel sound mellow our nervous systems before going to sleep.

"This world is not my home, I'm just a-passing through.
My treasures are laid up, somewhere beyond the blue."

A TRAVEL ROUTINE

A travel routine is not a schedule and should not be allowed to insidiously change into one. A travel routine is a loose plan that helps you enjoy a trip more by taking into consideration such things as the stamina of yourself and your vehicle, what you want to do with your time, how much money you have, etc.

"We usually splurge when it comes to a hotel room." "I don't like to hitch through deserts; I take the bus instead," "We stop whenever we see interesting pyramids, no matter where it is." These people have established at least a very basic travel routine and, though they may not be aware of it as a 'routine,' they do know that it makes their travelling more enjoyable.

Schedules, on the contrary, immediately put you into the position of *having* to do something.

Indulge yourself. If your true interests are lounging in sidewalk cafes or sitting on a warm beach, staring mindlessly out to sea, then do it. Throw away your guidebooks and lock the camera in the glove compartment. You can buy professional slides in a tourist shop and tell lies about your explorations and adventures; no one will know the difference.

WHERE TO GO

"Where to go and how to get there?" are decisions that reduce many would-be travellers to fits of map shredding and random dart throwing. Shall we drive to Mexico City, or fly to Veracruz or take the bus to Guadalajara? Or fly to La Paz and take the ferry from there to Puerto Vallarta? Or...? The choices and combinations seem infinite and the final decision may be made on a whim rather than logically. On my first trip to Mexico I went directly to Topolobampo, for the simple reason that its name stuck in my mind like a snatch of song and wouldn't go away until I'd actually seen the place.

Assuming that you haven't got the foggiest idea of a destination, the most important consideration should be what you want to do. My own answer to this is almost automatic: I want to go to the beach, skin dive, eat fish and drink beer. Chichen Itza, *fiestas* and the Museum of Anthropology can all wait until I've soaked up enough sun.

That's in the wintertime, when the beach isn't so hot that it grills the soles of your feet or the beer is so warm that it makes bubbles in your nose. In the summer I prefer mountains, the higher and cooler the better.

The first rule of thumb after deciding on a destination is *never take your decision seriously*: if something else comes up that seems better, drop plan A and try plan B. If you're relaxed and adventurous, you'll probably work right through the alphabet and hit plan Z: two months in a jungle hut, playing Humphrey Bogart and happily abandoning your original plan to study Aztec culture and Spanish.

Read guidebooks and ask friends for advice, keeping in mind, of course, that both the books and your friends are full of exaggerations, misinformation and white lies. I've often heard and read descriptions of places I've been to that sounded more like Shangri-La than reality. The disappointment may be great, but don't let it get you down. When we find that the super cheap colonial hotel with fine food is actually an adobe version of the Holiday Inn, or the picturesque sleepy village is staging a week-long brass band competition, we just move along knowing that something better isn't far off.

Look over the charts and maps in the appendices of this book for information on average temperatures, rainfalls and altitudes. Don't forget, however, that most of these figures are averages and can fluctuate considerably.

HOW TO GET THERE

One of your most important decisions is how to travel: bus or car? plane or train? hitchhike or tour group? People with cars or other vehicles often let habit make the decision and automatically plan to drive to Mexico. Others just as casually take the plane when a slower and less expensive train trip would have been more enjoyable. It is important to keep in mind that your trip begins the minute you step out the front door. Every effort should be made to enjoy all of it, from beginning to end.

If your trip will be for less than a month and you don't intend to camp out, consider going by public transportation. Mexico's public transportation system is very extensive and very cheap; some type of bus runs over almost every mile of road, including those you wouldn't want to take your car on. (See *Public Transportation* and *Prices*.)

Driving is not only physically tiring, but in Mexico it often leaves you feeling like a novice in a high stakes poker game. When you have to cover a lot of miles in a relatively short period of time, it's best to leave the driving problems to someone else.

If the thought of locking your loyal Edsel in the garage is just too much, it's time to get out the road map and compute how many miles lie ahead. You don't have to figure it out to the exact mile; a rough estimate will do, especially if ten percent is tacked on just to be safe.

Let's say that you live about 1,000 miles from the border. That's 2,000 miles coming and going, not counting travel inside Mexico itself. If you're entering the country any place west of El Paso you'll have at least another 1,000 (or more) miles to reach Mexico City. Double this figure to allow for the return trip and your total is up to 4,000 miles.

Optimistically assuming an average speed of 50 miles an hour, difficult to maintain, especially in Mexico, you're facing the prospect of 80 hours behind the wheel, not allowing for scenic viewpoints, waterfalls, rest stops and flat tires.

Eight ten-hour days, a full week of driving, can represent a large chunk of your vacation. These same hours will pass much more quickly from the seat of a bus or train, especially if some of them are at night and you can sleep. Reading, dozing or just gazing

JESUS
SAVES

out of the window are much more relaxing than staring at the white line, listening to the kids in the back seat chanting, "Aren't we there *yet*?"

An amazing number of people overlook the cost of operating a vehicle until their money is seriously low. By comparing your proposed itinerary with the cost-per-mile to operate the car—gasoline, oil, tires, insurance and general wear and tear—you'll have a better idea of basic, unavoidable expenses. (See *Appendices: Prices* for the cost of gas, oil and insurance.) On long trips it seems that half of your time is spent in gas stations, watching the pumps ring up the bad news as you curse the OPEC oil ministers.

There is an alternative to leaving the car at home that more travellers are discovering: drive to a city on or near the border and leave it in storage. The cost is low. Storage lots can be found in the yellow pages in the telephone book listed under Warehouses.

By just driving to the border you can take advantage of easy freeway driving in the U.S. This idea is especially useful for people who are only making a side trip into Mexico and don't want to bother with additional insurance, custom inspections and unfamiliar driving conditions.

Two or more people might consider one-way car rental to the border. It's easy to calculate if this will save you money: multiply the cost per ticket on the bus or train by the number of passengers, then compare this figure to the price of the rental car and gasoline.

Drive-away or delivery cars can save you a lot of money, too, especially if more than two people share expenses. Four of us drove one of these cars from Seattle to San Diego for less than the price of a single bus ticket. Our only problem on the trip was the attention we got from the highway patrol: someone had whitewashed the words TEXAS TURKEYS across the trunk.

Drive-away car dealers can be found in the yellow pages and in the classified section of newspapers. Call them well in advance and your chances of getting a good car on your particular route will be much better. A deposit is required and the driver may have to be over 25 years old. The requirements vary quite a bit so check before making plans.

People offering rides or wanting them, often advertise in newspaper classifieds under the Travel and Personal columns. Check these out carefully; if the driver plans to visit half a dozen aunts and uncles along the way or to make a side trip to Yellowstone, the expenses may add up to more than the ride is worth.

Rides and riders can also be found on bulletin boards, especially in colleges, outdoor equipment shops, community centers, food co-ops and laundromats. Some towns have share-a-ride centers that will refer you to people going your way; look in the classifieds or call Information.

If you will be travelling to Mexico by public transportation, check out prices and alternatives very carefully. Competition has driven bus and air fares to wonderful lows, but many of the best offers can be complicated and confusing. You may find, for example, that a special half price flight departs only on alternate Mondays at two in the morning for people over the age of 40 willing to fly standby in the cargo hold.

Travel agents can be very helpful, but many of them tend to mention the more expensive flights, withholding information on the real deals unless the customer is willing to badger them. I once got a bargain by turning down the suggestion to fly, telling the agent I'd already checked on the bus and knew it was far cheaper. He rooted around in a huge schedule book and managed to 'discover' an air fare that was actually cheaper than the bus (taking into consideration food on the 50 hour ride).

Many low-cost air fares are for round trip, minimum stay. The advantages of saving money may not justify the limits imposed on your itinerary, especially if you like to take things as they come rather than in a neat plan. Tempting side trips and diversions have a way of appearing in Mexico and it's a shame to have to pass them up.

The option of going wherever you please and by any means is one of the greatest advantages of travelling without a car. On a recent trip we drove a pick-up truck to the border, put it in a storage lot and then travelled by train, switched to a bus, then to a local *cooperativo* truck (see *Public Transportation*) and from that to a small boat. The boat dropped us off in the middle of nowhere and we finally reached another bus after a great deal of hitching and walking. Trips such as this require a complete *lack* of schedules. The sense of freedom more than compensates for any inconveniences encountered.

TRAVELLING WITH FRIENDS

Unless you prepare for your trip with the utmost secrecy—load the car at night and leave without a word—you might very well be faced with whether or not to take along a friend (or friends).

Let's imagine that you are standing in your driveway, looking critically at the packing job you and your girl, Linda, have just completed. A friend approaches.

"Hey man, you actually got all of that junk in there! Might even have room for another person. Heh! Heh!"

You stand mute; Linda is making noncommittal motions that indicate the decision, 'take Harold or leave Harold,' is up to you.

"Hey Phil," he says, "I could pay part of the gas."

That does it; you aren't exactly loaded with money.

"OK. How much have you got?"

"Twenty seven bucks!" Harold says, grinning from ear to ear at the thought of making the trip. Money is no object; he's willing to blow the whole wad.

Later: "Hey, Phil," Harold says with a slight look of embarassment, "I'd like you to meet Laura..."

"Sure, OK. Just try to be here by nine tomorrow. I want to get on the road before lunch."

Harold sighs with relief and as they're leaving he shouts back eagerly, "Laura's got some money, too! About seventeen dollars!"

As you're walking into the house to tell Linda, she meets you and says, "Robert just called. He's changed his mind. They'll be by this evening so we can go over plans."

You look back at the car, a '53 Buick Roadmaster that is beginning to blow oil, and you mentally cram in six people, thinking of all the things you will have to leave behind.

"Oh, well!" you say, "might as well start repacking."

Travelling with a group of friends can lead to problems, but it doesn't have to.

If you'll be travelling with other people, everyone should participate in trip planning. This avoids the inevitable, "Well, you said..." when things don't go exactly to plan.

Final decisions should be made while everyone is sober, relaxed and feeling good. Soft music and loose, comfortable clothing, sharp pencils, clean maps, good lighting and snacks will all contribute to successful planning sessions.

Common goals or interests are important. Your friends may not share your passion for collecting orchids or touring whorehouses. So, *before* leaving, agree to what everyone vaguely wants to do and absolutely doesn't want to do.

Money can destroy even the best travelling relationships. When everyone in the group has a more or less equal amount and attitude towards money, sharing expenses and being economical will be much easier.

A good system of sharing or pooling funds should be devised so that no one pays an unjust portion of the bills. The most accurate and reliable method is to appoint a bookkeeper to keep a written account of all expenses and periodically conduct a settling up.

We do this in a small notebook, tied by a string to the dashboard of the car or carried in a shirt pocket. Whenever anyone spends something for the group, the person who paid it records it in the book or tells the bookkeeper. Every few days the entries are totalled and divided by the number in the group. Individual contributions are then compared to the average debt and those who paid in less make it up to those who paid in more.

If you take a car tell your passengers how much you estimate will have to be spent on gas and oil. People who have never driven long distances usually don't realize how expensive it will be. If you expect them to help pay any repair bills, let everyone know before you leave, not after the engine has blown and the car is in the shop.

Passengers should do as much as possible to ease the burden on the car owner. They can do this by sharing the driving, changing the oil, cleaning the windshield, etc.

Let's imagine once again that you're Phil. You have been unofficially designated as group leader because you are the owner of the car and have two years of high school Italian.

The trip to the border has been uneventful; several gallons of oil needed and a few flats fixed, but nothing major has gone wrong. Now everyone has finally stopped holding their breath each time you pump the brakes. After the border crossing, you've made a straight shot into central Mexico.

The scene opens at breakfast time in a small restaurant. Everyone is discussing what to do that day.

"I'd like to look for that hot springs someone told us about!"

"How about visiting a few churches?"

"Let's drop!"

"Why not check out the market?"

"Let's just go somewhere and relax!"

"I thought we were going to head over to Veracruz today?"

The suggestions get thicker and more insistent, but nothing has been resolved by the time the bill arrives.

It is customary for one person to pay for everything and settle up later, but some of the group have other ideas.

"I had one egg and coffee and that's all."

"You ate my beans, but I had some of your eggs. How much is that?"

"Who's paying for the *tortillas*?"

"I ate four of those rolls. How much are they?"

"You owe me for lunch yesterday, but I owe Phil for gas. Let's see, if you pay Laura for the suntan oil and I'll pay Harold for..."

In desperation you pay the entire bill and tell everyone to forget it. On the way back to the car discussion of the day's plans continues.

"He said ask near the *plaza*. Everyone knows where the hot springs are."

"I just know this is a good place to drop," someone insists.

"I really want to get one of those baskets."

"Oh, wow, I can just feel that sand and that water!"

Harold and Laura have gone ahead and are standing by the car, attempting to converse with a cop.

"What's up?" you ask, fearing the worst.

"I think he wants us to move the car."

Everyone piles in, trying to find somewhere to sit amidst the sleeping bags, packs and old potato chip bags. The inside of the car is like a furnace and before you can reach into your pocket for the key, the usual comments fly from the back seat.

"Let's get moving! I can hardly breathe back here."

"Hey, would you mind opening your window, Phil?"

"I think that cop is trying to take our license plate off."

The last comment speeds you along, but instead of the mighty roar of the engine, all you hear is the whir of the starter.

"Not again!"

"I thought you fixed that before we left!"

"He *is* taking our license plate off!"

After convincing the cop with a bank note that you're not parked illegally, you delve into the engine, getting grease all over your last clean shirt.

"OK, where to?" you ask agreeably, after you've got the beast started.

"I don't care," comes the chorus.

"Well," you say, somewhat piqued at the sudden lack of interest in the day's events, "*someone* decide."

"It's up to you, Phil," someone says, magnanimously throwing it all in your lap.

"Whatever you say, man."

"Doesn't matter to me."

Harold makes the decision when he announces that he has to take another crap, his second in the last 15 minutes. It is pushing 11 a.m. and you notice a tic in your left eye.

Harold comes out of the gas station, wobbling slightly, and sags into the front seat.

"Wow," he gasps, "that place was enough to gag a maggot!"

You decline comment. Harold has become extremely fastidious since crossing the border.

A few hours later everyone has cheered up (after a nap while you were driving) and they are eagerly discussing your decision to visit Veracruz. Even Harold seems to have revived and he actually mentions eating again.

Laura hands you a warm beer and you tune in a good radio station from the States. It's hotter than hell in the crowded car, but everyone suddenly feels really glad to be there.

"Oh, well," you say to yourself, "I suppose we'll work it out."

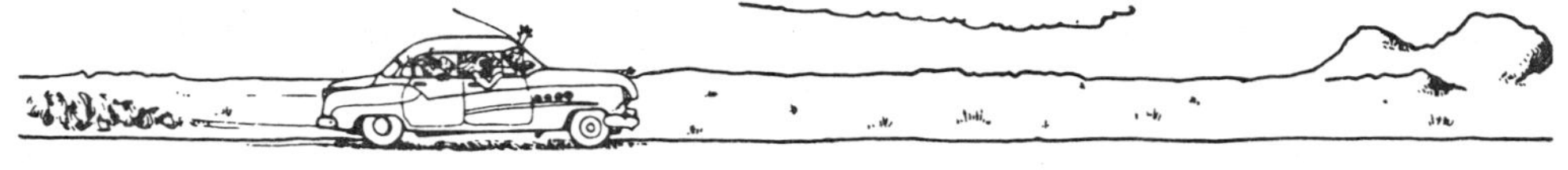

Travelling in groups of more than one vehicle can be extremely frustrating.

For example: You stop to take a leak. You're just about finished when your friends overtake you and stop.

"What's wrong?" they ask.

"Taking a leak," you say, discreetly leaning against a back fender.

"Oh, OK," and off they go.

A few miles later you see them in a gas station.

"Don't you need gas?" they ask.

"Not yet, still got half a tank."

You wait impatiently for 15 minutes while they check the oil, wash the windows and fill the tank. Ten minutes after leaving the station they pull over.

"What's wrong?"

"Taking a leak," they say.

"Oh," you say. "Why didn't you do it in the gas station?"

"Forgot."

Using signals between vehicles while driving is a good method of maintaining communications *if* you can work out a reasonably fool-proof system.

Our experiences with signals between vehicles usually go something like this:

Steve: "Dammit! Why don't they stop? I signalled four times."

- They finally pull over.

Steve: "Why didn't you stop when I signalled?"

- "I thought you were blinking your lights to speed up."

Steve: "No, I was giving you the 'rest stop' signal."

- "I thought that was two honks and a left turn signal."

Steve: "No, of course not! That's the 'stop at the next gas station' signal."

- "Oh no it isn't! 'Stop for gas' is four fingers pointed up and a right turn signal."

Steve: "Is it? I thought that was 'are you hungry?' "

- "I'm not hungry. We just ate."

Steve: "Do you know what this signal is?" He is beating his fists on his forehead.

- "No, what is it?"

Steve: "It's the 'meet you in Oaxaca in a month' signal."

 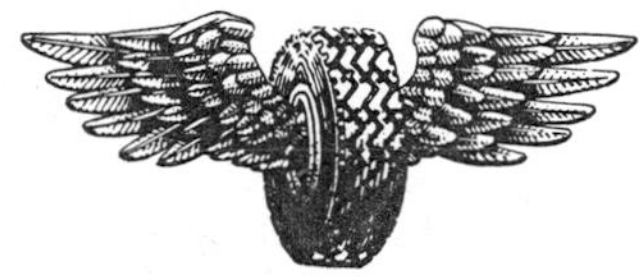

If you are travelling in more than one vehicle and find that it isn't working as smoothly as you'd planned, there's just one sensible thing to do—part company.

Since most of the problems arise while driving, it's easier to meet somewhere than to stick close together on the road. The meeting can be at the end of each day, at the end of a week or at some specific location with no definite time.

If you agree to meet in or near a town, just leave a stamped letter or postcard at the post office, advising your friends where to find you (see *Services*). The standard devices used to signal friends in the States—paper plates nailed to trees, flashy signs, etc.—are apt to be taken down by curious kids as soon as you're out of sight. Messages left at bars, stores and gas stations rarely get delivered.

When travelling with people you don't know very well, don't be afraid to strike off again on your own. Travelling can strain even well-established relationships and it's far better to face the problem rather than to ignore it in the hope that it will just go away. Friends of ours, for example, found that their long awaited 'dream trip' turned into a minor nightmare because their two teenaged children wouldn't give them a moment's peace. The problem was solved by a simple arrangement: the parents would escort the kids to the bus station and see them off to the next town along their route, agreeing to meet at a hotel they'd selected from a guidebook. When their kids were gone, the folks drove by themselves, trying to arrive at the meeting place within a few hours of the kids. The parents got privacy and peace and their children learned to be more independent and self-reliant.

Some people are natural loners and refuse to travel with others, but it is also not unusual to meet people on their own who really wish that they weren't. They have a tendency to latch onto a companion like a second shadow. The most casual conversation can suddenly turn into a partnership.

"Where you headed?"

-- "South."

"Gee, me too."

-- "Hmmm."

"How far?"

-- "Never can tell. Mmmm."

"You said it. Got your ticket?"

-- "Well..."

"Me either. I'm just hanging loose. You know?"

-- "Hmmm."

"Hey, I've got an idea! Why don't you and I...?

Ordinary, normal looking people may suddenly display completely disagreeable or bizarre behavior. I once travelled, briefly, with a fellow who claimed that his body hardly required any food. We were travelling by bus down the length of Mexico and I took advantage of the opportunity to re-discover regional dishes. We always took a table together, though my new friend would never order so much as a glass of water. His routine began when my food appeared.

"Hey, wow, what is that stuff?"

"It's called an *asadero*," I said, plunging my fork into the long flour *tortilla* rolled around strips of grilled beef. His eyes fastened on my plate as though it were a crystal ball.

"Hey, do you mind if I taste that thing?" he asked as if the food were some sort of laboratory specimen that required identification. I pushed the plate across the table.

"That's not too bad!" He took a second huge bite to confirm the analysis. "Kind of spicy, though," he said, casually sucking down half of my beer in one greedy swallow.

"You could order one," I suggested. "They aren't expensive."

"Oh, no!" he said, "I'm not hungry. It's not the money, it's just that I don't require as much food as most people." His hand worked idly across the table and began plucking at the chopped lettuce. I quickly stuffed my fork into the salad, but not before he'd filched the sliced tomato.

This scene repeated over the *mole* sauce, which took several bites before he reached a final verdict—"weird stuff!", the breakfast of *chilaquiles*, the lunch of *enchiladas*, various samplings of bread, *tortillas*, hot sauces and whatever drink I'd ordered. When he said, "Hey, does that taste like *real* coffee?" and reached for my Nescafe, I realized that our paths were about to separate.

Another apparently normal person turned out to be a walking collection of worry and paranoia. "Sure hope this train doesn't derail and kill us all. If it does I hope I die instead of being maimed. Which would you prefer?" The simple act of drinking a beer and watching the sunset from the dining car brought on dire comments on alcoholism, food poisoning, excess cosmic ray exposure, night blindness and the futility of hope.

We parted company soon after. His final comment when I told him where I was headed was: "Well, sure hope you make it." Doubt was heavy in his voice, though my alleged destination was no more than a few blocks away.

We were driving through a tiny village on the remote Gulf coast of Yucatan several years ago when the sound of our car brought people scurrying from their houses. One of them, tall, bearded and obviously not a Mexican, ran to the car and shouted desperately, "Are you Americans? Do you speak English?"

We hesitated before answering, fearing that he might be totally insane. All the others in the village looked happy and calm. "Right out of an old late-evening jungle movie," I thought, expecting to hear a voice in a heavy British accent say, "Gone starkers, I'd say, jungle madness."

We told him that we were Americans and he cried eagerly, "Thank God! Can you get me out of here?"

The prospect of being stuck with a madman didn't appeal to us so we stalled a bit and asked what was wrong.

"I'll tell you," he said. "I came here several months ago looking for privacy. A village like this seemed to be perfect; no other Americans, none of the things that distract you from reading and thinking and relaxing. I rented a house and moved in."

He paused and surveyed the group of smiling faces around him, his neighbors. "Then these people," and he indicated the crowd, "started visiting me, bringing food and inviting me to their homes and *talking* to me day in and day out. Finally I couldn't take it any more. I started hiding in the house during the day. But they pounded on the door to ask if I was sick. It's no use; they just won't let me alone. I hate to be unfriendly to them, but I have to get out of here!"

A few minutes later, he threw a hastily packed bag into the car and we left, followed by a pack of friendly children, chased by friendly dogs and waved sadly away by friendly villagers.

TRAVELLING ALONE

When you want to travel with someone but can't find a companion, don't let the prospect of travelling alone in Mexico stop you. Don't be afraid, you really will be safe. Lots of people do it, from high school kids to elderly ladies.

If the thought is still too much for you, you can be reasonably sure that you'll meet someone else who is alone and who will want to combine forces.

Travelling alone has many advantages. It is much easier to learn and speak Spanish and to become involved with Mexicans when you're alone.Most attractive to me is the sense of freedom and independence that comes with being entirely on your own. It is, quite frankly, a feeling of power; there are no arguments, even from loved ones. You are sole boss-of-the-games. If you don't like the looks of a place, you just move along and if you're feeling lazy you stop, even though the world's most unbelievable tourist attraction may be just up the road.

When I'm travelling alone it seems that I involve myself in side trips that I'd otherwise pass up. "Do you want to visit my uncle with me for a few days?" Why not? There's no one else to consult or consider and I don't much care where I sleep. Changing my mind is also easier if I don't have to convince anyone but myself that it's a Good Idea. When I step off the bus during a brief rest stop and suddenly feel compelled to grab my bag and stay for a while, it's entirely up to me; the bus driver certainly doesn't care.

Travelling alone requires a certain degree of self-reliance and levelheadedness that some people have most of the time and the rest of us have some of the time. When by myself I am much more careful with my money and personal possessions. I even pay more attention to what I eat: after all, getting sick when you've got someone there to cool your fevered brow with damp cloths and to hustle fresh orange juice can be almost pleasant; when you're alone it isn't so nice.

There are disadvantages to travelling alone. Single travellers tend to be more susceptible to emotional stress and you may feel an exaggerated sense of strain from normal problems in dealing with a foreign language and customs. A tiring day may become an exhausting one. Throw in a long train ride and a case of indigestion and the lone tourist may wonder if it's all worth it or not.

Single travellers often complain that they don't have anyone to bounce ideas off of or to compare impressions with. "Am I the only person in Mexico who thinks *tortillas* taste like cardboard?" "Should I blow my money on this handwoven blanket or save it to visit Monte Alban?"

Doubt usually leads to conservative decisions, but it may just as well go the other way: "Ah, the hell with it, you only live once!" The latter reflects my attitude for decisions that don't directly affect my health or sanity. If, for example, I get a sudden whim to change my route and visit a new place, I do it. What's the difference? On the other hand, if it's whether or not to have just one more little drink before walking back to my hotel through dark side streets, I pay up and leave.

Should things begin to get too weird while you're alone, it's time to slow down or stop completely. Don't panic; everything will be all right after a nice session of Traveller's Meditation: locate a pleasant place to spend the night and rent a room. Don't fret over the price even if it seems a little steep.

Now go up to your room and take off your clothes. Get into the shower or tub and use up all of the hot water. Dry off and move to the bed. Lie down. Put the pillow over your head. Breathe deeply. Scream a little if you must, but don't overdo it.

Lie in this position for at least an hour, thinking of clouds, ice cubes or gentle breezes. When you're ready to face the world again get up, put on your clothes and stroll calmly out of the room. The secret is to move and think *slowly*, to respond to people and events with the same serene, deliberate manner that you do at home. When a shoeshine boy races up and begins tugging at your arm, banging his shine kit against your sore knee, don't shriek obscenities or raise your hand: just fix him with a benevolent stare and whisper "No."

Now glide on down the street, absorbing the scenery. Cross at the proper intersections to avoid nerve-shattering near misses. Find a pleasant cafe or park bench. Sit down. Let it all flow around you. Buy a newspaper. It doesn't matter what language it's in; it is just something to occupy your hands. Don't you feel better already?

This is a good meditation to perform before making any decisions about what to do next or where to go. Single travellers are prone to impetuous changes in location. It is not unusual to hear of people who spent their entire vacation riding buses aimlessly from one end of the country to the other, waiting for that flash of inspiration or chance meeting which would give them a reason to stop.

Any place that is regularly visited by tourists will have a hotel, restaurant or bar where foreigners congregate. This can provide relief from travelling alone: an opportunity to exchange news, advice, reading material and diarrhea remedies. You might also pick up a ride or a travelling companion. By asking others you'll learn of similar meeting places in other towns.

You can maintain independence but still meet other travellers and join them for short periods of time—a side trip or just a meal, for example. Women travelling alone will find the 'gringo circuit' helpful as an insulation against relentless *machismo* (see *Machismo*).

One of the hazards of travelling alone is encountered by those using public transportation. This is the dreaded Empty Seat. Unless precautions are taken it may be filled by a cigar-smoking octopus, a screaming baby, a drunk, a chatterbox or some other threat to your peace of mind.

The solution is quite simple: put something in the seat (assuming seats are not assigned), which gives the impression that it is already occupied. As the other passengers move down the aisle, wait until you see someone who looks compatible as a seat-mate. The others can be fended off with a combination of significant looks at the object in the empty seat, lies (yes, it's occupied...by my paperback novel), scowls, glares or leers. My beard usually protects me from the fearful mother-with-two-children-in-arms. When a likely prospect appears, just pick up the decoy from the seat and smile sincerely, luring them in.

TRAVELLING WITH KIDS

Travelling with children or babies in Mexico doesn't have to be more of a hassle than it is anywhere else.

After the initial shock of entering a foreign country has diminished, children are remarkably blase about where they are. It is important, however, that parents respect their children's interest as well as their own. The trip should be arranged for the amusement and benefit of all concerned, from the father's passion for *Mayan* relics to the child's interest in playing on the beach.

I am often asked by nervous parents if it is safe to take their children to Mexico. It's not only safe, but can actually make parts of the trip much easier for everyone.

Children are natural icebreakers; when you enter a small village, just send the kid out into the street and within minutes your welcome will be assured. Mexicans lavish attention on their children and are very considerate to gringo kids, especially if the child is timid or just plain scared.

A friend of ours recently made a long trip to Mexico with his eight-year-old daughter, the first time he'd ever tried travelling with a child. When I asked him how things worked out, he answered, "It was like having a diplomatic passport." He explained that all of the people he normally expected to be cool toward him (he is tall, with a fierce black beard and long hair) completely ignored his appearance and treated him like a loyal and devoted parent. He and his daughter were given special attention in restaurants, escorted to the head of the line in the train station and generally treated like VIPs.

"I even got a better deal on souvenirs," he laughed. "I just let her do the bartering."

This reaction to children is very common and the younger they are, the more helpful other people are. A woman travelling with a small baby told us that whenever she wanted to speed up a border crossing she gave the little tyke a pinch and his squalling was better than having a personal friend in the President's office.

Lorena and I had been camped on a beach for quite a while and one day we decided that it was my turn to make a trip to town for the mail. The minute I walked into the post office I realized that I'd made a serious error: weeks of sun and salt-water had been rather hard on my clothes and I'd forgotten to comb my hair for a few days. The clerk gave me a hard suspicious look and demanded my identification before he'd hand over our letters. I explained that I'd left my tourist card at camp, but his only reaction was to remind me that I was legally required to carry it at all times.

I wandered away, snarling and spitting; that long awaited check for a million dollars might be in there! What if it was returned marked NO FORWARDING ADDRESS!? I was leaning against a wall, racking my brain for a solution, when a voice said, *"Ola, ¿que tal?"*

I looked up to find a Mexican acquaintance and his wife smiling at me curiously. "Oh, I'm fine, thanks," I said, shaking hands and absentmindedly patting one of their older children on the head. We exchanged the usual pleasantries and were about to go our separate ways when inspiration struck.

"Hey, Francisco," I said, "Would you mind if...*pues*...would your wife mind if I, uh, held the baby for a minute?"

Francisco gave me a hard look; we'd drunk enough beer together to know our respective ideas on birth and population control. Had I spent a little too much time in the sun? His wife tightened her grip on the tiny bundle in her arms, looking to her husband for protection.

"*Un minuto*," I said, holding out my hands and giving them a big cheery sane smile I knew I was taking advantage of their politeness, embarrassing them into doing something that seemed strange, but I had to have that check! A million green ones; hell, I'd buy them a nursery school!

The baby didn't know the difference. I just hoped the guy with my letters wouldn't question the discrepancy in our complexions; little Tomasito was pretty dark. His parents were looking at each other with mixed amusement and fright as I ducked into the post office.

The clerk recognized me at once; his face congealed into an unyielding mask. I didn't say a word, just edged up to the window and gave him a quick flash of the baby. His mouth dropped open. I chucked it under the chin a couple of times. It drooled. The clerk's eyes came up and looked into mine. He smiled.

"Thanks a lot," I said a few minutes later, transferring the baby back to his anxious mother. I scanned eagerly through the packet of letters that had been forwarded from home: an invitation to join a book club, an appeal for donations to protect small rodents along a polluted river system and a seed catalog.

Single mothers will find that having a child cuts down on unwanted attention from men. Motherhood is sacred in Mexico; husbands and marriage licenses are just frills.

Most of the following advice and comments on travelling with children came from innumerable conversations with parents, children and letters from readers. The almost unanimous conclusion was that a child should not be left at home unless the parents are making the trip specifically to get away by themselves or if the kid has a serious health problem. Here then, is what they have to say:

Food and Health

Health problems are a major source of worry for parents, especially when travelling. Careful attention should be paid to small children, particularly those in the grab-all-eat-all stage.

Because infants can't move around much or get into mischief they are easier to travel with than toddlers. Keep babies off the floor and out of the dirt.

Health care is cheap in Mexico; if your baby gets sick you should have no trouble finding a doctor. (See *Health*.)

If you are expecting a child, you might want to have the birth occur while you're in Mexico. There are two good reasons for doing this: It costs substantially less for medical care and the child becomes a dual citizen of Mexico and the U.S. (As a citizen of Mexico, the baby can legally own land or a business, an idea the parents might find attractive— see *Tourists and The Law*.)

Children have a notorious reputation for being picky eaters. The change to Mexican food may be very difficult for them. There are many types of food, however, that will satisfy kids who insist on something familiar. (See *Restaurants and Typical Foods*.)

Baby bottles can be filled with fresh juices and most juice stand operators will make purees of fresh fruits and vegetables if you ask. People in restaurants will go out of their way to heat baby bottles or to prepare a special dish for your child. Small food mills that will make a puree of a single food or cooked dish are useful.

Baby foods of all types, from pablum to familiar brands of canned and bottled vegetables, meats and fruits are available throughout the country. Keep in mind that Mexico has a very high birth rate and the care and feeding of babies is a big industry. Baby formulas are available in drugstores.

Disposable diapers are sold in drugstores and supermarkets.

Carry a piece of mosquito netting large enough to drape over the baby's cradle or bed, particularly if you will be staying in cheaper, unscreened hotel rooms or camping out.

Toys

If you are on the road with a child, you'll find that simple games, puzzles and small toys will interest the kid much more than the passing scenery.

For those who are old enough a personal map can be a great treat. I recall one young boy who constantly pestered his parents with questions about what city they were in.

The poor kid really wanted to know, but his folks didn't realize that a simple road map would have more than satisfied him. "It doesn't make any difference" was their standard reply to his questions.

A good supply of comic books may not enrich the child's mind, but the same could be said for the father's copy of *Hustler*. Although children's books in English are available in a few of the largest cities, bring plenty if your child is an avid reader.

Children's books in Spanish are almost always translated from English and are an excellent aid toward learning Spanish (for the older folks too). Many familiar comic books are also translated into Spanish.

If your kid is addicted to a familiar object, such as the classic Peanut's blanket, take it along. A favorite cup, bowl or plate may make the difference when serving the child a piece of fried iguana.

Should your child find it difficult to play with Mexican kids, don't get upset, it will only crease the kid's apprehension. Simple toys and non-verbal games will usually bridge the communication gap.

Frisbees, puzzles, marbles, kites, balls, jacks, jump ropes, tops, coloring books, modeling clay, etc., are almost universal, in one form or another. Expensive toys may cause problems of jealousy. Large, unbreakable toys are good for smaller kids.

Toys are available in the marketplace and many of the handmade wooden ones make excellent gifts for adults as well. There are many types of plastic toys and small pottery imitations of regular dishes and other kitchen utensils.

Carnivals, circuses and fairs are common and inexpensive. Public playgrounds and amusement parks are located in most large towns.

Language

Sudden exposure to a foreign language can be unnerving for anyone, and children may be particularly baffled by the change. Fortunately they adapt very quickly. The speed with which most kids pick up Spanish is amazing; they'll learn in days what it takes the rest of us weeks and months to cram into our heads and we'll never match the natural sound and flow of their pronunciation. Tongue-tied parents may eventually have to rely on them for assistance with translations.

It helps, however, to give your children a push in the right direction by teaching them basic words and polite phrases. This will give them a feeling of independence and self-importance that helps to break barriers of shyness and timidity.

The learning process won't always be fun: one little gringo sobbed to his mother that no matter how many times he said something in English to his new friends, they didn't seem to hear him. He felt like the Invisible Boy until he began to pick up a few simple words and phrases.

Another child rebelled against his mother's efforts to teach him how to ask for food and yelled, "I can't speak Spanish! I can't say *tortilla*! I'll never be able to say *tortilla*!" Needless to say, he pronounced *tortilla* like a native.

Children often don't understand the concept of another language until they've heard it spoken and have time to accept that it is real. A three-year-old, after two days on the train, turned to her parents and said accusingly, "You didn't tell me *everybody* talks Spanish." By the end of their trip she didn't know the difference between the two languages and used half and half.

If your child's initial reaction to Spanish is negative, don't make a big deal out of it. I remember a little boy who had driven his parents to distraction because he absolutely refused to speak a word of Spanish. One day I saw him playing in the sand with some Mexican kids and decided to eavesdrop.

They were engrossed in their play, with the Mexican children babbling back and forth in Spanish. It took me a few minutes to realize that the gringo kid was completely involved in whatever game they'd invented, though he was acting out a private and entirely different fantasy than the others.

If you're staying in one spot for a while you might want to enroll your child in a Mexican school. (See *Appendices: Schools*.)

Babysitters

Many parents, especially those without partners, say that Mexico is like travelling in a vast day-care center. Mexicans are very casual about having another kid around the house. In homes that can afford a maid or cook, the children are often placed under their care and one or two more probably won't be noticed.

A woman travelling with her five-year-old son told us that after she rented a house in a small town and had met the neighbors, her kid all but disappeared. When she wanted him back she just walked down the street until she was directed to whichever family was entertaining him that day. Stories such as this are very common. And then there's the very strange-but-true story of the woman who decided that her children were happier in Mexico and left them with the neighbors...permanently.

Leaving your child with someone else doesn't mean that you're abandoning them. You may, in fact, be doing them a big favor. Kids tend to tire of travelling quickly, especially when hopping from one town or tourist attraction to the next. Many kids have told us that they'd rather have stayed at the beach and let their folks go off on side trips by themselves. Don't be afraid to consider this alternative just because you're in a new country. If nothing else you might find some gringos willing to babysit.

Cholla

PERSONAL STUFF

Take it or leave it?...Clothing...A Hidden Pocket...Health record...Cameras and film...Camping equipment: sleeping bags, backpacks, tents, cook kits...A travelling kitchen...Food from home...Odds and Ends...Don't overdo it...

●●

Watching people prepare for their trip is sometimes more enjoyable than travelling itself. It usually goes like this: "Hey, look at this nifty little heating coil, it's only a dollar!"

"What's it for?"

"Heating coffee and tea in hotel rooms. Neat! I think I'll get one!"

"Do you have a cup?"

"No, but here's one over here. Oh yeah, I better buy some tea bags. And some instant coffee."

"How about hot chocolate?"

"Good idea!"

"And bouillon cubes for quick soups?"

"Definitely!"

"You'll need a spoon, won't you?"

"Of course. In fact, I'd better get two. Never know when I'll be having company."

"Then you'll need another cup. And how about bowls?"

"Glad you thought of it! Maybe some of that instant pudding...dried milk and granola...a bit of honey..."

This type of chain reaction planning and buying not only destroys your budget but leads to suitcases and backpacks weighing in at the hernia range. For those travelling with a vehicle the temptation to take one more thing is especially great: how many cars and vans have you seen on the highway that looked like refugees from the collapse of the American Dream, loaded to the top and them some with "just the essentials."?

When preparing for your trip to Mexico keep in mind that you aren't going there as a colonist but as a temporary visitor. The length of your trip and your interests will have a certain influence on what you'll need, but in general it won't be anything more than what you would take to visit the next state or to go camping in Yosemite.

CLOTHING

Your clothes should be practical. When you drool mango juice over your white pants, you'll wish they were a darker, camouflaging color. Flimsy clothing will fall to pieces if washed on rocks very often.

Unless you're going to live high on the hog in the resort areas, you won't need to dress up. As in many warmer countries it is considered proper in Mexico to wear light and casual clothing. The *guayabera* shirt from Yucatan is suitable in place of a sport coat or jacket. Mexican politicians always seem to wear them, along with highly reflective sunglasses.

You'll be correctly dressed almost all of the time if your clothes aren't scroungy or overly fancy. Strange or bizarre clothing should be left at home if you are sensitive about stares. Pants on women still attract comments in some areas, mainly well away from the tourist circuits and large towns, but bare legs draw even more attention. Many women prefer pants for travelling and a dress for casual places.

Weather is an important consideration. (See *Appendices: Climate.*) It will be cold at night at higher altitudes and in northern areas during the winter. A jacket or sweater and warm footwear are desirable. Sandals and socks will do for short periods, but shoes of some kind are necessary for long visits to cold areas. A long-sleeved shirt will not only keep you warm when necessary, but will also protect your arms from sunburn and mosquito bites.

When I'm travelling fast or extra light (for example, just to the beach), I eliminate one pair of pants and shirt. The following wardrobe should be sufficient for reasonable neatness without requiring great washing efforts:

three pairs of wash and wear pants
three wash and wear shirts
underwear
socks
shoes or boots
shorts or cut-offs
jacket or sweater
swimming suit
hidden pocket (see following page)

Optional or to buy in Mexico:
sandals
hat
hatstrings (*barbiquetes*)
handkerchief
raincoat or poncho

Women might want to take one 'respectable' dress for border crossings, visiting formal places, social functions, etc.

Some sort of protection from rain is needed, particularly during the summer months. Most Mexicans carry a large piece of thin plastic in their pocket for afternoon showers during the rainy season. It is very compact, cheap and can be used in a variety of ways.

Because skilled labor is cheap in Mexico it is far better to have clothing made to order (*hecha a la medida*) rather than to buy ready-made. Stores that sell cloth can refer you to a tailor, or look for signs that say "*Sastre*" or "*Sastrería.*" The customer usually provides the cloth and takes the responsibility for pre-shrinking it, though other arrangements can be made if necessary.

Depending on the skill of the tailor, you'll usually get best results by having a copy made, instead of an original. The savings can be considerable, especially on such high mark-up articles as shorts, hiking pants and bathing suits.

Be cautious when buying clothing in Mexico. Inexpensive factory made clothes are of poor quality and don't fit well. Good clothing is expensive. If you intend to buy and wear handmade clothes, remember that they aren't wash and wear although many types are presentable without ironing. Some things, a Oaxaca shirt, for example, will be a dense ball of wrinkles after washing.

Most inexpensive handmade clothing shrinks considerably. Large people—either wide or tall—will find it almost impossible to buy ready-made clothing. (See *Apendices: Clothing Sizes.*)

Used clothing from the U.S. can be found in many markets. Some of it still has price tags and stickers from such places as Goodwill and the Salvation Army. If you're lucky you may find something from an exclusive shop or designer. This clothing is generally a good bargain.

Mexican shoe sizes seem to stop at about size nine. Custom made shoes and sandals cost less than factory made ones of equal quality. A friend says that children's shoes are an excellent bargain in Mexico.

When a piece of clothing becomes too worn, too dirty or just too much hassle, give it away or hang it on a bush. Someone will find it and certainly use it.

A Hidden Pocket

"Hey, has anyone seen my . . . .?" (traveller's checks, tourist card, passport, driver's license or other important paper) is a question all too frequently heard while travelling. The slight note of anxiety in the persons's voice quickly turns to panic when everyone nearby casually answers, "Nope!" There's nothing that can quite match the gut-numbing feeling that comes from being unexpectedly penniless, without a shred of identification and thousands of miles from home.

The steps that some people take to avoid this unpleasant situation are seldom more secure than an ordinary wallet or purse: pouches that hang around the neck (these bang against your chest and chafe until the string breaks), money belts (won't hold anything else), secret compartments in luggage (not much good if the suitcase is misplaced) and so forth.

Our solution to this problem was inspired by Papillon, a French convict-turned-writer. He wrote that prisoners on Devil's Island hid jewels and large bank notes in small stainless steel cylinders. These cylinders, called 'chargers,' were hidden inside a person's...well, it's enough to say that it was very difficult to detect and to separate a man from.

The Hidden Pocket (see illustration), is much easier to use than a charger, far safer than a pouch or wallet and more convenient than money belts or hidden compartments. It will easily hold a passport, traveller's checks and even small lumpy objects, if necessary. The greatest advantage, other than security, is that once you begin using the Pocket, you soon lose that nagging background fear of being separated from your valuables. At night it's a simple matter to put the Pocket in bed with you. Never leave it with your clothing when sleeping, showering or sunbathing; that's the first place a thief will look.

A belt, cord or stout string inserted through the top 'loop' of the Pocket allows it to be worn hanging from the waist, though placed *inside* your pants, shorts or skirt. In a very short time the Pocket and its contents will mold against your hip and be almost

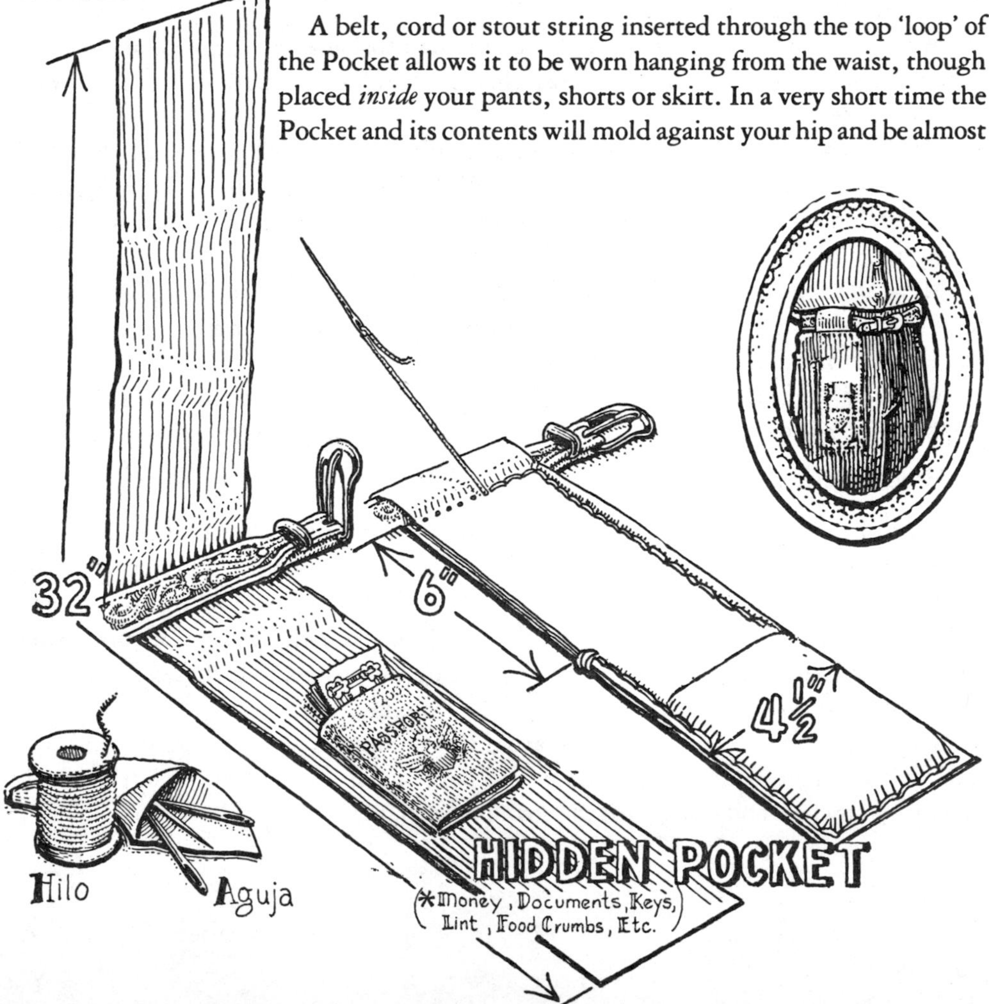

indistinguishable from the natural curve of your body and clothing. Variations are also possible: with elastic straps at top and bottom, the Pocket can be worn on your leg like a knife sheath; pins or sewn-on ties will attach it to the inside of a shirt or dress.

The important thing is that it be useable on all of your clothing. This not only saves the hassle of making permanent hidden pockets in every pair of pants or skirt but increases your awareness of where your valuables are at every minute. You should be as aware of your money and documents as you are of cigarettes and eyeglasses.

If you're carrying more money, papers or valuables than one Pocket will conveniently hold, another Pocket can be worn on the other side.

In the many years we've used the Pocket we've never lost a single thing from them (knock on wood). Once you've become accustomed to it, you'll probably find that a wallet isn't necessary at all. I always carry whatever cash I need for immediate use in a buttoned shirt pocket and spare change in my pants pocket.

Sewing Instructions: The Pocket should be made of a durable but lightweight material. Plain dark colors will be the least noticeable on your belt. It is important to have something safe, sturdy and inconspicuous rather than fancily made.

The material can be cut in a long strip, 6 inches by 32 inches or in a rectangle 12" by 16".

If you start with the 32" strip first fold it double, to 6" x 16". Leave 2 inches at the top for the belt loop. Now sew down one side, across the bottom and back up for about 6". The remaining gap is for inserting your passport and money. Leave an opening large enough to easily insert and remove valuables but not so large that they might work their way out.

If you want to have the stitching hidden on the inside, turn the pocket inside out; now sew another seam 2 inches below the top to form the belt loop.

If your fabric is squarish (12" x 16") fold it in half to 6" x 16". Now sew across the top and bottom and 6 inches up one side. Turn it inside out and sew the belt loop seam 2 inches below the top. Slice the fabric at the closed end of the belt loop. ***Remember: The Pocket goes inside your clothing, not outside.***

BEFORE YOU GO

Should you be involved in a serious accident or illness while travelling, a few simple preparations will make medical treatment quicker and more effective. A very brief medical record can be compiled on half a sheet of paper and kept with your passport or identification. *Be sure that it is legible.* Emergency information can also be engraved on bracelets and medallions. These are available from drug stores, jewelry shops and Medic Alert Foundation, a non-profit organization at P.O. Box 1009, Turlock, CA 95830.

Your medical emergency information should include any allergies or hypersensitivities and the names of all medications you are currently using; your blood type; chronic ailments; immunization history; eyeglasses prescription; type of health insurance and policy number; the name, address and phone number of your physician (arrange to have collect calls accepted in your name in case of emergency); your social security number, religion and dietary restrictions.

If you have health insurance check with your agent to see if coverage includes Mexico. Most policies do, though you may have to pay any bills and present receipts after returning home to recover the money.

A list of English-speaking doctors charging set fees in all parts of the world is available free (donations appreciated) from the International Association of Medical Assistance to Travellers, 350 Fifth Ave., Suite 5620, New York, NY 10001. Another list, not free, is available from Intermedic Inc., 777 3rd Ave., New York, NY 10017.

Blue Cross gives away a small booklet, *A Foreign Language Guide to Health Care*, that tells you how to say "I'm constipated" and other health-related phrases in four languages (French, German, Italian and Spanish). If nothing else you can look up your problem in English and then point to the translation. Write to Communication Department, Blue Cross and Blue Shield of Greater New York, 3 Park Ave., 27th Floor, New York, NY 10016.

CAMERAS AND FILM

Unless you're a hard-core photo snapper, don't buy an expensive camera just for your trip. Many people think that a fancy 35 mm camera is as essential as a bathing suit or sunglasses and, though they may use it only rarely, they've still got to have one around their neck. An albatross would be cheaper.

There are far too many types available to discuss specific cameras here, but in general anything that costs more than $20 and less than $50 should be quite adequate. If a simple record of your trip is what you want, keep your gear simple. Leave the light meters, filters, lenses, tripods and other paraphernalia for the professional or avid amateur. You'll save in initial cost, upkeep (such as the replacement or repair when you drop it in the Gulf of Mexico) and ease of operation.

If you do carry a 35 mm camera, protect the lens with a UV (ultraviolet) or skylight filter. I also like to use a polarizing filter for shots around water and for clouds. Carry lens paper and a camel's hair brush if you're fussy about spots in your slides or prints.

Film processing is best left until you return home. I've heard many complaints about the quality of processing in Mexico. Film is widely available but not a bargain. Buy a good supply at home; you'll often get a special price if you buy ten or twenty rolls at a time. (Mexico's import limit of 12 rolls per camera and one still camera and one movie camera per person is rarely enforced if you're a tourist.)

Change film out of the direct rays of the sun and never leave your camera sitting in the sun for more than a few minutes, especially inside a closed car. Heat will ruin the film and may melt or warp plastic camera parts. When travelling protect the camera from vibration by holding it in your lap or on a cushion of some sort. I wrap mine in a towel.

CAMPING EQUIPMENT

Keep your camping equipment as simple as you'd like your life to be while travelling. We've seen innumerable carloads of people submerged beneath mounds of canned goods, tents, sleeping bags, lamps, folding chairs and other paraphernalia that turned a two-week vacation into a nerve shattering pack-and-unpack marathon.

Camping is a time-consuming effort. If your stay in Mexico will be short, you won't want to spend it gathering firewood and setting up camp; you'll want to see and enjoy the country.

Comfortable, efficient camping does not require special equipment. Unless you're on foot or travelling by bicycle, most of your camping gear can be found right at home. By carefully selecting only what you need and will actually use, the difference in weight and space between special camping gear (cook kits, folding axes, etc.) and common household items will be minimal.

Begin assembling your stuff as far ahead of departure as possible, even when the trip isn't confirmed. If you need something, try to borrow it or buy it second-hand. Most camping equipment spends the majority of the year in the attic. When you have time to find a friend with a good tent and to convince him that it would not only be nice but morally strenghtening for him to loan it to you—you'll only be gone for a year—then you'll really save money.

New camping equipment, or 'new' used, should be tested before you leave, not after. One of the advantages of familiar used gear is that you'll already have an idea of its limitations and weaknesses and can anticipate them. The tendency to buy new stuff just for your 'special' trip should be resisted.

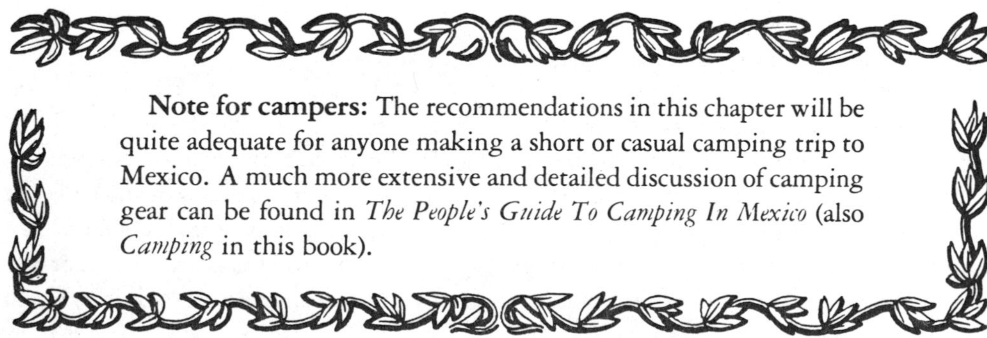

Note for campers: The recommendations in this chapter will be quite adequate for anyone making a short or casual camping trip to Mexico. A much more extensive and detailed discussion of camping gear can be found in *The People's Guide To Camping In Mexico* (also *Camping* in this book).

Sleeping Bags vs. Blankets: An astonishing number of people take Arctic type sleeping bags to Mexico. Unless you'll be sleeping directly under the stars in the mountains or in northern Mexico in wintertime, a light bag is more than adequate. If you're sleeping in a tent, under a tarp or roof or inside your vehicle, blankets should be considered. They aren't particularly lightweight, but they're cheaper and more versatile than a sleeping bag.

In warm or hot weather a blanket will keep the mosquitoes off your chest without roasting you and give sufficient protection from dew and early morning breezes.

If you find that your blanket or light bag isn't warm enough just go to the beach; you'll soon find someone selling their down-filled superbag for a bargain price.

Pack and frame: Your pack frame should be strong. A light frame won't survive being tossed from the top of a bus or out the back of a chili pepper truck. The bag should be strong, water resistant and not too large. It is an axiom of packing, from knapsacks to motor homes, that every available space will be filled, even if you have to take something totally useless.

Packs are for carrying on your back. They don't fit well into cars, vans or bus seats. If you're not a serious walker, don't bother to use one. A sea bag, although clumsier to carry, is more efficient for storage and doesn't take up much space when empty.

A medium-sized day pack carried inside your suitcase will usually be adequate for short hikes. A day pack works well as a shopping bag, lunch and book bag or for extra souvenir storage.

Tent: If you're travelling in a vehicle, don't splurge for an expensive lightweight tent; a good used canvas model will work fine, though it may smell moldy and look less adventurous.

Your tent should be easy to erect in sand, able to withstand a brisk wind, well ventilated and bug-proof. With good ventilation and bug screens you'll be able to lie naked on top of your Arctic sleeping bag without being eaten alive.

It is possible to improvise a tent for less than the sales tax on the one just described. Buy a piece of sheet plastic in tubular form about eight or nine feet long. Put your gear at one end and tie the tube off like a big sausage, then slide yourself into the other end. By running a cord lengthwise through the tube and tying each end to a tree or stake you have a real tent (available in hardware stores in Mexico by the meter—1.1 yards). While this is practical, it is about as cozy as sleeping in a plastic bag.

Sleeping Pad: Air mattress, foam pad or take your chances? None of these will cover the varied sleeping conditions you'll find on the road (and I have slept, literally, on the road). The final selection is mostly personal. I use a backpacker's air mattress: expensive, hard to keep patched and not much fun to inflate. Lorena prefers a foam pad: not expensive but in my opinion not very comfortable either. "It takes the edge off," she says, but that's about it. Foam pads are generally bulky and this can be inconvenient on a long trip. Pads should be covered with something washable; many miles of bus and train travel will attract dirt and grime.

Cooking Kits: If you must have one, get a good kit; cheap ones fall to pieces before your eyes and in the middle of a meal. Teflon coated cookware does not withstand washing with sand.

Cheap tin, aluminum and plastic plates, cups, utensils and cooking pots are widely available in Mexico and quite adequate.

Stoves and Lamps: Unless you're a fruitarian and prepare meals with a paring knife, you'll need a good stove. And while supper is cooking, a lamp will make rolling joints or studying the map much easier than by the flickering light of a candle.

Stoves and lamps should be sturdy, easily operated and cleaned and, most important, easy to supply with fuel.

The most practical fuel for use while travelling in Mexico is propane. It can be found almost anywhere and is very inexpensive. Propane is clean burning—essential if you're cooking inside a van or tent and don't want to look like a chimney sweep after every meal. Propane stoves and lamps are easier to maintain than other types and cheaper to repair when they do fail. Standard fittings for American made equipment are available at most propane stations.

Gasoline fueled stoves and lamps are undoubtedly the most common type in the U.S. However, white gas is expensive in Mexico and is a hassle to locate. Many campers burn unleaded (*Extra*) gasoline in their stoves and lamps. (See *Driving: Gas Stations* and *Services: Fuels.*) Though it stinks and gives a yellower, dirtier flame, it does work. This is hard on the generator so carry spares. They are easy to sell to other campers if you don't need them yourself.

Any equipment fueled by non-refillable cylinders, cans, cartridges, pellets or batteries is impractical for more than weekend camping. It belongs in the attic with electric socks, waterbeds and folding bathtubs.

Kerosene fueled camping and backpacking stoves are not cheap but they have many advantages: kerosene is very inexpensive in Mexico (and almost all of Latin America), easy to locate and not as dangerous as gasoline. Kerosene stoves and lamps are sold in Mexico but are not designed for travellers' hard use and constant knocks. Parts for Aladdin lamps are not available.

A TRAVELLING KITCHEN

Cooking isn't as easy on the road as it is at home. Eating well while travelling is very important and your cooking equipment should be selected with great care. By assembling your kitchen from your own home or long in advance from friends and junk stores, you will have utensils that you know and understand. You should like your cooking equipment and it should cooperate and fit together.

Our nomadic way of life requires us to carry most of what we need for easy, enjoyable living. Whether we're travelling by van, bus or hitchhiking, we prefer to do as much of our own cooking as possible. This saves money, increases our independence, cuts down on cases of indigestion and allows us to follow a more stable diet.

Few of our things go unused for long, no matter if we're in Quintana Roo or the Pacific Northwest. The following list reflects our own cooking and eating eccentricities, from Lorena's vegetarianism to my love for all things edible. Consider it as a model or a suggestion but never cease to evaluate each part of your own kitchen—old and new—with the idea of simplifying and improving what you use.

This list, or part of it, should cover everything from renting a house for six months to camping on the beach. When selecting what you'll need, use this rule of thumb: *when in doubt don't take it*. If you later decide that you need something and can't find it in Mexico, just put it on the list for the next trip.

Note: if you're a backpacker, boater or camper see *The People's Guide To Camping In Mexico* for a lot more on kitchen gear, cooking and food, including the *Suitcase Kitchen*.

plates
bowls
cups
forks (hard to find, take plenty)
spoons
table knives

pressure cooker
large skillet or dutch oven
small skillet
large kettle
medium saucepans (2)

butcher knife
paring knife
spatula
unbreakable juice container
assorted unbreakable food containers with lids
unbreakable egg containers

food mill
beating whip
small funnel
measuring spoons

measuring cup
small strainer
combination type can-opener
cutting board
pot holders

coffee pot
tea bob
vacuum bottle
old towels
cup hooks
liquid soap
dish pan or bucket

scouring pads
aluminum foil
wax paper
Baggies
paper plates

potato peeler
grater

fire grate
folding barbecue grill
blender
electric frypan
toaster
electric mixer
extension cord

Buy In Mexico:

bean and potato masher
juice squeezer
lime squeezer

fire fan
shopping bag
baskets (for food storage)

casserole dish
bean pot
salad bowl
wooden spoons and stirring paddles
tortilla press
milk can
mortar and pestle (for grinding bulk spices and making sauces)
comal

DISCUSSION

Pressure Cooker: A pressure cooker cooks things very fast. This reduces your work in the kitchen and saves fuel. (As an additional bonus, the food tastes better and is more nutritious.) Consider how you'd feel about cooking brown rice (45 minutes) after ten or twelve hours of driving. A pressure cooker will do it in a fraction of that time. Beef stew takes just 15 minutes and even Mexican beef will come out tender.

Food Mill: A food mill will help you convert those wonderful fresh fruits and vegetables into juices, stews, soups, purées and sauces. They are available in Mexico (as shown) for a few dollars. Junk stores and garage sales are the best place to find food mills and pressure cookers in the U.S.

Juice Container: Buying fresh juices 'to go' is quite common. A wide-mouth container is easiest to fill and clean. The lid should be leak-proof, even when the container is upside-down.

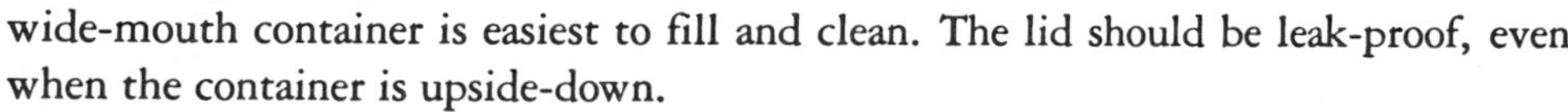

Egg Containers: Since eggs are sold loose or in flimsy plastic bags, you'll probably follow our example and break two per dozen before they're used. The neat collapsible wire egg baskets sold in Mexico aren't suitable for rough roads and casual handling, so buy unbreakable plastic egg cartons before you leave.

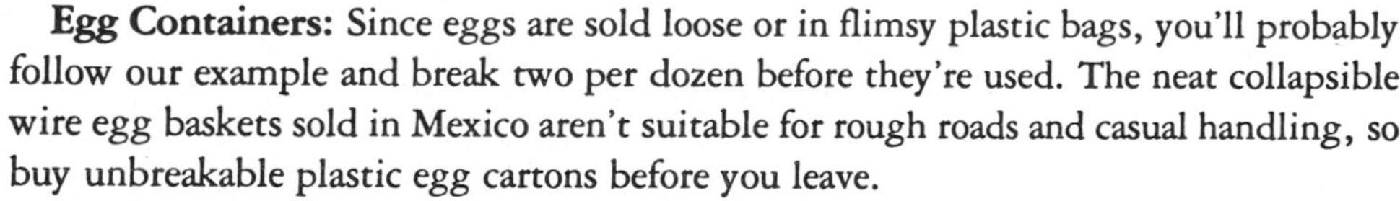

Aluminum Foil, Paper Plates, etc.: These are things that you should learn to do without by the time they're used up, but are nice to have until they're gone. A large package of very cheap paper plates is equal to a mountain of regular dirty plates and quite a bit of dish water. These are available in Mexico but you might as well have a stock on hand.

Old Towels: People love to give away old towels and they have a multitude of uses, from washing the windshield to blowing your nose.

Cup Hooks: For hanging things from posts and trees, especially while camped in sand, and for houses and huts not equipped with shelves.

Liquid Soap: Easier to handle than powdered soap and gives better results in salt water. Biodegradable liquid soaps are sold in health food stores, outdoor equipment shops and some supermarkets in the U.S.

Dishpan or Bucket: For washing dishes, clothes, yourself, the car, boiling lobsters, mixing adobe, etc. An aluminum bucket is not only very light but can be used to cook in. Galvanized buckets can leach dangerous substances and should not be used for food.

Fire Grate: The type with folding legs almost makes cooking over an open fire easy. Longer grates are best; a short one is difficult to use over a large fire.

Folding Barbecue Grill: Essential for grilling fish and meat over open fires. They are available in Mexico, but the heavier long-handled types sold in the U.S. are well worth the extra money. To clean the grill after use, scorch off any excess fat and then beat it against a tree or car bumper.

Blender, Frypan, Electric Mixer, etc.: If you plan on staying in trailer parks or want to rent a place, a few lightweight electric appliances can be very handy. Most are available used and are very inexpensive in the U.S. They make wonderful gifts or trade goods; because of high import duties, these same items are very expensive in Mexico, even well-used. Take a good extension cord along.

Juice Squeezer: Although juice squeezers can sometimes be found in junk stores in the U.S., they are much more common in Mexico.

Milk Can: A large milk can makes a great water jug and a good gift when you return home.

Comal: These round flat pans of pottery or metal are used for cooking *tortillas*. The metal type makes a good griddle for campfire cooking—fish, hotcakes, toast, etc. A *comal* is also handy for roasting chilies and tomatoes before peeling, and for reheating *tortillas*.

FOOD FROM HOME

What do you do when you're preparing your favorite dish, *Hin Nu Hwe*, in the middle of the highlands of Chiapas and there is not a spot of anchovy paste to be found? The answer is that you'd better have planned ahead and taken a supply from home.

If special foods (sugar or salt-free, etc.) or health foods are an irreplaceable part of your diet, consult a doctor or your favorite store for advice on what to take with you.

The following list, with the exception of pet food, represents what we consider important for our own varied and happy eating. Although we have located almost all the items during our travels in Mexico, none were common and many were very expensive.

See *Markets and Stores*, and *Cooking in Mexico* for more ideas.

Dried baking yeast	Scarce. Live yeast is sold by some *panaderías* (bakeries) and health food stores in larger cities.
Brewer's yeast	Available in some drugstores and health food stores but expensive and not very tasty.
Brown rice	Very hard to locate. You can easily sell or give away any extra you might have to people who didn't read this.

Dried fruit	Most are imported from California and expensive.
Herbs	Special herbs, such as golden seal and ginseng, are available only in a few places, if at all.
Mung beans, alfalfa seeds	Mung beans are seldom available and Mexican alfalfa seeds are almost always chemically treated for planting and should not be eaten. Lentils can be sprouted and they are common.
Olive oil	Much more expensive but good.
Peanut butter	More expensive and poor quality.
Pet food	Expensive.
Sesame oil	The concentrated type used for oriental cooking is not available, but regular *aceite de ajonjolí* is very common and good.
Sourdough starter	Not available. A few packages can be stretched out. Mexicans prefer sweet bread but most of them are pleasantly amazed at the taste of sourdough.
Soy sauce	We always take a good supply. Available but very expensive and of mediocre quality.
Spices	Those sold in bottles in the U.S. are very convenient for travelling. They are expensive in Mexico but you can refill your containers there with inexpensive fresh bulk spices as you find them. Bring ginger root if you use it.
Teas	Exotic teas (Chinese, Indian, etc.) are rare. Herb teas are available everywhere.
Vitamins	Not available at discount prices but otherwise easy to locate. One of the few pharmaceutical products that is not considerably cheaper than in the U.S.
Wheat germ	Found in some supermarkets.
Yogurt starter (dry)	Fresh yogurt is hard to keep while on the road.

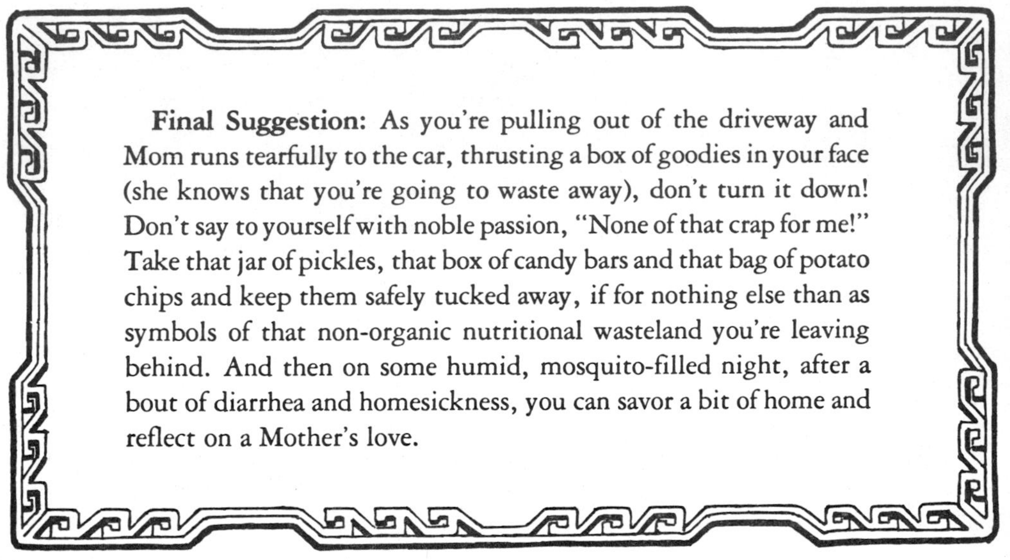

Final Suggestion: As you're pulling out of the driveway and Mom runs tearfully to the car, thrusting a box of goodies in your face (she knows that you're going to waste away), don't turn it down! Don't say to yourself with noble passion, "None of that crap for me!" Take that jar of pickles, that box of candy bars and that bag of potato chips and keep them safely tucked away, if for nothing else than as symbols of that non-organic nutritional wasteland you're leaving behind. And then on some humid, mosquito-filled night, after a bout of diarrhea and homesickness, you can savor a bit of home and reflect on a Mother's love.

ODDS AND ENDS

After having hauled unbelievable amounts of junk and nonessential weight to and from Mexico and Central America, we offer these sincere words of advice: Don't take anything that you aren't willing to give away, lose, sell cheap, carry in and out of Customs, explain the function of innumerable times, and pack and unpack continually.

If you're now thinking to yourself, "Well, hell! *Nothing* I have can pass that test!" you are on your way to travelling light.

In the fall of 1969, as we began the slow trip from Seattle to the Mexican border, we frequently heard the following type of comments when we stopped for gas or to visit friends.

"Moving out, huh?"

"What have you got in there, anyway?"

"Going homesteading?"

"Hey, you got a low tire."

After looks of amazement when they heard that we were headed for Mexico, there would be an inevitable, "Do you think you'll make it?"

When one wise gas station attendant asked, "Do you really need all of that stuff?" I immediately leaped to our defense, pointing out to him that in order to have a fully enjoyable trip it was necessary to anticipate *everything*.

"That's what the boat is for," I elaborated. "We decided we couldn't really enjoy diving and fishing without a boat."

"Well, what's that other crap?" he asked. "Don't all look like a boat to me."

I surveyed the top of our VW van, swathed in tarps and criss-crossed with a profusion of rope, bulging three feet over the roof rack.

"No, of course not," I agreed. "That lump there," and I pointed to a corner of old rug showing beneath a tarp, "is the outboard motor."

"Outboard! What the hell for?"

"The boat we have is inflatable, but we decided that with diving gear and our weight too, we'd need a motor to move it." I then went on to explain that after buying the motor, we realized that we'd need even more fishing and diving equipment to take full advantage of the boat. "So that bump," I indicated, "is the spearguns and fishing pole package and that sea bag is full of diving gear."

He looked at the huge mound in disbelief. "What are those boxes?"

"Oh yeah!" I coughed to cover a slight embarrassment. "The grey one has the extra food and the yellow case is full of spices. Those green things are stoves."

"Stoves?" he asked, barely concealing a growing sneer of amusement.

"Well, you see," I began lamely, "Steve felt that two stoves were necessary. He gets nervous without at least four burners to cook on."

"Oh, of course!" he agreed. "I can really see his point!" and with a final "Good luck!" he went back to pumping gas.

I stood by the car as Steve checked the tires for the hundredth time, wondering if we really were going to make it. I hadn't had time to point out the rest of the essentials we were going to be so glad we brought: "Let's see, there's still the tent, two gas cans, tackle boxes, water jugs and extra clothes on the roof." I peered into the back window: "Books (about 175), paint set, jewelry-making kit, air mattresses, typewriter, two gasoline lamps, more food and clothes, blankets, two turkeys (cooked, from relatives), half a gallon of whiskey..." I gave up and decided to cut down on weight by having a turkey sandwich and savoring a little booze.

Everything, except one stove, 150 books and the typewriter—profitably traded for a large *Mayan* drum—returned with us to Seattle several months later. The engine in the van, however, suffered a fatal stroke and remained in Mexico.

We now keep our Odds and Ends to a closely supervised minimum. We miss some of it, especially the boat and motor, but we don't miss the hassles involved from overloading.

If you are the fortunate person whose imagination can leap ahead to the havoc and chaos that may result from unrestrained and indiscriminate gathering of junk, you'll be able to use the following list properly: as a list of *possible things to select from*, not as a blanket suggestion to take it all. Although most of the items listed will fit into a carton box, don't take anything that won't be used.

Think ahead carefully to what you intend to do on your trip. If you want to skin dive, take only the basic equipment; chances are you'll find much to divert you from your original plans. *Don't let your trip be planned by your possessions.*

boat
bicycle or motorbike
diving gear
fishing equipment
art supplies
photographic film (take plenty, most people don't)
maps
first aid kit (see *Health*)

hammer
saws (hand saw, firewood saw, hacksaw)
nails
hatchet
crowbar
chisel
hand drill and bits
folding shovel
*sharpening stone
*machete
*rope
*twine
light tarp
baling wire
electrical wire
solder, flux
electrical tape
propane torch
assorted nuts, bolts, screws
epoxy glue
Elmer's glue
liquid wrench
rust preventive oil (WD-40)

knapsack
canteen
whisk broom
*wash basin
*mirror
water can with sprinkler head (for shower, see *Services: Bathing*)

cigarette papers
guitar strings
playing cards
checker set
Frisbee
volley ball, soccer ball
picture book
English instruction book

Gifts and Trade Goods:

clothing
toys
tools
flashlights
radios
cameras
ballpoint pens
picture postcards
seeds

DISCUSSION

Diving and Fishing Gear: Water sports equipment is just beginning to be manufactured in Mexico and it is available on a very limited basis. Larger beach towns usually have at least one store (often a hardware shop) that stocks fins, masks and the odd snorkel or speargun. The fins are adequate but the masks and snorkels are of poor quality

*Items marked with an asterisk are easily found in Mexico. Most of the things on this list can be bought in Mexico, but in general they're cheaper in the U.S. or easier to find.

and expensive. Spearguns are usually very expensive though of good quality. Mexican commerical divers prefer the French *Champion*, a real workhorse gun.

Many tourists sell their diving gear for one reason or another and hotels where younger travellers hang out are good places to find bargains.

Scuba gear can be rented in tourist towns and the same shops will offer diving tours. I've never taken a tour, but I've looked at their gear and it seemed to be of good quality. Air stations are scarce; once again the tour and rental people will be the only consistent source.

Mexican fishing equipment runs heavily to the basic hook, line and sinker, with perhaps an oversized swivel and a feather jig for the real aficionado. Rods and reels are prohibitively expensive. Lures are sold but almost entirely for heavy gear and big fish. A wire leader kit is good to have, especially if you prefer braided wire over single strand, the Mexican standard.

See *Appendices: Fishing and Diving* for more details.

Maps: see *Apendices: Maps.*

Hammer, Saws, Folding Shovel, Machete, etc.: These tools will not only be invaluable for camp construction projects but useful as well for repairing your car, digging it out of sand and mires, setting up a tent, hanging hammocks, cutting firewood and making adobe.

Regular hand saws are best for building things, but a folding wood cutting saw (Swede saw) is handy for firewood. Hacksaws are indispensible for jury-rigged repairs on cars and spearguns.

A sharp, three sided file is another valuable tool for repairs and for sharpening spearheads, knives and *machetes*.

Electrical Wire, Solder, Propane Torch, Tape, Anti-Rust Oil, Glue, etc.: With these miscellaneous items you can, and will very likely have to, perform miracles of improvisation and repair. They will be invaluable for lashing your car back together if it tends to loosen up on poor roads. (See *Preparing Your Car.*)

People in isolated areas believe that gringos can fix anything. You can often help them out by providing a few basic tools and parts that few of them can afford. In one day I was asked to repair a watch, solder two radios and analyze a couple of strange rocks. The watch and rocks were beyond me, but I fixed the radios by heating a nail with a propane torch and using it as a soldering iron. The solder was scraped from the seam of a milk can.

In payment for this simple job, we were given coconuts, *tortillas*, a sack of tomatoes and a large fish. We were also treated to several hours of blaring static-filled rock and roll music by the pleased owners of the radios.

A propane torch (non-refillable cylinder type) will last a long time if used sparingly.

Rust preventive oil is very important for lubricating metal that has been exposed to salt water and salt spray.

Knapsack and Canteen: Even if you're not a hiking nut, you may find a cheap knapsack and canteen very handy items for beachcombing or walking into the nearest village for supplies. Once camp is set up, it is often easier to walk or hitch a ride than to unearth your car.

Whisk Broom: For cleaning the car before crossing borders or between your toes before going to bed.

Mirror: Combing your hair or shaving in the rearview mirror of your car can be a drag. Get a small mirror that will hang on a nail. If you don't have a close friend along, you may also need a mirror to check your ass for ticks. Don't laugh...

Playing Cards and Checker Set: If you enjoy cultivating the friendship of people who might visit your camp or home, a deck of cards or game of checkers is a great way to establish communication. The Mexican checker game is considerably more difficult than ours, though the board is identical.

Frisbee or Soccer Ball: When you stop in the middle of some strung-out village and a huge crowd forms around your car, staring into windows and upsetting the more nervous members of your group, it is time for a diversion. A Frisbee or soccer ball will keep a lot of kids busy who were previously standing on the car hood driving your dog into fits. If you can afford it, bring extra Frisbees or balls to give away; they will be greatly appreciated. You might like to give them to the schoolteacher, priest or some village official to avoid jealousy.

Picture Book: This is a great thing to have when people ask questions about your home country. In the same day, two *campesinos* (country people) asked me, "Do the waves look the same in California as they do here?"

English Instruction Book: If you enjoy casual teaching, or if you meet a person who really wants to learn English, an instruction book is good to have.

GIFTS AND TRADE GOODS

When someone helps dig your car out of a sand trap or offers to give you Spanish lessons and refuses payment, it's nice to have something that can be offered in return.

Many Mexicans, especially those living outside the cities, still operate on a bartering and trading economy rather than cash. The person who refuses to accept money, either out of pride or generosity, will usually be delighted with a simple gift.

Clothing, toys and tools are always appreciated. We usually stuff a seabag with clothing donated by friends and family and either give it to someone to distribute for us (a teacher, priest or someone who knows who needs it) or offer it to those who look as though they could use it. Warm clothing is especially needed by poorer people.

Any toy, no matter now cheap or simple (and preferably durable) will delight some kid. Many poor children have no toys at all and a doll or rubber ball will become a treasure.

Tools, especially such basic things as hammers, pliers, chisels, screwdrivers, saws, scissors, adjustable wrenches, files and hacksaws are expensive in Mexico and of poor quality. They are excellent trade goods for small repair jobs; most Mexican mechanics will gladly exchange labor for tools.

Flashlights and transistor radios, if they work at all or can be repaired, are very good gifts. We usually look for them at garage sales and in attics.

Pens and pencils are appreciated by both children and adults, and color crayons and coloring books will delight them all.

Picture postcards, especially if they show cities, mountains, snow or farm animals are great for answering questions about what your home country is like. *Campesinos* love postcards showing prize animals and produce from county fairs.

Seeds, both vegetable and flower, are perfect traveller's gifts; they're light, inexpensive (buy at end of season) and greatly appreciated. Take practical rather than exotic vegetable seeds or the produce may go to waste; Mexicans are very traditional in their eating habits and reluctant to try new things.

Joshua cactus

NOTES

PREPARING YOUR CAR

Servicing and spare parts...Tools...Tires and tubes...Buying a car...Living in it: vans, campers, motor homes, school buses...Do-It-Yourself camper...Woody and Sonny go shell collecting...

●●●

Many people start off with no preparations at all, just as if they were driving to the corner store for a six-pack. If you're going to keep to the main roads and avoid punishing your car too much, you'll be OK. Mexico, after all, is a modern country. People who load up several spare tires, extra gas cans and paint "Mexico City or bust!" on the trunk just aren't with it.

First of all, take care of obvious repairs and servicing. It's easy to put off fixing a slight leak in the radiator because it was never much of a problem when you were driving short distances around home. On the road, however, when you're driving hundreds of miles a day, stopping every 50 miles to locate water and cool an overheated engine will be a real hassle.

For any car and for any trip, no matter how long it will be or where it will take you, I suggest the following basic precautions:

SERVICING AND SPARE PARTS

Complete tune-up and lubrication.
Check:

- tires
- brakes
- battery
- cooling system (clean air-cooled engines)
- steering, front end and suspension
- horn—you'll need it

headlights
windshield wipers

- A slight fender-bender accident will lead to much more trouble and expense than any safety precautions might cost you. Install, if possible:

    driving lights (replace VW headlights with *Lucas Quartz Iodide bulbs*)
    driving mirrors

- Labor is cheap in Mexico but parts—including tires, tubes and batteries—are not. (See *Car Repairs*.)

Spare parts:

tire
fan belt (be sure it's the right size)
motor oil (See *Driving: Gas Stations*)
oil filter (odd sizes are hard to find)
in-line gas filter
fuses
flare or reflector
repair manual (or jot down settings for plugs, points and valves)

Tools:

large, medium and small standard screwdrivers
medium Phillips screwdriver
vice-grip pliers
regular pliers
open-end wrenches
10-inch crescent wrench
jack and lug wrench
tire pressure gauge
electrical tape and wire
baling wire

- Driving conditions and roads are less than ideal in back areas. (See *Driving*.) If you're the type of person who doesn't care where you go or where you end up, more preparations for your car are advisable.

Tires: install tubes, even in new tubeless tires. Mexico is the land of the slow leak. Back roads are murder on steel radials.
Oil: enough to fill the crankcase.

Gas: a one-gallon can is sufficient. Never pass up an opportunity to top off your tank when driving in the boondocks.

Water: for drinking and filling the radiator.

Tire pump: someone else will need it if you don't.

Tube patch kit: for those awful multiple flats in the middle of nowhere.

Set of plugs, points, and condenser and feeler gauge for setting them and the valves.

Iron pipe or crowbar: for breaking loose jammed lug nuts, prying bent bumpers or for beating on the hood of your car out of frustration.

Folding shovel: to dig out of sand and muck.

Chain or heavy rope: for towing or being towed.

Booze: to offer people who help you out.

Books: to pass the time—hours or days, depending on how far off the main road you managed to get—while waiting for help or parts.

If you are the owner of a Kaiser, Edsel, Ferrari or other such off-beat, weird or very expensive car, you might be wondering what lies ahead. Since you are probably experiencing difficulty finding parts and reliable service for your car in the U.S., you are correct in assuming that the situation won't be any better in Mexico.

The following types of vehicles can be more than normal hassle if you need parts or major servicing: anything old, long out of production or of a limited production and distribution; most foreign sports cars or uncommon foreign cars of any type; high performance cars and motorcycles; and American luxury cars.

You may have problems finding parts for English cars, including Land Rovers, as well as Volvos, Saabs and Toyotas. Service and parts for many foreign cars, such as Datsun, Opel, Mercedes and Renault, however, are relatively easy to find.

Volkswagens are manufactured in Mexico and very popular. You should have no trouble finding service and parts in almost all areas of the country. Standard American cars, such as Ford, Chevrolet and Dodge are also common, though parts for very old and very new models may be difficult to locate outside of the largest cities.

Don't get discouraged. The one thing that can save you and your '39 Mercury is the unlimited ingenuity of the Mexican mechanic. Given enough time and motivation—usually money but sometimes just the challenge—he will figure something out.

Almost anything can be found in Mexico City if one looks long and hard enough and, if worse comes to worst, the part can always be ordered from your car's mother country.

If your vehicle or trailer has odd sized tires, you'll be lucky to locate replacements. Small trailer tires, 17" tires of the type used on many milk vans and 15" split rim truck tires are all scarce. Almost all Mexican pick-up trucks use 16" tires.

BUYING A CAR

When buying a car you should carefully consider operating expenses, ease and availability of service, and cost of repairs and parts. Repairs to large vehicles inevitably involve large bills, especially if parts are difficult to locate, which will be the case with many off-brand delivery vans and old buses.

Check tires closely, especially on a school bus or delivery van. If it hasn't been driven recently, the tires are probably worse than they look and will go to pieces or wear quickly when you suddenly start doing hundreds of miles a day on them.

Look at a map and figure approximately how many miles you'll be travelling, *at a minimum*. Compute gas consumption (see *Appendices: Prices*) and you'll have a good idea of how far you can go for your money. It cost us at least twice as much to operate a pick-up truck as it did our VW van. This can mean the difference between a short trip or a long trip if your money is limited.

Many of the newer model U.S. compact vans have large engines and are designed for freeway speeds (at least they are capable of them). However, transmissions that are geared too high for crawling up steep grades or over-powered vehicles with poor traction often run into trouble on back roads. This applies not only to towing a trailer but also to the fancy eight cylinder 'sport van' that easily does 120 mph on the freeway but can't gear down to 5 mph to hump over a large rock.

When considering buying an American van, remember that it was probably designed originally as a delivery wagon for use in town, not for travel on murderous back roads. American vans are often spot-welded together and go to pieces quickly when subjected to prolonged bouncing and pounding. Door hinges may not work quite so smoothly after a few thousand miles on the road and annoying rattles are inevitable.

Stick with a six cylinder engine unless you're a drag-racing fan; the economy difference between six and eight cylinders will be considerable. A standard shift plus heavy duty shocks and suspension are also advisable.

We have found that a VW, when properly serviced and given the recommended preventive maintenance, is more trouble-free and economical to run than any other van. General maintenance and servicing are not so difficult that you can't do them yourself. If you don't want to do your own work, there are VW agencies and unauthorized VW mechanics just about everywhere in the world. If something awful happens to the engine, it is reasonably easy to repair or replace. See *Car Repairs* and buy a copy of *How to Keep Your Volkswagen Alive, A Manual of Step by Step Procedures for the Compleat Idiot,* by John Muir, available from John Muir Publications, Box 613, Santa Fe, New Mexico 87501 (See *Appendices: Recommended Reading*). This book will not only tell you how to do everything to your VW yourself, but will also give you a good idea of what the mechanic should be doing if you don't care to do your own work.

The traction and clearance of a VW van are remarkable. We have driven ours over roads in Mexico which had been previously negotiated, according to local people, only by jeep-type vehicles and mules. We probably wouldn't make the same trips again, but they convinced us that our van could manage any road that we might want to attempt. Should there be anything left when you decide to sell or trade it in, the VW is noted for its high resale value.

LIVING IN IT

Selecting a vehicle that will be practical both for travelling and living requires careful thought and common sense. This applies not only to the person considering a new factory camper but also to someone with vague doubts about the practicality of taking their vintage school bus on a long trip.

What you'd like to do and where you'd like to go are the most important factors when examining the potential of a vehicle. Living arrangements can always be improvised, but if you can't drive your car or trailer to the places you'd like to see, your trip will be very frustrating.

Town driving, parking, narrow back roads and mountain curves can be a mental and physical nightmare if you're driving an extra-large vehicle. The vast majority of people who go to Mexico towing large trailers, in school buses or in self-contained motor homes are forced by the sheer physical size and difficulty of operating their vehicles to stick to the main roads.

Of the many people we've talked to who were living in such vehicles, most had the same complaints. Once they had found a good place to stay, they invariably began to feel confined by their living arrangements and began to spend a good deal of their time outside. Marketing trips or any attempt at local sightseeing were always major efforts.

Some friends equipped a school bus with all the comforts of home, drove to Mexico and parked for three months near a beautiful beach. Within a week of their arrival they had moved into a palm hut and their bus sat unused for most of their stay. The wife had made the most perceptive comment I've ever heard about travelling with such an elaborate set-up. "I don't like riding in buses," she said, "even when it's our own. For the money we've invested in gas and maintenance, we could have flown round trip and rented a palatial house here."

On the other hand, another friend drives his large school bus to the same spot every winter, parks and then uses a motorcycle to run around. He has enough propane to operate a stove and lanterns for months, plus stocks of staple foods. He uses the cycle for fresh food and water runs, trips to town for mail and general sightseeing. He starts the bus up every few days but it doesn't move again until he's ready to head for home.

Most factory camper set-ups are designed for showroom impact and mass appeal, not for long hard travelling and constant use. Appliances, parts and fittings such as stoves, water pumps, concealed water tanks, door hinges, interior lights and wiring can be almost impossible to repair or replace when and *where* they fail.

Factory campers aren't the only ones that lure you into believing that you're buying an efficient, durable and practical living arrangement. Many of the best looking home conversions have been done by people who've never spent more than a weekend at a time living in their vehicle.

A nice big over-stuffed Salvation Army chair in the back of a milk van has great appeal as you're tooling around town enjoying a beer from the home-sized refrigerator, but when you're careening down a steep mountain road, you soon regret the extra weight and the imminent possibility that you'll be crushed by your furnishings.

When selecting a used vehicle that has been converted into a camper the initial cost, if unusually low, may be a smokescreen to cover much needed and costly repairs. The smoke may be thickened by beautiful cabinet work or ingenious living quarters. Ignore superficial improvements and concentrate on examining it critically for mechanical defects.

DO-IT-YOURSELF CAMPER

Any living improvements, whether incorporated into a large bus or small van, should be kept simple. Some arrangements I've seen would boggle the mind of an Oriental puzzle maker. Complicated folding beds, seats and interlocking components require not only the most exact and careful construction but a good deal of patience and dexterity to use.

When you consider the size of an average compact van, it's rather amazing that people can travel and live in them for years at a time without going berzerk. The reason more people don't go insane is that they soon begin to live *around* their vehicle, rather than inside it. This is the key to the design of a really useable and enjoyable living arrangement in any small space.

Everything possible should be easy to remove and to use outside the vehicle. When we are travelling in a van, the interior is designed so that within minutes we can remove our food and dish cupboard, stove and icebox. This is all we need, in addition to a few folding stools and a hammock or two, to establish a comfortable camp or move into a hut or unfurnished house.

Removable units should be as light-weight as possible without being flimsy, and be able to withstand rough travel and handling without going to pieces. If building good cabinets is beyond your abilities, look for ready-made dressers, boxes, cupboards and chests in used furniture and junk stores.

Storage boxes and cabinets should be kept to a minimum. If you find yourself with an empty corner and are tempted to put some sort of storage container there, don't unless you *really* need it. The more empty space remaining after the essential things have been built in, the less confining your vehicle will seem. Remember that while in use the interior will be much more cluttered with clothing, fresh food, baskets, books and other junk than it is when neatly packed for departure.

If you've built boxes or are using apple crates for storage of miscellaneous odds and ends, you'll be able to empty a good deal of space quickly, both for cleaning and for comfort. By piling everything neatly outside, the interior can be quickly converted into a comfortable and roomy lounging area. A little leg room feels good after driving all day.

Built-in water tanks aren't worth the expense or trouble. When a hose for filling them is not available (often the case in Mexico) you'll have to do the bucket brigade trip, so you might as well start with portable jugs. Two five gallon cans should be a sufficient supply of fresh water for two or three people for a considerable length of time.

A sturdy metal-cased ice chest that can be easily removed for use outside is much more convenient than a permanently built-in one.

Don't forget to lash, bolt, or otherwise tie down all components until you are ready to take them out—or an emergency stop may send your furnishings flying.

To avoid dreading every night that you have to spend in your vehicle and to insure that you won't break down at the slightest excuse and spend money on a hotel, make the bed as comfortable as possible. This is very important. A comfortable bed will keep you from being bitchy in the morning and dead tired by noon.

The best material for a travelling mattress is two to four inch foam rubber. It should be covered to protect it from getting dirty and rancid.

When bugs or rain force you to close yourself in, you'll want as much fresh air as you can get. If your vehicle is short on windows, install a few more. Those that open will provide air to breath, in addition to light and a better view. Overhead ventilators of the type used on house trailers are a good source of air.

Some type of bug screening is essential. Rig drapes or curtains of mosquito netting over side and back doors. They should be long enough to prevent mosquitoes from crawling underneath and loose enough so that you won't punch a hole in them with a foot or elbow.

Some people prefer a rectangular canopy of mosquito netting rigged over the bed. This allows all doors and windows to be opened but without having to screen them too. The canopy arrangement, however, forces you to stay in bed when the mosquitoes are out. (This is not always an inconvenience but rather a good justification for reading, sleeping, etc.)

In many places where we've camped, bugs weren't a problem, *most of the time,* but when they decided on an attack it was merciless and all-out. This may happen during the day as well as night. A screened refuge can mean the difference between evacuating a nice campsite or holing up for a short time.

Unless you're an exhibitionist, you should have curtains on all windows or you'll be playing to standing room only audiences when camped in most areas of the country. This is especially true if you spend the night in a town, schoolyard, soccer field or other public place.

When you are sleeping by a highway, the lights of passing trucks can keep you awake with their near-lighthouse intensity. Dark curtains are especially good for blocking out unwanted headlights (and daylight too, if you enjoy an occasional *siesta*).

Curtains also protect your possessions from greedy appraisal by would-be thieves when you are not inside.

Small folding tables attached to the back and side doors of a van are much more useful than a single large table that can only be used inside. A door shelf of some sort allows you to move the stove and cooking outside.

Some counter or table surface should be easily accessible while cooking, either inside or outside. Using the stove outside may become a hassle instead of a convenience if you have to climb in and out to cut vegetables or to set down a hot pan.

All folding tables should be very sturdily supported when in use. I will never forget the full scale Chinese dinner Steve so lovingly prepared under the most unbelievable hardships. After hours of delicious anticipation, he gave the chow mein a final masterful stir. The stove, dinner and table crashed upside down on his foot. Screams and obscenities rang in our ears for weeks afterward.

Interior lights are important for reading and cooking. Lights from junked cars are inexpensive and quite easy to install.

A roof rack will help keep the inside clutter to a minimum and is an excellent way to carry all the junk you'll accumulate during the trip. At night, you can store things on top, preferably covered, that otherwise would be underfoot or sitting on the ground. This will keep them dry and out of the reach of stray dogs or curious kids.

For more ideas see *The People's Guide to Camping in Mexico.*

We were camped north of Mazatlan, enjoying the surf and conducting a full-scale van clean-up after driving almost non-stop from the Pacific Northwest. Suddenly a contingent of local police and army troops dropped in for an afternoon visit. They circulated among the campers, casually checking tourist cards and occasionally giving a car or backpack a brief search.

We had been following their approach rather apprehensively when a voice from the van parked next to us, drawled, "Well, Yeaup. Uh huh. Looks like it's 'bout time to move on down the line."

A few seconds later a figure eased out of the side doors, stretching and yawning. It was Woody, an exuberant hip-hillbilly who had pulled in next to us the evening before. Woody ran a long bony hand through his scraggly brown hair, squinting into the bright sun. As he hitched sagging Army surplus trousers over his narrow hips his partner, lounging inside, put another country classic into their powerful tape deck. Mother Maybell's quavering voice blared out to one and all. A group of California surfers camped a few hundred feet away shook their heads in disgust. Sonny remained hidden, his nose undoubtedly buried between the pages of the thick pocket book he'd been reading since they'd arrived. Both of them seemed oblivious to the ear-splitting noise of the recorder.

Woody gave another huge yawn, then suddenly bent forward, jamming his right hand into the sand beneath his bare feet. "A CLAM SHELL!" he crowed, holding it up for us all to wonder and marvel at. The shell was quickly slipped into his pocket, sagging heavily with similar treasures. He cast a sneaky look toward Sonny. They may have been buddies since childhood but Woody was taking no chances; let him find his own!

"Did you say you were moving?" Steve shouted, a look of disappointment on his face. He'd spent half the night with them drinking warm *Pacificos* and reviewing their extensive collection of country & western tapes at maximum volume. After many days of being subjected to recorded concerts of surfing songs from nearby gringo vans, Woody and Sonny's arrival had been Steve's salvation. He saw them as a cultural oasis in a teenybopper wasteland.

"Yeaup!" Woody called back, scuffing the sand in hopes of another rare find. "Me and Sonny need a little more elbow room. Too much competition 'round here. All the good shells are picked over." A tiny blond headed boy ran by, exictedly clutching half of a broken sand dollar to his chest. Woody scowled.

"Where are you headed?" Lorena asked.

"Yeah," Steve added, "We've been thinking of moving, too." He gave us quick looks.

Lorena and I just shrugged; why not? We had no particular affection for either the Mexican army or surfing music.

"Me and Sonny heard about a real good beach south of here a ways," he said, "lots of nice shells."

"Just *exactly* where?" I asked, familiar with stories of deserted beaches that in reality were lined with hotels and crammed with sunburned tourists.

"Oh, maybe a hundred miles from here," Woody answered vaguely, "give or take..."

When pressed for more definite information, he pointed to a group of people who had just returned from the beach and could give me the details. After checking the directions with them, I returned to find Steve and Lorena hastily breaking up camp.

"I've got the name of that beach," I said. "It sounds good to me."

"Great! Let's get the hell out of here as fast as we can." Steve urged.

"Looks like they're handling the heat pretty well," Lorena said, motioning toward Woody and Sonny. A crowd of slightly bewildered soldiers was gathered around their van, trying to interrogate our new friends over the mindnumbing din of the tape deck.

"You essmoke *marijuana?*" one of them shouted at Woody, ignoring the gifts of clam shells being pressed upon him. Woody gave the soldier a blank look, then turned to Sonny.

"Hey!" he yelled, "This turkey wants to know if you want to smoke some of that mary-wanna. Neat, huh?"

Sonny shook his head. He brushed this thick dark hair from his eyes and jammed his hands obstinately into the back pockets of his tattered Bermuda shorts. "Not me!" he snarled, glaring at the soldier suspiciously.

"*¡NO, GRA-CI-US!*" Woody said, grabbing the man by the shoulder and pushing him toward the open doors of the van. "Have some of this here tee-quila old buddy! It's a little rough but it does the job!" Woody thrust the bottle into the soldier's hands. He looked at it for a few seconds and then began to unscrew the cap. Loud Rebel yells pierced the air as Woody and Sonny urged him on, celebrating each swallow with a high pitched "Aieee! Aieee! Aieee!"

"You boys are all right!" Sonny laughed, passing the bottle to the next soldier with a wide toothy grin. As he raised the bottle to his lips, Sonny gave him a neighborly slap on the back, cracking the soldier's front teeth against the glass. "Here, bud, lemme put those things inside so you won't get sand in 'em!" Before they could protest Sonny grabbed their carbines and submachine guns and tossed them casually into the back of the van.

"Beats that marywanna doesn't it?" Woody laughed, handing the near empty *tequila* bottle to a stunned sargeant.

Steve grunted unhappily. "What are we going to do if Woody tells them where we're going?" he said. "At the rate they're guzzling that booze they may even decide to go with us!"

Fortunately, the soldiers soon tired of the overwhelming level of music. When the last swallow of *tequila* had been downed, they reached for their weapons. "Ya'll come back, 'ya hear?" Woody said, giving the sergeant another overly hearty slap on the shoulder. As the patrol wandered rather unsteadily toward the next group of campers, Woody flashed us a huge grin and a two-fingered peace sign.

An orderly repacking of the van was impossible; Steve kept one eye on the soldiers as he pitched our belongings into the open doors, urging us to hurry. Lorena looked at the chaotic mess and groaned.

"Ain't ya'll ready yet?" Woody yelled, leaping into the driver's seat of his van and motioning Delly, his somewhat moth-eaten terrier, onto his lap.

Lorena got into the back of the van, offering to restore some semblance of order as we drove.

"How 'bout going ahead?" Woody added, "Soon's it gets dark I have trouble seeing what's up front!"

To illustrate his point, he turned on a single dim headlight and grinned through the dirt and bug spattered windshield.

Steve decided that a brief strategy session was in order. After conferring with Woody for several minutes, he slid wearily behind the wheel. "He says would we please signal when we stop or slow down, because he only has one brake and can't stop to well. And if he has a flat," Steve continued, "would we please wait for him at the turn-off."

I thought grimly of the tubes protruding from two of Woody's tires that we laughed so hilariously over early in the afternoon. In the rush to leave he had volunteered to carry our precious stove and food box, and we had been only too eager to accept.

All went well until dark. Steve beat on the horn, blinking the headlights to frighten horses and cattle from the road, while lightly tapping the brakes to signal Woody that danger lay ahead.

But when our slow progress became unbearable, Woody would pass us recklessly, often on blind curves. After leading for a few seconds he would allow us to overtake him, then jerk into the left hand lane and drop back.

After a few of these passes, Steve became a total nervous wreck and asked Lorena, huddled in the back amidst our junk, to unearth the Emergency Booze.

He gurgled a tranquilizing mouthful and handed the bottle in my direction.

"Gaaaahh!" Steve sputtered, dropping the *tequila* in my lap and suddenly swerving into the opposing lane.

"What the hell?" I yelled, scrambling for the bottle. Could the *tequila* be so foul that Steve was having convulsions?

"Oh God!" Steve sighed, "he almost got us that time." I peered out the back window and saw the feeble candle flicker of Woody's single headlight a few scant inches from our rear end.

We drove on nervously, Steve and I with noses pressed to the windshield, peering into the darkness for unlighted trucks and livestock. The bottle made its silent rounds and the only conversation was an occasional position report from the backseat.

"He's about 50 feet back and gaining," Lorena said. Steve gunned the motor.

"OK, about a quarter of a mile," she reported a few minutes later, causing a general relaxing of tense muscles and white knuckles.

After an hour or more of relatively uneventful travel, the turn-off to the beach appeared. Steve made a dramatic sliding turn while holding the bottle between his legs.

Two or three miles later we gave a collective moan, "Oh, no! Woody and Sonny!" They weren't behind us.

Steve turned the van around and drove back as quickly as possible to the main road. We hung on as the van crashed into pot holes and bounced over ruts.

"I hate to say this," I muttered, "but I forgot to tell them where the turn-off was. Woody doesn't even know the name of the place, much less how to get there."

"What?" Steve shouted angrily. "Are you serious? They don't know?"

"Afraid not," I answered. "And from what we've seen of the way Woody drives, the only thing we can do is wait at the crossroads until he decides to start backtracking."

"*The stove*," Steve moaned, pounding the steering wheel in frustration, "I let him take my stove."

We sat at the crossroads for half an hour, then decided to continue south. Perhaps they'd had a serious breakdown or accident and we could overtake them.

After hours of driving and no sign of their van, not even a shredded tire on the side of the road, we decided to give up and wait for Woody to find us. Conversation ended with Lorena's prediction that we'd probably be there all night. Groaning miserably, we made ourselves as comfortable as possible and tried to sleep.

"Hey! Hey! Wake up!" I jerked up from a back-breaking slouch across the front seats Woody and Sonny were standing in front of our van.

"How come you didn't tell us you was stopping for the night?" Woody asked.

"We didn't just stop for the night. We've been trying to catch up to tell you the turn is back behind us. At least a 100 miles!" I added with a slight snarl.

"That's what I told ya, Grunt," Sonny said sarcastically, using Woody's endearing nickname.

"What the hell?" Woody said cheerfully, "Let's get going. We can be at the beach in time for sunrise. Get some good shells."

Steve peered into the *tequila* bottle and gauged that it would get us there, if we hurried. I took a few quick nips and recklessly volunteered to ride with Woody in order to guide him to the turn-off.

Steve looked at me sadly but didn't argue; he was too concerned with getting to the beach and safely into a hammock.

I jumped into the seat beside Woody. Delly immediately began to wash my face affectionately.

"Git down! Git down, you mutt!" Woody laughed, engaging the clutch with a tremendous lurch.

"Hold on there, Grunt!" Hold on, dang ya!" But Sonny was unable to reach a pot of coffee boiling unnoticed on the stove behind Woody's seat. With a crash and a cloud of steam, it landed on a pile of assorted junk.

"Sheeeyit!" Sonny cursed, rolling over on his strange couch-like bed in the back of the van and ignoring the dripping mess.

As we raced down the highway, Woody thumped enthusiastically on the horn in time to country and western music blaring from speakers suspended throughout the van. Sonny lit several candles perched precariously in holders glued to various parts of the interior and retreated into his book.

"What are you reading?" I yelled, hoping Woody might take the hint and turn the volume down on the tape. My head was reeling with *tequila*, gas fumes that seemed to be coming in through the floor and the thump! thump! of an electric bass.

"Russian Revolution," Sonny answered.

"Hang on!" Woody warned, hands and feet moving in a blur as he shifted madly and somehow steered through a group of wild-eyed horses.

A fat candle, still burning, landed on Sonny's chest. He flicked it onto a pile of books and clothing next to his couch. The candle snuffed itself out but Sonny didn't notice.

I looked back into the dimly lit rear area of the van. Psychedelic wall paper, huge paper flowers, strings of beads, beer signs, flickering candles and a gallery of Grand Ole Opry stars plastered the inside. The furnishings could have been lifted from Snuffy Smith's living room.

The ceiling, a strangely textured gory red-orange, caught my attention.

"Corduroy!" Woody yelled over the music, obviously pleased by my interest. "Sprayed it with Day-Glo and then fiberglassed it all over. Made quite a mess 'til I got her all finished up."

I re-examined the interior and realized that everything—ceiling, walls, doors and cabinets—were covered with a thick coat of fiberglass resin.

I turned my head away; it was just a little too much. The texture of the door next to me caught my attention. It appeared to be nothing less than a man's long-sleeved cowboy shirt fiberglassed to the door panel.

"Needs a few more coats," Woody said, noticing my stare. "Buttons fell off in Texas and the cloth is so hard that I can't seem to get 'em back on. Check this out," he said, "your friend and mine, E. Tubbs!"

I leaned over his shoulder and looked into the faces of several popular country music stars. Photos had been cut from fan magazines and glued over the instruments. Ernest Tubbs peered up at me from the speedometer, obviously the position of honor in the weird little Country Music Hall of Fame.

The decor continued over the rest of the dashboard; a nearly half inch layer of rippled and sagging fiberglass resin covered a choice selection of beer bottle labels, playing cards and photos of lesser country music stars.

"You ain't seen nothin! Watch this." Woody said, twisting together two wires that dangled beneath the dash. To his great delight a dim red light diffused through the photographs pasted over the instruments. Before I could comment on this latest marvel, he jerked the wires apart. A shower of gravel rattled under the van as we swerved onto the dangerously narrow shoulder of the highway.

"Gettin' pretty hot," he said casually. "That's how I blew out the headlights. Hey Sonny!" he yelled. "Show him the rest.!"

Without lowering his book Sonny stuck his hand into a hole in the side panel. The ceiling suddenly glowed with the flickering lights of a string of Christmas tree bulbs. Some even bubbled.

"Neat, huh?" Woody asked, his face creased by a huge smile.

"I've never seen anything quite like it, Woody," I answered sincerely, wondering what else he might have in store. Steve's comment that our new acquaintances were "out of their heads, country style" seemed to be something of an understatement.

The next surprise came in the form of a slowly plodding cow that refused to yield the right of way. As we skidded and slid from one side of the road to another, I marvelled at Woody's ability to keep the van under control, but always, it seemed on the very edge of disaster.

"Damn you, Grunt," Sonny said quietly from somewhere amidst a heap of fallen books, cookware, candles and bedding, "Gawd damn you!"

Woody chuckled, then yelled over his shoulder, "It's about time you got out of that rack! We haven't seen your scrawny neck all day!"

As Sonny attempted to restore some order to the disaster area in the rear, Woody gleefully outlined the difficulties of driving a van that had one brake, one headlight and no steering.

"No steering!" I gasped, taking a new and intense interest in the curves and abrupt shoulders of the road.

"Well," he drawled, "not exactly what you'd call 'no steering' but just *partial*. See this," he said, demonstrating what seemed to be an impossible amount of free play in the steering wheel.

"Happened up north in *Yaqui* country. Me and Sonny got lost at night out in the desert and before we knew it we'd smacked us into a big cactus. Screwed up something underneath.

Sonny chuckled from the back, amused at the thought of having no steering.

"How did you hit a cactus?" I asked. "Run off the road?"

"Oh no, we weren't on any road! We had us a load of drunk Yaqui Indians in the back and we decided to take 'em home, cross country."

"Don't worry yourself about it, Carl," Woody said, evidently noticing my drawn expression and clenched fists. "Why, it's been like this for two months and its still going, ain't it?"

My comments were cut short by the appearance of the sign for the turn-off. Several tense moments passed as Woody deftly negotiated a flying left turn into the deeply pocked road.

"Not quite as smooth as the main stem!" he shouted, his voice barely audible over an incredible metallic crashing and banging as he attempted to maintain our previous speed. "Have to slow her down a bit, got a lot of weight up there," Woody finally conceded, dropping the speed a few miles an hour.

The weight he referred to was one of the more incredible 'improvements' to his van: two rectangular steel water tanks, each with a capacity of forty-five gallons, mounted precariously on either side of the roof.

Woody had been told by well-meaning friends that drinking water was unavailable in Mexico. He had left his home in North Carolina carrying enough fresh water for a three month trip.

"Hope Steve doesn't get too far ahead of us," Woody said, futilely attempting to avoid a bone crunching series of deep holes that sent us crashing against the ceiling. I waited for the inevitable sound of a multiple blowout or broken axle.

As we hopped from rut to rut, he morbidly ticked off the remainder of the van's varied ailments, from ragged tires to burnt valves. He expected, he said, a major breakdown any minute.

"Hope she lasts a spell longer, though," Woody added thoughtfully. "Me and Sonny are down to about 30 bucks and we gotta make it home on that. Can't afford any sort of trouble."

Before I could share any gloomy predictions, we spotted Steve in the road ahead, warning us to stop by waving a flashlight.

"Whoooeee!" Woody howled, "Here we are!" A few minutes later, after doing a series of deep knee bends and push-ups, he rummaged beneath the sagging driver's seat and pulled out a battered 3 cell flashlight. The lens was badly cracked and the case had been swathed in black electrical tape. "Not much, but it'll do." he chuckled, aiming the light toward me. It glowed like a cat's eye.

"Let's go get some shells!" Woody called, pointing the flashlight at the long dark expanse of beach. The surf was tinged with a faint pinkish glow from the east; sunrise was at least an hour away. Delly leaped and barked excitedly, then threw himself onto the damp sand for a few refreshing rolls.

"What'sa matter? Feelin' a little tuckered out?"

Steve answered Woody with an exhausted wave of his hand. His head sank slowly down onto his arms, crisscrossed over the steering wheel. I staggered over to our van and began dragging my sleeping bag from the debris in the back. Lorena was collapsed across the bed, obviously well into a state of deep meditation.

Woody shook his head. "Well golleeeee!" he sighed, "Guess I'll just have to get 'em all for myself! Come on mutt!" He smacked his hand against the flashlight a few times to increase it's output.

"Well T for Texas!" Woody sang, moving off into the darkness, "and T for Tenne...THERE'S ONE!...and T for Tenneesseeeee! THERE'S ANOTHER! Golleeeee!

It took Woody ten days and often part of the nights, to fill the rooftop water tanks on his van with a tire-squashing quantity of seashells, driftwood and miscellaneous beach treasures.

"Man, the Customs people at the border are going to love that smell," I warned him.

Woody just shrugged. "That's their problem, not mine."

"Ya'll be careful now, ya hear?" Woody shouted, forcing the van into first gear. Sonny was lost somewhere in the rear, still an inch or so from the end of his book. We sadly waved goodbye to the 'country and western freaks.' Although they had two flat tires within half a mile of leaving the beach and less than 25 dollars, Woody and Sonny departed as cheerful and undaunted as ever.

Thorny Heart

DRIVING IN MEXICO

Hazards...Close encounters of the worst kind...Smerge...Flagmen...Road conditions...Speed bumps...City driving...Glorietas...At night: Don't!...Traffic Signs...Toll roads...Cops... Parking...Finding your way...Green Angels...Breakdowns... Gas stations...Steve takes us for a ride...

Driving in Mexico, as in all other parts of the world, is a constant battle for survival. Roadside crosses and shrines mark the fatal confrontations and commemorate the losers.

Many common driving hazards and annoyances found in the U.S. are also there, though usually in a slightly altered form.

The omnipresent teenager, for example, hunched birdlike behind the wheel of his 400 h.p. candy-colored, air-foiled Supercar, passes you dangerously close at 140 mph as he calmly munches a DoubleBurger and squeezes an annoying pimple.

In Mexico he's still the same basic teenager, apparently oblivious to other traffic; mesmerized by the blaring radio and the dangling ornaments that festoon mirrors and knobs. But there is one difference: he's behind the wheel of a hurtling semi-truckload of bananas. And he's passing you on a blind mountain curve. You glance over, afraid to imagine what is about to happen. He grins, flashes a peace sign and cuts you off as he swerves to miss an oncoming bus.

HAZARDS

The number and variety of driving hazards are incredible; from the ever present trucks and buses to homemade wooden carts loaded with logs, steered down precipitious mountain grades by grinning old men.

Tiny motorbikes with heavy loads (firewood, kitchen sinks, baby goats, beer cases, children) teetering dangerously on the sagging back fender appear as you roar over the crest of a hill. Relaxing country boys can be seen lying in the road, taking a little sun after a hard day's work.

And everywhere, from the coastal lowlands to the highest mountains, a constant traffic in dumb beasts—cows, pigs, horses, children and burros—parade alongside and in front of you. Nerves strain as you attempt to anticipate their next few steps, your foot poised over the brake pedal.

Low flying buzzards are a very real hazard, as are piles of drying corn, beans and chili peppers placed on the hot pavement by enterprising farmers who prefer the smooth road surface to the dusty shoulder.

As you fly around a curve and find yourself unexpectedly in the middle of a small village it seems that everyone suddenly leaps up and crosses the street, forcing you to brake madly. Pigs that haven't moved from gooey wallows for a week lurch frantically to their feet and stumble in front of the car, followed by reckless children beating them with twigs.

But of all hazards none can compare to the other driver. By American standards, many Mexican drivers are not only wild and unpredictable, they are dangerous and a threat to personal safety.

People who have travelled in foreign countries like to play a one-upmanship game about the driving conditions and dangers found in various places they've visited. The standard comment to someone totally freaked about driving in Mexico is, "If you think this is bad you should see (Beirut, Paris, Tokyo, etc.)..."

"They may be wild but they're damn good!" is another comment you'll hear about Mexican drivers. The professionals—truck and bus drivers—are undoubtedly good. But if *good driving* involves *good sense*, they are among the worst. Most would be disqualified from a destruction derby on grounds of excessive zeal and disregard for human life.

While driving you must be continually alert. To see trucks and buses pass each other on blind curves or just before the crest of a hill is not at all unusual. After witnessing and participating in innumerable near collisions between trucks, cars, buses and motorcycles, I maintain that for the majority of these 'good drivers,' it's only a matter of time.

It is dangerously easy for tourists to fall into the same driving habits they see demonstrated by other drivers. When stuck behind a slow diesel truck in a mountain pass, the temptation to follow the example of a huge bus and pass on a blind curve can be very strong. At this point, you should seriously consider what the consequences are if you don't make it. And if you decide, as many do, to play their game, you'll find that it doesn't end until you've passed them all.

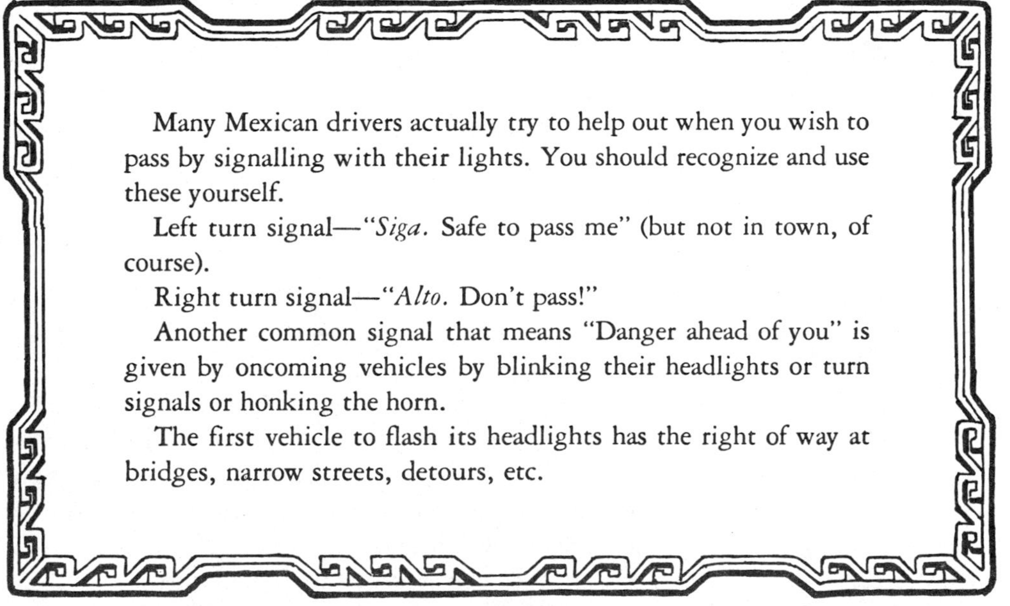

Many Mexican drivers actually try to help out when you wish to pass by signalling with their lights. You should recognize and use these yourself.

Left turn signal—"*Siga.* Safe to pass me" (but not in town, of course).

Right turn signal—"*Alto.* Don't pass!"

Another common signal that means "Danger ahead of you" is given by oncoming vehicles by blinking their headlights or turn signals or honking the horn.

The first vehicle to flash its headlights has the right of way at bridges, narrow streets, detours, etc.

Patience, as well as alertness, should be constantly maintained while driving.

A second-class bus passes you at 70, belching smoke and looking for all the world like an Express to Hell. As soon as he's around you he spots an old lady with a chicken standing on the shoulder of the road and slams on the brakes. You madly pump your brakes, but are forced by your speed to go around him. The race is on. Thirty seconds later he passes you again. In a few more minutes you pass him while he loads more bodies and inevitably he passes you within a mile. This can go on for hours.

When you're stuck behind a smelly bus or truck, the best thing is to drop back out of the exhaust cloud and open a beer. Don't let other drivers or your passengers goad you into doing something stupid.

Many sections of major highways and boulevards are not marked off into separate lanes. You will then have to join in that exciting Mexican game I call 'Smerge.' This is a nerve-tingling mixture of courtesy, cowardice and intimidation. This game is so popular, in fact, that most drivers practice it even when lanes have been marked. A friend calls this type of driving, 'Close encounters of the worst kind.'

Let's say that you're driving innocently across the desert on a two-lane highway, mindful of the buses that appear out of nowhere and roar past at high speeds. Suddenly you're close behind two large trucks. One of the trucks has broken down and is being towed to the shop. A tow bar wasn't available so the enterprising drivers got together and felled a tree. It is now lashed from the rear bumper of the front truck to the front bumper of the second. It's not too safe but they're only doing 60 miles an hour.

You move to pass this unlikely combination. When you're just about even with the first truck, the bark of a bus horn raises the hair on the back of your neck. You look nervously into the rear view mirror, but all you can see is the word 'ANID,' in huge chrome letters. That's DINA, the company that made the bus.

The driver honks insistently and begins to edge around you. Five seconds later you're the middle vehicle of 'three-abreast.' It's time to play smerge: ease very cautiously to the right—just enough to let the bus get by without forcing you into the trucks—and apply your foot ever so gently to the brake pedal. Now drop back about a quarter of a mile behind the trucks and let your pulse rate return to normal.

Mexican pedestrians are notorious for forcing cars to avoid hitting them. It is not uncommon to have people step nonchalantly in front of your car and then appear startled when you come to a screeching stop a few inches from them. The average Mexican, with no driving experience, cannot appreciate the difficulty of stopping a fast moving vehicle. Having to travel on foot, they tend to think of roads as footpaths.

Road improvements involve a whole new group of hazards: the repairs themselves. Piles of dirt, gravel and sand neatly line the highway for mile after mile. A two-lane road turns into a one-lane or a one-and-a-half-lane ordeal as you are forced off the road time after time by trucks and buses. Some neat piles have waited so long to be used that they've dissolved and weathered into lumps. These are often marked with regular road signs portraying piles of dirt.

If road repair hasn't progressed to the point of using the dirt piles, you may see large rocks, often whitewashed, placed hazardously in the roadway, apparently marking future work areas. Surveying crews mark the roads with rocks, as do paving crews, chuckhole fillers and truck drivers who've parked to eat a watermelon.

A single white rock on the crest of a hill can mean anything awaits you on the other side, from a full-scale road crew with graders and dozers to a broken down pickup truck with a dismantled engine. A rock, a stick with a rag tied to the top, a row of beer bottles—any of these can be an important warning signal.

Sections of road being attacked by full-scale repair crews can be frustrating areas to drive through. It seems that trucks and buses never move over enough to allow you to pass easily. Strange, unintelligible hand signals and flag waving from irate traffic directors may have you tearing out your hair with rage. As traffic behind you impatiently leans on the horn to speed you up, the repair crews frantically motion you to slow down.

The secret to driving through this maze is simple: go slow and keep calm.

If an oncoming vehicle refuses to yield the right of way and you know that it can, or should, it's much easier to give in quickly than to become involved in an ugly confrontation that you'll probably lose anyway.

Mexican flag signals are a complete mystery, to them and to us. A waving flag *usually* means 'keep moving': a stationary flag *usually* means 'stop.' If the flagman uses his hand(s) with the palm(s) down, pumping up and down as if giving someone artificial respiration, it means 'slow down.'

If he waves you back and you stop and then he keeps waving you back so that you back up and stop, only to have him wave you impatiently even farther back, it means 'come ahead.' One of the most confusing and most common gestures you'll run into throughout Mexico is the waving motion that would seem to mean 'go back' but instead means the exact opposite.

Confusion can become quite hysterical. You back up as you suppose you should until bumper to bumper with a semitruck. You motion him 'back' (actually forward) until he gets pissed off and inches forward. You interrupt a mutual exchange of insults and horn blarings with the truck driver long enough to check the flagman. Sure enough, he's still motioning you back, but by now frantically and assisted by half the road gang.

Someone finally runs to your car and shrieks unintelligible instructions and points—ahead! You put it in gear, shake your fist at the truck driver, and go triumphantly forward. The flagman, hoping to encourage you, begins to wave you 'back'...

What happens if worse comes to worst and you are involved in an accident? Stay calm and turn to *Tourists and The Law.*

ROAD CONDITIONS

Driving on secondary roads requires alertness and caution. The same hazards found on main highways are compounded by poorer road surfaces, which rarely slow down the other drivers.

You should be aware of weather conditions. During the rainy season (May to September in most areas) the back roads can go to pieces in hours. Dirt roads literally melt before your eyes and become rushing streams. If this happens before you get back to the pavement, you'll be stranded until things drain. At the beginning of the rainy season or after unseasonal showers, paved roads will be slick with accumulated oil.

Mudslides and falling boulders are common in the mountains, even on main highways. Fog often reduces visibility in mountain passes and is common in some lowland areas, especially early in the morning. Driving in fog in Mexico is the ultimate combination of hazards.

If you are exploring remote mountain areas and aren't driving a four-wheel drive vehicle, or something of equal capability, it is advisable to check the condition of steep grades closely before attempting them. This is true going uphill and downhill.

We and many others have had the experience of barely getting up a hill we casually drove down. On the other angle, going up, we once slid *back down* a road that we attempted without checking the grade or surface. The van refused to stop, even with the brakes locked and large rocks under the back tires. The loose surface of the road gave way beneath the car's weight and we slid a considerable distance before stopping. A drop of several hundred feet on the immediate right added drama to the situation.

Some very common year 'round conditions are real hazards, usually because they appear so rapidly. A broad, paved two-lane highway suddenly narrows to a single-lane bridge and you're faced with the uninviting prospect of playing chicken with an oncoming bus.

The Rules of the Road say that the first vehicle to flash its headlights has the right of way in such situations. But when you've given the signal and the other driver is still barreling along, you know that the real rules of the road are determined by size, speed and recklessness.

Sudden chuckholes in an otherwise good road are common on the main trucking routes, particularly on the coast where roadbeds are often soft and deteriorate rapidly in the rainy season. Bad holes are sometimes marked. But the markers (usually a large boulder or pole) are hazards themselves.

Road conditions are particularly treacherous in areas where sugar cane is grown. A friend who hit an unexpected series of deep chuckholes says he now keeps in mind that sugar cane leads to cavities in the road. Heavy truck traffic during the cane harvests raises hell with highway surfaces. These trucks, always overloaded, are hazards Most are very slow and suffering from overuse. Watch out for them.

Most Mexican roads do not have shoulders, especially those built more than a few years ago. The edge of the pavement drops six to twelve inches and may be very uneven. New roads, however, may have hazardous low curbs which prevent a safe, fast emergency exit.

In areas where seasonal rains wash out small bridges and chunks of roadway, the pavement may suddenly end, turning to a short section of dirt and rocks that will rattle your teeth and nerves. If the washout is a yearly occurrence, as many are, the road will be graded to form a *vado* (dip), allowing the high water to pass over the roadway without destroying it completely. *Vados* may be dirt or surfaced with cobblestones, pavement or cement.

Some *vados*, especially along Baja's Transpeninsular Highway, are marked with depth indicator poles. The idea is that you'll note the depth of the water and base a decision to cross or to wait on the size of your vehicle. When in doubt, wait! I know of cases where small cars (especially a good tight VW Bug) were swept away.

Often a village will tire of high speed traffic racing through town and erect one or more sets of speed bumps (*topes, tumulos, vibradores* or *boyas*) to slow things down. If the *topes* aren't marked, you may hit them fast and hard. Watch for them closely.

A friend who deliberately ignored *topes* and delighted in hitting them at a fair speed, learned his lesson one day when the impact caused the front bumper to fall off. As if that wasn't enough, the bumper was caught under the car and wreaked additional havoc.

CITY DRIVING

Driving in town can be nerve-wracking, though the speeds involved are *usually* less than those on the open highway. While you're desperately craning your neck to spot road signs, you must also watch for other cars, pedestrians, cops and legless beggars skateboarding through traffic. In town chaos seems to reign. People ignore traffic lights completely or only slow down slightly for them; they drive three abreast in streets clearly marked as two-lane; and there seems to be no control over right-of-way at cross streets.

What do you do in a situation like this? The best procedure is to *drive slowly* and keep your eyes on the road ahead. Let the guy behind you worry about what you're going to do, because the driver ahead of you is the most dangerous (and he's not paying attention to you, either). Unexpected stops for double-parked cars, jay walkers and slow carts are common.

Don't let other drivers sweep you up in their lemming-like enthusiasm for speed and reckless lane changing. When you get in a good lane, stay there until you're certain that you have to turn or move over.

At cross streets and intersections not controlled by traffic lights or police, assume that you *don't* have the right-of-way. This doesn't mean that you have to stop, just decrease your speed a bit and look in all directions. Even if you have the right-of-way, it may not be recognized by your opponents.

If an intersection is regulated by a cop the position of his body will determine right-of-way. Facing you or with his back to you means 'Stop!'; when he is sideways to you, it means 'Go!'

The *glorieta* (traffic circle) is one of the more confusing and nerve-straining aspects of driving in larger cities. It is essentially a circular 'free zone' established around a grotesque statue or fountain. Several streets feed into the traffic pattern that is wheeling around the circle. When you spot a street that you'd like to exit to, you merely shoot through traffic and are on your way. Unless, however, you ignore the cars speeding around you and nail one as you try to break out of orbit.

Should you get confused in a *glorieta*, grab the inner lane and maintain an orbiting pattern until you've figured out what the hell is going on. Have another beer and observe the traffic; eventually you'll get the hang of it. The nice feature of the traffic circle is that it allows you to make a few reconnaissance loops if you aren't sure which street to take.

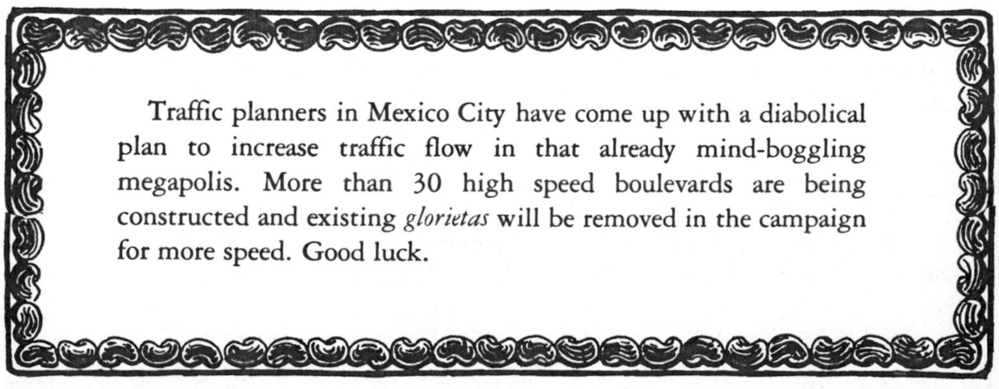

Traffic planners in Mexico City have come up with a diabolical plan to increase traffic flow in that already mind-boggling megapolis. More than 30 high speed boulevards are being constructed and existing *glorietas* will be removed in the campaign for more speed. Good luck.

NIGHT DRIVING

Anyone with any sense who has driven more than a few weeks in Mexico will tell you that driving at night is stupid, insane and downright suicidal.

Stories of cows and horses in the road don't seem to justify the intensity of the warnings so you find yourself incined to say, "I'll try it for myself." And you probably should. But remember, the basis of the entire 'don't drive at night' scare is that all of the hazards you'll encounter during the day will still be there at night but they'll be much harder to see. (Because of the heat retained by asphalt roads, livestock and wild beasts are drawn to them at night for warmth.)

Unless you have good night vision, quick reflexes and an important appointment, leave night driving to those who do.

Mexicans often deliberately drive at night without lights. The logic behind this, or so I've been told, is that they can see better without the glare of headlights. They can see, for example, the lights of oncoming cars, especially over hills and around mountain curves. This doesn't work quite so well, however, if two oncoming vehicles are both doing it.

When headlights are used it's invariably on highbeam, which they won't dim until the last moment, if at all.

Night driving on the outskirts of cities and even villages is especially hazardous due to the concentration and variety of traffic there.

TRAFFIC SIGNS

Traffic control signs, such as speed limit signs, stop signs and yield right-of-way signs, are open to liberal interpretation by the driver.

Once you've mastered the decimal system and realize that a kilometer per hour is just six-tenths of a mile per hour, you'll be perplexed by Mexico's low speed limits. No one seems to take these signs seriously and speeds are determined strictly by the driver and the limits of the vehicle. Eighty kilometers per hour (50 mph) is the usual speed limit for a good two-lane highway where the average truck is doing 70 mph and cars are going just as fast or faster. The best toll highways have top speed limits of 110 kph (about 70 mph) and secondary roads often have speed limits as low as 25 to 35 kph (15 to 20 mph).

There is a campaign in Mexico to get drivers to slow down to 95 kph (60 mph). It's called *95 Y VIVE!* It remains to be seen if '95 and Live!' will overcome the 'Floorboard it and pray!' attitude most people seem to drive by.

Similarly, stop signs (*ALTO*) will appear in the most unlikely places and may be completely ignored by traffic,. Stop signs which appear to have no logical reason for being where they are can usually be taken to mean 'caution.' For the driver conditioned to the much more rigid traffic laws of the U.S., casually running a stop sign can be a traumatic experience. If this is the case, it is best to obey all signs, at least until the feelings of guilt have subsided.

Yield right-of-way signs, *ceda el paso*, should read 'someone yield...' because you're mistaken if you think that a fast moving semitruck is going to let a little VW and a tiny sign stop him.

Remember that the laws of the highway are made by the drivers and there's no one to complain to if you feel that you've been wronged. (See *Appendices* for translations of other traffic signs.)

CIRCULÀCION

One Way Street

Traffic arrows: These are commonly posted on buildings to indicate traffic flow and right-of-way. They are equivalent to traffic lights, though some Mexican drivers take them casually. General rules for traffic arrows are:

A red arrow facing you means *stop*; a green arrow, *go*.

The direction in which the arrow points is the direction in which traffic may flow.

A two-headed arrow means *two-way traffic.*

The designations *Transito, Circulación* (both mean Traffic) and *Preferencia* (through traffic) written on a traffic arrow also determine right-of-way. These designations, in combination with red, green and double arrows are confusing and other drivers interpret them to their own advantage. Until you're accustomed to driving in Mexico, it's best to assume that you must stop or slow down at all dubious intersections.

TOLL ROADS

Toll highways have been built around Mexico City to facilitate traffic flow to neighboring cities. These highways are good but they are not cheap and they often bypass interesting villages and scenery. Toll roads are also appearing in other parts of the country, especially in industrial cities and major tourist areas.

Though the proper name for a toll road is *autopista*, everyone actually calls them *cuotas* (tolls). After you've paid several you'll understand why. In a VW the toll costs as much as the gas, doubling expenses on these roads.

When approaching an *autopista*, you'll have a choice of going *cuota* (toll) or *libre* (free). Both roads may run very close together but in most cases the *libre* road will follow a more circuitous route.

There are advantages to toll roads, even for people who don't want to miss the scenery (or the *pesos*). Toll roads are usually fenced, preventing livestock from wandering onto the highway. This is very helpful when driving at night. The road surface tends to be better (though some of the two-lane 'freeways' are just regular roads with toll booths), and there are few or no intersections. All of these factors contribute greatly to driving safety.

The toll rates are clearly posted. After paying the attendant, watch the electric sign in the booth; it will record your toll in lighted numbers.

Warning: Many of the most heavily travelled freeways leading in and out of the capital pass through areas that are plagued by fog. If you see a flashing sign (most toll booths have them) that says *MANEJE DESPACIO NEBLINA* (Drive Slow, Fog) take it seriously. Be on your toes for other drivers who do not heed the warnings.

COPS

One of the greatest driving 'hazards' on highways in the United States is the all too familiar flashing red light in the rear view mirror and the icy smile of a seven foot cop as he slips a fresh carbon paper into his ticket book. Mexico seems to rely principally on the Law of Averages and the Grim Reaper to control drivers on its highways.

You will rarely see a police car on the highway that is there for the purpose of enforcing traffic laws. When not escorting dignitaries, highway patrolmen are almost always found parked beneath large shade trees, reading comic books or gossiping with ice cream vendors.

Newspapers in Mexico City recently ran bitter articles damning the entire system of federal highway police for corruption and inefficiency. The papers even went so far as to suggest that they be abolished.

A survey of Mexico City's traffic cops, those using cars and motorcycles, revealed that only 40 percent of the officers had driver's licenses themselves. I'm sure that someone was immediately sent off to the printer to correct the situation.

Although speeding is acceptable on most highways, it is not considered proper in town. Watch your speed closely for both legal and personal safety. City traffic police, in contrast to the highway patrol, are annoyingly efficient.

Larger cities, especially the capital, have discovered that traffic police can literally pay their own way and 'mounted' cops are much more common. Mexico City has fleets of VW bug police cars and lots of motorcycle cops, too.

When you are stopped by city police for a minor violation, you can expect to receive a routine lecture and perhaps a fine. Either the lecture or fine, or both, may occur on the spot or at the station.

When the thought of facing the cops frightens you, there is an alternative. If you've been signalled to stop by a cop on foot, usually by tweeting a whistle, waving, yelling or pounding on your car with a nightstick, simply keep going. 'Haul-ass' as the saying goes. It's a solution that may land you in hot water if you don't pull it off, but we have tried it ourselves on occasion and it can work.

If the thought of 'resisting arrest' appalls you even more than a possible fine, the next best method is to play very dumb. Unless you speak Spanish better than 99 percent of the tourists, you won't have much trouble erecting barriers to communication. If you absolutely refuse to understand even the most obvious words, right down to the cognates (*policia, pistola,* etc.), the cop will often give up in disgust and let you off with a sneer and a wave of the hand.

If he happens to speak English, as sometimes is the case in larger cities, don't make a complete ass of yourself by speaking pig latin or imitation German. He'll look at your driver's license or license plate and figure out what is going on.

In Mexico City English-speaking cops may wear a piece of red cloth on their shoulders and then again, they may not.

The best strategy, safer than running away and more dignified than affecting deafness, was given to me by a friend who advised, "Place the burden of communication on the other person."

With a cop, do this by asking for an explanation of whatever he's doing: removing the license plates, reaching for his handcuffs or writing a ticket. The motive behind this isn't necessarily to wear down his patience but to make certain that *you know what is happening.* Don't let a cop snow you with a torrent of Spanish and then walk away with a fat 'fine' if you have no idea of what it was for. When you have to pay, at least get your money's worth and a short Spanish lesson. You may discover that he just wanted to ask if you knew his brother in Los Angeles. For more on bribes, cops and traffic accidents see *Entering Mexico: Red Tape* and *Tourists and The Law.*

PARKING

Driving in larger cities often takes an unacceptable toll on nerves and fenders. I much prefer to park and use cabs, buses or shoe leather to get around. If you're not staying in a hotel that offers parking, look for signs that say *Estacionamiento.*

A parking lot may be as fancy as anything you'd see in the U.S., with uniformed attendants and underground parking. Or, it may be as basic as an empty dirt lot guarded by scruffy kids. Whatever it looks like, a parking lot is usually safe as long as someone is on duty. After that, especially late at night, it's just another parking space. Never leave your car unlocked, even if the attendant swears the place is absolutely secure.

Rip-offs of parked vehicles usually occur at night or on side streets in Mexico City (and on some main ones, too). The best protection against thieves is not to leave valuables in the car. When this isn't practical, keep them well out of sight.

Car mirrors, hubcaps, gas caps and radio antennas are the first to fall prey to casual rip-offs. Take them off, secure with tamper proof screws or carry spares.

Uniformed 'play cops' or 'rent-a-cops' often supervise parking on city streets. These men wear quasi official uniforms. (I've seen several wearing old Boy Scout stuff and surplus U.S. Army.) Each has their own small territory. If one of these men assists you with finding a parking space, a tip is customary. It's the way they make a living. They will also guard your car.

As you're parking a play cop or shoeshine boy may begin rapping his fist on a rear fender of your car. This rhythmic 'tap-tap, tap-tap, tap-tap,' will continue as long as it's safe for you to keep backing up. A sudden hard single tap means 'Stop!'

The reassuring call of "*¡pasa! ¡pasa!*" (Go ahead! Go ahead!) that often accompanies the fender slapping has led to parking attendants being nicknamed *Pasapasas*.

Should you leave your vehicle unattended and return to find a rent-a-cop or enterprising kid who claims to have guarded it for you unasked, give them something for the favor. The "I didn't ask you so I don't have to pay" routine is completely unjustifiable when compared to the small sum it takes to satisfy them.

Kids, usually boys between the ages of 3 and 18, may approach in a howling mob, all making offers, warnings and pleading for guard duty. Pick a strong aggressive one, capable of at least shouting for help should it be needed. Fix his face or clothing in your mind to avoid conflicts when you return. "They looked the same so I paid them all" is a frequent complaint when trying to recall which kid actually did the job.

ILLEGAL PARKING

If your car is in an illegal zone or overparked, don't be surprised to see a cop with

screwdriver in hand removing your license plate. This ingenious substitute for the so often ignored paper parking ticket is a common method of enforcement.

Should you return to your car and find the plate missing, wait before rushing off in search of the police station until you've given the cop who removed it time enough to find you. This shouldn't be long because he'll probably be lurking nearby waiting for you. He might chew you out and make a few feeble motions toward the police station, but these can be quickly stopped by the display of money, usually not very much. If he expresses total outrage at such petty bribery, it's best to up the ante or drop the matter and go along. (This however, would be very unusual; in fact, quite remarkable).

The legal procedure for recovering the plate involves locating the police station and paying a fine. You will then receive your license plate as a 'receipt.'

There are devious ways to avoid having your plate removed. One is to fix it to the car in a more or less permanent fashion. This can be done with non-removable screws or by judicious welding. If your state issued you two plates, remove one of them and carry it inside the car. It can be displayed in the rear window if you wish.

Should your license plates expire, it doesn't matter while you're in Mexico. Don't let the cop who removed your plates squeeze you for more money because he noticed that it was out-of-date.

FINDING YOUR WAY

The Mexican government is making an effort to take some of the surprises out of driving by an admirable program that includes traffic lights and road signs. Until recently, most directional signs were cryptic, hand-lettered, phonetically spelled and hard to spot.

One could spend hours wandering through large cities with no idea where the main road was or sit perplexed at a crossroad until forced to flip a coin. Things are changing and now you'll be aided throughout your trip with a variety of handy international road signs. (See *Appendices*.)

It's off the main road where the trouble lies. It is advisable to ask for directions often, if for no other reason than to confirm that you're really going where you think you are. If you are travelling to a town some distance away—ten miles, for example—ask directions to intermediate points if you know their names. In rural areas, it's not uncommon for people to be ignorant of towns several miles away. Try to keep your questions within the range of their normal travel, usually just a few hours walk.

When a choice is possible I prefer to ask men rather than women, both for directions and information. First of all, men tend to travel far more than women (some never leave the vicinity of their villages) and are therefore more likely to be accurate about local geography. *Campesinas* (country women) are often timid of strangers and unexpected questions may well fluster them. It is not uncommon to see a look of real fear on a woman's face when confronted by a gringo spouting fractured Spanish.

When approaching anyone for information, don't just leap into the questions but give them a chance to size you up by leading off with a friendly and polite greeting. This not only relaxes the encounter but is considered very impolite if not observed.

Children are handy guides, mainly because they are so attracted to any passing traffic (especially tourists) that they usually know where it comes from and by which way it leaves. When you're faced with a choice between two roads and all of the kids are shrieking and pointing at one in particular, you'll be better off taking it rather than following your own intuition. The roads sometimes follow strange paths around obstacles that you can't possibly anticipate—fallen trees, washouts, landslides or a new house.

Asking for more detailed directions (i.e., "Where is the road to San X?") can be quite frustrating. Simplify the questions, thus simplifying the answers you'll get. Use hand signals; country people often wave their arms for a few explicit seconds when others would spend five minutes on detailed explanations.

When you think you're on the right road and headed in the right direction, simply point ahead and look at the person questioningly. If he smiles and nods his head, you're OK. If he scowls, frowns, laughs or shakes his head sadly, it is time for a more detailed question. Point in the general direction you think is correct and say, *"¿A San X?"* (To San X?). This should take care of it; he'll either say *"Sí"* or point in another dirrection.

Beware of irrelevant questions such as "How far is it to...?" Answers will be purely subjective, varying from "very close" to "very far," and will rarely be based on driving experience. A truck driver will say "three hours" and that means that if you get in his truck you'll be there in approximately three hours, which may include lunch and a siesta or just three hours of solid kidney-jolting driving. A man carrying a heavy bundle of firewood may say "two days," and you'll know that he could get there in two days with his load.

You may be tricky and ask the actual distance to the next point but five miles over a terrible road can easily become hours of travel, often not much faster than walking. And if you've asked anyone but a fellow motorist, you may get the distance by footpath, invariably shorter and more direct.

As if this isn't enough, you must be very careful in your choice of words to denote 'road.' The common translation for road that you've probably learned in high school is *camino*. But outside of the city *camino* means 'path' and is used almost exclusively for any type of trail or path that is not travelled by cars. Cars travel on the *carretera*, the 'highway,' even though this highway may be nothing more than a rutted rock-filled driver's nightmare.

The final frustration to finding your way is that usually no two answers are the same or even similar. Villages often have two (or more) names and the distance given may have been in leagues. *Leguas* (leagues) are a common unit of measure in back areas, particularly among *campesinos* (country people). A *legua* corresponds, roughly, to an hour's walk. This varies with the individual, the terrain and the load on one's back. Three to five kilometers (1.8 to 3 miles) is a rough average measure of a *legua*.

Should you ask a direction by saying, "Is this the road to La Victoria?" and the person doesn't know, he might well say, "*Sí*" rather than worry you or himself any further. This reaction may be, as some say, an effort to please you but I believe it's based on something vaguer and not so sentimental.

First of all, if you're in the back country, you have undoubtedly blown his mind by asking him anything at all. He probably doesn't completely understand the question or your strange accent, so to get rid of you he answers in a more or less positive manner. He might assume that although he's never heard of the place, it must be close or why else would you be looking for it?

Contrary to tourist bureau propaganda, not all of the picturesque Indians in Mexico enjoy being gawked at, photographed and generally treated as subjects of an anthropological field trip, with everyone waiting expectantly for them to do something 'ethnic.' Ask one of these people directions to his village and he'll possibly think to himself, "*¡Madre de Dios!* Another afternoon of quiet ritual drinking about to be ruined by these *turistas* with cameras!"

He smilingly directs you to another village; not the one you want but it'll probably do.

Maps: see *Appendices*.

GREEN ANGELS AND BREAKDOWNS

On major highways, particularly those frequently travelled by tourists, you'll see green government-operated pickup trucks whose purpose is to aid stranded or injured motorists.

The driver and his assistant are trained in auto repair, first-aid and English. They'll help you out in any way possible, including supplying directions or gasoline. There's no charge for 'Green Angel' Service, but you will have to pay for any parts, oil or gas that they provide.

If you see a Green Angel truck and then your car craps out (always the way it happens), don't worry, they should be by again soon. Each truck tries to cover its route four times daily, that is two round trips, one in the morning and one in the afternoon.

Never leave your car unattended if it breaks down on a highway. Unattended cars are good targets for thieves, vandals and the police, since any empty vehicle is considered abandoned, even if the hood is up or a tire flat. If there is no Green Angel service where you are and no friend to stay with the car, wait for another motorist (or even a pedestrian) to come along.

Ask them to get you a *mecánico* (mechanic), *grúa*, or *remolque* (tow). If there is no other way than to go yourself, try your best to hire a guard. Offer a fair amount, enough to maintain their interest, and most any kid, or adult for that matter, will gladly watch the car until you return. Think of it as very cheap, short-term insurance.

FERRIES

Although most ferries are being replaced by bridges or by-passed by new roads, many still operate, particularly in tropical areas. Ferries rarely run at night, even if they are large, and the first trip of the day is around dawn. You might like to plan around this and avoid spending a night on the landing—usually a good place for bugs. During the holiday seasons, you can expect a long wait for ferries on roads between large towns or between any beach and the main road.

Ferries that are being used to replace washed out bridges or to cross small rivers run on very loose schedules. They often operate only when they have a full load, or if they carry just one vehicle at a time, they'll take you across whenever they get around to it.

Some ferries are free of charge but most aren't, and the fees may seem exorbitant, especially to cross a river that you could *almost* drive through.

Foot passengers pay less or nothing at all, depending on how inconspicuous they make themselves. The passengers of any and all vehicles, from cars to buses, have to get out while loading and unloading. If the ferry runs aground, you'll probably have to help push it free. (For long distance ferries see *Public Transportation*.)

GAS STATIONS

Selection of a *gasolinera* (gas station) is quite easy. *PEMEX* stations (a government monopoly) are the only ones to choose from. Although new *Pemex* stations are opening all the time, the best rule to follow is never pass one up if you can't make it to the next town.

Pemex stations are generally located at the edge of towns. Some large towns have a station on each side and possibly one in the middle for good measure. Stations are also located at important crossroads between cities and at points where major roads branch. However, you won't find the familiar American scene of four gas stations at each corner of a crossroad. Other stations will occur at irregular and unexpected intervals, making it necessary to watch the gas gauge when travelling away from main highways.

Very few *Pemex* stations stay open all night; even those located in large cities often close before midnight. On main trucking routes, however, there are some large all-night stations.

In December of 1973 *Pemex (Petroleos Mexicanos)* replaced its three standard grades of gasoline *(Super Mexolina, Gasolmex* and *Pemex Cien)* with two grades: *Nova* in the blue pumps and *Extra* in the silver pumps. Diesel fuel is widely available and so cheap you won't believe it. (See *Prices*.) A third type of gasoline, as yet unnamed, has recently been announced by *Petroleos Mexicanos*. According to *Pemex* this gas will provide "more efficient ignition for engines and reduce air contamination." The new gas is blended with methanol. It will be introduced "gradually" so it's difficult to say when and where it will be available and at what prices.

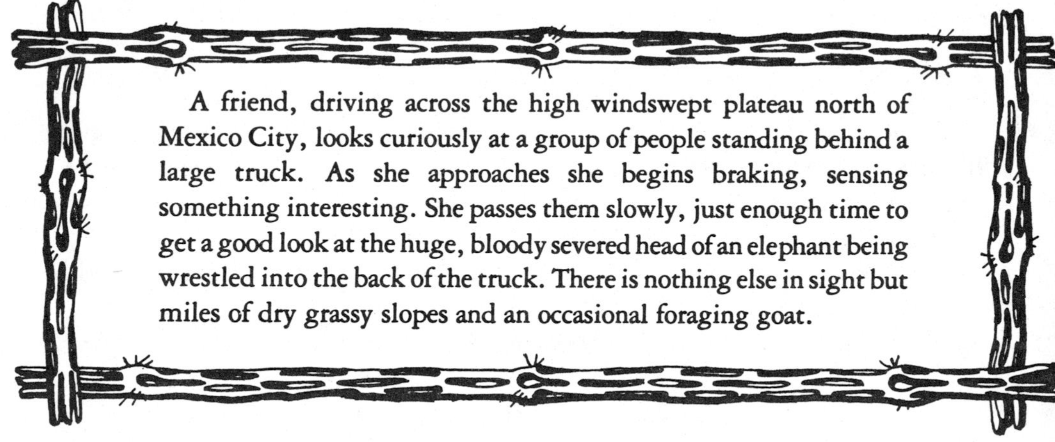

A friend, driving across the high windswept plateau north of Mexico City, looks curiously at a group of people standing behind a large truck. As she approaches she begins braking, sensing something interesting. She passes them slowly, just enough time to get a good look at the huge, bloody severed head of an elephant being wrestled into the back of the truck. There is nothing else in sight but miles of dry grassy slopes and an occasional foraging goat.

Government regulation of the petroleum industry guarantees supplies and considering Mexico's newly discovered oil reserves, any shortage of gasoline is highly unlikely. Individual stations do run out, however, so don't be shocked if you're told that one or more pumps are dry. In small towns and in the country a gas station may have just one pump of *Nova* and nothing else, not even oil.

The prices of both oil and gasoline are controlled by the government and vary just slightly, usually a few *centavos* more per liter in remote areas. Although the price of gas has almost doubled in the past few years, the octane ratings have been decreased. *Nova*, rated at 81, is contemptuously referred to by many drivers as "*No—va*" (doesn't go) and *Extra* supposedly tests at several points lower than its rating of 94 octane.

Many people mistakenly believe that the price of gas has something to do with quality. Using this logic, they burn high octane gasoline in engines designed and tuned for lower octane. This is a waste of money. Try a tank of *Nova* in your car (assuming you're not driving a Ferrari) and if it runs OK, keep using it. If it runs badly or pings like a pinball machine, have a mechanic retime the engine (retard the spark, *retardar la chispa*).

Extra is non-leaded and designed for use in cars equipped with catalytic converters. It is not just a higher grade of gasoline. If your car uses leaded gas you're stuck with *Nova.*

Engine performance is affected by altitude. If you're making a significant change, either up or down, and will be doing a lot of driving at a new altitude, it might be wise to have the timing adjusted accordingly.

Many people use mixtures of *Nova* and *Extra*, increasing the octane above *Nova's* 81 but diluting the lead content. (Start at 50-50 and then change the proportion according to performance. More *Nova* means less knock.) Opinions vary wildly from one so-called mechanic to another on the advisability of blending gasolines. Many prefer to use gasoline additives, sold in larger stations and auto parts stores.

Water in the gas is not uncommon in hot coastal areas, where the high humidity can condense into problems for your carburetor. Alcohol additives should be used occasionally; they blend with the water and allow it to burn. I prefer to avoid the expensive commercial additives and use drinking alcohol instead. (See *Booze.*) A liter or so every once in a while is a vague enough guideline. Mixes well with grapefruit juice.

An in-line filter will trap both water and dirt. Check it often for clogging and carry at least one spare. (See *Preparing Your Car.*)

Running out: I've run out of gas enough times to have developed a healthy respect for a spare gas can. If you have to ask for the use of a gas can from a *Pemex* station, be prepared to be turned down; very few of them have gas cans on hand. In a major station near Mexico City I was offered a large plastic detergent container, complete with a half inch of hardened soap. It took me an hour to get the soap out and the suds nearly engulfed the station. After all this I was asked to pay a very hefty deposit.

Mexican motorists are very good about stopping to give a stranded tourist a helping hand. For that reason you can usually save yourself the hassle of hitching to a gas station if you can produce a siphon hose and ask the favor of a slight drain from someone's tank.

Lorena and I were driving down a deserted highway when we noticed a police car parked in the road in front of us. As we slowed down four cops jumped out of the car and began to flag us down, indicating that we should pull off the pavement.

"I sure don't like the looks of this," I said to Lorena, rolling down my window as one of them came running over. He looked very hot and impatient.

"Where are you going?" he demanded, standing beside the car with hands on his hips. The cop kept glancing over at the others as if for support. They acknowledged his glares by drifting around our car, looking in the windows and staring at the license plates. It didn't feel like a search but it didn't feel very comfortable, either.

"We're going to . . . ." I answered. "Why?"

He ignored my question. "Do you have enough gas?" he asked, throwing me off guard.

"Of course," I said, now thoroughly confused. "Why?"

He continued to ignore my questions, turning to the others with a shout of "Get the hose!"

A cop hustled back to the patrol car and dug around in the trunk for a few moments, taking out a short length of pink plastic hose and a small galvanized bucket. I got out of the car and began to protest.

"*Señor*, wait a moment!" I said, "*¡No es posible!*" I started to protest again, trying to explain that it was impossible to siphon from this particular tank due to a dent we'd picked up in Baja.

"Don't worry, *amigo*," he interrupted, "We'll leave you enough to get to the next *gasolinera*. We'll pay you, of course, for the gas."

Truck bumper graffiti: The King; Speedy Eagle; All for Nothing

The guy with the siphon hose was ordered to his knees and quickly began the job of sucking up the gas. He gave several valiant trys but couldn't quite manage to maintain a steady flow. The gas would start to run and then trickle down to nothing.

"*SUCK ON IT* you idiot!" the first cop roared, slapping his holster impatiently. The other two exchanged wary glances. I wondered how long they'd been stuck out here and who's fault it had been. I began to enjoy myself.

The man on the hose finally wobbled to his feet and ran off to the ditch, falling to his knees and retching up raw gasoline.

Without being told another took his place. When the bucket held two or three cupfuls he followed the first to the ditch, pitching forward onto hands and knees, his back heaving up and down as he gagged convulsively. The third cop went down to the hose like a man kneeling before the chopping block. He didn't bother to join his companions but vomited instead into the bucket, spoiling what pitiful little gasoline they'd managed to accumulate.

Without a word the first cop pulled the hose from the filler neck, threw it into the dirt and stomped back to the patrol car. He climbed into the front seat, slammed the door and sat staring off into the distance. We waited a few moments, then started the car and pulled slowly away. I took a quick look in the rear view mirror; three of Mexico's finest lay sprawled on the ground, puking, a fourth trying to fight off a fit of apoplexy It had been an interesting interlude.

Pemex stations offer three types of oil: *Pemex Sol, Ebano* and *Faja de Oro. Pemex Sol* and *Ebano* commonly come in SAE grades 20, 30 and 40, but 20W may be difficult to find. In general, Mexicans prefer 40W oil.

This oil is not of the best quality. It tends to break down, especially when subjected to the high operating temperatures of an air-cooled engine. If your trip will be a short one, try to carry enough oil to last until your return to the U.S. Should you run out, it is possible to buy oil made in Mexico under the license and specifications of U.S companies. Of these, Quaker State is the best. These oils are sold in auto parts shops, garages and some large *Pemex* stations. If you buy oil in a garage, they will often change it for you as a bonus.

When you order a can of oil, always check the SAE weight before you or the attendant dumps it in. The attendants often grab the first can of oil in sight. A young kid did this

Truck bumper graffiti: Bird Without Direction

to us after we'd ordered a can of 30W and all he could find was 50W. He said it was "more or less the same" but we insisted on 30W, which he eventually found.

Gas and oil additives, car wax, fuses and all the other little goodies so commonly found in gas stations in the U.S. are sold only in the larger and shinier *Pemex* stations. Small stations have nothing more than one or two grades of gas, a haphazard selection of oil and a broken tire pump. Auto parts stores are the best source of automotive odds and ends. Road maps are usually not available. (See *Appendices: Maps*)

Repairs and Servicing

Grease jobs, routine lubrication, oil changes, tire repairs, car and motor cleaning and minor repairs are done at average-sized *Pemex* stations. The quality of the work and the price will vary from station to station. (See *Car Repairs* and *Preparing Your Car.*)

Air and water are available in almost every station, though it is best to *ask about the water before drinking it.* (See *Services*)

Because air gauges may be calibrated in kilograms instead of pounds (*libras*), it is best to have your own tire gauge and to check the tire pressure yourself. Standard tables used to convert kilograms to pounds *cannot be used for air pressures.*

Restrooms in *Pemex* stations vary from as bright and clean as an operating room to as dark and funky as a sewer, which they often lack. No matter what they look like from the outside, bathrooms are rarely equipped with toilet paper. A wad of *papel sanitario* should be your constant travelling companion.

The restaurants that often adjoin gas stations vary as much as the restrooms, from psuedo-Howard Johnson's to stomach-knotting. If there are two restaurants near a gas station, the one farthest away is almost always independent of the station and more reasonable in price and quality.

Ripoffs

Anyone who has heard anything at all about driving in Mexico has heard stories of ripoffs in gas stations.

Mexican gas station attendants are not as dishonest or conniving as most tourists believe. *Pemex* attendants may make an occasional error when figuring your change, but it is usually an honest error. The people who work in gas stations are not generally renowned for their mathematical wizardry, so don't jump down some 14-year-old's throat because he shorts you 20 *centavos.*

The type of stations that commonly cheat tourists are almost always easy to spot. The routine usually goes like this: as you pull in, a mob of kids surrounds your car, elbowing away old men selling yesterday's *tamales* and soggy sandwiches. The kids try to get you to agree to a wash job or to clean the windows.

Before you can force your way out of the car, you hear the pump dinging away. By the time you've got the brats from under the hood or prevented them from greasing the windshield with their dirty rags, the gas tank is full. Or at least they say it is. Sometimes it really is full, more gas, in fact, than you have ever seen crammed into it before, perhaps as much as ten gallons over capacity.

The first precaution is: observe the attendant at the pump and make sure that he rings the pump back to all zeros. If he leaves ten or twenty *pesos* from the previous purchase, he's going to try to soak you for it. It is this ploy that results in tanks that have apparently had more gas pumped into them than they can hold.

If this happens, just calmly point out that the tank isn't that large. (*No cabe*—It doesn't fit.) If this isn't enough, ask to see *el dueño* (the manager) or take down the number of the station and the reading on the pump. The attendant assumes that you're going to complain officially (which you can do with success—to both the *Pemex* company and the Mexican Tourist Bureau) and he will almost always rectify his 'mistake.' Don't get violent or nasty until he's had time to pretend it was all an error.

A very handy way to avoid this type of cheating is to put a reminder of the tank's capacity in liters on top of the gas cap or near the filler neck. This can be done with labelling tape or paint. *Capacidad 40 litros* (capacity 40 liters) is a very straightforward way of letting people know that *you* know what's going on.

Another ploy in this type of station is charging the normal price for a can of oil and then only pretending to put it in or not actually emptying the entire can into the crankcase. To avoid this, do it yourself. You should anyway, since even honest attendants often read dipsticks incorrectly and tell you that you need a liter of oil when you don't.

Similarly, attendants frequently forget to replace the gas cap, so check it at the same time. A locking gas cap will save you many a filched or forgotten cap. Put the key on a ring with the ignition key. This means that the cap can only be opened after you've stopped the engine and gives you time to check the pump. The engine cannot be restarted until the attendant hands back both keys.

Shortchanging happens on occasion but may be done so subtly that you'll never be quite sure if it was tried intentionally or not.

The sneakiest method is for the attendant to count your change back very rapidly, then suddenly stop counting short of the correct amount. In many instances, the person receiving the change assumes the final count is correct and pockets the change with no suspicion of what's happening. When the customer does notice that the change stopped too soon, the attendant just pauses as if checking the count mentally and then forks over the rest.

Another method, not nearly so cool, is to wait you out hoping that, rather than search or ask for the person who owes you five *pesos* change, you will give up in disgust and leave. This is usually tried by a younger attendant in stations where large groups of people make him hard to recognize.

When you aren't given enough change say, "*Me falta*" (I lack). If you know how much you're short, give the amount, "*Me falta cien pesos*" (100 pesos).

The solution to any type of dishonest money changing is to have the correct change or so close to it that it won't bother you if they get away with a two or three cent 'tip'.

Once you're familiar with the capacity of your tank and what it costs to fill it, you can order gas by the amount you wish to pay, e.g., 50, 100 or 200 *pesos*. This saves time and hassles with small change.

Sometimes you will be assaulted by a screaming horde of ragged kids who want to wash the windshield. I have rarely seen them do anything but smear more dirt or even oil from their filthy rags on a window they were supposedly cleaning. Their intentions are good; they just do a lousy job.

Whether it's window washing, tire repair or a lube job, always determine the price before agreeing to have anything done or the charge may be rather astounding.

We had been driving for several hours through the jungle, alternately marvelling at the scenery and the unexpected bonus of a brand new two-lane blacktop road. What showed on our map as unimproved dirt was actually one of the best stretches of highway we'd yet found.

"So you realize that there's not even any traffic?" Steve said, putting the van into a near slide as he cut a sharp corner. I could hear Lorena cursing in the back as she tried to stop the avalanche of books, clothing and miscellaneous pottery that Steve's racing maneuver had loosened from the overloaded cabinets.

"Take a look at those Tarzan vines!" Steve continued, sticking his head and most of his upper body out of the side window. He was in his full tourist/driver position, glancing at the road ahead for occasional course corrections while maintaining a running commentary on the passing sights. If I failed to exclaim over the beauty of a large tree we'd narrowly missed colliding with, he'd repeat, "Did you see that tree? Did you see

Truck bumper graffiti: Only God Knows Where I'm Going; Savage Wind; What's the Value of Hurry?

that tree?" until I admitted that I had, that I found it not only beautiful and amazing but perhaps even spectacular. This same routine was applied to large leafy plants, streamers of moss, unusual boulders and any form of wildlife larger than a grasshopper. Requests that he give at least equal attention to the road were useless, for like Mexican truck drivers he fully believed that the Great *Chofer* in the Sky was lending a helping hand.

"Look out!"

Steve's head snapped down, his hands clawing at the steering wheel as a huge bull lumbered across the road directly in front of us. My foot pumped at an imaginary brake as the van swerved wildly around the unfazed animal. I was still trying to catch my breath when Steve slouched back in his seat and said, "Beautiful cattle around here, don't you think?"

I gave him a hard look; he was picking idly at some colored bits of tape stuck to the steering wheel, the remnants of his homemade wrap job. Lorena and I had agreed that pink and yellow crisscrossed tape looked wonderful, just like a Mexican semi in 'full dress.' The problem was that the cheap adhesive backed tape he'd used soon wore through and driving was like grappling with flypaper.

"Yeah," I answered. "A bull would make a great hood ornament. If this van had a hood, that is." His eyes narrowed; on a previous trip he'd lashed the sunbleached skulls of a large sea turtle and a long horned cow to the bumper and draped a small but vicious set of shark jaws over the rear view mirror. He glanced wistfully into the mirror; the bull was safely off the road and into the bushes. One of those ears would have looked nice flapping from the radio antenna...

"Hey, Carl," Steve said, turning his body to face me, his left thumb hooked into the steering wheel, eyes focused vaguely over my head, "Remember the old *Pato de Paz?*"

"Hey, watch the road...!" I yelled, trying to shake off the feeling that we were about to become another roadside shrine. "Why don't you let me drive for a while?" I added, knowing this would bring him back to earth if nothing else would. It seemed to work; he turned his head for a few seconds, then slowly let his eyes drift back toward me.

"Yeah, the good old Peace Duck," he sighed, "I should never have let those creeps at the border touch her."

He went off into a long monologue, reminiscing about past trips as though narrating a mental slide show.

"...and then we stopped for lunch, remember? I had the best refried beans there. You had a chicken *torta* and a *Pacifico.* Remember?"

"No."

"Yeah, you do. That was the place with the parrot in the bathroom. His name was Lorenzo. Remember now?"

"No."

"Are you serious? It was just down the highway from where we ran over that giant black and green snake. Remember?"

"No."

"Aw, come on. Lorena had scrambled eggs with Oaxaca cheese in them. That was the day after I changed the oil in the van. It took an extra quart and I adjusted the valves. Number three was tight. Now you *have* to remember!"

"I don't."

"You gotta be putting me on." He ran a hand through his hair, straining for more details. "We were listening to that Johnny Cash tape, the one with Ring of Fire. I had on a blue shirt and..."

"Oh hell!" I interrupted. "What possible difference does it make if I remember or not?" Steve turned to me with a look of complete astonishment. "Why, well...because...what if you wanted to stop and see Lorenzo some day? How would you know where to go?"

"Steve," I sighed, turning to stare into the jungle, "I don't even remember the parrot in the first place so how could I..." Oh, what was the use? We tore around another sharp curve.

"Well, you *must* remember what we had for dinner that night. I had a piece of barbecued..."

"DID YOU SEE THAT!" He jammed the brake pedal to the floor, interrupting himself with a shout and the shriek of tires burning against pavement. I braced against the windshield as the van shuddered to a stop.

"That was *unbelievable!*" he said, sticking his head out the window and slamming the gear shift into reverse. Before Lorena or I could register the proper degree of curiosity at whatever had prompted our nerve fraying stop, we were backing down the highway at 30 miles per hour.

"There it is!" Steve cried, standing on the brake pedal again, throwing us violently back against the seats. He pointed into the jungle and I strained to see this latest marvel.

"See it? See it?" he asked, banging his hand on the edge of the window sill. I looked harder: jungle, trees, bushes, not a rhino or gorilla or giant condor in sight.

"See what?" Lorena and I asked in unison, squinting now to sharpen our vision. It might be a rare miniature deer or a purple spotted tree frog.

"Right there!" Steve cried. "Right in front of you! Are you *blind*?"

"I give up," I said, knowing he'd have us sitting there for an hour if that's what it took to make identification. He looked aggrieved; what was it about us that we could not remember what we had for lunch last year, or perceive these fantastic natural wonders that literally surrounded us? He gave an enormous sigh of defeat and disgust.

"The vine! The Tarzan vine!" he yelled, tracing its length with his fingers, following the greyish twisted form from treetop to ground level.

"Oh! I see it." I said. "You mean that thick vine over there all tangled up with those other thick vines. The one that looks like those thick vines we saw a couple of miles back?"

Steve didn't say a word; he just put the van into forward and pressed the gas pedal to the floor. Pearls before swine! A genuine Tarzan vine, one capable of swinging an entire family and no one around to appreciate it but Steve.

The deeper Steve delved into memories of past trips the less he was aware of the present one. Our speed began to drop, mile by mile, until the van was barely moving. I looked nervously behind us, watching for fast moving buses or trucks. The lack of traffic was a real godsend.

"I picked up this crippled hitchhiker just this side of Tuxtla and..." The monologue continued, dipping here and there into various memorable trips and experiences, most of them very familiar to both Lorena and me. Those we hadn't been involved in ourselves had been told and re-told over the years.

"...had a huge dog, a mean S.O.B., that could sing, well, *howl* actually, Jingle Bells. Offered me a half interest..."

I yawned. The van began to buck and lurch as our speed fell to about 15 miles an hour.

"You're lugging it down!" I said, not missing the chance to get one on him. When I drove he watched every move, as though I were an astronaut training on a lunar lander.

"...the fat guy with the .45 had a carved jade mask you couldn't believe..." Steve's hand slipped to the gear shift and he dropped it into second. "No, I'm not," he said, breaking his account of tomb robbers.

"You aren't now but you were before," I said.

"Was what?" he countered.

"Lugging it down!" I yelled.

"I'm not lugging it down," he answered, putting the gas pedal to the floor and winding the engine up to a scream. I groaned and turned to stare into the jungle. The van immediately slowed as the travelogue resumed.

"...about 25 cents between us and I said, 'Take a chance, you never know' and so he put it on number 7 and...picked up a turtle poaching boat just this side of...she said, 'Where'd you get that hat' and I said...maybe a broken leg, but it was only a sprain so the driver...couple of gigantic bats, vampires I'm sure..."

"Hey, look out!" I said as we came around a tight curve. Steve's eyes turned to the road and his foot moved to the brake pedal. A group of workmen blocked the highway, standing around two battered dump trucks loaded with broken pieces of cement. One of the men flagged us down.

"We got just beyond the outer reef when..." Steve continued his story, waving irritably at the flagman. The van kept moving. Either he hadn't really noticed the signal to stop or just didn't care. The flagman gestured frantically and then waved us on with a 'What the hell?' motion.

"...got a little choppy and the captain said..."

The road ended in a massive washout. Steve stopped the van.

"...the damned oil line broke and sprayed hot oil on the supercharger..."

A huge concrete bridge lay twisted and broken in front of us, surrounded by mountains of splintered trees and debris. It looked quite new, as new as the highway, but was obviously beyond repair. The flagman came jogging up from behind us.

"...ate this thing that looked like a peach but..."

The flagman was next to Steve's window, motioning at him insistently. Steve brushed him off with a quick smile.

"couldn't believe the taste, man, it was fantastic!"

The flagman said something to Steve and pointed at the bridge.

"*Sí, sí,*" Steve muttered absentmindedly, rolling his eyes at me as if to say, "Catch the jerk with the flag, would 'ya?"

"...lit the incense and the candles and took this poor chicken..."

The flagman's head was turning quickly from us to the bridge and then back again. He opened his mouth, paused, then was gone.

"...the fog rolled in and you could still smell the hot lava..."

I glanced out the rear window and then toward the bridge. Where had everybody gone?

"Hey," Lorena said, looking out of her window and toward the ground, "There are legs and feet sticking out from under the van."

"...the damnedest thing you ever saw, feathers and bones..." I stuck my head out the window. There were several pairs of boots and *huarache*-shod feet on my side, too. How did they get there? What were they doing, sleeping?

"...girl started chanting these weird words kind of like..."

"Hey, Steve!" I interrupted, "There's a bunch of people under the van!"

He stopped in mid-sentence, turning to me with an angry scowl. "Can't I just tell this *one story* without you guys breaking in all the time? Is that too much to ask?" I started to answer but he cut me off, eyes glazing over as he sorted through his memory for the thread of the story.

"...oh yeah, it was just after midnight but still hot..."

"Something's going on here!" I yelled, reaching for the door handle. "That flagman must..."

KA... WHAM!... WHAM!... WHAM!... WHAM!

I stopped, stunned by the tremendous blasts. The bridge in front of us quivered... KA... WHAM!... WHAM!... WHAM!...twisted upward... KA... WHAM!... WHAM!... then seemed to lift itself slowly from the streambed... KA... WHAM!... WHAM!... as clouds of dust shimmered around it and chunks of cement... KA... WHAM!... WHAM!... WHAM!... tumbled high overhead like huge softballs lofted into center field...and...

"OH NO!" Steve screamed, eyes bulging as the van rocked against the terrific concussions. Twenty quick explosions, then suddenly a series of five, a ripple burst, then five more, thirty, forty, fifty!

"LOOK OUT!" he cried, cramming himself between the front seat and the steering column. The softballs were coming down now, shattered meteorites of jagged cement, some the size of grapefruit, others even larger, thudding into the ground around us like a mortar barrage. A hailstorm of smaller pieces rattled against the top of the van.

The explosions continued, WHAM! WHAM! WHAM! WHAM!, completely obscuring the bridge in clouds of dirt and smoke. We held our arms over our heads, eyes tightly closed, waiting for the inevitable impact. There was no chance of running, we could only pray that the van's thin roof and overhead rack would take the main force as the cement tore through.

And then a sudden silence, punctuated by the thump of a last volley of fragments. My ears rang with the after-shock. The bridge was gone, transformed into a long mound of blasted concrete and steel rods.

Steve worked his way back up onto the seat, his face white and sweating.

"You OK?" I croaked, looking in the back of the van for Lorena.

"Fine," a voice said. She had somehow managed to crawl into the long cupboard beneath the bed. A few hours earlier she'd sworn it wouldn't hold another thing and Steve had been forced to put his extra shoes on the roof.

The flagman's grinning face was suddenly at Steve's window.

"Did you enjoy it?" He asked pleasantly.

Steve gave him the Black Death stare.

What do you mean, enjoy it?" he snarled, flexing his hands on the steering wheel as though they were around the fellows neck.

"I asked if you had parked in the danger zone on purpose," the flagman said, "and you said that you had. You said, *'Sí! Sí!'* "

Others were crawling from beneath the van, laughing and dusting off their clothing. They looked at us as if we were completely insane.

Steve rubbed his face with the heels of his hands, muttering low curses. The flagman grinned nervously, backing away with a final, "You can wait for an hour, if you want, and there will be more to watch." He didn't wait to hear Steve's colorful reply but turned instead and began walking back to his post.

We sat for a few minutes in a heavy silence. Steve finally reached for the gear shift and put it in low, edging the van carefully down the rough, temporary road bypassing the fallen bridge. We came to the edge of a shallow stream.

"You know, this kind of reminds me of a place in Peru," Steve began, "I'd just got back from a trip up towards..."

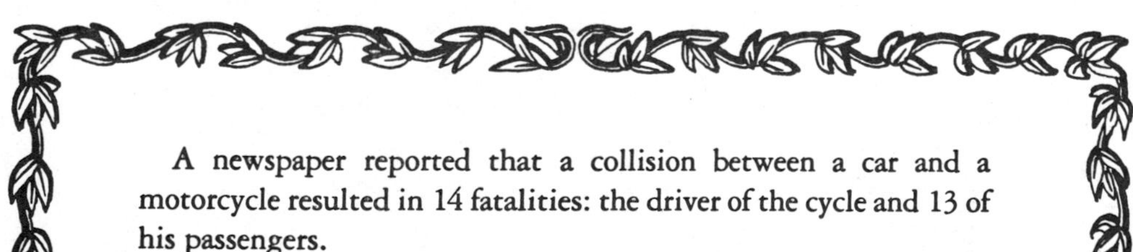

A newspaper reported that a collision between a car and a motorcycle resulted in 14 fatalities: the driver of the cycle and 13 of his passengers.

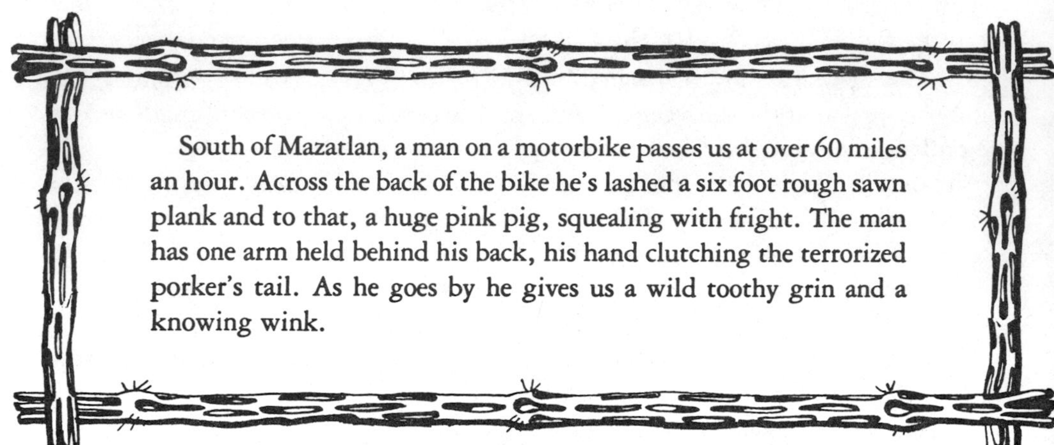

South of Mazatlan, a man on a motorbike passes us at over 60 miles an hour. Across the back of the bike he's lashed a six foot rough sawn plank and to that, a huge pink pig, squealing with fright. The man has one arm held behind his back, his hand clutching the terrorized porker's tail. As he goes by he gives us a wild toothy grin and a knowing wink.

PUBLIC TRANSPORTATION

Bus service...First and second class...Terminals, tickets, baggage... Crossing the border...Travel hints...City buses...Trains: tickets, reservations, baggage, food, sleeping, general information...Taxis...Rental cars...Navigating in Mexico City: buses, cabs, subway...Airlines... Ferries...Boats...Animal back...

Mexico's public transportation networks are so extensive that almost no point or area of the country is totally inaccessible to the traveller.

BUSES

Bus service is truly remarkable, and the common expression that "wherever there's a road, there's a bus" is no exaggeration. There are approximately 700 separate bus lines and though service may vary from air-conditioned luxury to open stake trucks, they'll get you there somehow. For those few places inaccessible to even the most determined bus driver, transportation will almost certainly be available in some other form: by small airplane, canoe or burro.

The excitement of visiting remote villages is sometimes overshadowed by the experience of the bus ride to it. The condition of the bus and the road and the general condition of the other passengers (particularly around *fiesta* time) make each bus ride a unique adventure.

Travellers who use buses often will find that they become totally immersed in Mexico. There is no other method, short of walking through the country, to establish such close and continual contact with the people.

The cost of travelling by bus is remarkable low. (See *Prices* for cost per mile.) The expense of operating your car will buy an incredible number of bus tickets. Unless we're on a camping trip we almost always travel by bus (or train) and notice a substantial savings.

There are two types of bus service: second class and first class. Second class buses vary from relatively comfortable to positively back-breaking, depending on where you're going and the age of the bus. In recent years, many companies have begun to replace their old second class buses with newer models and first class retirees. Once a bus becomes too funky for first class passengers to tolerate, it is sent into second class service. (From there the only place for it to go is into the junkyard or over a cliff.)

As the ancient wrecks are gradually replaced, some of the color and excitement has gone out of second class bus travel, but enough remains to overwhelm most tourists when they ride one of these mobile adventures.

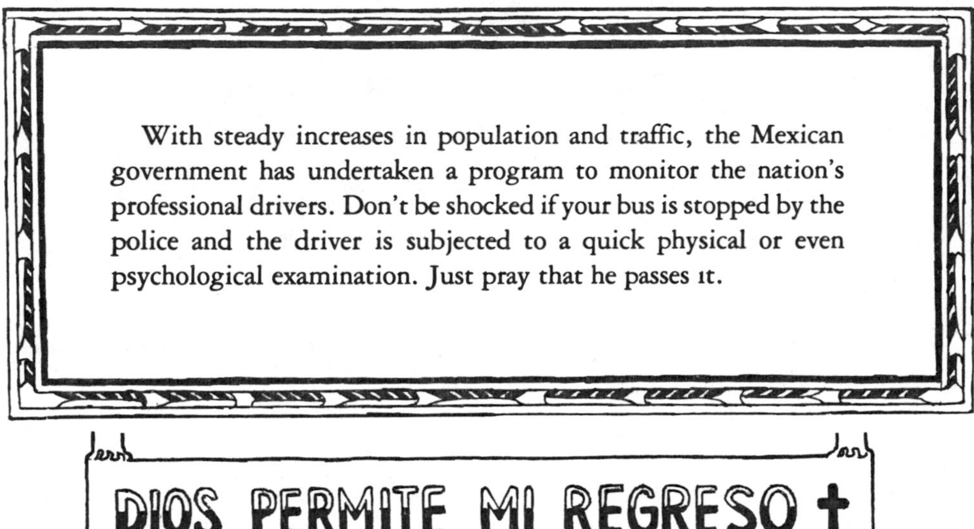

With steady increases in population and traffic, the Mexican government has undertaken a program to monitor the nation's professional drivers. Don't be shocked if your bus is stopped by the police and the driver is subjected to a quick physical or even psychological examination. Just pray that he passes it.
DIOS PERMITE MI REGRESO †

The initial shock of being crammed into a rusty tin box with 50 other people, a variety of market goods and domestic animals, soon moderates to a feeling of warm camaraderie.

You smilingly agree to a woman's request that you hold her baby while she whips up a few *tacos* from ingredients extracted from a greasy piece of newspaper. When she's managed to assemble her lunch she takes the baby back and offers you a rag for the mess on your lap.

Beads of sweat are breaking out on your upper lip but the window is frozen shut by years of rust. You take a deep breath or two and find a *taco* under your nose. You've been invited to eat.

Truck bumper graffiti: God Allows My Return

You want to decline the invitation, but from the thrusting motions she is making with the *taco*, it is clear that it would be grossly impolite to refuse. No matter, it turns out to be your favorite: steamed goat head with lots of chili pepper. The air you suck in through tightly pursed lips sounds like ripping cloth and you attempt to cover your embarrassment at reacting to the pepper by staring out the window.

Through tear-filled eyes, you gaze over a thousand foot precipice, but the *taco*, stuck halfway down your throat, blocks a scream of fear.

The lurching of the bus is considerable, very similar to that of a boat foundering on a storm-tossed sea. The ringing in your ears almost drowns out the voice behind the hand that is holding a crude pottery mug under your nose. You look up, eyes filled with a plea for mercy, but the smiling face insists. You tip the mug back, determined to do a chug-a-lug and have done with it. It is *pulque*, the fermented sap of the *maguey* plant, and it is distinctly slimy. It hits your stomach like warm mustard water.

Your apparently experienced manner of tossing down the *pulque* brings admiring remarks from other people jammed in nearby. They appreciate the fact that you're trying to be sociable and to show this appreciation, they contribute little delicacies they're bringing home from market. A piece of deep-fried pig skin, a cactus fruit, some incredibly sour berries and two old *tortillas* with something brown smeared on them are offered up for your enjoyment.

You are just about to go under when the bus lurches to a stop. Everyone piles out to see what's gone wrong and you gratefully stagger into the fresh mountain air.

A front tire has blown, the second flat of the trip, and there doesn't seem to be another spare. After a quick look at the other tires, the driver decides to remove one of the rear duals and put it on the front. As he does this, his assistants, a motley collection of boys about eight years old, fill the leaking radiator with water from a nearby ditch. They're using one beer bottle and a leaky oil can so they have to make several trips.

When the repairs are finished, everyone crowds back into the bus and in the confusion you lose your seat. You're grateful, however, because you can now assume a position in the aisle near the front door. The body of the bus is so low that you have to stand with your neck slightly bent. Every really bad bump gets you a crack on the back of your skull. At least there is air to breath—since half of the windshield and the entire door are missing.

When you've settled into a more or less tolerable slouch, you begin to take a new interest in the driver and the road ahead. Before entering the mountains, the road had been reasonable. Now, however, with occasional boulders to dodge, half filled washouts, and vertical drops of hundreds of feet just scant inches from the edge of the road, you wonder seriously if the bus will make it.

The driver is shifting like a madman; something is wrong with the clutch and he's having trouble on the steeper grades. You notice anxiously that the brake pedal goes very close to the floor when he throws his weight on it. You wonder then about the motto painted on the front bumper, the one you and your friends had laughed about before you left: "Guide Me God, For I Am Blind."

It's anyone's guess just how much is getting through those opaque sunglasses and the heavily decorated windshield to the driver's eyes. The garlands of plastic flowers, intertwined with blinking Christmas tree lights, have sagged so low that he has to lean forward to peer over them on particularly tight corners.

A large crucifix is mounted between the two front windshields and each point of the cross lights up to correspond with a particular gear. As he shifts, you follow the lights: white...green...red...red...green...white. The ceiling is plastered with an unlikely assortment of faded pictures. The Virgin Mary peers from between an old Marilyn Monroe magazine photo and a rather obscene playing card.

In addition, a variety of dangling objects, evidently amulets and charms, swing in crazily distracting patterns in front of the driver, occasionally whacking him on the forehead. Between shifts he idly fondles the gearshift knob, a blindly staring doll baby head that winks conspiratorially at each bump. Before you can determine the significance of this macabre object, the bus arrives at your destination and you gratefully jump off.

Because second class bus rides that last more than a few minutes invariably become social affairs, it's nice to have something to offer people who offer something to you.

This can be nothing more than a piece of candy, a cigarette or a turn with a newspaper.

I usually carry a small bottle of liquor, both for socializing and for numbing tired muscles and brain cells. A large bottle involves the danger of getting smashed. There's nothing more agonizing and awful than a hangover on a rattling second class bus. The driver will rarely object if you drink but it's best to be discreet, at least until he smells the fumes and looks thirsty himself.

It is not customary to offer your seat to anyone standing unless they are ill or very old. This conflicts with what most of us had drummed into our heads as children but standing for hours in a bouncing hot bus can do a great deal of attitude changing. In most cases, you'll find that after you've offered a lady your seat, she takes it gratefully and then gets off within the next mile. You then continue standing as some guy elbows past you and drops into the vacant spot with a big sigh of relief.

If you don't feel like giving up your seat, it is polite to offer to hold something for people who are standing. Children seem to be the most common bundle, though you maybe given a chicken or a bag of groceries.

Should the cozy atmosphere get to be too much for your stomach, ask the driver or his accomplice for permission to ride on the roof or rear bumper. The roof is not only much safer than the bumper but offers a better view with less chance of fume poisoning.

The only time I've ever driven a fast car in Mexico, I was passed by a second class bus travelling at over 80 mph. This wasn't unusual, nor were the three young men on the rear bumper. The one reading a comic book, however, *without holding on,* seemed abnormally blasé.

After you've ridden a few genuine second class buses you'll understand why Mexicans refer to them as *matasanos* (health killers) and *doctorsanos* (sarcastically: doctorhealth). It should be kept in mind, however, that on a statistical basis—miles per accident or something like that—Mexican buses have an excellent survivor record.

When the bus stops in a terminal, the driver will yell out how long you have before it leaves again. If you don't understand rapid Spanish you may be afraid to leave the bus in order to avoid being left behind. This happened to me on my first trip and I was thoroughly sick of the bus after several hundred miles of confinement to a hard seat.

In general, you can expect 15 minute stops in terminals and 5 minutes or more elsewhere. On side roads, the stop may be long enough for the driver to take a bath, shave, have a good lunch with a few beers and do a little gossiping.

During long rest stops the driver may tell everyone to get off so that the bus can be locked up. On all stops it's best to leave something in your seat—a book or hat—as new passengers may not have been assigned a specific seat and will go for yours. Valuables, needless to say, should be carried with you if the bus is left open.

Second class buses leave the terminal with amazing regularity and you'll rarely have to wait more than an hour. In fact, it is quite common to make connections so quickly that you don't have time to find a place to eat.

Whenever a bus slows down, someone will be there selling cake, *tacos*, sandwiches, pop, beer and fruit. Vendors will often board the bus and sell their wares between stops.

Most of this food is relatively good but it is wise to be especially cautious of greasy food while bus riding. We have found that almost every problem we have had with diarrhea or upset stomach occurred after eating something greasy. If you get sick on a bus, it is a real hassle. I always carry a handy supply of emergency medicines, at the very minimum some type of pills or liquid (see *Health*) to prevent uncontrollable diarrhea. If you absolutely must request an unscheduled stop, the bus driver will oblige, though perhaps with a ribald comment.

In addition to regular vendors, bus passengers are the favorite targets for a variety of enterprising hucksters, offering everything from Salvation to Kleenex. They often work in cooperation with the driver, who allows them aboard during regular stops or picks them up along the way, giving them a long enough ride to reel off their pitch.

The best are groups of musicians; they pile onto the bus with beat-up guitars, accordions and flutes and bang out a few discordant tunes as a hat or tin can is passed for donations. Unfortunately their routine is now being imitated by groups of aggressive young men who play insipid Gospel songs and then make a plea for donations to aid the poor. Since they're usually dressed better than most of the passengers, they often get a chilly reception.

Deaf mutes selling miniature key chain screwdrivers and sign language cards are also common. They have it down to a profitable science: they prefer buses that are making five minute stops as most of the passengers stay aboard. The deaf mute hustles down the aisle, dropping the item for sale in each person's hand or lap. The card invariably translates as "Give generously." Once he's reached the rear of the bus he starts back, collecting donations. If you don't want a pot metal miniature screwdriver or are just tired of all the deaf mutes, hand it back or put it on the seat beside you. They seldom argue.

In addition to musicians and mutes you'll often see men selling books on medicinal herbs (some are good). Other people may give short impassioned speeches, recite epic poems or gasp out a heart-rending tale of woe that ends with the inevitable open palm.

You may be offered merchandise rather than an appeal for charity. Regional variations can be very interesting: homemade molasses in *tequila* bottles, honey, bottles of *rompope* (like alcoholic eggnog), bags of trimmed sugar cane, live iguanas and armadillos, birds, beadwork, guitars, Huichol Indian God's Eyes and other irresistables. It's a far cry from the Greyhound and "Please do not speak to the operator while the coach is in motion."

High speed, air-conditioned buses, equipped with restrooms and stewardesses serving refreshments, travel the same routes as many of the second class lines. These buses are called Pullman, although this means that they offer toilets, not beds.

Stops are infrequent on first class runs and occur only at terminals or occasional rest and refreshment points. A ride on a first class bus doesn't have quite the atmosphere of a second class junket through countless villages but you certainly get to your destination in a hurry.

Some people say that they prefer to ride second class because of the white knuckle speeds that the first class buses attain and maintain for such long stretches. In reality, second class buses are no slower than first class over the same roads. To make up for time lost loading passengers, the second class bus driver will do anything to keep his average speed ridiculously high.

This means that he'll pass on curves and hills, race 'chicken' fashion to beat other vehicles to narrow bridges and generally make a complete fool of himself. This, of course, isn't to say that the first class bus driver is slow or cautious in comparison.

Truck bumper graffiti: Punisher of The Highway (Road Whipper)

I once rode a first class bus through a mountainous area because I assumed that it would be safer than second class. This involved some inconvenience because the service was not as frequent as second class. I was sufficiently impressed by the narrow road and steep mountains, however, to prepare myself in a nearby *cantina* through the hours before departure.

As an added precaution, I bought a small travelling bottle to use as a sleeping potion; the bus left at midnight and I certainly didn't relish the idea of having to watch the highway all night.

I discovered as soon as I boarded that I had made a critical mistake when buying my ticket by not specifically asking for a rear seat (though the swaying motion is much worse in the back). Instead I found myself behind the driver.

An hour after take off, we entered the mountains and I opened the bottle. The driver, nattily attired in a crisp white shirt, black tie and official looking cap, seemed to think of himself as an airline pilot rather than a mere bus herder. As the assistant driver watched with obvious respect, the pilot went through a complicated series of 'in-flight' systems checks. Had the bus suddenly lifted from the road and shot gracefully into the sky, it appeared that the driver would have been fully prepared and not at all surprised.

From my nervous vantage point, I followed his little training lecture with more interest than the real student. Neither driver or assistant seemed to notice that most of the maneuvers involved in demonstrating brakes, engine revs and complicated shifts were taking place along blood-chilling stretches of narrow mountain road.

We would accelerate to breakneck speed and then the driver would suddenly remember another detail: the fire extinguisher under his seat or the nifty map case near his left foot. With one hand on the wheel and paying no attention at all to the road, he would give a quick demonstration of each new item, then turn back to the chore of driving just as we crossed the road or were about to run over a cow.

He drove purely by instinct, pushing the bus to the limit on every curve, passing trucks and then cutting them off so close that the face of the driver behind us seemed to be just another passenger in the rear seat.

For the final demonstration, he began to flick his headlights from one intensity to another, at times blinding oncoming drivers with bolts of light from special high beams, then suddenly dropping to fog lights, then back to normal intensity. By then I was on the edge of my seat, feeling a deep gut fear of what I knew had to be coming as the finale, the ultimate test of his driving abilities.

He chose a long curve skirting a high rock cliff for the closing act, casually flipping off all the lights after a final demonstration of maximum illumination that had lighted the area in front of the bus as if for a night football game. The plunge into utter darkness surprised even the driver. Not the slightest feeble ray of moonlight could be seen. It was as if the projector light had gone out and the film stopped: the driver frozen at the wheel, unable to reach the switch in time to make the curve but unable to see the curve without the lights; the assistant staring into the windshield, as black as the Grim Reaper's cape, and the passengers suddenly instinctively aware of danger, a tense audience to the driver's dilemma.

As the front tires hit the ditch, the assistant, a pimply-faced kid of about sixteen, leaped to the light switch and flipped it on. At the same instant, the driver turned the wheel desperately and we slid for several heart-pounding seconds down the side of the highway, scant inches from the rock cliff.

Once we'd straightened out, the driver settled comfortably into his seat and turned to his white-faced companion saying casually, "That's the way it's done, son."

The combined sighs of relief from 60 passengers sounded like a communal "Amen!" I emptied my bottle.

All bus drivers aren't maniacs or fatalists. One in particular stands out in my mind as extremely level-headed and reasonable. He was in charge of an old American-made bus and the sign over the aisle read in English: "Your Operator—Safe, Courteous, Reliable—*Jesús Cristo.*" A small ID type photo of Christ attached to the sign left no doubts as to who was really in the driver's seat.

Terminals

There are so many bus lines, often each with its own station, that locating the right terminal can be a problem. (Many towns are combining all bus lines and offices into one central terminal, usually called *Central de Autobuses.*) If your Spanish is weak or your destination unpronounceable, write down the name of the place you want to go or say, "*A Oaxaca, A Morelia*," etc. (The *A* means 'to' and is pronounced as in "Ahhh hell!") A

Truck bumper graffiti: Free and Clean; They Criticise Me From Jealousy; Flavor of Death bus driver, passenger, shoeshine boy or ticket agent will then tell you the name of the bus line that you want.

Although the terminal you're looking for may be conveniently located next door to the one you're in, chances are that it will be on the other side of town. Wandering aimlessly in search of a bus station, particularly in the middle of the night, is an almost futile effort. Bus terminals seem to delight in being obscure and hard to locate. A cab is a worthwhile splurge in this case.

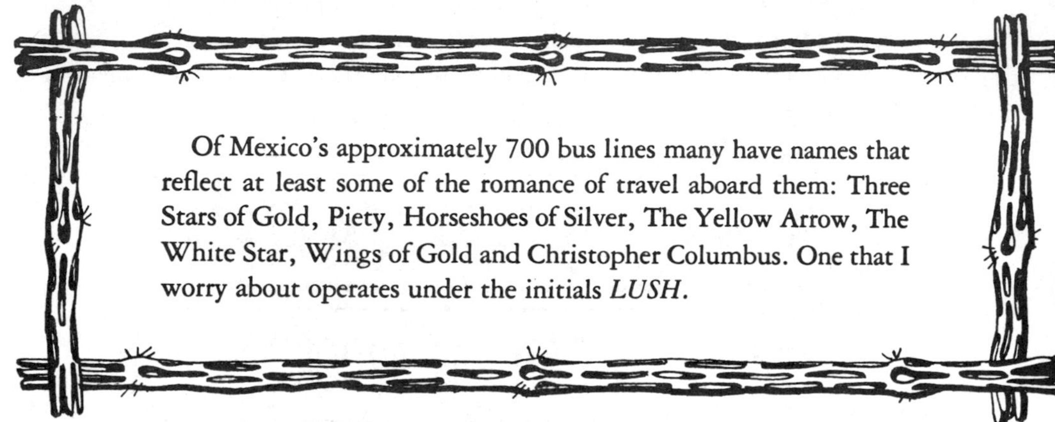

Of Mexico's approximately 700 bus lines many have names that reflect at least some of the romance of travel aboard them: Three Stars of Gold, Piety, Horseshoes of Silver, The Yellow Arrow, The White Star, Wings of Gold and Christopher Columbus. One that I worry about operates under the initials *LUSH*.

Repeat the name of the bus line to yourself as you walk slowly to the street and to the cab. Repeat out loud the name of the bus station as the cabbie opens the door to let you in. Keep repeating it to yourself until you actually arrive, because the cabbie may forget it if he starts bullshitting with other passengers.

If you cannot afford a cab, follow the same procedure, but with passersby, as you wander for hours through town.

The biggest terminals offer a variety of services: bar, restaurant, bank, post office, telegraph, newsstands, souvenir shops, long distance telephone and so on. Information booths, some staffed by English-speaking attendants, will be prominently located in the main lobbies.

There will also be booths selling taxi tickets (see *Taxis*) and others selling *Andenes* tickets (admission to platform). Everyone entering the platform area has to have one to get in, even if they already have a bus ticket. These are very cheap. In some terminals, however, the bus ticket will serve for admission. It all depends on the whim of the management.

In the larger terminals you will be told which of the *Andenes* (platform or departure slot) you will be leaving from. If it isn't marked on your ticket or ticket envelope and you've forgotten the number, just ask any employee, from floorsweeper to bus driver. Most of these people will go out of their way to give you a helping hand.

Arrivals and departures will be announced in echoing and unintelligible Spanish that is best ignored. Your ticket has the vital information about bus number and departure time and it is more reliable than your translation of loudspeaker announcements.

At night in larger terminals you'll often see people sleeping on chairs, benches and the floor. Most of these are worn out travellers or street people avoiding another night in an alley. If you choose to sleep, arrange your baggage securely or check it at the ticket or baggage office.

Mexico is an excellent example of how a mass transit system can move literally millions of people. A recently built terminal in Mexico City is designed to handle 3,000 buses and 100,000 passengers *daily*. This is just one of several major terminals within the capital, and part of a nationwide program to build 31 new terminals throughout the country by the year 1982.

The *Central de Autobuses* in Mexico City *Magdalena de las Salinas, Avenida de los 100 Metros, No. 4907)* offers free tourist information. They will assist you in buying tickets and making reservations for no extra charge. This is the northern station. (See *Navigating Mexico City*.)

Tickets

The cost of a first class ticket is often little more than second class. The greatest difference is that first class lines operate mainly between terminals, while second class buses will stop almost anywhere and accept all passengers, from pigs to drunks. They stop so often that it seems the bus does nothing but begin to accelerate and then immediately start braking again. (A few lines now have big modern second class buses which run only between large cities and stop only at terminals and *Parada* (bus stop) signs, located at frequent intervals on these routes.)

Tickets for first class buses are purchased at the terminal and they assure you of a seat. During the holiday seasons, especially Christmas and Easter, it is wise to make reservations. Everyone wants to travel at these times and you can easily be stuck for days waiting for a seat. When you can't get first class, try the second class lines. You may have to stand but you'll almost certainly get on.

You can buy your second class ticket in the terminal, which may be very tiny if there is one at all, or just get on the bus and wait for the conductor (often a young kid) to collect fares. This is generally done after the bus gets under way. Tickets are good only for the date of issue stamped on them and do not guarantee a seat. Be at the terminal at least half an hour before departure time if you want to be sure of getting a seat; otherwise you may be left behind or have to sit on the roof with the pigs.

On long trips, you can buy a ticket all the way through to your final destination but you may have to wait in the terminal for connections. If you do not have a 'through' ticket, you can avoid waiting by finding another bus line.

Stop-overs are not allowed. If you'll be stopping, buy a series of tickets: city A to city B; then B to the next stop or final destination.

Mexican Student Card discounts can be substantial. (See *Appendices: Schools*.)

Your ticket is also your claim to insurance in the event of an accident. I've never known anyone who had to use it for that but it's worth holding onto just in case. This is true of almost all modes of public transportation. Collecting this so-called insurance would probably be an incredible stroke of luck.

If you lose your ticket, you may have to buy another, so be careful.

Tickets cannot be exchanged or refunded though if you plead and whine they may relent and let you trade. If you've got a ticket that you can't use, the only reliable solution is to sell it.

The first time I found myself in this situation I lurked around the doorway of the terminal, hissing "Guadalajara? *¡Oiga amigo!* Won't you buy a ticket to Guadalajara?" My furtive approach sent prospective customers hustling away as fast as their legs and luggage would allow them. As the moment of departure approached I dropped the "Psssst! Hey!" routine and went right to the ticket counter, buttonholing waiting passengers. The ticket agent groaned and rolled his eyes but did me the favor of directing two Guadalajara-bound people to me. They looked puzzled at having to buy tickets from a bearded gringo but smiled when I gave them a one-*peso* discount.

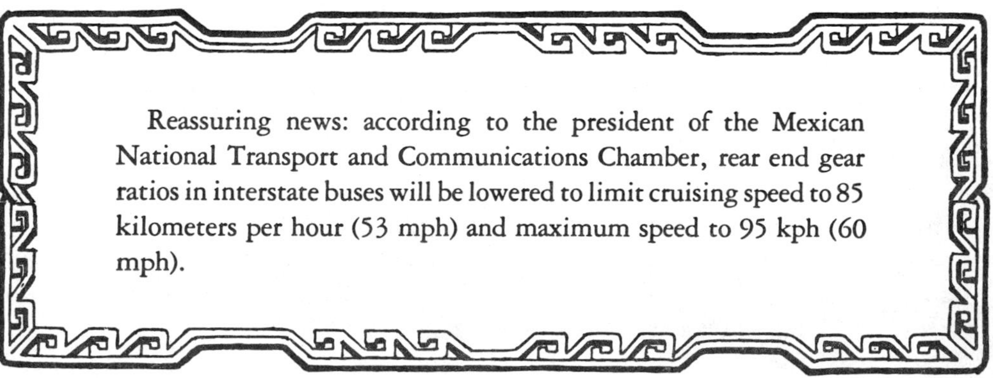

Reassuring news: according to the president of the Mexican National Transport and Communications Chamber, rear end gear ratios in interstate buses will be lowered to limit cruising speed to 85 kilometers per hour (53 mph) and maximum speed to 95 kph (60 mph).

First class tickets are for assigned seats and many second class lines operating newer buses also use numbered seating. Look on the ticket for the word *Asiento* and a number. You may be offered the chance to select your own seat number at the ticket counter. The diagram is similar to those used at airlines.

I always choose a seat in the teens, 13 to 19, give or take a seat. This puts you in the first half of the bus, handy for quick rushes to the front door at rest stops, but far enough back to avoid having to watch traffic. When riding on buses equipped with bathrooms, (almost all first class and many second class) avoid the last few seats. Bus bathrooms are smelly and the odor and slamming of the door will distract you from the scenery.

Your ticket for first class should be marked with the number of the bus, the hour of departure and the destination. Check them closely; if you or the agent makes an error it should be cleared up immediately or they'll assume you've just changed your mind about when you want to leave and are trying to pull a fast one. The departure is marked *Salida* or *Hora* and the bus number is under *Camión* or *Autobus*. The *destino* may be printed right on the ticket or stamped or scribbled across it.

For details on which bus companies serve specific cities and towns see *Appendices: Transportation*.

Baggage

On first class and long haul second class buses, baggage can be checked through to the final destination. You should be given a claim stub and if you aren't, ask for one. Baggage handlers on a few lines tend to be sloppy about checking claim stubs, but on most they are efficient and dependable.

Some second class lines expect passengers to take care of loading and unloading their luggage. This can be preferable to having a twelve-year-old kid slam it into the cargo compartment and bury it beneath a crate of overripe tomatoes. When loading your own, beware of spilled oil or grease. I once took my suitcase out of a second class bus and found it soaked with motor oil. Complaining is a waste of time and air.

The standard baggage allowance is 25 kilos (55 pounds), but unless you're carrying something extra bulky, they'll rarely hold you to the limit. I once travelled with five enormous baskets loaded with handicrafts, a full-sized backpack and a portable typewriter. It took a major conference between the bus driver, ticket agent, baggage handler and myself, but I got that nightmarish quantity aboard for a very reasonable 'adjustment' fee.

Hand carried luggage can be taken aboard, but if it won't fit on the overhead rack the driver has the right to insist that it go below: either between your feet or in the cargo hold. If you really object to this, the alternative is to buy your luggage a seat of its own (which is frowned upon) or to offer a tip to let it ride on the steps or in the aisle. On second class buses, especially older ones, baggage is put anywhere and everywhere and size and weight are rarely problems. If your baggage requires special handling or extra muscle, you may be prodded for a tip by the driver's helper. This is standard practice, though tourists often aren't asked to pay.

On buses that are loaded with *campesinos* coming to or from market, you'll probably observe lively bartering between the driver and his *ayudante* and goods-laden passengers. The discussions over baggage charges can get quite animated. On one bus I rode it took longer to hassle over fares and tips than it did to drive to our destination. The people who had baggage on top of the bus were especially hard hit; the *ayudante* would literally dangle things from the roof over the heads of the passengers, threatening to keep their stuff aboard if they didn't pay what he asked. The driver was helpfully gunning the engine at the same time.

Always label your baggage, including an extra label inside just in case it is lost or misplaced. When travelling long distances I keep my camera and valuable small personal items in a bag or box between my feet. On short rides I carry valuables on my lap or in the rack directly over my head. Rip-offs are not common but it's easier to take a few simple precautions than to chance a loss.

Upon arrival you can wait for the baggage to be taken inside the terminal or take it directly from the handler yourself. On second class *expect* to carry your own.

The largest terminals may have *Andenes de Equipaje* (baggage claim platforms) but if not, your baggage will be taken to the baggage office of the bus line you came in on. If you're confused ask at any ticket counter.

Big terminals will have porters and some offer free baggage carts *(carretillas)*. Porters have a way of whisking you to the more expensive taxis. When I'm loverloaded, however, I always use them; it's far better than losing track of something. Once I'm out on the sidewalk, I can then find whatever transportation I want.

Baggage can be left at the ticket counter in small terminals or in storerooms in larger terminals. Look for signs that say *Guarda Equipaje.* Some charge a small fee, others don't. If it's the storage room for the bus line you're using, your ticket should be sufficient, though a tip isn't a bad idea. Ask if there's a time limit if you expect to be gone for a day or more. I've found that even in larger terminals the ticket agents will usually let me dump my luggage on them for a few hours without bothering with claim stubs or payment.

If by any chance your baggage is lost, *don't panic.* Remain calm and polite; the outraged customer routine rarely gets better results. If phone calls from one depot to another seem to be in order, offer to pay for them. Communication between terminals is usually via messages carried by the drivers, not by expensive phone calls.

The polite offer of a tip (don't act as though you're bribing) can make some underpaid and overworked baggage handler take a sudden interest in digging through a dark storage room.

Border Crossing By Bus

First class tickets for destinations in Mexico can be purchased in the U.S. through Greyhound (affiliated with *Tres Estrellas de Oro, Transportes Del Norte* and *Transportes Chihuahuenses*) or Continental Trailways (*Omnibus de México* and *Estrella Blanca*).

There are several advantages to this: first, a ticket between the U.S. and Mexico includes the border crossing (but you'll first change to a Mexican bus). This saves a cab fare. The bus driver who takes you across or a baggage handler will see that your baggage gets through Mexican customs since the bus he's connecting to can't leave until this happens.

At the station in Mexico, he'll also point out which bus you'll be travelling on. If you're unfamiliar with Mexican bus stations, you'll probably find them slightly mind-boggling at first. They are places of great activity, not at all like the somber dentist-waiting-room atmosphere of American depots.

By being directed to the proper bus, you'll avoid having to find the ticket office and fend off porters and shoeshine boys while taking in the scene: beggars, *taco* stands, tear-filled partings and reunions, and other wide-eyed tourists madly thumbing phrasebooks for the correct pronunciation of "Please direct me to the ticket agent offering connections to Ixtznitlapoapan."

When returning to the U.S. buy your ticket all the way through or to the first border town on the other side. Once again, this takes care of the crossing. Because Mexican ticket agents may not be aware of special fare offers in the U.S. I would wait until north of the border to buy a continuing ticket.

Should you drive to Mexico, you may encounter people who think that *you* are public transportation. A Mexican may mistake a distant gringo van for a regular bus and try to flag it down, assuming it to be one of the small vans that operate as second class buses in many parts of the country.

We often give rides to these people and they invariably offer to pay, even after they find out that we're not operating a bus line. People carrying loads of food to market may offer to pay in goods. We've taken a bunch of onions or a piece of fruit rather than cash.

Whether you accept payment or not, don't brush the offer away too casually or you'll offend the person offering. When the offer is made quite firmly, accept it. If they're just hitchhiking and not seriously eager to pay, you'll be able to tell by their attitude.

Bus Travel Hints:

After many years and many thousands of miles of riding on Mexican buses I've developed several survival skills that make trips much easier.

•Don't hang back when the mob charges a bus without assigned seating or you'll end up standing. Go over the top like a Marine after the Congressional Medal of Honor; that's the way it's done.

•If your assigned seat is taken and the person occupying it doesn't understand your polite request to find the correct seat, just take another. In a short time someone will ask you to move. Keep smiling and shrugging and the driver will soon straighten it all out or leave you where you are.

•When the driver slides behind the wheel and puts the bus in gear, *relax*, he's a professional with a large loving family and a strong desire to retire in one piece. If you backseat drive you'll soon be reduced to a slobbering wreck. Stick your nose against the window or inside a book, chat with your seatmate, drink a beer or nap; you'll be there before you know it. This took me a long time to accept but it's true; even on the awful bus ride when the lady next to me started staying the rosary. Or how about that night when I looked up over the driver's shoulder and saw another bus coming at us head-on at high speed, six feet away My scream didn't even wake the others. It took me several minutes of deep breathing to realize I'd been frightened by the reflection of our own bus in the windshield

•If you have to get off to take a leak or to be sick, don't hesitate to tell the driver or his helper. They may grumble but they'd rather stop than mop.

•Fix the bus number in your mind and if necessary write it on the back of your hand. When the driver calls out "*Quince minutos*," don't expect to come back in 20 minutes and find the bus there. It probably will be, since the driver often stays longer than he says, but if the bus is gone, it's your problem, not his. Meal stops are usually a minimum of 25 minutes and may run close to an hour. Keep an eye out for the driver. If the announced 25 minutes comes and he's ripping into a piece of fried beefsteak you can bet you've got more time.

•Be nice to the driver and his assistant, smile at them and say "*Buenos días.*" If they notice you they'll probably take extra care not to leave you behind. Some, but not all drivers, will take a head count before leaving a rest stop. If the bus starts to pull out and your friend isn't aboard call out *¡Falta uno!*" and they'll wait.

•When travelling with others make a contingency plan in case you become separated. This is an unlikely stroke of bad luck but it doesn't hurt to take precautions. If you or a friend miss the bus go immediately to the ticket counter and tell them what happened. They'll get you on another as fast as possible but don't be surprised if you're charged for another ticket.

•Take first class on long hauls; it costs just slightly more than second class and will make fewer stops and detours.

•If you're in a hurry and in a small town, take a second class bus to a larger town and then catch a first class.

•At night sit on the right hand side of the bus and you'll avoid the glare of oncoming headlights. During the day I always select a seat that won't get the glare and heat of the afternoon sun. Heading south, for example, I would sit on the left (east) side and going north on the right. Mexicans generally avoid exposing themselves to wind even if the wind is a blistering 90 degrees. (See *Superstitions.*) You may be asked to keep your window closed and if so, the shaded side of the bus will be much cooler.

City Buses

City buses are just as hard to figure out as in any part of the world. A city bus usually has *Servicio Urbano* written on it somewhere. The destination is often painted on the windshield with whitewash but it could also be the destination of yesterday's route that the driver didn't bother to clean off. Trial and error and asking for help are the best ways to use city buses.

The cost makes them economical enough to be worth the effort. If you're hitching, you might want to ride one through town.

Buses in big cities stop only at *Parada* signs in the downtown area but on side streets, get on wherever you can and don't hesitate to board one that is stopped at a traffic light.

These buses are often crowded, so crowded that you'll lose track of where you are or be trapped inside and unable to force your way to the door. That's the way it goes; at least you'll see parts of the city that you might have missed otherwise.

You may have to show your ticket to an occasional inspector. If you've thrown it away, he will sell you another.

As on any type of bus, the city transit bus will not stop unless you ring the buzzer over the door, speak to the driver, or beat on the roof with your fist. You may have to say, "*¡Baja! ¡Baja!* (Down) *¡Por favor!*" or "*¡Aquí, por favor!*" If you just yell, "Stop!" in Spanish or English, it often pisses them off and they won't.

Get off through the back door if you can; the driver may not let you out the front unless it's too crowded to do otherwise.

TRAINS

High speed buses are convenient, but they don't have the easy-going style of a train, rattling through the mountains, stopping at what seems to be every other *pueblo*. The lazy traveller lounges in a seat or bed, reading a book or just staring out of the window, wondering how long it will take the beer man to make another round. Some young gringo on his way to Tierra del Fuego is strumming a guitar, a yawning businessman from Mexico City reads the sports section of *Excelsior* while his wife, daughters, mother and two older sisters have tea in the dining car. *El portero* pokes under the seats with his broom, then sweeps the trash overboard from between the cars.

Mexico has a very well developed train system. In spite of stories that a Mexican train is inevitably hours off schedule you will find them reasonably punctual. Delays do occur but not often. The railroad system is not nearly as extensive as buses but train travel has many advantages.

For travellers not in a rush to get where they're going, the leisurely pace of the train becomes a positive factor. The fact that they don't pass each other on curves makes travel by train more relaxed and restful.

Trains often follow routes where there are no roads and stop at villages that are otherwise accessible only on foot. The countryside along the track is likely to be unspoiled, without the usual gas stations, cafes and tire repair shops one constantly sees alongside the highway.

See *Appendices: Transportation* for a map of major train routes.

Tickets

Train travel is very inexpensive. (See *Prices*.) A first class train seat costs about three-fourths of the price of a first class bus ride. A second class train ticket is about half as much as a first class bus. A berth on the train just about doubles the cost of first class. On long trips having a bed usually means the difference between arriving tired or rested. This is especialy nice if you have trouble sleeping sitting up or like privacy.

The comfort of train travel is largely dependent on how much you're willing to pay. Second class is very cheap and very uncomfortable: poorly padded seats (if at all), ancient cars which are crowded, dirty, noisy, hot or cold according to the weather outside and generally picturesque, like most uncomfortable situations when viewed from a slight distance.

Young travellers are often attracted to second class, both for the savings and for the atmosphere. In most cases they usually regret not going first class; the price difference is small and if you need excitement you can always visit the second class cars. The bathrooms in second class are rough, to say the least.

Regular first class may be unheated and unairconditioned, with seats that aren't very comfortable. One car I rode in had *Primera Clase* painted over a still legible *Segunda Clase.* The only difference was the degree of crowding.

Most people will want *Primera Especial*, or *Primera Numerada* (sometimes called *Turismo*). Seats are assigned, though this isn't enforced if the car isn't full. These cars will have restrooms, men's and women's, and on most trains they are kept reasonably clean. Drinking water and paper cups are also provided. Air conditioning and heating may or may not be in operation. One trip we made started with the temperature so high that passengers had to ride between the cars until the wind cooled our car down. And on another trip, in wintertime, Lorena and I sat wrapped in sleeping bags, watching less well equipped passengers slowly turn blue.

Tickets in smaller stations may not be sold until the train arrives or shortly before. This can lead to crowding and confusion at the ticket window, but if you decide to board the train without a ticket, you'll have to pay the *auditor* an additional 25 percent above the regular fare.

If tickets are sold out and you're desperate, ask a porter if there isn't *some way* to get aboard. We've done this and although it took a few extra dollars, a friendly porter conjured up two first class tickets for us. A friend calls this "Mexican witchcraft."

Round trip tickets cost double one-way and are valid for only 30 days. There are no special deals for groups although students holding current Mexican Student Cards (see *Appendices: Schools*) can get a 50 percent discount during three vacation seasons *(ciclo especial de vacaciones)*. These are: 15 to 31 December
15 to 30 May
1 July to 31 August

The student discount is for seats only, not beds.

If you lose your ticket, tough luck; buy another.

Children under five are free; over five and under twelve, half fare; over twelve, full price.

Refunds on tickets are given only under the following conditions: if the trip is interrupted or cancelled by fault of the railroad company itself; if the passenger cancels 24 hours in advance of departure; or if the passenger cancels three hours in advance of departure when the ticket is bought on the same day; in all cases by writing a nice letter explaining the circumstances in English or Spanish to: *Jefe, Departamento de Tráfico de Pasajeros, Gran Estación Central de Buenavista, Av. Insurgentes Norte, México 3, D.F.* He can also be approached personally. Most railroad officials speak English.

If you get into a dispute over a ticket or are confused, pay what is asked, get a receipt *(recibo)* and write or speak to the people in the office mentioned above.

Exchanges of tickets come under the same rules as for refunds.

Reservations

Whenever possible buy your tickets in advance. This will save standing in line or not getting aboard at all. Train travel is popular and trains are sometimes full. During the Christmas and Easter holidays, if you don't have a reservation you'd better forget it entirely.

The railroads advise tourists to make reservations by mail, one or two months in advance. Send them a letter (in English if you wish) giving all details, including number of children and their ages, etc. (For addresses of Railroads, see *Appendices: Transportation*.) They will write back and tell you how much it will cost. You then send a cashier's check or certified check payable to National Railways of Mexico. No other form of payment can be used. They'll either send you the tickets or tell where they can be picked up.

Railway offices will also send information on schedules and fares in English upon request.

Baggage

Adults are allowed 110 pounds each, children 55 pounds. We've often taken more and gotten away with it. It pays to hire a porter if you've got more baggage than can be easily carried in two hands. They'll find your seat and help you stow your stuff.

When you're coming into Mexico, baggage will be inspected by Mexican Customs officials at the train depot, as the passengers are being boarded. Tourists are usually hustled right through but if you have something unusual in your luggage you may be questioned about it. A porter makes a good middleman. Porter service is available in larger stations and their rates are determined by the railway company.

Baggage cannot be checked on some trains. First class cars, however, have extra space behind the last row of seats and most have an additional cubby hole or two for excess baggage.

If you're riding second class keep a sharp eye on your baggage. I've heard of a few cases where departing passengers took more than their share. Quick thieves may also hop into second class during stops. The first class cars are watched by the conductor and porters so the danger of rip-offs is much less.

Larger stations have baggage rooms *(Guarda Equipaje)*. There is a small fee charged for each 24 hours. Baggage can be left for longer periods (weeks) but this is a private enterprise, not a service of the railway company; they take *no responsibility*. Don't lose your claim ticket!

Food

Dining car service is available on long distance runs but the food isn't especially good. It isn't especially bad, either, but by preparing a substantial picnic basket before the trip you'll save money and avoid indigestion.

Meals in the dining car are announced by a man in a white jacket playing a small chime.

Fruit is sold at almost every stop, as well as the usual *tacos, enchiladas, gorditas,* chicken, rice, candy, sodas, and miscellaneous junkfood. For those unaccustomed to Mexican food I would advise caution.

If you're travelling south stop in a supermarket at the border and stock up on cheese, nuts, bread, vegetables, canned juices, crackers, condiments and magazines. A bottle of wine or liquor is nice to have; beer sold on the train is not cheap. Travellers heading out of Mexico City's Buena Vista station can buy a box lunch there (standard fare: two ham sandwiches, one hardboiled egg, one banana, one orange and a piece of cake).

A better picnic, however, is available by shopping at the supermarket half a block from the station. Go out the front doors to the old railroad engine planted near the boulevard. From there you can see the sign of a huge supermarket-department store across the street. It has an excellent selection of cheeses and other picnic ingredients, as well as beer, wine and liquors.

Beer, soft drinks, canned juices and candies are sold on the train by men carrying buckets and boxes. Their prices are not a bargain but it is convenient. In the morning they will bring around hot sweet coffee, calling out "*¡Café!*" It is usually stronger than hell.

Sleeping

I love to sleep on a train, at least when we can afford some sort of bed. When we can't it's a matter of trying to imagine I'm in one, instead of slouching in a seat, fighting off a stiff neck. If you're lucky and the train isn't crowded it is possible to flop across two seats. In spite of her height Lorena somehow manages to make this look comfortable. I'm less flexible and have to be content with sitting upright. Fortuntely pillows *(cojín)* can be rented at night from the porter. They reduce head-knocking against the window.

Sleeping in second class is difficult to impossible. The lights are left on all night and there's usually an assortment of wailing children, loud drunks or bragging soldiers to contend with. Second class passengers who attempt to sneak into the first class cars for a quick nap are inevitably caught and sent back by the conductor. Pretending to be asleep is no defense; they have almost infallible memories and won't hesitate to shake you awake to check your ticket.

The cost of a bed is not bad, especially if shared by two people. We've found that the rest and privacy are usually well worth the extra expense. Beds are available in the following categories:

Upper and lower berth (*cama alta* and *cama baja*): two adults and one child can sleep in a berth or up to four adults and one child in a section (upper and lower). At night a section is surrounded by a heavy curtain, during the day it is made into opposing cushioned seats. These cars have restroom facilities and are generally quieter and better maintained than regular first class.

Roomettes (*camarín*) are for one or two intimate persons. They are equipped with toilet, sink, mirror, small cupboards, fan and a door. These accommodations closely resemble a tiny ship's stateroom, a feeling which is enhanced once the train is underway and begins rocking back and forth. The bed makes into a seat during the day and at night the toilet is hidden beneath the bed. The bed is comfortable but cramped for two people. With the bed down there's very little floor space; just enough to get your shoes on.

Bedrooms (*alcoba*) have upper and lower berths, toilet facilities and more open space than the *camarín*. A double room, *alcoba doble*, can be made by opening the dividing wall between two bedrooms. It's very nice for couples travelling together and families. A *gabinete*, when available, has three beds.

The following regulations are taken from the National Railways information bulletins. Like all regulations they can change under the influence of friendly persuasion accompanied by *propinas* (tips).

In addition to the cost of whatever type of bed or room you're occupying, National Railways requires the purchase of one adult seat ticket per berth; one adult and one half fare for a section, two adult tickets for an *alcoba*; and four adult tickets for an *alcoba doble*.

Because some stations cannot sell sleeping space, you may have to make a reservation in advance and pay the full price from the train's point of origin, in order to insure that you get a bed. You can take a chance, however, and try for a bed after you're aboard the train. If the conductor says that they are full, ask him if you can have a bed when one becomes vacant. Some people get off in the middle of the night and you can at least have a bed for part of the trip. Tips help considerably.

General Information and Advice

Passenger trains are generally made up of older cars retired from service in the U.S. The staffs also seem to have stopped the clock about 30 years back; they wear traditional railroad uniforms and are very fussy about their jobs and responsibilities. The average train consists of the *maquinista* (engineer), the *fogonero* (fireman), *conductor* (the over-all boss), three *garroteros,* (conductor's signalmen-helpers), one at the front, middle and rear of the train, one *portero* per car and the *auditor*, in charge of checking and selling tickets aboard the train. If there's a dining car it has about ten cooks and waiters (*cocineros* and *meseros*).

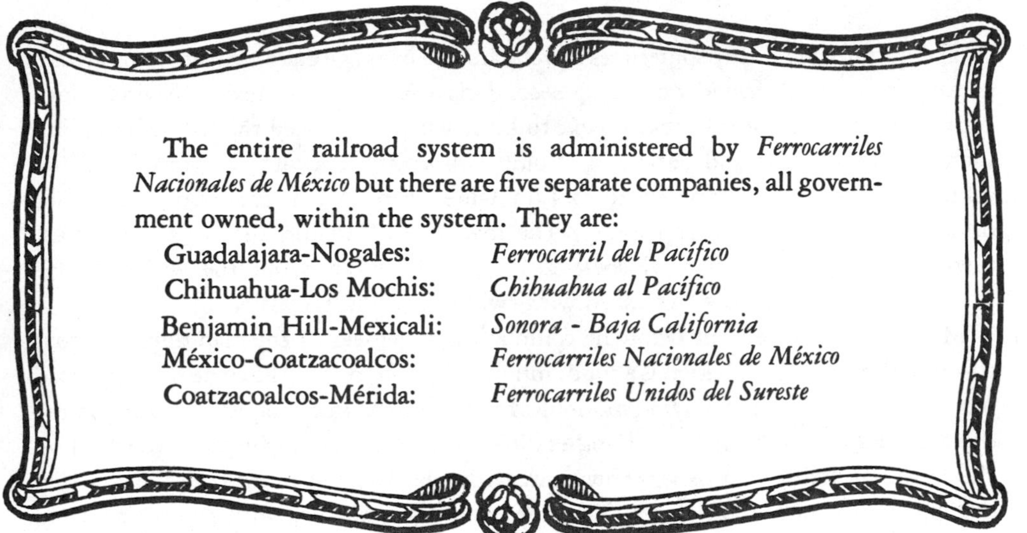

The entire railroad system is administered by *Ferrocarriles Nacionales de México* but there are five separate companies, all government owned, within the system. They are:

Guadalajara-Nogales:	*Ferrocarril del Pacífico*
Chihuahua-Los Mochis:	*Chihuahua al Pacífico*
Benjamin Hill-Mexicali:	*Sonora - Baja California*
México-Coatzacoalcos:	*Ferrocarriles Nacionales de México*
Coatzacoalcos-Mérida:	*Ferrocarriles Unidos del Sureste*

Stops are frequent and vary in length from seconds to hours. The best way to determine how long you'll be at a station is to observe the other passengers: if they flock to the food vendors, it's usually a long stop. Be careful of being left behind. The conductor may know how long they'll be there but then again, he may not. On some routes trains are shuffled around at stops and it's easy to get confused and lose track of your particular car. Note its number carefully.

It will be cold at night on northern routes in wintertime. Have a jacket, blanket or sleeping bag handy.

Dollars are not normally accepted aboard the train and if they are, the rate of exchange won't be good. Change enough money into *pesos* to last the entire ride.

Have toilet paper handy; there won't be any in second class and it sometimes runs out in first class.

If you're getting off at an intermediate point be sure to get your things ready well ahead of time. Even though the porter may promise to wake you up, don't count on it.

Lorena and I were once sound asleep in a *camarín*, engulfed, as usual, in our excess baggage, when the porter yelled that we had about three minutes to get dressed, sorted out and off the train. He and the conductor formed a baggage brigade and shortly after waking from deep dreams, we found ourselves standing knee deep in boxes, packs, and bags, on a dark, deserted platform, still buttoning up our clothes.

The *federales* and Army sometimes search cars and baggage en route (the Army always travels by train). A friend was riding second class in southern Mexico, having a nice conversation with the man seated next to him, when he noticed the fellow becoming increasingly agitated and nervous. "Would you do me a favor?" the man suddenly asked, forcing the window next to him wide open. My friend said "Yes," not understanding what was happening. The man looked around the car a few times, obviously frightened, then whispered, "Throw those boxes out the window!" He pointed to three large cartons lashed with twine sitting in the aisle.

My friend hesitated but before he could ask any questions, the man dove headfirst through the window. There was a thud, followed by a short cry. When he stuck his head out my friend saw the man lying motionless alongside the track, rapidly receding in the distance. He turned his head in the other direction and saw a group of *federales* signalling the train. Realizing that he was now stuck with whatever was in the boxes, he quickly dumped them out of the window. The other passengers watched without comment and when the cops searched the car, obviously looking for someone in particular, no one said a word.

Pets

Dogs and cats must ride in the baggage cars. If they aren't in a cage, box or other container they should have a collar and leash. The fee is small but the railroad takes no responsibility for the conditions under which the pet travels or in which it arrives. They recommend giving the baggage handlers aboard the train a good tip. Pets can also be shipped express. Birds must travel in cages.

TAXIS

Taxi service is relatively inexpensive. A town or village of any consequence will have at least one cab, even though it may be a wreck of a car or pickup truck with broken seats and no fenders.

Because the cost and maintenance of even an old car are far beyond the means of most Mexicans, taxis are more commonly used than in the U.S. If a special Sunday outing, picnic, wedding, birthday party or social visit requires the use of a *coche*, it will be hired, along with the driver. What seems at first to be an extravagance is actually quite the opposite: rather than use private cars casually Mexicans ride buses, trains and cabs.

Tourists would often save by doing the same. The cost of insurance, for example, would hire a taxi for a good many miles, without the responsibility of driving or ownership.

Meters are used in larger cities but in smaller towns taxi rates are determined by distance and bargaining, though some cabs post the rates per kilometer or per hour in the window. Bus stations may also have signs announcing what should be paid to specific destinations.

In rural areas private car owners or licensed cabbies will make irregular runs between towns, charging by the head and amount of baggage. They'll often wait until they've got a full load before leaving. If the driver sets a flat price, the passengers may beat the bushes for other riders to share the expense, sometimes bringing it down as low as a bus ticket. (See *Navigating in Mexico City*.)

Border Cabs: When crossing into the United States from Mexico you may find it convenient to take a taxi across the border rather than trying to figure out city buses or walking. Certain Mexican cab drivers are licensed to drive into the U.S. They'll charge a flat rate, subject to haggling. Because the cabbie will have to wait until you are checked through U.S. Customs, his fare depends somewhat on the amount of baggage you're carrying. If, for example, you've got half a dozen boxes, bags and baskets—our usual load—he'll expect more money while waiting out what may be a long inspection. Agree on a flat rate for the trip and inspection time or on a flat rate plus an additional amount per 15 minutes or half hour spent at Customs.

Set rates are posted in some bus stations and train stations along the border but cab drivers will rarely hold to them.

RENTAL CARS

Car rental agencies can be found in Mexico City and towns of any size. Look for familiar names: Hertz, Avis de México, Budget Rent-A-Car and others, Combi Rent SA, Auto Rent, etc. Most rental agencies have someone around who speaks English.

Rates are government controlled but special offers and requirements vary from one company to another. In general, however, you'll have to be 25 years old, have a valid driver's license and passport (or tourist card) and a credit card or enough cash for a substantial deposit. Check requirements versus rates before deciding: Combi Rent, for example, has low prices but does not accept credit cards (for rates see *Appendices: Transportation.*)

Rental cars can be driven one way for an additional charge per return kilometer.

Before renting a car make a rough estimate of how much driving you'll be doing and what the basic charges will be. You may well find that it's cheaper to hire a cab for shorter trips and to fly for longer jaunts. Cars are considered a luxury in Mexico, not a necessity.

NAVIGATING IN MEXICO CITY

Mexico City is literally the crossroads of the country and anyone tavelling south of the capital will almost certainly have to pass through it. Just how complicated that will be depends not only on where you're going or coming from, but by what means you arrive and how much you're willing to pay for connections. If this already sounds confusing just wait until you're actually there. Mexico City has a predicted population of 35 to 40 million by the year 2000 and it feels as though most of them are already in town, just waiting to be counted.

Four main terminals and several minor ones control first and second class bus traffic in and out of the city.

Terminal Central del North, Avenida de los Cien Metros, 4907. This terminal is huge. Anyone arriving from or heading north of the city will pass through the *Terminal del Norte.* (The most southerly cities served are Manzanillo on the Pacific Coast and Poza Rica on the Gulf.)

Terminal Central del Sur, Avenida Taxqueña 1320. For those going to Cuernavaca, Taxco, Acapulco, Zihuatanejo and vicinity.

Terminal Central del Sureste, Zaragoza 200 (near the airport). Opened in late 1978 to serve the southeast and Yucatan peninsula.

Estación Cristóbal Colón, Blvd. Gral. Ignacio Zaragoza 38. To Oaxaca, Tehuantepec, Tapachula, San Cristóbal de las Casas and Guatemala (you must change to the *Galgos* line within Guatemala).

The size and complexity of the city make it impossible to explain all the ins and outs of getting from one point to another. If you just want to get it over with as quickly as possible, here are connections travellers frequently need to make.

Terminal del Norte to:

•**Terminal del Sur.** Take *Delfín* bus 7D either way from in front of the terminals. The bus going to the Southern terminal has a blue stripe running along the side of the bus and the one going to the Northern terminal has an orange stripe. No standing is allowed but baggage is. It's about a 45-minute ride in light traffic.

For a faster trip (without baggage only) take the *Metro, Línea 2, Dirección Taxqueña* to *Estación Taxqueña* and you'll be right near the Southern Bus Terminal. (See *Subway*.)

•**Buena Vista Railroad Station.** Take the same bus, 7D. The railway station isn't too far from the Northern terminal and is quite obvious. (Ask the bus driver for *estación del tren*). This also works in reverse; 7D will take you from the railroad station to the *Terminal del Norte.* The bus has an orange stripe along the side when going north. It also says *'Cien Metros.'* To go to *Terminal del Sur* from the train station you would have to ride the 7D orange striped bus to *Terminal del Norte* and from there take the blue striped 7D to the southern terminal.

•**Airport.** Bus 12 goes back and forth between the airport and the *Camino Real* Hotel, via the downtown area, along the *Reforma* and *Alameda.* To get to the airport from the northern or southern terminals or train station, take 7D to *Insurgentes Metro* station, (which is where this bus route ends) and ask for *Avenida Reforma* or *Hotel Camino Real.* They are both within walking distance if you don't have much luggage. Get Bus 12 there. To get from the airport to the train and North or South bus stations, get off Bus 12 as it crosses *Insurgentes* and take the 7D north with the orange stripe for the train station or *Terminal del Norte.* To reach the Southern bus terminal go first to the Northern terminal and from there catch 7D with the blue stripe going south.

For other destinations ask at the tourist booth in the airport. The bus driver will usually signal when you reach your destination if you ask him on boarding: *"¿Me puede avisar cuando pase la calle ________?"* ("Can you tell me when you pass ________ Street?") Sit near him if you can or occasionally remind him you're still on board.

Bus 12 leaves the airport every 15 minutes and baggage is allowed. The airport is otherwise difficult to get to and from without taking some type of taxi.

•**Other stations and points.** Ask at the information booth in whatever terminal you're at. As of press time the *Zaragoza (Sureste)* station was brand new and no definite inter-connections had yet been established.

Mexico City Buses

I like to climb on a city bus and ride to the end of the line, then grab another and ride it out, and then another, until I've seen half of Mexico City and am hopelessly lost. It's a cheap tour, one that's usually full of surprises.

There are three basic types of city buses in the capital: *Delfín* (Dolphin), *Ballenas* (Whales) and *Metro* (they look like the underground *Metro* cars). They're all very cheap, plentiful and convenient.

Delfín buses will not allow standing passengers or bulky luggage (except from the airport and bus stations). Look for a silver dolphin on the side and orange or blue stripes.

Ballenas are less discriminating; they'll haul all they can hold and then some, including your guitar, backpack and pet chicken.

The destination of the bus will be shown on the front. *Parada* signs (bus stops) will identify a bus by number and destination. These buses stop only at *Parada* signs and loading and unloading is done quickly. Have small change on hand if possible. When you've got your ticket move as far to the rear as possible. Passengers must exit from the rear unless the bus is too crowded.

Some buses have signal cords and others have a button over the rear door to let the driver know you want off. Fortunately the days when transit drivers didn't make full stops have ended so you won't have to bail out until the bus has actually come to a halt. Don't dawdle, however, or he might take off when you've got only one foot on the ground. There is no transfer system.

Taxis in Mexico City

There are cheap cabs and expensive cabs. The most inexpensive are the *peseros* or *colectivos* but these operate only on main streets. They will have a small *colectivo* sign on top and though they prefer to stop at designated spots they can sometimes be flagged down. A *pesero* may or may not have the end points of its route whitewashed on the windshield or scrawled on a piece of cardboard among the plastic saints and flowers. They will cram in as many passengers as possible, to the point of sitting on each other's laps. Though the days when a *pesero* ride actually cost only one *peso* are long gone, they're still a bargain.

Metered cabs come in various sizes and colors. The cheapest are *mini-taxis* (VW bugs).

Absolutely insist that the meter *(taxímetro)* be turned on or you'll be overcharged and outraged. A boarding fee, called a *banderazo*, is already included on the meter's reading when you get in. This varies according to the type of cab.

The most expensive cabs are *Turismos*, usually big American cars with an onimous black hood over the meter, which means they'll take both you and your budget for a ride.

Taxi tickets are sold in the biggest bus terminals. Look for a booth with a sign saying *Boletos de taxi*. A large map shows concentric rings, or *zonas*. Locate your destination or tell the ticket person where you're going. You'll be sold a cab ticket for a particular zone. Give it to one of the drivers outside. The trip is now completely paid for.

At the airport the system varies according to the type of taxi. In some the money is given to the driver in advance and he buys the ticket at a booth near the exit ramp. Metered cabs operating out of the airport are expensive. There are also those that charge a flat rate, per person, while others, called *colectivos* or *semi-colectivos* charge by the trip, dividing the cost among the passengers. The *colectivos* will wait until they have a full load before leaving.

If you don't have very much luggage ask for *Boulevard Puerto Aéreo*, (only a couple of blocks away) where you can catch a taxi that charges regular metered fares.

There are also radio call cabs, listed in the phone book under *Sitios*. (These cabs have *SITIO* marked on the side.) They use meters but charge an extra fee for the call service on top of what the meter marks at the end of the ride. If a cruising *Sitio* cab picks you up in the street, remember that you'll be charged something extra, even though you didn't use the radio call service.

Any meter reading not in even pesos is rounded off to the cabbie's benefit.

A 10 percent night-time charge is added to meter readings between 11 p.m. and 7 a.m.

Tips are not required unless the cabbie has performed a special service—such as getting bus tickets or taking you to his favorite whorehouse.

A cab is available when the *Libre* (free) flag on the meter is horizontal.

Hourly rates are available in *Turismo* cabs, some operated by English-speaking drivers, and in other cabs on a haggling basis. You can ask someone, a desk clerk for example, to inquire about the price and to make the deal if your Spanish is weak. Ask for *precio por hora* or *por día* (by the hour or by the day). If done by the day ask how many hours the driver considers a day to be; it might be only three or four.

Any cab going to the airport, city limits or beyond will charge a *tarifa convencional* (convenience rate) which literally means "to the drivers' convenience"; he will name a price and you can bargain until you reach a mutual agreement.

In the event of a hassle, take the cab number and report the incident to the tourist bureau, or call a cop.

Subway *(Metro)*

The *Metro* in Mexico City is a fast and fun way to get around. By color codes, symbols and maps found in stations and cars you can more or less figure out where you are and where you are going.

A ticket is very cheap and even cheaper if you buy five at a time.

Bulky baggage (backpacks, guitars, boxes, even large shopping bags) are definitely not allowed aboard the *Metro.* Exceptions were made in the past but crowding has reached such proportions that this rule is now strictly enforced.

The *Metro* stations alone are worth the price of a ticket. Many have interesting displays, including archaeological finds from the excavation of the subway tunnels, and it's fun to watch people getting on and off.

The *Metro* closes at midnight and after that you'll have to rely on an occasional bus or cab. It opens again at 6 a.m.

See *Appendices: Transportation* for a map of the *Metro* routes.

AIRPLANES

Air service to and within Mexico is good but it costs several times the price of a first class bus or train ticket.

With increasing competition between airlines it is inevitable (or hopeful, anyway) that fares to and from Mexico will decrease. At the present time two airlines offer cut rate nighttime flights from the west coast and more discount deals are expected. Check with a travel agent for details.

Domestic flights (within a country's borders) usually cost substantially less than International flights of the same distance. For this reason you can often save by waiting until you've crossed the border into Mexico before catching a plane. Once again, check with a travel agent.

Mexican planes which carry passengers to or from the U.S. must conform to U.S. standards. Mexican airlines are very proud of their safety record.

Small planes are widely used in Mexico for trips into isolated areas. Many small airlines also operate regular or sort-of-regular flights between large cities and tourist towns. Their prices are usually quite reasonable.

FERRIES

Have you ever had the desire to take a sea cruise but couldn't afford the price? If so, consider a passage on one of Mexico's large car/passenger ferries. These ships travel between points on the Baja California Peninsula and the mainland of Mexico. They are made in Europe, quite modern, comfortable, and equipped with a cafeteria and bar. The price of a crossing of the Sea of Cortez is relatively low, especially for foot passengers. (See *Prices*.)

There are four routes: La Paz to Mazatlan, La Paz to Topolobampo, Cabo San Lucas to Puerto Vallarta and Santa Rosalia to Guaymas. Another route between Puerto Escondido (near Loreto) and Topolobampo was cancelled before it even began due to hurricane damage to the docking facilities in Baja.

Schedules may vary slightly depending on the tides, weather and amount of traffic but they are otherwise quite reliable. (See *Appendices: Transportation* for sailing times.)

•Gulf of Mexico and Caribbean: In spite of official announcements that a car ferry service was opening between the Yucatan Peninsula and Florida, this has never gone into actual operation. Other than the ferries in the Sea of Cortez and along some highways (see *Driving*) there are no regularly scheduled ferries that I know of in Mexico.

Tickets and Reservations

Passengers have a choice of four classes of accommodations (except on the routes to Guaymas and Topolobampo, where only the first two classes are available). These are: *Salon, Turista, Cabina* and *Especial.*

Salon class is a bus-type reclining seat. *Salon* compartments are large, with lots of walking room (except at night when many passengers spread out for a nap on the deck) and plenty of windows. *Turista* consists of cubicles with bunkbeds and washbasin. *Cabina* is a tiny cabin with two single beds and a bath. *Especial* is an even larger 'suite,' also with two beds and bath.

If you are travelling alone and take a cabin, you may have the room to yourself for the price of a single ticket. However, if the ferry is crowded, you will be given a roommate of the same sex. The price of a berth in any category includes your passage.

Infants travel free and children 11 years and younger are half-fare.

Salon class tickets are sold on a first-come first-served basis but anyone desiring a bed or travelling with a vehicle should try to make reservations in advance. This is especially advisable during the holidays, when most of the ferries are completely filled. The easiest way to make a reservation (for those already in Mexico) is to visit a large travel agency or apply directly at the ferry office in one of the ports. The ferries, known as *Transbordadores*, are operated by *Caminos Y Puentes Federales de Ingresos Y Servicios Conexos*. These offices and the ferry docks are well known and easy to locate.

Reservations and information are easily available in the U.S.through the International Travel Service, 3130 Wilshire Blvd., Suite 502, Los Angeles, CA 90010, phone (213) 381-7707. The travel agent will call Mexico (billed to your phone), confirm a reservation and then issue you a ticket voucher. There is also a service charge; the Mexican government absolutely refuses to pay commissions to travel agents, a fact that severely limits the number of travel agencies handling Mexican reservations.

When making a reservation be sure to give the exact length of your vehicle (and trailer), including extensions to the front and rear and the height if it is unusually tall.

Vehicles and Pets

Many people take advantage of the shortcut across the Sea of Cortez to avoid the long and often traffic-filled coastal mainland highway. Baja ferries can carry just about any vehicle, including semi trucks and passenger buses. The fare is based on length, though extra large vehicles may also be charged for height and weight. Motorcycles pay a flat fee.

Your vehicle will be measured by a *Transbordadores* employee before boarding. If you have extended the length by adding a spare tire to the front bumper or other piece of equipment, it might well put you into the next size category. (See *Appendices: Transportation*.) When in doubt, remove any extensions if you can.

A charge is made for each vehicle, including those carried or towed by others. A dune buggy or motorcycle, for example, will be counted separately.

Once aboard you will absolutely not be allowed inside your car until the trip is over. This means you'll want to have your camera, toothbrush, picnic basket and other personal stuff ready in advance.

Pets must stay in the vehicle and no care is provided. Don't feed your pet too heavily before boarding unless it has exceptional powers of self control. Allow adequate ventilation; the cargo compartments are tightly sealed during the crossing and get very stuffy. Give your pet plenty to drink in a stable container—if it tips over, that's it.

Tourist Cards, Car Papers and Customs Inspections

When crossing from Baja to the mainland of Mexico you must have both a tourist card and a car import permit. The latter is available at the dock in Santa Rosalia and Cabo San

Lucas and in the Aduana office in La Paz. For more details see *Baja California* and *Entering Mexico: Red Tape.*

When leaving Baja by ferry all passengers and vehicles are subject to inspection by Mexican Customs. This may take place either before boarding or as you disembark. Foreign tourists are almost always given the briefest treatment; it's the Mexican tourists who are carefully looked over. Since La Paz is a free port, it is a popular shopping place for mainlanders. Goods purchased by them in Baja are dutiable. In recent years, however, drug smuggling via Baja has led to an increase in searches of gringos and their cars. Dope sniffing dogs are sometimes used, both in Baja and on the mainland.

BOATS AND BEASTS

Small boats aren't commonly used for travel within Mexico by tourists, though many Mexicans depend on them for transportation. It is very difficult to get accurate information about boat service. The canoe someone told you about may have gone to the bottom by the time you get there or will be loaned out to a relative.

In spite of a lack of schedules regular boat service (and by boat I mean anything that will float, from dugout canoes to modern fiberglass *pangas* with big outboards) does exist on many rivers, lagoons and coastal areas. All it takes is determination, patience and a desire to see parts of Mexico that are rarely visited by tourists. It is just about our favorite mode of travel.

One other type of transportation deserves mention—animal back. Many people would like to make long treks in search of Adventure. If it's done by *bestia* ('beast' as the people call them, from horses to burros), the real adventure may be surviving the agony of sore muscles and a blistered butt.

One problem of long trips by *bestia*, or even by foot, is that they are often made into areas considered slightly taboo by the government. In Yucatan, local authorities would not allow us to visit an area of the coast because they suspected we might be buying or looking for artifacts.

In other areas, dope might be suspected as the reason for your trip. Even if you aren't a dealer in artifacts or opium, without legitimate credentials as an archaeologist or permission from the government, you may be discouraged from making the trip.

If you go ahead with arrangements for this type of travel, get someone, preferably the owner of the animals, to go with you as a guide. He probably won't rent them to you alone if you don't know how to handle and care for the animals.

For more details on Boats and Beasts see *The People's Guide To Camping In Mexico.*

HITCHING

It's legal and common...Don't push yourself...Finding a good ride...In the boondocks...A handy survival kit...Alone...Hazards...A ride to remember...

Hitching rides is socially acceptable in Mexico. Don't think that you'll be the only person with your thumb out; there are many Mexicans, from laborers to students, doing it too. Truck drivers and middle and upper class Mexicans will give hitchers a lift. Their curiosity will quickly overcome any shyness they may feel toward a foreigner, especially if your appearance or equipment is distinctive.

I once asked a Mexican friend, after a long discussion of what he called the 'hippie problem,' what he really thought of *turistas* who hitched around the country with just a few dollars. He paused for a few moments and then said, "Well, they don't contribute anything to the economy but...well...you have to admit that they travel *con valor mexicano*" (with Mexican courage). This rather grudging respect is common.

Many of the people who pick you up will offer to buy you a meal, put you up for the night or show you something of interest. Remember that when Mexicans make such an offer, *they mean it* and it's difficult to refuse without giving offense. The best payment you can give for a favor is a polite 'thanks' or another favor in return: wash the windshield or tell a funny story.

Hitching involves almost total immersion in Mexico. For the person with a poor knowledge of Spanish or not experienced in hitching or travelling, this can be traumatic. It is important, therefore, to break into things gradually and to know *when to stop*.

Pushing yourself too hard, whether it's by eating poorly and sleeping very little or by trying to see and experience everything all at once, will lead to trouble. Marathon travel by any means leads to exhaustion. Exhaustion leads to grouchiness, irrational thinking and eventually to illness.

Although it is possible to live incredibly cheaply in Mexico, really economical travel, especially hitchhiking, takes a great deal of restraint, common sense and planning. Why hitch a ride for 1000 miles and then spend more money on a room for the night and a big meal than it would have cost for a ticket on an air-conditioned bus? You enjoy the trip less and after you've arrived you must spend both time and money recovering.

We've met many people who travelled like this and who actually spent more money by hitching than if they'd gone exclusively by public transportation. For those who had the money it didn't matter, but for those who didn't it means a shorter trip. (For more ideas on cheap travel and living see *Travelling Cheap* and *The People's Guide to Camping in Mexico.*)

We also met a guy travelling on almost nothing, eating quite well and having a very good time. His technique was to take whatever came along, whether it was a ride to a town he'd never heard of or an offer of a free dinner. Rather than free loading, he made an effort to be useful to anyone who befriended him. He taught campers how to hang their hammocks, pick coconuts or helped them on marketing trips. The meals and rides he received in return were given gratefully and people soon began to pass him on from one friend to another as a sort of *major-domo.* He never stayed long with one group and his visit was never an imposition.

There are a few tricks that can make hitching much easier: if you've been dropped off at the edge of a town that has to be crossed it's often more convenient to take an *urbano* (city bus) rather than wait for a ride that is going through. *Pemex* stations are excellent places to pick up a ride and the management rarely objects if you wander around asking drivers for *un ride* or *aventón.*

Trailer parks are good places to get rides with gringos but keep in mind that the most conservative people in Mexico are not Mexicans, they're other tourists. Gringos can be buttered up by offering to translate for them or by making it quite clear that you want a ride only for a certain time or distance. Anyone who has had the common experience of getting stuck with a hitchhiker tends to be leery when approached by another.

If you or your gear are exceptionally scroungy, your chances of a ride will diminish. Friends who have tried hitching with such things as surfboards, large musical instruments, wheelchairs, goats and monkeys, found them to be liabilities.

Hitching rides on cargo trucks is usually easy, but women are technically prohibited from riding in many company trucks. The management of these firms assumes that the female hitchhiker will be unable to restrain herself and will distract the driver's attention with panting and pawing. Don't be upset, therefore, if the driver asks a woman hitcher to get out of the truck or to hide when reaching a town or trucker's check point.

Children almost always make hitching easier. We met a family in Guatemala who had been hitching together for two years. They found it both a wonderful way to travel and also quite economical. There were five of them, including an infant. "We don't get many rides in small Volkswagens," the mother said, "but there's nothing like several hours in the back of a truck to keep the family spirit high."

Although hitching on main roads is generally quite easy, travelling by thumb into more remote and less populated areas can involve waiting or walking. You should definitely be prepared to do some waiting if you don't have enough money for bus fare or are one of those people who absolutely refuse to pay for a ride.

The length of time you'll wait for a ride usually depends on just one thing: luck. It is true, however, that most traffic in the back country occurs in the morning and evening, when people are off to town or just returning. It's best to ask someone nearby; most country people know every vehicle in the area and more-or-less where it's at and what it's doing.

If you're told that the prospects of a ride in the next eight hours or two days are very low, relax; it's time to take a good rest or to make your stop into a side trip of its own.

When hitching in areas with very infrequent bus service or none at all (rare), you may be asked to pay for your rides. This is common practice; any tourist who has driven into the boondocks has undoubtedly been approached by people who not only expect a lift but expect to reimburse the driver for it.

The owners of flatbed and pickup trucks are accustomed to filling extra space with paying bodies. If you flag or thumb down a ride on one of these, ask the driver what it's going to cost; it may be surprisingly high, though a bargain in comparison to no ride at all. With rising gas prices, drivers are forced to charge a fare based on expenses rather than a large volume of passengers. In almost every case the price will be fair.

Anyone interested in penetrating deep into the back country without backpacking will find these trucks to be a perfect, if sometimes hair-raising, means of transportation. (See *People's Guide to Camping in Mexico.*)

Riding in the back of a truck over unimproved dirt roads can be exhausting. This means that when it's hot, you'll want something to drink. You can carry sodas or beer, but water is easier to stretch out and a canteen is more practical to refill and carry in a pack. Nothing is worse than having half of a grape soda soak your clothing.

If your hat doesn't have a chin strap (called *barbiquetes*), lash it to your head with a bandanna or piece of twine. Your head may feel cool from the breeze as the truck is moving, but the sun will still be roasting your nose and forehead.

While a hat is the most convenient way to block the sun, I met a hitchhiker who found an umbrella quite useful for protection both from the heat and aggressive dogs. (Mexican dogs are trained by experience; bend over as if you're looking for a good throwing stone and they'll back off.)

Several hours in the heat can be quite dangerous; if you don't have a hat put something, even your undershorts, over the top of your head. Should a ride appear just as you're vomiting from too much heat or crawling into the bushes to collapse, you'll be out of luck.

Hitchhikers will find that an emergency stash of food will be invaluable for long waits or long rides without stops. Bananas are good, but I inevitably squash mine inside my day pack. Nuts, chia seeds, dried fruit (though it's expensive in Mexico), cheese, oranges, chocolate and granola are good for moments of low morale, sickness or ordinary hunger when nothing else is available.

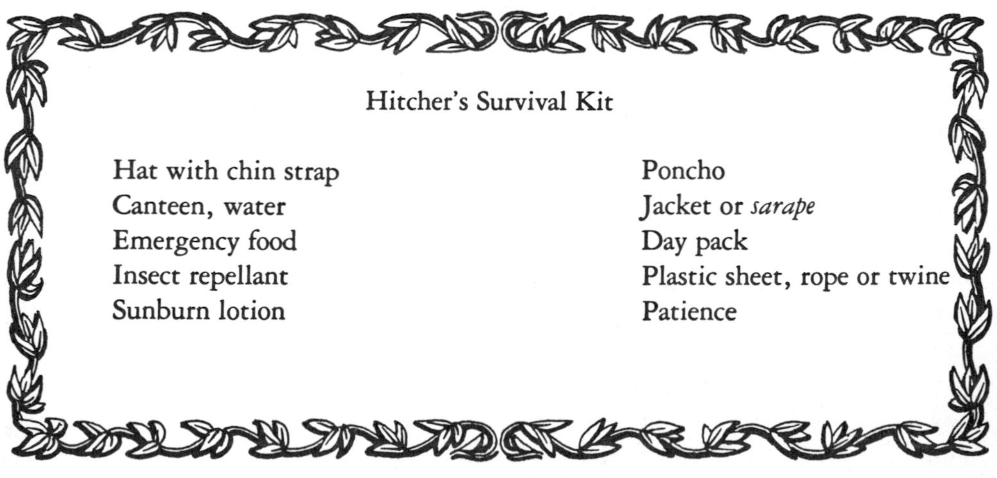

Hitcher's Survival Kit

Hat with chin strap	Poncho
Canteen, water	Jacket or *sarape*
Emergency food	Day pack
Insect repellant	Plastic sheet, rope or twine
Sunburn lotion	Patience

When travelling through the high deserts or mountains, be adequately prepared for a night in the open. Most people on foot will have a sleeping bag, but if you don't, a warm *sarape,* jacket or sweater is advisable.

Protection from rain is essential. A poncho or piece of plastic large enough to cover both you and your possessions will save you a great deal of discomfort and the hassle of drying things.

Because you'll be spending a certain amount of time in the open, bottles of bug repellent and sunburn lotion should be taken.

One disadvantage of hitchhiking is that is is very inconvenient to be ill. If you do get sick don't hesitate to take a bus to the next town or the first cheap hotel and hole up until you're well enough to travel again.

Anyone hitching in Mexico should be aware of the hazards of driving there. When you're standing on the edge of the road, always keep a close eye on traffic. Mexican drivers don't consider the shoulder of the road to be a safe zone for pedestrians; it's just another foot or two used for passing on the right or three abreast. If you aren't ready to jump out of the way, you may get a ride on a fender.

The police rarely harass hitchhikers. They might, however, search your things on occasion, particularly in areas where large numbers of young people are congregating. Have your tourist card ready at all times to avoid prolonging any routine identification checks. It's best to be ready to dump anything you're holding that will get you into trouble. The police rarely search a woman's person.

Keep knives and *machetes* out of sight or packed in such a manner that it doesn't appear as if you're ready for action. Open knives might upset people who give you rides. The police will confiscate even small penknives. A *machete* on the belt might be acceptable in the back country, but unless you're trying to go completely native, keep it out of sight. The natural distrust that some *campesinos* feel toward strangers, including both Mexicans and foreigners, will only be heightened if they see that you are armed.

Your luggage often suffers damage from rough truck trips. We always make an effort to put our backpacks in a secure spot, away from any slopping kerosene barrels or puddles of motor oil. Most cargo trucks are well coated with the dirt, grease and grime of past trips. The responsibility to avoid getting it on you and your gear is entirely your own. I'll never forget a five hour trip in the back of a stake truck which was carrying four leaking barrels of kerosene, an overweight pig with diarrhea, and two loose truck tires and rims. On the first bump my leg was smashed against the sideboards by a shifting tire and on the second bump the pig squirted on Lorena's pack.

Knife blade inscriptions: He Will Tell You Who Your Father Is

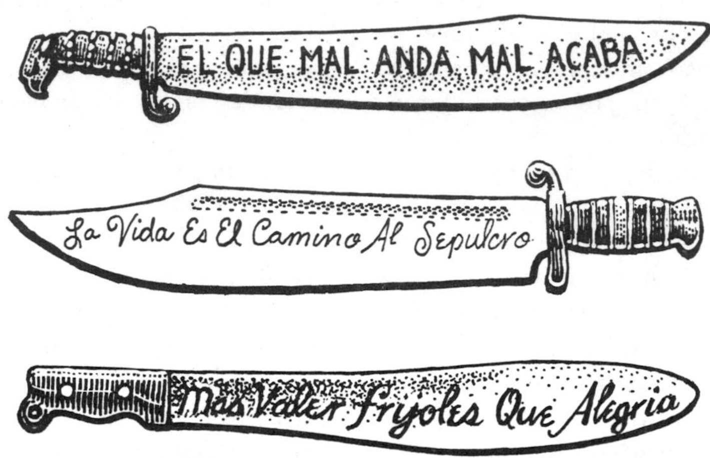

We now carry a small square of plastic to cover our packs with and a length of rope or heavy twine to lash them down. Be especially careful of other passengers who like to flop down on a backpack and may break the frame or contents.

Hitchhikers should be very careful about forgetting or losing gear while travelling. When you are awakened in the middle of the night at a dark intersection and the driver says, "This is where you get off," it is easy to absent-mindedly leave behind a camera, hat or handbag. For this reason we always keep our loose odds and ends under control by carrying them in a shopping bag or daypack. A daypack that can be securely closed is best; I've found that when mine is left unzipped it can easily dump out smaller objects like flashlights, eyeglasses and notebooks.

If you're riding with someone who looks like they might forget *you* when you've gone into a restroom or behind a bush, carry valuable possessions with you at all times. This doesn't mean that you have to remove your luggage at every stop (if you're that worried find another ride or hold your water). Just keep your camera, money, papers and other hard-to-bear-loss-of articles close at hand, whether it's for a brief rest stop, a meal or quick shopping trip.

Hitching Alone

While hitching alone, particularly if you're a woman, take the same precautions about accepting rides as you would anywhere. Remember that it's easier to refuse a ride than to talk your way out of any situation that may develop after you're in the car.

Knife blade inscriptions: He Who Acts Bad Ends Bad; Life Is the Road to the Tomb; Beans Are Worth More Than Happiness

We've met quite a few women travelling alone in Mexico and none of them felt that it was dangerous. They did say, however, that constant attention from men became very tiring. (See *Machismo.*) Women may prefer hitching rides with other tourists, usually quite easy to do.

For anyone who is alone and a bit nervous, travelling with a large dog can be a great help to morale. Of the several people we've talked to who hitched with dogs, none felt that it cut down significantly on the number of rides they were given. A woman travelling with a large well-trained dog should be able to handle any situation with a few growls. Dogs, however, are complications themselves. (See *Pets.*)

The biggest disadvantage of travelling by thumb is that not all drivers are models of skill and self-control. Don't hesitate to bail out when things get strange or scary.

Lorena and I were once riding in the back of a new pick-up truck on a curved-filled highway. Before we'd gone a mile my heart was in my throat and my knuckles were white from clutching at the side rails.

"It must just be an illusion of speed," I said to Lorena, trying to convince myself that the wild lurching and the howl of the tires was as natural as a Sunday drive. "I'm probably scared because we haven't been in a truck for so long. When was the last time we rode in a truck?"

She gave me a long look.

Didn't she realize that after a few months without riding in a motor vehicle that one lost their perspective? A sharp curve appeared a short distance ahead. The driver went at full speed, then began braking madly in the middle of the curve.

"I think the last time was the day before yesterday. When you went to town for food, remember?" She grabbed for her hat, fending off an old man who had lost his footing and was lurching back and forth, arms flailing for a handhold. He flopped to a safe landing over a bulging sack of corn. "Very windy," he said, tipping his hat politely to Lorena as she worked her boot from beneath the small of his back.

I clambered over other passengers and cargo to the cab of the truck, determined to check our speed.

"Hey," I yelled back to Lorena, "It's really not so bad after all. We're only doing 90 to 100 kilometers an hour. That's fast but not so dangerous." I took another peek through the rear window; a curve was coming up and we were slowing to 70. I was just about to turn and work my way back when I noticed a small MPH beneath the speedometer needle.

MPH! I felt the blood drain from my face and go roaring through my ears and down to my feet. Seventy into a curve! One hundred on the straight-away!

"Let me off! Let me off!" I screamed, pounding the roof of the cab with my fists. I got a glimpse of the driver's startled face turned toward the rear of the truck.

He obligingly slammed on the brakes, pitching most of the passengers to their faces as we slid to a halt. I grabbed my pack and tossed it onto the side of the road, madly clawing at the grain sacks and miscellaneous boxes that had shifted over Lorena's gear. The other passengers watched in bemused silence as we leaped out.

"*Perdóname,*" the old man finally said, sweeping his eyes over the dense jungle that surrounded us, "But where are you going?"

I caught enough breath to gasp, "Camping...take pictures...pretty birds...*adiós, que le vaya bien!*"

He looked at us incredulously. "Here?" he asked.

"Sure," I answered, "it's a perfect place."

The driver gunned the engine.

"What do we owe you?" I called. He looked at me in the rear view mirror, shook his head impatiently and then slammed the truck into gear. It lurched forward, spraying us with dust and gravel. The old man grabbed for his hat with one hand, waving farewell with the other. The exhaust had not yet cleared when we heard the protesting squeals of tires and brakes on the next curve.

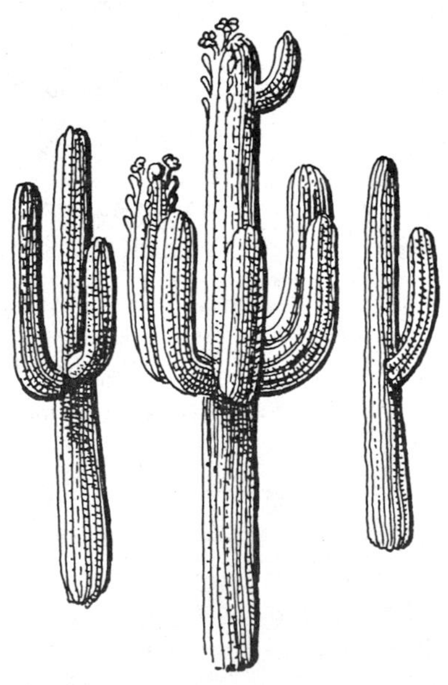

Saguaro

HOTELS

Economical and comfortable...How to choose: old, new, fancy or cheap?...Inside parking...Hammocks and beds...Rates...In small towns...Supercheap...A survival kit...Boarding houses...Rip-offs... A Memorable Night...

How do you go about choosing a hotel that is both economical and comfortable?

We've found that outward appearance is the quickest and most dependable way. If a hotel looks old (and this doesn't mean that it has to be a mouldering ruin), it will probably be inexpensive. An older hotel is not necessarily located in a run-down area of town. There are innumerable nice old hotels located in any city, often right on the *plaza* and next door to newer places that cater to wealthy Mexicans and tourists.

Some older hotels look deceptively fancy, but keep in mind that flourishes which went into the construction 200 years ago probably won't affect today's prices. Look at the windows of the rooms from the outside; if they are about ten feet tall you can bet that the ceilings inside are high. Very high ceilings are a sign of old-fashioned construction.

Many tourists try to economize by looking for places that fit their idea of a sleazy cheap hotel in the U.S. This type of hotel actually costs *more* because it does look like an American hotel.

Older hotels have other advantages besides economy. First, and most important, you're in Mexico to experience the country and its people. What better way to capture the flavor of Old Mexico than to sleep in a huge, high ceiling room, furnished with massive mahogany artifacts, genuine handmade tiles in the bathroom, though perhaps faded and cracked; a squeaking overhead fan; wrought iron grillwork on the windows and a octogenarian at the desk. This is what travelling is all about. Leave the ironed bedsheets, the wrapped water glasses, sanitized toilets and Astro Turf carpets for your trips at home.

Large groups and families can take advantage of the Mexican custom of putting everyone into one room; it not only saves a considerable amount of money but makes every moment a social event. Newer hotels have reduced room space to an absolute minimum, part of the effort to make more *pesos* per square inch. Older hotels, however, will almost always have a few rooms designed to accommodate parents, children, grandparents and their guests.

Many hotels include a cafe, restaurant and bar. The prices in these will vary considerably, but as a general rule, the best bargains and often the best food and service, will be in older, less expensive hotels. Many of these hotels cater to long term guests and budget-conscious local business people. They are always the last to raise prices.

Older hotels almost always offer more personal service than their flashier competitors. If you just have to have a piece of laundry done on short notice, the desk clerk is more likely to have the time and personal interest to find an unoccupied maid or laundress to help you out.

Employees in smaller and older hotels will usually be happy to help you unravel bus schedules, make phone calls in Spanish, direct you to the local sights and generally assist in whatever way they can. The manager of one hotel helped me plan a two day eating itinerary designed to include the best regional dishes. When I told her that my money was limited, she said, "I'll tell you about the places that we take our friends to, not the tourist spots."

The most dramatic example of personal attention that I have experienced occurred when I was travelling alone in northern Mexico. I suddenly fell very ill while visiting a small, nowhere town. My one night stop soon became a week, fighting off a fever in a hotel room. The family who ran the place brought me tea, soups and little delicacies from the kitchen (no charge) and did their best to keep me content and alive. When I took a turn for the worse, they insisted on bringing me home for closer care. I spent another week with them, treated like ailing royalty, and when I'd recovered I left with great regret.

CHEAP AND COMFORTABLE

Finding a good inexpensive room sometimes takes a lot of leg work, but there are clues besides the appearance of the hotel that should help. Asking is always the best way to find anything.

Inexpensive rooms can be found near bus and train stations. Ask a bus driver, ticket agent or at the information booth; you may well find a hotel within easy walking distance and avoid the additional expense of a cab. Your heavy luggage can be checked in the baggage room until you've located a place to stay. (See *Public Transportation.*)

Cab drivers are classic sources of information and advice. Many will have friends or relatives in the hotel business and, though their natural tendency may be toward a specific one, they'll seldom attempt to bamboozle you into something too expensive or too funky. I always say "*algo económico y comodo*" (something economical and comfortable).

Ask in the market; the local merchants usually know of something cheap. Hotels in the market area cater to a large influx of people at least once a week and these people, usually small time merchants, aren't about to pay more than they have to.

If you're looking for a basic room, ask non-prosperous looking gringos for leads. The 'hair people' often congregate in one hotel and it's likely to be a bargain. Asking also gives you a chance to find something that isn't advertised—such as a room in someone's home.

When leaving a hotel that I've enjoyed, I always ask for a recommendation in the town I'm headed for. If someone on the staff doesn't know of a good hotel, they'll often find a guest who does. This can save a great deal of searching.

Check It Out First

After you've spotted a likely looking hotel and have asked the price, look at the room before agreeing to take it. Quality does not necessarily vary according to cost. Of two hotels with identical rates, one might offer comfortable beds, a fan, a beautiful patio and free inside parking; while in the other you get a broken bedspring in your side, exhaust fumes pouring in through a missing window pane and a toilet that overflows on your feet.

Unless hot water appears when you first check the room, don't expect to see it at all, though they may advertise it and swear to various saints that it will be running copiously "in a moment." Some hotels will have hot water at specific hours, usually early in the morning and in the evening. Others may produce hot water upon request (or demand), though you'll usually have to wait while someone stokes up a wood-fueled hot water heater.

Ask for a room facing the back or in the center of the hotel if noise bothers your sleep. The din of early morning traffic, particularly near the market, can be incredible.

If you have a car, you'll feel less uptight by selecting a hotel that has its own parking lot or can direct you to one nearby. You might like to inspect the parking lot before agreeing to take the room. Some hotels park cars right inside the patio, which is safe; others may have a vacant lot nearby that wouldn't be any safer than the street unless there's a *velador* (night watchman).

In hot areas ask for a room with a fan (*ventilador* or *abanico*) and check to see that it works. If the weather is warm, there will probably be mosquitos around. Some hotels offer mosquito nets over the bed, but to be sure, carry your own or a supply of repellent.

Hotels in Yucatan and other hot parts of the country often offer a special rate to guests who bring their own hammocks rather than using beds. Hooks are fixed in the walls to hang them (the hammocks) from. Groups of people can rent one large room and fill it with hammocks—a bit crowded but very cheap.

Rates are government controlled and should be posted in the lobby and in each room. A hotel can charge less than the posted rate but cannot legally charge more. Since devaluation of the *peso*, however, many of the rate sheets are hopelessly out of date and you can't expect them to stick to pre-devaluation prices. Until the exchange rate has been fixed once again, price sheets will tend to be unreliable. This is particularly true in older hotels and in towns off the main tourist routes, where changes of any kind occur at glacial speeds. Newer hotels will probably make the extra effort to keep their rate sheets current.

The rate sheet also tells you the check-out time: *Su cuarto se vence a* . . . . . and then the hour, usually 2 p.m. but sometimes noon. Failure to check out in time means you are legally obligated to pay for another night.

Bartering over the price of a room is quite common, particularly in hotels that aren't obviously designed for gringo tourists. Though sometimes even fancy places are willing to make a deal, especially hotels that suffer from a chronic lack of business. Hotels spring up in Mexico like mushrooms after an autumn rain and many of them are white elephants, the result of unrealistic planning and boondoggle spending. If the management has any interest in survival, they will often give reduced rates.

Bartering for a room isn't quite like haggling over a wood carving or a handmade blanket. The counter offer is best made in the form of indecision: "Well...I don't know... that sounds a little expensive..." or the classic "Don't you have a smaller room. Something cheaper?" Don't rush; it may take the desk clerk five minutes or more to recall that there's an alternative to the Bridal Suite.

In older hotels, with a wider variety of room sizes and types, there will be a correspondingly greater range in individual room rates; for example, there may be an upper floor with small simple rooms, with or without baths.

If the price doesn't drop far enough, don't hesitate to ask for a recommendation to a cheaper hotel. This is not only the ultimate bartering maneuver, but is a good way to get directions. Mexicans are very casual in this regard and desk clerks will usually offer advice quite freely.

Most hotels lock their front doors after a certain hour and in small towns it can be surprisingly early. If you have any plans for staying out late, ask if someone will be on night duty or if there is a master key. Night watchmen in small hotels usually sleep on duty and if they're sleeping off a drunk, you might find it difficult to rouse them. If the owners are old fashioned, you may have to give a good respectable excuse for staying out late. The strictest will set a flat curfew after which you'd better find another room or a warm alley.

Once I told a landlady in a small town that I planned to go out and have a few drinks at the local *cantina*, she marched me to another room, pounded on the door and handed me over to a visiting priest for a stern lecture. He recognized my plight and we shared brandy in the privacy of his room.

SMALL TOWN HOTELS

In small towns the difficulty of selecting a hotel will be greatly simplified; usually it's a choice of one or two. Take it or leave it. This might sound a bit grim, but I've found that these places almost inevitably provide the basic material for good stories and memories. The gigantic rooster tethered outside our window, loudly protesting its captivity every 30 seconds; the insane elderly aunt locked in a spare room who demanded Coca Cola 24 hours a day; the landlord's barking dog, stunned into temporary silence by an occasional firecracker lobbed from the front desk; a boardinghouse television tuned to incomprehensible quiz shows until midnight; being rousted at five a.m. by a desk clerk who invited me to visit his avocado orchard and watch him blow up a boulder with dynamite; blocking the door against a drunk who insisted on kissing me goodnight; opening the wrong door and finding a sheer four story drop, and so on—an adventure or an anecdote waiting every night.

If a town is so small that it doesn't have a hotel at all, go to someone official—the mayor, priest or school teacher—and ask for a place to stay. You may get a night in jail (hopefully with a key to your cell), or a place to crash in a church or public building or even a real bed in a municipal guest house. In one town we slept in the armory, a cell-like room filled with old furniture and antique weapons, which had to be locked at night (with us in it) to protect the guns from thieves.

Whatever you get will be interesting. You may be asked or expected to perform in some way as payment for the hospitality. This might involve answering hundreds of questions about yourself and where you're from, showing off your possessions, eating gifts of weird food, drinking the local booze and perhaps being subjected to a 'concert' on the mayor's Victrola.

SUPERCHEAP

Super cheap rooms are almost always to be found near the market place. They tend toward the very basic; perhaps just a wooden frame for a bed and a rough straw-filled sack that symbolizes a mattress. The communal bathroom may be quite funky, with magazines or other types of shiny paper instead of regular toilet paper. One hotel had old bank ledgers in the bathroom and I spent many interesting minutes checking out withdrawals and deposits.

The cheapest hotels and boardinghouses may double as bath houses. In these places a bath is an additional charge, sometimes even for guests.

Casas de Huéspedes and *Pensiones* (boarding houses) will rent rooms for one night, though they specialize in long term guests. No matter how low the price of a room may be, and some are quite cheap, ask if it includes meals. Tourists are sometimes confused by the low prices in these places and miss getting meals that they have paid for.

A *casa de huéspedes* may be quite nice or it may be nothing more than a flophouse. They are always economical and should be investigated if you are trying to save money.

The best bargain may be no hotel at all. Houses, apartments, bungalows and furnished rooms are usually cheaper than equivalent accommodations in a regular hotel, especially for two or more people. (See *Renting a Place*.)

Along the coasts you can sometimes sleep in restaurants, especially if you eat there before you ask for lodging. You might do as I once did and sleep on a table or if there's room, hang your hammock on the porch. You'll be awakened very early to get your stuff together before the customers arrive. This is a very pleasant way to meet people and many travellers 'adopt' a restaurant, eating there and using it as a boarding house. You should offer something in payment, but usually buying meals there will be considered sufficient. We slept in one restaurant for over a month (waking up occasionally for beer and food) and it was one of our most enjoyable experiences in Mexico. When you are broke or bored, help out with the basic chores and you'll probably get free or bargain meals in return.

A final suggestion: If you're desperate for a room and can stand the excitement, go to the red light district and stay in a whorehouse. They may balk at renting a room without 'services,' but if you're with a woman (or are one) they will usually relent and let you in. The posted rates are for the room. Or it could happen that you unsuspectingly choose a cheap hotel and find out that it's a whorehouse. This may not matter, but if you're in a group (and our group once included my mother, to the manager's dismay), keep it in mind.

The dangers of staying in a whorehouse, especially for a single woman, are pretty obvious. When you're worried about the respectability of a hotel, ask someone if it is "*familiar.*" This means politely, "family hotel, not a whorehouse." Many hotels have this word prominently posted to ease customer's minds.

A Hotel Survival Kit

Hotel services and accommodations vary so much in Mexico, especially for those who stay in less expensive places, that it's best to anticipate possible shortages. When I'm travelling from one hotel to another, I always carry my 'survival kit' in my day pack or in a small sack in my suitcase. It consists, more or less, of the following:

- Flashlight: for power failures and midnight trips to the bathroom.
- Bug dope: cheap hotels rarely have screens or mosquito nets.
- Soap: I always drop those tiny hotel bars down the drain.
- Towel: a small one, just in case. I usually carry an extra t-shirt for a towel. It's not very absorbent but it works. It also doubles very well as a pillow case and in emergencies can be worn as a shirt.
- Toilet paper: always carry toilet paper.
- Heating coil: this is a little device that plugs into the wall and heats up a cup of water for tea, instant coffee or bouillon. I wake up very early, before most cafes open, and the heating coil saves me from coffee withdrawal.
- Tea, instant coffee, bouillon, Postum, etc.: saves money if you make it yourself. Nice for times when you can't or don't want to leave your room.
- Cups: cheap hotels rarely provide drinking glasses or cups.
- Drink: soft or hard. A bottle of soda, can of juice or dram of rum. Don't expect purified water in cheap hotels.
- Good Book: for bad nights.

If details bother you—no water, no mattress, a smelly toilet, someone coughing in the next room—staying in very cheap hotels may be tough. However, if you enjoy the Mystery and Excitement of never knowing what is coming next, you're going to be able to live very economically.

We once stayed in a hotel that featured a giant tortoise that roamed through the corridors all night, shuffling and scratching its claws against the tiled floor. The door to our room was missing and the beast spent an hour or two under the bed, butting its head against one of the brass bed legs. This same hotel was arranged around an overgrown patio, with all rooms opening onto a balcony without railings. One faulty step and the unfortunate guest could plunge into statues and decaying lawn furniture several floors below.

While preparing for bed in another hotel of this caliber, we noticed that there was an upside-down bucket in each corner of the room. Too tired to investigate, we went to bed. In the middle of the night we were awakened by strange sounds: squeaks, scratchings and other rodent-like noises. It seemed to come from the buckets. Rather than risk uncovering some horror and completely ruining our rest, we compromised by hiding under the blankets. By morning the awful sounds had increased and we decided something would have to be done.

Steve solved the problem by tying a long string to the handle of one of the buckets and trailing it out the door into the corridor. We all gathered outside and he jerked the string, tipping the bucket onto its side. A mass of tiny yellow bodies ran peeping and squealing into the middle of the room. The buckets were homemade chicken incubators. We spent the next half hour rounding up the newly hatched chicks and returning them to their nest. The manager explained later that our room was the warmest in the hotel and was used to hatch eggs, whether it was rented or not.

Better Safe Than...

There are disadvantages to super cheap rooms and these not only include cardboard thin walls and the occasional bedbug, but also a lack of privacy and even rip-offs. For the cautious traveller I heartily recommend the following precautions:

Keep small valuables on your person at all times. I take my money to bed with me and unless there's another person in the room, I also take my money into the shower when bathing or using the toilet. One of the classic rip-offs in cheap hotels (and this is worldwide) happens while the unsuspecting victim is in the bathroom. When the shower is turned on, the door opens and within seconds wallet, money, camera and other goodies disappear. "I can't believe it! I was only in there for five lousy minutes!" That's also all the time it takes for two strong men to move a refrigerator from a kitchen to a moving van.

When you're going out for a stroll, leave larger valuables at the desk, even if the clerk protests that it's not necessary.

At night, or when sleeping, make sure that the door is securely locked. In most really cheap hotels with flimsy or improvised doors, this is difficult, if not impossible. We sometimes carry small padlocks, but even this is a poor defense against a hard blow or a well wielded screwdriver.

If you're a light sleeper rig an 'alarm' that will signal if the door is moved. I usually have a few empty beer or soda bottles on hand and arrange them to topple over with an ear-splitting racket when the door is opened. I know this works because when I wake in the middle of the night and stumble out to the bathroom, I always crash into the bottles myself.

If you sleep or worry heavily, move the entire bed to block the door. If it's too heavy, find something else: table, bureau, chairs, etc.

Precautions such as these are rarely necessary, but I consider them to be like health care: it never seems important until things have gone wrong. *Precautions are not paranoia; they're good common sense.*

Woman travelling alone should be particularly careful when selecting a cheap room. Many women have told us that saving money on a room was sometimes offset by hassles from other lodgers or desk clerks looking for a one-night romance.

Because the cheapest hotels are usually located in less than elegant neighborhoods, women should exercise caution when walking alone at night. (See *Machismo*.)

When a man and woman travel together but are sleeping in separate beds, it doesn't hurt to give the impression of being a couple. It not only avoids offending straight-laced people who may refuse or balk at letting two people share a room, but also cools down those on the prowl. This is especially true in small towns where tourist's eccentricities are unfamiliar.

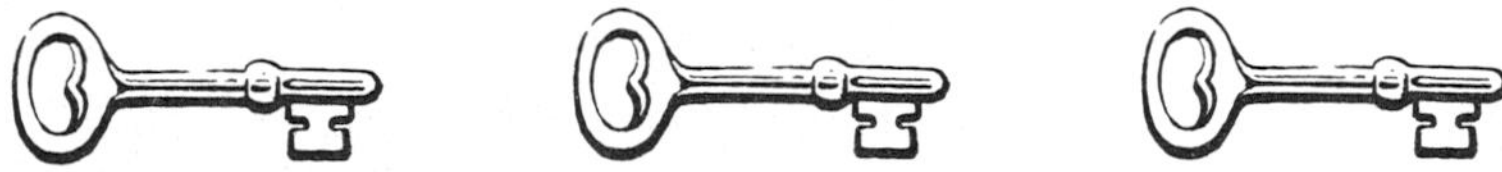

It was the end of a day of long tiring travel; the type of day that you desperately hoped would not end in a Memorable Experience. We had decided, against our better judgment, common sense and other weak notions to stay in a hotel as a 'break' from camping. We reasoned that the cost wouldn't be bad if we looked for something slightly scroungy, a hotel of the type soon to be a vacant lot.

Steve sagged over the steering wheel as we entered town, his eyes slightly glassy.

"There's a good one," he said gloomily, pointing to a psuedo-American motel, not quite concealing his true feeling about those soft, expensive gringo beds.

"How about that one?" Lorena suggested, turning to look at the darkening ruin of a large building, obscured by weeds and fast growing vines. "It looks like a Hilton to me," she added, referring to the joke we'd picked up from a hitchhiker who often stayed in abandoned or unfinished buildings that he called 'Hiltons.'

Our fatigue and foul humor were not at all eased by the traffic which literally jammed the streets. The blare of irate horns made argument impossible. Steve stuck his head out of the window in order to back into a side street, the only avenue of escape. I watched disbelievingly as a mob of kids approached us, lobbing balloons filled with water at the stalled cars.

"Look!" I yelled, and Steve turned his head to receive a fat balloon square in the face. It burst quietly, soaking him with water that smelled more than slightly of stale urine.

"You gawddamn *pendejo*!!!" he shrieked, losing what little was left of his composure. The kid who had thrown the balloon laughed uproariously and his accomplices added their apologies by launching a general attack. Balloons burst over every square inch of the van, showering us with water through open windows.

"We aren't the only ones," I said. "Look at that poor guy." The driver of the car in front of us was mopping large quantities of water from his dashboard while his wife dried their screaming baby.

"God, must be some kind of weird *fiesta*," Steve groaned, for by now it was obvious that the water fight was of city-wide proportions. The streets were flooded gutter deep.

As traffic crawled toward the *plaza*, the bombardment continued without mercy; the sight of a gringo vehicle inspired even greater and more desperate feats of daring. We soon found ourselves trapped under a waterfall of baloons and emptying buckets.

"There! There!" I yelled, pointing to a hotel that had the look of a badly neglected flophouse.

We squelched to a stop directly in front of the entrance.

"How do you propose to get in?" Steve asked sarcastically, pointing toward the eager horde of water ballooners anticipating our next move.

"I'll open my door like I'm making a run for it and then you duck into the hotel while they attack me."

Steve looked rather dubious, but agreed to my proposal.

"Go!" I yelled, pretending to jump from my side of the van. A wave of kids launched an immediate attack, but I slammed the door before the water hit. Steve leaped to the hotel entrance, followed by a few late balloons. The manager anticipated our predicament and opened the front door just as Steve was about to break it down. A few minutes later, Steve's face appeared at an upper window and he motioned us to come up.

"What about the birds?" Lorena asked me, looking at our parrots, Arturo and Farout. "One of those balloons could really hurt them."

We pondered this additional problem for a few moments and then the sight of a slightly reeling attacker inspired me to a solution.

"We'll negotiate," I said, reaching under the seat for the bottle of *tequila* we'd been using to maintain our mental equilibrium.

I opened the window just far enough to extend the bottle into sight of the group dedicated to drowning us. One of them immediately rushed over.

"*Oye, amigo*," I said, "if you'll let us take our parrots into the hotel without soaking them, I'll invite you all to a drink."

After consulting his friends, the pact was sealed with a round of healthy slugs from the bottle. We quickly gathered a few things together and raced safely into the lobby. The manager, dripping slightly, directed us to the room in which Steve was hiding.

"What about the car?" I asked, "Do you have a parking lot?"

"Oh yes! Certainly!" he said. "But do it quickly or they'll flood the lobby." The parking lot was in the center of the hotel and we would have to drive through the large front doors of the lobby and into the patio.

"Take this, it's your 'Safe Passage'," I said, handing Steve the bottle of *tequila*. He looked at it sceptically, then chugged an enormous swallow.

While Lorena and I watched from the balcony of our room, he made his peace with the mob. At a signal from Steve, the huge double doors swung open and the van raced into the lobby, barely missing an end table. The balloon squad could not resist the temptation and a hail of missiles followed. A rather sour looking bellboy caught the force of the attack.

"The manager told me this is the annual Water *Fiesta*," Steve said, returning from his mission looking slightly soggy.

"How are we ever going to get out for dinner?" Lorena asked. Confusion in the streets had reached panic proportions, with hundreds of people madly throwing buckets of water at each other. The cop directing traffic at the next corner stood stoically under a continual shower of water balloons, turning occasionally to glare at traffic as water dripped from his nose, obviously enjoying the entire scene. Fire hoses had been connected and pumped thousands of gallons into the surrounding traffic and passersby. A tank truck, stalled in the middle of the street, gushed forth great fountains of water from various valves and pipes as lines of dripping people waited to fill their buckets, balloons and washtubs.

The manager luckily appeared as we were debating whether to eat or not and offered to arrange our entry into a nearby restaurant; tonight their doors opened only by appointment.

We stepped out of the hotel door with the air of dignity that quells riots and calms rabid mobs. The crowd on the street looked at us expectantly, waiting for some noble word. I turned to Steve and Lorena to say, "This is how it's done," but my words were drowned in a fussilade of balloons and a cascade of water falling from the balcony of the hotel. I looked up and thought that I saw the face of the manager behind a large washtub.

"Bastards!" Steve muttered, running for safety.

The door of the restaurant opened magically in front of us and we burst into a room crowded with soaked and chattering diners. The waiter bolted the door securely before taking us to a table. I noticed that several groups seemed to have finished eating and were merely waiting for the tide to change before leaving.

We ate dinner in relative peace, though wavelets of water lapped under the door and screams and laughter from the street confirmed that the insanity was not abating. We asked for the bill and then sat back to relax for a few moments before braving the return trip. I absently noticed that another group had left without being escorted out by the waiter.

"Yaaahhh!" With a scream of triumph, the mob burst through the front door, now unlatched. Water sprayed everywhere as balloons burst on heads bowed reverently over food and tubs emptied into diner's laps.

"No!" someone screamed as one of the crowd grabbed a tablecloth and whisked the plates and *tacos* into a crashing heap. Tables were swept clean, chairs overturned, water flowed, waiters cringed and we ran.

Back in the hotel, dripping but safe, we listened politely while the manager apologized profusely for the entire *fiesta* and Mexico. As we slogged off to bed his *"perdóns"* and *"lo siento muchos"* rose above the sound of falling water and bursting balloons.

"At least we have a nice room," I said surveying the cave we had been given for the night. The beds were cots, scrounged from some unsuccessful revolutionary camp, and the blankets looked as if they had covered untold numbers of obscene acts. The ceiling, far above our heads, gave off a light snow of plaster and paint, dislodged, I imagined, by bats unable to sleep because of the clamor in the street below.

Bam! *¡Señor!"* Bam! *"¡Señor!"* We leaped out of bed just as the manager burst into the room, lugging a huge washtub and followed by the entire staff of the hotel, all carrying containers of water.

"Excuse me, please!" he said, "I have a little matter to take care of." They were all drunk and soaked to the skin.

Before we could manage to ask what was happening a bucket brigade had been established between the bathroom and the balcony. Curses and screams from the street below affirmed that the counterattack was taking its toll.

I looked at Steve and Lorena and then at the scene in the room. A bellboy was drinking our *tequila* while the desk clerk and maid delivered tubs of water to the manager. An ancient cleaning lady assisted him in lifting the heavy containers to the railing and then dumping them in cascades onto the crowd below.

"Shall we?" I asked, reaching for an empty bucket.

RENTING A PLACE

Why rent?...Life in a Mexican town...Meeting the neighbors...House hunting...Types of houses...Furnishings...Housekeeping hints...Wood fueled hot water heaters...Renting a room...Maids...Mary of the Light...

We'd been travelling in Mexico for several months, following our usual routine of camping out, with occasional periods in hotels or trailer parks, when we came upon the long sought after Perfect Spot. Almost perfect, that is, but there was no place to camp and no nearby convenient, inexpensive hotel. An old farmer kindly agreed to let us park in his alfalfa field for a night but could give no suggestions for a better, long term site. We looked over the small valley, criss-crossed by neat stone fences and carefully tended vegetable gardens, bordered on one side by forested hills and on the other by a clear stream and thought, "There's got to be a way!"

The old man was sympathetic but explained that there just wasn't room in their valley for camping. Every inch of flat or fertile ground was planted in a food or cash crop.

"The only way to live here," he said, plucking a green stem of alfalfa and chewing it idly, "is in a house." His eyes followed a billowing mass of clouds hanging over the foothills.

"A house?" Lorena said doubtfully, as though she were a gypsy suddenly faced with a 20-year lease.

"*Sí, una casita*," he continued, "Like that little house of mine just over there on the edge of the trees."

We looked at each other for a few moments and then at the van. If we could live in that thing for months on end...

"How much?" Steve asked.

Ten minutes later we were residents, having agreed to rent for a month. The price was low enough that even if we got the itch to move on before the rent was up we wouldn't really be losing anything. We shook hands with our new landlord and got a brief run down on the village a quarter of a mile away—where to buy food and supplies, who sold the best moonshine and other domestic facts of life.

The difference between being members of the community, though only temporary, and just passing tourists was remarkable. Steve quickly struck up a friendship in the market and had long conversations on the merits of the Pacific versus Gulf Coast mango. Lorena met the landlord's wife and was soon learning to make *tortillas*. I had a favorite stool in *Mi Oficina,* the town's only *cantina*, a perfect spot to pick up odd bits of information and the sutleties of Spanish. People greeted us on the street and from their fields, inquiring after our health; the local dogs quit barking at me; Lorena traded *Kaliman* comic books with the children's literary society and low level gossip with their mothers and older sisters.

Our acceptance by the people was gratifying and for the first time in our travels, we felt that we were really getting beneath the surface. Our understanding and appreciation of how the people thought and lived increased by the day. We also noticed something else: we were relaxed and rested, thoroughly enjoying a slower pace.

Many tourists don't consider a trip to be a success unless they log a great number of miles and take in the better known sights and attractions. Art Buchwald described this rapid transit tourism as 'The 3-Minute Louvre.' The Museum's record for viewing the Winged Victory, Mona Lisa and Venus de Milo was won by the Japanese, Buchwald said, because of their superior track shoes.

This is two dimensional travel: impersonal, tiring, unsatisfying and expensive.

Life in a Mexican Town

In smaller towns the arrival of a new neighbor is always an event of great interest. They'll want to know where you're from, what you're doing and why, where you're headed next, what work you do, how many kids you have and so on, right into the details of your health and sex life. This can get tiring, especially if your Spanish is shaky, but it has its rewards.

In one small *pueblo* we barely had time to hang our hammocks before the neighbors began arriving with gifts of food. "This is like the Welcome Wagon," Lorena laughed, accepting yet another 15 pound squash from a blushing woman. By the time we'd bade the last of our new friends good night, we had enough fruit and vegetables to open a stall in the market. We soon learned that the neighbors were literally in competition to see which could give us something even tastier than the others.

A few nights later we came back from an evening stroll to find an anxious group of children on our doorstep. "Where have you been?" one of them cried. "We're having a wedding *fiesta* and everyone is waiting for you!" We were hustled to a nearby house and greeted as if we were the bride and groom.

Participating in the daily routine of the people around you can be extremely interesting. Rather than just talking you'll often find yourself actually doing something with someone. Your neighbors might be a little startled when you offer to help with the corn harvest, but they'll soon get over the shock. There's nothing like shared work to make you one of the family.

While we were living in a beach town I overheard a conversation between several tourists, complaining that the cost of hiring a boat for fishing was beginning to add up to more than they could afford. The man they'd been hiring for several days turned out to be our neighbor. Whenever I wanted to go fishing, which was often, all I had to do was show up at his house early in the morning, ready to go. He refused any payment, even for gas and oil, but did let me help paint his boat and clean fish.

Another neighbor in the same town offered us the use of a rich, irrigated garden patch after I spent a day helping him spread rock salt on a tobacco field. He also gave us an open invitation to pick fruit and avocados from his orchard.

Whenever something exciting comes up, you'll probably be told of it and invited to participate. A neighbor once stopped by to ask if I wanted to go fishing in a nearby river. I accepted and we set off, enlisting a few more people along the way. When we were half a mile out of the village and no one had yet produced any fishing equipment, I asked my friend how they intended to fish. He gave me a sly grin and began to unbutton his shirt. "Special Mexican bait," he said, revealing several sticks of dynamite stuck inside the waistband of his pants.

On other occasions I've gone hunting for jaguars, deer, rabbits, treasure (all with notable lack of success) and visited illegal *mezcal* stills, uncatalogued ruins, hidden waterfalls and other local sights that the tourist rarely has the opportunity to see.

Lorena has learned about medicinal herbs, folk remedies, *tortilla* making, cooking, gardening and general facts of family life in Mexico.

Many practical and valuable skills can be picked up, either on a casual basis or by working as an apprentice. I know gringos who have worked with sandal makers, weavers, potters, jewelers, blacksmiths, cabinet makers, brick layers, commercial fishermen, divers and even mule skinners. Many of these trades and their techniques have succumbed to automation and technology in the U.S., but are practiced in Mexico as they have been for generations. You'll learn very basic and time tested skills along with a lot of Spanish. Don't be shy about expressing an interest in what someone is doing; this is just about the best possible way to break the ice and, at the same time, give yourself something interesting to do.

Renting a place for a couple of weeks or more doesn't mean that you're stuck; in fact, it can mean the opposite and give you much more freedom. We use a house or room as a center for side trips, a place where we can leave the bulk of our luggage while we explore by car, bus or on foot. Side trips can be anything from an afternoon stroll in the country to a few days visiting a nearby city. When you get back you've got a place to rest and relax, without the strain of constant packing and unpacking and searching for a good hotel room.

Another consideration is cost: unless you don't care about money, you'll want to keep expenses within reason. Compare the daily cost of restaurant meals and hotels to the cost of renting a house, room or apartment and cooking for yourself; you may well discover that you can afford to rent a fairly fancy place and still save. (See *Travelling Cheap*.)

HOUSE HUNTING

Although there are rental agencies (*Agencia de Renta*) and real estate agents (*Agencia de Bienes Raices*) in larger cities and tourist towns, most house hunting turns into something of a snipe hunt. There is no great surplus of dwellings and most towns will have very few newspaper advertisements for housing. The grapevine seems to be efficient enough for spreading the information about vacancies to satisfy most landlords.

The best way to find a vacancy is to ask a resident gringo for advice. If you want a nice house, ask a prosperous looking gringo; if you want a humble hut, ask people (like us) who look as though they live in one.

When there seem to be no resident foreigners, you'll have to look for yourself. Find an agreeable looking neighborhood and begin searching for vacancies.

If you are lucky, you may see signs advertising a house or apartment for rent. The key words on such a sign will be *Se Alquila* or *Se Renta* (for rent). Houses that are for sale (*Se Vende*) are often for rent if you inquire.

After you locate a beautiful house with a *Se Renta* sign in the window, ask someone in the neighborhood where the owner lives. Should luck be with you, the neighbor will know the owners and where they can be found. Our experience, however, has been that tracking down the *dueño de la casa* is usually even more difficult than finding the house.

You must be patient and persistent. When you've finally got your hands on your prospective landlord, you may find that the house for rent is not the one with the sign. It was put up on a friend's house, one that was in a better location and therefore easier to spot.

Small stores, supermarkets, drugstores and *cantinas* are centers of local information. In small villages or outlying neighborhoods the local *tiendas* (grocery stores) are especially helpful in locating landlords.

Because the search may become long and difficult, you will be tempted to give up or to take the first thing that comes along. Avoid either alternative if you can; a patient search usually uncovers wonderful surprises. And you get an interesting tour of Mexican homes.

Types of Houses

The types of houses available fall into four categories. The first category is usually rented to rich Mexicans, tourists and foreign residents. These houses have furniture, modern appliances and conveniences, plumbing and high rents. By U.S. standards, however, they can still be a bargain.(In towns with a large tourist trade or gringo community, rents will be higher than average but good deals can be found.)

The second category includes a variety of dwellings, from little two room places to defunct *haciendas*. The old places often have more rooms than you know what to do with, huge overgrown gardens with fruit trees, pools for fish, stables and servants' quarters. In general, they cost about the same to rent as a much smaller but newer house of psuedo-motel design.

Older houses may have some disadvantages: an occasional leak in the roof or falling tile, drafty rooms, erratic plumbing and ghosts guarding the inevitable buried treasure from the Revolution, but living in them is much more interesting than a modern house.

These places rarely have furniture or appliances. Most have electricity but no light bulbs and few electrical outlets. Gas lines for a propane stove or water heater may be installed, but often the previous tenants will have removed the gas tanks, stove and heater. When Mexican families move, they do a complete job of it and when they get to their new home, they don't expect to find much more than a starkly empty house. Furnishings and appliances are not left behind but treated as lifetime possessions.

Very inexpensive furniture can be purchased in and around the market place and occasionally from wandering vendors. Chairs, tables, cupboards and beds of unfinished pine are reasonably priced and can be re-sold to the neighbors or given away when you leave. Some landlords will give credit toward the rent for furniture and other improvements. By using bricks, boards, wooden crates (also sold in the market), mats and your imagination, you can furnish the barest house quite adequately for very little money.

If you're travelling with your own vehicle it is easy to carry a few basic furnishings and utensils. You may not have much more than a stool to sit on and a fruit crate for a table, but it's better than nothing. See *Personal Stuff* and *Preparing Your Car* for suggestions on things to bring from home to make life easier.

The Mexican custom of packing up the entire family for a Christmas or Easter vacation at the beach has created a large number of rental houses and apartments designed for groups. These are generally known as *bungalos* and *cabañas*. Because most are fully equipped, from linen to kitchen utensils, they can be ideal for the foreign tourist. This is especially true for people with children, who don't want to be cooped up with them in a hotel room or forced to rent two rooms to get a little privacy.

Bungalows are usually available by the day as well as by the week and month. They are almost always cheaper than an equivalent hotel room, not counting the savings that can be made by doing your own cooking. Maid and laundry service will probably be optional, but it's best to ask to avoid paying twice. An extra charge may be made for additional beds, linen and kitchen utensils if you require them.

Large bungalows can be shared by several people and the cost per person will drop rapidly to the bargain level. If you have any doubt about the number of people allowed, ask before making any agreement. Some owners will set a limit, others could care less if the tenants are stacked in the rooms like cordwood.

Most bungalows are booked in advance for the Christmas season (mid-December to about January 7) and around Easter Week (*Semana Santa*), so don't expect to find one then without a search. Rents also tend to inflate during these traditional beach holidays.

The fourth category includes what most people call hovels, shacks and shanties. After a few months of camping, they look like mansions. They may be below suburbia standards but hopefully by the time you want to rent an adobe hut, you'll be beyond such unrealistic judgments. A simple house or hut of local materials (boards, bricks, rocks, sticks, fronds) is inexpensive to rent. Monthly rates range from very little to nothing; a particularly friendly landlord might allow you to use a house for free.

A basic hut will have a dirt floor, few if any windows, a crude adobe stove and fleas. (See *Housekeeping Hints*.) Water will have to be carried from a communal faucet or well. Sanitary facilities will be the most basic and may be positively unhealthy. Garbage is usually thrown out back and picked up by dogs, pigs and the wind. Privacy is also minimal; children and animals will wander in and out when they are bored and want to see what you're up to. Neighbors will drop in at all hours, especially if you're doing something odd, like cooking, reading, writing or painting. All of these factors make your life very interesting, especially if your neighbors are friendly—almost always the case.

Housekeeping Hints

•Insects, particularly ants, fleas and scorpions, can be discouraged from moving in by regular mopping with water and kerosene. Add one cup of kerosene to a bucket of water. The smell won't last long. When used on brick floors this mixture gives a slightly waxed look and eventually darkens the bricks. Detergent can also be added.

•Sprinkle kerosene around doorways and where floor and walls meet. Kerosene can also be painted on table legs, bed legs and woodwork to suppress termites and other insects.

•Bed legs can be placed in dishes or tin cans filled with kerosene and water. This stops travelling visitors.

•A chicken will scratch and probe for insects and is said to be an excellent scorpion hunter.

•Bed bugs can be repelled by smearing the pulp of *calabaza hedionda* (Apodanthera undulata, also known as *calabasilla*) on the bed frame. This is a wild gourd or squash, about the size of a baseball. If you make the mistake of tasting it you'll understand why bedbugs can't stand it.

It is not uncommon, particularly along the Pacific coast, for a family to build a small hut or room in the back yard (or on a nearby lot) especially for renters. One town we stayed in had carried this to the degree that a family without a gringo was like a family without a pet cat or dog.

"How's your gringo?"

"Oh, fine, yesterday he cut his foot on the beach. How's yours?"

"Fine, too. She got a letter from her mother. Money, I think."

"It's about time, I'd say. Did you hear about Eugenia's?"

"No, what happened?"
"He won't eat meat! Can you believe it?"
"*¡No me digas!* Is he sick?"
"Who knows? He certainly eats enough of her sweet *tamales!*"
"Some people! *Pues*, Cona says her gringa won't eat sugar."
"*¡Ay! ¡Imposible!* That one I don't believe!"
"Well, *¿quién sabe?* With these gringos anything can happen!"

We heard this sort of banter all around town.

Renting a place in this village was as easy as stopping the first little kid you saw on the street and saying, "*Quiero un cuarto*" (I want a room). It would hardly take more than an hour or two to find what you wanted.

Check the roof of your prospective home. Can you see through it? During the rainy season, you'll want a tight roof. Be wary of houses located in a low spot if rain is imminent. The saying that shit flows downhill is quite true.

Check the walls for indications of a waterline; we once had to leave a house early because dark stains near the floor turned out to be a high water mark.

I was sitting in front of a adobe house we'd just rented, admiring the huge black clouds that had been piling up steadily, hour by hour. My daydreams were interrupted when an old man approached. He was staggering under a load of crude homemade bamboo crucifixes adorned with beautiful wild flowers. Without a word he handed me three of the crosses and pointed to the darkening sky. The look on his face was ominous.

"What do I do with these?" I asked, holding the crosses rather nervously.

He leaned toward me confidentially and said, "When the rain comes, burn one inside the house." He paused and looked at the hut. "It will prevent the roof from caving in." I looked up at the sagging beams and heavy tiles, then back to the old man. He chuckled knowingly and said, "Here, better take three more." When he'd gone I burned two in each room though the rains were a week away.

Bartering over the rent is common. It is wise to look at more than one or two places in the same area to get some idea of what the going rate seems to be.

The less you pay for a house the less hassle you're likely to have with the landlord. Along with expensive houses, you will often get such familiar things as damage deposits, rent in advance, lease requirements and snoopy landlords. This most often happens when the landlord has had some experience with foreigners. If the house you're renting isn't worth more than a few month's rent, the landlord probably won't give a damn about anything. Fortunately, the most nosy and uptight landlord is positively relaxed and unconcerned in comparison to those in the U.S.

Establish exactly what you are renting before agreeing to anything. Does the deal include the right to pick fruit and vegetables from the garden? Some landlords reserve the right to plant the land surrounding the house. Can you use the outbuildings? Should you neglect to ask, you might find that one of the buildings or even one of the rooms of the house is rented out to someone else. The landlord might reserve some rooms for use as granaries or for tool storage. This probably won't seem unreasonable—until he drives a bunch of pack mules through the patio every Sunday at four a.m. to load up corn for market.

Interested in buying a house? See *Tourists and the Law.*

What to Expect

After you've settled in don't be shocked or outraged if something comes up that wasn't quite in your plans. People who rent cheaper places should be especially open to unexpected developments.

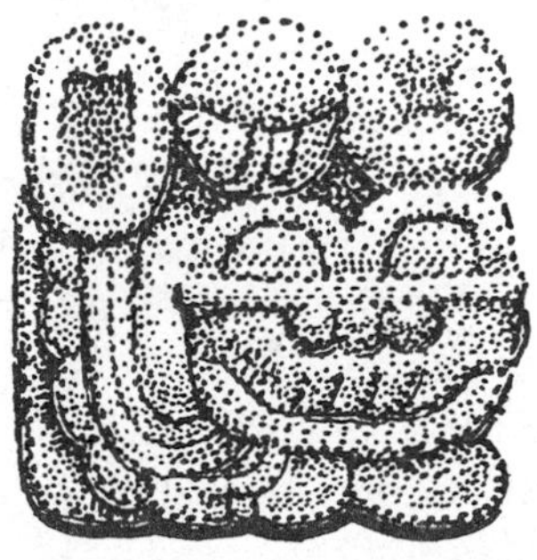

Lorena and I once looked at a small apartment located on the third floor of a large building. It had a tiny open patio with an interesting view of the neighbor's roofs, windows and gardens. While our prospective landlord was showing off the positive points of having to climb steep flights of stairs, *"La vista es*...gasp...*maravillosa!"*, I noticed several one inch galvanized pipes sprouting from a corner of the patio floor. They extended several feet into the air, quivering slightly in the breeze like a stand of metal bamboo.

"What are those pipes for, *señor?"* I asked several times, never quite getting an answer as the man suddenly darted into the phone-booth sized kitchen to demonstrate the stove or into the bathroom to flush the toilet.

When we finally agreed to take the place, he disappeared like a shot, nervously consulting his watch. "Must have an appointment," I thought, putting aside a vaguely uneasy feeling as Lorena urged me to begin unpacking.

By the time we'd put away our clothes, a few books and slopped a mop around the living room, it was time to have a drink and admire the sunset.

"This is perfect!" Lorena exclaimed, arranging two chairs behind a low wooden stool that would serve as our patio table. I brought out a bottle of *tequila,* mineral water, glasses and slices of lime, easing into my chair with a deep sigh of satisfaction.

"What's that?" Lorena asked, her head turning toward the corner of the patio.

"The pipes are rattling, I think," I answered, reaching for the *tequila*. I began to pour and then stopped: there was no doubt about it, the pipes were emitting a chorus of pops, groans, and hisses. Strange, yes, but certainly nothing to worry about.

"Well, here's to our new place," Lorena said, lifting her glass for a toast. I moved to clink my glass against hers when one of the pipes let out a loud "whoooosh!" spewing a column of steam and scalding water into the air over our heads.

"Ahhhhhh!" I screamed, "Quick! Inside!" We ran into the kitchen dodging large drops and splots of hot water. The pipe geysered two or three more times and then went silent.

"It's the overflow from one of those damned wood-fired hot water heaters downstairs," I guessed. This was immediately confirmed as a second pipe began a violent rattling, soon imitating the scalding gushes of the first. While we waited in the kitchen each of the pipes took it's turn showering the patio. I checked my watch: "It's just about the time when everybody getting off work would want their evening bath. I have a feeling this may be a regular performance." I was right but I'd underestimated the other tenants' fondness for showers: after the morning crew bathed and set off to school and jobs, the stay-at homes took their turns. Then came the night shift preparing for work, the early-to-home school kids and last, the returning day shift.

A few days later I cornered the landlord on the stairs and invited him for an evening drink. He fidgeted nervously but I insisted that we wanted to share the view with him for a few minutes. He trudged into our apartment like a man with something heavy on his mind and took a chair Lorena offered him next to the pipes.

When the first pipe began gurgling I raised my glass to his and said, "To the view, *señor*, to the marvelous view!"

Determine who pays the utilities. Water is generally free but electricity is usually paid for by the tenant. Some landlords prefer to charge a flat rate for electricity, almost always reasonable, in order to avoid the paper work involved in changing the name on the bills at the electric company's office. Because the electricity bills are almost invariably out-of-date or not paid up, it is wise to ask the landlord to handle this for you.

Faulty or inoperative wiring, broken windows, missing door latches, leaky faucets and all such minor discrepancies fall into the category of 'nonessential details' for most landlords. They may make sincere vows to repair things or replace them, but don't be so foolish as to count on it. They feel that when you rent the house, you are accepting it as it is, not as you want them to make it later.

When everything has been agreed to and the money handed over, you will usually be given a dated receipt (*recibo*). If not, ask for one, as a reminder to both you and your landlord of when the next rent is due. A receipt is especially valuable if the transaction is being handled by an agent for the owner of the house. An agent may not be above adding a little something to the rent for himself. If the owner shows up, you can avoid disagreements by having a receipt.

Wood-Fired Water Heaters

If you rent a place or live with a Mexican family, you're likely to run into a classic Mexican appliance, the wood-fired hot water heater. Gas stoves and water heaters are widely used in Mexico, but many people still use the basic wood-fueled ones. They are cheap to buy and install and cost little to operate.

The water heater is made up of a tall metal fire box, cylindrical in shape, surrounded by a coiled water pipe. It is simple, durable and foolproof. Or so it seems at first glance. But as with all foolproof devices, it takes the proper kind of fool to make it work.

The best fuel is small pieces of dry hardwood. Corn cobs are also good and make excellent kindling for wood when soaked in kerosene. *Carbón* (charcoal) can be used but it burns too slowly to give best results. (For sources of fuel see *Services*.)

The idea is to build as hot and roaring a fire as possible. When the overflow pipe spouts off it's time to strip and jump into the shower. Adjust the water for the minimum flow; most heaters have a small capacity and by the time you're ready for a rinse, it might be quite cold.

Problems arise when the fuel is not dry enough or the draft is fouled by gusts of wind, excessive smoke, sooting up of the exhaust pipe and so forth. Be patient, these heaters all look alike but most have individual characteristics that make them seem almost alive. Anyone who has passed through the trials and tribulations of learning to operate a wood or coal cookstove will understand. (Many people are buying wood water heaters to take home; they are perfect for use in remote cabins, houses without electricity and as back-ups to gas and electric heaters.)

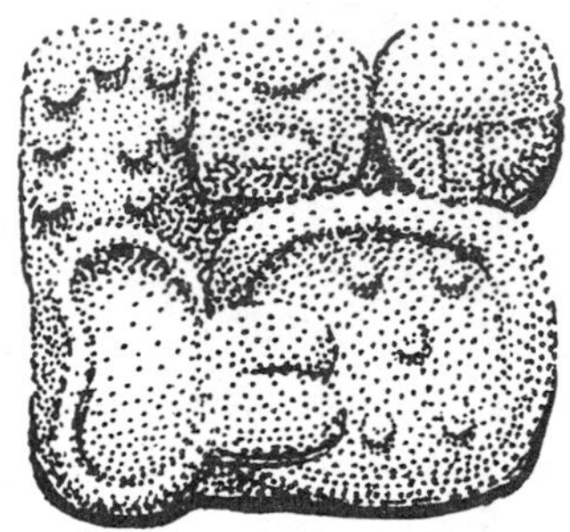

My battles with Mexican heaters have been long and bitter. The worst took place with a heater that absolutely refused to produce anything but choking clouds of smoke from every opening and crack. I tried everything from dangerous amounts of kerosene to hours of fanning and got nothing for my efforts but watering eyes and clouds of pollution.

On the seventh morning my frustrations rose to the boiling point, though the shower water still ran ice cold. I shredded old newspaper, magazines and added oven-dried corncobs and slivers of *ocote* (pitch pine). I cracked every twig of firewood to insure that it was dry and arranged it in approved Scout fashion over the tinder. Then came a liberal slosh of kerosene. I stood by the small firebox door with a fan in each hand, inhaling deeply, prepared to add my own breath to the draft, even if it drove me to my knees.

I struck a match and touched it to the newspaper. Flame shot up, igniting the cobs, then the pitch pine and then the.....smoke began billowing out the firebox door in great choking clouds. I fanned furiously, trying to protect my eyes from the oily stinging smoke. It spread throughout the patio; I could hear Lorena muttering as she closed all windows and doors, trying to keep the awful smell from the house. I fanned even harder, my lungs burning painfully as I went down to my knees for an occasional emergency breath of air. It was no use; I was just creating more and more smoke, rising now in a column over the roof.

I dropped the fans and ran for the nearest exit: the stairway to the roof. Choking and spitting on the awful taste of scorched cobs and kerosene, I burst up out of the smoke and stood, chest heaving. Across the alleyway our neighbor was crouched in front of one of several small cages, talking to a fighting cock. It was part of his evening and morning ritual, haranguing his team of chickens into a state of lethal aggression.

"What are you doing, having a barbecue?" he called, giving me a friendly wave.

"Heating water!" I snapped, swabbing my eyes with a sooty handkerchief.

"I can tell you, *amigo,* that you'll have to wait for that." His voice was knowing and sympathetic. I swallowed my irritation and decided to ask for his advice; I must be making a basic error in the operation of the heater.

"What do you mean?" I asked, "Wait for what?"

He leaned over to whisper into a cock's ear, probably a threat about chicken *enchiladas* if he didn't win his next fight. "You see," he said, "that heater will only work properly when there is no wind. It's always been that way. Wait for the wind to calm and then heat your water."

"Well, OK, thanks," I said, suddenly aware that the wind was indeed quite strong. Come to think of it, the wind had been fairly steady for days.

"When does the wind stop?" I asked, hoping it wouldn't just be in the middle of the night.

He slipped the bird back into its cage, straightening up with a laugh. "Oh, it usually ends in May but sometimes not until June."

I headed back downstairs. More newspaper, more corncobs, kerosene...it was not yet March.

Warning: When using kerosene in a heater, don't slop it onto hot coals. The kerosene will instantly vaporize and form a very explosive gas. If the fire dies down but is still hot, dip a newspaper roll into the kerosene, light the end and put it into the fire box.

Never use gasoline. The trapped vapor inside a water heater can turn it into a bomb.

Living With Mexicans

Although some landlords will rent out houses for short periods most prefer that you stay at least a month. If your time is short consider renting a room in someone's home.

Mexicans are, by average American standards, very casual about taking someone in for a week, a month, or even longer. Unannounced visitors, either friends or relatives, are put up without great fuss, though it may mean six kids to a bed instead of three or four. This custom makes it relatively easy for them to understand why a gringo would like a place to stay; hotels are used only as a special treat or last resort.

A young Mexican sitting next to me on a bus once asked what cities I had visited on my trip. I mentioned several and his eyes widened. "You must have a very big *familia, señor,*" he said, "to be able to visit so many places." When I explained that I had no relatives at all in Mexico and stayed in hotels, he looked doubly surprised and exclaimed, "*¡Caray!* It must be very lonely for you to travel like that!"

He was hoping that a cousin would move to Acapulco so he might go there for visit. When I suggested that he go on his own, he just laughed.

Living in a Mexican home is a standard part of what language schools call 'total immersion.' The immersion can sometimes be so complete that you have to come up for air. Unless you're very reserved or a militant loner, you'll be treated as part of the household and not just a paying lodger.

This can create problems, especially if the family has traditional concepts of morality and conduct. Single boarders will probably find themselves tippling in the outhouse. If the situation becomes tense, consider finding a more relaxed place to live; another family might be completely casual about everything.

The main problem we've experienced when living with a Mexican family is that they are overly solicitious and concerned about our well being. Anyone not at least 50% overweight is considered to be in imminent danger of death by malnutrition.

"Please!" the lady of the house cries, approaching the table with yet another bowl of *sopa de arroz!* "You've got to keep up your strength! You read so much!" This isn't Woody Allen doing a Jewish mother routine; it's the landlady who forces you to eat five meals a day and worries that the neighbors might think she's starving you.

You'll undoubtedly be introduced to new customs and superstitions. Whatever you do, don't sneer, laugh or otherwise indicate disrespect for their beliefs, however bizarre they might seem. I once made the mistake of taking a shower after eating a huge afternoon meal. I'd barely gotten soaped up when there was a frantic pounding on the bathroom door. "Carlos! Carlos! What are you doing?" A voice cried. I turned off the water and called out, "Taking a bath. Why?" The voice begged me to reconsider so I quickly rinsed, dried off and dressed, afraid that I'd done something to offend them or had used up the last of the household water.

When I emerged from the bathroom the landlord and his family apologized for bothering me, but I evidently didn't know that bathing after eating was certain death. It was only their quick intervention that had saved me from a heart attack. There are many superstitions of this type that you should be prepared to deal with. (See *Superstitions*.)

Always ask what the price of your room will be and if it includes one or more meals and laundry service. The price is usually quite fair but it is customary to ask and good sense besides. Inquire also about any particular rules of the house: no smoking, drinking, radios, late visitors, etc.

Living with a family cuts down on personal privacy, but the experience is well worth minor inconveniences. There are side benefits, too, that are difficult to place a value on: you really learn about daily life in Mexico; you eat foods that aren't served in most restaurants; pick up Spanish if only through contact and osmosis, and make meaningful friendships with people who would otherwise be just another face.

When it's time to move on consider asking for an introduction or recommendation to a family in another place. The more contacts you establish the more you'll save on both time and money. And, of course, you'll be dealing with people who will be predisposed to help you out.

HIRED HELP

As soon as you've moved into a house, someone will come to the door offering to be your maid, cook, gardener, washerwoman or general helper. When faced with camping and doing all the chores yourself, the temptation is great to hire a replacement. Because the wages for even full-time help are very low, the temptation often becomes irresistible.

There are occasionally problems, however, involved in hiring someone to do housework or washing. Unless they have worked for foreigners before and thoroughly understand their idiosycracies, things will be done according to their ways, not yours. Most problems we've had were the result of over-enthusiasm. You want the house quickly swept so you can relax and do some writing, but before you know it, buckets of cold water are flying through the air, furniture is being hauled outside and you have to retreat to the back yard.

Determining what is fair pay can be difficult for those not accustomed to the Mexican system. Basically, it goes like this: (legal minimum) salaries are for eight hours a day, six days a week. Most people who work part time or for a few weeks at a time get less than the minimum, depending on the bargain that is made with their employer. Meals and a place to sleep can legally count for no more than one-half of a salary, but often they're figured as more than this. When Mexicans are hiring household help they drive a very hard bargain. I've never heard of a maid or gardener who preferred working with Mexicans instead of foreigners.

Unless your house of family is large you probably won't need more than a few days of help each week. Most of the people who apply to tourists for jobs have an incredible ability to expand their duties—and wages.

Even though you insist that the woman come and wash your clothes just twice a month, she miraculously appears every day on one pretext or another. Before you know what's happening, she's moved in. Should you value your privacy highly or be a marginal poverty case yourself, this can pose a problem that is difficult to solve.

Happily the minor problems involved with hiring help rarely outweigh the advantages. An intelligent cleaning woman can teach you more Spanish in a week than most formal courses do and she doesn't expect extra pay for tutoring services. You'll get instruction in cooking, how to buy food, where the best bargains are and countless other bits of domestic information very helpful to the ignorant and uninitiated. Many details in this book were supplied by such people.

A few hints about where to buy firewood or which store sells the cheapest beer can easily save you a good portion of the wages paid.

Unless the person you hire is really a loser, you'll almost certainly become great friends. The only problem you'll have then is leaving; there always seem to be great amounts of weeping involved, not to mention final parties, hangovers and the mutual exchange of useless gifts.

Lorena and I had been loafing on the west coast of Mexico, catching up on hammock time after a long damp winter in the Pacific Northwest. With summer approaching we decided to move to a higher altitude, to a climate more conducive to writing than the oppressive heat of the beaches. Early one afternoon we caught a second class bus, relieved to know that by sundown we would be back among the cool pines and oaks of the mountains. We had no exact destination in mind, preferring to rely on intuition and luck.

A few hours later the bus was winding its way up the side of a long narrow valley heavily planted with sugarcane. The air had thinned noticeably. I was anxiously waiting for the first glimpse of evergreen forests when my stomach made some sudden and very unpleasant noises.

"Hey, Lorena," I said, clutching a cramp as beads of sweat popped onto my forehead, "Remember that hot dog I just couldn't pass up outside the bus station?" She turned with a curious stare, comprehension dawning as she noticed my hand massaging the front of my shirt.

"You mean...?"

"Yeah," I groaned. "I gotta get off right away or there's going to be a very embarrassing scene."

Lorena immediately began gathering up her 'extras': a knapsack, a string bag filled with yarn, a yarn bag filled with fruit, a cloth bag stuffed with notebooks and pens, a hat, a small cardboard box of shells and stones and a fat green coconut.

The other passengers watched with interest as we worked our way to the front of the wildly swaying bus with repeated, "*Con permisos.*" One old man bowed back courteously as I doubled over with a cramp, his dark face breaking into a grin at what he took to be my excessively formal farewell.

"We want to get off at the next *pueblo*," I gasped to the driver's helper, a ten-year-old boy who stared at us blankly over the top of an *Hermelinda* comic book. He barely had time to relay this message to the man at the wheel before we reached the crest of a ridge and bumped into a small town.

"Where are we?" I asked as we braked to a stop in front of a tiny open *plaza*. *"Funerales Lopez, Servicio Dia y Noche"* was cast into the backs of four cracked cement benches, facing outward from a forlorn wooden bandstand and two very dry pine trees. At least we were out of the hot banana country.

"Where are you going?" the driver countered, his hand resting on the door lever.

"*Here*," I said, "What is the name of this place?"

"How can you go here when you don't know where you are?" he answered suspiciously, the door held tightly closed. I felt a slight buzzing in my ears and mopped my forehead with a shirtsleeve.

"Because...because..." I took a deep breath, willing my guts to hold off on anything drastic for just a few more minutes. "Because...my mother lives here!" I blurted, "I'm going to visit my mother!"

The door banged open as the driver muttered sarcastically, "Then go ask your mother where you are!"

The bus had hardly pulled away before we were surrounded by a horde of children, asking eager questions about our backpacks, our birthplaces, our hometown and its proximity to Washington, D.C. and the North Pole.

"Where are you coming from?"

"Where are you going?"

"What is your work?"

"Do you have a camera?"

"Hey! Wait a minute!" I yelled, trying to fend off an industrious youngster who was either polishing my left hiking boot or stealing the shoelace. "Where is a place to eat?" I knew that my best chance of finding a tolerable toilet fast would be in the nearest *comedor*.

"Over there! Over there!" several voices cried as the children began jumping up and down, little hands clutching at our gear, vying for the privilege of helping us across the street. Lorena began laughing as she handed her odds and ends to the kids. Only a few of them were taller than her waist. A small girl hissed urgently and Lorena bent down so that her blond hair could be stroked for good luck.

We moved en masse to the doorway that they pointed to and entered a dark cool room, crowded with oilcloth covered tables. I explained my urgent need to one of the larger children. While Lorena draped her bags over the back of a chair, I was rushed to the rear by my sympathetic retainers. "*¡Baño!*" I explained to the startled grey haired lady stirring a large earthen pot of beans as we hurried through the kitchen and into the patio.

Two small boys stood guard in front of the bathroom's flour sack covered doorway. Behind it I drifted gratefully into a Zen-like state of diarrhea detachment, my mind barely registering the low babble of speculation and laughter outside.

Fifteen minutes later, after washing my face and hands in a bucket of refreshing cold water brought to me by a blushing little girl, I wobbled back to the dining room.

"Feel better?" Lorena asked sympathetically, while slurping from a large pottery mug. "Try some of this; it'll fix you up," she said, offering me the cup.

"What is it?" I asked, edging away. Her travelling medicine bag included combinations of powders and leaves capable of gagging *Don* Juan.

"Why don't you just try it?" she urged, smacking her lips encouragingly.

"What's in it?" I stalled. "Anything weird?"

"Do you want to feel better or not?" Lorena demanded, increasing my suspicion.

"Well...I don't know..." I said, my resistance weakening at the twinges of another cramp.

"It's just golden seal, a little cinnamon, some cayenne pepper, a pinch of garlic powder and a squeeze of lime juice," she said, as casually as if it were Constant Comment.

Before I had time to reject this ghastly potion, the lady I'd surprised in the kitchen bustled into the room bearing a similar steaming mug.

"Té de perro, joven," she smiled, setting the cup of 'dog tea,' a classic Mexican stomach remedy, on the table in front of me. I sniffed it warily; Lorena might have convinced her to add a little something extra, just for the sake of my health. The tea was bitter but good and its warmth soon relaxed my tense muscles. The combination of bus trip and diarrhea had been exhausting. I began to drift off, calling upon my Navy training to allow myself to doze sitting up, eyes open wide, my face making occasional twitches, falsely signalling mental activity. In the background I vaguely heard Lorena and the lady discussing our plans, lifestyles, families and finances. My eyes closed slowly...

"Carl? Hey, Carl!"

I snapped awake, my hand jerking convulsively, spilling the dregs of tea across my lap.

"Yeah? What? What is it?" I yawned, realizing that we were alone, actually completely alone, not an adult or kid in sight.

"I rented a house," Lorena said, her voice charged with excitement, "from the *señora* here. It's really cheap and she says that it has a good view of the valley."

I considered this news quietly, staring out at the deserted street. "Well, why not?" This looked like as good a place as any. If nothing else the children were friendly. I yawned, easing down into the chair and stretching my legs. Somewhere in the distance a radio blared and dogs barked lazily. The air was fresh and clean; smelling vaguely of pine needles and cooked beans.

Our first view of the house Lorena had rented was something of a disappointment.

"I've seen worse," I lied, wondering if the sagging roof was holding up the crumbling adobe walls or vice versa. I surveyed the few remaining patches of whitewash, obviously applied before the Revolution, the rotting roof beams, and the cracked tiles. I could see three small cell-like windows, barred with weathered sticks.

It was a scene of quaint and picturesque neglect. Picturesque, that is, to a passing artist and not a new tenant.

"At least we won't have to buy a padlock," Lorena said, pushing aside the curtain of burlap sacks covering the front doorway.

"Or lightbulbs," I said, pointing to the kerosene lamp and candle stubs set in niches in the thick walls.

"What about the furniture and the decor?" Lorena laughed, testing a midget-sized pine chair. Her chin just about reached the level of the table top, barely large enough to hold a checkerboard.

There was another elf-sized table, two crudely hewn wooden stools, a few empty crates and a stove, a massive affair of adobe bricks and hardened mud. "I'd call it Late Cortez," I said, crossing the small living room and moving into the even smaller kitchen.

"Everything is so *small*," Lorena sighed, easing her backpack onto the single narrow canvas cot that we would cling to like mountain climbers in the nights ahead. "But at least she wasn't exaggerating about the view."

I turned to look. The boundary of our front yard was a nearly vertical drop of almost three thousand feet to the next village.

While we sat there, soaking up the sun and tossing pebbles over the edge, I privately wondered what we'd gotten ourselves into. Suddenly a boiling mass of thick clouds appeared at the foot of the valley, swelling and surging upward until we were engulfed in an eerie golden fog. The temperature dropped immediately and we hurried into the house to pull jackets from the bottoms of our packs.

"That's what I'd call a ten dollar sunset," I said. "I just wish it had come a couple of hours later." It was four in the afternoon.

That night we again sat on the edge of the cliff, watching the dim twinkle of lights below and listening to the music from the village loudspeaker echoing upward, like passengers observing the earth from a silent dirigible. When I later asked a neighbor for the quickest route down, he laughed and said, "By parachute."

The waves of interest created by our arrival eventually subsided and within a week we were tentatively accepted as members of the community. Our status floated somewhere between that of the schoolteacher and the village idiot. When it became common knowledge that I spent the mornings writing, several people began greeting me as *"Profe,"* short for *"Profesor,"* Others who might have seen us flinging a Frisbee with the kids or flying homemade kites, treated us with the cautious respect reserved for the non-criminally insane.

The quiet routine we established ended abruptly on the morning of our eighth day. I had just finished writing and was about to begin the usual argument with Lorena over who had to wash dishes, when a woman's voice called a cheery, "*¡Buenos días!*" from the front doorway.

"*¡Pase usted!*" Lorena called back, expecting to see another of the neighbors.

The curtain was pushed aside and a small middle-aged woman marched into the room. "I am *Maria de la Luz*," she announced brightly, "And I have come to do your housework." Lorena and I looked at each other, startled, as 'Mary-of-the-Light' disappeared into the kitchen.

"Did you see her face?" I finally asked.

Lorena nodded, stunned. There was no light in one of Maria's eyes, it was lost in the milky blindness of vast cataracts. A tingle ran up the back of my neck. The blankness of that eyeball, in contrast to her lively smile, had somehow seemed menacing.

"Did you ask her to come?" I said.

"Never seen her before in my life!" Lorena answered, astonished.

I didn't know what to say, but judging from the sounds that came from the kitchen, Maria was wasting no time asserting her employment. I got up from my chair and took a deep breath, squaring my shoulders: the woman would have to be shown the door!

"I'll take care of this," I said, moving toward the kitchen. I barely avoided colliding with Maria as she bustled into the room, wiping her hands on the front of her full length apron.

"Where is the soap?" she demanded, fixing me with that lopsided blind stare, a numbing psychic laser beam that left me stammering, "Er...it's on the shelf...by the stove."

"It should be by the bucket," she answered, turning her back and returning to the kitchen.

"You handled that really well," Lorena chided.

"Well, what do you want me to do?" I yelled. "Drag her out by her braids and throw her off the cliff?" I moved warily to the kitchen doorway, determined to clear up this misunderstanding without further delay.

"Ah...er, Maria?" I said. "We're sorry but we don't want you to..." Her sarcastic bark cut off my dismissal speech. "*Señor*," she laughed, "Everyone in the *pueblo* says that you, a *man*, wash your own clothing and cook and even..." she hesitated, peering at me uncertainly with her blank eye. The impropriety of my next offense was almost too terrible to mention aloud, "...and even *sweep the floor*!"

I blushed.

"*Señor*," she continued, "That is not *la costumbre* here!"

Guilty of violating local custom by helping with the housework! How could I explain to her that if I forced Lorena to do all of the chores, I would be violating *our* custom and she would probably be leaving on the next bus, without me?

"*Pues...*" I conceded. "If it's *la costumbre*...but how much will it cost to have you work? We don't have much money." I added this hurriedly, certain that our emaciated budget would make the decadent practice of having a 'domestic' unthinkable.

Maria's stare fixed on me for several long moments. She then announced a salary so fantastically low that I all but rubbed my hands together with glee. Visions of never having to touch a dishrag or mop again brought a flush to my face, erasing guilty thoughts of exploitation of the working class.

"*¡Cosa hecha!*" I cried. "It's a deal!"

"Of course," she answered, smiling indulgently as she turned back to the bucket of dishes.

During those first idyllic days, writing, hiking, or just loafing on one of the funeral parlor's uncomfortable benches in the *plaza*, trading gossip with the kids, I had formed an image of village life tht went something like this: early in the rosy pre-dawn chill the jolly woodcutters and farmers tumbled from their cozy cornhusk mattresses to eat a simple but nourishing breakfast of beans and *tortillas* before tramping off into the surrounding mountains, whistling along the pine needle covered slopes to their picturesquely steep woodlots and fields. There they engaged in honest labor until late afternoon, when they returned, still whistling, to a simple but nourishing supper of beans and *tortillas* and a quiet evening around the blazing hearth, relating folk tales and earthy wisdom to their attentive and well-mannered broods.

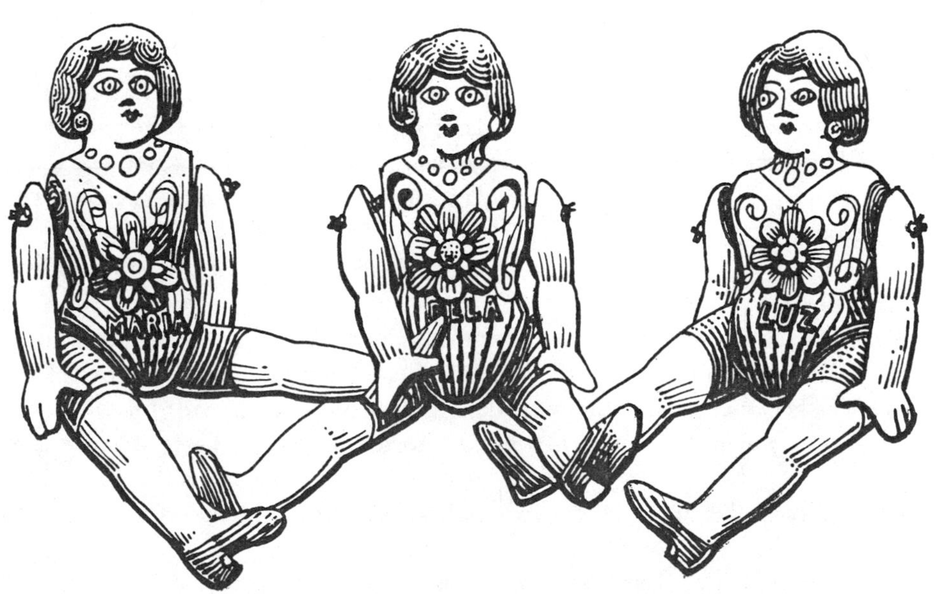

When not busy preparing simple but nourishing meals of beans and *tortillas*, the womenfolk were scrubbing brightly colored hand-loomed clothing and arranging it picturesquely along the banks of burbling mountain streams. Children laughed and gambolled on the grassy hillsides nearby as their older brothers and sisters tended flocks of prancing goats.

Maria changed all this with daily reports as lurid as The Evening News.

"That *pinche* ox Celestino borrowed the axe of Juanito and broke the handle and now the old *cabrón* says that...and when Lupe got home his old lady was drunk on *ponche* and burned the *tortillas* again, that *tonta*...and let me tell you how Rosamunda went into Iguala to visit her sister and came back *embarasada* and..."

"Wait a minute," I said. "What was she embarrassed about?"

Maria looked at me blankly for a few seconds, then gave an ear-splitting shriek of laughter, *"Embarasada,* you fool!" She formed her hands over her belly and began clomping around the kitchen as though in the last stage of a grotesque pregnancy. "No wonder you have no children!" she added, wiping a tear from her blind eye. "Don't you know how to..."

"Ok! Ok!" I said, edging toward the door.

"Wait!" she cried, casting a lopsided glance at the window for eavesdroppers, "You know what those dirty little *esquincles*, those brats next door, did to Pedro's chickens yesterday?"

"No, no, that's enough!" I protested, holding up my hands and backing out of the room. "I have to work now. You can tell me later, after dinner.

"¡JOVEN!"

Maria's shout brought me crashing to my feet, jostling the table. My half-filled coffee cup slopped across a stack of notes. I raced into the kitchen, expecting to find her cornered by some lethal serpent or rabid hound. To my surprise, however, she was only standing in front of our small brass backpacking stove, hands on hips, her face set in an angry scowl.

"How can I cook you a meal with this..." Maria hesitated, at a rare loss for words, "...this piece of gringo garbage?"

This was the last straw! I'd taken her through the operating procedures a hundred times, patiently demonstrating the various steps required to light the stove. Hell, I'd even heard her brag to the neighbors, describing it as '*moderna*' and '*preciosa*.'

"I've told you many times, Maria," I retorted angrily, "that this stove is very simple."

Her bad eye rolled upward as she twisted her shoulders in a classic Mexican 'Don't kid me' shrug.

"All you have to do," I continued, ignoring her deep self-pitying sighs, "is to put this thing on here and twist this." I opened the air valve, raising my eyebrows at her.

She sighed heavily and nodded.

"Oh, yeah," I said, reaching for the cleaning tool, "I forgot to tell you that you have to put this little wire in here and do this." I worked it up and down a few times. "Then you just put some of this alcohol in here, twist this back...no, wait, light the alcohol first, *then* twist this back. *¿Está bien?*"

She nodded silently.

"Ok, then, after 30 to 40 seconds open that and pump this." I couldn't resist adding, "It may take longer at this altitude because the fire isn't as hot."

"Fire isn't as hot here?" Maria snorted. "I didn't know that!" I chose to ignore her tone of voice. "When this is hot, *calientita*, you can adjust the fire by opening this *¿Entiende?* It's very simple."

She threw her hands into the air. "When *Doña* Lorena returns I will go for firewood," she said, turning her back on me and reaching for a banana.

I ground my teeth. "*Doña* Lorena!" Here I was just *Joven*, young man, while Lorena was the equivalent of 'Lady Lorena.' And this business of waiting for Lorena to return before Maria could leave the house, as though I were under protective custody—it was too much. I stormed out and headed for the village.

"*¡Ay, qué milagro!*" *Don* Antonio cried as I stepped through the door of his shop. His deep brown face was creased by a wide grin and as usual his hand automatically went to his chin, stroking the scraggly white whiskers he was cultivating in my honor. "What a miracle!" was *Don* Antonio's standard greeting to me, though we saw each other at least once a day.

It was to *Don* Antonio's that I escaped each afternoon, to sit on a fat grain sack among the pickaxes, *machetes,* broad bladed hoes and stacks of empty five gallon cans. I would sip warm Cokes laced with moonshine *mezcal* as we discussed the state of the world. He had patiently explained the politics and poverty of the local turpentine industry, and I in turn helped him to understand that Holland and Canada were separate countries and not parts of the United States. In spite of his age *Don* Antonio was a quick student. Our tattered Exxon road map of the United States was now tacked prominently behind the zinc topped counter, sandwiched between a rusting tin *Faros* cigarette sign and a faded and flyspeckled calendar for the year 1959. He used the map to conduct impromptu geography lessons for his younger customers.

"You're early today." He smiled, dusting a bottle of Coca Cola with a shirt sleeve and wrenching off the cap with his front teeth. I winced, another part of the daily ritual, and accepted the bottle. "*¿Con piquete?*" he asked, hooking a thumb toward the small wooden cask of moonshine that hung from the wall.

"*No, gracias,*" I said. "I'll wait until later for the stinger." I took a sip and added, "I can't work today. There's too much noise in the house."

He nodded sympathetically. *Don* Antonio invited your confidence and respected it; few decisions of any importance were made in the village without first seeking his opinion.

"Perhaps you should get rid of the noise?" he suggested, his voice completely neutral. Maria's antics were well known to him; our daily conversations often centered on her past and present exploits, sending us both into choking fits of laughter. *Don* Antonio had known her for more than 40 years and whenever I was telling a new 'Maria Story' I felt that he was reading my mind. His words of caution and advice had been invaluable.

"I can't send her away," I answered, "You know how poor she is."

He nodded. In a village where poverty was endured with heroic stoicism, Maria's plight might one day become legend.

"I asked her what she had for breakfast this morning and she said 'Beans. Six'." *Don* Antonio roared with laughter, his forehead touching the counter top as he beat it with his right fist.

While he waited on a man interested in a dozen nails, I worked on the Coke and pondered what to do about Maria. I glanced at my watch: almost one o'clock, time for *comida*.

"*Con permiso,*" I called, laying a few coins on the counter, "But I have to eat." *Don* Antonio waved, an amused grin on his face. He knew that I did not dare be late. Even if Maria had 'forgotten' to prepare the afternoon meal, as she often did, I was still expected to appear.

"What are we eating?" I called as I entered the house, praying it wouldn't be one of her eye-watering specialties. Maria's love of chilies was beyond belief; she snacked on them like peanuts.

"*¡Menudo!*" She answered cheerily, sweeping into the living room with a large steaming earthen *olla*. The bowl was placed on the table with the reverence of a sacrificial offering.

"Maria," I groaned, "We told you that we don't like to eat meat, remember?" She stared at me coldly. "Lorena *never* eats meat." I continued, knowing that whatever the *Doña* wanted the *Doña* would get, "And even if I wanted meat I would not want *menudo*." I tried to smile, to soften the blow a bit, but the thought of a bowl of hot tripe brought a shudder instead.

She snatched the *olla* away, giving me a withering glare with her blind eye that said "Pearls before swine!" and marched back to the kitchen.

Lorena returned five minutes later, just as I was beginning my meal of barely warmed beans and stiff *tortillas*. I explained the lunch situation and she rushed off to soothe Maria's feelings. I soon heard laughter and the sound of pans being rattled. Lorena came back bearing a plate covered with piping hot *quesadillas*, a fresh single serving of salad and an attractively sliced avocado.

I labored grimly over my beans as Lorena laughingly told me how good old Maria had accidently made *menudo*, thinking it was my favorite dish. Her extreme mental anguish had been assuaged somewhat when Lorena told her to take the stuff home.

"These are delicious," she added, munching on a *quesadilla*, "Like to try a bite?" I tore savagely at my day-old *tortilla*.

"Where are you going?"

"Out."

"Where?"

"In the mountains."

"What for?"

"To relax."

"Why? You can relax here."

"I need some air."

"When will you be back?"

"Soon."

"How soon? Don't forget dinner."

"I won't. What are we having?"

"Your favorite. *Pozole*."

"Oh, wonderful."

"What's wrong? Don't you like *pozole*?"

"Yes, Maria, I love it. If we didn't have it every day I think I'd die."

"Well then, get going, you need some air."

"Yes, Maria, thank you. *Hasta luego*."

"*Hasta luego, joven*. Be careful. Don't get lost. Or drunk."

I had been working for three weeks on a handwritten manuscript, making good progress in spite of Maria's repeated warnings about certain blindness from eyestrain. I finally shut her up one morning after she predicted that I would go insane from an "attack of brain pressure." I looked up at her, bugged out my eyes, and wheezed: "But Maria, my love, I went insane years ago!" A maniacal giggle sent her scurrying to *Dona* Lorena for protection.

Despite her morbid warnings Maria secretly approved of my writing. More than once I was approached by people who asked when I would be finished chronicling the life and times of Maria de la Luz.

And then my manuscript disappeared.

"What's wrong with him?" Maria asked, edging past Lorena with a shopping bag full of yet more *pozole* ingredients.

"He lost his papers," she answered.

"I DIDN'T LOSE THEM!" I shouted. "They were STOLEN! Robbed! *ROBADO! ROBADO!* I flopped onto the cot, grinding my fists into my forehead. The ultimate nightmare come true! Who could have possibly wanted those pages? Who in the village could even read them! It was senseless, absolutely senseless. Hell, they didn't even use paper around here for...oh no! Anything but *that!*

I was struck by the awful image of an Indian casually tearing the yellow legal pages into quarters, squatting behind a bush with his pants around his ankles, puzzling at the funny scribbles. I moaned.

"Oh, *those* papers!" Maria laughed, digging into the deep pockets of her apron. "I have them here. I just borrowed them for a few hours. *¡No te preocupes, joven!*"

"Don't preoccupy myself?" I cried, leaping from the bed and snatching the pages from her hand. I tore away the piece of grass that bound the tightly rolled sheets and riffled through them quickly. They were all there.

"Are you *loca*?" I stormed. "Don't you understand what this...this..." I gasped for breath as Maria watched with a knowing smile: only a matter of time now; I was throwing a classic 'brain pressure fit.' Such a lovely ceremony they'd have, carrying me to the local *panteon* in my whitewashed pine box, spilling over with plastic gardenias. *Doña* Lorena would look so nice, her blond hair over black.

"Why?" I asked, trying to calm myself, "Why did you take them? What did you do with them? *You can't even read!*" She puffed up like a game hen, turning as usual to Lorena: "*Señora*," she said, "I took the papers to show to my friends. To prove that the *joven* was writing the story of my life. They didn't believe me before. Now they do." She gave me a triumphant grin; my secret project had been revealed to all.

"*¡Bueno!*" she said, fluffing her apron busily, "Isn't it time for you to begin work?" Maria gave Lorena a motherly pat on the arm, "Come *señora*, it is the hour for us to take a cup of your delicious tea."

"*¡Kaaaalimaaaaan!*"

I shot up from the table, the noise striking like a cold dental probe on a tender nerve. I kicked the chair away, pulling wildly at the crude door I'd fashioned from raw pine boards, my final line of defense against Maria's constant warnings, questions and sly suggestions about her assumed biography.

"*¡KALIMAN! ¡HOMBRE INCREIBLE!*"

I threw the door aside, determined to put a final end to this ultimate irritation. The radio crackled:

"*KALIMAN approaches the Forbidden City in the company of little Solin...*"

"Yeah, maybe so," I thought, edging across the living room, "But this time he's had the course."

"*Go with patience and serenity Solin, for only the coward dies twice!*"

I flattened myself against the wall and reached for the curtain Maria had rigged over the kitchen doorway. Kaliman's platitudes boomed out into the house over a background of hissing and popping static. It was a complete mystery to me how Maria could coax such volume from her cracked and patched transistor radio, let alone how she understood the distorted words. She often worked with the radio held inches from her ear.

"KALIMAN ATTACKS!"

I threw the curtain back and leaped into the kitchen, raising my hand to snatch the radio and hurl it out the window. Let Kaliman entertain the people at the bottom of the cliff!

"The coward dies by his own hand! Take that you..."

"Oh, Carl! What are you doing?" Lorena asked, looking up from the radio she held in her lap. Maria gave me a wicked grin, winking her bad eye deliberately.

"Would you like to listen to the program with us?" Lorena continued, "Kaliman has just approached the Forbidden City and..."

"I'm going to miss this place, but I have to admit that I'm getting a little bored." Lorena said one evening as we sat on the edge of our front yard tossing pebbles into the pine trees below.

We'd hiked almost the entire network of trails surrounding the village. I knew Maria's jokes well enough to anticipate the lurid punch lines and conversations at *Don* Antonio's were as predictable as the price of turpentine.

"When Maria saw me looking at the map this morning, she just about flipped," I said.

Lorena sighed; leaving was going to be difficult. Maria seemed convinced that we had come to the village for good and had begun to say things like, "When you buy your *parcela* of land..." and "I think your new house should have a fireplace." It was useless to try to explain that we'd come to the village on a whim and would leave on another. In Maria's world, life was as regular as sunrise and sunset, with very few surprises in between.

"I gave her a good reason for our leaving," I said. "I told her I wanted to write about witches and magic herbs and that we were going somewhere to look for them.

"What did she say to that?"

"Not much," I answered. "She just gave me a funny look and then left. Said she'd see us tomorrow. Come to think of it she looked sort of horrified."

We both laughed; I'd finally gotten one over on her!

Maria disappeared. When she didn't show up the day after I'd told her we would be leaving, we assumed she wasn't feeling well or was busy at home. The next day, however, we began to worry.

"We've got to leave by tomorrow," I said, "But if she hasn't shown up, we can get one of the kids to take us to her house." Lorena agreed, though I could tell she was ready to begin the search immediately.

I woke early the next morning, shifting carefully for a more comfortable position on the 'Ledge,' as we'd come to call our narrow bed. A noise from the kitchen caught my attention. I heard the blowtorch roar of the backpacking stove and the rattle of the tea kettle. Maria?

"Hey, Lorena," I yawned. "Time to get up. I think we'll be able to catch the morning bus after all. Maria is in the kitchen." I eased out of bed and began pulling on my clothes, relieved that this final complication was now resolved. Our backpacks were almost ready; we could just eat breakfast and be on our way. A cup of coffee, first, that's what I really needed.

"Maria," I said, pushing aside the kitchen curtain, "Is the coffee...?" I stopped, recoiling from the sickening odor that filled the kitchen. Maria stood over a small pot, stirring it with...a turkey feather? Her mouth was set in a hard line, her nose seemed to be trying to crawl away of its own accord, struggling to escape the obnoxious steam that poured upward.

"What are you doing?" I cried, fanning the air before me and trying to catch a glimpse of the pot's contents. Something caught my eye. Turning to the pine table I saw a pair of scraggly dead birds, their pitiful feet tied together with bright yellow yarn, surrounded by leaves, roots and dried bark. A large basket of assorted mushrooms, some a vile pulpy red, sat on the chair. I looked up, just in time to catch Maria's dark eye fixed on mine. The lid of her blind eye closed slowly in a sly, calculated wink.

"*Joven*," she croaked, and I immediately caught the theatrical tone, the exaggerated old crone whine, "I have many things to show you." She lifted the pot from the stove with one of her asbestos hands and poured the scalding liquid into a pottery mug. "Drink this!" she commanded, "and it will protect you from *El Mal Ojo!*"

I gave a tentative laugh. 'The Evil Eye?' Was this for real? She pushed the cup toward me, ignoring the boiling hot tea that splashed over her fingers.

"What is all this?" I stalled, waving my hands at the strange display on the table and chair. Was it my imagination or did she pull her head down into her shoulders and bend into a witch-like crouch?

"There are certain secrets I possess," she answered cryptically, fingering a small cloth bag that hung at her throat.

"What's that?" I asked, moving in for a better look. She immediately stuffed the bag inside the front of her dress. "I will explain," she repeated, "but now you must drink this." I took one more whiff of that awful tea and retreated to the other room.

"Lorena," I said, reaching for my boots, "I think you'd better have a little talk with Maria before she tries to change herself into a crow." I went to the front door, "I have to say goodbuy to *Don* Antonio. Watch out for that thing she's got in there, it'd kill a werewolf with one sniff." She looked up from the bed, puzzled. As I walked by the tiny kitchen window I heard a stifled cackle.

"That about does it," I said, giving the kitchen a final once-over in case we'd forgotten something. Maria's unidentified herbs and mushrooms were now scattered in the trees below the house, along with the unfortunate birds. She had taken her unmasking as a phoney witch quite well, laughing openly as she described to Lorena how she'd gathered everything she could find that looked even vaguely poisonous or weird. "But I was very afraid," she said, "that the *joven* would actually drink that..."

The awful brew had been her undoing. When Lorena had gone into the kitchen she'd called Maria's bluff by not only accepting a cup, but by actually raising it to her lips for a drink. Rather than see the *Doña* poisoned, Maria had grabbed it away and dumped it onto the floor. A confession of quackery was not far behind. "The *joven* said he wanted to write about a witch so I thought..."

"Well, here we go," I said, raising my pack and slipping my arms through the shoulder straps. Maria hurried to help Lorena, clucking disapproval at the weight of her pack. She gave me a look that said, "Brute! How can you make the poor thing carry *this*?"

We parted in front of the house, shaking hands in the Indian fashion, a gentle mutual stroke that somehow conveys so much more than a gringo knuckle-buster. In spite of her great pretensions as our *mayordoma*, Maria was too shy to accompany us to the bus stop. She issued her final warnings and instructions from the yard.

"Don't sit by open windows on the bus, you'll get a bad wind and die."

"Go to the market when you get to Guadalajara and buy thicker eye glasses."

"Drink lots of *atole*; you're too skinny."

She stopped for breath, searching her memory for another bit of folk wisdom. "Remember, a closed mouth catches no flies!" We started down the trail, waving back to her. "*Señora*!" she called, her voice breaking, "*Señora* don't forget to...forget to..." Maria gulped, tears pouring down her cheeks, "Don't forget to listen to *KALIMAN!*"

We stumbled down the tree covered ridge, following the red dirt path to the tiny *plaza. Don* Antonio waved and called from the doorway of his store. Somewhere in the distance a radio blared and dogs barked lazily. The air smelled vaguely of pine needles and cooked beans.

NOTES

CAMPING

Why go camping?...Privacy: next to impossible...Learn to adapt... Where to camp...Where not to camp...Exploring...The Perfect Campsite... Mosquitoes, coconuts and shade trees...Rainy season...Bandits!... Camping skills...Building a thatched hut...Machete sharpening...

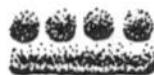

For many people a trip to Mexico means one thing: camping. There is an almost irresistible attraction in Mexico's 6,000 miles of coastline, the vast majority of it open and undeveloped, plus countless square miles of jungle, mountains, deserts and forests. *Norteamericanos* who are tired of having to make campsite reservations up to a year in advance, are finding that Mexico offers the chance not only to get away from the crowds, but to actually explore country that has seen few campers.

This potential is just beginning to be realized by foreign tourists as well as Mexicans. Trailer parks and campgrounds are much more common than a few years ago and new ones seem to spring up every day. Some enterprising people have found that if they stick a sign in the ground that says "*Campamento*" or "*Parque de Traylers*" that campers will play to cluster around it.

Facilities may range from tiled bathrooms, hot showers, laundromat and shuttle bus service to the nearest town to none at all, just an open pasture and an outhouse. Those who prefer less organization and the excitement of the Unknown, will find innumerable side roads to follow, empty beaches, trails, jungle rivers, remote canyons and no one to talk to but the occasional passing fisherman or mule skinner.

Camping in Mexico is different in many ways from camping in the U.S. and Canada. Many Mexicans live all of their lives on a scale that we would consider 'camping.' Chopping firewood; hauling water; hunting; fishing; gathering herbs, wild fruits and vegetables; and sleeping on mats or hard cots are all part of the normal daily routine.

Unsolicited Plug

"How's the revision going?" Lorena asked, perhaps noticing a certain glow of insanity in my eyes.

"Great. Just great!" I sighed. "I'm up to almost twenty pages just on the Camping chapter." I threw my pencil across the room.

"So what's the problem?" she said, "You must be about finished, right?"

"Not quite," I answered. "That's twenty pages of outline. I haven't even started re-writing!"

It was true. I had enough new material on camping to do another...Oh no! Not that! I looked over quickly at Lorena. She was staring off into space, thinking. A dangerous sign.

"Carl...?"

"Hold it!" I interrupted. "Don't even say it! We're *going* camping remember? Not writing any more about it! Just as soon as this revision is done we can hit that old dusty trail."

I turned back to my notes. It would be difficult, to say the least, but they'd have to be compressed into one chapter. There had to be a way! We couldn't keep expanding this book forever.

"You could do a chapter on boating and dugout canoes," Lorena persisted, "Remember that time we rented a *panga* and went down the coast to..."

I waved the memory away. I couldn't afford to daydream. Temptation could easily become torture.

"Or that hike we did to...? You could write about that, too."

I groaned.

"Or how about that *palapa* we built near the lagoon? Remember that coral reef?"

"Stop!" I pleaded, "You're killing me!" I could almost feel powdery white sand crunching beneath my bare feet, the sun hot on my shoulders. Cotton fleece clouds slid across the sky, the fragrant breeze rustling through the palm fronds. I'd better get my diving

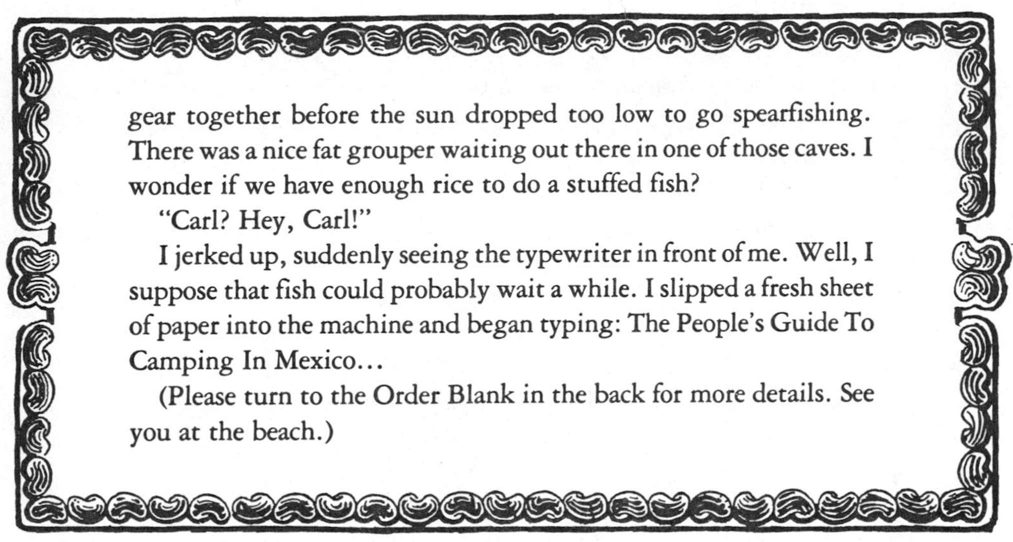

gear together before the sun dropped too low to go spearfishing. There was a nice fat grouper waiting out there in one of those caves. I wonder if we have enough rice to do a stuffed fish?

"Carl? Hey, Carl!"

I jerked up, suddenly seeing the typewriter in front of me. Well, I suppose that fish could probably wait a while. I slipped a fresh sheet of paper into the machine and began typing: The People's Guide To Camping In Mexico...

(Please turn to the Order Blank in the back for more details. See you at the beach.)

Most Mexicans finds it difficult to understand why rich people—and we *are rich* by their standards—deliberately regress from luxury to 'roughing it.'

Camping is therefore a rather unusual activity, something to be curious about. This curiosity makes 'getting away from it all' almost impossible. The farther you go from cities and tourist areas, the more interesting you become to the local people. Your arrival in a remote area will not go unnoticed—the inhabitable areas of the country are all inhabited. People—curious, questioning, staring—are everywhere. You're mistaken if you think that all of those interesting natives are just going to stand there like natural formations while you point and take pictures. You'll find, instead, that the interest is mutual. They'll soon be outstaring you and even taking *your* picture.

Privacy

Unless you camp in trailer parks and organized campgrounds, your camping trip will turn into a 'people' trip. There are ways, fortunately, to increase your privacy without hiding inside a tent or camping on the edge of an active volcano.

Children are the worst intruders. To avoid them, camp a long way from the nearest village or ranch. This certainly won't eliminate their visiting, but it will keep the smaller and less adventurous away. Large kids are notoriously difficult to avoid and if they have to walk five hot dusty miles to see you (which they will do), they'll probably make a day of it.

Avoid camping near trails, usually the major travel routes for local people.

Don't camp near obviously popular swimming holes. Half-used bars of soap, discarded scrubbers and picnic garbage near an inviting pool of water are sure indications that weekends and evenings will find it full of people.

After you've chosen a campsite, you can expect visitors within hours. On the coast and in the lower mountain areas, people are generally more open with strangers than the Indians of the high mountains. You can expect them to stare. Silent staring can be unnerving (to say the least), especially if you're alone or don't speak Spanish. Paranoia may have you packing up and heading to a city if you don't understand—and try to accept—the reasons for this mute intrusion.

Natural curiosity is obviously part of the reason that people want to stare at you. You look funny. Your hair is weird, your clothes are strange, your car and all of your possessions are wonderful to look at and you talk and act like no normal person in the village. Curiosity itself isn't difficult to understand, but the open staring, pointing and excited talking over everything you unpack or do can be infuriating, and for some, quite frightening.

Why do they do it? How can they be so blatant and unembarrassed? The answer is that they have no feeling of "each man's house being his castle" and no concept of being rude or impolite merely because they are observing what you are doing in your house, i.e., car or tent.

You will probably notice that this open curiosity doesn't normally reach the point where visitors will walk uninvited into your camp or actually handle your things. When you want someone to 'come in,' you'll usually have to invite them (women are especially shy). It's as if invisible boundaries marked off the area of your camp from the general community.

This attitude can best be understood by visiting one of your curious visitor's homes. Communal activity isn't restricted to work in the fields. The same people who sat twenty feet from your car for hours on end will crowd around the house you're visiting, hanging on every word of conversation between you and your hosts.

You'll inevitably have people around camp at mealtimes. I personally find it difficult to eat in front of a staring crowd. Remember, however, that your guests do not feel embarrassed by eating in front of others. This, too, is just another aspect of village life.

When the food supply or budget is limited, a polite offer to share a meal with ten or fifteen others could lead to a food crisis in your camp. We often invite Mexican visitors to eat and they almost always politely refuse or accept only a token bite as a gesture of appreciation. It's the other tourists who eat you out of house and home.

Maintaining normal activities (eating, reading, writing, lying around in your underwear) can be difficult with a group of people looking on but it can be done. Present a rather unexciting appearance and don't do anything hilarious or unexpected. Your visitors will eventually drift away or at least relax the intensity of their stares. Keep high interest items such as radios, tape recorders, cameras, fishing and diving gear and tools out of sight. This will greatly reduce their interest once visitors have recovered from the initial shock of your presence. If you decide, however, to do a tune-up on the car, you'll undoubtedly have them on the edge of their seats—if not right in the engine compartment with you—for the entire fascinating procedure, no matter how long it may take.

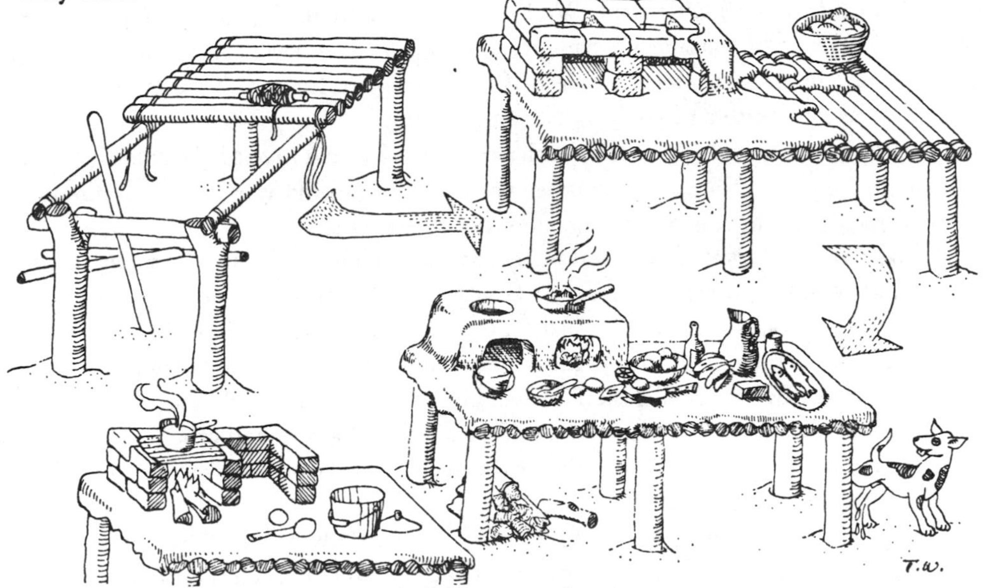

Building a mud stove

Once you've accepted the fact that there are going to be people around, you can take advantage of their curiosity to satisfy your own curiosity about them. I've found that there's no better way to get into an area than to select some likely looking person and suggest that I'd like to do something: go fishing, hunting, exploring, collect water or gather firewood. The response is almost automatically enthusiastic. This quickly changes the relationship from frustrated curiosity about you to a desire to demonstrate something that they can do, whether it's climb a coco palm or lead you to an interesting ruin.

By doing this, you'll soon have real friends among your guests. Rather than feeling a slight sense of dread at their visits, you'll begin to look foward to them.

We once camped in a very remote spot on the Pacific coast where food was extremely scarce. There were several of us, all big eaters, and the nearest market was three hours away over a barely passable road. We hiked to a few small villages nearby but there wasn't even an onion for sale. We had just about given up and were reluctantly planning to move on (the area was incredibly beautiful, which made leaving all the more difficult) when, as usual, visitors began wandering into camp.

The first, a surly looking cowboy with a rifle casually held in one hand, rode his horse to within a few feet of our group and then just sat there, staring at us for several minutes. Our friends thought this was the prelude to a bandit raid.

I finally said, "*Buenas tardes*," and wandered over near him. He answered my greeting with a curt word or two and offered me a large bundle wrapped in a spotless white cloth. I hesitated, but he thrust it at me insistently and muttered, "Open it."

Inside was a large pile of homemade *tortillas*, a few eggs, onions and a couple of rather limp tomatoes. Before I could ask if it was a gift or for sale, the cowboy said, "From my wife," and rode away. His visit was the first of many by him and other local people. Their gifts of food continued steadily for the entire month we were there and, in fact, made it possible for us to stay.

Being offered gifts of food is quite common, particularly when you're camped in an area where the local people themselves don't have very much. Their sense of sharing can be very touching. If there is any doubt in your mind whether something offered is for sale or a gift quietly ask, "*¿Cuánto le debo?*" (What do I owe you?) or just say questioningly "*¿Regalo?*" (Gift?). You'll almost always get a response indicating that it is a gift.

We always accept whatever is offered to avoid offending anyone. When you are given a piece of odorous dried fish, a few half rotten bananas or some other unappetizing little treasure, accept and then carefully tuck it away somewhere, as if you're reserving it for a tasty midnight snack.

When you wish to give someone a gift in return, remember that it really is the idea that counts, not the value or quantity of what you're offering. A very poor Mexican friend came to our camp almost daily for several weeks, always bringing some type of food: *tortillas*, fruit, a few vegetables or an especially huge fresh fish caught just for us. Since previous offers of money had seemed to offend him, I would give him an orange, a fish hook or some equally small present in return. His thanks, made with great emotion and sincerity ("God will pay you, friend," was his favorite), would have been quite sufficient if I'd given him a gift worth hundreds of dollars.

Where To Camp

Camping in Mexico is easier after you accept the fact that almost anyplace can be a campsite, if only for a short time. Here are some common choices:

Wide spots: It's the end of a hot day and you have mild diarrhea. You haven't eaten enough and would like to cook a good dinner, but you've fought off hunger with a few hits of cheap *tequila*. Suddenly you feel the crushing hand of exhaustion descending on your mind and body. Your companions are getting bitchy because they spotted a good place to stop forty miles back but you casually said, "I feel like I could drive all night."

The smartest and most logical thing to do under these circumstances is to find a wide spot—any place wide enough to get safely off the highway—and to forget about plugging along until something better shows up. It probably never would anyway, so you might as well stop before you're totally done in.

Side roads: These all lead to that mythical Perfect Camping Spot, or at least they would seem to. Of the hundreds of side roads that we've followed, most led to sand traps, mud holes, ranches and towns. Unlike secondary roads in the U.S., which seem to go everywhere—and nowhere in particular—Mexican side roads almost without exception lead to a group of houses or a small town. If you park your car so that it blocks the road, even though you'll swear it's a long abandoned trail, you can almost count on being blasted out of bed by someone leaning impatiently on the horn of a bus or truck.

Schoolyards and Soccer Fields: You may be driven by desperation to stop near a town or village. The edge of a schoolyard has the advantages of being reasonably level and away from noisy *cantinas* and drunks. The big disadvantage, however, is that schoolyards, playfields and soccer fields are frequented by packs of children and there's no place to take a crap. Don't park in front of the goal posts of a soccer field or you might block (as we did) an early morning game.

Dumps: I personally rate camping in dumps over all other desperation campsites. Unlike dumps in the U.S., full of rotting food and rats, Mexican dumps are usually dry and pest-free. This is undoubtedly because few Mexicans throw away food. Dumps are usually just flat areas close to the road and easily spotted by swirling heaps of plastic bags. Not AAA approved but very convenient.

Gas stations: You can try this but it doesn't always work: buy some gas and then ask the attendant if you can park behind the station for the night. Noisy, bright and smelly but better than nothing.

Cemeteries: Don't drive right into the cemetery, but don't make yourself conspicuous by attempting to hide. Park openly near an entrance and you won't arouse suspicions of grave robbery. I enjoy an early morning tour of the graves and have never met with any resentment or hostility from caretakers or visitors. Cemeteries are quiet, peaceful places with very few curious children hanging around, especially after dark.

Police station: Some people seem to think the police (being public 'servants') should know of good camping places and they make a point of going to the station to ask where they can park. The usual answers seem to be: 1) a motel, 2) a parking lot or 3)nowhere, get out of town. But there is a sneaky way to avoid actually going to the station while still enjoying its protection. (I don't recommend this if you look very freaky.) Find the police station and then park on the street, just around the corner. The logic to this is that criminals and drunks won't be lurking so close to the cops. I prefer the cemetery or a good dump.

Street: When you have to park on a city street, do it very near the *plaza* in a small town or on a side street in the business district of a larger town or city. If anyone asks what you're doing, give them a simple honest answer—sleeping *(durmiendo)*. Believe it or not, even the police won't think that this is an unusual answer.

Bridges: Most bridges are of fairly recent construction. Some replace smaller bridges and ferries and others have been built to replace damaged or washed-out bridges. At one or both ends of many newer bridges, you should see the remains of a road leading to the old bridge or ferry landing. These roads are often quite indistinct, particularly at night. They are good camping places, especially as many lead right to the water's edge.

Quarries and dirt pits: Found along many highways, especially if they are new or recently repaired. Be very careful when driving into one of these places; some are soft, others have huge pits and trenches that you could easily fall into at night. If it has been raining, send someone ahead to check the firmness of the ground. But don't forget that a human foot may not make a dent where a heavy car would sink.

Friends of ours almost lost their van when the wife walked ahead into an old excavation, on what looked and felt like wet grass. It turned out to be a bog, covered with a very thick layer of floating weeds. It took a passing team of oxen and a large gang of men to save the van from sinking.

The desert: Many unfortunate travellers reach the desperation point and say, "Hell, let's just pull off into the desert!" And there they remain, stuck in sand or dust, until help comes along.

The desert is occasionally made of rocks, but more often of something softer. In winter, when rain is extremely rare, the ground dries out quite hard in some spots—and quite soft and dusty in others. During the rainy season it may be surprisingly soft, even after a light sprinkle.

Always check the ground directly in line with where you're moving the vehicle before leaving the road. Once off the road, don't get carried away and race a quarter of a mile onto the desert just because the ground is solid; it may suddenly change to a sand trap.

Among the worst hazards of off-the-road driving in the desert are cactus spines and thorns. They are all over the ground and will play hell with your tires.

Trailer parks: Common on the tourist circuits but few and far between elsewhere. If you prefer to camp in trailer parks, try to learn their exact location ahead of time. Tourist literature (both from the U.S. and Mexican tourism offices) may help, but the most reliable method is to ask other travellers. Some trailer parks are that only in name and have no real facilities; others have everything from hot water to neatly trimmed lawns. Many trailer parks charge an unhealthy rate, but they're still cheaper than a motel room if you need a night of 'civilization.'

Motels: Camping in a motel? Many tourists, particularly the nervous types, prefer to camp on the grounds of a motel rather than in dumps or under bridges. Some motels offer various conveniences for campers, just as trailer parks do. The price isn't exactly a bargain, but once again, it's cheaper than actually taking a room.

(Camping in either a trailer park or motel, especially on the Pacific coast, may be very crowded during the tourist season.)

National parks: Camping facilities within parks, reserves and national monuments are very rare. Most are closed at night and camping is not allowed. If you are told that you can't camp, it is occasionally possible to make a 'special arrangement.' This means you pay the guard or caretaker and agree to leave early in the morning.

Where Not To Camp

Note: The following suggestions about places *not to camp* are included to help you sleep better and not because they involve any real threat to your safety. If you camp in one of these places, as we often have, you will be quite secure.

Hills: Because of the incredible number of large trucks and buses on the highways at night, most without mufflers, a hill is a lousy place to get any sleep. We once camped in a place even worse than a hill—a tiny valley between *two* hills. The little valley, so peaceful in the early afternoon, was just one-eighth of a mile long and represented over twenty shift points for the trucks and buses, which passed at the rate of one every thirty seconds. Each shift brought forth a great diesel blast and awful rasping of gears.

Markets: If you find yourself forced to camp in town, don't park near the market, even if it appears to be deserted and quiet. In the very early morning all of the trucks that kept the people camped on hills awake will roar into town and head for the marketplace. If the sound doesn't ruin your sleep, exhaust fumes will.

Archaeological sites: These used to be favored campsites and for very good reasons: they are interesting to visit, especially at the crack of dawn or during the full moon when camera-toting, children-dragging tourists are safe in their hotels. These sites are often near water or on a prominent hill.

Recently, however, the government has been cracking down on camping in or near ruins. The reasons are not without justification. Vandalism, theft and amateur efforts to make midnight archaeological discoveries really irritate authorities and authentic archaeologists. Another reason, particularly exasperating for the cops, is having people in various states and stages of 'non-ordinary reality' tripping around, over and off of pyramids, temples and tombs. It may be groovy to get stoned and play *Mayan* priest at the full moon, but the caretakers and police never seem to quite appreciate what you're doing.

Camping is still allowed in some sites, but in general it is either officially prohibited or really frowned upon (which means you may or may not be run out in the middle of the night, depending on the local attitude and your behavior).

Exploring

When you're looking for a place to camp for more than one night, and eventually even the hardest travelling people do, you'll want something better than a wide spot or a dump. What's the best method for locating a good campsite? There's only one sure way: *explore*.

Your guide books may rave about fabulous diving or sparkling rivers but when you get to the place they've recommended, you might find an ugly hotel or cold rain. Because of extremely variable weather, bug and building conditions, the only way to be sure that a place is good for camping is to go there and look at it yourself.

Don't let others scare you off or delude you.

A very common problem when asking people for advice, either old friends or someone you've met on the road, is that few of them can describe a place objectively and accurately. Their well-intentioned advice frequently turns out to be a case of four blind men describing an elephant. I've heard some of the best camping areas in Mexico described as "full of cops," "bug infested," "absolutely no food or water" or "really nothing much to see there."

Should you meet another traveller who seems reliable, frame your questions about a particular spot around your particular interests. When I ask someone about skin diving conditions, I ask specific questions: whether or not they have done any diving there themselves, if there are local fishermen (always a good indication of fish being available) and if the water is clear and easily assessible. One person might recall each detail of a reef while another who spent two months in the same place will say vaguely that "the beach was nice" or "the people were friendly."

Once you've found the area you'd like to camp in the decision of just exactly where comes up. The more people there are in your group the more difficult this final selection can be. With Steve and Lorena along it invariably went something like this, a complicated three way battle of wits.

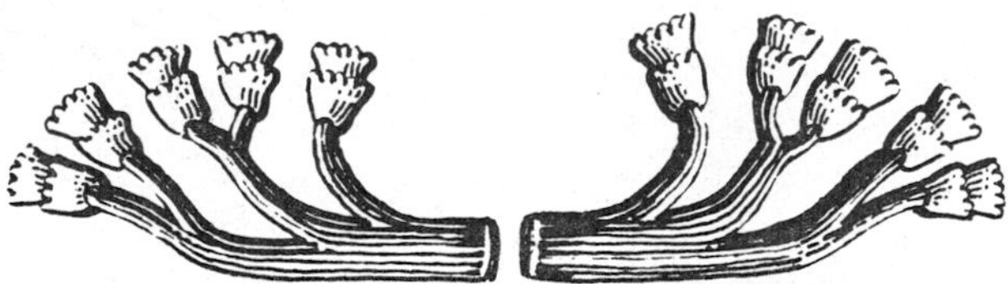

"I vote that we stop here," Steve says as we reach the outskirts of a small fishing village. "There doesn't seem to be much point in going on," he adds cleverly. "The road is getting too soft; we may get stuck."

He neglects to add that we've just driven several hours on an identical road and could easily keep travelling if *he* wanted to.

"Don't you think we're just a little close to town?" I ask sarcastically, pointing to several nearby huts. Steve is obviously worried about just four things: stop, eat, drink beer, meet people.

Each of us is willing to sacrifice the wishes of the others to satisfy their own requirements. The problem becomes one of convincing them that this would be a Good Thing.

"Let's just keep going for a few more minutes," Lorena says, "We may even come to a river."

She has just played her most powerful card, the mythological River we've pursued for years, where the clothes wash themselves and the water is whatever temperature you wish. We all know this is a pipedream but we can't resist. I give us another five miles of driving just on this one ploy alone.

"There! There!" I yell enthusiastically, pointing to a group of jagged rock pinnacles outside the surf line. "Good diving!" I am almost in tears at the thought of fish and oysters waiting there patiently for the harvest. Both Steve and Lorena moan their disagreement.

"We're five miles from the nearest beer or food," Steve complains, momentarily forgetting that we are supposed to be living on the fruits of our own labor and ingenuity.

"It's awfully windy here," Lorena says. "Don't you think we ought to look for a spot with some shade?"

I might admit that the barren windswept beach is a bit bleak and sunburnt but the thought of those oyster covered rocks causes me to stand firm. "What do you want, anyway?" I sneer. "Palm trees? Grass to lie on? A burbling brook?"

"That's it!" she cries. "That's exactly what I want and I'm sure we'll find it if we just go a little bit farther."

Steve and I now groan in unison; this is going to be a tough one.

A tin can oven

Everyone wants both a beautiful and a comfortable campsite. Unfortunately the most comfortable places are not always the most aesthetically pleasing. You may find yourself—and your group—torn between camping in a grove of trees, with lots of shade and places to hang hammocks, or on the beach with beautiful sunsets and the sound of the surf. I advise you to chose in favor of the most *comfortable* location. You'll find that you will be able to enjoy everything much more: sleeping, the weather, the food and the view. If you have to stake your sleeping bag down to keep from sliding over a cliff, the fabulous sunrises and sunsets will soon begin to pale in comparison to a good night's sleep.

Camping on the beach means camping in sand. Sand can drive you crazy. It will soon be in your hair, food, clothes, crotch, books and toothbrush. In addition to the sand, there's the salt mist from the spray and from the wind blowing over the sea. This mist soon has everything either damp or feeling slightly greasy and salty. Avoid this by camping back from the beach if possible. You'll be amazed at how much easier and more enjoyable your camp life will be.

Camping away from the beach often means, however, that you lose cooling breezes that keep the temperature more reasonable and act as a barrier against mosquitoes. We've found that some beaches were made unlivable by mosquitoes unless we camped right on the edge of the water. What little wind there was kept the bugs from harassing us. Trees and brush are favorite mosquito haunts, even on cool windy days.

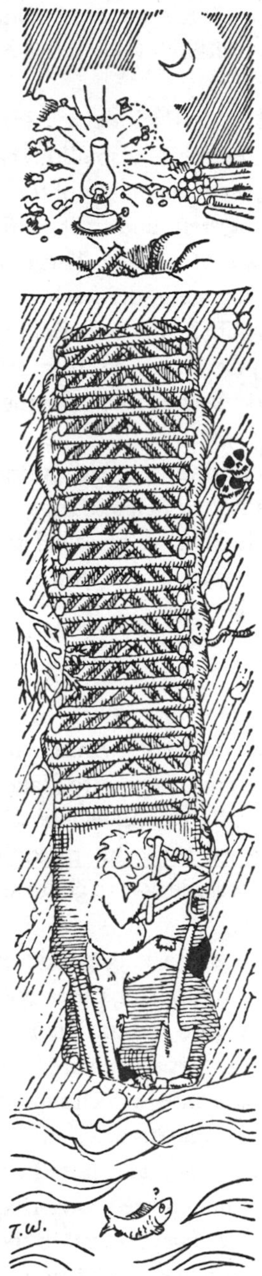

Digging A Well

If mosquitoes bother you, avoiding them is the most important thing you can do for your comfort and peace of mind. This is a good example of finding the proper balance between you and Mother Nature.

A good camping place also requires access to food and water. Long hikes for a few tomatoes and a canteen of water tend to get longer and less desirable, even though the campsite itself is a perfect little Garden of Eden.

Since you're going to save money by living on fresh rather than canned foods, you'll want to be able to buy at least such basic things as eggs, tomatoes, onions, beans, bananas, oranges and cooking oil. Ask local people if they will sell you fruits, vegetables and eggs from their own homes if there are no stores nearby. In isolated areas, it may take you a week or more to establish good contacts. Allow for this by carrying sufficient food, booze and water to carry you through. (When water is not readily available you can always dig for it. See *The People's Guide to Camping in Mexico*).

No matter where you camp, if you have a car, park with the assumption that it won't start when you decide to leave. Assume that the battery will be dead, either from too many hours of bedtime reading or too many tapes played on the recorder, or that it will just be 'one of those things' and will need a push. In many cases, it's best to play safe by parking near a road and establishing the camp away from the car.

Protection from the sun is very important. If you can't build a sunshade, you'll have to look for some sort of natural protection. Finding a shady spot involves locating a large tree or overhanging cliff. First of all, if you've found an overhanging cliff, examine the possibility that it may quit hanging one day and start falling, either in pieces or all at once. It's better to look for a tree and on the coast this almost always means a coconut palm.

When I first went to Mexico, I spent a lot of time sleeping and lounging under coconut palms, not considering the obvious danger until a coconut fell one night, narrowly missing my head but knocking some sense into it. On calm nights when there isn't the slightest breeze to disturb them, you'll hear *coco* palms dropping their heavy nuts. The thudding impact will give you an idea of what they can do to your head or the roof of your car. Fronds that are brown and obviously dead also have the disturbing habit of falling when there's no wind. One missed us by inches on a quiet afternoon, splattering into the middle of our kitchen, destroying our lunch and a great deal of pottery.

Another potentially dangerous tree, the *Manzanillo,* is found on the Pacific coast. It is large, offers excellent shade, and bears a distinctive fruit that resembles a small green apple. The fruit and the sap of the *Manzanillo* are poisonous. If you break off one of these 'apples' you'll notice a milky white fluid exuding from both the stem and fruit. This fluid will raise blisters on your skin and on your tongue if you taste it (as I did). This tree occasionally drips its poisonous sap onto the ground. Woe to anyone underneath.

In places where palm huts (*palapas, ramadas*) are built for Christmas and Easter, traditional times for Mexicans to visit the beach, you can often just move into an empty one during the off-season and nothing will be said. It is always best to ask someone, however. You may be told to move out or more likely, to pay rent.

Abandoned houses are uncommon, but you may occasionally find one that can be used as a camp. When asking permission to use an old house or hut, it helps to suggest to the owner that you plan to improve it a little. The people that we've asked for permission to live in old houses have been very casual; unless you burn or tear down the building, they usually don't pay any attention to what you do with it.

The Rainy Season

The rainy season usually occurs between May and September. When it is approaching, select a campsite that won't be inundated or made unlivable. Anticipate that a lot of rain, even for a short time, can turn a creek into a river and a pond into a lake.

If your camp centers around a car, you'll want to be especially careful where it's parked. This doesn't just mean preventing it from being washed away but parking where you won't be isolated by the first heavy rain. Be sure there is some way to get to an all-weather road once the rains begin.

In many remote areas, the arrival of the rains is the beginning of a long period of isolation, when the only contact with the rest of the world is by foot or canoe and sometimes only by radio. Food becomes scarce and the people who are too poor to stockpile ahead have to endure real hardship until the roads and bridges are repaired. In some places even the beer runs out during particularly bad rainy seasons—which should give you an idea of the seriousness and extent of the isolation that has to be endured.

The rain may begin quietly with a few weeks of occasional afternoon drizzling, telling you it's time to move on. Or it may come dramatically with an unexpected torrential downpour, cutting you off before you've had time to get away. We always question the local people closely when the rainy season approaches and establish: 1) the condition of the roads after the rains begin, 2) alternate routes out of the area, 3) the earliest date that the area has been isolated, and 4) if it was cut off temporarily or for the entire rainy season.

Fortunately, there are many places to camp during the rainy season that have year 'round access to all-weather roads. With adequate protection from the rain and a good parking place, camping in the rainy season is quite enjoyable. (In most cases, it only rains for a short time in the afternoon, even at the height of the rainy season.)

Violent rainstorms are usually preceded or accompanied by strong gusting winds. By anticipating the wind, you can avoid having your camp stirred up and blown around.

Late summer and early fall are the usual months for *ciclones* (hurricanes). Hurricanes frequently strike very close together and large areas of the coasts are often flooded. Roads are cut, food is scarce and you may actually face the possibility of danger to yourself and your car.

Listen to the radio for hurricane warnings, but don't absolutely depend on it to warn you; they often bungle their predictions. *The News*, an English language paper printed in Mexico, gives weather forecasts, but the paper is available only in tourist areas and larger cities.

Should you be caught in the path of a hurricane, go to high ground or as far from the beach as possible. A palm hut will not survive a hurricane, so don't decide to lie in your hammock with a bottle of rum or a lid of grass and ride it out. A hurricane will uproot trees, particularly coconut palms, and flying limbs, roofs and junk will be in the air. (See *Appendices* for average temperatures and rainfall.)

Bandits! Rip-off!

As long and as hard as I've tried to be captured or confronted by bandits, all of my efforts have been in vain. The only thing my searches produced was a prodigious number of hangovers. Most bandits, it seems, lurk in *cantinas* and my research involved a considerable amount of exploratory drinking.

Bandits do exist, but fortunately for the tourist interested in a good time, they confine their activities to the 'big time.' Banks, kidnappings and miscellaneous assassinations keep them occupied and out of tourist campgrounds.

Criminal types who lack the glamour and style of the moustachioed, bullet adorned *bandido* are called *ratones* or *ladrones* (rats or crooks). They do have an interest in the unsuspecting tourists who leave their car unlocked or fishing gear outside all night. These rip-offs almost always occur in crowded or very popular tourist spots, from trailer parks to archaeological sites.

The most popular method is what I call the 'swoop.' It goes like this: Two young people with packs finally reach the ocean after three weeks of dusty hitching from New York. With cries of glee, they race past other campers, drop their packs and their pants and plunge into the water. Ten minutes later they return to find themselves ripped-off.

No one saw a thing, even though there were plenty of people around. Avoid this hazard by asking someone to watch your stuff. Most bar, restaurant and small store owners will gladly do this for you.

A group of tourists invariably attracts dope dealers, thieves, trinket sellers, beggars, curious kids and the police. This type of situation is common along the Pacific coast (especially *Mazatlan, Barra de Navidad, Puerto Vallarta* and *San Blás*). It can easily be avoided by steering clear of camping communities which periodically spring up and then drift slowly away to reform elsewhere. Escaping the attention of thieves, dope dealers, cops and the irritating sales pitch of hammock salesmen (they always approach just as you doze off on the beach) is often just a matter of moving a mile or two from the main group of campers.

Camping is very safe, but it can and very probably will, make you nervous until you've become acquainted with the country and with new night sounds and activities. You don't expect a burro train of firewood to pass by your sleeping bag at three a.m., so when it does it might freak you out. It's hard not to be jumpy and tense when you don't fully understand what everyone else is doing.

Relax Your Mind

There are many strange things, at least strange to the newcomer, that can turn a perfectly normal, happy day into a bad experience. You must learn to accept the unknown and to wait for an explanation until morning. Don't allow yourself to be scared off by your imagination.

One of our most unsettling experiences took place while camped on a lonely beach on the Gulf of Mexico. We were sleeping in the sand around the remnants of a campfire when we all simultaneously awoke at the sound of approaching hoofbeats. As they grew louder, we raised ourselves from our beds and waited apprehensively for the attack.

Suddenly we were surrounded by several armed men on horseback, silhouetted dramatically against the moonlit sky. Rifles were slung casually over their saddles. They seemed barely able to keep their prancing horses from trampling us.

Steve called out shakily, "*¡Buenas noches!*" but there was no reply. After a minute or two of blood-chillng scrutiny, one of them grunted and they rode away, yelling and whooping into the night. Badly shaken, we stoked the fire and spent a restless night wondering what else might happen.

The next morning the horsemen reappeared and with a great commotion of yells and laughter gave us a large fish. They were sorry, they said, to have disturbed our sleep the night before, but they'd spotted our camp while returning from a hunting trip and wanted to see if we were OK. They had been worried that the tide would wash us away.

On another occasion we had camped on a high mountain road overlooking a sinister fog-shrouded canyon. We were sure that it held some lost tribe of Indians who would emerge at night to perform strange pagan rites. Leo, a young hitchhiker we'd picked up the day before, would be sleeping outside so we entertained him with stories of human sacrifice as we huddled around a blazing campfire.

Before going to bed, we unloaded most of our things from the van. In the morning we planned to hold a major cleanup and reorganization. Leo crawled into his sleeping bag and pulled it over his head; our stories had been very descriptive.

I woke hours later to hear Lorena whispering excitedly in my ear; "Carl! Look outside! Hurry!"

I lifted my head and peered through the side window. Nothing much, just a large group of Indians squatting on the ground neaby.

The three of us peeked furtively from the windows at the figures in our camp. Their flashlights illuminated a blood-chilling scene: men in strange costume—turban like head dress, white tunic coats, knee length baggy pants and colorful sashes—were making packs and bundles of our worldly goods.

"Oh good God!" I hissed. "What have they done to Leo?" He was nowhere to be seen and had evidently been disposed of. I hoped it had been done with a touch of mercy and that he hadn't been saved for some later, leisurely performed atrocity.

"What are we going to do?" Steve whispered fearfully.

I thought for a few moments and then proposed that we hide; perhaps, I figured, they assumed that poor Leo was alone.

As we lay inside holding our breath, I wondered vaguely how we would notify his family. Leo had been such a cheerful person, so unaware of danger and so quick to laugh at our fireside stories.

"There they go!" Lorena said. "Oh, I hope they didn't take my shawl!"

When the last of the group had gone, staggering beneath heavy loads, I slipped quietly outside. Hopefully Leo had only been clubbed unconscious and not diced with a *machete*.

"Pssst! Leo? Leo?" I whispered anxiously, "Leo?" Where the hell could he have gone? Then from behind me came a low moan. I raced around the van and fell over Leo's body, still up to the ears in his sleeping bag.

"Hey, watch it!" he yelled, "I'm trying to get some sleep and people keep shining lights at me!"

"How did you get over here?" I asked, suddenly realizing that our Indian attack must not have been quite what it had seemed.

"I moved to get away from the fire; thought I might roll into it," Leo said matter-of-factly. "Then a bus stopped and a bunch of guys with loads of junk got off."

"You mean they came on the bus?" I gasped. "I distinctly saw them coming out of the woods; we thought they'd murdered you."

"Oh, man!" he snorted, "you guys are so damned paranoid! They were coming back from market. They took their stuff and made it into packs and then went off into that canyon."

I looked again and realized that we'd all been turned around. Our things were still there, on the opposite side of the van from where the 'looting' had taken place.

"Why don't you go back to bed?" Leo yawned, "there ought to be a good sunrise from here."

CAMPING SKILLS

One of the most enjoyable aspects of camping is the opportunity to resume fantasies normally restricted to children: building crude shelters, digging in the sand, lashing sticks together and so on. A sampling of various projects has been included from *The People's Guide To Camping In Mexico* not only to tempt you into buying the book, but to give you an idea of how pleasurable camping in Mexico can be.

A Thatched Hut

A *palapa* (hut, also *ramada, choza* or *jacal*) is basically a shelter made of sticks and palm fronds (also called *palapas*). They are very common on all the coasts of Mexico. Although many *palapas* are torn down when not in use to prevent the theft or natural loss of the poles, you may find one ready built.

Building a hut that will be waterproof and long lasting is not simple. A *palapa* of your own construction will be adequate as a sun and wind shelter, but if you're hoping to live in it for several months, it's quite easy and inexpensive to have a really good one built for you. A good hut builder can finish a small one in four or five days. In most cases the only tool he'll use will be his *machete*—even for digging the holes—and all of the materials will be gathered in the surrounding coconut groves or jungle.

Building a *palapa*

If you are building the *palapa* yourself, you should determine its size; spectators and their endless suggestions are to be ignored completely. When they become persistent, go swimming until the heat changes their attitudes.

Begin by finding four sturdy poles about eight feet long and forked on one end. Shorter poles can be used but eight feet will give about six foot head room inside. Dig four holes, two or more feet deep and place the poles. If sand keeps filling the holes, use water to moisten and firm it up as you dig. The easiest shape to use for a *palapa* is a square. It is even easier if the distance between the poles is the length of your palm fronds. It takes a lot of fronds to cover both roof and walls so keep the size within reason. *Petates,* mats, can also be used if fronds are scarce.

When the corner posts are in place, find at least four more poles for the roof rafters. These do not have to be forked, but they must be sturdy enough to support the weight of the frond roof; usually considerable. Place the four rafters between the upright corner posts and lash them together. Additional rafters spanning the roof area will be a considerable help to supporting fronds that are small or broken.

Next locate some coconut palm fronds. **Warning!** If you are building a hut from fallen fronds or from materials scrounged from another hut, watch for snakes and scorpions! They like to sit in piles of fronds, leaves and coconut husks and will often be in the walls and roofs of old huts. Move heaps of fallen fronds with a stick and don't thrust your hands or feet into these piles. Never carry an old frond or piece of dry firewood on top of your head. A scorpion may pop out and nail you on the nose. When cutting fresh fronds, check first to see if there might be a snake resting his weary bones on top.

The worst hassle of gathering fronds isn't scorpions or snakes, but ticks. Check yourself carefully, including your clothing, after rooting around in the coconut groves or bushes. (See *Health*.)

Dry, rather than green fronds, are best for building as they are lighter and much easier to split. Don't try to split them from the large end. Slip the blade of a *machete* into the thin end and use it to keep the split even and to avoid breaking the frond off short.

Begin roofing by laying the half-fronds (whole ones aren't as neat or efficient) at a 90 degree angle to the roof rafters, overlapping them as closely as you can afford to. The center rib of the frond should be up. In this way each rib acts as a weight for the leaves of the frond beneath it, preventing your *palapa* from looking like a wild head of hair. Alternate large and small ends of the fronds to keep the weight evenly distributed. It is not necessary to lash the fronds down as you do the roofing. However, it's best to determine the direction of the prevailing wind (if there is one) and to begin roofing at the side facing into the wind. When it blows hard, the resistance will be less and the weight of the fronds alone should keep them from blowing away.

During the rainy season, sheets of thin plastic *(plástico)*, available in the market and hardware stores, laid under the roof and behind the walls (preferably before placing the fronds) will give reasonably good protection from water.

To make walls, just lash frond halves between the corner posts, starting at the ground. Your *palapa* will look very neat and trim if you overlap the fronds with the loose leafy side facing inward. This works fine for three of the walls but if you'd like a fourth to be covered too, you'll have to allow for a doorway.

A doorway and window can be made by adding just two more poles to the framework. This can be done after finishing the roof and three walls.

Plant another upright pole (it doesn't have to be forked but should at least be lashed to the roof rafter) about two and a half feet from any corner post. This is the doorway. The remaining wall space can be completely covered with fronds or a long window can be left in the wall by lashing another pole, horizontally, between the door post and the other corner post. (If this crossbar is about waist-high, it can also be used as the main support for a table or counter, inside and outside the *palapa*.) Lash fronds beneath the crossbar from the ground up.

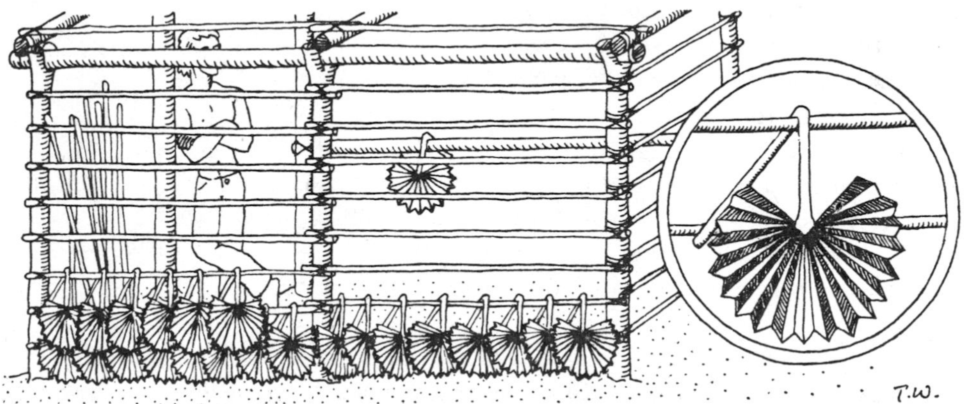

Palmetto leaf hut

Sharpening a *Machete*

The usual temptation for the tourist is to buy the biggest, heaviest, nastiest looking blade he can find. This is a real mistake; those without long experience of handling a *machete* often injure themselves seriously with these wicked knifes. Unusually long *machetes* and those with unique shapes are designed for specific uses—cutting sugar cane, husking coconuts, clearing brush, etc. The tourist who buys one of these special-use *machetes* is greatly increasing his chances for an unfortunate accident. For general camp use—cutting poles, firewood, opening coconuts—the most practical type of *machete* is short with a broad blade, and not *razor* sharp. *Machetes,* especially long ones, have the nasty habit of ricocheting when you least expect it. A very sharp blade is not essential for the occasional use it will be put to while camping.

New *machetes* are as dull as butter knives. By far the easiest way to sharpen them is to have it done by a metal shop or wandering knife sharpener. He can put a good edge on it in just a few minutes.

To do it yourself, a file will be needed and a six-pack of beer or a fat joint. It is a long laborious process.

Brace the *machete* against something solid with the edge of the blade toward you. Holding the file at a low angle to the blade, run it in long even strokes from the handle to the tip. Do this three or four times and then turn the *machete* over. Now repeat the same number of strokes, running the file from the *tip toward the handle*. You should always be filing toward the blade, a slightly risky motion but necessary for a good clean edge. By keeping the strokes even in pressure and number on each side, you'll avoid a lopsided or wavy edge.

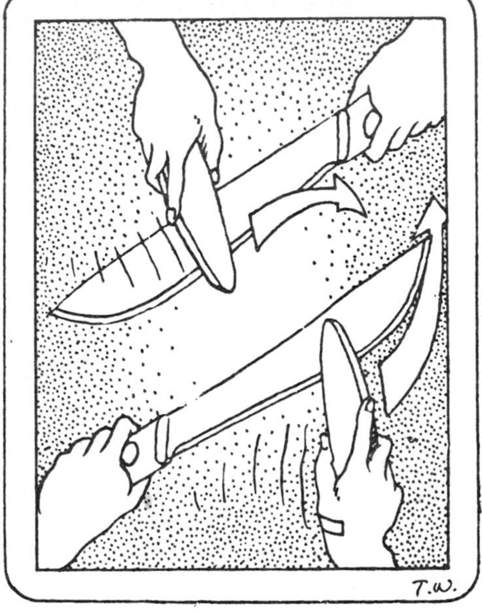

Once you've got the edge to the point where it might just cut something, you are ready for the sharpening stone. I use a regular *machete* stone, the type sold in every market and hardware store. (See illustration.)

Pour a shot of cooking oil, beer or water on the stone and drip the excess onto the blade. Smear it around on both. Hold the *machete* as you did while filing and repeat the same motions with the stone. Always keep the stone at a very low angle to the blade. When the beer runs out or your head gets straight, it's time to quit.

Work the *machete* over with the stone every time you use it and it will never degenerate to the point where it must be refiled. When the blade gets black from oxidation, slice a lime in half and rub it vigorously over the metal. Before the juice dries, wipe it off with a rag.

TRAVELLING CHEAP

Attitude is the answer...Budget Breakers...Finding the minimum...Plan ahead...An expense record...Time really is money...Learn from others...Travelling poor...Eating economically...Totally broke...Rescue money...An order of shrimp spaghetti...

Travelling cheaply in Mexico—or anywhere else for that matter—isn't just a question of learning tricks that will save you money. Attitude is more important than a list of inexpensive hotels and restaurants.

Where does this leave you with your $478.65 income tax refund and no definite plans for the rest of the year? It all depends on how economically you can travel and still *enjoy* it. Even with unlimited money travelling can be difficult and many people never manage the adjustment to travelling economically. If the trip becomes too much of a strain, our advice is to drop it; blow what's left and go home. The important thing is to enjoy your trip, not to suffer. Better to go out in a blaze of glory than to keep at it on the principle: "We planned this trip for so long, we've just got to stick it out."

We once gave a ride to a couple who bragged that they'd hitched from the U.S. into Mexico eating nothing but oranges for three weeks. They spent most of their time in a stupor in a tent or drinking beer at a nearby restaurant. They steadfastly refused to eat anything but oranges in order "to save money" but between them they drank up several dollars a day. It was not surprising that they soon decided to return to the U.S. rather than continue their ordeal.

It is important to establish your basic limits and personal requirements as quickly and as honestly as possible. "We won't have to stay in hotels—I can sleep anywhere" and "Forget restaurants; as long as they have bananas I'm fine," are typical hard-to-live-up-to statements from travellers about to embark on some shoestring odyssey. If you really aren't happy without an air-conditioned room, private bath and an evening tumbler of

12 year-old scotch, take it into account before you commit yourself to a hard cot in a *pension* and a tin cup of cheap rum.

We met a guy who spent every *centavo* as though he'd earned it slaving in the salt mines and would be doomed to return there when he was broke. About once a month, however, he'd do something outrageous: hire a small plane for an hour or two, order a fantastic dinner with French wine or spend the night in a luxury hotel. "I guess I do it to blow off steam," he said. We were eating lunch in a small cafe and he'd just stuck the leftover *tortillas* in his pocket. I watched as he twisted up a tiny packet of salt into a piece of napkin. He looked around and then put the napkins in his pocket, too. "Cheaper than handkerchiefs and toilet paper," he laughed.

Many people learn to travel economically the hard way: by gradually realizing that their money is evaporating much faster than they want it to. You begin your trip feeling like what-the-hell-it's-only-money and by the time it's almost gone, you've decided the trip has really just begun. Southern Mexico is often as far as many eager South American-bound travellers get before facing financial realities. You will see them drinking coffee around the plaza in Oaxaca, kicking themselves for buying $500 worth of souvenirs and trying to sell their unused copy of the *South American Handbook.*

Budget Breakers

The expenses that will devastate your budget in short order are a car, liquor, luxury foods, splurges in hotels, restaurants or tourists traps, and souvenirs.

"Oh, look at that!" you cry to your friend, reaching for a stuffed armadillo encrusted with opals, seashells and shiny copper 5 *centavo* coins. "Wouldn't that look nice on one of our Early American end tables?"

The clerk moves in beside you and demonstrates the clever lamp concealed in the unfortunate armadillo's head. "Oh! I've just got to have this!" you exclaim, reaching for your traveller's checks. Two years later, when you find it in the attic, gnawed by mice, you'll wonder why in the world you even looked at the damned thing.

The sourvenir splurge is perhaps the most difficult to avoid but it can be done. Take pictures instead, they're cheaper and usually longer lasting. I always ask myself, "Is this thing really necessary?" It rarely is.

It's possible to live a year in Mexico on $100; in fact, friends of ours scraped by on just $5 for six months by doing odd jobs. Another friend blew more than $2,000 in two weeks and didn't even have a souvenir to show for it.

It is a common misconception that travelling cheap is strictly for the young and adventurous, those willing and able to endure flop houses, hitchhiking and skimpy meals. This is far from true. In fact, the most accomplished money savers I've met have almost always been older, retired people. When you've got a relatively low fixed income and the rest of your life to travel, economy can mean the difference between wintering in a drafty apartment in Minneapolis or a beach cottage in Zihuatanejo.

Deciding to travel cheaply is one thing, doing it is another. Attitude is critical, especially for those who want to enjoy getting by on the absolute minimum. No need to despair just because you've hit a temporary low. One of the best times I've had in Mexico was when we were down to 80 cents. For complicated reasons we found ourselves forced to live on this meager sum for a month.

Fortunately we were on the beach and I was able to scrounge for food. The routine was quickly established: up at dawn with a handline, flogging the water for an early fish; then breakfast (always beans and fish) and back to fishing or diving. We traded work on a house and clearing brush for rent, fish for onions and beans, and learned to do without cooking oil and other luxuries. When a Mexican friend offered us a handful of slightly mushy bananas, we accepted them with genuine appreciation. Our odds and ends suddenly became a treasure trove; needles and thread were traded for eggs, an old screwdriver was worth some chilies and a rusty knife brought a sack of coconuts. I'll never forget how I felt when our Rescue Money arrived: disappointed (though not exactly heartbroken).

Although travelling cheap doesn't have to mean hardship and privation, it does require constant attention and a certain amount of planning. For example, how much money do you have to spend on your trip? How much time, allowing for possible extensions? (My first two week trip to Mexico lasted two months.) Divide money by time and you've got your budget per day, week or month.

Decide how you want to travel and how far (See *Travelling In Mexico*) and deduct the approximate cost. If this now leaves you with no money at all, it's time to backtrack and do some changing. Instead of flying you'll hitch, or instead of hitting every good archaeological site in Mexico you'll visit one or two. Or maybe you'd rather drive down, rent a house and stay in one area of the country.

A friend flew from New York to Yucatan with his bicycle, pedalled to a small village, and then sat there quite happily for two months. The cost of living in the village was about equal to the tax on his airplane ticket. He not only had a wonderful time but was able to keep his *overall* expenses within his limits and still enjoy the luxury of flying to and from Mexico.

To begin with, don't spend money on unnecessary preparations and equipment. I know people who automatically buy every available book on whatever country they're planning to visit. They could save this money by a few trips to the library and blow it later on lobster dinners. New cameras, new shoes or new luggage are not going to make your trip a success; in fact, their cost will probably shorten it or otherwise limit what you can afford to do and see.

Expense Record

Buy a pocked-sized notebook and keep a detailed record of all expenses. Add them up, by categories (food, transportation, souvenirs, booze, lodging, etc.), every few days. This will give you an excellent idea of where the money is going and at what rate. An expense record is like a portable conscience: merciless and unforgiving, just waiting to hit you with guilt when you add up the 'Beer' column. It will also show trends in spending, which in turn can be used to help devise economy measures.

We find that the faster we travel the more we spend. *Time is money* is another of those old cliches that still rings true, especially for the traveller. You hop off the bus, dying of hunger; there's no time to find a market or store, so you grab a meal in the nearest restaurant. The FOOD column suddenly shows a startling increase from those lazy days when you ate out of a well stocked picnic basket. A can of juice, for example, costs two or three times as much in the bus terminal as it does in a nearby *tienda*, but if you're dying of thirst and pressed for time (or lazy), you'll pay. Don't suppress those guilt feelings or fail to enter this into your expense book. Once the money has gone, it has to be faced up to.

Your expense record may be unforgiving, but don't let it get you down, just change your style or level of travel. Are you willing to spend an hour walking to a museum or half an hour waiting for the city bus or will you continue to take cabs? Time or money? Is it worth it to spend the time to search for a cheaper room and stay longer or would you rather spend the time at some especially interesting ruins and leave the next day? Impatience is expensive and is an attitude that low budget travellers cannot afford to indulge.

Learn From Others

Pay close attention to what other people, especially residents, are doing. If the majority are riding buses, then it's almost a certainty that that will be the most economical way to move around. Whatever is common or customary is invariably the best bargain, whether it's the afternoon *comida corrida* (daily lunch special) or riding the train instead of flying.

Ask for advice. Many people won't do this, either out of a misplaced sense of pride ("I can take care of myself!"), embarrassment ("What if they laugh?") or laziness ("It doesn't matter that much anyway."). Such simple questions as "Do you know where I can get a good cheap meal?" or "Isn't there something less expensive?" can not only save money but lead to invaluable advice and tips.

A good way to learn what your absolute minimum requirements are is to study a poor Mexican household. If they don't have it, you probably don't need it. This, of course, is rock bottom basic living, probably more basic than you'll ever care to go. But by cautious elimination of your extra 'necessities' (clothes, cooking gear, air mattresses, etc.) you will soon learn the difference between the true essentials for living and what you had always *believed* were essentials. You'll be amazed at how well and how happily you can get by on almost nothing.

Mexicans seem to delight at the sight of gringos trying to live like themselves. Since they are accomplished and experienced masters at basic living, you'll never go wrong by learning from them. The faster you adapt to your new life, the sooner you'll be able to pursue other interests with a minimum of hassle. It's difficult to relax when you don't know what's happening around you.

Camping is a good imitation of the way most Mexicans live: cooking over a wood fire, no electricity or inside water, simple cots or mats on the floor, the most basic furniture and utensils. A very simple house still costs about as much per month to rent as a single night in a good hotel.

The transition to a one room adobe hut with absolutely no 'conveniences' can be disturbingly abrupt, whether it's made from a well organized commune or a suburban home. Certain important aspects of daily living may be obscured by the shock of a total change in physical and cultural surroundings. To minimize 'cultural shock' and also maintain your health and good spirits, you should establish a few basic security props. The most important of these, at least at first, are eating and sleeping. Your first days or even weeks in Mexico are no time for a fast. Eat well and save food economizing until you are comfortable and confident that it won't disrupt your life.

Sleeping is important and a good night's rest means a comfortable bed or hammock. A mattress might seem to be an unreasonable splurge, but if you can't sleep without it don't jeopardize your whole trip by suffering on a hard cot. Get a good mosquito netting and, if it's cold, warm blankets.

Living 'poor' doesn't have to meal living in squalor. The dirt and disease associated with poverty are often the result of ignorance rather than a lack of money. If water is available, along with soap, neither you, your clothes or your living area should be dirty. Lorena and I have often lived in small houses that barely qualify as shacks in the U.S. With a broom and a determination to keep clean, however, these places were always quite adequate *for our needs*.

When we're really down and out financially we first decide what activity we'd like to get involved in that costs little or nothing.

"Gosh, Lorena!" I moan, "We're in *big trouble!*"

"You mean?" she answers, raising her hand to her throat.

"Yes!" I say, closing the little black book with a snap.

"Then it's..." she gasps, sinking back into a chair.

"It looks that way," I say, pacing back and forth.

"I'll...start packing at once!" she cries bravely, putting the tiny bars of hotel soap in her bag and dumping her clothes into a suitcase. We are off to the beach, to sit in idle poverty on some sandy shore until our expense book can recover its delicate balancing act.

It's astonishing but true that many people, particularly younger travellers, get bored stiff with basic living in Mexico. Once they work out a daily routine—shopping, cooking, cleaning, sleeping—they say to themselves, "Well, what now?" Life in a small village is not all excitement, even if it is in a strange and exciting country. Local people tend to do and discuss the same things over and over again. To avoid boredom you must either invent or discover a project.

For some this might be drawing, writing, touring museums, mural gazing or studying Spanish wherever it can be picked up. Many Mexican craftspeople are eager to teach their skills and many of their skills can be profitable when you get home.

Eating

Eating is a major expense for most travellers and also one of the easiest to save money on. Those not familiar with Mexican food should first find a few common and simple dishes that can be ordered whenever there's doubt about the menu or your appetite is shaky. On my first trip I lived on *tortas* and plain broiled chicken. I later graduated to beans, *tortillas* and *milanesa* (breaded meat). Ignore people who say, "You mean to tell me you haven't eaten goat noses in chili sauce? How dull!"

Always have snacks, preferably nourishing rather than unsatisfying and expensive junkfoods, for times when a meal might be unnecessary or expensive. While staying in hotels, for example, we keep fruit in the room. When I get up in the morning, instead of going out and subjecting myself to the torture of sniffing frying bacon and fresh sweet rolls, I gnaw on a few bananas. If that doesn't do the trick, I'll either eat some bread and cheese or give up and find a nice cafe. Once again, it's important to realize your limits. A good breakfast is important to health and sanity; starvation is not the answer.

Eat what is readily available or in season. One apple, imported all the way from Washington State to Mérida, can cost more than an armload of local fruit. If all the restaurants you look into are serving big bowls of *pozole*, it's a sure bet to be a bargain.

Mexico is becoming a country of involuntary vegetarians due to the high price of meat. If you can imitate people who eat meat infrequently, or not at all, you'll save money. On the other hand, some vegetarians can't be content without expensive vitamins, special foods and expensive substitutes for meat (cheese in particular).

Can you do your own cooking? When Lorena and I travel for more than a few days at a time, we carry enough cooking gear, including a backpacker's stove, to maintain independence from restaurants. There are numerous quick, inexpensive and nourishing meals that can be prepared right in your hotel room (See *The People's Guide To Camping In Mexico: The Suitcase Kitchen.*)

Later...

Let's assume that you successfully lived on a very low budget for a few months and want to move on again. This is where most people blow it. The first town they hit usually means a restaurant meal and a hotel room. In one stroke they spend what it cost them to live for two weeks on the beach. Throw in a few souvenirs, a few hours drinking beer and you have a month's (or more) budget gone.

The only effective way to economize is to *economize on everything, all of the time.* Spend every *centavo* as if it were your last. It's a hell of a lot easier to stay another month or two than it is to go home, rake together a few more bucks and return—all because you lost your self-control a few times and spent money frivolously.

Economizing, no matter how difficult or petty it seems, will buy time. After long practice, one day you will reach the point where a new magazine, a fancy meal or the thought of a soft hotel mattress won't even occur to you. When this state of mind has been reached, you'll find that your Mexican trip has changed your entire outlook, both there and at home. It's a good feeling.

Searching for bargains can be time consuming. One way to save time is to talk with other travellers and pump them for information on good places to eat and sleep. Unfortunately most people don't bother to write down specific addresses and names so it's usually a case of, "Well, let's see, I think it was two blocks from...no, it was three or four..."

The hazard of misinformation requires a flexible attitude. When the dollar-a-night hotel you were told of, complete with swimming pool and color t.v., turns out to be an empty lot behind a bus station, don't take it too hard, something almost as good will show up somewhere.

On the other hand, always looking for and demanding the absolute cheapest, whether it's food, lodging or transportation can be a mistake. A ride in a second class train car, for example, costs little less than first class but is far more uncomfortable. To the majority of those riding in second, that small difference is very important, the price of quite a few *tortillas*. But to the traveller, even the very budget conscious, the search for the super cheap may cost more in the long run in aching muscles than a relaxed but aware attitude.

Beyond Poverty

What happens when you find yourself sitting in a small village without any money at all or on the verge of total bankruptcy?

If you've lived in the area for long, store owners will usually be glad to give credit to tide you over. This is also true of most landlords. Unfortunately some people who have been given credit leave without paying up. This makes it unlikely that the next tourist who runs out of money will get much sympathy from anyone who has been ripped off.

Although this credit will tide you over for a few days, you're going to have to send for more money, sell something or find a job (the most difficult choice). See *Appendices: Money*.

Once your 'rescue money' arrives you must decide what to do with it. Before spending a cent of your newly received wealth, especially if it's more than five dollars, consider very carefully what you want to do. Most people who go broke far from home decide that the trip is over and it's just a matter of getting the money to return with. If you figure what it will cost to get home and you have a bit extra, why not stay until the difference is gone? Living on this narrow edge, believe it or not, can be very enjoyable. Will I make it home or won't I? Am I going to have to sell my shoes?

I flung open the front door and staggered across the room. "That's it!" The end! Never again!" I fell backward onto the cot, trying to massage away the headache that raged behind my inflamed eyeballs. Lorena crouched over the make-shift stove we'd rigged from a five gallon tin can, stirring the daily pot of beans.

"Was it that bad?"

I sat up. "Bad? Bad? Are you kidding? You're lucky to see me alive! Do you know what it's like to drive 50 miles over a washboard dirt road with a load of slopping gasoline drums?" I could still taste the fumes, the awful mixture of dust and raw gas clogged my nostrils and coated my tongue. "It wasn't the gas spilling all over the van or crawling along at five miles an hour" I said, "Or the 150 degree heat or the flat tire," I paused, groping under the cot for a warm beer. "It wasn't even Vicente's damn kid playing his radio full blast the whole way." I took a long foamy swallow, "It was Vicente smoking one cigarette after another, not two feet from the gas, laughing that they'd see the explosion in Guadalajara if anything went wrong!" It was still almost too much to believe; I'd risked my life and the van just to earn the price of a tank of gas with maybe enough left over for a few kilos of *tortillas*.

"Did you say anything to *Don* Alfredo?" she asked, slowly chopping an onion.

"Of course not!" I snapped. "He did us a favor getting me the job in the first place. It would make him feel bad if I griped." *Don* Alfredo, landlord and friend, had offered to help us ride out a long period of poverty by getting me jobs *fleteando*. 'Arrowing,' more commonly known as 'light hauling,' could be a lucrative sideline for the discreet tourist who didn't sweat such trivialities as breaking the law by working in Mexico or delivering dynamite, gasoline, not quite mature bulls, bananas, squealing porkers and other local freight. The messes left were indescribable. Fortunately it wasn't our van; we'd borrowed it for a few months from my brother.

"Actually," I continued, "I'd like to find something that doesn't require so much driving. It's been interesting but the wear and tear are really terrible. Rob will kill me if we have to push his van over a cliff somewhere."

Lorena got up from the stove and moved across the room. "You know we might be able to help out in the restaurant," she said, easing into the hammock with a great sigh of relief. "*Don* Alfredo keeps saying that Christmas is a real mob scene. He knows we can cook. In fact, he said something the other day about wanting to learn some new recipes."

"That's not a bad idea," I yawned, "What could be easier than cooking?"

"Three shrimp spaghettis, two plates of garlic bread, a vegetarian poor boy, one bowl of beans and a large fried fish!" *Don* Alfredo called out the latest orders as he edged through the crowded kitchen toward the beer cooler. He plunged his hands into the dark icy water, muttering, "*¡Hijole!*" as he lifted out the brown bottles of beer, wiping them carefully on his white apron. When the round enameled tray had been filled, he hoisted it over his head in approved waiter fashion. With a cry of "*¡Ay voy!*" he shooed a path through to the low doorway.

"Was that three orders of shrimp spaghetti or two?" Lorena reached for a large earthenware bowl brimming with shrimp and began peeling them expertly.

"Three," I answered, giving the Coleman stove a few extra pumps. "Build up that fire Carmen," I ordered, "and someone cut more bread." The girl slipped out the back door to the woodpile while her older brother, Ramon, began slicing *bolillos*. His younger brother, Juanito, complained that Ramon was crowding him from the table. "Just clean the fish," I said, "and then cut more garlic." The boys fell silent and worked obediently side-by-side.

"Carlitos!" *Don* Alfredo called, sticking his head just inside the doorway, "*Lo siento mucho*, but those gringos changed their order. Now they want three orders of beef stew instead of shrimp..."

"Oh, hell!" I sighed, going to the refrigerator for the pot of stew. *Don* Alfredo shook his head sympathetically.

The sound of quarreling voices suddenly rose from near the stoves. "How can I heat the bread if you take the stove?" Carmen wailed, trying to push past her sister, Ofelia.

Ofelia stood firm, brandishing a large spatula. "Use the fire, *tonta!*" she hissed, "I need this one for the fish."

Carmen turned angrily, "*Señor* Carlos, Ofelia won't let me..."

"OK! OK!" I said, "Just wait a moment. There's plenty of time for everything." I searched through the littered table, finally unearthing my beer behind a cluster of hot sauce bottles. I drained it in one long gulp and rolled the empty bottle beneath the counter. It clinked against several others.

We'd presented our scheme to help out in the restaurant just one week ago, the same afternoon I'd hauled the leaking barrel of gasoline. *Don* Alfredo himself provided the opening I needed.

"Even at Christmas time," he said, "we get very few of the gringos in here. They always ask for things we don't have. Then they drink a beer or two and leave."

"Please don't be offended," I said. "But the fact is that many tourists get tired of eating *tacos* and refried beans after a while. Most of them would get very excited about something familiar, like a hamburger or a hot dog."

"Really?" he answered, running a hand over his chin, scratching thoughtfully at his perpetual three-day stubble. "But if they won't eat something as delicious as *camarones rancheros,* what can we possibly offer?"

As if on cue, Marigeñia, his wife, set a long platter on the table between us. It was covered with large pink shrimp, smothered in onion, tomato and chili sauce. As usual he couldn't stand to have us visit without a *botana*, though by his reckoning a snack might be two kilos of shrimp or fried fish.

"*Don* Alfredo," I said, spearing a tasty morsel with my fork. "If you put this on spaghetti as a sauce it would be perfect."

He looked sceptical; turn ranch-style shrimp into spaghetti? No, it just didn't add up.

I went into detail, explaining how the noodles were cooked and the sauce poured over them. He grinned. Leave it to these crazy gringos to come up with impractical ideas. I became insistent; the more he resisted the more I realized that with shrimp spaghetti on the menu, his business would enjoy an immediate boom.

"Garlic bread!" I said. "That's what you need to go with the spaghetti!" As I explained how he could produce this additional treat, Lorena chimed in with: "And three-bean salad. We've got the beans, all we need is a little celery and..."

"*Bueno,*" *Don* Alfredo interrupted, a look of genuine interest spreading over his face, "But do you think others...other gringos would like those things?"

"Certainly!" Lorena and I answered in unison.

He began to smile, "Would it be possible...could you perhaps teach *me?* One day, God forbid, when you are gone from here, I would have to..."

I interrupted him with a friendly laugh and a pat on the shoulder. "Don't worry, *Don* Alfredo!" I said, "This will be child's play!"

I sagged against the counter, trying to ease the shooting pains that stabbed through my legs and lower back. My eyes streamed with tears; no matter how often I chided her, Carmen could not seem to keep the wood fire burning properly. Smoke hung beneath the blackened rafters in a thick acrid fog, cutting down on the normally weak light until it seemed that we worked in perpetual twilight. We had tried candles but they toppled into the salad or gave off crazy flickering lights that were worse than none at all. *Don* Alfredo had promised a lamp but first it was necessary to locate his brother-in-law...

Lorena collapsed onto one of the beds jammed into the narrow room, to sip a cup of tea and chat with *Don* Alfredo's wife. Marigeñia had been ill during most of the two weeks we'd been cooking in their restaurant. It was frustrating for a woman who normally commanded the operation of the restaurant and the practical management of their large family to be confined to her bed. When things got especially hectic or one of the children balked at the task we had given them, her voice would rise over the general din, striking the offendors dumb with her wrath. "Juan, when Carlos tells you to go to the village for more chili YOU GO IMMEDIATELY! *¿Entiendes?* Ofelia! Chop those carrots the way *señora* Lorena wants them or I'll...

These instructions carried sufficient weight to whip everyone into line for at least an hour. It was only rarely that a situation arose that required direct intervention by *Don* Alfredo himself.

"Ramon, bring Carlos a beer, he looks nervous!"

Ramon hustled to the beer cooler. Though it was only ten in the morning *Don* Alfredo believed that without a beer in my hand I could not cook. I took the bottle, shocked to see that Ramon had another in his hand and was taking a tentative sip. He grinned at me proudly, wiping the mouth of the bottle with the palm of his hand.

"*¿Que? ¿Que? ¿Que?*" *Don* Alfredo shouted, confronting the 15-year-old boy with an outraged glare. Ramon dropped the bottle from his lips, backing away a few steps, giving us a guilty smile.

"What are you doing?" his father roared. "Put that beer down at once!"

Ramon set the bottle on the table, turning back defiantly. "Why does he drink beer all the time and I can't?"

I struggled not to laugh. *Don* Alfredo caught my eye and winked. He grabbed Ramon by the shoulders and gave him a few hard shakes.

"You're just a child, that's why. Carlos is a gringo and gringos drink beer all the time. You're not a gringo. It is very simple, *¿entiendes?*"

I started to protest.

"Beer is a vitamin," he continued, "And you are too young to need vitamins."

Ramon's face cleared. Here was something that made clear sense! He grinned bashfully and went back to his morning job of cleaning fish.

As *Don* Alfredo returned to the dining room he stopped for a moment and called back, "I don't know how children get these crazy ideas!"

The orders were coming too fast; *Don* Alfredo dispatched one of the kids to the village for more supplies and a pair of idle nieces. Marigeñia had risen from her sick bed and now sat near the stove, making garlic bread. *Don* Alfredo hustled in and out, passing along orders and shouting encouragement to the kitchen crew. The jukebox raged near the doorway, blasting out a *mariachi* rendition of White Christmas. I could hear drunken voices demanding more beef stew, more shrimp spaghetti, more garlic bread. Carmen burned her hand on a hot coal and began crying; Juanito complained that he wanted to go play soccer and the grandmother, drafted back to work after years of undoubtedly well-deserved retirement, sang Revolutionary tunes in a shrill quavery voice as she labored over a *tortilla* press.

I caught occasional glimpses of Lorena hustling from one table to the next, taking orders in a mixture of Spanish, English and sign language. She had found it easier to help *Don* Alfredo in the dining room than to decipher the garbled orders he took from tourists. The sight of a six foot gringa waiting tables left most of the customers gaping until they realized it wasn't a joke and began clamoring for service.

The suffocating heat from three stoves and an open wood fire finally drive me to the doorway of the kitchen for a gasp of fresh air. As I leaned against the door and sucked at my beer, I caught the attention of two Mexican men at a nearby table. I had barely registered their amazed stares when Carmen called out for help with the spaghetti pot. I waved to them and dove back into the maelstrom.

"Know what day this is?" Lorena asked, mopping her forehead with a damp dishtowel. She had taken advantage of a lull to catch up on the pile of dirty dishes that threatened to avalanche into the family living area.

"I give up," I yawned, wishing that it was quitting time and we could stagger back to our house for a few moments of peace and quiet. Was it weeks or months since we'd come to the beach for a vacation?

"It's Christmas Eve," she said, reaching for another bucket of water. "You know, the night before Christmas and all through the house...?"

I shook my head; no, it couldn't be! Christmas? I looked around the room, suddenly noticing the bits of colored paper and tinsel. The family alter, perched precariously on top of the refrigerator, was decorated with fresh flowers and sprigs of pine. And there, right in full view on the door I'd opened at least 200 times that day, were big paper letters spelling out "*Feliz Navidad*".

"We ought to be sitting around a tree, opening presents in front of a crackling fire," I sighed. "And thinking about a big turkey dinner tomorrow afternoon." Lorena brushed a strand of hair from her eyes and began laughing wildly.

I was about to start singing Jingle Bells when *Don* Alfredo rushed into the kitchen, crying, "Two orders of...two orders of...of..." he stopped, looking around the room in confusion, "Two orders of..." He slapped his forehead with the palm of a hand, trying to dislodge the words. "Two orders of...*¡ay pues!*" he groaned, "Let's have two orders of beer!" He walked wearily to the cooler and stuck his arm into the freezing water, not bothering to roll up the sleeve of his shirt.

"Here we are!" he said, handing us each a beer and then suddenly grabbing more, popping the caps off with a vigorous snap and passing them around the room, to grandmother, children and all. When everyone had a bottle he raised his arm dramatically and shouted, "*¡Feliz Navidad y dos ordenes de espaghetti!*"

NOTES

RESTAURANTS AND TYPICAL FOODS

The joy of eating...Choosing a restaurant...Specialty foods...Street food...Ordering a meal...Menus...Tips...Vegetarians...What you'll eat...Regional dishes...Seafood Sunday...Junkfood...Beverages...A Substantial Meal...

One of the greatest pleasures of travelling in a foreign country is encountering new foods and eating customs. This is especially true in Mexico, where at times you'll feel inundated with food smells, food vendors and raw food materials themselves.

Memories of a trip often focus not on bullfights or a group of loud *mariachis* but on eating. "Do you remember that blow-out we had in Mexico City for only a hundred bucks, complete with imported champagne and Napoleon brandy?" "Or how about that side street in Oaxaca, sitting by the smoky charcoal brazier as that little Indian woman popped *quesadillas* into the snapping oil of her soot blackened tin *comal*, tossing an occasional scrap of *tortilla* to one of the scarecrow dogs browsing at our feet?"

There is an incredible range not only in what to eat but where to eat it. The search involves surprises; those who will be the most successful must be adventurous and have a love for the unknown. My motto is: When in doubt, close your eyes and chew.

How do you go about sampling all these savory new dishes without also trying some indigestible bacteria? Mexican restaurants, especially the less expensive ones, are not as easy to categorize by appearance as MacDonald's or Howard Johnson's. Many popular restaurants don't have the time or staff to scrupulousy wipe down each table between groups of customers. A crowded seafood place, for example, will be in a state of pandemonium, with waiters slipping on shrimp shells and discarded limes, diners demanding more fish soup and beer and crackers, beggars looking for a kind face or a forgotten bread roll, kids spilling sodas and crying, and a couple of hungry tourists standing hesitantly in the doorway, wondering if this is some kind of crazy private *fiesta* or just normal lunch time disorder.

The best criteria for judging a restaurant are the same as at home: personal experience, intuition and optimism. Clean floors and ironed tablecloths don't tell you a thing about what's going on in the kitchen. If the place is full of customers hungrily diving into their food and savory odors bring eager rumbles from your stomach, it's probably a good place to eat.

Keep in mind that *all of the food comes from the market.* A white jacketed waiter, a Diner's Club card in the window, or an impressively printed menu do not sterilize the lettuce or disinfect the ice cubes. Once you've adjusted to the initial sensory overload of most Mexican restaurants you can begin to notice details. The tiny market stalls serving refried beans is quite clean, though a whiff of overripe fruit from the next aisle might have first led you to believe otherwise.

TYPES OF RESTAURANTS

Expensive restaurants are most easily identified by their clientele: Mexicans wearing wrap-around sunglasses and shiny suits and tourists shaking their heads in confusion over the menu or poring over maps. Credit card signs in the window also indicate large bills.

Always check the *menú* (expensive restaurants are the only type that consistently have one, often posted outside) before committing yourself; it may send you running to the market.

The humble appearance of many **seafood restaurants** doesn't prevent them from charging relatively high prices. Check before you casually order a lobster dinner, though even obviously expensive seafood restaurants often have side dishes (fish soup, seafood cocktails, etc.) for reasonable prices.

Mexicans love seafood. It's a touching experience to see an entire family, from grandma to tiny children, move into a restaurant for several hours of intense seafood gorging. The bill for one of these feasts would feed a Korean village for a month. (See *Seafood.*)

The next category, **businessmen's restaurants**, are very similar throughout the world: good food, quite a bit of it and reasonable prices. They are most commonly located in cities and usually near the *plaza.* The service in the early afternoon may be slow as this is their most popular hour. If you order anything other than the *comida corrida* (daily special), your meal may be delayed while the ready-made food is served. The *comida* is usually served between one and five p.m. and is a good bargain, even in many expensive restaurants.

In large restaurants the *comida* will be posted on a signboard or inserted in the menu; in other restaurants you'll have to ask. There may be a choice of main dishes and side dishes. If there is, you'll select something from each category, i.e., main dish, side dish, dessert and beverage. Don't expect to get everything on the list.

The ***lonchería*** or ***comedor*** is another very common type of restaurant. It doesn't offer comfort, atmosphere or an interesting view, just a constant production of good inexpensive food. The service may be slow, the portions unequal and the selection very limited (they rarely have a menu), but this type of restaurant is the wise traveller's most frequent and reasonable choice.

Specialty restaurants such as Chinese, Italian, European, Middle Eastern (there are many Lebanese living in Mexico) and vegetarian are found in larger cities and tourist towns. The advertising pages of the phone book will give you their addresses but whenever possible ask someone for a recommendation.

I'd advise every traveller, penny pincher or not, to allow themselves at least one 'blow-out' meal.

Many very fine restaurants will serve memorable meals for surprisingly reasonable prices; once again, keep in mind that a fancy decor isn't necessarily a reflection of what's going on behind the kitchen door. The cost of a splurge will be vastly inflated by expensive cocktails and bottles of wine, especially if from imported stock. Try a Mexican cocktail, wine or beer instead. (See *Booze*.)

Be especially wary of places that imitate American style restaurants. Mexican food is becoming popular all across the United States, and in retaliation many gringo fast-food chains are opening in Mexico. Their hamburgers, pancakes, fried chicken and pizza should be avoided both for taste and price. Unless you need something to cure a severe case of culture shock (see *Health*), stick with *real* food: Mexican.

Older hotels and boardinghouses often provide good bargain meals, especially the *comida corrida*. Some boardinghouses, however, will only serve their own lodgers.

Fondas, the restaurants or eating stalls found in the market, are another good choice for the adventurous eater. (In some areas small restaurants are called *Fondas* even if they're outside the market place.) As you wander past the *fondas* and their rows of steaming kettles, cauldrons and giant plates heaped with rice, chicken and other goodies, don't be embarrassed to ask prices and move on until you've found just exactly what you want. It's customary to peer into the pot, ask what is cooking and what it costs, and then do the same at an adjoining stall.

Because the cooks will often collar you and insist that you sample something, this can turn into a very enjoyable pastime. Getting away after a sip or a bite is the difficult part. I have been all but dragged to a table after expressing interest in the contents of a bubbling pot.

In the *fonda* you are usually faced with a choice of several main courses. Beans, rice and soup are also available, as are *tortillas*, bread and beverages. If you order a main course, you'll get it and nothing else. This probably won't fill you up so you'll order a plate of rice and *tortillas* and perhaps soup too. When you first asked the price, it sounded like the bargain meal of the year. However, after adding on the cost of your other dishes and a beer, you may find that the bill mounted up considerably. It was still an economical meal but it was certainly no cheaper than a restaurant.

The answer to eating a filling and inexpensive meal isn't a secret word to the cook that will get you an extra leg of chicken; it's the *tortilla.* (See *Tortillas* under *What You'll Eat.*)

Temporary or improvised restaurants often appear on the edge of carnivals, fairs, large weekly markets and in city streets. Business is brisk in the evening, with tables and benches appearing out of nowhere to block traffic. Old ladies and little girls furiously cook up chickens, soups, *tacos* and all of the other good things to be found in simple restaurants.

Prices vary considerably from one temporary restaurant to another, as does the selection and quality of food, so look around before sitting down to a meal.

Street Food

Street grunting is our favorite way to eat out. It covers everything that doesn't have to be eaten while sitting at a table, truly a vast and tasty area.

Anyone who stops at a sidewalk stand and drinks an orange juice or buys a *taco* and then eats it while wandering through the market is indulging in street grunting. To many people this is just grabbing a snack, but when done systematically it can be the source of your every meal. This doesn't mean that you'll have to live on popcorn, orange juice and *tamales.* Street grunting is an entire system of eating that eliminates much of the hassle and time involved with ordering, menus, tips and other restaurant rituals.

My introduction to street food came during my first visit to Mexico in a small town in Yucatan. A Mayan friend asked me if I wanted something for lunch and I said, "*Sí.*" Without consulting me further he went to a nearby street vendor selling meat from a glass box. The sides of the box were encrusted with spattered grease and the meat inside looked absolutely disgusting. I couldn't believe that I was going to have to eat it.

My friend smilingly handed me a fat *torta* (sandwich made with a french roll) wrapped in a piece of newspaper, dripping grease and pepper juice. Before I could make an excuse, I smelled the delicious aroma of barbecued pork. From that moment on, I was hooked.

Economy is a very good reason to dine on the street. The *torta* I ate on the sidewalk would have cost two or three times as much in a restaurant. If you aren't overly concerned about comfort, you can buy the various parts of a meal from vendors and then find a bench or doorstep to eat them on. When a park or *plaza* is handy, your meal can become a very pleasant picnic. It is considered quite normal to eat in public.

Select street food as carefully as you'd select a restaurant. If it doesn't look good, don't eat it. Indigestion rather than diarrhea is the street grunter's most common complaint. Eating pastries, a pig meat *taco*, then a warm beer followed by a fried banana will have your stomach crying, "take it back," and leave you a quivering wreck for hours.

Once you've developed a sixth sense for sanitation, broaden your eating horizons by sampling unknown foods. The worst I've tried was fried worms and the best a strange avocado paste served on a sweet roll. Avid street grunters should study the foods described in the *Market* section for more eating possibilities.

Warning: It grieves me to report that studies of what bureaucrats call 'ambulatory food stalls' show a high incidence of nasty bacteria. The Mexican government is trying to educate food vendors in the rites and rituals of sanitation but it's a big job. Street grunting involves a risk, if only indigestion from greasy food. Use caution and lots of lime juice and chili. (See *Health.*)

Ordering

One of the most difficult things about eating in Mexico is understanding exactly what you are ordering and what you're likely to get. Direct translations of menus may be misleading. The words might be correct but often the resulting food won't be anything like you expected.

You want coffee with cream before breakfast. Your friend sees *café con leche* (coffee with milk) on the menu and says authoritatively, "That must be it. They just don't have cream."

Not being a sceptic you agree. You order and begin waiting impatiently; you want your coffee immediately and can't understand what the delay is about.

When your breakfast arrives, there's still no sign of the coffee. Finally a waiter sets a tall glass in front of you. He begins to pour hot black coffee, watching you expectantly.

When the glass is half full and he's begun to look at you rather oddly, you smile nervously and nod your head. He immediately stops pouring.

As you're reaching for the coffee the waiter grabs your wrist and quickly fills the glass to the brim with hot milk from a teapot.

"What the hell is this?" you moan. "He's just ruined my cup of coffee!"

What happened? This is the way *café con leche* is served. The problem was the assumption that coffee with milk would come out looking like coffee with cream in Dayton, Ohio.

The coffee came with the breakfast rather than immediately after ordering because that too is the custom. Very few Mexicans would think of drinking coffee on an empty stomach.

The menu may be more enjoyable than the meal; there's nothing I love more than reading garbled translations like "Dreaded meat with potatoes," "Eggs with Fool," "Fruit with ice cream—5 pesos, Fruit withnot ice cream—3 pesos," "Cheeselies," "Smacked Pork Chops," "Black coffeecup—5 pesos," "Chicken Car Cold," and so forth. (If you've got any good ones, please send them along for future editions.)

RECUERDO
MENU
PEPSI
N.Y. N.Y.
DECEMBER

Eating in a Mexican restaurant, from the most lavish to the most humble, is never a cut-and-dried experience. An element of the unknown lingers about everything, from the hygiene to what you're going to be served. Like a magician the cook will change your order of *tacos* to *enchiladas*, your tea to coffee and your bread to *tortillas*.

Steve and I once decided to splurge and order a seafood plate. We were literally drooling at the thought and waited very impatiently for over an hour. The waiter assured us repeatedly that dinner was just about to be served. Finally it came with a great clatter of bowls, plates and cold beer.

"What," I howled, "do you call *this?*"

Steve stared blankly at the meal in front of him.

The waiter caught our looks of hatred and whisked to the table, "Oh!" he said calmly. "There was no seafood, just this."

Steve gave me his 'Well, after all this is Mexico' look and dug into a bowl of tripe soup while I attacked a boiled shoulder of goat.

Order slowly; never subject the people serving you to a long blast of imperfect Spanish that cannot possibly be understood completely. If they don't understand everything, chances are they'll delete the vague parts and not worry about it. This means that you may get coffee and bread instead of coffee, fried fish, rice, milk and bread.

Even if you're given a menu, it's best to ask "*¿Qué hay?*" (What is there?), before making any agonizing decisions. Menus, especially in small restaurants, often reflect what the owner would *like* to offer rather than what is actually available.

In a small village restaurant we learned another quirk of ordering a meal. Our mistake was asking if they had chicken instead of just asking what was available.

"Oh, yes!" the owner said, signalling to his teenage son. While they went into a whispering huddle in a corner we sipped at our beers and wondered what was up.

"*¡Momentito!*" the man called encouragingly. A few seconds later the son flashed by the open doorway on a clattering bicycle.

"Steve," I said, "Do you get the odd feeling that..."

"Yeah," he answered, staring sourly at the table. Half an hour later the kid was back, a squawking rooster clutched under one arm, it's feet lashed with a piece of red cloth. The boy gave us a wink as he ran into the back of the restaurant.

"Was that chicken you ordered?" the owner asked, hovering over us anxiously, worried that we'd changed our minds. Steve shrugged his shoulders; why not? We'd already waited this long.

"*Sí,*" he answered.

The man turned, yelled out "*¡Si!*" and before the word had echoed off the high ceiling, a brutal *Chop! Squawk!* and a convulsive rustling of feathers was heard from the kitchen.

I looked at Steve; the last swallow of beer seemed to have stuck in his throat. "Well," I said, "At least we didn't order a steak or a porkchop."

The really relaxed and adventurous diner can simplify ordering by saying "*Lo que sea*" (Whatever there is). It might be quite interesting and tasty. We found, for example, that while living with a family that operated a restaurant, we could do much better by asking for servings of what they themselves were eating rather than the unappetizing dishes they prepared for the customers. I tried to convince them that they should throw out their menu and just serve traditional family recipes, but they thought I'd lost my mind. "Everyone *asks* for this type of meal!" the lady of the house protested. "It's not my fault if I can't cook it well. Anyway, they eat it!"

It is risky to discuss your order in Spanish in front of the person serving you: you may get everything you read off or whatever sticks in the person's mind. If you're with a group, one person should give all of the orders and attempt to combine them; for example, three orders of fried meat, two coffees, one salad, etc. The waiter or waitress rarely writes down the orders, no matter how complex they may be. It is quite common to be served one dish and then to be asked again what else it was that you wanted.

One of the most frustrating results of confusing the person who takes your order is that everyone may be given the same thing, no matter what was requested.

Imagine that you're in an ice cream stand in the U.S. There's a big sign that says, "27 Flavors!" You ask what the flavors are and the person behind the counter reels them off as one long word. Chances are you'll catch about 50 percent of what is said and order vanilla. Now imagine yourself in a tiny restaurant near the market in Tapachula. You ask "*¿Qué hay?*" Against a background of traffic noise, blaring jukebox and a shoeshine boy tugging at your sleeve, you hear ten completely strange dishes as one long word. You smile weakly and say "*¿Mande?*" (What?) and the list comes at you again.

This time you catch one word that you recognize and say "*Bueno, déme...*" (Ok, give me...). Hopefully, it will be good because until you understand more you'll probably be eating it quite often.

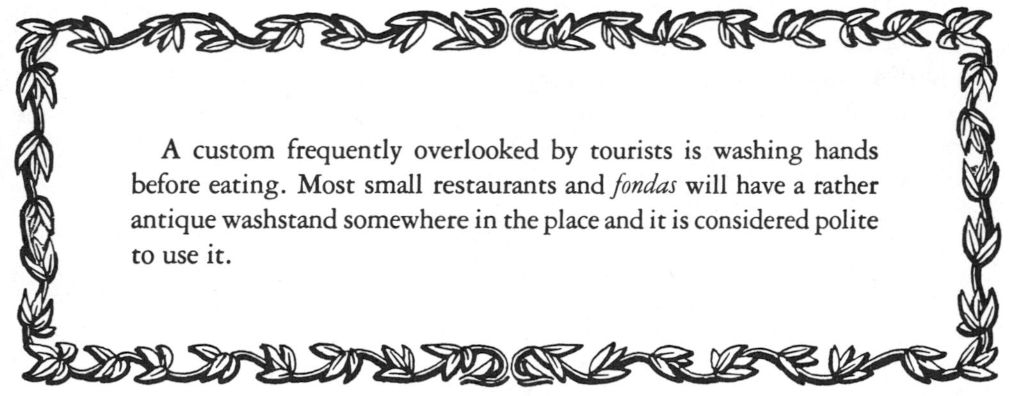

A custom frequently overlooked by tourists is washing hands before eating. Most small restaurants and *fondas* will have a rather antique washstand somewhere in the place and it is considered polite to use it.

We sat down in a typical *lonchería* for a relaxed meal. A young guy took our orders, then asked what we wanted to drink: Coke or Pepsi?

"*Coca,*" I answered clearly.

"There is none," he said without smiling.

I hesitated for a second and changed my order to Pepsi.

"Warm or cold?" he asked.

"Cold," I answered.

"There are none cold," he said.

"Then give me a warm one," I answered, suddenly very weary of the whole thing.

"*Sí, señor,*" he said very politely and brought me a *cold* Coke.

Paying Up

Paying the bill can lead to hassles as long and complicated as ordering. This is especially true when dining in groups and one or more people want to see an itemized bill or pay individually.

It is the custom for one person to pay the entire bill though they may settle up later. Among Mexicans there is almost invariably a big show of whipping out the money and paying for everyone. People who do the "I had the rice and you had the beans and you had three *tortillas*..." routine often find that in the confusion they've created, they actually pay more than if they'd settled on one communal bill.

Tips

If you are eating in one place often, an occasional tip can make it much easier to order, especially when you're having difficulty with the language. The distracted seven-year-old waitress who barely listened before will suddenly take a new interest in your welfare if she decides it's worth the effort.

Tourist bureau literature says that tipping is similar to the U.S.: 10 to 15 percent. In most of the restaurants where we eat, any tip at all would be considered something of an event. The nicest tip I've seen was given by two produce truck drivers who met for lunch at a roadside cafe. One driver left a cantaloupe, the other a cabbage.

When you honestly enjoy a meal, say so: *¡Estuvo muy buena la comida!* Once again, this may help when eating often in one place. Compliments can work wonders on the size of the portions. We have even been given free dishes to sample and appreciate because we had previously praised the food.

VEGETARIANS

The eating potential for vegetarians is almost unlimited. The variety and quality of fresh fruits and vegetables in the average market are excellent, as are the nuts, seeds, fresh juices and dairy products.

Unfortunately, all the wonderful food you'll see in the market doesn't look quite the same after it's been processed through a typical restaurant kitchen. Mexicans believe in well cooked food and few vegetables are served raw or even steamed.

Fortunately (for vegetarians), the Mexican craving for meat is strongly tempered by its cost, and many dishes are almost all vegetable. This is especially true in cheaper restaurants where the so-called meat dish may not be recognized as such by either vegetarian or carnivore. *Tortillas*, both at home and in a restaurant, make up the bulk of a poor person's meal.

The majority of Mexicans practice what I call "reluctant vegetarianism," eating meat only when they can afford it, which is often never. Others are giving up flesh for loftier reasons and vegetarian restaurants are opening across the country. Unfortunately they are often expensive and until vegetarianism is accepted as a reality rather than a fad, the best bargain meals will still be found in places that omit the meat because of its high cost.

If you're a hard-core vegetarian and won't eat anything that has even touched meat, you'll have trouble avoiding *manteca* (lard). Lard is used extensively in Mexican cooking and is responsible for the distinctive flavor of refried beans, a dish that many gringos live on when trying to avoid meat. If you ask the cook, "Has this been cooked in lard?" the answer will often be "Yes," even if cooking oil was used. Lard is considered *good.*

Eating a cheap non-meat meal is quite easy; corn, beans, rice, tomatoes, onions, chilies, eggs and cheese are all commonly served. This diet is nutritious but many travellers soon tire of it. At this point, salvation lies in the direction of the market.

Juices, nuts, raw vegetables and fruits should keep the vegetarian well fed and content.

Travellers who are prepared to do their own cooking will find that it's quite easy and inexpensive to follow a vegetarian diet. Travelling in remote areas, however, often means that food of any type is harder to find and more expensive. High in the mountains, for example, the food will be mostly staples (corn, beans, rice and chilies).

Health food stores and strictly vegetarian restaurants are found only in the largest cities and in a few smaller tourist towns. Vitamins and brewer's yeast are available in most drugstores but cost more than in the U.S.

Because few Mexicans voluntarily give up meat they find it amazing that anyone else would either. Lorena's best explanation, though not the most accurate, is, "It's my religion." Even hardheaded meat eaters accept that as legitimate. In restaurants we usually don't have the time or energy for long explanations and confusion reigns.

"She would like something without meat," I say to the waitress, completing my order and Steve's and ending with Lorena's since it will be a hassle.

There is a long silence. The waitress doesn't understand.

"What do you have without meat?" I repeat. "Anything?"

"Beans?" she asks, looking utterly confused.

"Don't you have anything besides beans?"

"One moment, please!" she says, rushing off to the kitchen. A few minutes later she returns triumphant.

"We have *menudo!*" she says, eyeing Lorena expectantly.

"What's *menudo?*" Lorena asks.

"Tripe," Steve says.

"Please," I beg the waitress, "that is meat. She wants something without any meat, without any meat *at all.*"

"*¿Tacos?*" the girl asks, obviously beyond reach but trying to please us, to end this ordeal so she can get back to her comic book.

"What kind to you have?" Lorena asks.

"Pork, chicken and sausage," she answers calmly.

"But those are meat!" I say, wishing Lorena would accept beans and forget this circus.

"One moment, please!" and she runs off to the kitchen. She returns in a few minutes, again triumphant but obviously cautious.

"*Mamá* says she has *tacos* without meat!"

"What are they?" I ask. "Chicken?"

"No," she says proudly. "Beans!"

"Look," I say. "How about an order of chicken *tacos* but without any chicken or meat or *menudo* in them. Just chicken *tacos* without the chicken, OK?"

"*Sí, señor,*" she says politely, drifting from the table with looks of distrust. Then, when a safe distance away, she runs into the kitchen for the final time. Half an hour later she throws a plate in front of Lorena and retreats quickly.

"She did it!" Lorena says happily, "Cheese, beans, cabbage, cooked potato and chili sauce but not a bit of chicken."

When the meal is finished, we ask for the bill. The waitress computes out loud, adding it up on her fingers as she goes around the table from plate to plate. She stops at Lorena's plate—a look of panic crosses her face.

"One order of chicken *tacos*," she says.

"Wait!" I protest. "There was no chicken in those *tacos*; they can't cost as much as ours."

She stands staring at the empty plates until her mouth opens and she shrieks, half hysterically, "*¡MAMA!*"

Mamá comes trucking out of the kitchen wiping greasy hands on a newspaper, preparing to do battle with the gringo maniacs who are destroying her tranquility and her daughter's tenuous grip on sanity.

"Something wrong?" she says sweetly. "Was the food alright?"

"Delicious!" I answer. "I just thought that chicken *tacos* without chicken," and I motion to Lorena's plate, "should not cost the same as chicken *tacos* with chicken. Right?"

"Wrong, *señor!*" she says firmly. "I only took the chicken out as a favor to the *señorita*," and she smiles heavily towards Lorena. "They were still chicken *tacos*. Do I charge less if you ask me to leave out the *chile?*"

We stare at our plates as mother and daughter beam happily. As an afterthought the *señora* says, "And anyway, everyone knows that chicken is not meat at all! It isn't red!"

WHAT YOU'LL EAT

First time visitors to Mexico are often boggled by the variety of dishes offered from one restaurant and region to another. If your idea of Mexican food is *tacos* and *enchiladas*, be prepared for a pleasant surprise.

One of the main reasons that true Mexican dishes are not available outside the country is the incredible amount of work and time that go into their preparation. A good *mole* sauce, for example, might take as long as a week to prepare and contain 30 ingredients or more. Special utensils and processes, such as the time-consuming and wearying grinding of corn with a *mano* and *metate* (stone hand roller and grinding stone), make it impractical to serve genuinely Mexican dishes in the U.S. In fact, most Mexican restaurants will only offer things requiring elaborate preparation on certain days of the week. Look for signs hanging in the window or on the door that say *"Hoy Mole"* (*Mole* Today) or the name of some other special meal.

Tourists often make the mistake of ordering the same dishes time after time. This is an easy habit to fall into, especially if your Spanish is weak or your palate is having a difficult time adjusting. On my first trip to Mexico I lived almost entirely on broiled chicken and sandwiches and it took a major effort to plow through an order of *chiles rellenos*.

You will notice that menus change from area to area. Many regional dishes and styles of cooking are quite different from each other and should be tried: look for *platos regionales* (regional dishes) or for dishes identified by the name of a city or state, (*a la oaxaqueña, a la veracruzana*, and so on).

Tortillas

Tortillas have been around for thousands of years and are the Staff of Life in Mexico. *Tortillas* are round cooked cakes of corn or wheat flour, about as heavy as blotter paper, which is what I thought they tasted like when I first tried one. They range in diameter from a few inches across to what seems to be a few feet, but the standard size is about five inches across.

The best *tortillas* are made by hand, a long and laborious task that occupies many of the waking hours of legions of Mexican women. The rhythmic "pat-pat-pat" as the cakes are formed has been called Mexico's heartbeat. The traditional process involves soaking kernels of corn in lime water to form *nixtamal* (like hominy). This is ground on a stone *metate* into dough, called *masa*. The *masa* is shaped into small balls and then patted out by hand into *tortillas*, which are then cooked on a *comal*, a round flat earthenware or metal griddle. It seems very simple, at least until you try it for yourself.

Did you know that the two apparently identical sides of a *tortilla* are actually quite different? One side is much thinner than the other and is called the *pancita*, the belly. When rolling a *tortilla* around a filling or piece of food, the *pancita* faces inward and the *espalda*, the thicker 'back' is on the outside. To the woman who explained this to us, it was as obvious as the difference between crust and bread.

Tortilla technology has advanced to the point of mechanized factories, churning out *tortillas* that taste as bland as enriched white bread. Some short cuts, however, don't noticeably affect the quality of a well-made *tortilla:* power operated *nixtamal* grinders and small wooden or metal presses. Among good Mexican cooks, though, anything ground by machine is considered of poorer taste and quality.

Corn *tortillas* commonly come in two colors: white and yellow. White *tortillas* are made from lighter shades of corn and are generally preferred over the yellower ones. A Mexican friend explained to me that yellow corn is associated with the poorer classes, especially Indians. Some people, myself included, prefer the yellow *tortillas*, much as some prefer dark whole grain breads to those made from bleached flour. It is not uncommon, when eating with poorer people, to have them apologize for serving yellow *tortillas*. When I tell them that I prefer the darker *tortillas*, they usually admit that they have more vitamins and "give more sustenance."

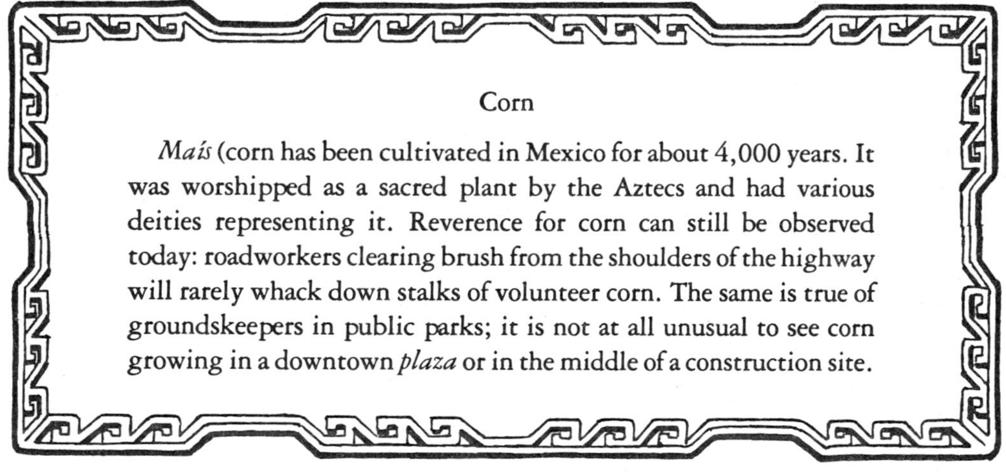

Corn

Maís (corn has been cultivated in Mexico for about 4,000 years. It was worshipped as a sacred plant by the Aztecs and had various deities representing it. Reverence for corn can still be observed today: roadworkers clearing brush from the shoulders of the highway will rarely whack down stalks of volunteer corn. The same is true of groundskeepers in public parks; it is not at all unusual to see corn growing in a downtown *plaza* or in the middle of a construction site.

Blue and red *tortillas*, called *prietas*, are made from naturally colored corn and considered a special treat. They are rarely served in restaurants. Food coloring may also be added to the *masa* for a special *fiesta*. There's nothing like beans and pink or green *tortillas* to fill you up fast.

Tortillas that are only about three inches in diameter and quite thin are served on special occasions, to be eaten with tasty snacks. They are also served in the type of ostentatious restaurant that doesn't allow common *tortillas* to cross the threshold.

Flour *tortillas*, usually white but sometimes made of whole wheat, are typical of Northern Mexico and are rarely seen in the south, except at altitudes where corn will not grow. Flour *tortillas* are now commonly sold in supermarkets, prepackaged and frozen.

Tortillas can be purchased from *Tortillerías* (*tortilla* factories) or in and around the market from women and girls who bring them from home to sell. You can find the most appealing and then barter. They are sold individually and by the dozen. These *tortillas* are almost always far superior to factory made, though watch out for women re-selling factory *tortillas* if you want handmade.

Tortillerías must legally close for one day a week but they try to stagger it so that a constant supply is assured.

A *kilo* will feed several tourists or one or two Mexicans. Fortunately, they can be purchased in smaller amounts such as a *medio* (half *kilo*), *cuarto* (quarter *kilo*) or by the *peso.*

In *fondas* (market eating stalls), the *tortillas* are generally supplied by little old ladies who go from stall to stall, insisting that the diners feel the texture of the *tortillas,* test them for proper warmth and buy more than they can possible eat. Other restaurants usually include all the *tortillas* you can eat in the price of the meal. Don't hesitate to ask for more.

Portions served in most restaurants often seem very small to the tourist. When you order pork and get one thin rib, you begin to wonder how you're going to get full. The answer is *tortillas.* By making a *Poverty Taco*—slivers of meat or tiny amounts of other foods wrapped in three or four *tortillas*—you'll find the most meagre dishes filling and satisfying.

Tortillas are not only cheap but they turn a simple bowl of beans and chilies into a very nourishing and balanced meal. (See *Beans.*) Poor people often have to forego the luxury of even the beans and will make a meal of nothing but *tortillas* and salt.

Learn to use *tortillas* as eating utensils. It is quite proper to tear meat apart with your fingers to make *tacos.* Watch other people; the techniques vary throughout the country. A really basic restaurant will offer only spoons and *tortillas*; forks are unknown.

Bread

Pan, the Spanish word for bread, usually refers to the *bolillo*, a french style roll (called *pan francés* in Yucatan). Sliced bread (*Pan Bimbo*, a brand name) is also served in some restaurants. Plain toasted bread is called *pan tostado* or *pan dorado. Pan dulce* (sweet bread or cake) may be served in the morning. If a basket of sweet rolls or cake is placed on the table, you will pay only for those that are eaten. (There's rarely any charge for *bolillos* or *Bimbo*, except in *fondas.*)

Butter (*mantequilla*) is seldom offered except in fancier restaurants and even then you may get margarine.

Chilies

Because many tourists tend to overemphasize that they don't want anything *con chile*, many restaurants automatically hold back the delicious sauces that they customarily serve with meals. It's a shame not to give them a try. The majority of people who add *chile* to their food eventually become quite fond of it. (Chilies are an excellent source of Vitamin C. See *Markets* for more on chilies).

If you want chilies or sauce, ask for *chilies, salsa* or *salsa picante* (hot sauce).

When you're given a bottle of hot sauce (some of the regionally brewed concoctions are very good) and prefer something made fresh, ask for *salsa casera.*

Mexicans firmly believe that chilies improve the appetite and aid digestion. However, experience has taught me to go easy until my body has built up a tolerance for them. Some of the milder varieties, such as the *chile poblano*, can be eaten in quantities that fool the mouth but devastate the stomach and lower regions. Don't get over confident just because it doesn't burn at first. For a flaming mouth, the best cure is to eat salt and bread.

Pimienta negra (ground black papper) is rarely on the table but they will probably have it in the kitchen if you ask.

Meats

The most common meat (*carne*) dish is *bistec* (also called *bistek* or *biftec*), a general term for anything resembling a steak even if cut from the side of a tuna. You must specify what type of *bistec* you wish: *bistec de res* (beefsteak), *bistec de puerco* (pork steak), *bistec de pescado* (fish steak), etc.

A *bistec de res* is not at all similar to a typical beefsteak in the U.S. It is thin, cooked well done and usually tough.

Steaks served with sauces of tomato, chilies and other ingredients are called *bistec de res ranchero* and *bistec de res estilo mexicano.* A steak may be named after an area of the country (*bistec tampiqueño, bistec norteño,* etc.) but most of these just have a variation in the sauce.

Filet mignon is sometimes offered, even in smaller places, and will be called *filete mignon* or *minon.* Don't confuse filet mignon with *filete*, another term for ordinary *bistec.* Tenderloin is called *lomo* or *lomito.* These finer cuts rarely cost much more than regular steaks and are almost always better eating. One of the best steaks I've ever tasted was served to me in a small middle-of-nowhere town. When I saw *filet minon* on the menu it seemed so unlikely that I immediately had to try it. When it came, wrapped in bacon and beautifully grilled, I could hardly believe my eyes.

The other *bistecs*—pork, fish, venison and turtle—are served in forms similar to those of beef. *Bistec de venado* (venison) is very common in the Yucatan peninsula. *Bistec de tortuga* (turtle, also *caguama*) is sold by seafood restaurants when available. Although it tastes good, eating a piece of turtle meat definitely contributes to their extinction. Mexican fishermen are killing turtles indiscriminately—and illegally—because of the demand in restaurants. *Huevos de tortuga* (turtle eggs) may also be served. I think the practice of eating turtle eggs is particularly stupid because they really don't taste very good.

"Save a turtle: eat a fish."

Whenever I am in doubt, either about the food or my appetite, I order a *milanesa* Breaded beef, pork and veal cutlets (*milanesa de res, puerco* and *ternero* respectively) are usually much more tender than a plain fried steak and are equivalent to an American 'chicken fried steak.'

A *torta de milanesa* is a french style roll (*bolillo*) and a piece of batter fried steak made into a wonderful substitute for a hamburger or steak sandwich. Even if it's not on the menu, they'll usually whip one up.

Carne asada is grilled meat, usually a beefsteak, though once again it may be pork, goat (*cabrito*), venison or turtle. Meat prepared *asada* is often tough but flavorful. When grilled over charcoal, it is called *al carbón*.

Chuletas de puerco (pork chops) taste better than pork chops in the U.S. *Chuletas de puerco ahumadas* (smoked pork chops) are very delicious.

Carne de chango (monkey meat) has fooled many tourists and travel writers into thinking they were dining on some unfortunate primate. It is actually cured ham. The best is cured in a kind of tropical fruit jam and then smoked. It's outrageous.

Guisados are stews of various types of meat, cooked with or without other ingredients (chilies, vegetables, etc.) and served either wet or dry, hot or cold. The meat is usually much more tender than a *bistec*.

Caldo de olla and *puchero* are stews that might be compared to New England Boiled Dinner, if you aren't from New England.

Salpicón de venado (or *de res, puerco* or *tortuga*) is cold cooked meat mixed with chilies. A variation of this, usually made with ground beef, raw or cooked, is called *picadillo* The first time I blithely gorged down a dish of *salpicón de venado*, I almost fainted from lack of breath. This was long after I considered myself quite immune to such embarrassing scenes as pouring sugar or jugs of water into my mouth to quell the flames My downfall in this case was the dreaded *chile habanero* from the Yucatan. It's known to the Maya as the 'crying tongue' chili and should be considered dangerous.

Carne adobada, adobo and *cecina* are meats cured with chilies and other spices. *Cecina* may be dried quite hard and then fried before serving, usually in a sauce. These dishes can be tough on a tender stomach.

Carne machaca is cured and dried meat, usually beef, shredded and served in sauces and with eggs.

Albóndigas are very elaborate and tasty meatballs.

Carnes en alambres, sometimes called *carne en brochete* (shish-ka-bob), is usually made of beef or lamb (*carnero*).

Barbacoa (barbecued meat) is not prepared as in the U.S. The meat is placed in a container, covered with *maguey* or banana leaves, then buried beneath a slow fire or with hot stones. (Our idea of barbecued meat is much more similar to *carne asada* or *al carbón*).

Cochinita pibil (barbecued pig) is a specialty of Yucatan. The meat is coated with a sauce of oranges and spices before it is interred and this gives the *pibil* meat a delicious and distinctive flavor. Turkeys and deer (*pavo* and *venado*) are also cooked *pibil* style.

Birria (*carnero* in some areas) is goat or mutton barbecued Mexican style. Most stands serving it will display the skull (usually with horns) to let the customers know that the meat isn't pork.

Carnitas are made by rendering a pig, from tail to snout, in a huge cauldron. After a batch of *carnitas* has been prepared, it is arranged in a pile with all of the skin, intestines, ears and odds & ends heaped over the lean meat. Ask for *carne maciza* (lean meat) and the vendor will root through the stuff (avert your eyes if you must) and extract a delicious loin or shoulder. You can also ask for *pura carne* (pure meat) or *carne sin grasa* (meat without fat) to get lean meat.

If you don't care what you get, ask for *surtido* and you'll be given a selection of everything from ears to ribs. It all costs the same.

The meat is prepared with great care and is cooked at a high temperature, usually just hours before it is sold. By avoiding large pieces of fat, meat that is obviously old or a particularly dirty stand, you should never suffer from indigestion after eating *carnitas*. (Unless, of course, you follow my example and overeat.)

Carnitas can be ordered by the weight (*kilo, medio kilo, 100 gramos*, etc.) or by the *peso*: '*Dame diez pesos, por favor*" (Give me ten *pesos*, please). There is no savings by buying large quantities.

Start by ordering *cien gramos* per person and keep in mind that combined with *tortillas*, it will make several *tacos*. If you eat chilies the vendor will usually throw them in, free of charge. They help digest the grease. Ask where you can buy *tortillas* and get about *un cuarto* (one fourth of a *kilo*) per person or less if you're not really famished. Those who don't care for *tortillas* can buy *bolillos* instead. If you'd like something to drink with your meal, it is considered proper to take your food into a small restaurant, *fonda* or *cantina* and order beverages. They will often offer you a plate, napkins and salt for your meal.

Around a *carnita* or *barbacoa* stand you'll frequently see ladies selling *tortillas, chiles, salsas* and *nopalitos* to those buying meat. *Nopalitos* are chopped cactus leaves often mixed with onion, garlic, herbs and lime juice. They are naturally slimy but have an agreeable flavor and mix well with *carnitas*. They also make a nourishing vegetarian *taco* by themselves.

Chicharrones (pig skins or cracklings) are sold in meat shops, *carnitas* stands and on the street by wandering vendors. I prefer to buy *chicharrones* from the *carnitas* stand, on the assumption that they were probably cooked with the meat and therefore should be fresh. A large piece makes a handy improvised plate for your *carnitas*. When you've finished the meat, you can eat the plate, salty and soaked in chili juice and pork drippings.

There are many other kinds of meat sold for immediate street eating. One of my favorite choices is to visit a stand with a charcoal brazier over which the vendor or the customer cooks raw meat, usually strips of beef.

Armadillo, venison, fish and other less identifiable animals are also sold precooked, most commonly in markets and small towns with a strong Indian influence.

In southern Mexico you may be offered *tepescuintle*. It is a delicious meat, even if it is from the *agouti*, a racoon-sized rodent. I've yet to meet a hungry carnivore who didn't love it.

Liver is served as *hígado encebollado* (liver with onions) or *hígado entomatado* (with tomatoes).

Menudo, a very popular dish, might best be translated as the 'interior odds and ends' of whatever poor beast fell under the axe, along with its feet, paws or hooves. This stuff is put into something, usually a piece of intestine, and cooked. *Menudo* is a classic Mexican hangover cure and is often sold by vendors around *cantinas*. It is gaining immense popularity in the United States, for reasons completely beyond my understanding.

Mondongo is stomach and intestines, often filled with blood and spices. *Tripas* are tripe.

Pollo (chicken) is much better than chicken sold in the U.S., which usually, as Steve's father used to say, "tastes pasteurized." Mexicans serve chicken in many ways: *Pollo asado* (grilled), *pollo frito* (fried), *pollo con arroz* (with rice), *pollo en mole* (in *mole* sauce) and *caldo de pollo* (soup).

Cold cuts (*carnes frías*) are usually offered in sandwiches or *tortas* but are sometimes served on a snack plate. The most common are *queso de puerco* (head cheese), *jamón*, (pressed ham) and *salami*.

Chorizo, the famous Mexican sausage, may be served as a side dish but it usually comes with eggs or in *tacos*.

Patas de puerco are pig's feet. They gain a lot when fried in a thick batter.

Seafood

The Aztec emperor, Moctezuma, set a precedent for Mexican seafood lovers when he established a system of runners from Tenochtitlan (Mexico City to us) to the Gulf of Mexico. Life for these relay teams must have been like perpetual Olympic Games, with the runner's baton substituted by red snappers, fresh mangrove oysters and steamer clams.

The tradition continues, though the runners have been replaced by fast trucks. *Mariscos* (seafood) are extremely popular and towns of any size, even far from the coast, will have at least one seafood restaurant.

Because of these fast trucks, many refrigerated and other using ice, there's rarely any worry about being served something spoiled or overripe. If you're in doubt, however, don't eat it. This is especially true when eating seafood from street vendors.

As a general rule I only eat street vendor's seafood when within sight or smell of the ocean. Even then I avoid the less prosperous stands (which can't afford to throw anything away if it's marginal) and prefer to eat seafood before the heat of the afternoon. Most *mariscos* are delivered early in the morning and several hours out of water or ice is more than enough to reduce their flavor and increase the chance of spoiling.

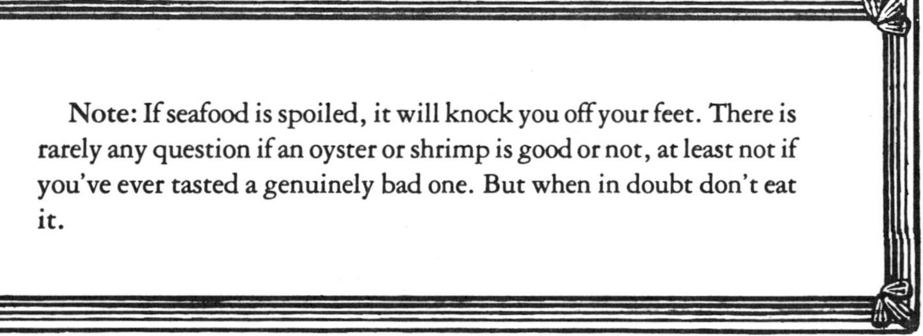

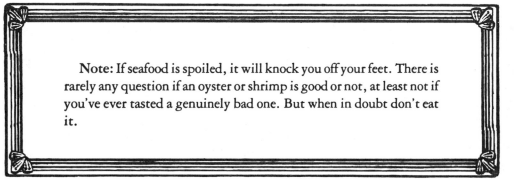

Note: If seafood is spoiled, it will knock you off your feet. There is rarely any question if an oyster or shrimp is good or not, at least not if you've ever tasted a genuinely bad one. But when in doubt don't eat it.

Pescado frito (fried fish) is usually a whole fish, head and all, deep fried. Unfortunately, Mexicans tend to overcook fish and some positively cremate them. Look at what someone else is eating before you order and you'll get a good idea of what's going on in the kitchen. If they are eating a fish and it sounds like the crunching of potato chips, you'll probably want to order something else, like *mondongo*. (Watch out for stale grease. You can smell it.)

Filete de pescado (filet) is fish without the head, tail and most of the bones. It is served *frito* (fried) unless you order it specifically cooked otherwise. *Pescado al mojo de ajo* is fish fried in butter and garlic. It is fabulous.

Huachinango a la veracruzana (red snapper Veracruz style) is justifiably famous. Anyone who can eat a whole red snapper smothered in an elaborate tomato sauce (with olives too) and not groan with pleasure needs help.

Other fine fish are also served: *pargo* (sea bass or snapper), *mero* (grouper), *cabrilla* (excellent rock fish) *robalo* (snook, among the best), *sierra* (mackerel) and *mojarra*, a general word used for any perch-like fish, usually pan sized.

Camarones (shrimp) are available throughout the country, in both restaurants and sidewalk stands. They are most often served in a cocktail (*coctel de camarones*) that is doused with sauces and various condiments. If you don't want your cocktail *con todo* (with everything), just point to the things that you want or take it *natural* ('natural,' naturally). Some of the sauces are quite *picante* (spicy hot).

Boiled shrimp are often sold by street vendors on the coast and are called *camarones naturales.* They are sold by the *kilo.* The price of shrimp in Mexico has skyrocketed in recent years due to the insatiable demand from the American market. This is a point of great distress to Mexican seafood lovers and justifiably so.

Camarones gigantes (prawns) are prepared in various delicious ways; among the best are *camarones en alambres* (shish-ka-bob), *camarones al mojo de ajo* (garlic and butter sauce) and *camarones a la diabla* (fried, devilled shrimp). Great! *Camarones en gabardinas* are batter fried.

Ostiones (oysters) are almost always eaten raw, in cocktails (*coctel de ostiones*) or on the half shell (*en sus conchas*). They are spiced up the same as shrimp.

Langosta (spiny lobster) is served steamed, broiled or *al mojo de ajo. Langostinas* are small crayfish. They are sometimes called 'river shrimp' (*camarones del río*) and *cucarachas* (cockroaches).

Many seafood restaurants offer fish and lobster by the size, with the price varying accordingly. Keep in mind, therefore, that fried snapper may be low priced because it's really just a red minnow. If you're in doubt, ask before ordering. Seafood cocktails also vary in size and condiments. Some of the more elaborate cost as much as a full meal.

Caracol (conch) are usually prepared in soup or *ceviche. Ceviche* is any type of raw seafood marinated with lime juice, chilies, onions, tomatoes and garlic. The best *ceviche* is made from *sierra* (mackerel) and young shark (*cazón*). It's a popular snack in *cantinas.* (Beware of wandering *ceviche* vendors; their wares are often half spoiled.)

Calamares and *pulpos* (squid and octopus) are most often served *en su tinta* (in their ink). They are tasty but something like eating tough spaghetti soaked in India ink. Both are also popular when served as cocktails.

Almejas (clams), *abulón* (abalone) and *lapa* (giant limpet similar to abalone but not as tasty) are not widely available, but when they are, they're usually served in cocktails or as *ceviche.*

Jaibas are very small crabs that make excellent soup. *Cangrejos* are larger crabs often served in rice, cooked whole.

Tiburón or *cazón* (shark, baby hammerhead) is served in tomato sauce and is very good.

Tortuga and *huevos de tortuga* (turtle, also known as *caguama*, and turtle eggs) are sold in many restaurants and cocktail stands. (See *Meat: Turtle.*)

SEAFOOD SUNDAY

During the Christmas season, Lent, and especially Easter Week, millions of seafood hungry Mexicans head for the coasts. Their minds are dazed with visions of golden fried *huachinango*, tall cocktail glasses brimming with *camarones* and *pulpo*, topped with slices of fresh lime and thick chunks of avocado, bottles of cold beer sweating damp rings onto the tablecloths...oh, it's almost too much to bear!

I used to observe these seafood orgies with mixed awe and admiration, tempered by a good measure of disbelief. How could they eat so much? How could they afford the bill, usually running to several pages? Why did they even do it, especialy those who drove hundreds of miles to the beach and then spent most of their time in a restaurant?

I decided to find the answer to these mysteries. I knew that like any strange custom, it wouldn't be solved by logic: I'd have to try it for myself. First, a group of people with a similar curiosity had to be assembled, since it would be impossible to round up enough members of my own family to create the crowd needed. And money...lots of money...

"Do you want shrimp in garlic sauce or devilled?" Steve asked the group seated at our end of the assembled row of enamelled metal tables.

"Both," I answered, "and a few orders of *ceviche* and some *tostadas* and a bowl of fish soup..."

"Hey!" he interrupted. "Isn't that an awful lot?"

"...and a plate of oysters and..." The waiter was scribbling furiously, "...and a round of cold *Corona* and some ice for this brandy and..."

"And some crackers," Steve added, eyes glazing over, "and a shrimp cocktail, *large*, and let's see...oh yeah, another menu, I want to be able to study it in detail."

Our friends soon succumbed to our mood and began barraging another waiter with similar orders. A group of *mariachis* wandered over and were immediately hired.

"Not bad, eh?" Steve asked, giving me a big wink as he drained the last drops of his second shrimp cocktail and waved the band to continue playing. A large family of Mexicans at a nearby table engaged another group of *mariachis* and the sound level soared. The long table was littered with dishes and cocktail glasses, empty beer bottles, cracker wrappers and a row of assorted liquor bottles. We'd sent out for strong spirits and a few pineapples before embarking on the main courses.

"I think I'll have a..." Steve's voice faded into indecision, "...a medium, no, make that a *gigante* fried snapper and maybe I ought to..." He looked over at me and added, "Carl, do you think I ought to have a lobster, too?"

"Sure, have *two*." I said, "Why be so conservative?"

His eyes widened. "Gee, I don't know...two lobsters all by myself?" The waiter stood patiently, tapping his order book with a pencil. "*Bueno*, give me the fish and lobsters!" Steve said, "and better bring us another round of beer."

We'd been in the restaurant for almost three hours, eating and drinking steadily, gossiping and enjoying the music, hiring small boys to dash off for side goodies from local stores, having our sandals polished and watching the passing crowds when it suddenly struck me: I was completely and absolutely relaxed, well fed, slightly drunk and euphoric, surrounded by good company and entertainment. What more could a person want? That was it, the secret of Seafood Sunday!

"The bill, *señor*," the waiter said, laying a sheaf of papers in front of me. I took a tentative peek.

"What's wrong?" Steve asked, waving the band to play another tune. "You look like you just saw a ghost!"

Potatoes

Many dinners, especially orders of meat or fish, are served with *papas fritas* (fried potatoes). Baked, boiled or mashed potatoes are unknown in most restaurants.

Eggs and Breakfast

Huevos (eggs) are cooked in a variety of styles. *Huevos estrellados* or *huevos fritos estrellados* are eggs sunny-side-up. *Huevos fritos duros* are eggs fried hard. Eggs 'over easy' are almost impossible to order. However, you can always try; the suspense of waiting to see what you'll get can brighten up your morning. (Ask for *huevos estrellados volteados*.)

Eggs are usually fried in oil rather than butter and may be somewhat greasy. If they are you can do the same as a man I once observed in a small cafe, carefully wiping his fried eggs with a napkin.

It is common to order eggs, especially scrambled, 'by the egg.' When listed on the menu, the price is almost always for two eggs.

Huevos revueltos (scrambled eggs) are very common but the name is something of a tongue twister. I learned to remember it by thinking of *"huevos revoltos"* which was my impression when I once had them served floating in an inch of cold grease.

Scrambled eggs can be ordered Mexican style mixed with onion, tomato, garlic and chilies (*Huevos revueltos estilo mexicano*); or mixed with refried beans (*huevos revueltos con frijoles*) or mixed with sausage (*con chorizo*). Eggs mixed with *chorizo* are often greasy and spicy.

Huevos rancheros (eggs ranch style) consist of two sunny side up eggs placed on *tortillas* and smothered in sauce. The sauce will be red or green tomatoes mixed with the usual combination of garlic, onion and chili. Although it will occasionally blow the roof off your mouth, this dish is quite tasty and usually tolerably spicy.

There are many variations on *huevos rancheros:* a *tortilla* may cover the eggs and be sprinkled with cheese or with a ladle of beans on top, my favorite.

Regional variations in egg dishes are common and usually quite good. One of the best I've tried was *huevos albañiles* (bricklayer's eggs), a sort of omelette smothered in a flaming hot sauce. If you're leery of spicy foods, ask before ordering; *chiles* are often used in egg dishes.

Omelettes may be called *omelet* (or some variation of that spelling), but are most commonly known as *torta de huevo. Huevos batidos* (beaten eggs), usually shortened to just *batidos*, are whipped eggs fried without stirring.

Chilaquiles are a scrambled combination of left-over *tortillas,* eggs and chilies. They are usually quite spicy. There are many variations on this dish and it is one that restaurant-goers would call 'dependable.'

Huevos tibios (soft boiled eggs) should not be ordered if you absolutely insist on a properly timed egg. They are sometimes called *huevos pasados por agua* (eggs passed through water) which is the way they generally come out: raw.

Steve once spent several minutes explaining in detail how he wanted his eggs boiled for four minutes. The cook personally heard the instructions and agreed that it could probably be done.

The eggs arrived and were opened with great ceremony. They oozed, raw but warm, into the dish. The waitress, seeing our looks of disbelief, explained that the cook had placed a pan of cold water on the stove, added the eggs, then 'cooked' them for just four minutes.

Huevos hervidos duros (hard boiled) are not common but easier to explain than soft boiled. If you don't want to rish confusion, order *huevos crudos* (raw); many Mexicans eat them this way. They are another of the classic masochistic Mexican hangover cures, especially effective when served in orange juice with a large dollop of searing hot sauce.

Tocino (bacon) and *jamón* (ham, usually pressed) are common but may be served scrambled into the eggs. If you want them (or anything else) separate, say, *al lado* (on the side).

Hot kakes (you can guess this one, can't you?) are rarely seen in typical restaurants but are common at fairs and *fiestas.* They are sold individually and are considered a treat rather than a regular food.

Breakfast cereals can be found in some restaurants, especially those catering to tourists. *Atena* or *hojuelas de avena* (oatmeal) is served much thinner than in the U.S. The preferred form for oatmeal is as *atole.* (See *Beverages*.)

Beans

Frijoles (beans) are served with almost every meal, including breakfst. *Frijoles refritos* are made by mashing cooked beans and then frying them in lard. They are often served with a piece of cheese.

Frijoles de olla (boiled beans, 'of the bowl') may be served drained or floating in a delicious broth.

When beans are combined with corn or flour *tortillas*, the essential amino acids are balanced and provide a complete protein. Add a chili for Vitamin C and you're ready for a long day of sightseeing.

Soups

Sopas (soups) are considered a very important part of both the afternoon and evening meal. They are always served with the *comida corrida* (daily special).

Soups are either *seca* (dry) or *aguada* (wet). The very common *sopa de arroz* (rice soup), for example, is more similar to fried rice. *Sopa de fideo* (noodle soup) is another common dry soup.

Consomé is broth and does not have any solid ingredients. The dish which most closely corresponds to our idea of soup is called *caldo* or *caldillo*. This is a catchall term for anything from pea soup to beef stew.

Although Mexico is noted for its fine soups, many restaurants have degenerated to serving canned. Ask "*¿Es sopa de lata?*" (Is it canned soup?) and if it is, you might prefer to pass.

Sandwiches

A *torta* is a sandwich made on a split *bolillo* (french roll). They are most commonly made with ham, chicken, cheese, lunch meat, cooked potatoes, beans or *carnitas* (pork). Most *tortas* contain one or more hidden chilies. Americans with a heavy hamburger habit usually find *tortas* to be a good substitute.

Take all of the ingredients of a good *torta* and place them between two slices of *Bimbo* white bread. You now have a *sanwich* that could have come out of a vending machine in a gas station on the L.A. freeway. A toasted sandwich is called a *sanwich dorado.*

Tacos, Enchiladas, etc.

Tacos are basically one or more *tortillas* wrapped around one or more ingredients and served either hot or cold. The strangest *taco* I ate was filled with *mondongo de sangre* (fried blood from the loser of the previous day's bullfight). It went down stubbornly, even under a flood of beer, but I eventually managed. The taste was actually quite good.

While street grunting, it is wise to buy *tacos* from someone who is making them on the spot. This is especially true of fried *tacos*, which tend to get very funky when allowed to stand for several hours after cooking. If the *tacos* are being fried in old grease—which makes them very dark—move on until you find something more digestible.

Enchiladas are *tortillas* dipped in hot sauce (the name literally means 'chilied'), filled with goodies and then fried. After cooking the *enchilada* may be served smothered in sauce or sour cream (*enchiladas suizas*) and sprinkled with cheese.

Quesadillas are made by frying various ingredients inside raw *tortilla* dough. Two of the most delicious are *flor de calabaza* and *huitlacoche* (squash flower and black corn fungus). The latter type looks disgusting but tastes great. A very common *quesadilla* is *queso y rajas* (cheese and strips of chili). A *taco de queso* is made with a precooked *tortilla* and often will be called a *quesadilla.*

Tostadas are crisply fried *tortillas* heaped with a variety of chopped vegetables and meat or cheese. When served as *antojitos* and *botanas* (snacks) in *cantinas,* the *tostadas* are invariably quite spicy. It sells beer.

Gorditas are round cakes of raw *masa* (*tortilla* dough) stuffed with various goodies and then fried. The most basic *gordita* is fried with no stuffing and then smeared with refried beans.

There are many variations and improvisations on the *gordita* and *taco* and one of my favorites is the *empanada*, a baked or fried *taco*-shaped tart (made with wheat flour). They are filled with everything from canned sardines to meat to sweet sauces and cream cheese.

Chalupas are similar to large *gorditas* and in some areas are similar to cupped *tostadas.* *Flautas* are like tightly rolled *enchiladas*, fried.

Tamales are steamed corn dough wrapped in a dry corn husk or a banana leaf and filled with meat, vegetables, beans, chili or a sweet candy-like mixture. Some are solid dough and eaten like bread. A single tamale is a *tamal*. Some are so big that they're a real meal in themselves.

Burritos are found only in northern Mexico, and if you ask for a 'little burro' in the south you'll probably end up with something with two large ears. *Burritos* are large and very thin flour *tortillas* wrapped around meat and beans. One or two make a full meal.

Mole is a dish that is distinctly Mexican. The most famous type, *mole poblano*, is a mixture of unsweetened chocolate, chilies and a great variety of spices. *Mole con pollo* (with chicken) or *con guajolote* (with turkey, also *pavo*) can usually be found in *fondas.* Turkey in *mole* sauce is considered the national dish.

Chiles rellenos are large *poblano* chilies (mild to hot) stuffed with cheese, meat or seafood, dipped in egg batter, deep fried, then stewed in a sauce of tomatoes, onion and garlic. Eat a *chile relleno* from the small end up. The stem end will be the hottest part and it helps to work into it gradually.

Salads and Snacks

A typical restaurant *ensalada* (salad) is rather disappointing. It rarely consists of more than a small pile of grated or chopped cabbage or lettuce, a slice or two of tomato, a few rings of onion and half of a lime. The lime is squeezed over the salad as a dressing.

Note: Lime juice has been proven to be highly effective against bacteria and should be used liberally on salads and street foods. (See *Health*.)

If you're desperate for a salad of fresh vegetables and can't seem to find one, try ordering *un surtido de verduras crudas* (an assortment of raw vegetables). We've found that this often brings better results than trying to describe how to make a "real" salad to someone who has never seen one. We discovered this accidentally, when a frustrated woman brought out a large plate of neatly arranged vegetable pieces and said "Show me how you make a salad." I picked up a slice of lime and squeezed it over the vegetables and said "Like that!" Her comeback was the solution to our ordering problems: "That's not a salad; that's a plate of raw vegetables!"

Guacamole is one of the few salads typical of Mexico. It is basically (as invented by the Aztecs) a mixture of chopped or mashed avocado, onions, and chilies. Tomatoes may be added as well. Some people throw in mustard, spices, and who-knows-what.

Many restaruants offer a delicious *coctel de frutas* (fruit cocktail) that just about makes up for the skimpy vegetable salads. Lime juice is also squeezed over fruit salad as a dressing.

Street vendors sell many delicious peeled and prepared fruits and vegetables. Most are served garnished with lime juice, chili powder and salt. By all means, try them *con todo* (with everything). The chili powder is rarely too hot, even for a tourist, and does interesting things to the flavor of an orange, cucumber or slice of pineapple. If the vendor has a large selection, try those things that are not familiar at first. The *jícama,* for example, resembles a potato in texture and an apple or pear in flavor.

Elotes (cooked ears of corn) are sold dripping with lime juice and chili powder. They are tougher than sweet corn sold in the States but the flavor is excellent. Some vendors smear mayonnaise on their *elotes* but considering that it is unrefrigerated, I would advise against it.

During the corn harvest season (summer and fall) it seems that everyone on the street is chewing on a *elote.* They are sold boiled and roasted, the price depending on the size of the ear.

Chick peas, (*garbanzos*) are also sold steamed. They are served in brown paper cones, covered with lime juice and chili powder. Pop one in your mouth, suck off the spice and then work out the bean with your tongue and teeth. They are as addictive as the peanuts you'll also find on the streets either roasted or raw, cured in vinegar. It's another of those habits you'll acquire in Mexico and then never be able to satisfy at home.

Pepitas are squash and melon seeds, toasted and sometimes salted and sprinkled lightly with chili powder. They are a national pastime and a favorite of movie goers. The seed in popped whole into the mouth, sucked briefly and then cracked open with the front teeth. A good *pepita* snapper can eat them as fast as peanuts, one handed.

Mangos, when in season (spring through summer), are sold on sticks, like ice cream bars. Try one with chili. While still green they are eaten with lime and chili, an interesting and tart combination.

Desserts, Junkfood and Candy

The national *postre* (dessert) is *flan* (custard). It is sold and eaten everywhere, from restaurants to street corners. Because street *flan* is prepared under rather dubious hygienic conditions (most is made at home by poor people), think twice about it.

Gelatinas are similar to Jello. Once again, street *gelatinas* should be avoided by those people wary of possible contamination (they are made with water).

Nieve (snow) looks very much like ice cream (*helado*) but it's actually made from flavored water. The street vendor who sells *nieves* is popularly known as *"El abominable hombre de las nieves"* (the abominable snowman).

In most towns you can hardly walk down the street without being run over by a *paleta* cart. A *paleta* is a piece of flavored ice on a stick. If you are nervous about water, *paletas* will give you uncontrollable palsies. The best flavor, in my opinion, is *tuna*—not tuna fish but *tuna* cactus fruits.

You'll see *paleta* salesmen pushing their heavy two-wheeled carts *everywhere*, from beaches to deserted stretches of scorching highway to fog shrouded mountain passes. The distribution of these carts is something to marvel at, which I do whenever I see one sitting on the side of the road, hundreds of miles from nowhere.

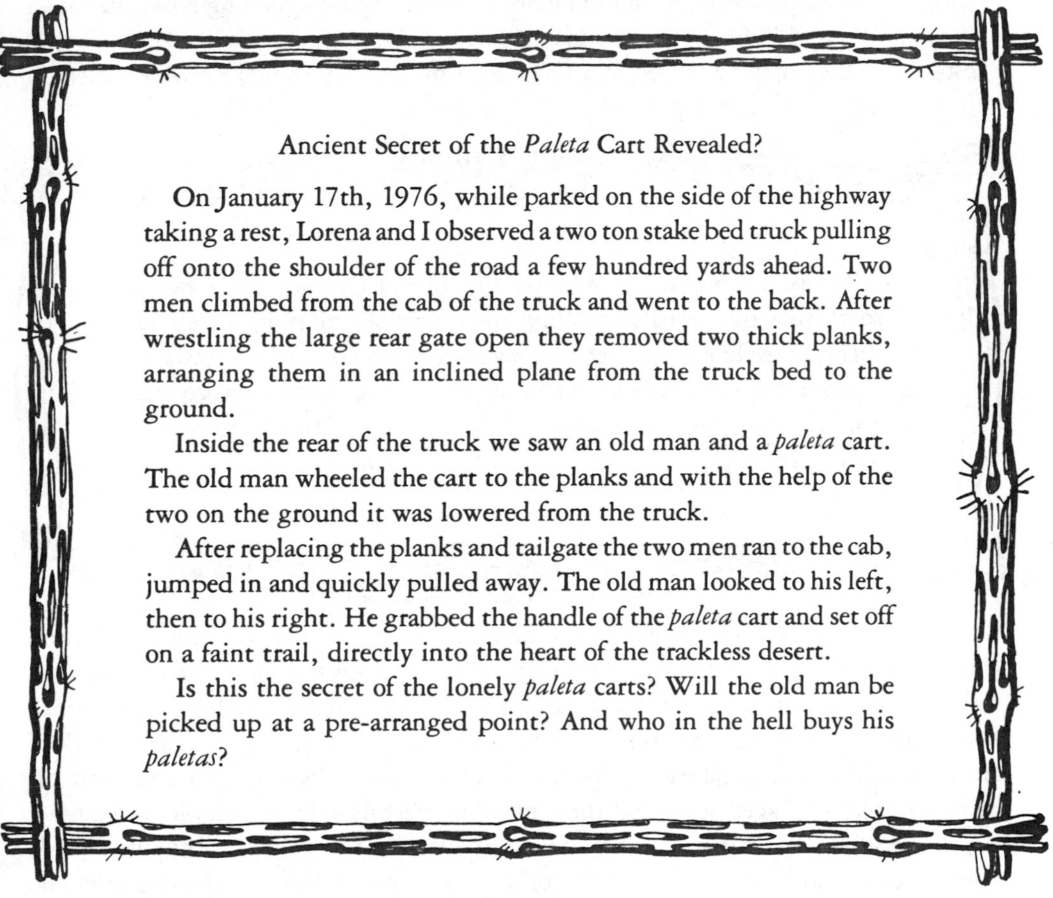

Ancient Secret of the *Paleta* Cart Revealed?

On January 17th, 1976, while parked on the side of the highway taking a rest, Lorena and I observed a two ton stake bed truck pulling off onto the shoulder of the road a few hundred yards ahead. Two men climbed from the cab of the truck and went to the back. After wrestling the large rear gate open they removed two thick planks, arranging them in an inclined plane from the truck bed to the ground.

Inside the rear of the truck we saw an old man and a *paleta* cart. The old man wheeled the cart to the planks and with the help of the two on the ground it was lowered from the truck.

After replacing the planks and tailgate the two men ran to the cab, jumped in and quickly pulled away. The old man looked to his left, then to his right. He grabbed the handle of the *paleta* cart and set off on a faint trail, directly into the heart of the trackless desert.

Is this the secret of the lonely *paleta* carts? Will the old man be picked up at a pre-arranged point? And who in the hell buys his *paletas*?

Ice cream is very popular and the flavors made with fresh fruits are outstanding. Large ice cream shops are becoming quite common.

Pastel (cake) is common but *pay* (pie) is not.

Buñuelos are molded fried dough served hot or cold, sprinkled with sugar or honey. They come in various shapes and sizes. Pastry lovers often lose their self control over fresh *buñuelos* and suffer from indigestion. This rarely stops them from doing it again and again.

Churros are also made of fried dough but the shape is quite different: long, narrow and usually ruffled. The raw dough is squeezed through a paper tube or metal pastry shaper and fried in long coils. These are cut into smaller lengths, dusted with sugar and sold like tiny stacks of cord wood by street vendors.

Polvorones are crumbly cookies, often made with lard, easy to overdose on.

Camotes (sweet potatoes) are a Mexican favorite; they are sold everywhere, from the market to travelling vendors who announce their passing by signalling on a flute. Most *camotes* are cooked in brown sugar and sold hot or cold, to be eaten with the fingers. In restaurants they may be served in a bowl with milk. They come in a wide variety of shapes, sizes and colors; my favorite is bright purple.

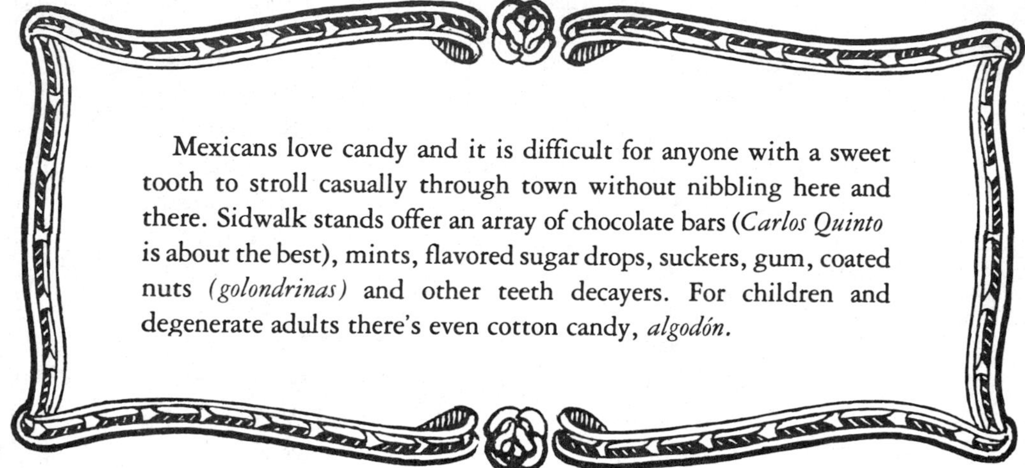

Mexicans love candy and it is difficult for anyone with a sweet tooth to stroll casually through town without nibbling here and there. Sidwalk stands offer an array of chocolate bars (*Carlos Quinto* is about the best), mints, flavored sugar drops, suckers, gum, coated nuts *(golondrinas)* and other teeth decayers. For children and degenerate adults there's even cotton candy, *algodón.*

Many excellent candies are homemade or unpackaged. These are commonly sold from large stalls. Among the best of these are *ates. Ates* are jellied fruit bars (some as big as an adobe brick) and are sold by the weight and by the piece. Some have been cooked until hard and broken into lumps, others can be sliced like cheese. They are usually made of tropical and semi-tropical fruits. You may be offered a sample; if so, try it. Some stands offer sampler packages of *ate* and these make interesting gifts for people back home.

Along with *ate* you'll see bricks, bars and balls of *cocado,* an incredibly sweet candy made from shredded coconut. There's nothing more pitiful than a tourist strung-out on *cocada,* constantly licking sugar from their fingers and probing cavities to dislodge bits of coconut. *Cocada* comes in a variety of colors; try the pink.

Cajeta is a toffee candy made in the city of Celaya and sold in many parts of the country. It usually comes in jars and has the consistency of cold honey. *Cajeta* is also made into candies. Anyone travelling near Celaya will see *cajeta* stands, *cajeta* signs, *cajeta* shops, *cajeta* hawkers and discarded *cajeta* candy wrappers at every turn. Needless to say you will want to try some.

Obleas come in various sizes and shapes but are basically a sandwich of *cajeta* between two thin flour wafers. A Mexican version of the Eskimo Pie. *Pepitorias* are thin flour wafers folded over a filling of *cajeta* and *pepitas* (toasted squash and melon seeds).

Chongos are a custard-like sweet similar to *flan* but usually of a thicker consistency. They are not too common.

Mezcal is not only the name of a liquor but is also a type of homemade candy. It is the heart of the maguey plant, cooked in brown sugar. It is sold by the chunk. Chew the fibrous stuff until you've got the sweetness out and then spit it out.

Peeled sugarcane (*caña de azúcar*) is sold by the length or in bags of small sections; another chew and spit candy.

Dulce de tamarindo is tamarind fruit combined with sugar or with salt and chili powder. It is sold in flat cakes or long rolls. The sugar variety is mixed with water to make a refreshing drink, *agua de tamarindo.* The fruit is high in vitamin C.

Platanos prensados (pressed bananas) are cooked bananas (*machos*) that have been steamed and pressed together in blocks. The natural sugar content of the bananas makes the candy very sweet.

Dulce de tojocotes en almíbar is a favorite mouthful at Christmas time. It is squash, cooked in *piloncillo* (crude brown sugar). *Tojocotes* is often served in *fondas*, usually drenched in sweet cream or milk.

Curtidos are candied fruits soaked in alcohol. They are sold in jars or individually. Kids love them.

Fruits crystallized with sugar are called *frutas cristalizadas.* Candied fruit peels are *cascaras.* Among the more common candied fruits are oranges, limes, mangoes, pears, peaches, apricots, apples, figs and *arrayones* (a type of berry). *Calabaza* and *chilacayote* (squashes) are also candied. Candied plums (*ciruelas*) are called *jobos.*

An interesting variation of crystallized fruits is *limones rellenos de coco,* an entire candied lime, hollowed and stuffed with shredded coconut or *cocada.*

A candy that is very similar to peanut brittle is called *palanqueta.* Peanuts are formed into bars and blocks by cooking them with *piloncillo* (medium hard texture), sugar (very brittle) or honey (very flexible). Some vendors make large blocks of candy and then saw them into smaller pieces.

Candies of this type are also made from melon and squash seeds. Another type, called *alegrías*, looks almost identical to sesame seed bars (and cakes) but is actually not a seed at all. Whatever it is, it has a rather bland flavor.

Anyone with a real sweet tooth should try *jamoncillo.* It is something of a cross between a milk candy and a fruit bar. A friend calls it "Mexican halvah."

Gaznates (gullets) are for hopeless junk food fiends: a pastry tube or cone plugged with stiff sweet cream. Not far behind are *merengues,* a very hard mixture of sugar and egg whites formed into a lump.

Morelianas are pastry-like *tortillas* smeared with milk candy.

Trompadas are similar to taffy though made from *piloncillo* and anise seeds. I'm sure you can see the connection. Another taffy candy, very popular on the Day of the Dead, is called *charamuscas.* It is sold in twisted lengths, sometimes covered with nuts.

Beverages

Café (coffee) is almost always drunk heavily laced with sugar. If you want it black, ask for *café americano, café solo,* or *café negro.* Unfortunately, many restaurants buy their coffee with sugar already added to the beans and you don't have any choice.

Nescafé (instant coffee) is far more common in restaurants than ground coffee. A jar of *Nescafé* sits on the table and customers are served cups of hot water, then add their own instant coffee. Some restaurants serve *cafe con leche* as described in *Ordering,* but others just bring a glass of hot milk to the table and let the customer add the *Nescafé.* Coffee with cream is called *café con crema.*

Your coffee will come with the meal or sometimes after it. To get it sooner say, *"El café ahorita, por favor"* (Coffee now, please), but don't be surprised if this doesn't work, especially in restaurants unfamiliar with the eccentricities of tourists.

Té negro (black tea) is not a common in small restaurants as *té de manzanilla* (camomile) and *yerba buena* (mint). If you are a heavy tea drinker, it is best to carry your own tea bags and order a cup of hot water. Don't be surprised if they charge you for a cup of coffee; after all, they have no way of knowing whether you used the *Nescafé* on the table or not.

Chocolate is a very popular drink but is not always available in cheaper places. An excellent drink can be made by adding instant coffee to hot chocolate.

Before ordering fresh cow's milk (*leche de vaca*) or goat's milk (*leche de cabra*), read *Health* and *Stores: Dairy Products.*

Fresh fruit juices (*jugos*) are very popular among tourists; they are inexpensive and don't carry the evil associations of impure water or milk.

A juice stand may offer more flavors and combinations than one could sample in a lifetime: things like alfalfa and carrot or beet and grapefruit, all the old favorites. Before ordering a *jugo,* give the stand a quick appraisal. Many just rinse used glasses in a bucket of funky water before refilling them. Even worse, some juice sellers don't wash their fruit or vegetables. I've seen carrots covered with dirt being pushed into a juicer. Look before you order; there are plenty of stands that understand the value of basic health precautions.

Licuados are very similar in taste and texture to a fresh fruit milkshake. The standard *licuado* will be one type of fruit, water and sugar all blended together. Milk is optional and gives a richer texture than water. Ask for anything else you'd like added (fruit, eggs, ice, etc.). You'll be charged accordingly.

Licuados can also be made from a base of orange juice. This is my favorite: orange juice, one raw egg, banana and ice. For variations add vanilla, papaya, strawberries, pineapple and a dash of cinnamon. You'll never want to go home again.

Chocomil is a powdered-milk-based drink that vaguely resembles a milkshake. It comes in various flavors but the most common are chocolate and strawberry.

Esquimales are thicker and creamier than *licuados* but otherwise very similar. An *esquimal* is made by adding a prepared dry mix (chocolate, strawberry or vanilla flavored) to milk and blending it with chunks of fresh fruit.

Atole and *horchata* are distinctly Mexican drinks. *Atole* is basically fresh ground corn or corn starch, water and sugar. It is served hot or cold with a variety of spices and flavorings. *Atole* is quite nourishing and inexpensive, two good reasons to learn to like it. (*Atole* is also made from wheat flour, rice flour or oatmeal.) *Horchata* is ground melon seeds and water. It took me a while to get used to *horchata* but once I did, I was hooked.

Pinole is ground, toasted corn mixed with water, sugar and cinnamon. *Aguas* or *aguas frescas* (fresh waters) are made by adding a small amount of fresh fruit juice and sugar to a large amount of water. Most of the water used is not purified. *Aguas* made from flowers, cactus fruits and other exotic ingredients are especially worth sampling. They are refreshing and ridiculously cheap.

Many tourists have found that by making *agua fresca* at home (cantelope is great), they can wean themselves and their children away from expensive and unhealthy soft drinks.

Cocos (coconuts) are sold both as a drink and as a snack. The milk of the coconut is naturally pure and tends to plug up your bowels but don't eat too much of the meat, it has the opposite effect. After drinking the liquid, hand the nut back to the vendor who'll whack it open and remove the meat for you.

Soft drinks are very common. Those that are *not* made by large American companies are the best. Soft drinks are generally known as *refrescos* but they may be referred to as *aguas* or *gaseosas*.

Some of the better *refrescos* are *Sidral, Manzanita, Imperial* (all apple flavored and much like cider) and *Sangria* (mixed fruit). Mineral water with fruit flavors is sold under the brand names *Tehuacán, Del Valle, Lourdes* and others.

Some other common brands and flavors are:

7-Up	*7-Up* or *Seven*
Coca Cola	*Coca Cola, Coca* or derisively, *Choca Chola*
Pepsi Cola	*Pepsi Cola* or just *Pepsi*
Squirt	*Squirt* (pronounced *Esquirt*)
Orange Crush	*Naranja* or *Crush*

Lemonade	*Limonada*
Lime	*Limón*
Grapefruit	*Toronja*
Pineapple	*Piña*
Strawberry	*Fresa*
Cherry	*Cereza*
Cream soda	*Cebada*
Banana	*Sidra negro* (Yucatan)
Mineral water	*Agua mineral* (*con gas* or *sin gas:* without gas.)
Quinine water	*Agua quinina*
Pure water	*Agua puro, sin gas* (noncarbonated)

If none of these excite you, almost every restaurant, gas station, grocery store and sidewalk food stand will have *cerveza* (beer. See *Booze.*)

There are a wide variety of mildly alcoholic drinks that are often served at street stands, *fiestas* and fairs. For details see *Booze.*

When ordering a *refresco* or *cerveza,* specify if you want it cold or warm. Many Mexicans drink beverages *al tiempo* (room temperature) rather than *fría* or *helada* (cold). For this reason Mexican soft drinks and beer usually taste good warm.

The road south, a one lane sand trail, wound through huge coconut plantations and seemed always on the verge of leading to the beach but never did. We were involved in one of our periodic wild goose chases, searching for the mythical road through the mountains that only a select few knew of. The inside of the van was incredibly hot and dusty; we were generally agreed that the trip had become uncomfortable enough to rate as an Adventure. As darkness fell, our thoughts turned from exploration to food and rest.

"There's a village!" Steve yelled, pointing to a vague cluster of buildings in the distance. "We can get something substantial to eat!"

"Yeah, like a plate of beans," I muttered. If, after eating, Lorena pointed out that the meal had been nothing compared to what could have been scrounged from the food cupboards of the van, Steve would invariable answer, "But that's different." I was about to remind him of this for perhaps the hundredth time when we suddenly lurched to a stop.

"Take a look at that," Steve said. A broad smoothly flowing river apparently marked the end of the road and his hopes of finding a substantial meal. After taking a flashlight and wading carefully across the stream, I motioned to Steve that it was safe.

The van plowed into the water and splashed across. The wake drenched me to the waist, to the great amusement of a group of children standing on the opposite bank.

A few minutes later, we drove slowly into town, pursued by excited kids and carefully followed by the curious stares of their parents. The large dirt *plaza*, littered with paper, garbage and sleeping pigs, was surrounded by low adobe buildings well on their way to becoming part of the general erosion.

We parked in front of the only lighted building, a hardware and grocery store filled with men drinking warm Cokes (liberally laced, I discovered later, with locally made alcohol).

I asked them about a restaurant. The men looked at each other mutely; then an arm raised and indicated a nearby doorway. Steve made a beeline for it, eyes glazed with the thought of food.

Two huge wooden tables almost filled the room, packed with people eating by the light of dripping candles. While the owner shooed a pack of children and dogs from the doorway, his wife escorted us ceremoniously to a bench in a dark corner.

No one missed a bite but we felt every eye following us, every ear tuned to hear what we would say. After an uncomfortable silence, a man across the table asked politely if we were travelling clothing salesmen. We said that we were just *turistas.*

"Doctors?" he asked, ignoring the previous answer or not understanding it.

"No, just tourists, travellers."

"Missionaries!" he said proudly, turning to his friends with a smile, having called their unspoken dare to talk to the strangers.

We looked at each other and shrugged. We had been through this routine before.

"Yes," I answered. "We're missionaries."

Satisfied with this lie, they returned to their food. Soon the only sounds were those of bones being sucked and bowls scraped clean with oversized tin spoons.

We asked what was for dinner and found the decision as simple as the menu: sweet potatoes and milk or *pozole.*

Pozole, a dish we'd only heard of, or sweet potatoes, something even I didn't consider too substantial. Lorena, leaning toward a definitely vegetable meal, chose the sweet potatoes.

"*Pozole?*" I asked Steve questioningly, implying that I would if he would too.

"Yeah, guess so." he said rather dejectedly, realizing that once again the Substantial Meal was going to be a letdown.

Our orders were quickly filled and I tried to look eager as I peered into the bowl in front of me. Several hideous joints of bone and gristle were floating in a thick white gruel. "Oh, for a sweet potato," I thought silently.

Steve interrupted his eager gobbling of the gruesome stuff to say, "pig spine," as a means of reassuring me that it was edible.

I swallowed a spoonful of the liquid, determined not to be one of those shameful people who order food and then act as though it were a strange scientific curiosity, to be poked and probed, but certainly not eaten.

"Uurrghh!" I croaked.

"What the hell's wrong?" Steve hissed, looking anxiously around the room to see if anyone had noticed my impolite gurgling.

"What is that stuff?" I said, pointing in horror to the white gooey mass in my bowl.

"Hominy," Steve answered casually, slurping down huge mouthfuls with apparent gusto.

"Well, try mine." I said, sliding my plate toward him as I rearranged the plastic flowers and hot sauce bottles to form a protective screen against possible spying from the kitchen. Steve put the spoon to his lips and sucked noisily.

"Urrkk!" he gagged.

"What's wrong?" I asked. "Just a bowl of hominy. Right?"

"Yeah," he said ruefully, guzzling a bottle of warm orange pop, "with about a pint of hot sauce for flavoring."

The owner, sensing that something was amiss, rushed over to ask if the meal suited us. I wondered how the hot sauce had come to be added to my bowl of *pozole* and not to Steve's.

"Great! Just great!" I answered, determined not to offend their cooking. While he watched with obvious concern, I quickly shoveled down the remainder. Beads of sweat stood out on my forehead as I licked the last of the hog spine clean and casually chug-a-lugged a large container of water that might have been a vase.

"A very good meal, *señor*," we assured him, noticing that all of the others in the room had ordeed sweet potatoes and milk.

"Should have said we were doctors," I thought to myself. "Evidently they are trying to discourage missionary work or get rid of the extra chili sauce."

"I'm still hungry," Steve said, eyeing a plate of *tacos* being carried from the kitchen. Business was picking up and the menu was expanding. The *pozole* had been a slow mover.

I had to agree that my dinner had been more flavorful than filling and impetuously offered to split an order of *tacos* with him. Steve motioned to the owner and he and his wife bustled to our table. We immediately became involved in a four-way conversation that ended in utter confusion.

"Did we order?" I asked, completely bewildered by the entire discussion.

"Oh, God!" Steve said, burying his face in his hands. "I don't know! I don't have the slightest idea!"

We sat silently, wondering desperately if we had ordered and if we had, what?

"Maybe we just ought to get up and make motions as if we're leaving," I suggested. "If we did order, they'll certainly tell us something like '*un momento*' or else give us the bill."

"We can't do that!" Steve said. "It wouldn't be polite."

Before a solution could be devised our order arrived: two steaming bowls of *pozole* and a huge plate of *tacos*.

"Oh no, please no!" I moaned, unable to contain my grief at the sight of the *pozole* and the realization that we had to eat it, every bit of it.

"What have we done?" I cried, counting the *tacos* and finding that we had to follow our *pozole* with 16 of them.

"We ordered two dinners, which includes *pozole*," Steve said as he gazed fondly at the heap of golden *tacos*, spilling forth great quantities of lettuce and cheese.

"Everyone else is being served three *tacos* with their *pozole*," I pointed out. "How come we have 16?"

"I don't know!" Steve snapped. "Maybe I ordered four dinners; maybe they just like us! Whatever we did, here it is. Eat up!" And with no further comment, he fell upon his dinners with obvious pleasure.

Half an hour later we staggered onto the street, our plates left clean. I clutched my stomach in agony; barely able to keep it under control. It had been, I readily admitted, a very Substantial Meal.

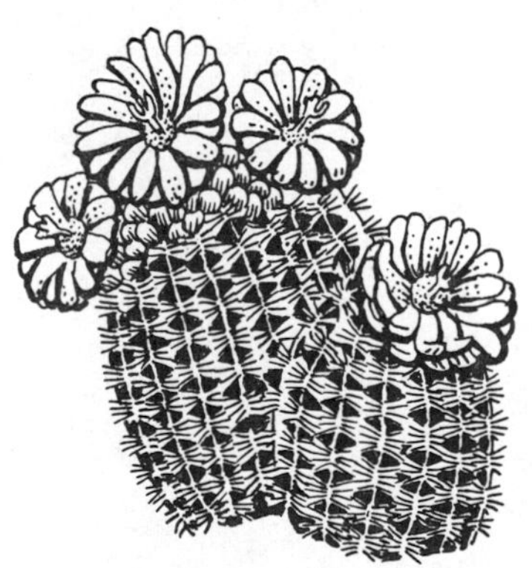

Hedgehog cactus

NOTES

MARKETS AND STORES

Markets and tianguis...Ins and outs of bartering...Shopping suggestions...Weights and measures...Stores: tiendas, Conasupo, supermarkets...Shopping lists: Alfalfa to Zucchinis and everything between...A typical marketing trip...

There are two types of markets: permanent buildings that have no other function and temporary markets that spring up like nomadic tent cities.

Large permanent markets are jammed with people from surrounding towns and villages on one or two days of the week. They do not close completely on less active days and many stalls remain open to accommodate regular customers and wholesale dealers.

Temporary markets are found in small towns, rural areas, on the outskirts of large cities and occasionally at major crossroads. Temporary markets are especially active during the holiday seasons (Christmas and Lent) and on special *fiesta* days. However, even an average market day is something of an event, with a festive, carnival mood.

Shipments of fresh fruits and vegetables are scheduled to reach the market just before large crowds of shoppers, so quality and selection vary greatly from one day to the next, with the best offered on market day.

Market day may be called *día del mercado, día de plaza* or just *tianguis.*

Many tourists mistakenly believe that they must be in the market at the crack of dawn. This is far from true; the main hours of business are later, from about 9 a.m. to 1 p.m. It is at this time, when the food is still fresh and not picked over, the sun not too hot and both vendors and customers feeling friendly and energetic, that the market is at its peak.

The best markets for variety and quality of food are those located in large cities or towns with a resident gringo community or prosperous tourist trade. Small markets, on the other hand, away from tourist influences, are often much more interesting in themselves. This is particularly true of *tianguis* (Indian markets).

Locating the market is usually not difficult; just walk or drive near the central *plaza* and look for concentrations of buses and trucks, or pedestrians carrying shopping bags and baskets. You can ask for directions to *el mercado*, but in some areas the market is more commonly known as *la plaza* or *la plaza comercial.* In smaller towns and villages the old custom of gathering in the central *plaza* to buy and sell is still observed. If you are driving, park a few blocks from the market. When all parking places have been filled, the heavy cargo trucks will still be rolling in with loads of corn, bananas and chilies. You might be hemmed in for hours.

Bartering

Bartering is a form of social contact. It does not necessarily have to be a long involved process. Unless you enjoy drawing it out by diverging into friendly conversation or exchanging tales, the average transaction will take only a few seconds.

The common rationalization that bartering is not worth the effort is completely erroneous. The person who barters competently can easily save 10, 20 or even 30 percent on an average shopping trip.

Bartering will earn you a certain amount of respect from the people you deal with. First, and most important, you are not disdaining social contact with them; you are willing and eager to communicate and to acknowledge their customs. The person who pays the first price without question may be laughed at, sometimes to their face. Vendors have little respect for the customer who throws money away.

Bartering in a tourist-town market can be frustrating; vendors often have a "take it or leave it" attitude that is difficult to break through. Bartering will still be done, however, by people in from the country for market day, by vendors in smaller stalls and those dealing in damaged or slightly inferior goods (which in Mexico often just means 'small').

Bartering is not an argument—it is a polite discussion of the price—and should be conducted calmly and with respect for the other person. As it is not an argument, you will not offend anyone by trying to barter.

Truck bumper graffiti: At the Glitter of Gold I Won't Come Down

Begin by saying something as a greeting; remember that Mexicans are polite to an extreme, even if they hate each other's guts. Examine whatever it is that you're interested in. Squeezing, smelling, hefting and even tasting are all acceptable.

The next step is to ask the price. The most easily remembered and overworked word is "*¿Cuánto?*" (How much?). Try other expressions like: "*¿Cuánto cuesta?*" (How much does it cost?); "*¿A cómo la da?*" (At what price do you give it?); "*¿Cuánto vale?*" (What is it worth?) or "*¿Cuánto es?*" (How much is it?). Each of these should be followed by, "*por favor,*" (please).

After you're told the *asking* price, it's time for the counter-offer. This can be the amount you're willing to pay or less, "*¿Seis pesos?*" (Six *pesos*?), or you can use such expressions as: "*No sale en*...amount?" (Won't it go for....?); "*No me da en*...offer?" (Won't you give it to me for...?) or "*Lo llevo en...pesos,*" (I'll take it for...*pesos.*)

When shopping for food, the markups are usually much less than those for handicrafts. Shop around various stalls. I generally offer two-thirds of the asking price and see what happens. If you are given a sad smile and a wagging forefinger, you were too low, but if you are handed the item instantly you were too high. With practice you'll soon learn to quickly judge the proper offer and selling price.

Never try to lower the price by acting as if the merchandise is so foul, so inferior or so unappetizing that the vendor would be better off giving it to you for nothing. This is true for both the craftsman who takes a great pride in his crude wood carvings and the old *campesina* who laboriously grew a crop of withered squashes on a dry mountain side.

Let's imagine that you want to buy a papaya. An old man seems to have read your mind because he's winking suggestively at several large ones heaped in front of him, attractively ringed with bananas and oranges. This is to be the first test of your newly acquired bartering skills.

You approach with a friendly smile and a greeting. He smiles back. You wipe the smile from your face and become inscrutable. His hand stops stroking the papaya and comes to rest on a pile of potatoes. You make an offer after hearing his initial demand. appears to think it over as you stand there patiently, humming the theme from Exodus.

The old man rubs his chin reflectively, then turns to another customer with a cheery, "*¿Qué le damos, señora?*" The woman scowls at a heap of carrots, selecting only the best. You consider the possibility that negotiations have been broken off, but notice that his eyes are following you craftily.

You reach into your pocket and pull out a handful of change. His attention becomes fixed on the money. Are you giving in or just checking for rare coins? He takes money for the carrots, distractedly shovelling them into a plastic sack. You give the coins in your hand a tempting jingle and quietly repeat your last offer. There is a questioning note in your voice, as if you might have mistaken his counter-offer for acceptance.

He sighs out a, *"No es posible,"* but you signal by a cynical twitch of your lips that he'd better deal fast. You lean toward the next stall, squinting toward a competitors's display of fruit.

He makes another counter offer, good but not quite good enough. You slip the money back into your pocket with a shrug. There are other papayas, your attitude tells him, and other vendors who understand profit and loss.

You wonder what to do next, he is matching you shrug for shrug. If you smoked you might light a cigarette. The dilemma is solved when he points to a slightly smaller papaya and repeats your last offer. You quickly accept, wondering if he'll go home and gloat to his grandchildren that he took you for a ride. He drops the fruit into your shopping bag, then tosses in an orange. You exchange more smiles, silently vowing to try him another day, perhaps over a pineapple or a watermelon.

Many people believe that walking away after the last rock bottom offer has been made is the best technique. This is often effective, but in some instances it's best to hang around, waiting for the vendor to make a decision. If you leave too soon, they may not bother, especially on small purchases, to yell after you and accept. Always say *"Gracias, adiós,"* as you leave. This brings attention to your departure. Drag your feet a bit; the vendor knows that many customers have turned back and given in first.

Haggling can involve a complicated juggling of number, size and quality of the items being discussed rather than a sum of money. You offer two *pesos* for three large oranges. The vendor says she'll give you two oranges for that price.

"No," you say. "I'll give you just one *peso* for two." She laughs and says, "*¡Bueno!* I'll let you have three oranges, but small ones, for two *pesos.*"

You smile. "Oh, no! You give me four small ones or three large ones for one *peso* 50 *centavos.*"

She laughs and says, "I'll give you three small ones and two handfuls of peanuts for 2 *pesos.*"

You accept.

Shopping Suggestions

- Always carry a good supply of change when shopping for food, particularly in Indian markets where few of the vendors have much money. When they can't come up with the proper change, you'll get it in merchandise. This isn't desirable if you've already got as much as you need.
- Don't be surprised if your money is carefully scrutinized or subjected to the classic counterfeit test of dropping coins to hear them ring. Torn or extremely dirty bills may be rejected, even though the person waving the money away could obviously use your business. Mexicans, especially poorer ones, are extremely suspicious of being cheated

with counterfeit money. A vendor once refused to accept a brand-new bill from me because it was a design that he had not yet seen. Although a helpful passerby assured the man that my money was perfectly good, he just apologized and said, "I can't afford to take any chances." Which was undoubtedly true.

Damaged or dirty money must be exchanged at the bank or foisted off on a harried supermarket cashier or gas station attendant.

If someone tries to pass *you* a ripped or badly worn bill just shake your head and point to the damage. You'll be understood. You'll do small time merchants a favor, however, by accepting damaged money; few of them ever have reason to visit a bank.

•One of the most common mistakes made by people unfamiliar with marketing is buying too much. Weights are measured in *kilogramas* (2.2 pounds) and volume in *litros* (1.1 quarts). This system confuses many tourists and they tend to buy in units larger than they normally would.

"*¿Un kilo?*" the lady asks, filling the measuring tray with twice as many tomatoes as you actually need. With a flick of the wrist she balances out the scale and you pay obediently.

Your greatest protection against this is to think in terms of *medios* (half *kilos*, 1.1 pounds). It is much easier and quicker to compute one and a half *kilos* into three *medios*—which you can think of as three pounds—than to multiply 2.2 by 1.5. *Un cuarto* (one-fourth *kilo*) is very close to half a pound.

Since few foods are sold in packages, this also confuses those accustomed to buying a box of this and a bag of that. How many grams of bulk macaroni are equivalent to the amount you used to get in the local supermarket in a plastic sack? The only way to relearn how to buy correct amounts is by trial and error and a heavy dose of self-restraint.

When I'm in doubt about how much I want of something I always start low. No sensible merchant will be offended if you change your mind and ask for more.

•Many vendors sell their goods by their own system of measures. The most common of these are the *mano* (handful) and *manojo* (bunch or handful). *Manos* range in size from tiny piles to large handfuls. Any food arranged in small heaps, piles, mounds or pyramids is probably being sold by the *mano*, from seeds to melons.

"*Son manos de un peso,*" (They're *peso* piles) a vendor says, noticing your interest in his peanuts. Closer inspection reveals that another pile of equal size costs two *pesos*. In this case, it's the quality that changed, not the basic *mano* measurement.

Other common measures are by the can (usually a liter or fraction of a liter), the *jícara* (gourd bowl or dipper), the piece, the bundle (especially herbs and fresh greens), the bunch, the length (sugar cane) and the *montón*. *Montón* means a pile or heap and can vary from a handful to a truckload.

The word *bola* (ball) may be used when discussing any fruit or vegetable that remotely looks round or rounded. The term *bola* is frequently heard in Indian markets where many of the vendors do not know the proper Spanish names themselves.

When measuring something a vendor may say "*¡Ya cabal!*" to indicate a full or completed amount. This is an old fashioned term most often encountered in *tianguis* and rural areas.

If a vendor cannot afford a fancy scale to weigh goods a homemade *balanza* may be used. Your purchase is put in one side of the balance (a pair of baskets or matching tin cans) and a known weight in the other. This 'known weight' can be anything from a rock to coins to scraps of metal.

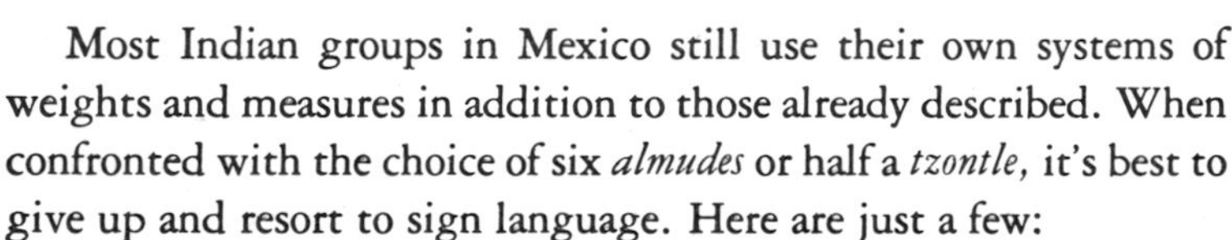

Most Indian groups in Mexico still use their own systems of weights and measures in addition to those already described. When confronted with the choice of six *almudes* or half a *tzontle,* it's best to give up and resort to sign language. Here are just a few:

carga—42 kilos
almud—3.5 kilos
fanega—12 *almudes*
cuartillo—1/4 *almud*
yankabal—one meter

borcelana—large cup (1/2 kg. corn) or small cup (1/4 kg. corn)
quartilla—8 borcelanas
tzontle—400 corn ears
xiquipil—25 *tzontles*
maquila—5 liters

•Because Mexican foods are seldom treated with artificial coloring agents and preservatives, the customer must learn to judge the ripeness. A papaya vendor will ask you, "*¿Para hoy?*" (For today?) or "*¿Para mañana?*" (For tomorrow?). Other commonly used terms are *madura* (mature, ripe) and *tierna* (tender, soft). A coconut that is *tiernito,* for example, is one with tender meat inside rather than hard. (The diminutive ending -*ito* means it's really soft.) *Suave* and *suavecito* (soft, smooth) are also commonly heard.

Once untreated foods reach maturity, they go quickly. When a vendor says that something is ripe be prepared to eat it immediately. Large bunches of bananas, for example, all seem to ripen on the same day and begin rotting on the next. Banana bread is the answer (see *Recipes*).

Overripe fruit is not considered rotten or at all inferior by most Mexicans. To gringos, however, a melon or pineapple that is judged to be *bien bien madura* (well matured) may appear downright soggy. The wise shopper will buy some produce that is ready for immediate eating and some that isn't, for tomorrow.

•Waste not, want not: Smaller stores and markets have yet to adopt prepackaging to the point where you must buy a tube of six tomatoes in order to get one (all you need and want) or two pounds of dry pasta to make a single serving of spaghetti. Many stores will even break open packages to sell a single razor blade, a couple of cigarettes or a *peso's* worth of saltines. This makes it easier to avoid over-buying. When you just need a small amount don't be afraid to ask for it. Many foods are deliberately packaged in small jars, cans, bags or boxes. This not only keeps the individual price tp within a poor person's means, but eliminates left-overs, an important consideration for those who do not have refrigerators.

•Plastic bags: *Bolsas de plástico* are proliferating in Mexico like some sort of modern plague. They drift across the countryside, hanging up on cactuses, fluttering and flapping until a curious burro mistakes them for a snack.

When any other container is not available, a plastic bag will be used. Do you need a few ounces of grain alcohol to see you through the day? Sack it up! Large orange juice? Into the bag for just a small additional charge. Flavored ices, sliced fruit, dried paint powders, coffee, honey, milk, bulk cough syrup, cloth, birdseed and—why not?—a sack of baby chicks to take to the *rancho*. When it rains a plastic bag makes a fine hat and a full raincoat for the kids. If it gets deep, buy two more and wear them for boots.

•When buying produce keep in mind that to Mexicans big is beautiful—and therefore more expensive. Large tomatoes and potatoes, for example, will cost more per *kilo* than equally tasty smaller ones.

Produce is not only sold by the piece but also by the part: a quarter of a cabbage, a slice of melon, half of a papya, etc. Many stalls offer plastic sacks stuffed with grated cabbage, carrot, onion and radish: a pre-mixed salad; just buy a lime and squeeze. You'll also see bags of assorted raw vegetables for soups. Buying portions or bags of produce can make shopping much easier and cut down on waste.

•Hard-nose shopping will save you money but it can also backfire, particularly if you want to save money and eat well at the same time. Beans, for example, vary in price depending on age and quality. The cheaper beans are often last year's crop, tough, require long cooking (more fuel), not as tasty and proably not as nutritious as the more expensive ones. The expensive beans are still cheap but considering the factors previously mentioned, they become even more of a bargain than you might have first thought.

Child Labor

While shopping you may be approached by children who will offer to assist you with your bundles, "*¿Ayudo? ¿Ayudo? ¿Ayudo?...*" (Help?). Most of these kids hardly look able to carry a sack of bread. Your first tendency will probably be to say, "No!" or to ignore them.

Before you do, however, don't forget that your shopping bag will get heavier by the minute. When your shoulders start to ache and your feet are swelling, it's time to remember that Mexicans consider these kids to be as normal a service as using a shopping cart or hiring a cab. No self-respecting affluent housewife would carry her own groceries.

These children can serve a better purpose, however, than just acting as bearers. They will guide you to the best bargains (they want a tip and won't get it from the vendors), search out foods you can't seem to find, teach you a little Spanish and anything else they can think of to please you. The money saved as the result of this advice will pay for their services.

Restrooms

Permanent market buildings are equipped with restrooms, most of which aren't places you'd care to visit except out of real necessity. They are usually located near rear loading docks. Ask for *sanitarios, excusados, baños* or *mingatoria* (pisser). The fee to take a piss is very small and not much more if you want paper, usually enough to cover the palm of your hand.

STORES

The average shopping trip in Mexico often turns into a snipe hunt. You go directly to the marketplace and load up two bags of fresh vegetables and fruit. A piece of beef would be nice, but there was something about the meat stalls along one dark wall that...well, there's always a butcher shop nearby, one with better air circulation. You dash across the street, arms straining, deftly avoiding speeding handcarts loaded with crates of carrots, bulging sacks of grain that seem to stagger by on legs of their own and cargo trucks that back up carelessly to the loading docks.

Without once slipping on the assortment of discarded fruit peels and blackened lettuce leaves, you cross the street. After side stepping an old man sitting Buddha-like next to half a dozen scrawny chickens you duck into the doorway of a small *tienda,* a grocery store. At first it appears that there's a run on the stock, but after a minute or so you realize that it is just the general confusion of impatient customers and harried clerks.

"Give me two kilos of tar!"

"I would like 17 eggs and fresh ones!"

"Put ten *pesos* of elbow macaroni on my bill!"

"I want a razor blade and two aspirin!"

You manage to buy your rice and candles in less than ten minutes. You call out "*¡Gracias!*" and slip back outside, pocketing the change. There's a shop selling fresh chicken a few doors away, not too crowded so you forget about steak and buy a fryer instead.

"Don't you want the feet?" The lady wielding the cleaver asks, raising her eyebrows in surprise. You tell her to keep them—and the head, too—and push back onto the sidewalk. By the time you locate the bakery your shoulders are sagging. Did it use to be this exhausting at Safeway?

•For translations of food terms and more information and advice on specific items please turn to *The Shopping List* later in this chapter.

Tiendas

To find things that are not available in the market place, you'll almost always go to small grocery stores, called *tiendas*, that stock everything from fresh capers to firewood. *Tiendas* are everywhere but those with the best selection and prices are usually found near the market place and central *plaza*.

Many *tiendas* serve multiple functions, especially in small towns where the most prosperous store owner is also the local government, bootlegger or professional man (or all three). He is assisted in his duties by a confusion of relatives, friends and loungers.

Like the popular image of the American general store, with its group of local characters seated around a glowing potbelly stove, the *tienda* also serves as a social center. Instead of a stove, the gossiping is done around the beer cooler.

One of the most enjoyable ways to learn Spanish is to find a nice neighborhood *tienda* and become one of the loungers that use it as a headquarters. Sit on a rough wooden bench or a sack of dried corn with your soda or beer and watch the neighborhood file in and out for their daily purchases. Before long, you'll be an accepted fixture, included in the jokes and conversations and turned to for authoritative comment should the topic under discussion drift outside of Mexico.

After you've spent some time sitting in the corner, sipping your warm drink and saying, "*¡Buenos días!*" about 100 times a day, you'll notice something very important: much of the stock isn't in plain view. Customers frequently ask for whatever they want. The owner reaches under the counter, into a bag, box or can or disappears into the back room to produce the item requested. It may be something quite startling: a leg of venison, a car muffler or an umbrella. Always ask, even though you are *almost* sure that they won't have what you are looking for.

Produce and eggs are more expensive in the *tienda* than in the market. This is because the store owner isn't paying much less for these items than you would. The quality of fresh food is often poorer; the owner is reluctant to throw anything to the pig unless it absolutely can't be sold.

Bartering does go on in *tiendas,* but it's not common. You might try to get the price lowered if the item is damaged or spoiled, but in general the owner sets the price.

Prices vary between these stores, sometimes dramatically. Most have regular clients and a good customer will stop in a favorite *tienda* even though it might cost a bit more than in another place.

Conasupo

The Mexican government provides an alternative to shopping in private stores by operating its own *tiendas*, called *CONASUPO* (which is the name of the agency: *Compañia Nacional de Subsistencias Populares).*

Conasupo stores were originally designed to handle basic staples at controlled prices. Their success, however, has led them to expand into *ConaSupers*, offering a much larger variety of goods. In areas too remote or thinly populated to make a permanent store practical, the govenment dispatches mobile *Conasupos*, usually a large stake truck or semi trailer rig. Tourists may also shop in these travelling stores. Considering that stocks are limited, it would be polite to buy only what you absolutely need. Local people may rely on the *Conasupo* for their only relief from beans, *tortillas* and Coca Cola.

Prices are almost always lower in a *Conasupo* than in any other store. Their stock, however, often varies greatly from one week to the next and from one store to another. Most things are either the cheapest available or major brands packaged under the *Conasupo* label.

These stores are privately managed under a franchise basis, much like the government regulated gas stations. This does not prevent them from keeping bureaucratic hours, closing on Sundays and holidays and for obscure reasons which escape prediction. Because of the substantial amount of money that can be saved in a *Conasupo*, it is worth the effort to locate them and learn their hours. They are often found near the market.

Supermarkets

The term *supermercado* is loosely applied to any store that allows you to pick groceries off the shelves yourself. The so-called supermarket may be nothing more—or even less—than a large *tienda*, or it may have a cash register, bag boys, free cups of coffee and Musac.

Supermarkets are becoming relatively common, especially in large cities and tourist towns. The biggest are veritable shopping malls, offering everything from sporting goods, clothing, drugs, hardware and books to furniture; not to mention food and drink too: fresh seafood, imported wines, smoked ham, cheeses, cold beer, canned frog legs and other staples.

Prices for fresh food are almost invariably higher in a *super* than in the marketplace. Canned foods, dry goods and booze, however, may be a better bargain. Sales are often run; look for signs saying *"OFERTA," "GANGA"* or *"ESPECIAL."*

I always make one reconnaissance pass by the cheese and packaged meat section; they frequently give away tasty samples. Samples are also offered if you appear to be interested in a particular cheese.

Prices are usually marked, but check them closely if you're in doubt, especially if the item is imported or could be considered a delicacy. A small can of smoked salmon, for example, may cost as much as an entire cartload of groceries. Wealthy Mexicans love to splurge and the prices they pay for treats can be absolutely astounding.

Most supermarkets do not allow shoppers to carry bags (other than purses) into the store. Look for a check stand near the entrance. The person behind the counter will keep your things while you shop. They usually issue a claim ticket or marker.

It is customary to tip bag boys if they help you beyond the check-out stands.

•For a sampling of actual prices see *Appendices: Prices.*

THE SHOPPING LIST

Alfalfa	***Alfalfa:*** Fresh alfalfa is popular in mixed juices. Alfalfa seeds are sprouted for ornament, but almost all are chemically treated and should not be eaten.
Allspice	***Pimienta gorda***
Almonds	***Almendras***
Aluminum Foil	***Papel aluminio:*** Supermarket
Anatto	***Achiote***
Anise	***Anís***
Apples	***Manzanas:*** The best are imported from the U.S. and very expensive.
Apricots	***Chabacanos, chavacanos***
Artichokes	***Alcachofas***

Asparagus — ***Espárrago***

Avocado — ***Aguacate:*** Avocados were cultivated by the Aztecs and were believed to be an aphrodisiac. Judging from some people's reaction to *guacamole* salad this may well be true.

Avocados come in many shapes and sizes, from plum-like to as fat as grapefruits to long crooked-neck types. Some varieties have paper thin skins that are eaten along with the pulp. This type is preferred for a favorite Mexican snack: smeared like butter on bread or *tortillas*, then doused with lime juice and a pinch of salt.

The price of avocados is relatively high due to the export market to the U.S. They tend to be cheaper in late summer, when backyard trees begin to produce. I once met a traveller who claimed to live on nothing but avocado sandwiches: cheap and nourishing.

Baby Food — ***Alimento infantil:*** American brands of baby food are sold in supermarkets. Many types of baby food and formulas are available in drugstores.

Baking powder — ***Polvo para hornear:*** More commonly known by the brand name ***Royal.***

Baking soda — ***Bicarbonato sódico, bicarbonato de sodio*** or ***de sosa.***

Banana — ***Plátano*** or ***banana:*** There are several types, including one that must be cooked, ***platano macho.*** Stalks of bananas (***racino***) are sold in roadside stands in the lowlands. Always ask what type of bananas they are to avoid accidentally buying ***machos.*** The ***Colima*** is an average banana, ***Tabascos*** are large and ***Dominicos*** are quite small, what we call 'finger' bananas. A very sweet and plump reddish purple variety is called ***platano morado.***

In Yucatan, bananas are called ***manzanas*** or ***manzanos.*** Since ***manzana*** means apple in the rest of Mexico, this often leads to confusion.

Basil — ***Albahaca, albahacar***

Bay leaves — ***Laurel***

Beans — ***Fríjol:*** The word for cooked beans, *frijoles*, is often mistakenly used by gringos for dry beans. Beans have been cultivated in Mexico for about 7,000 years, so it's not surprising that there are so many types and ways of preparation. Mexicans rate beans according to subtle differences and preferences that are difficult for a gringo to detect or appreciate. In some areas, for example, black beans are considered to be *corriente* (common, mediocre) while in southern Mexico and the Yucatan they are preferred over all others. White navy type beans (***fríjol blanco***), thought to be ordinary in the U.S., are reserved for special occasions in Mexico.

The most common beans (other than black beans) are ***Bayo*** or ***Bayo Gordo***, similar to kidney beans, and ***Flor de Mayo*** (May Flower). The *Flor de Mayo* costs more but has a tendency to break down if cooked too long. Another tasty variety is called ***Ojo de Liebre*** (Hare's Eye).

When shopping for beans avoid *fríjol viejo* (old beans). This is last year's crop, tougher, takes longer to cook and not so flavorful as *fríjol nuevo* (new beans). When two apparently identical bins of beans are different in price, the cheaper will be *viejo*.

Always clean beans thoroughly before cooking and watch for small stones, even in packaged beans. (See *Recipes*.)

If you don't have the time or the patience to cook whole beans you might like to try instant, ***fríjol instantaneo***. With a bit of practice it is possible to turn this unappetizing brown dust into quite tolerable *refritos*. Look for boxes of instant beans in the supermarket. A good emergency food.

(See *Lima beans* and *Garbanzos*.)

Bean sprouts — ***Nacidos:*** Available in some health food stores, but if you eat them often plan to grow your own. (See *Recipes*.)

Beef — ***Carne de res:*** See *Mea..*

Beets — ***Betabeles, remolacha***

Bell pepper — ***Pimienta, pimienta dulce:*** A Mexican chili, *chile poblano*, is often confused by gringos with bell peppers. (See *Chilies*.)

Berries — ***Frambuesas, fresas*** and ***fresas del monte*** are commonly used to describe various berries, whether accurate or not.

Black pepper — ***Pimienta negra:*** Sold in tiny cellophane packets in *tiendas*. Peppercorns are ***pimientas***. They are sometimes sold in bulk. Cans and small bottles of ground pepper are found in the supermarket.

Bleach	***Blanqueador*** or ***cloro***
Bouillon	***Cubitos de Maggi*** (brand name) or just ***cubitos:*** Chicken bouillon cubes are as common in Mexico as *tortillas.* Beef bouillon is scarce and plain tomato is becoming very popular. Cubes are sold individually, in boxes, cans and plastic jars.
Bread, Bakeries	***Pan, Panaderías***

Many tourists are pleasantly surprised to find that although *tortillas* are a staple food, *pan* (bread) is also common and very good. *Panaderías* (bakeries) can be found in almost every town.

Bolillos (french style rolls) are the most common type of bread. Most other baked goods, regardless of their appearance, are slightly sweet. Ask, "*¿Es dulce?*" (Is it sweet?). *Panaderías* generally bake only in the morning and offer fresh things in the early afternoon. It's best to be there just after the baking has been done or you may go without. They rarely prepare more than can be quickly sold that same day. Other than American style products, baked goods do not contain preservatives and should be eaten within a day or two.

Shopping in a *panadería* is very simple; just grab a tray or basket and a pair of tongs and select more than you can possibly eat. Baked goods are very cheap.

Some bakeries prepare special things on certain days of the week. *Empanadas* are a favorite. They are made by cooking a tart-like shell of dough filled with fresh fruits, vegetables, fish or meat.

At fairs, carnivals and *fiestas* you'll see vendors selling an incredible variety of special cookies, breads and cakes. Those that aren't sold will be repacked and taken to another town. This is why most of these baked goods look a hell of a lot better than they taste. Free samples are frequently offered to passersby, which is probably a mistake on the vendor's part.

Bimbo is the trademark for a variety of baked goods that are faithful imitations of the stuff manufactured in the U.S. Their sliced bread probably has even less food value than it does flavor. *Bimbo's pan integral* is a feeble attempt at whole wheat. Other products include *bollos* (hamburger buns) and *medianoches* (hot dog buns, 'midnights').

A better mass produced bread bearing the unfortunate brand name of *Filler*, tastes like a cross between rye and pumpernickel.

A delicious french style bread, *pan francés*, is baked in the Yucatan.

Broccoli	***Brécol*** or ***brócoli***
Brussels sprouts	***Col de Bruselas***
Butter	***Mantequilla:*** see *Dairy products.*
Cabbage	***Col*** or ***repollo***

Cactus

Nopales, nopalitos: The young leaves of the nopal cactus are a very popular food in Mexico. They are sold fresh in the market cleaned of their spines. Canned *nopalitos* are available in supermarkets and *tiendas*.

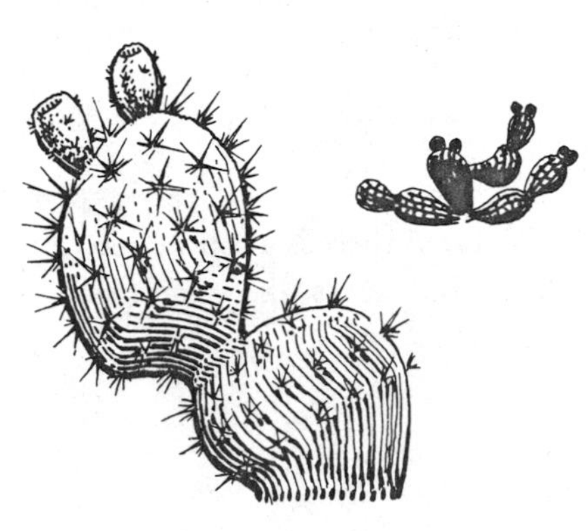

The fruit of the nopal is also an importan food, especially to those who live in arid areas and cannot afford imported fruits ***Tunas*** (also known as ***higo de nopal, higo de chumbo, chumbos*** and ***xoconostli***) come in a variety of colors, including yellow, green, red and purple, the most common The fruits are covered with tiny hair-like spines that must be removed with a sharp knife before eating. Anyone who has tried to eat a *tuna* complete with spines (me) can testify that it is a painful experience. The flavor, a tasty sweet-sourness, is very refreshing. The fruit is high in vitamins and mineral salts.

Tunas are widely used in candies, *agua fresca* (flavored water) and ices.

The ***pitahaya*** is a similar fruit from another type of cactus. It is reddish purple with spines.

Cactus fruits have a lot of seeds inside; they are swallowed or spit out, depending on how hungry you are.

Cake mixes

Harina preparada para pasteles

Camomile

Manzanilla: Té de manzanilla is a classic Mexican drink. It is widely used to calm upset nerves and stomachs. Sold everywhere in tea bags, bulk dried and fresh.

Candles

Velas: Very ornate candles are sold in funeral parlors and coffin shops (often a lumberyard). They make interesting souvenirs. Real beeswax candles can sometimes be found in *tianguis* (Indian markets). Candle lanterns of glass and tin are sold in and around the marketplace.

Candy

Dulces: Sold individually and in bulk. A Mexico City newspaper warned parents that caramel eating was a sure sign of drug addiction. Be careful. (See *Restaurants and Typical Foods: Junkfood.*)

Cantaloupe	***Melón:*** This word is used for all types of melon except *sandias*, watermelons. The peak of the harvest is mid to late spring, when cantaloupe lovers are struck with melon madness.
Capers	***Alcaparrones:*** Sold in bulk in most large *tiendas*.
Caraway seeds	***Semillas de Alcaravea***
Cardamom	***Cardamomo***
Carrot	***Zanahoria***
Cashew	***Marañon***
Catsup	***Salsa de tomate catsup:*** In Yucatan there is a concoction called ***Catzuut*** that looks like catsup but tastes like mincemeat pie.
Cauliflower	***Coliflor***
Celery	***Apio***
Celery salt	***Sal de apio:*** Supermarket
Cereals	***Corn flakes:*** Dry breakfast cereals are sold by their English names. The most common cooked cereals are oatmeal (***ojuelas de avena***) and Cream of Wheat (***crema de trigo***). Read the cooking directions carefully; many people make *atole*, a watery drink, from these cereals.
Chayote	***Chayote:*** This vegetable looks like a hairy squash. They are vaguely obscene in appearance but taste great. (See *Recipes*.)

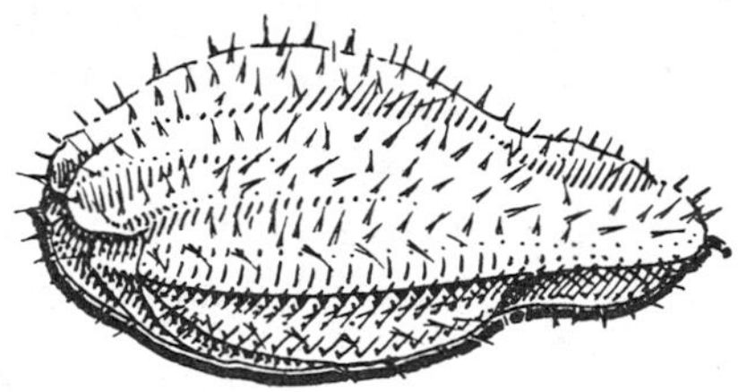

Cheese	***Queso:*** See *Dairy products*.
Cherries	***Cerezas:*** There is a small native cherry called ***capulín***.
Chervil	***Perifollo***
Chia seeds	***Chia, semillas de chia:*** Chia seeds are used in breads, candies, *agua fresca* (freshwater drinks) and medicinally for diarrhea and to calm upset stomachs. *Chia* was used as a quick energizing food by the Aztecs and is being rediscovered by modern day athletes and hikers. One or two teaspoonsful is said to be a hefty portion. portion.

When mixed with liquids the seeds produce a sticky gelatin that is soothing to the digestive tract. This gelatin is so thick that I once plugged a soda bottle by dropping in a teaspoonful of chia seeds.

Chia is also known in English as the lime leaved sage.

Chick peas — See *Garbanzo beans*.

Chicken

Chicken and turkey are prized by Mexicans and most private *fiestas* and celebrations require the sacrifice of at least a few birds. If you want to give someone a simple gift and can't imagine what they'd appreciate, try a chicken, dead or alive. You'll probably be invited to help eat it.

Dressed poultry is sold in meat markets and in small shops specializing in birds and eggs. Live birds can be purchased in and around the market place, but it takes an astute type to avoid getting something old, skinny or tough as rubber. Bartering with *campesinos* for a hen or rooster requires skill; it helps if your Spanish is good enough to say, "His wattles look a little pale."

A few shops sell live birds at fixed rates. The first time I visited one of these I noticed that a nice impersonal, already plucked chicken was displayed on the counter. It lay 'in state' on an attractive bier of shaved ice, surrounded by sprigs of bright green parsley. It looked good.

"I'll take that *pollo*," I said to the man behind the counter.

He looked at me for a few moments. "A chicken *like* that one?" he answered.

I hesitated. There was a row of wooden cages behind him, crowded with live chickens, clucking and cackling contentedly. Some sort of minor egg laying operation, I assumed.

"Sure, like that one," I said.

With no further comment he stepped to a nearby cage, flipped open the door and grabbed a startled chicken by the neck. Before I could protest he turned the squawking bird upside down and jammed it, head first, into a metal cylinder mounted on the wall. The cylinder ended in a funnel-like device. The instant the bird's head came out of the opening, the man drew a razor sharp knife across it's throat.

There was a crimson spurt of blood, neatly funneled into a metal trough already running with water, and a final frantic rustling. With equal efficiency he removed the chicken, stripped off the feathers and reduced it to a cut fryer in a few strokes of his cleaver.

"Just like that one," he smiled, nodding toward the peacefully resting display bird. I took the body and hurried away; other customers were waiting their turn.

Pollo (chicken) is sold whole and then cut up upon request (make hacking motions with your hand). Some vendors also sell individual parts, usually for about the same price per kilo as an entire bird. These parts are *pechuga* (breast), *pierna* (thigh and drumstick), *alas* (wings), *hígado* (liver) and *cabeza* (head). If you don't want the feet and head to eat, take them anyway and bestow them upon some beggar; they'll be delighted.

A chicken that has a golden tone to the skin is considered superior to a pale bird. A ***pollo de oro*** (gold chicken) usually gets that way by being fed marigold flowers rather than by lounging around in the sun or eating an especially good diet.

Pollo de leche (milk chicken) is for frying or broiling.

Chilies

Chilies are a very important food in Mexico. A fresh ***chile*** is an excellent source of vitamin C and minerals. They are popularly believed to stimulate the appetite and improve digestion, at least when eaten in moderate amounts.

Mexicans take their *chile* fresh, dried, pickled, cooked or raw in sauces, stews, soups, desserts (*capirotada*), mixed drinks, with fruit and in a variety of ways for medicinal purposes. The ways of preparing and eating chilies are as numerous as the types: chilies have the ability to cross-fertilize themselves, making the variations infinite.

Contrary to popular belief, chilies are not peppers. They are actually Capsicums. Columbus made the initial error in identification when he spotted what he thought was a pepper in Haiti.

Chilies are not only a source of food and vitamins, but play an important role in Mexican humor. *Chile* is synonomous with penis and the jokes are limitless. A classic song *La Llorona*, the Weeper, has gradually evolved verses far spicier than the original:

"Soy como chile verde Llorona,
Picoso pero sabroso."

"I'm like the green chili Weeper,
Hot but tasty."

A brand of canned chilies is called "*El Lloron*"; the label shows a Mexican *charro* (cowboy) biting a large chili as tears stream down his face. The double meanings are as interwoven as a basket.

•General chili lore: The tip of the chili is the coolest part. A particular type of chili can vary greatly in spiciness depending on what stage of growth it was picked at and the conditions it was grown under (temperature, humidity, etc.). One *poblano* in a batch of *chiles rellenos* might go down as easily as a bell pepper while the next will snap your neck.

To impress your friends without searing the skin from the throat, bite off the whole chili just above the stem and quickly move it to the rear molars. Use only the back teeth to keep the hotness away from sensitive taste buds in the front of your mouth and tongue.

Now chew it up quickly, with great ecstatic smacking sounds, and swallow. If you did it correctly the burning sensation will be within tolerable limits. Your friends will be impressed and want to match your feat.

A chili can be cooled by removing the seeds and veins. When using them for cooked dishes or sauces, try soaking the chilies in hot milk or water first; they should cool down even more.

A pinch of salt taken on the tip of the tongue and allowed to dissolve before eating a *chile* will raise a protective coating of saliva that helps resist burning.

A person who has overdosed on chili is *enchilado(a).* The symptoms are a noisy, desperate sucking of air, head thrown violently backwards, copious sweating, runny nose, and hands clawing at the throat or groping frantically for water. There is no certain cure, but the symptoms can be relieved by eating salt and bread. If this isn't sufficient, try sugar, then milk, sodas and/or beer. Mexicans purse their lips when *enchilados* and inhale forcefully.

For chili in the eyes (I won't bother to describe the agony) immediate and liberal washing with cold water is advised. Lightly rubbing or brushing human hair over the eyes will also give relief.

Cooks often get chili burns on their fingers. This doesn't sound serious unless you get a genuine case of fingers *enchilados.* I once spent three hours with my hands in a bucket of ice water after cleaning a large number of fresh *jalapeños.* It felt like an acid burn. The Mexican women I was helping almost fainted from laughter; their ribald comments got downright boring.

Chilies are *picante* (spicy hot) and not *caliente* (warm, hot temperature). "*¡Sí, pica!*" means "Yes, it bites! It's hot!" *Picoso* is also commonly heard in place of *picante.*

Poblano A reasonably mild dark green chili, 4 to 5 inches long. It is preferred above all others for making *chile rellenos. Poblanos* are what I call a 'Mexican bell pepper'; compared to others they are downright cool. When dried the poblano is called an ***ancho.***

Jalapeño The most commonly canned and pickled chili. Up to 2 inches long, fat and meaty, and tolerable to scorching. Often sold in bulk in *tiendas.* A favorite Mexican snack consists of a fresh *bolillo* with a pickled *jalapeño* stuffed inside. *Jalapeños en escabeche* (pickled) should be stored in a glass container. *Jalapeños rellenos* are stuffed, usually with mackerel or shrimp, and canned. *Rajas de jalapeños en escabeche* are strips of chili without seeds. They make excellent tidbits for those not up to biting into a whole one.

Fresh *jalapeños* will be green, yellow or reddish.

Dried and smoked *jalapeños* are called ***chipotles.*** They are fairly mild and have an excellent flavor. Canned *chipotles* are also tasty.

Serrano Smaller and thinner than *jalapeños* and preferred by Mexican cooks for sauces, *guacamole* and *ceviche.* Red or green and quite hot, with a sharper bite than *jalapeños.* They are often served fresh in restaurants. Start with a tiny nip off the small end. *Serranos* are commonly prepared *en escabeche.* When buying canned peppers try the tiniest size of both *jalapeños* and *serranos*; most gringos prefer the former.

Habanero The dreaded and deadly Yucatan killer, known by the Mayans as 'crying tongue.' The hottest chili in Mexico and not one to fool with lightly. A piece the size of a pea will transform your soup into liquid fire. I once overdosed on *habaneros* in a small restaurant in Quintana Roo. I fainted right into my plate of food.

I like to keep some around to offer friends who brag they can eat anything. Instant humility.

Bottled sauces made with *habaneros* are popular in Yucatecan restaurants. Handle with care.

Habaneros are red, green and yellow and generally small.

Chile del árbol The 'tree chili' is small, green or red and quite hot. They are sometimes offered fresh in restaurants.

Piquín Also known as ***tipín.*** Quite small (berry sized), quite hot and red in color.

Güero The 'blonde' is a light green or yellow, similar in shape and size to a *poblano* and hotter. They are sometimes used as a substitute for *poblanos* when preparing *chile rellenos.* Seasonal.

Cambray Small, green or red and quite hot.

Guajillo Long, narrow and light red. Mild.

Chiltepiquin Small, green and very hot.

Chile negro Also called ***chilaca.*** It is long and dark and hot. Dried it is called ***pasilla.***

Ancho Dried *poblano;* very popular for sauces. Not too hot.

Chipotle Dried, smoked *jalapeños.*

Pasilla	Dried *chile negro (chilaca).*
Cascabel	Two to three inches long, dry, red and medium hot. Excellent for hot sauces. (See *Recipes.*)
Chili powder	***Chile molido:*** Many types of chilies are dried and ground, but for all-purpose use the *cascabel* and *ancho* are best. The *ancho* isn't as hot as the *cascabel.* Both blend well into sauces. ***Pipian*** is a ground mixture of squash seeds, cornmeal and *chile.* ***Chile molido con especias*** is like the ground chili sold in the U.S. Various ground chilies are sold in bulk in the market; when in doubt ask for a taste before buying.
Chili sauce	***Salsa picante:*** Bottled hot sauces of various types and blends of *chiles* are very common. Try local concoctions, some are quite memorable. Canned sauces of chopped chilies and other ingredients are also very good. Our favorite is called *salsa casera* (homemade sauce). It is reasonably spicy and inexpensive.
Chinese parsley	***Cilantro*** or ***culantro:*** Very important in Mexican cooking, particularly soups and sauces. Many people can't stand the stuff.
Chirimoya	***Chirimoya*** (Anona glabra): A greenish fruit that appears to be covered with large scales. The inner pulp is white with many black seeds. Tasty.
Chocolate	***Chocolate:*** A sacred Aztec beverage. Hard chocolate is sold in *tiendas* and the market, cut with crude sugar.
Cigarettes, Cigars	***Cigarros:*** A pack is a ***cajetilla***, a carton is a ***cartón.*** You can buy waterproof cigarettes in Mexico. Dunk one in a glass of water to simulate the rain falling on a farmer's head, then light up. The paper won't burn but the tobacco will—well almost. More conventional cigarettes are also available. U.S. brands made in Mexico include Winston, Salem, Camel Filters, L&M,

Raleigh, Commander and Newport. Mexican brands are cheaper, some of the more common are *Fiesta, Baronet, Del Prado* and *Record.* Non-filters are even cheaper: *Alas, Casinos* and *Delicados.* And cheaper yet are *Faros* (Lighthouses), worth the price just for the picture on the package.

Both *filtros* and *sin filtros* (non-filtered) come regular and *mentolado.*

Cigars (*puros*) are good and relatively inexpensive but common only in larger towns. Very crude cigars are sold in Indian markets. The classic coffin nail.

Cinnamon

Canela: Sold in powder (*molida*) and stick form (*canela en rama*). Very common.

Cloves

Clavos de especia are whole cloves and ***clavos molidos*** are ground. If you ask for just *clavos*, the word for nails, that's what you'll get.

Cocoa

Chocolate: The chocolate that comes in cakes is excellent. ***Chocomíl*** (flavored powdered milk) is very popular but don't be misled by the name; it comes in flavors other than chocolate: *Chocomíl de fresa* (strawberry), *de vainilla*, etc.

Coconut

Coco: Sold dried and shredded in supermarkets. Much better quality coconut is available in the market and from street vendors. All you need is a straw—to drink the *agua* (water, not milk as we call it)—and a shredder. Whole *cocos* are sold throughout Mexico, usually pared down to the hard inner shell. If you don't want a whole one just ask for *carne* (meat).

Cocos that are grown especially for drinking are *coco de agua.*

Coffee

Café: Many large stores grind coffee beans. If the beans are very dark and shiny, they have been coated with sugar. Ask for *café sin azúcar* or *café estilo americano* if you want sugarless coffee. Have it ground *regular.* Coffee that has been ground *fino* is like flour and will go through a perculator. Instant coffee is called by the most common brand name, *Nescafé.* The best buy in instant coffee is the *Conasupo* house brand, said to actually be *Nescafé.*

Coffee is sold in one pound cans, almost always ground *regular.* Look for *estilo americano* on the label.

I always stock up on whole bean coffee (cheaper) when heading back to the U.S. Try to give it a taste test before buying a quantity; flavor varies from one area to another. Most large towns have shops that carry fresh beans from around the country.

When asking for a blend the safest is *export* if you prefer American style.

Coffee is also sold in small packets, just enough to make a couple of cups. It is finely ground and usually mixed with sugar; don't mistake it for instant.

Coffee, canned or in bulk, can legally be imported into the U.S. Don't forget, however, to declare it at Customs.

Cookies — ***Galletas:*** Sold in bulk in *tiendas* and the market. Animal crackers are very cheap when purchased in the handy economical gunnysackfull. Probably not very nutritious but you can make a lot of kids happy. Fancy cookie assortments are sold in supermarkets.

Coriander seeds — ***Semillas de cilantro:*** Fresh coriander (Chinese parsley) is caled ***cilantro*** or ***culantro.***

Corn — ***Maíz***

Corn on the cob — ***Elotes:*** They tend to be tough but tasty. Ask for *tiernito* (tender) and you might get one that is. Try an *elote con todo:* lime juice and chili powder.

A hard dried ear of corn is a ***mazorca.***

Cornmeal — ***Harina de maíz amarilla:*** Supermarket. If you want cornmeal to make *tortillas* see *Masa.*

Cornstarch — ***Maizena,*** the most common brand name.

Crackers — ***Galletas saladas*** (salted cookies): Crackers are very big in Mexico. A favorite snack, available from street vendors and in most *tiendas*, is a saltine doused with bottled hot sauce or a squirt of juice from the pickled *chile* jar.

An excellent and addictive brand of crackers is called ***Pan Cremas.***

Cream — ***Crema:*** See *Dairy Products.*

Cream cheese — ***Queso crema:*** See *Dairy products.*

Cream of tartar — ***Crémor Tártaro***

Cucumber — ***Pepino***

Cumin seeds	***Cominos:*** Indispensable in creating authentically flavored Mexican bean dishes. Most common whole.
Currants	***Grosellas***
Curry powder	***Polvo de curry:*** Supermarket
Custard	***Flan:*** The national dessert; sold as a mix everywhere.

Dairy Products

There have been so many hysterical scare stories about food and drink in Mexico that many tourists approach dairy products (***productos lacteos***) as if they'd been handled by Madame Borgia herself. People who categorically refuse to touch any milk, cheese or cream are not only unrealistic, but putting themselves into the position of not being able to eat much of anything typically Mexican.

Dairy products are perhaps more important to Mexican cuisine than chicken and beef. For many meat is a luxury, but milk (for *café con leche*), cheese (for *enchiladas*) and cream (to pour over strawberries) are vital necessities.

This doesn't mean precautions shouldn't be observed. Unhealthy animals do occur, but they aren't the only reason dairy products can be hazardous at times. A piece of cheese may be perfectly safe until the woman in the market cuts off a slice for you with a knife that hasn't been washed with soap and water for a week. Milk may be contaminated by dirt on the cow, in the milk can, in the cup it is measured out with or by adulteration with impure water.

The Mexican government is attempting to educate people, especially those in rural areas, to handle dairy products with care. This means that a homemade cheese may be made under very hygienic conditions or then again, it may not. It all depends on the awareness and attitude of the person who makes it. Which also means that you can never tell.

When in doubt about any dairy product, cook it well. This should make it safe. The so-called dangerous dairy products are those that have not been carefully pasteurized (cooked) and packaged. You should have no problems at all if you avoid uncooked ranch cheeses and raw milk or cook them yourself. Mexico's dairys and processing facilities are generally modern and sanitary; pasteurized products, from butter to cheeses to yoghurt, can be found in most towns.

Butter	***Mantequilla:*** Sold in *tiendas* and supermarkets in *barras* (sticks, bars). Bulk butter sold in some markets and *tiendas* is usually unsalted and sweet and may not be pasteurized *(pasteurizada)*.
Cheese	***Queso:*** Many cheeses are sold under familiar names: Camembert, Gouda, Parmesan, etc. Mexicans prefer to buy cheese in bulk, rather than packaged. Samples are offered in

Cheese (cont.)

stores that sell cheeses. Just say *"Quiero probarlo"* (I want to try it) and you'll be given a small piece.

Chihuahua cheese is one of the most well known cheeses and also among the best. It was originally introduced by Mormon immigrants, many of whom still live in isolated farming communities in the northern states. *Chihuahua* is pale (Mexican cheeses are rarely dyed) and tastes much like a mild cheddar. When comparing two pieces of *Chihuahua* I prefer the flavor of the darker yellow. This is a good cheese for *tacos, enchiladas,* toasted sandwiches and other cooked dishes. It keeps well, even without refrigeration, though it should be carefully wrapped in brown paper or cloth.

Oaxaca cheese is also very well known throughout the country. It is sometimes called ***quesillo.*** It is a very white cheese, formed into balls about the size of a fist and stringy. It is sometimes shaped into small round cakes and can be confused with ranch cheese. *Oaxaca* cheese that is homemade is cooked. If the vendor handles it properly it should be safe even if not labelled pasteurized. *Oaxaca* is a good substitute for mozzarella.

White or ranch cheese (***queso blanco*** or ***queso del rancho,*** also ***queso ranchero***) is almost always homemade. It is commonly sold in the market, wrapped in fresh green leaves or door-to-door. Much of it is made from goat's milk. Ranch cheese has a crumbly texture and is very white. It is rarely cooked in processing. Ranch cheese should be avoided until it has been well cooked.

Queso amarillo, yellow cheese, is more commonly known by the brand name ***Queso Club.*** I call this stuff rat cheese; compared to *Chihuahua* or *Oaxaca* cheeses it just doesn't seem worth the *pesos*. Kids love it.

Other yellow cheeses are either Mexican cheeses that have been dyed, or imported and very expensive.

Queso suizo, Swiss cheese, is found in larger stores and is both safe and costly.

Queso estilo parmesano or just ***parmesano***, Parmesan, is fairly common and quite good. Much of it is imported from South America. The type sold grated in cans is much more expensive than bulk. It is sometimes called ***queso añejo*** (aged).

Queso crema, cream cheese, is sold in the same bright foil wrappers as in the U.S. It is expensive. An excellent bulk cream cheese, ***doble crema***, is far superior to the packaged variety but not easy to find. It is made in the Uruapan area.

Requesón, cottage cheese, is found in some supermarkets and is expensive.

Cream

Crema, crema dulce: Bulk cream should be avoided unless you intend to cook it. Mexican cream is very thick and sweet, some of it has to be spooned like butter. Pasteurized cream is sold in *tiendas* and supermarkets in small bottles.

A phoney cream is also commonly sold in stores that handle bulk cream. It is cheaper but doesn't taste very good.

Sour cream (***crema ácida*** or ***crema agria***) is sold in supermarkets.

Ice cream

Helado: Ice cream sold in stores should almost always be safe. It is often flavored with fresh fruits and I prefer it over American ice cream. Try combinations like mango and chocolate; they'll drive you mad.

Street ice cream is usually good but you never can tell; few ice cream addicts have enough self control to resist it. When eating street ice cream I purify it by quietly chanting, "Pure! Pure! Pure!" It hasn't failed me yet.

Milk

Leche, leche de vaca: Bottled and carton milk is widely available. The best is produced by Italian dairy families, the descendents of immigrants who came to Mexico around the turn of the century. They still live in Italian style villages and speak an odd dialect of Italian and Spanish. The original village is called Chipilo, also the brand name of their milk.

Raw bulk milk is sold in the market, in the street by wandering vendors carrying galvanized milk cans on their backs or on burros and direct from small farms.

To make raw milk safe bring it slowly to a boil, stirring constantly to avoid scorching. Some people prefer to cook the milk twice, reheating it to the boiling point after it has been allowed to cool. This is far beyond the legal pasteurization limits set by health agencies in the U.S. Milk served in the market in *licuados* is almost always boiled; after all, if their customers get sick, they lose business.

Powdered milk, ***leche entera de vaca en polvo***, is fortunately known more commonly as ***Nido***, a brand name. *Nido* is a very high quality powdered whole milk. A glass of it is said to be more nutritious than a glass of boiled whole milk.

There are two types of *Nido*, regular and instant. The instant has *instantánea* printed in red on the can. It costs a little more, is said to be less nutritious and mixes much more easily than the regular.

When mixing *Nido* remember that the resulting milk will be no more pure than the water used to prepare it.

Condensed milk (***leche evaporada***) is quite common. ***La Lechera*** (Milkmaid) is a heavily sweetened evaporated canned milk. A favorite snack for Mexicans is *Lechera* over saltines. Kids buy the stuff and suck on it like a candy.

Goat's milk (***leche de cabra***) should always be cooked. It is usually made into ranch cheese rather than sold for drinking.

Buttermilk, ***jocoque***, is not common.

Yogurt — ***Yogurt*** or ***Bulgara:*** Becoming very popular in Mexico. It is sold plain (*natural*) or with fruit. See *Recipes* if you prefer to make your own; it's much cheaper.

Date — ***Dátil***

Detergent — ***Detergente***

Dill — ***Eneldo***

Eggs — ***Blanquillos, huevos:*** Buying by the kilo is more economical and for that reason vendors may refuse to sell eggs other than individually. Some *tiendas* have brown eggs, ***huevos rojos*** or ***huevos del rancho*** (red or ranch eggs), but they are more commonly available from little old ladies in and around the market. Eggs often become scarce in the dry season. Ranch eggs cost more than mass produced white eggs but are far superior in taste and food value.

Buying eggs sometimes leads to unexpected complications, which is why *blanquillos* is the preferred word rather than *huevos*. (See *Speaking Spanish*.)

Eggplant — ***Berenjena***

Endive — ***Escarola***

Epazote — Wormseed: The fresh leaves are used for flavoring in soups, *tacos* and beans. This plant has very important medicinal properties. (See *Health*.)

Fennel — ***Hinojo***

Figs	***Higos***
Fish	***Pescado:*** See *Seafood.*
Flyswatter	***Matamoscas***
Flour	***Harina:*** White flour is called ***harina de trigo.*** Wholewheat flour is ***harino de trigo integral, granizo, semitilla*** or ***salbado***, depending on where you buy it. It is commonly sold in *tiendas* for pig food and in this form is most often called ***salbado.*** (*Salbado* should be mixed with white flour.) You can buy whole wheat (***trigo***) in the market and have it ground. *Tortilla* flour is called ***masa harina.*** Some *tortillerías* (tortilla factories) allot one day a week to grinding other types of flour.
Fruits	***Frutas:*** You will undoubtedly discover many strange and tasty fruits while exploring different markets. The names for these are difficult to remember and their translation into English doesn't make it any easier. *Chirmoyas*, for example, are known in Guatemala as *Anonas* and are called both Sour sops and Anonas in English. Eat around, ask questions and take notes. Don't pass something up just because you don't know what it is.
Garbanzo beans chick peas	***Garbanzos:*** Sold fresh in season, in small bags. Try them with chili powder and salt. Dried garbanzos are sold in stores and markets.
Garlic	***Ajo:*** Mexicans eat a great deal of garlic and esteem it for its medicinal properties. (See *Health*.) Garlic is sold by the handful, by the head (*cabeza*) and even by the clove (*diente,* tooth). For the true garlic lover there are beautifully woven chains of garlic (*ristra*). These make great gifts. If you eat as much *ajo* as we do, you'll want to carry a *ristra*, if only a short one, in your suitcase or backpack. Garlic can be taken back into the U.S.
Garlic salt	***Sal de ajo:*** Supermarket.
Ginger	***Jengibre:*** Ground ginger is sold in supermarkets; fresh can sometimes be found in the market, but don't count on it. We always bring some from home.
Grapefruit	***Toronja***
Grapes	***Uvas:*** Mexico produces a quantity of grapes, most of which are converted to brandy and wine, far more civilized than making jellies and juice. The grape season is late summer to fall, at other

times they are expensive. Pale green grapes are called ***blancas*** (white) and dark grapes are ***negras*** (black).

Fresh squeezed grape juice (***jugo de uva***) is available in grape growing areas during the harvest.

Greens — ***Quelites:*** Includes a wide variety of green leafy vegetables, many of them gathered wild. Among the most common are ***verdolagas*** (purslane), ***romeritos, tintoniles*** or ***quelites***, a general term that covers many plants with regional names. When in doubt ask how they are prepared.

Green beans — ***Ejotes***

Groceries — ***Abarrotes***

Guava — ***Guayaba:*** This tasty fruit looks very much like a yellow or pink crab apple, but is soft and sweet. It makes good wine.

Herbs — ***Hierbas, Yerbas:*** Herbs and spices (***especías, olores***) are available in most *tiendas* and from vendors in the market place. Some stalls have an amazing variety of fresh herbs and spices, including various medicinal teas.

Imported spices from the U.S. as well as U.S. brands made in Mexico are sold in most supermarkets.

The best way to find spices is to ask for them. Many are sold in bulk or fresh and are not easily recognizable. A *tienda* often has several types of spices in tiny cellophane bags and others growing in the back yard. It is common to see people ask for a particular spice in a *tienda* and then wait while the woman of the house scrounges through her garden to see if the plant can be trimmed for the customer.

Hibiscus — ***Jamaica:*** The dried flowers are sold in bulk in *tiendas* and the market. They make an excellent tea or *agua fresca*; very refreshing.

Honey — ***Miel de abeja:*** The Yucatan is famous for its honey, most of which is sold long before it is even harvested. Local honey is available throughout Mexico. It is sold in bulk in some *tiendas* or direct from the beekeeper. Take your own container.

Honey sold in the market by *campesinos* will vary in color, quality and price. Some people aren't above cutting their honey with cheap sugar. Good honey should be fragrant and clear, though even the best does crystallize.

The word *miel* is a general term for honey, molasses and syrups. When buying honey be sure to specify ***miel de abeja*** (honey of bees). If the label on a jar of honey doesn't say *de abeja*, it may well be molasses.

Jam, Jelly — ***Mermelada, Jalea:*** Btecause sugar is kept cheap in Mexico by government control, the price of jams and jellies is fairly reasonable. The best bargains are in *Conasupos*. Jam lovers will be particularly attracted to types made with tropical fruits.

Jicama — ***Jícama:*** A very popular root vegetable (it grows like a potato) that can be used as a substitute for water chestnuts. It is eaten raw or cooked. Jicamas are a very common street snack: try one peeled and doused with lime juice, salt and chili. The flavor is something like a cross between an apple, pear and potato. Excellent in salads.

Juice — ***Jugo:*** Excellent fresh juices are available in the market, (see *Restaurants and Typical Foods*). Canned juices (***jugo de lata***) are sold everywhere, almost as commonly as Coca Cola. They are cheapest in the *Conasupo*. Try the tropical fruits: *guayaba* and mango are especially good. *Jugo de fresa* (strawberry) is the only one I don't like; it is very sweet.

Bottled fruit juices are sold in *tiendas* and supermarkets. They aren't too expensive and are sometimes on sale in the *super*.

Carton juices, usually orange, are actually just water and flavors. *Anaranjada* (orange colored) is a good description of how they taste.

Lard — ***Manteca de cerdo:*** Sold in bulk by the *peso*. ***Cebo*** is beef lard, i.e., grease.

Lavender — ***Espiliego, lavanda***

Leek — ***Puerro*** or ***poro***

Lemon — ***Lima:*** This word is forever being confused with *limón*, (lime). The yellow lemon used in the U.S. is not common in Mexico. Almost all of the many types of limes and lemons are collectively called ***limones.***

Lemon grass — ***Té de limón:*** Looks like large pieces of grass and makes a very tasty tea. Try a combination with hibiscus.

Lentils — ***Lentejas:*** Good for making sprouts. Clean lentils carefully; even packaged ones are rocky.

Lettuce	***Lechuga:*** Includes both head and Romaine lettuce (***lechuga romana***).
Light bulbs	***Focos:*** Same wattage as in the U.S. and cheapest in the *Conasupo.*
Lima beans	***Habas verdes:*** Usually sold dried. A traditional Lenten soup is made with lima beans.
Lime	***Limón:*** There are sweet limes and sour limes (***limones dulces*** and ***limones agrios***). They may look exactly like a lemon but the taste is definitely lime. The standard lime is small and either green or yellow. Very important medicinally. (See *Health*.)
Macaroni	***Macarrones, fideos, pasta: Fideos*** covers many types of macaroni, from elbows, stars and clams (***codos, estrellas*** and ***almejas***) to a very thin, vermicelli-like noodle that is just called *fideo* or *fideo delgado. Fideos* are very common in Mexican cooking, usually served as a dry soup (*sopa*). Thicker noodles are not too commonly used. The soft Mexican wheat works best in thinner macaroni. Supermarkets sometimes have good quality spaghetti and fettucinni noodles, though they are much more expensive than the average *fideo.* *Fideos* are usually sold by the weight rather than the package.
Mace	***Macis***
Mamey	***Mamey:*** An oval shaped fruit with a brown pebbly skin. The pulp is reddish purple around a large seed and has a very exotic flavor.
Mango	***Mango:*** Whoever introduced the mango to Mexico from the East should be canonized. Mexicans talk of mango season (late spring to fall) in reverent but slightly hysterical tones. In their eager anticipation, in fact, they even eat green mangoes. The hard fruit is speared on a sharp stick, sliced petal-like and covered with lime juice and chili. Slices of similarly garnished mango are sometimes served as snacks in *cantinas.* Never have cheap *mezcal* and *tequila* been more delicately mellowed than with a sour mango. There are more than 500 types of mangoes. The most commonly eaten in Mexico is the *Manila.* The *Manila* is green on the outside or yellow with black spots, depending on its maturity. It is not stringy (coarse varieties are). An average *Manila* is about 4 inches long. They are best when firm. The finest *Manilas* come from Veracruz.

The *Manila de Guerrero* is orange on the inside rather than yellow.

The *Petacón* (from *petaca* - buttock), also known as *Criollo* or *Indio,* brings blissful sighs from mango fanciers. It is big, as the name implies, red to reddish orange, very sweet and not at all stringy. A *Petacón* is large enough to carve, like a small melon.

The latest rage in areas of Mexico where mangoes are grown is the *Tome Arkins.* This mango, perhaps named after some dedicated gringo grower, is even bigger than the *Petacón*, which it resembles.

Another huge mango, as large as a cantaloupe, is called *Kent.* It comes in a range of pastels: pale green, yellow, pink and red. The *Kent* has a dreamy perfume flavor that goes well with sunsets and liqueurs.

In contrast to the big mangoes, there's the tiny *Obo*, sweet but stringy.

•For those not yet indoctrinated into the Mango Mystique, here are a few suggestions:

Don't eat different types at the same sitting or you'll get a gut ache.

Watch our for overripe mangoes; they don't digest well.

Don't try to eat the skin; it's bitter.

Mangoes are best eaten in the nude or wearing a bib and rain gear. Better yet, in fact the absolute best, is to eat them chin deep in the surf, just as the sun is coming up or going down.

Margarine — ***Margarina:*** very common.

Marjoram — ***Mejorana***

Masa harina — *Tortilla* flour: sold everywhere.

Matches — ***Cerillos:*** The Spanish word *fósforo* is rarely used in Mexico.

Mayonnaise — ***Mayonesa:*** A good fake mayonnaise that is much cheaper is called ***aderezo para ensaladas*** (salad dressing).

Meat Shops

A trip to the average ***carnicería*** (meat shop) separates the true carnivores from the vegetarians.

If meat markets were graded as movies are, on the basis of the acts portrayed in them, al those in the U.S. would be rated 'GP' or 'family entertainment.' The average Mexican meat market would get an 'X' rating, 'for hardened adults only.' The one stage of the meat cutting process not usually done before your eyes is the killing.

To select a meat shop (most are actually tiny stalls) use your eyes and nose. The stalls inside the market place itself are frequently the goriest and least appetizing.

Large markets will often arrange the stalls by the type of meat they are selling. Ten stalls in a row will have beef, the next ten pig meat and the rest goat, chicken, etc.

Although the appearance of the raw meat and the shop itself might be disturbing to those unaccustomed to the sight of pig heads lolling from iron hooks or coils of entrails draped like Christmas decorations over the counter, the meat is almost always very fresh. In fact, it is often *too fresh.* When an animal is butchered, it is not hung in a cool room or locker to be aged; it's sold that very day. Unaged meat is tougher and may taste stronger than most tourists are used to.

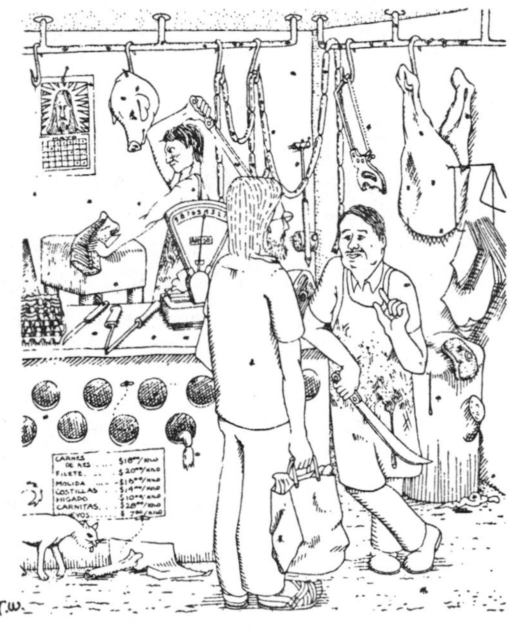

Anyone can become a qualified meat cutter in Mexico as long as they have a strong arm and a big knife. 'Cuts' are made by repeated blows on the meat; when it has reached manageable proportions, it's ready to be sold. Although butchering is more refined in shops that cater to foreigners and particular Mexicans, there are just a few basic cuts: steaks, chops, ground meat and stew meat.

Such things as roasts and t-bone steaks are not used by the average Mexican cook. To get them, you'll have to find a butcher who understands the subtleties of meat cutting or else explain it yourself. This can be very difficult.

My first experience with ordering a specific cut ended in disaster. We were having a birthday feast and decided to splurge with a barbecue. I was elected to buy the meat.

After touring the market and looking over the selection, I finally located a good slab of pork ribs. The butcher weighed the meat, then shoved it over the counter for a closer inspection.

"Perfect," I drooled, "I'll take it."

He picked up the ribs and flipped them onto a large wooden block behind him. Before I realized what was happening, he grabbed a razor-sharp *machete* and dexterously reduced the meat to bite sized pieces.

As the butcher wrapped the ribs in newspaper, I explained that I wanted to have a barbecue, not a stew. His face darkened. Before I could say more, he walked into the rear of the stall and dragged a freshly killed pig from a dark corner.

Fifteen minutes later, after an exhibition of savage meat cutting, he handed me another sizable slab of ribs. "*¡Pedazo entero!*" (whole piece!) he said emphatically, using the words that I could have avoided trouble with in the beginning.

When ordering meat, fish or poultry specify that you want it whole (*pedazo entero, trozo* or *entero*) or it may be chopped up.

Because the distinction between cuts of meat is vague, there is no great value attached to specific pieces and parts. The loin may be ground into hamburger rather than cut into more expensive tenderloin steaks. When you do pay more for a particular piece, the extra cost is small.

Prices are government controlled and should be posted in the shop.

Meat is sold by the *kilo*, but it is more common to order by the amount you wish to spend. The average customer doesn't buy very much; 50 cents worth of stew meat is a typical order. This is an excellent way to shop as you tend to spend less.

To make meat shopping less complicated, buy all of your meat in one place. Tell the butcher how you want it cut; before long, certain cuts will be saved for you, especially if you spend as much money as most gringo carnivores do.

Meat — ***Carne:*** Always specify what kind of meat you want: *carne de res, carne de puerco*, etc.

Bacon — ***Tocino:*** Mexican bacon is delicious. Sliced, it is called ***tocino rebanado.***

Beef — ***Res, carne de res***

Cecina — This is a curing process used on many types of meat. It is spicy but very tasty.

Chop — ***Chuleta: Chuleta de puerco*** is the familiar pork chop. Smoked pork chops are ***chuletas de puerco ahumadas.***

Dog bones — ***Huesos para perros:*** This is just stew meat with bones.

Goat — ***Cabrito:*** Tourists are usually shocked to see cute little goats trussed together by the hind feet and thrown over a man's shoulder or the handlebars of a bicycle. They aren't being sold for pets, either.

Ground meat — ***Carne molida, pulpa:*** Once again, it is important to specify ***de res*** if you want hamburger or you might get ground pork. Unlike American hamburger, Mexican hamburger is made of meat. Ask the butcher to add a bit of *grasa* (fat) to the meat being ground or it may be too lean to make a proper pattie. If the meat is tough, and much of it is, the hamburger will be coarse and pellet-like. Avoid this by asking for *carne de res doble molida* (beef ground twice).

Ham — ***Jamón:*** This usually refers to pressed ham rather than a whole piece of pork.

Organs and innards — As in the U.S., some of the more nutritious meats are also the most inexpensive.

liver	***hígado***	kidneys	***riñones***
heart	***corazón***	brains	***sesos***
tongue	***lengua***	tripe	***tripas***

Lamb — ***Carnero***

Pork — ***Puerco, carne de puerco***

Ribs — ***Costillas:*** About as expensive as pure meat.

Roast — ***Trozo:*** Any word or gesture that communicates 'whole piece' might result in a roast. Some butchers actually recognize the word *rosbif.*

Sandwich meat — ***Carnes frias*** (cold meats): The most common types are pressed ham (***jamón***), ***queso de puerco*** (head cheese) and ***salami.*** Virtually all sandwich meats are made by the *FUD* company. A better brand, when available, is *ZWAN.* They make especially good hot dogs (***salchichas vienés, perros calientes, salchichas coctel*** or just ***ot dog***).

Sausage — ***Salchicha:*** Salami is the only common sausage that does not require cooking. Supermarkets may have locally made sausages or imported. The standard Mexican sausages are ***chorizo*** and ***longaniza.*** Both must be cooked and cheaper varieties are very greasy. *Chorizo* comes in links and *longaniza* is long. They are sometimes quite spicy. Some restaurants and meat shops offer their own *chorizo.* The best are smoked or specially cured and invariably quite tasty. Beans with *chorizo* is excellent.

Steak — ***Bistec*** or ***filete (de res, de puerco,*** etc.): The meat is thinly sliced, usually without a bone. It is almost always pounded flat for tenderizing. If you don't want your steak *aplanada* (flattened), say so immediately or you'll get it that way. Some butchers convert all of their chunks of meat to flattened *bistec* and

	sell almost nothing else. To order a gringo style beefsteak, ask for *bistec de res muy grueso* (very thick—indicate how thick with your fingers). A steak with bone is more commonly referred to as a *chuleta* (chop). Should you order a *chuleta de res*, you'll probably get a rib steak of whatever thickness you indicate.
Stew meat	***Carne para caldo:*** Stew meat is sold *con hueso* or *sin hueso* (with bone or without). It is usually quite tough and stringy.
Tenderloin	***Lomo*** (also ***filete***): This cut costs a bit more but it's usually well worth it.
Veal	***Ternero***
Venison	***Venado:*** Yucatan is famous for its venison. It is often the only meat available in small towns and villages.
Meat tenderizer	***Suavizador*** or ***Ablandedor de carne:*** Supermarkets. Papaya juice is a natural meat tenderizer.
Melon	***Melón:*** A general term used for all melons other than *sandias*, watermelons.
Milk	***Leche:*** See *Dairy products.*
Mint	***Menta*** or ***Yerba buena***
Molasses	***Melaza*** or ***miel de sorgo***
MSG	***MSG*** or ***Glutamato monosódico:*** Supermarket
Mushrooms	***Champiñones*** or ***Hongos:*** The type of fresh mushroom sold in U.S. supermarkets is available in some Mexican markets. *Avoid odd mushrooms*, even those sold in large markets. Canned mushrooms are common.
Mustard	***Mostaza:*** Dry mustard is ***mostaza molida en polvo. Mostaza amarilla*** is prepared in a jar. If you love mustard as much as I do, bring some from home. The common Mexican prepared mustard is vinegary and sharp.
Napkins	***Servilletas***
Noodles	***Fideos:*** Sold in bulk in *tiendas* or packaged in the supermarket. (See *Macaroni.*)
Nopal cactus	***Nopales*** or ***Nopalitos:*** Cactus leaves, flat, thin and broad with the spines carefully shaved off, are sold throughout the country. (See *Cactus* and *Recipes*.)

Nut — ***Nuez*** (plural—***nueces***): Cleaned nuts, salted nuts and nut and seed assortments are sold in grocery and liquor stores. Some are surprisingly inexpensive. Nuts and seeds are excellent travelling food; they keep you occupied and are nice to offer to fellow passengers on buses and trains.

Nutmeg — ***Nuez moscada***

Oil — ***Aceite comestible:*** Bulk cooking oil is sold in *tiendas* by the *peso* or by the measure. It is slightly cheaper if you have your own container; if you don't want to pay the bottle deposit, get it in a plastic bag. Sesame oil (***aceite de ajonjolí***) is very common and costs about the same as other oils. ***Cartamo*** (safflower) is widely available but usually not in bulk.

Olive oil (***aceite de oliva***) is expensive but good. Be very careful that you don't buy ordinary vegetable oil that has been packaged in what looks exactly like an olive oil can or bottle. This unscrupulous packaging is very common.

Olives — ***Aceitunas:*** Green olives with seeds are sold in bulk and are inexpensive. Always taste bulk olives before buying them and be careful to sample one from the jar you are actually given. Crafty owners of roadside stands sometimes save on vinegar by using only water to pack their olives. Others put a layer of cured olives on top and plain ones underneath. Stuffed or pitted olives are very expensive.

Onion — ***Cebolla:*** When buying large onions by the kilo, select those without large green tops or you'll get as much stem as onion. Purple onions are very mild and not as tasty as lighter colored types.

Onion salt — ***Sal de cebolla:*** Supermarket

Oranges — ***Naranjas:*** Oranges are not dyed and they are rarely a bright orange color. A green or yellow orange will be as ripe and sweet as anything painted up for the A & P. Very juicy oranges (***naranjas para jugo***) are sold for squeezing. In Yucatan oranges are called ***chinos.*** Discounts are usually given if you buy them by the dozen or by the *costal* (gunny sack).

Orange Leaf Tea — ***Hojas de naranjo:*** Made of fresh leaves from orange trees.

Oregano — ***Orégano:*** Common in bulk form.

Papaya — ***Papaya:*** To avoid buying an over or under ripe papaya, you can buy just part of one. Most vendors open up a papaya or two to

	show how nice the inside is. Papayas are especially good covered with lime juice and salt. They aid digestion.
Paper plates	***Platos de cartón:*** Supermarket
Paper towels	***Toallas de papel:*** Supermarket
Paprika	***Pimentón dulce***
Parsley	***Perejil, peregil:*** Sold dried and fresh.
Paw Paw	***Papaya***
Peach	***Durazno:*** They tend to be small but tasty.
Peanuts	***Cacahuates:*** Peanuts are priced according to quality. It's usually worth it to buy the best, called ***bolas*** (balls). ***Crillos*** (Creoles)cost much less. They taste good but have a higher rate of rotten nuts and are much smaller. (See *Nuts*.)
Peanut butter	***Crema de cacahuates:*** Supermarket. Bring some if you're hooked; Mexican peanut butter isn't very good.
Pear	***Pera***
Peas	***Chícharos:*** Often tough but they taste good.
Pecan	***Nuez:*** The word *nuez* (nut) covers many nuts, similar to the use of the word *bola* for rounded fruits and vegetables.
Peppers	***Pimientas:*** Chilies are not peppers. (See *Chilies*.)
Peppercorns	See *Black pepper*.
Pet food	***Alimento para perros, gatos*** and ***pajaros:*** Food for dogs, cats and birds is sold in supermarkets, *Purina* stores and veterinary supply stores. Bird food is also sold in *tiendas* and in the market.
Pickles	***Pepinos:*** Supermarket, ***pepinos dulces*** (sweet pickles), ***pepinos agrios*** (dill pickles) and ***picados aderezados*** (pickle relish).
Pineapple	***Piña:*** A ripe pineapple will smell very sweet and aromatic and the inner top leaves should come out with a light tug. Darker skinned pineapples are often sweeter than pale skinned ones.
Pine nuts	***Piñones***
Plum	***Ciruela***
Pomegranate	***Granada***
Popcorn	***Maíz palomero:*** Sold in bulk in *tiendas*. It is called ***palomitas*** (little doves) when already popped.
Poppy seed	***Semillas de amapola:*** Hard to find these days, perhaps because of what they use the rest of the plant for.

Pork	***Carne de puerco:*** See *Meat.*
Potatoes	***Papas:*** Large potatoes cost more than small ones.
Poultry	***Aves:*** See *Chicken* and *Turkey*
Prickly pear	***Tuna:*** See *Cactus.*
Prunes	***Ciruela pasa:*** Many types of dried fruits are sold in bulk in the market, on the street and in *tiendas.*
Pumpkin	***Calabaza***
Pumpkin seeds	***Pepitas***
Purselane	***Verdolagas:*** See *Greens.*
Quelites	Greens
Quince	***Membrillo:*** Makes excellent wine or jelly.
Radish	***Rábano:*** Oaxaca is famous for an Xmas radish *fiesta.* Giant long radishes are common in the south.
Raisins	***Pasas:*** Usually sold in bulk.
Razor blades	***Hojas de afeitar:*** Can buy them individually if you prefer.
Rice	***Arroz:*** Brown rice is very difficult to locate. It is called ***arroz moreno*** and is sometimes available right from the mill (*molino*). When buying rice, get the best. Cheap rice may be old full of rocks and bugs and not very nutritious.
Rosemary	***Romero***
Saffron	***Azafrán española***
Sage	***Salvia***
Salad dressing	***Aderezo para ensaladas***
Salt	***Sal***
Sauerkraut	***Col agria:*** Supermarket
Savory	***Ajedrea***
Seafood	

Most large markets have a ***mariscos*** (seafood) section. It is wise to do your seafood shopping early in the morning, both on the coast and inland. Fish that have been properly iced for shipment will be almost as good as those freshly caught and dressed. During Lent seafood may be sold from the back of trucks. This is the best time of year for the Mexican fisherman.

Fish tastes better and is more nutritious when fresh, but it won't kill you if it's slightly old. Bad seafood smells ghastly, but it all smells slightly. I've seen people sniff a fish and say, "Smells kind of fishy to me, probably no good." What do they want, lilacs?

Abalone	***Abulón: Lapa*** are similar and much more common.
Barracuda	***Barracuda, pecuda***
Catfish	***Bagre, gato***
Clams	***Almejas***
Cod	***Bacalao:*** Usually sold dried and salted. Imported *bacalao* is very expensive.
Conch	***Caracol***
Crab	***Cangrejo*** or ***jaiba:*** Sold live with their claws tied with twine or pieces of grass.
Crayfish	***Langostinas, cucarachas***
Fish	***Pescado:*** A live fish is a ***pez.*** Whole fish is ***pescado entero,*** filets are ***filetes.*** The price of fish is most often for whole uncleaned fish. It will be cleaned free of charge after weighing. Ask them to remove only the guts and gills. A fish will last much longer if the scales, head and fins are left intact. Poke the fish with your finger. If the flesh springs back, the fish is probably good. However, should the dent remain or should your finger go into the flesh, it isn't so good. Look at the gills. They should be dark red. If they are greyish or white, it is a good indication that the fish is old. Now give it the sniff test. If the fish fails again, move on to the poultry shops. Dried, salted fish, especially shark and ray, are very popular. They are generally called ***pescado seco.***
Lapa	Giant limpet
Lobster	***Langosta:*** Mexican lobsters are the spiny variety, without the huge front claws of the Maine lobster.
Mackerel	***Sierra:*** A premium fish for *ceviche.* (See *Recipes.*)
Mullet	***Lisa***
Octopus	***Pulpo***
Oysters	***Ostiones:*** Oysters should be purchased alive, in the shell, whenever possible. If you can partially open the shell with your fingers, the oyster is either dead or dying. A live oyster keeps its shell firmly closed when handled.

Many seafood vendors sell cleaned oysters in bottles, plastic bags and jars. We often buy these when we can't find live ones and they are usually reasonably fresh.

Prawns — ***Camarones gigantes*** or ***azules:*** very expensive.

Red snapper — ***Huachinango:*** Includes many types of snapper.

Salmon — ***Salmón:*** Common canned but not often seen fresh.

Sardines — ***Sardinas:*** Canned are most common and very popular.

Sea bass — ***Mero***

Shark — ***Cazón, tiburón***

Shrimp — ***Camarones: Camarones secos*** (dried) are excellent and very common.

Fresh shrimp are sold by the kilo, with or without the heads. Vendors may remove the heads as they tend to spoil faster than the bodies. Many shrimp fishermen do this on the boat. With or without heads, the best indications of the freshness of shrimp are general appearance and smell. They should be brightly colored and not mushy.

Shrimp are priced according to their size: ***azules***, the most expensive, are huge prawns. ***Cristales*** are large and ***Regulares*** are average. The price of these will increase if they've been beheaded.

Tourists sometimes buy shrimp direct from the boats, but this is actually illegal (for the fisherman). The price may or may not be a bargain. I've found that a trade is preferred over cash: fresh fruit, booze or tools. One crew gave me a crate of shrimp in exchange for a crate of fruit. If they refuse to sell or trade shrimp, be gracious—they may be low or worried about the authorities.

Squid — ***Calamares***

Tuna — ***Atún:*** Sold fresh and canned. Canned tuna is a favorite *cantina* snack.

Seafood, canned — Canned seafood makes good travelling food. Canned mackerel is often sold in cans labeled ***Salmón*** in large letters with a picture of a salmon completing the deception. Look for the microscopic words ***macerel estilo salmón*** (mackerel salmon style). The most common canned seafoods are ***atún*** (tuna), ***sardinas*** (sardines), ***almejas*** (clams) and ***camarones*** (shrimp). Canned seafood is becoming more expensive because of the demand from the States.

	A Mexican picnic or impromptu celebration is not complete without a can or two of some seafood and salted crackers.
Seasoned pepper	***Pimienta condimentada:*** Supermarket
Seasoned salt	***Sal para sazonar:*** Supermarket
Seeds	***Semillas***
Sesame seeds	***Semillas de ajonjolí***
Shampoo	***Shampoó: Jabón de coco*** (coconut soap) is sold in *Conasupos, tiendas* and drugstores. It makes great shampoo and lathers in salt water. American brands are expensive. If you have a favorite shampoo take a supply with you.
Soap	***Jabón:*** (See *Shampoo.*)
Soups, canned and dry	***Sopa en lata:*** Campbell's soups are sold in most stores. Dried soups are sold under the brand name *Maggi.* They are inexpensive and pretty good. Bouillon cubes are very common. (See *Bouillon.*)
Sour Cream	***Crema ácida*** or ***crema agria:*** See *Dairy products.*
Soy sauce	***Salsa soya, salsa china*** or ***salsa japonesa:*** Supermarket. Expensive and not very tasty.
Spaghetti	***Spaghetti, macarrones delgados*** or ***pasta:*** See *Macaroni.*
Spices	***Especias, olores:*** See *Herbs.*
Spinach	***Espinaca***
Squash	***Calabaza:*** Covers all types and sizes. ***Chilacayote*** is a common primitive squash. ***Calabacitas*** (little squashes) is used for small zucchinis.
Squash flowers	***Flores de calabaza:*** Excellent in soups, deep fried in egg batter or in *quesadillas.*
Squash seeds	***Pepitas:*** Covers almost all seeds, including pumpkin and melon. *Pepitas* are sold roasted in the market and on the street.
Strawberries	***Fresas:*** Very common and inexpensive in some parts of the country. *Fresas con crema* is a popular dessert, usually associated with the wealthy. "They eat *fresas con crema*" can be a sarcastic put-down of someone who is stuck up.
Straws	***Popotes***
Sugar	***Azúcar:*** Brown sugar is sold in molded chunks called *piloncillo* or *panucho.* The price is controlled by the government to keep people happy. Raw sugar is ***azúcar moreno.***

Sugar cane	***Caña, caña de azúcar:*** The harvest is called "*la zafra.*"
Sunflower seeds	***Semillas de girasol:*** Most easily located in bird food stores in and around the market. Many good eating seeds are sold as bird food. Ask if they can be eaten in case they're chemically treated, "*¿Se puede comerlas?*"
Sweet potato	***Camote:*** Some are purple.
Swiss chard	***Acelgas:*** You can also use the general term for greens—*quelites.*
Tamarind	***Tamarindo:*** This fruit looks like a giant brown bean pod. The seeds inside are covered with a brownish stuff that is sour but tasty. Good with *tequila.*
Tangerine	***Mandarina:*** Very cheap around Christmas.
Tarragon	***Estragón***
Tea	***Té:*** Snobs call it *the.* Black tea is ***té negro.*** Imported teas are sold in supermarkets.
Thyme	***Tomillo***
Toilet paper	***Papel sanitario:*** It's easier to ask for it by the most common brand names, ***Pétalo*** and ***Regio.***
Tomatoes	***Jitomates:*** Big beefsteak tomatoes cost more than good quality small tomatoes. Small green tomatoes (the ones encased in a leafy membrane) are used in sauces (see *Recipes*) and are called ***tomates.*** To avoid confusion remember that *tomates* are not tomatoes.
Tomato purée	***Puré de tomate:*** Thinner than purée sold in the U.S.
Tomato sauce	***Salse de tomate:*** It will be hotter than hell if the can has a picture of a chili on it or warnings such as *estilo español* or *estilo mexicano.*
Toothpaste	***Crema dental:*** Very cheap in the *Conasupo.*
Tortillas	See *Restaurants* and *Typical Foods.*
Turkey	***Guajolote:*** The Indian name is more commonly used than the Spanish ***pavo.*** Turkeys are usually sold live.
Turmeric	***Cúrcuma***
Turnip	***Nabo***
Vanilla	***Vainilla:*** Mexico is famous for its vanilla.
Vegetables	***Verduras*** or ***Legumbres***

Verdolagas	Purselane: See *Greens.*
Vinegar	***Vinagre:*** Homemade vinegar is sold in bulk in some *tiendas.*
Walnut	***Nuez castilla*** or ***Nogal***
Watercress	***Berro***
Watermelon	***Sandía:*** If you are going to travel back in the sticks and have the opportunity, buy several *sandías.* They keep well, are usually inexpensive and make wonderful treats to offer guests.
Waxed paper	***Papel encerado***
Wheat germ	***Germen de trigo:*** Sold in some supermarkets and health food stores.
White pepper	***Pimienta blanca***
Worchestershire sauce	***Salsa inglesa:*** Supermarket.
Worm seed	***Epazote:*** The leaves of this plant give excellent flavor to soups and are important medicinally. (See *Health.*)

Yam	***Camote***
Yeast	***Levadura:*** Dry yeast is sold in supermarkets. Bakeries will often sell cakes of fresh yeast if you ask. Brewer's yeast (***levadura de cerveza***) is sold in some drugstores and health food stores, but if you use it often bring some from home.
Yogurt	***Yogurt*** or ***Bulgara:*** See *Dairy products.*
Zapotes	***Zapotes:*** A very common and interesting fruit. Both the *zapote blanco* and *zapote borracho* have sleep inducing properties. The *borracho* (drunken) zapote is yellow on the outside and reddish inside with a few large seeds. The seeds are supposedly narcotic, though they don't have to be eaten to get the sleep inducing effects of the fruit.
Zucchini	***Calabacitas:*** Mexicans eat an amazing amount of this squash. It is harvested young, when no more than 3 to 6 inches in length.

I never cease to be amazed at how much time and effort marketing requires, no matter how much experience the marketer has. You don't just run down for the week's groceries. You form an expedition. As Steve says, "Let's make a foray to the market." To me the implication is that one or more of us may not make it back.

Before we enter the market, Steve issues the shopping bags. (Food is seldom packaged and you're expected to provide your own containers.)

"Who's got the list?" He asks impatiently, drawn like a magnet to this great mine of food.

"Not me," I say. "Lorena must have it."

"Where is she?" Steve asks, looking wildly from side to side. She has disappeared, as usual, before the plan of attack can be drawn up.

"I don't know but before I look for her, we'd better agree on a meeting place."

"How about the *fondas?*" He suggests, thinking ahead as usual to lunch and a beer. I agree and set off in pursuit of Lorena.

The main building of the market place is very old, the roof and supporting beams darkened by hundreds of years of smoke from the cooking fires below. It is a huge structure and today, on market day, it is literally jammed with people and their goods. Vendors are crammed into every available corner and some have usurped space normally used for walking. Tiny Indian ladies seem able to occupy no more space than could be covered by a handkerchief. Their inventory is worth perhaps 50 cents, if anyone were expansive enough to buy it all. It's doubtful, however, that they would part with everything at one blow; there's far too much gossiping to be done with neighbors to justify that.

An old man stumbles by, pushing an ancient wheelbarrow loaded with freshly butchered meat. He forces his way through the crowded aisles, shouting warnings to ladies haggling loudly over a few cents worth of onions or *chiles*. They sidestep his gory load without a glance, a bloody joint of meat barely missing a clean white dress. On a front corner of the wheelbarrow, the old man has bolted the left arm of some long discarded baby doll. Its hand waves grotesquely at the crowd, fingernails bright with fresh polish.

Following in the wake the old man has cleared through the mass of shoppers, vendors, delivery boys and beggers, I plunge into the long narrow entrance. It is hot and stuffy, smelling of blood, onions and oranges, and I have a hangover. Steve is skirting the main building, confining his purchases to the vendors who have erected their temporary stalls in the surrounding streets.

I see Lorena a short way ahead but we are rapidly being separated by the crowd. As usual, I cannot bring myself to employ an elbow against these women who use it so liberally on me. Lorena towers over the people around her, attracting a good deal of attention and a stream of comments.

"Hey, blondie, buy my tomatoes!" a cackling old shrew yells at her. "Give them a squeeze!"

"Look at that tall one!" the woman in front of me says to a friend. "She looks like a *Tehuana** to me!"

Lorena is rapidly moving ahead, so I shout over the crowd and ask her what I should buy. "Tomatoes and onions!" she yells back, ignoring a few friendly mocking cries from the stalls nearby. Then she spots a tiny bunch of fresh herbs or rather is stopped by a bunch of herbs thrust into her face by a grinning Indian woman. She smiles and asks the price. Five fingers are displayed, two times. The old woman evidently does not speak much Spanish. Lorena looks at the herbs, sniffs them, then nods her head.

The bundle is laboriously wrapped in a piece of old newspaper and tucked safely in the huge shopping bag. Lorena hands her a small coin and politely accepts a very withered green onion as a bonus. As she begins to move on, the old lady grabs her long blonde hair with a giggle and gives it a tug for luck. Everyone laughs. I am hit in the back with some type of tiny fruit. More laughter.

**Tehuana* women, from the Isthmus of *Tehuantepec*, are famous both for their stature and matriarchal society. They are, perhaps, the only women in Mexico who enjoy a form of 'Women's Liberation.'

A few feet further on, I spot a likely looking heap of tomatoes and try to approach close enough to ask the price. Before I can inspect them, however, someone pushes me and I find myself standing next to a lady selling neat little piles of green onions. Rather than push my way back, I ask the price of the onions.

She shyly names a price, three times more than the going rate, as she carefully observes my face for a reaction.

I make a much lower counter-offer but she just grins and turns her head slightly. She would probably let them go for that but she is too embarrassed to talk to a foreigner. Her stubborness irritates me slightly but before I say anything, someone grabs my ankle and shouts, "Buy my onions, *marchante* (customer)! Smell them! Fresh today! I picked them myself!"

The other vendors giggle at this hard sell approach but the lady with the onions is not about to be fazed by her neighbors' comments. She thrusts a bunch at me and waggles them seductively.

After a quick exchange of offers and counter-offers, I stick them in my bag. Heads nod and shake as the price I paid is passed on, both behind me to tell others what they missed out on and ahead to warn of what I'm willing to pay. In seconds, every onion in the area is converging on me. I escape down a side alley into Tomatoland.

Everyone in this row is selling tomatoes; there are tens of thousands of them and all look and cost about the same. The vendors loudly proclaim the merits of their wares, as if all the other tomatoes were fakes, only skins wrapped cleverly around hollow frames.

After buying half a *kilo* from a very serious and dignified elderly gentlemen, I make my way slowly to the fruit section. There are a hundred more vegetable stalls but I am willing to leave them to Lorena; she enjoys searching out strange tasting treasures packed in from distant farms.

The odors in the fruit section are almost obscenely rich and heavy, fragrant with memories of the hot coastal country and bubbling asphalt roads. Even the vendors look slightly dissipated, as if the goods they sold corrupted them with ripeness and thick maturity.

In a large market such as this one, the selection is excellent, even though many of the fruits available are grown hundreds of miles away. Pineapples seem to be particularly abundant today, their heavy sweet fragrance masks even the strong scents of bananas and papayas. Almost every vendor is busily stacking them in attractive mounds.

Pineapples are being peeled dexterously with razor-sharp knives, sliced, then arranged on trays of ice to attract customers. One nearby vendor spears a juicy piece with the tip of his blade and extends it toward me. As I reach for the sample, momentarily forgetting the rush of people, a young boy piled high with crates of bananas crashes into me. One of the wooden slats hooks my shirt and tears it slightly.

¡Aguas! ¡Aguas!" (Careful! Careful!) he shouts, swaying dangerously under the tottering load. I curse at the hole in my shirt but apologize for being in the way; the responsibility to avoid such collisions always rests on the shopper.

When I turn back, the sample is still being offered and the vendor is laughing with amusement over my clumsiness. After tasting the pineapple, pale and slightly sour, I tell him, "*No, gracias,*" and move on. He shrugs his shoulders; there will be more customers and the fruit will ripen.

After a tasty sample in another stall, I finally select a large ripe pineapple and begin to barter.

The huge smiling woman behind the counter asks for a price that seems quite reasonable. I offer her quite a bit less, hoping against hope to get a real bargain. She shakes her head impatiently. I increase my offer. Another head shake. I raise my offer once more, almost matching her original price.

The pineapple is handed to me without a word, though she scans the surrounding crowd quickly to see if anyone has overheard the final price and will know beforehand how far down it can be pushed.

As I slip the pineapple into my shopping bag, I notice a deep bruise on one side. Rather hesitantly I point out this previously unnoticed defect to the woman who had so deftly juggled it out of sight during the bartering. I half expect her to tell me to go to hell but instead she smiles good-naturedly and indicates that I can select any pineapple I want.

The damaged fruit is being waved brazenly in another customer's face before I am ten feet away.

Once out of the fruit section, I steer a course toward the hardware and leather goods area. Real treasures can often be picked up there for just a few *pesos*. Junk, secondhand tools, comic books, antiques that almost work, bags hand woven from string and grass and all the other essential things we can do so well without are arranged in tempting displays.

Walking past the leather stalls, I inhale the earthy odor of cured hides and oil. *Huaraches* (sandles) hang in pungent rows, their tire tread soles turned to display such names as *B.F. Goodrich, Atlas* and *General Popo.*

Quickly scanning the various soles for real gems—a particularly good white sidewall or a name that has been accidently altered by the cut of a sandalmaker's knife (*...rich Tire Co., Fire....,* etc.)—I spot a pair of *Michelin's.* The owner of the stall quickly seats me on a tiny chair, whips the sandals off the wall and lays them in front of me. Unfortunately, they are too small and he regrets to say that the only thing he has in my size is a white-walled *General Popo.* He, too, appreciates a *huarache* with more class than just a plain black sole.

Next I enter the narrow alleyways of metalware. There are hammers made from iron reinforcing rods, lamps from beer cans, dust pans from oil cans, stoves from gas cans; anything, in fact, made from cans, rebar, scrap tin or license plates that you might imagine.

A few stalls farther on an old man is meticulously arranging keys, broken scissors, a light bulb, bits of iron and tin, washers, nuts, screws, bent nails and other such valuable stuff in neat piles and rows. While watching him, I spot an ancient clothing iron.

It is solid metal, obviously an antique but not long out of use—the bottom is still smooth and shiny. This is just what we need, I think to myself guiltily, hefting the heavy iron and wondering how I can justify it.

The old man takes his business seriously. He begins to describe exactly how to use the iron; there's no doubt in his mind that I really need it. We discuss the temperature it should be heated to, the best type of fire to warm in on, how to dampen the clothing properly, etc. He is willing to tell me all this valuable information and include the iron for just 50 cents.

I add two very camp looking old comic books to the deal and we part friends, the old man still muttering about ironing and charcoal as I wander on.

Around the corner, I see Lorena examining something on the ground in front of her, at a similar junk stall. By craning my neck, I am just barely able to see past the crowd to the object that is attracting her attention. It is an iron, identical to mine.

The people jammed in front of me make it impossible to force my way through. Now she is bending intently over the iron and I can tell that she has made an offer because the vendor is wagging a forefinger back and forth in front of his nose.

This signal means, "No deal," so I still have time.

Just as I manage to attract her attention, the iron disappears into a piece of newspaper. She turns to me with a grin of triumph and say, "Do you have a dollar in *pesos*?"

On the way to the *fondas*, we decide to tell Steve that antique irons are worth a fortune in the States. He'll fall for it if it seems we stand to make a huge profit, but we'll have to be convincing; both irons together weigh several pounds. Overloading the van—or how to avoid it—is one of his favorite sermons.

He is sitting impatiently in a dark food stall.

"How'd it go?" I ask sympathetically, ordering a cold beer.

"Oh, God! What an ordeal!" he moans, chugging down half a bottle in one gulp. "Did you see Lorena?" I almost caught up with her once near the oranges but she disappeared again."

"She just stopped to buy some pottery."

"Great!" Steve says. "It'll probably be hours before she shows up."

Lorena emerges as if on cue from a nearby stall. She is carrying a new piece of pottery, a handful of candles and what appears to be a full sack of fresh parsley.

"What did you get, Steve?" I interrupt hastily. "It looks to me like you've got quite a bit of stuff there."

"Just the usual," he sighs, "onions, tomatoes, potatoes, cabbage, lettuce, a small squash, mangoes, rice, limes, greens, milk, oranges, bananas, half a papaya, some peanuts for the birds, a few chilies, bread, cooking oil, avocadoes, half a *kilo* of green beans..."

"Forget anything?" I interrupt sarcastically. "Sounds to me like you did pretty well even without the list."

Steve looks up, a mixed expression of bewilderment and injury on his face. "We can't go hungry," he says quietly. "These are *just the Basics*; you know that."

Lorena looks at the list and checks a few things in Steve's bag against it. "You got it all," she announces.

"Get a pineapple?" I ask casually.

"Yeah," they answer in unison.

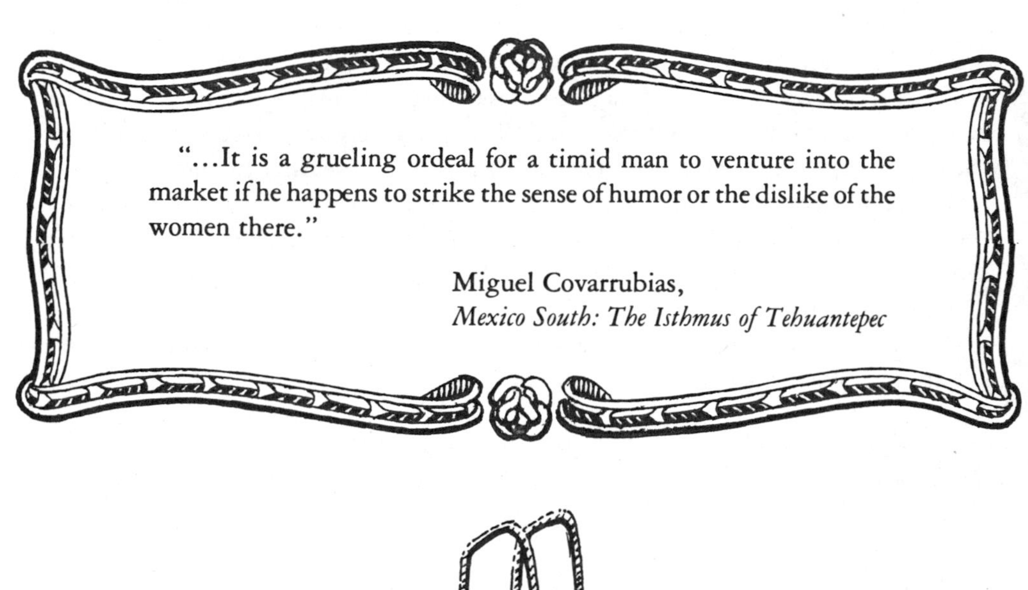

"...It is a grueling ordeal for a timid man to venture into the market if he happens to strike the sense of humor or the dislike of the women there."

Miguel Covarrubias,
Mexico South: The Isthmus of Tehuantepec

COOKING IN MEXICO

Cooking hints...Too many tacos?...What's cooking?...Recipes: Eggs to Cactus and more...The Great Grunt-A-Rama...

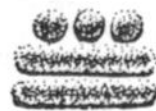

The qualifications for a good travelling cook, especially while in a foreign country, are numerous. The person who fits them is a combination of Houdini, Adelle Davis and J. Krishnamurti.

If this person exists, and it is doubtful, he or she must even now be hunched over a stove on some remote road, slicing onions in the darkness of a crowded van, calming friends' raw nerves and slavering appetites. While they lounge around drinking beer, listening to tapes and hinting about dinner time, the cook is rooting through huge shopping bags, looking amongst the food (bought almost single handedly that day) for some tasty ingredient. Someone is sitting in front of the only light, engrossed in a *Pato Pascual* comic book (Donald Duck). The cook cuts a finger while slicing green peppers. Patiently lighting a candle, the cook chops stoically on.

When the meal is served the cook supervises the division of the food, reprimanding greedy hands and encouraging hesitant appetites. By careful planning no food is wasted and enough remains for the next meal.

With the meal over and digesting, the cook now accepts, with painful modesty, the applause and compliments of well-fed friends. And while they sleep, lies awake, planning breakfast.

Cooking while on the road demands a dedication to keeping your stomach full that few of us possess. My tendency at the end of a long hot day of driving is to forget the hassle and go to bed. Breakfast always seems easier to cope with than supper.

Skipping meals, however, is dangerous. You must eat well to enjoy your trip. The snack foods which most people tend to use to keep starvation away are usually so low in nutritional value that they might as well fast.

Cooking Hints

•Buy a simple cookbook. *The Joy of Cooking* by Rambauer and Becker is hard to beat. Use it as a general source of advice, not as an inflexible set of rules. Good meals involve a certain degree of spontaneity and surprise. If there's not enough of one ingredient, substitute another. Cookbooks and recipes are like sex manuals: they can only provide directions, you do what feels right to make them work.

•Shop as often as possible. The food you serve will not only be fresher but you will feel less inclined to buy huge amounts.

To keep food stocks to a convenient size and to minimize clutter and waste, you should do a certain amount of advance planning.

Avoid cooking more than can be eaten in one or two meals. Leftovers are not only hard to handle while travelling but they also don't keep well. (Some foods, however, make very delicious and practical leftovers. Mashed potatoes can be eaten for dinner, then refried for breakfast.)

Whenever practical, prepare a meal in advance. This usually means a great deal of work for the cook at one meal and a nice rest at the next. We often make fried egg sandwiches at breakfast to eat at lunchtime.

•Use paper plates when necessary. Washing the dishes is one of the worst aspects of any cooking situation and on the road it can really be a drag. Dirty dishes just don't seem to pack well; they are forever underfoot and sprouting moldy growths.

•Keep a good selection of fruits, nuts and vegetables that can be eaten raw on hand at all times.

•Purify fruits and vegetables. When water is called for in recipes requiring less than 30 to 40 minutes of cooking, use purified.

•Do not used glazed pottery for acidic foods and beverages. If you use a glazed bowl for salads don't add the dressing until right before serving or, better yet, after the salad is on the plate. (See *Buying Things: Pottery.)*

•Whenever possible, take a container to the market and have it filled with fresh juice. Juice tastes much better while travelling than a lukewarm cola. When fresh juice is not available or cannot be kept for as long as you wish, stop at a CONASUPO store or *tienda* and stock up on canned juices.

•Go to eating stalls in the market or small restaurants with a container and buy cooked rice and beans *para llevar* (to go). This pre-cooked food will form the basis for a great number of meals, all quick to make and quite good. Ready made *tortas* (see *What You'll Eat*) are inexpensive, and are perfect for lunches or a quick dinner before going to bed.

Fresh bread, cheese and *tortillas* are available almost everywhere and are good supplements for beans, rice and eggs.

Very good quick meals can be made using *bistec de res aplanada* (flattened beefsteaks) and *carne de res molida* (ground beef). Both can be made into *tortas,* cooked with beans, rice, macaroni, spaghetti, potatoes or served with fried eggs.

•Cook all raw dairy products well.

•Eggs are a perfect travelling food; they keep well and can be used at almost every meal. We often eat them for breakfast, a very important meal while on the road.

•You will inevitably feel tempted on occasion to eat in a restaurant rather than cook for yourselves. We resist this by figuring out how much food we could buy in the market with the money.

Remember that even the most basic restaurant meal costs several times the price of the ingredients. When you feel yourself wavering, reach for some kind of nutritious buffer against imminent starvation—a banana or *licuado*—and read over *Prices* in the Appendices. If that doesn't do it, the hell with it; find a nice restaurant.

•For much more on cooking while travelling, camping, backpacking and boating see *The People's Guide To Camping in Mexico.* There's information on foraging, cleaning and preparation of seafood, drying and smoking meat, cheap and lightweight foods, drying fruits and vegetables, a kitchen in a suitcase, recipes and who-knows-what-else.

Taco-itis

People who are equipped to do their own cooking can easily avoid rapid changes in diet which can be disastrous to both morale and digestion. There's no reason to give up all the old familiar foods just because you've crossed the border into another country.

My introduction to Mexican food came several years ago. One day I was happily grinding away on a cheeseburger and an order of fries, the next I was desperately trying to smile at a plate of *enchiladas.*

Although my previous eating habits had been purely Middle American, the thought of eating in Mexico had never bothered me, mainly because I never really thought about it at all.

"Steve," I said one afternoon in a restaurant, giving my plate of greasy *tacos* and beans a sickly stare, "I have got to have some mashed potatoes or I can't go on any longer."

"Hummpff?" he said, spooning hot sauce over his lunch. "Mashed potatoes? Why? Where? What the hell are you talking about, anyway?"

"I just have to have some mashed potatoes," I said. "Let's find a restaurant where they fix them."

"Forget it!" he laughed, reaching for the remainder of my food. "You could sooner find a hamburger in this town; they don't even know what mashed potatoes are, much less care."

"O.K." I said, "A hamburger then! Anything, just so it isn't another order of *tacos* or chicken and rice or..."

"Hold it!" Steve yelled. "What's wrong with any of those things? We've been eating them for weeks and they taste fine to me."

"Look," I pleaded, "I'd just like to have a dish of mashed potatoes for a change."

We walked around town, looking for a likely place to find mashed potatoes. There was none. Finally we drifted toward the market place. Hundreds of women were haggling noisily over colorful heaps of fresh food. Steve stopped and began to stare at one old lady hypnotically. "Hmmmm," he muttered, "potatoes. She's selling potatoes! Nice ones, too."

The light suddenly dawned. "Are you thinking of making our *own* mashed potatoes?" I asked.

Steve turned to me with a strangely greedy look. "Exactly!" he cried, "make our own mashed potatoes...and gravy!"

"Gravy?" I gasped. "Real gravy? Gravy with milk in it? Gravy and mashed potatoes? Not gravy and *tacos*?"

With a regal gesture, he nodded to the old lady and said, "Give me a *kilo* of potatoes, please!"

Using a battered Boy Scout mess kit and a campfire, Steve managed to turn out a splendid meal, guaranteed to cure homesickness and lagging appetites: mashed potatoes, gravy *and* hamburgers. From that moment on, we never suffered from dietary boredom.

As our experience broadened, we learned that it's possible to eat almost anything you want in Mexico, prepared in any way, from Chinese food to Jewish dishes. Just use your imagination.

What's Cooking?

Selecting the recipes that would be included in this chapter was something like the indigestion nightmares that come from eating *enchiladas* and mango ice cream at midnight. Friends, however, insisted that help was needed: "Just a few basic dishes," someone said.

Steve's eyes glazed over. "You mean like some nice Campeche style duck stewed in sherry, followed by tongue stuffed with truffles and *capirotada* pudding smothered in honey and raisins and..."

"No! No! Something *easy*!"

"A Yucatan barbecue?" He continued, wiping at a fleck of saliva, "First you dig a giant pit and then you get a big pig, 2 turkeys, a fresh deer, some..."

"I've got it!" I interrupted, "What you really want are recipes that are simple, reliable, nourishing, cheap, not too exotic, flexible, don't require much time or equipment and...what else? Oh yeah, they have to taste good."

"Of course, that's just what I was trying to give them," Steve said, obviously peeved, "...after you dig the pit and find the banana leaves you take the first turkey and..."

These recipes are intended to be very flexible. Since individual tastes are different, it would be unreasonable to inflict our preferences in spices, especially garlic, on you.

Inexperienced cooks have a tendency to dump a bit of everything on hand into what they are cooking. This usually results in a multiflavor that may taste good but it always tastes about the same, whether the dish is scrambled eggs or fried rice. Try using unfamiliar spices one or two at a time. You'll soon learn to appreciate each of them individually and to anticipate to a better degree what a dish will taste like.

Most of my favorite eating memories are of dishes prepared with gut feelings about the ingredients rather than from a recipe.

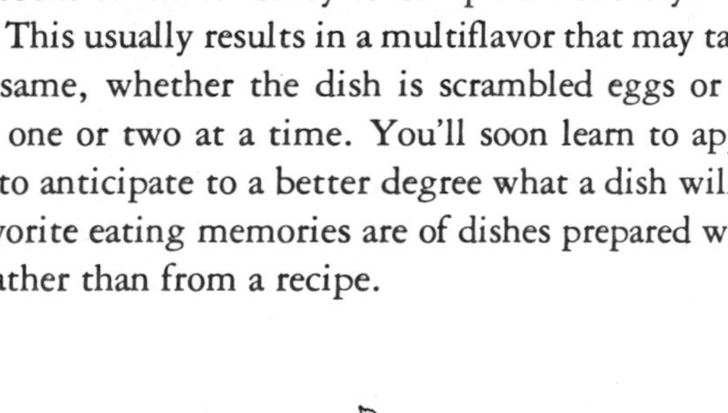

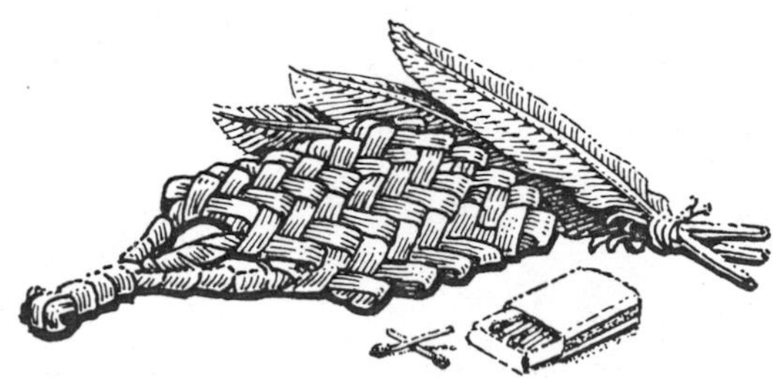

1. Scrambled Eggs
2. Ranch Style Eggs
3. Eggs and Gravy
4. Mashed Potatoes
5. Potatoes Baked without an Oven
6. Beans
7. Refried Beans
8. Lentils and Split Peas
9. Bean Sprouts
10. Steamed White Rice
11. Steamed Brown Rice
12. Rice with Vegetables (and Meat)
13. Mexican Quick Fried Rice
14. Gorditas
15. Quesadillas
16. Tortillas: Snacks & Leftovers
17. Steamed Vegetables
18. Fried Vegetables and Gravy
19. Cactus and Squash
20. Creamed *Chayote*
21. *Chayote* with Cheese
22. Soup
23. Garlic Soup
24. Salad
25. Tomato Salad
26. Salad Dressing
27. Fruit Salad
28. Stew
29. Fish
30. Grilled Fish
31. Fried Fish
32. Deep Fried Fish
33. Seafood Tempura
34. Grilled Conch
35. Fried Conch
36. Deep Fried Conch
37. Other Seafoods
38. *Ceviche*
39. Chop Suey
40. Macaroni, Cheese and...
41. Fast Spaghetti
42. Clam Spaghetti
43. White Sauce
44. Red Sauce
45. Green Sauce
46. Rattlesnake Sauce
47. Gravy
48. Yogurt
49. Coconut Banana Bread
50. Toasted Seeds
51. Tepache Wine
52. Fruit Drinks

•When in doubt: use *more* butter, cream, cheese, eggs, garlic but *less* cooking oil, heat, salt, chile, cumin.

•Olive oil is very tasty but expensive. Dilute it half-and-half with sesame oil; they'll never know the difference.

1 Scrambled Eggs

Eggs don't have to be monotonous. The possible variations of cooking methods and ingredients should prevent you from retreating to corn flakes.

Heat a small amount of *margarine* or *oil* in a frying pan. Break two eggs per person into the pan, keeping the heat low. Add one tablespoon of *milk* for every two eggs and a bit of *salt* and *pepper*. Stir this all together gently. Don't stir any more than necessary to mix the ingredients. Reduce the heat to very low, cover and cook for about ten minutes.

To make scrambled eggs more interesting, add, individually or all together, any of the following:

cheese (grated or thinly sliced)
fresh tomatoes
mushrooms
onions
chopped meat or fish
capers
nopales
parsley
garlic
asparagus, cooked
beans, mashed or boiled
all types of herbs
olives
greens
bean sprouts
tortillas, chopped

2 Ranch Style Eggs (*Huevos Rancheros*)

Fry eggs up or over, place on one or two warm *tortillas* and cover with heated *Red* or *Green sauce* (see *Sauces*). If you fry the *tortillas* lightly in oil and then dip them in the sauce, they will be softer and more flavorful. Options: cover all this with another *tortilla* and sprinkle *grated cheese* over everything. My favorite variation is to smother everything in beans.

3 Eggs and Gravy

This is an excellent travelling breakfast. We often use it for dinner too, especially when we're too tired to cook anything lavish.

Hard-boil two eggs per person. While the eggs cook, make a thick brown gravy (see *Gravy*).

Cut the hard-boiled eggs into the gravy, mix well and serve over warmed *bolillos* (rolls).

For variations, cook *vegetables* into the gravy or add cooked *meat* or *fish*.

4 Mashed Potatoes

Wash the potatoes thoroughly or peel them. (Mashed potatoes including peels are very good and also more nutritious.)

Boil in salted water until you can easily pierce the potatoes to the center with a fork. Beware of overcooking.

When done, pour off the water or save it for soup. Unless you have fresh or canned milk, use part of the water to mix with powered milk. (We often boil eggs along with the potatoes to eat the next day.)

Mash, stir and whip the potatoes as you add *milk*. If you don't have *milk*, just use raw *eggs*. Be careful; once you've made them too soft there's nothing to be done. Add *butter, margarine, lard* or *cooking oil* as you mash, along with *salt, pepper*, and one or two *raw eggs*. For variations add *parsley, celery salt, mayonnaise, onion greens, garlic* and anything else handy.

5 Potatoes Baked without an Oven

Scrub potatoes well and coat lightly with *cooking oil* or *lard*.

Preheat a heavy skillet or other utensil that can be covered. Place the potatoes inside, preferably on a rack, upside-down tin plate, heavy aluminum foil or even on small stones, and cover tightly.

Cook over medium heat for about 45 minutes or until the potatoes can be pierced easily with a fork.

If you don't have a stove or a pan, you can still bake potatoes.

Build a good sized fire and allow it to burn down to coals. Scrub and oil the potatoes and wrap each individually in aluminum foil.

Place the potatoes on top of the coals. *Do not bury them.* They can be turned after 20 minutes and should be done in less than an hour, depending on their size and the heat of the coals.

You'll find that cooking on top of the fire makes baked potatoes a much more practical operation. There is nothing more frustrating than interring half a dozen potatoes and having one burn up, one raw, one lost and one destroyed by the shovel.

Any vegetable can be cooked in this manner; *onions* are especially good, as are *squash, corn* and *carrots*.

6 Beans

One cup of dry beans is a reasonable amount for one meal for three or four people. Wash the beans thoroughly and remove sticks, stones, pieces of brick and all of the other junk that comes with them.

Soak the beans in cold water overnight to decrease cooking time. If you don't have a pressure cooker, put the beans in a kettle or pottery bean pot, cover with water, bring to a good boil, then turn down to simmer. Watch them carefully or they will go dry! Once they've gone dry and hard, you might as well start over or resign yourself to eating pellets.

When more water is needed to keep the beans from going dry, add *boiling water*. The beans will get hard if they are subjected to rapid temperature changes.

Simmer the beans slowly until they are done. This may take an hour or it may take several; it all depends on the beans. Start them early; they can be reheated as the rest of the meal is being prepared. Add salt after the beans are cooked, not before, or it will make them tough.

Add a few pinches of *ground cumin* and a couple of *epazote* leaves for authentic flavor. We also throw in *garlic, chopped onion, chile* (try one dry *ancho* without seeds) and *oregano*.

When the beans are soft, take a few spoonfuls out of the pot, mash them up well or run them through a food mill with a bit of the juice and dump them back in. This improves the broth.

Refried Beans

The following technique for refrying beans was given to us by a Mexican woman; it's simple and really outstanding.

Heat a couple of tablespoons of *lard* (or *butter, margarine* or *oil*) in a frying pan. Drain cooked beans well and save the liquid. Now fry the beans over a hot fire, mashing and stirring constantly. Use a fork, or better yet, a potato or bean masher. After a few minutes add a few tablespoons of the bean broth and don't stop stirring. Fry until almost dry and add more broth. Continue this process until at least one or two cups of liquid have been used and the beans are the consistency of paste, not runny.

Serve them smeared on tortillas and garnished with chopped tomatoes, onion, garlic and lettuce. A lifesaver!

8 Lentils and Split Peas

Both of these make excellent soup or stew. Cook lentils or peas the same way as beans. When they begin to get tender (about two hours) start dumping in *vegetables*. Add *meat* or *seafood* at the same time. A little (1 tsp.) *curry powder* is good. Thyme goes well with split peas.

9 Bean Sprouts

Bean sprouts are a nice addition to almost any dish with vegetable ingredients. Fried rice, chop suey and salads are especially suitable for a handful or two of sprouts.

Almost any type of bean or seed can be sprouted. Mung beans are most commonly used in the U.S., but are rare in Mexico. We use lentils instead. They are cheap, easy to locate and give delicate and tender sprouts.

Line the bottom of a pan or dish (baking pans work best) with several layers of paper towels, toilet paper or napkins. If you use newspaper, the ink may come off and discolor the sprouts.

Moisten the paper and sprinkle a good handful of lentils evenly over the surface. Cover with another layer or two of paper and a piece of aluminum foil or heavy cloth. This last layer should keep out light. Moisten the lentils once or twice a day until the sprouts are as long as you'd like them. This should take 3 to 5 days.

Another method: Put whatever will be sprouted into a jar or plastic food container. Cover with water and soak for 12 hours. Now secure a clean cloth (handkerchiefs work well) over the opening with a string or rubber band. Turn the container upside down and drain it well. Rinse with fresh water at least 2 or 3 times a day, more if it's hot and dry outside.

Try to keep the sprouts in the dark, but if you're like us and can't remember to rinse them if they're hidden away, just wrap the container in a shirt or towel.

People on foot can sprout beans in their packs or even their pockets. Soak a few tablespoons of beans (or whatever you have) overnight in water. This helps them sprout but isn't essential. From then on keep them in a cloth or screen covered jar (use foil with holes, mosquito netting or wire screen), washing the sprouts two or three times a day to keep them moist.

When sprouting beans larger than lentils, you may prefer to remove the beans from the sprouts before using them raw.

10 Steamed White Rice

Like all simple foods, rice is easy to prepare and just as easy to screw up. Wash rice until the water is clear. This removes some nutrients, but Mexican rice is very starchy and often turns pasty.

Add enough water to the pan so that the rice is about half an inch under. To measure the amount of water, place your thumb with the tip just touching the rice. The water should be just over the thumbnail. A Japanese friend taught us this method, it works in any size pan, with every normal thumb. How? *¿Quién sabe?*

Cover the pan, bring to a boil, then reduce the heat to low and steam for about 20 minutes. Don't peek. Keep the lid on and pray.

Give the cooked rice a few strokes with a wooden paddle and serve.

One cup of raw rice will be enough for two or three people.

11 Steamed Brown Rice

Use a 2:1 ratio of water to rice. Add the rice slowly to boiling water. Cover pan, reduce heat and cook for about 40 minutes.

12 Rice with Vegetables (and Meat)

This recipe has countless variations. The only constant ingredient is the rice.

Steam one cup of rice (white or brown). When the rice is cooked, sauté *garlic* (we use lots) and *ginger* (powdered or whole, but not too much) in *oil.* After a few minutes, turn up the heat and when the oil is hot, add the following:

large onion, chopped or
green onions, including stalks
celery, 2 or 3 stalks, chopped
green pepper, chopped or a mild poblano without seeds
jicama, 1 cup, chopped
salt
soy sauce
other vegetables, sliced or chopped

Fry quickly and keep stirring. When the vegetables look shiny and translucent (should take less than five minutes) dump in the steamed rice. If your vegetables are tough or extra firm (carrots, green beans, etc.) either cut them smaller or start frying them first, adding more tender ingredients later. Add a good shot of *soy sauce* and cook slowly for a few more minutes.

Finally, add two *raw eggs* and stir well. Cook until the egg is congealed—no more than a few minutes—and serve.

Variations and additions are many. *Meat, poultry* or *seafood* should be cooked first and added while the vegetables are being fried.

We have made rice and vegetables with the following additions and enjoyed them all thoroughly: *ground beef*, thinly sliced *bistec de res*, slided *lomo de puerco,* fresh steamed *fish, oysters,* well pounded *conch*, steamed *iguana* (cook until the meat falls off the bones), *chicken, venison, dried beef*, canned *clams* and *shrimp, liver, tongue* and others.

Almost any vegetable that you can think of is also good, but none should be used that must be cooked for more than a few minutes to be edible.

13 Mexican Quick Fried Rice

This is truly a classic, a delicious and versatile one pan meal.

1/2 cup dry rice
2 tbsp. oil
1 small onion, chopped
1 cup of water
salt
1 handful of peas
1 carrot, diced or sliced
1 tomato, chopped
celery, green pepper, mushrooms or whatever you have, chopped

Heat the oil and fry the uncooked rice until the grains are golden. When you think the rice is almost done add the vegetables, stirring constantly. Before the rice gets too dark add the water, cover and simmer. The rice will be done in about 20 minutes. If it looks too gummy, leave the lid off the pan, stirring occasionally, for the last few minutes of cooking.

This recipe serves 2 people quite generously or up to 4 if eaten with fair amounts of *tortillas*.

14 Gorditas

Go to the marketplace and buy several *gorditas* from one of the women hawking them from cloth covered baskets. Gorditas look like small, very thick 'pocket' *tortillas* and may come with refried beans already stuffed inside or smeared on top.

Heat each *gordiita* and stuff or heap on top: *chopped lettuce, cheese, refried beans, cooked potatoes* and *carrots, slices of onion, hot sauce* and...

Variation: after stuffing the *gordita* fry it in a small amount of *oil* and garnish with *fresh lettuce* or *thinly grated cabbage.*

15 Quesadillas

tortillas
oil or butter
cheese, grated
onion, chopped
tomato, chopped
epazote
salt
lettuce, cabbage
chile sauce

Purists will argue that these are actually *tacos de queso*, but while they talk I suggest you eat their share. Mix the cheese, onion, tomato and epazote (several sprigs). Put two heaping spoonsful in a *tortilla* and fold it over. If your *tortillas* are stiff they can be sprinkled with water and wrapped in a warm cloth for a while. Fry the filled *tortilla* in 1/8 to 1/4 inch of hot oil until golden, turn, and fry the other side. Drain on paper and garnish with lettuce or cabbage and hot sauce.

16 *Tortillas:* Snacks and Leftovers

Until you develop a Mexican's awesome appetite for *tortillas*, you'll undoubtedly have leftover *tortillas* kicking around. They very quickly turn hard, but don't think they're not still useful and tasty. Here are some suggestions:

●Keep *tortillas* wrapped in cloth or paper, not plastic. If they can't breathe they'll go sour.

●Sun dried *tortillas* can be used for snacks. Garnish with refried beans, hot sauce, cheese, vegetables or even peanut butter.

●Bake *tortillas* in a warm (not hot) oven until brittle.

- Fried chips: sprinkle the *tortilla* with salted water and dry. Cut or break into pieces and fry until golden in hot oil. Fried *tortilla* 'chips' require lots of oil and are less nutritious than baked or sun dried.
- Sauté hard *tortillas* in butter. When soft, sprinkle grated cheese on top, roll tightly, and eat like a breadstick.
- Add hard *tortilla* pieces to soups just before serving or bake in casseroles

17 Steamed Vegetables

Vegetables that have been steamed just until tender are much more nutritious and flavorful than if boiled.

Slice or chop the vegetables into bite sized pieces. Place them in a saucepan with a small amount of water (one inch or less of water depending on the amount and texture of the vegetable), cover and bring to a boil. Reduce heat and steam until tender, keeping a close eye on the water level or you will end up with a burned mess. Greens can be steamed without putting any water into the pan at all; the water adhering to them after washing will be sufficient.

Steamed vegetables are excellent with *butter, olive oil, salad dressing* (serve them cold), *cream, yogurt, soy sauce* or other sauces and gravies.

18 Fried Vegetables and Gravy

Although many kinds of vegetables can be fried we generally use *tomatoes, zucchini squash* or *eggplant*. All three are soft, juicy and quick cooking.

Tomatoes can be fried when green, but firm red tomatoes are not so sour.

Slice the vegetables about one quarter of an inch thick. Roll in *flour* that has been salted and peppered. You might want to add *paprika*, too.

Fry in hot *oil* or *margarine* until brown. It takes a fairly large amount of oil, especially if you want enough left over to make gravy.

Serve the vegetables over rice and cover with gravy (see *Gravy*).

19 Cactus and Squash

Slice a few *nopal* cactus leaves (without spines) into thin strips. Drop into boiling water along with *garlic* and a sliced *onion*.

Cook for ten minutes and then drain well. Wash and drain again to remove the slime

Chop:

1 small zucchini squash or chayote	*garlic,*
2 tomatoes	*herbs (oregano, basil, thyme are all good)*
1 onion	*salt*
	pepper

Mix everything in a saucepan.

The tomatoes should provide sufficient liquid, but if they don't, add a little water Simmer until all the vegetables are tender.

20 Creamed *Chayote*

Peel *chayotes* if the spines are tough and sharp or just scrub well with a brush or scraper if the spines are small and hair like.

Always use the seed.

Chop one medium *chayote* into bite sized pieces
and steam with:

1/2 onion, sliced or chopped	*garlic*
herbs (rosemary, basil)	*salt*

When tender serve with *sweet cream, yogurt* or *white sauce* (see *Sauces*).

21 *Chayote* with Cheese

Cut the *chayote* into slices about one quarter of an inch thick. Fry in *butter* or *oil* until tender. Take two of the slices and make a sandwich' with cheese Round slices of *Oaxaca* style cheese taste best, but any cheddar type cheese will do.

Chop and mix:	*garlic*
2 tomatoes	*thyme*
1 medium onion	*oregano*
	salt

Arrange alternate layers of *chayote* sandwiches with the tomato mixture in a saucepan or bean pot. Simmer or bake for 20 to 30 minutes.

22 Soup

Soups made from fresh vegetables are so superior in taste to canned soups that you might regret making them. It is almost impossible to enjoy canned soup after making your own.

Select a vegetable. About a double handful, chopped, will make a reasonable pot of soup. Steam (see *Steamed Vegetables*) until tender with *garlic* and half of an *onion.* Blend to a more-or-less even consistency. Add milk (powdered or fresh) or cream to taste.

Heat this mixture and add *herbs, spices, salt* and *pepper* to taste. We usually just throw in a little *bay leaf* and *thyme* or *basil.* Too many spices will mask the flavor of the vegetables.

My favorite soup is tomato. Peel four or five medium to large *tomatoes.* This can be done by dipping the tomatoes briefly into boiling water (10 seconds or more) and then into cool water. The skins should come right off. (This step is optional.)

Chop the tomatoes up and cook them over a low fire in 2 tablespoons of *oil* or *margirine* with 1/4 to 1/2 finely chopped *onion* and a little *garlic.* Cook the tomatoes for ten or fifteen minutes (until the onion is soft) and remove from heat.

Force the cooked tomatoes and onions through a sieve or food mill. This is not absolutely necessary but will give the soup a smoother texture.

Now add two cups of either *water* or *milk* and one teaspoon of *cornstarch* (optional). Mix the cornstarch in a cup or so of the liquid before dumping it in or it will be lumpy. Add *spices* and chopped *tortillas*.

23 Garlic Soup

This is a Mexican favorite; eat enough of it and it will protect you from stomach troubles, mosquitoes and unwanted company.

garlic, 1 cup!
2 Tbsp. butter or oil
1 liter of water
1 or 2 tomatoes, chopped
1/4 onion, chopped (optional)
2 bolillos

Sauté the whole, peeled cloves of garlic with the onion until tender. Add the tomato and water. Simmer for ten minutes. While the soup cooks, slice the *bolillos* (bread slices can be used) and toast them well. Cut into bite sized pieces and float them on the soup when it is served.

24 Salad

You'll find that cabbage is more common, cheaper and of better quality than the average head of lettuce in most parts of Mexico. It will also keep much longer.

If you already know how to make salads with lettuce, just substitute cabbage and you're on your way.

If you don't know, here's how: Chop one half of a small head of cabbage into a bowl. Add any or all of the following:

tomatoes, quartered
celery, sliced
green pepper, sliced
garlic
cold boiled beans
jícama, thinly sliced
nuts
seeds
raisins
carrots, shredded or thinly sliced
raw cauliflower, small pieces
beets, grated
onions, finely chopped
zucchini squash, sliced
herbs (basil, thyme, oregano, dill, parsley, marjoram, tarragon, etc.)

Lime juice or *vinegar* can be used alone or in combination with oil. Add a few squirts of *olive* or *cooking oil, salt* and *pepper*. Mix well and serve. Mayonnaise can be used instead of oil.

25 Tomato Salad

Cut several ripe tomatoes into quarters or sixths. Mix with 1/4 cup of *salad dressing* and allow to marinate for at least 15 minutes. Vinegar and oil dressing with lots of *garlic* and *oregano* is very good with this dish, but any kind of salad dressing can be used.

26 Salad Dressing

The amount of vinegar or lime juice you use for this dressing depends on individual taste. Olive oil makes the best salad dressing, but unless you're able to restrain the amount you use, it will be quite expensive. Mix together:

1/4 cup lime juice (or vinegar)
3/4 cup oil (mix in some olive oil for flavor)
1 small chicken bouillon cube (optional)
salt and pepper
mashed garlic
1Tbsp. oregano, preferably unground, or other herbs and spices

Note: Lime juice is sourer than vinegar, so add it carefully, using less than 1/4 cup unless you like very tart dressing.

27 Fruit Salad

Fruit salad is a good travelling snack and very tasty when served with fish, especially tempura style.

Cut up different kinds of fruit into bite sized pieces. *Pineapple, papaya, bananas, oranges, tangerines* and *melon* are very good together.

Squirt *lime juice* over the cut up fruit and *salt* lightly. For a reasonable quantity of fruit, add one tablespoon of *sweetened condensed milk (La Lechera)* and one tablespoon of *mayonnaise.*

Mix well and chill if possible before serving.

If you don't have mayonnaise on hand, more *La Lechera* can be used. Avoid adding too much, however, or the salad will be runny and unattractive.

Nuts, (coconut, peanuts, etc.) can be added to the salad if you wish.

Plain fruit with *yogurt* is excellent and very nutritious.

28 Stew

Stew can be made with about any kind of meat and vegetables you can think of. It is very good with *iguana* or *conch.*

The proportions for stew ingredients are determined by personal choice and appetites. If you have several vegetables on hand, it is quite easy to make too much. By the time you've thrown in one or two of everything, the stew will fill a washtub. Stew fortunately tastes better on the second or third days.

Cut meat into chunks. Bones give flavor so don't automatically toss them to a dog. Sprinkle the meat with *tenderizer* (if it's tough) and *black pepper.*

Heat a few tablespoons of *oil* in a large skillet. If you like *garlic*, brown it just before browning the meat. Remove and discard the browned garlic. Brown the meat well.

As the meat browns, chop vegetables. We prefer to use vegetables in large chunks, but this makes it very easy to cook too many. Anyway, use such things as *potatoes, carrots, onions, celery, bell peppers, green beans, fresh peas, corn, squash, chayote, parsley, epazote,* etc. *Cabbage* is also good but its flavor tends to mask the flavors of other vegetables. If you use cabbage, add it 15 minutes before the stew is done.

When the meat has browned, remove it from the pan and brown the vegetables in the fat for a few minutes.

Now put the meat back in with the vegetables. Add *salt* and other *spices*, a shot of *Worcestershire sauce* if you have it, a cup of *water* or *broth* and half a cup of *dry red wine* (optional).

Turn the heat down, cover the pan, and cook until vegetables and meat are tender. If you are using cheap Mexican stew meat, it's best to give up when the vegetables are tender; the meat probably never will make it.

●Vegetarians: Prepare the vegetables as if they were pieces of meat (flour and brown).

When you think the vegetables are about ready, mix two tablespoons of *flour* or one tablespoon of *cornstarch* in half a cup of broth from the stew. Stir it up well and dump it back into the stew. This will make a nice thick gravy. If it doesn't, repeat the procedure.

Note: Very tough meat can be parboiled or pressure cooked to tenderize it. Be sure to brown it first. If you use a pressure cooker, the meat and vegetables can all be cooked together together in a short time. If you're using something with a great number of bones and prefer not to have them in the stew, cook whatever it is—iguana, chicken or stew bones—until the meat can be easily removed from the bones. Use the broth for the stew.

29 Fish

Most people overcook fish and other seafood. This makes them dry and tasteless, like the fish sticks served in cafeterias and chow halls.

It is far better to undercook a fish. Fish is not cooked to be tenderized as are most other flesh foods. Congealing the protein (like hard-boiling eggs) is the object of cooking a fish. This doesn't take very long.

Undercooked fish is not dangerous to eat; in fact, there are many delicious dishes made from completely raw fish. (See *Ceviche*.)

30 Grilled Fish

This is the easiest way to cook a fish while camped on the beach.

Build a fire, not too large, of the hardest wood available. While it is still flaming, place your grill (if it's metal) in the fire to preheat it.

If you don't have a grill construct one of green branches and be careful not to burn it down.

Small fish should be grilled whole, with head, tail, skin and fins intact. This prevents the loss of juices from the flesh. Large fish (over a pound or two) can be cut into filets, steaks or just split in half lengthways.

Brush the fish all over with *oil* and place it on the red hot grill. The wires should sear the fish and thus prevent it from sticking.

When the fire has burned down to a good bed of coals, start cooking. Two or three minutes per side should be sufficient to cook a small whole fish, depending on the thickness of the skin and the heat of your fire. Larger fish will of course take longer. Don't get impatient and place the fish too close to the fire or the outer layer of flesh will harden.

31 Fried Fish

Roll whole small fish, filets or steaks in any kind of *flour* (including *tortilla.*) Dip into a *batter of egg* beaten with a shot of *milk* or *water, pepper* and *paprika.* Now back into the flour.

Fry in about 1/2 cup of hot *oil* (not so hot that it smokes) until brown. Do not overcook.

or

Dry the fish or pieces well and fry gently in a small amount of *butter, oil* or *fat.* Dip in flour first if you wish but this requires a hotter quicker cooking.

32 Deep Fried Fish

This is more of a hassle and requires a hot stove and lots of oil. The oil can be reused, however, if it is strained after cooling and placed in a sealed container.

Prepare fish, in pieces or whole, as described for frying in flour.

Place in at least two inches of hot oil and cook until browned. Drain well on paper.

33 Seafood Tempura

A Japanese style tempura batter makes really superior tasting deep-fried fish. The batter and methods can be used for tempura vegetables or other seafoods.

The ingredients for the batter are very simple:

1 cup white flour
1 tsp. salt
1 heaping Tbsp. baking powder (optional)
1 cup cornstarch (optional)
1 or 2 egg yolks (optional)
water

Sift flour and cornstarch together, then add the other ingredients. Mix with enough water to form a batter the consistency of light pancake batter. If you find that you haven't added enough at first, you can always water it down after you've started cooking. It takes one to two cups of water, depending on how heavy you like the dough.

Beer can be used instead of water and *flour* can be used instead of cornstarch. Cut fish into chunks about two inches by one inch. Dip into the batter and then drop carefully into hot oil. Use enough oil to prevent the pieces from touching the bottom of the pan.

Deep fry *vegetables* with the seafood or make tiny shish-ka-bobs of fish, vegetables and fruit on twigs or toothpicks and cook after dipping in the batter.

If your batter doesn't puff out well when it hits the hot oil, add more baking powder.

Large shrimp and strips of conch should be sliced thin and flattened to reduce the cooking time.

Cooked tempura is excellent when dipped in *soy sauce, hot mustard* and then coated lightly with *sesame seeds.*

I also like it with catsup, but this is not considered too cool.

34 Grilled Conch

Cooking time is critical for conch; overcooking makes them tough and chewy.

Dip well flattened and pounded conch into a mixture of *oil, pepper, garlic* and *paprika.*

Place them on a hot grill over coals. Cook no more than 30 to 45 seconds, *total time.* This means you'll have to work fast. Try overcooking one piece and you'll see the reason for such a short cooking time.

35 Fried Conch

Conch are good fried but the cooking time necessary to brown a flour coating toughens most of the flesh. Fry dried unfloured pieces of conch in *oil* or *butter* with *garlic* and *onion.* Eat them as they come out of the pan. This helps keep cooking time to a minimum, especially if you're feeding a group.

36 Deep Fried Conch

Cook exactly like fish. Conch in tempura batter are really a delicacy. If they tend to become tough while deep frying, add more *baking powder* and/or *water* to the tempura batter. This should make it lighter and faster cooking.

37 Other Seafoods

Clams: Steam living clams in a couple of cups of salt water until the shells open. Don't drown the clams, steam them! Dip in *melted butter* mixed with *garlic* and *parsley* and eat.

Use them in rice, spaghetti, macaroni or scrambled eggs. Clams are good with almost everything.

Crabs: Boil in salt water until the shell turns red (no more than 5 to 7 minutes). Small crabs can be used whole in soup or rice.

Lapa: Prepare as conch.

Limpets: Prepare as conch or clams.

Lobster and Crayfish: Boil, living or dead, in salt water until the shell turns red (don't overcook), or extract the uncooked meat from the shell and cook in tempura batter. Lobster can be grilled. Split the entire lobster lengthwise (leave it in the shell), coat well with *melted butter, margarine* or *oil* and grill the same as fish.

Oysters: Cook as clams or eat raw, garnished with lime juice. Heaven!

Shrimp: Bring a large pot of salted water to a boil. If you're using sea water dilute it half and half with fresh or it might be too salty. Drop the raw shrimp, heads and all, into the water. They should be done before the water comes back to a boil. When in doubt, remove the pot from the heat and start testing: remove a shrimp, peel and eat it. If it isn't done, remove and eat another. The shrimp will still be cooking in the scalding water. When you decide they're done, drain them quickly and rinse with cold water. If you don't rinse the shrimp, heat retained by their bodies will continue to overcook them. *It is a sin* to overcook shrimp!

38 *Ceviche*

This dish is an excellent snack, often prepared by Mexican fishermen right at the water's edge. It is usually accompanied with salted crackers and *tequila.*

Many types of seafood are used to make *ceviche.* It never seems to be the same twice.

Before committing yourself to a large batch of *ceviche,* experiment with a modest amount, noting the proportions of the ingredients. I've often prepared *ceviche* for Mexican guests and have found that they can be embarrassingly honest in their criticism.

Cut into bite sized pieces about two cups of either skinned and boned *raw fish* (an oily fish such as *mackerel (sierra)* is good but any kind will do), *oysters,* pounded *conch, lapa, clams* or whatever else you scraped off the beach. Place in a bowl and cover with *lime juice.* Stir and set aside.

Chop very finely:

1 white onion
1 tomato
salt
2 seeded jalapeño peppers (canned or fresh)
2 cloves of garlic

Add this to the seafood. Optional: a shot of *bottled hot sauce, pepper,* and if you wish some *oregano and parsley.*

Allow the *ceviche* to marinate for at least ten minutes before serving. Many people recommend hours of marinating, but this is usually impractical; no one seems willing to wait that long. *Ceviche* is customarily eaten with toothpicks.

39 Chop Suey

Chop suey can be made from almost any type of vegetables and meat, though meat is not essential.

Advance planning will allow you time to assemble the best ingredients. The following things are what we *try to use,* but we seldom find them all at once.

celery, sliced thinly on the diagonal
onion, including green tops
jícama, very thin slices (almost like water chestnuts)
bell pepper, in long thin slices (or mild seeded chile poblano)
meat, chicken or seafood, cooked and thinly sliced
mushrooms, canned or fresh
bean sprouts
garlic
tomatoes: slice into quarters and add just before the liquid. The taste of the chop suey won't be as authentic but it is very good.

Cook the meat in a *small amount* of *hot oil.* Remove and set aside.

Heat two tablespoons of *oil* in a skillet until very hot. Fry one bud of *garlic* and a slice or two of *ginger* until crisp. (Use 1/4 to 1/2 tsp. of *ground ginger* if you don't have fresh.)

Remove *garlic* and *ginger* and add the vegetables, keeping the fire high. Fry, stirring constantly, until the vegetables are shiny and translucent and *still chewy.* Soft, mushy vegetables won't taste as good.

Stir in the meat or seafood.

Add one half to one cup of *liquid* (water, broth or the juice from canned shrimp or clams) mixed with one tablespoon of *soy sauce* and one tablespoon of *cornstarch.* Stir well and cover pan for two or three minutes. Serve over steamed rice or noodles.

40 Macaroni, Cheese and...

Place about 1/2 pound (250 grams, *un cuaruto*) of macaroni or noodles into two quarts of salted boiling water. Add a tablespoon of *cooking oil,* stir well to separate all of the macaroni and boil over high heat for five to seven minutes. (Mexican macaroni, noodles and spaghetti are often starchier than those sold in the U.S. and take longer to cook.) When still slightly chewy, it is ready. Avoid overcooking or it will be like a pot of paste.

After cooking drain and wash the macaroni thoroughly. (Before draining add a pint of *ice water* if you can; this will take almost all of the starch out and make your macaroni much nicer.)

While the macaroni is cooking, heat a can of *condensed milk* (or a cup of other milk) in a saucepan.

Add:

1 onion, finely chopped
1/2 green pepper, finely chopped
2 stalks celery, chopped
garlic, minced
salt
pepper

Simmer all of this over low heat until the vegetables are about cooked. If you prefer your vegetables slightly raw, as we do, watch the cooking time closely; it doesn't take long.

Add grated or finely chopped *cheese*—a cup or more if you have it—of any kind that will melt. Homemade ranch cheese, the crumbly white type, will not melt properly but it can be used if there's nothing else. Add enough to give the sauce the consistency of thick cream. Avoid scorching the cheese; it is murder to clean out of the pan.

Add the sauce to the drained macaroni, place over a low fire and stir well until good and hot.

Add just about anything you can think of to make the macaroni more interesting: a can of drained *tuna, olives, canned clams, oysters, hamburger (cooked), iguana* or any other precooked meat, fish, or flesh.

Fresh *tomatoes* are good, but they tend to make the macaroni soupy.

If there is any left over, mix it with eggs and fry for breakfast.

41 Fast Spaghetti

Cook 1/2 pound of spaghetti, macaroni (see *Macaroni and Cheese or fideos.* see *Macaroni* in *The Shopping List*). As it is cooking, sauté in two tablespoons of *oil:*

1 to 6 buds of garlic
1 onion, chopped
1/2 to 1 green pepper, chopped
2 stalks celery, chopped
salt
pepper
oregano
thyme
marjoram

When the onion is transparent or beginning to brown, add 1/2 pound of *meat,* ground or chopped. Dried beef or venison is good. Cook until browned.

Dump one medium sized can of *tomato sauce* or five to six chopped fresh *tomatoes* into the pan. Stir well, cover pan and simmer for at least half an hour and serve.

42 Clam Spaghetti

With practice, you will be able to crank out a delicious meal of clam spaghetti in a very short time. The same basic recipe can be used with other seafoods as well. *Conch* is particularly good in spaghetti when well tenderized.

Cook 1/2 pound of spaghetti, noodles or macaroni (see *Macaroni and Cheese*).

While the spaghetti is cooking, sauté in one cube of *butter* or *margarine* or 1/2 cup *olive* or *cooking oil* the following:

1 onion, finely chopped
1/4 cup fresh parsley, chopped (2 Tbsp. dried)
1 to 6 buds garlic
salt
pepper
basil, oregano (optional)

When the onions are translucent, add 1/2 cup of canned *clam juice* or some of the water used to cook live clams in. Add the clams too, the more the better. We usually use just one can of clams if we have to buy them.

When the sauce is well heated, pour over the drained spaghetti and warm the entire mixture.

43 White Sauce

This is actually a gravy but we use it primarily as a sauce for steamed vegetables.

Make a gravy using *butter* or *margarine* for the fat and *milk* for the liquid. Add *paprika* if you have it.

Pour the sauce over steamed vegetables and heat both together for a few minutes.

44 Red Sauce

This sauce is good over just about anything. If you're interested in making Mexican food, you'll find Red Sauce indispensable—and not too spicy.

Chop and mix:

2 red ripe tomatoes
1 medium onion
garlic (to taste)
chili (to taste)
salt
squirt of lime juice

I recommend using canned *jalapeños*, carefully cleaned of seeds. Try one to begin with and then increase the dosage according to your tolerance.

Red Sauce can be served just as described or simmered until the ingredients have cooked, then served hot or cold.

45 Green Sauce

This sauce will keep for several days without refrigeration. It can be served hot or cold on fish, eggs, potatoes, rice, meat, beans, etc. Green sauce has a distinctive tart taste and does not have to be spicy unless you wish it to be.

The mashed ingredients are most easily prepared in a stone mortar and pestle, called a *molcajete*. The *molcajete* is indispensible for grinding fresh peppercorns, seeds, nuts and other ingredients for typical Mexican dishes.

Cut and mash:

6 to 10 green tomatoes (the small type covered with a leafy membrane)
1 medium onion
1 jalapeño, canned (optional)
2 to 3 buds of garlic
salt
pepper

Simmer for half an hour and serve.

46 Felicia's Rattlesnake Sauce

Sauces made with dried *chiles* are quite different from those calling for fresh. This sauce is called Rattlesnake because it uses *chile cascabel,* not because it is unusually deadly or spicy. With practice you can make a batch in just a few minutes. It keeps for weeks if refrigerated.

10 dried cascabel chiles (a handful)
6-8 green tomatoes (tomatillos, membrane covered)
salt to taste
garlic, several cloves

Toast the chiles over an open flame or in a pan. Avoid breathing the fumes, they are quite irritating. Remove the seeds. Peel the husk from the tomatoes and drop them into boiling water. Cook for 3 to 4 minutes or until soft, remove and drain.

Blend everything in a *molcajete,* bowl or blender. If a *molcajete* is used grind each ingredient for several seconds, add another and grind it and so on until everything is mixed together. This is said to improve the flavor.

The green tomatoes can be roasted instead of boiled. If regular unripe green tomatoes are used be sure to cook them well (they can be slightly poisonous).

Variations: use red tomatoes or fresh chiles. If fresh chiles are used, decrease the number to about two or three.

47 Gravy

Heat 3 to 4 tablespoons of *fat* (bacon grease, meat drippings, cooking oil, butter or margarine) in a frying pan until it is quite hot but not smoking. Meat drippings or boullion stock make the most flavorful gravies.

To the hot grease add 2 to 3 tablespoons of *flour* (any kind). Stir the flour into the grease until well browned, then slowly add *milk* or *water* to the pan.

The first half cup or so of liquid may just disappear into the flour and form a thick goo. If it does, keep stirring without adding more liquid until the mess is hot again. Once the gravy is bubbling, add more liquid until the desired consistency has been reached.

The first time I made gravy, it took one gallon of milk to thin down the amount of flour I'd used. Never use more than four tablespoons of flour unless you want ungodly amounts of gravy.

Boil the gravy at least five minutes after adding the liquid to cook the flour. The hot gravy, still in the pan, should be thin enough to make little wavelets when you splash around in it.

Milk makes a thicker, richer gravy than water. Add *salt, soy sauce, pepper* and *herbs* (thyme, oregano, rosemary, etc.) just a few minutes before taking the gravy off the fire. A *raw egg* can be added and stirred in with the spices.

48 Yogurt

Dry yogurt cultures (available in the U.S.) provide the most convenient way to start your own yogurt. Most Mexican supermarkets carry fresh yogurt which can also be used as a starter. The best type is Bulgarian yogurt.

Mix up:

1 cup boiling water | *1 cup powdered milk (Nido)*

1 cup cold water | *1 culture or 1/4 to 1/2 cup fresh yogurt*

Pour into glasses or jars. Place the jars in a pan of warm water. Keep the pan warm by placing it over the pilot light of a stove, in the sun, near a fire, or wrapped in a sleeping bag.

The yogurt should form within 3 to 12 hours. If it turns sour, it has been kept warm too long. Do not shake the jar; test for solidness with a knife.

Refrigerate the yogurt if you can or make smaller amounts if you can't.

Plastic containers used for keeping *tortillas* warm are excellent for making yogurt

49 Coconut Banana Bread

Stir up the following in a bowl:

2 cups flour (we prefer whole wheat)
1 tsp. salt
1 tsp. baking powder or soda

Chop up one cup of *coconut meat* (hard or soft, it doesn't matter) or 1/2 cup of any other type of nut. Add the nut and milk to the other ingredients.

Mash three or four overripe *bananas* and add them to the mixing bowl along with:

3 Tbsp. vegetable oil
1/2 cup honey or molasses

Line the bottom of your baking pan with heavy paper. When you burn the bread, this will make it much easier to pry out. Grease the inside of the pan, including the paper. Dump in the mixture. Bake for about 45 minutes at 350 degrees. When using an adobe oven, tend the fire carefully to maintain a constant temperature. To test the bread stab it with a toothpick—it's done if the toothpick comes out clean.

50 Toasted Seeds

Pepitas, toasted squash and melon seeds, are a favorite Mexican snack. They're not only very nutritious but also quite inexpensive. To make your own either buy seeds in the market or scrape them from a squash and clean thoroughly. Mix one cup of seeds with 1/4 cup of heavily salted water. Fry in an unoiled pan over a hot flame, stirring constantly. The *pepitas* are done when brown or popping open. I cook mine until even the shell can be eaten; it's lazier than opening them with your teeth.

Variations: add garlic or chili powder while cooking or after.

51 *Tepache* Wine

This mildly alcholic brew is easier to make than it is to digest. The longer it ferments, the more potent it will be. Most Mexicans wait a few days before drinking their *tepache,* but I prefer a two to four week vintage.

We usually carry a large jug of *tepache* while travelling by car. When the level drops, we just add more water, sugar and a few pieces of miscellaneous fruit.

Tepache can be used in cooking.

Chop up the skin of a pineapple that hasn't been washed in any type of disinfectant solution. (This kills the natural yeasts necessary for fermentation.) If you're extravagant, you can also use the rest of the pineapple, too.

Add about a *gallon of water* to the skin. Stir in one *kilo* of *sugar* or 1/2 liter of *honey*. Brown sugar (*piloncillo*) is preferable to white sugar as it gives the *tepache* a richer flavor.

If you wish add *stick cinnamon, cloves, apples, raisins,* etc.

Cover the container with a cloth and let it ferment for a few days. Strain well, allow time for most of the yeast to settle and drink. An excellent cure for constipation.

Warning: If your container has a tight-sealing lid, don't close it down completely. Gas given off during fermentation can explode even a thick-walled glass jug.

'52 Fruit Drinks

These drinks, called *agua fresca*, are very easy to prepare, more healthful than soft drinks and quite cheap. They go great with a hot day at the beach.

1/4 ripe pineapple or
1 small melon or
1/2 pound of strawberries or
10 limes

honey or sugar
pure water, 2 liters
ice

Blend or mash the fruit you've choosen (combinations are good, too). If you're using limes, oranges or grapefruits peel them first, then use both pulp and juice.

Sweeten to taste. Mexicans drink it lightly sweetened, which is more refreshing, especially if ice is added.

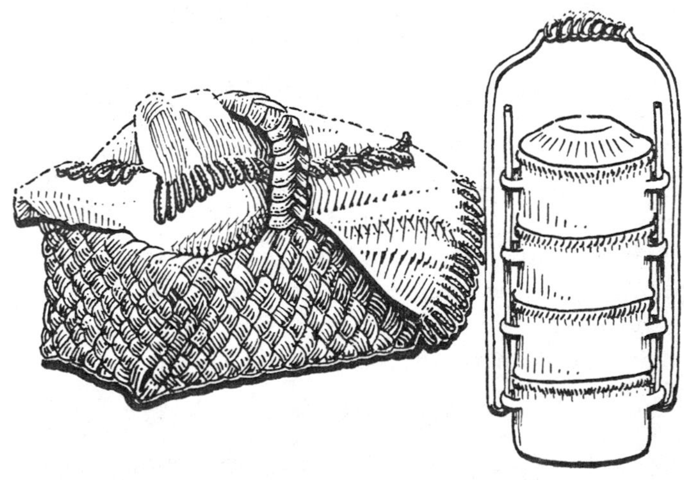

The day began typically enough with bright probing fingers of sunlight urging me out of my hammock. After a short struggle with tangled blankets, I managed to extract myself from my swinging nest. Vague thoughts of an early swim, of fishing, of making coffee, of going back to the hammock were abruptly ended by the sound of curses from our nearby *palapa*.

"That sonnofabitching rat ate my last tomato! I'll kill that bastard if he keeps this up! Aw hell! My very last tomato!"

"Well," I thought grimly, "looks like Steve is in for a good day."

"I've got to go to town," he said. By the tone of his voice, I knew that arguments were out of the question. He *had* to go to town, even though there was enough food to scrape by for a day or two more.

"Yeah, well..." I muttered. "I guess I'll probably stay around here and go fishing or something." The thought of a 150 mile round trip drive on dirt roads just for food didn't excite me greatly.

"Maybe Fred and Kris would like to go in," I suggested, hoping that our neighbors would accept the wonderful opportunity to make a day long shopping expedition.

Steve left the hut muttering about family loyalty but I was glad to notice that he headed directly for Fred's van.

He was back within a few minutes, already chanting the food list: "Naturally we need onions, tomatoes, potatoes, bananas, garlic, *chiles,* oranges, cooking oil, flour, rice, sugar, salt, a papaya, a watermelon if they have it, a couple cans of juice, a..."

"Wait, I interrupted. "For God's sake, is this a shopping trip or the end of our budget for two months?"

Steve looked at me sadly, "Would you prefer to go instead?"

"Well...errh...I...ah...guess not," I answered, shocked that he would say such a cruel thing. "I just thought you might sort of take it easy on the money, you know...?"

"Yeah!" Steve muttered. "Well, at least Kris has some appreciation for food; she said she'd be glad to go."

As he rummaged through the kitchen area, collecting shopping bags and checking supplies, Lorena wandered in.

"Going to town?" she yawned.

"Thinking about it," Steve answered with forced casualness. "Need anything?"

"Well," she said vaguely, "if you see any purple sewing thread or any of those little brown fruit things or maybe a bunch or two of that greenish herb that lady told us about or..."

"O.K.!" Steve said, scuttling toward the van. "See you guys in a few hours."

As I was about to flop back into the hammock, I heard Steve yelling for me.

"What is it?" I asked, hoping he wasn't going to try to enlist me at the last moment.

"I was thinking that we ought to have a really *substantial* meal when we get back," he said. "Why don't you and Fred see if you can round up a good batch of fish?"

"Sure, Steve!" I agreed, freed now from any lingering sense of guilt at staying behind.

The Great Grunt-A-Rama

"OOrrrfffhh!" Steve moaned, sagging into a hammock and dropping two shopping bags stuffed almost to bursting with food. "God, what a trip!" he sighed, eagerly accepting the beer Kris offered him.

"Blew a tire...gasp...six inches of dust...slurp...no tomatoes except on some *rancho*... cough... slurp... slurp... slurp... Kris had diarrhea... stopped 2000 times... slurp... must have been 150 degrees... slurp... got another beer?... Oh!... get any fish?...no white onions, got purple instead...back killing me...slurp, slurp, slurp..."

Steve belched hugely, heaving himself out of the hammock. "Time to start cooking!"

"Can't I do something?" Kris yelled after him. "Chop something or..." But before she could finish, he disappeared through the low doorway, caught now in the spellbinding thought of intense food fondling and preparation.

"Looks like an impending Grunt-A-Rama to me," I said to Lorena. "Better stay clear of the kitchen."

"What's a Grunt-A-Rama?" Kris asked curiously, for although we had lived side by side for weeks, neither she or Fred had yet observed this impressive cooking phenomena. "Why do we have to avoid the kitchen? Can't I help?"

"Look, Kris," I said, "when Steve is in a state that we call a 'food frenzy' he's like a vicious feeding shark. Anything within range is subject either to dicing, slicing or intense cursing. My advice is to wait until you've seen him in action before deciding to help."

Kris couldn't help looking rather sceptical, so I said, "Let's take in the groceries, have a beer and watch what happens."

"Here you go, Steve," I said, easing my heavy burdens to the ground.

"Yeah, thanks," he muttered absent-mindedly, eyes travelling back and forth over the array of foodstuffs strewn about the hut.

"Oh!" he said suddenly, "How about the fish? Did you get any?"

"Of course," I answered. "Fred speared a really nice hog nosed snapper and we got several smaller fish too. Also, half a dozen good sized conch and a lobster."

"Then how about some conch soup for starters?" Steve asked. "Sound good?"

"Yeah, sure. Sounds great," I assured him, knowing that on other days he would make it a full meal but now he considered a huge soup just openers for a larger, more adventurous foray into gluttony.

As I retreated outside I heard him muttering, like strange incantations, the ingredients that would go into the full Grunt-A-Rama.

"Half a cup of onions for the soup...better make it a full cup...oil...lots of garlic...I wonder where Lorena put the parsley?...ought to have tempura...cornstarch...stuffed snapper with olives...where'd I put the olives?...better have Carl fix up this knife, getting dull...need another stove.."

This last comment caught my attention and I whispered to Kris, "Would you mind getting your stove? This looks like at least a four or five burner meal." While she was gone, I began to gather wood. I knew that he would also want a hot campfire for deep frying.

By the time I'd started the fire, Steve had entered into a full food frenzy. Lorena and Kris, giggling as they sipped warm beer, watched furtively from the doorway of the *palapa* as Steve performed before the stoves.

Chopping, cursing, dropping, searching, tasting, sipping, hacking, stuffing, mincing, measuring, burning, smearing, dipping, sticking and making an incredible mess of the kitchen, Steve whipped untold quantities of raw food-stuffs into a symphony of grunting.

With his spatula held baton-like in his left hand and a beer clutched greasily in his right, he induced skillets to musical sputterings and spatterings of hot fat. To add dimension and depth, pungent buds of garlic sent heavy penetrating odors and crisply sautéing sounds out of the hut and into nearby camps.

The stacatto chopping of onions, the melodious grinding of peppercorns, the light bubbling of sauces, all held together and given coherence by Steve's rhythmic chanting: "fry, you bastard.. why won't that stove get any hotter?... oh, hell! I cut myself ...where's the hot pad?... use my shirt... ouch! damn that thing!... wonder if that's going to be enough?...where's Carl?...need the fish...need another beer...how many of us are there?...looks like a lot...should have got more onions...where's the garlic press?...my back is killing me..."

"Shall I invite those people down the beach?" I asked quietly, dodging a handful of potato peels being thrown blindly away from the cooking area.

I don't know!" he cried, furiously opening a can of pickled peppers. "If you think there's going to be enough..."

"What all are we having besides conch soup, fruit salad, cole slaw, stuffed snapper, vegetable and fish tempura, french fries, lobster, *tortillas* and banana nut bread?" I asked. "Of course, if that isn't enough for five of us, we could always cook up some beans."

"Beans?" Steve said. "Do you think there's time?"

"No," I answered. "I do think, though, that there'll be plenty for a few extra people."

"Whatever you say," he agreed, obviously pleased at the thought. "Just so there's enough for everyone to get *really full.*"

Lorena had overheard our conversation and was already on her way down the beach to the many camps hidden among the palms, spreading word of the impending feast. Odors had preceded her and within minutes hungry, undernourished travellers were drooling toward our hut.

"This is going to be a good one," I thought ruefully, "and I can imagine who will end up doing the dishes."

The Eating

"Did you try any of this?" I dodged a hot dripping spatula just as Steve dropped a huge piece of deep fried fish onto my already overflowing plate.

"Oh man!" I complained, "I can't eat all that!"

"Well, at least give it a try," he urged, moving on to another person who had paused to breathe between bites, encouraging, cajoling and even whining in order to increase the per capita consumption.

The uninitiated loudly praised each bite and were rewarded with unasked for portions while Lorena and I, veterans of many overfeedings, confined our praise to those dishes we knew were running low or were already exhausted.

As the bottoms of pans were scraped for the final morsels and plates dropped empty into the sand, Steve sagged like a bloated walrus, his beer drooping dangerously from a limp hand, eyes wandering vaguely in search of a resting place.

When his grease spattered bulk had been eased into a vacant hammock, he uttered the immortal words that signal the end of the Grunt-A-Rama: "I don't know why I feel so tired all of a sudden!!"

And with that, he lapsed into a state of semihibernation that would last until breakfast.

The Cleanup

There was nothing funny about it at all.

NOTES

BOOZE AND CANTINAS

Drinking customs...The borrachera...Vino or wine?... Liquor stores...Contraband...Wine...Beer...Tequila and Mezcal...Pulque...Hard liquors...Homebrews...Cantinas... She who went away...

Although present day Mexicans freely enjoy an occasional drink their predecessors, the Aztecs, took a dim view of alcoholic beverages. Recognizing the destructive power of over-indulgence, they restricted drinking to the ruling priest class and old people. Everyone else was automatically included in what must have been the world's most successful chapter of AA: drunks were simply strangled or clubbed to death. A tough thing to face with a hangover.

The *Conquistadores* were horrified by this savage custom. Once they had completed the subjugation of the native population (and burned emperor Cuahtemoc alive) booze was made available to the survivors. The Spanish could point out both the humanity of such a reform and the economic good sense: Spain produced vast quantities of wines and spirits. The market potential of the New World was considerable.

Today the thirsty traveller is offered cold beer at gas stations, bus depots aboard the train, from sidewalk stands, in innumerable small stores, supermarkets and liquor stores and even on the beach, from dripping buckets lugged by enterprising vendors.

In addition to beer there's a wide variety of imported wines and liquors, not to mention such Mexican specialties as *tequila, mezcal,* rum, brandy and *Kahlua*.

Local concoctions fill any gaps that might remain in your thirst: *pulque*, *tepache, coco locos* and many others.

No good *fiesta*, celebration or public rally will be without liquid refreshment, though it may be sold discreetly in a temporary covered bar in a side street. Sporting events, in particular bullfights, just aren't the same without ice cold beer in paper cups and *botas* filled with everything from wine to *margaritas*.

DRINKING CUSTOMS

Even though alcoholic drinks are widely available, Mexicans do not generally approve of public drinking or public drunkeness. In between *fiesta* and bullfights drinking is done mostly in *cantinas,* bars and at home.

Women sometimes drink in the company with men, but only in bars (not *cantinas*), restaurants and at private parties. It is rare to see an unescorted woman drinking except at more sophisticated bars and clubs in big cities and tourist towns. A man who occasionally ties one on is considered *macho*; a woman who does the same is a disgrace.

The minimum drinking age is 15 years of age. I have seldom seen anyone that young drinking, other than a glass of beer or *pulque* at a private *fiesta*. (Mexico City, which cannot be considered typical, supposedly has a problem with teenage drunkeness.) Mexican parents tend to be very strict; their kids wait until they are a safe distance from home before drinking.

Drinking customs are closely tied to economic and social levels. As in most societies, rich Mexicans do pretty much as they please and the poor blindly follow tradition. A typical day in the country, for example, has the men sitting under a shade tree, passing the moonshine *mezcal* jug while the women huddle in the kitchen, preparing *tortillas* and sneaking an occasional sip from a hidden bottle.

One of the most disturbing customs encountered in Mexico (and Guatemala) is called ritual drinking. Ritual drinking is practiced by the Indians in conjunction with *fiestas*, religious and civil ceremonies and celebrations such as harvests, deaths, and births. At these times it is not only considered proper *but necessary* to get rip-roaring drunk. At a wedding, for example, it may be expected that everyone drink in order for the marriage to have a successful beginning. Failure to drink would be like a gringo ceremony without a clergyman or a shower or rice.

Public officials in Indian communities are often expected to drink while performing their duties. Because terms of office run for a year, it is said that many are alcoholics by the time they've served their time.

Tourists will rarely have the opportunity to participate in this type of drinking. Those who visit Indian towns to observe a *fiesta*, however, should be aware of it. At times it seems that whole villages are determined to drink themselves into the ground. As one anthropologist wrote, "...A *fiesta's* success is determined by the number of drunks jailed."

In the rest of the country ritual drinking is more likely to come in the form of the classic Mexican *borrachera*. Unlike the Indian system, the success of a 'spree' is measured by the amount of money spent, time spent intoxicated, days of work missed and the severity of the hangover. This type of drinking is considered more normal than a regular

intake of several cocktails each evening. A typical man might be a model of sobriety for 6 months and suddenly jump off the wagon and "*¡Agarrate a la borrachera!*" (Grab onto the binge!)

Experience has taught me to treat this phenomena with the same respect I would a hurricane at sea. Inexperienced drinkers, like inexperienced sailors, often miss the signs of an impending *borrachera* and find themselves unable to reach shore.

It usually goes like this: you're drinking with Pedro, a Mexican acquaintance and are slightly tipsy. You feel it's about time to stop, but he insists that you continue. In spite of your protests Pedro orders more drinks. The bartender ignores your cries of, "*¡No, por favor!*" and sets them up. You sigh but reach for the glass.

"*¡Salud!*" and down the hatch.

Pedro then makes an amazing discovery: buying an entire bottle of brandy eliminates having to wait for the bartender to serve you. Several of Pedro's *cuates* (buddies) gather and drinks are freely distributed. Someone begins yammering into your ear, something about visiting another *cantina*. The jukebox blares, then suddenly dies out, immediately replaced by a band of *mariachis*. Pedro calls out for a song. Whoever is hanging on your shoulder is still talking, but you've had a little bit too much to drink; is he speaking Spanish or Chinese?

Pedro finally staggers over to pay off the musicians, peeling off bills as if they had no end. He turns, grabs you by the elbow, and says, "Let's go to another place and get *borracho,* eh?" Since you're already drunk you decline, telling him you have to go.

"*¿Que?*" he answers, stepping back with a shocked expression on his face. "Go? Go? You can't go!" From the looks the others are giving, you realize that you've been challenged. Is this guy *macho* or not? Can he take it or can't he? You don't believe in that *machismo* stuff, it's just not good common sense. But after all, if anyone thinks you can't hold your own...

Everything slowly dissolves into an expensive blur as you visit Pedro's favorite *cantinas*, friends, relatives, more *cantinas* and perhaps—you can't quite remember—a whorehouse or two. Then come more drinks and *tacos* and more friends. By dawn you're either unconscious or on the verge. It's time to rest—either in a bar, someone's car or maybe even a bed.

"*¡Vámonos!*" Pedro cries after a few brief hours of coma-like sleep, dragging you into the next round of wine, women and song.

When your bodies fail to respond any further and your money and credit are totally exhausted, the *borrachera* ends. Now the dreaded *cruda* (hangover) begins. A really determined Mexican *macho* may delay this moment of awful truth for days or weeks.

Después de los celos queda la duda,
Y después de la borrachera, la cruda.
After jealousy remains doubt,
And after a *borrachera,* the hangover

A *borrachera* can be pre-meditated, such as the celebration of someone's Saint Day (see *Customs and Superstitions*) or it can begin casually, "Let's stop somewhere and have a couple hundred beers." This is the most difficult type to avoid. I once gave a man a lift on a lonely back country road.

"What can I pay you?" he asked when I let him out. We had stopped in front of a small palm thatched store and I was thirsty. I didn't want money so to be polite I suggested a beer. Twenty hours later I continued my trip. My passenger departed for home on a mule, safely lashed to the saddle by his three young sons. He spent more money repaying a ten mile ride than he would have on a chartered plane.

Para agarrar borrachera,
Bueno es el vino cualquiera.
To grab onto the binge,
Any booze is good.

VINO OR WINE?

On my first trip to Mexico I strolled into a *cantina*, clouched against the bar and confidently ordered myself "a glass of wine." I'd read Steinbeck's *Tortilla Flats* and knew that Mexicans love a good big tumbler of wine.

"What kind?" the *cantinero* asked, raising his eyebrows at the other patrons as if to say, "Hey, catch this one!"

I hesitated. "What kind?" I didn't know brand names, but rather than show my ignorance I said, *"Blanco.* Give me a *vino blanco!"*

The bartender reached down and held up a tiny shot glass. I shook my head. I wanted a *glass* of wine, not a sniff! He noted my look of disdain and exchanged the shot glass for one just slightly larger. I groaned dramatically. Up came a tall tumbler with a colored reproduction of the Virgin of Guadalupe painted on the side. Now this was something you could get your hands around.

"¿Todo?" he asked, giving the other drinkers another of those annoying eyebrow signals. "Yes, Yes!" I answered, "Fill it up!" I sighed, shaking my head sadly. Evidently those poor folks just didn't understand *thirst.* Steinbeck would have been disappointed

"There you go, *amigo*!" the bartender said, sliding the glass across the bar toward me. It was filled right up to the brim. I carefully lifted the wine to my lips. I took a mouthful, allowing it to trickle down my throat to catch the flavor. Suddenly my lungs and chest convulsed, forcing the wine back through my nose in a searing atomized sneeze.

"Gaaaahhhh!" I cried, hacking and coughing in a desperate struggle to replace fumes with oxygen. The bartender watched impassively. I threw my sunglasses onto the bar, swabbing my eyes with a shirt sleeve, croaking and gurgling a good imitation of someone drowning on their feet. "Wha...is...this?" ...I gasped, drumming on my chest in an effort at self-resusitation.

"Vino blanco," he answered calmly, reaching for the bottle. The label was turned toward me: *tequila*. For the next half hour, while I gingerly nursed down the remainder of the booze, the bartender helpfully explained to me that in Mexico, *vino* means liquor and *vino blanco,* though also the correct term for white wine, is actually the common name for any clear liquor, including, heaven forbid—pure alcohol.

To order 'real' wine ask for *vino de uva* (grape wine) and then specify *blanco* or *rojo*

Liquor Stores

Liquor stores are called *licorerías* and *vinos y licores. Licores* translates both as liquor and liqueur. A store with a sign saying *Ultramarinos* will sell liquor and snacks, a sort of Mexican delicatessen. Liquor stores often have interesting names. My favorite is *"El Exorcisto."*

Supermarkets are excellent places to buy liquor and wine; they often run sales (*¡Oferta!*) which include a bottle of booze, drinking glasses, ashtrays, sodas and whatever else it takes to attract a customer.

We've found that a town usually has one store that consistently undersells others. In one village, for example, the best buy was in the post office, which also sold the tastiest home roasted coffee.

Cantinas will sell beer and hard liquor to go at very steep prices.

Another source of booze deserves mention: contraband liquor and wine. Smuggling is a very popular and profitable business. The Mexican National Chamber of Commerce estimated that in one year more than 2,000,000 bottles of whiskey, 1,900,000 bottles of cognacs, brandy, and wine and 600,000 bottles of vodka were smuggled into the country. Such apparently vast quantities of tax free booze doesn't mean, however, that tourists will find it easy to buy. It is a hit-or-miss affair, at best. The best way to tap into contraband is through a Mexican friend: chances are that without an introduction or go-between, you'll never run into smuggled liquor.

WINE

The average Mexican seldom drinks wine. In spite of excellent grape growing conditions, the production of Mexican wine was severely limited by the Spaniards, fearful of competition in the lucrative European market. As a result, the Mexican wine industry has never approached its potential. Even today wine is considered an upper class drink.

Although many Mexican wines are good, few, if any are great. The cheapest are not a bargain, particularly when compared to jug wines from California. One wine is actually called *California*, which must bring a sour smile to anyone who appreciates wine from that state.

Mexican wines tend to be sweeter than American or French wines, though sometimes they are too sour. Quality control is loose. Some producers are actually not above adding sugar or alcohol to adjust flavor and potency. This doesn't mean that good wine isn't available, but that a variation from one bottle to the next can be expected. Wine lovers should buy several bottles when they happen upon a particularly good batch.

The following wines are widely available and moderately priced (see *Prices*). Remember: when ordering wine in a restaurant, you'll pay premium prices, especially for imports.

Los Reyes: both red and white. Produced by *Pedro Domencq*, one of the largest and most reliable companies, for brandy as well as wines.

Santo Tomas: Burgundy, not their *Vino Tinto* which is overpriced and very sharp.

Marquis Del Valle: both red and white

Hidaldo: white

There are many others, from sauterne to *Sangre de Cristo* (Blood of Christ). Homemade fruit wines are sold in various parts of the country. These are often better than a run-of-the mill commercial grape wine, though usually sweet.

BEER

Much has been said about the excellent quality of Mexican *cervezas* (beer). I love them all, from high class *Bohemia* to proletarian *Victoria* (also known rudely as *Pee-toria*).

Most Mexican breweries are operated under strict Germanic guidelines and their products often compare favorably to fine European beers. Americans who develop a taste for Mexican beer usually find it difficult to readjust to the lighter and less tasty brews back home.

Beer is sold by the *cartón* (case), *canastilla* (six pack), *bote* (can) and the *botella.* A standard tall bottle is a *media.* Liter-sized bottles are a good buy. They are called *caguamas* (sea turtles) in some areas and *ballenas* (whales) in others. I once ordered a *caguama* in central Mexico and was treated like a nut case. The bartender finally handed me a liter of beer, advising me with great seriousness that it was a *ballena.*

Regular and large bottles come in both returnable (*retornable*) and throwaway (*desechable*). *Cerveza de bote* (canned) is more expensive than bottled. Many Mexicans consider it classier to drink from cans.

Beer by the case is cheaper than singles or six packs, though case prices are given only at authorized agencies (*agencia* or *deposito de cerveza*). Everyone pays the wholesale price at the agency, whether a tourist or store owner. Beer agencies are very common; a small town may have three or four. In large towns there will be many agencies and subagencies (*sub deposito*). The *sub deposito* may have a smaller selection and probably won't offer blocks of ice.

Agencies have both canned and bottled beer. A bottle deposit is required and you should ask for a *recibo* (receipt). You'll probably have to buy a full case before they'll bother to write out a receipt. This piece of paper authorizes you to sell the bottles back, without it you're stuck. Bottles are not interchangeable between companies (though they may be identical in shape). Agencies of the same brewery may balk at refunding a deposit from another town. Be patient and insistent, but if they absolutely refuse to take the bottles, it's easier to give them away than argue.

Ask for a case of cold beer (*cerveza helada* or *fría*) when you buy it at the agency. Some have beer in large coolers and others will give away chunks of ice.

Delivery trucks sell beer at agency prices or just slightly higher. If you're renting a place or are camped in one spot for more than a few days, ask the driver to put you on his route. Beer trucks usually carry ice but they prefer to sell or give it to regular customers.

Beer agencies also handle soft drinks by the case and the price is a bargain. If you're hooked on mineral water (which is my favorite soft drink next to beer), buy it at the agency.

The following comments on taste are strictly subjective and should not stop you from trying every different type of beer you can lay your hands on.

Bohemia: The 'quality' Mexican beer, though in my opinion its reputation may come from a similarity to light American beer. After many years of exhaustive testing, I find *Bohemia* somewhat over-rated.

Tecate: Formerly a regional brew (Baja and the border), *Tecate* is now mass-produced and mass advertised. It is the *macho's* beer, customarily taken with lime juice and salt (on the top of the can). It is darker than average and also more expensive. The bright red cans are a familiar sight on the edge of Mexican highways.

Carta Blanca: Although most common in the north, *Carta Blanca* is gradually appearing in other areas. It comes in bottles, one type called *Quitapón*, which translates as "Take the top off." Each bottle has an indented socket in the bottom that is used to wrench the top off another. Be careful when opening a *Quitapón* with a bottle opener; the glass is rather weak. *Carta Blanca* is a light beer with a distinctive flavor.

Corona: A very popular light beer, sold in both clear and brown bottles. It is usually called *Corona Clara* or just *Clara* to distinguish it from the company's dark beer, *Negra Modelo. Corona de Barril* (draft) comes in bulbous throwaway bottles. *Modelo*, from the same brewery, is a light canned beer.

Superior: Also known as *Super, Chuper* and *Chuperior* (from the verb *chupar*, to suck or drink). *Superior* comes in tall brown bottles and non-returnable stubbies. It is a light beer and very popular. *Dos Equis* (XX), from the same brewery, is fairly dark. *Tres Equis* (XXX) is canned.

There are many regional beers, among them: *Sol, Indio, Pacifico, Liston Azul, Carta Clara, Leon Negro, Montejo* (these last three are from the Yucatan and excellent). *Noche Buena* (Christmas) is a bock beer that appears only around Christmas time.

When ordering a beer specify *fria* (cold) or *al tiempo* (air temperature). Beer is automatically served cold only in bars and restaurants catering to tourists. In other places you'll probably be asked how you want it.

You may also be asked, "*¿de bote?*" (canned) if you order a beer without specifying a brand.

Beer bottles are generally called *envases* rather than *botellas*, though the latter is certainly understood. A common slang term for bottles is *cascos*.

The slang terms for beer that can be used (again, some are regional) to impress your friends and the bartender are *chelas, chupes, cheves, eladas, elodias* and *las frias*.

TEQUILA AND *MEZCAL*

There is as much myth and misinformation floating around about these two liquors as there is about the fall of Mayan civilization. Because the English spelling of *mezcal*—mescal—is just three letters short of being 'mescaline,' it has been attritubed with broader properties than it rightly deserves. Although it's quite true that drinking a liter of *mezcal* will induce states of 'nonordinary reality,' the same can be said of drinking a liter of peppermint gin. *Mezcal*, in reality, is nothing more or less than hard liquor and basically the same drink as *tequila*, though the taste is quite different. The rumors, however, persist. For more see *The People's Guide To Camping In Mexico: In Search of the Magic Mezcal.*

To be an instant expert on *tequila* and *mezcal* you have only to memorize these few facts:

●*Tequila* is a type of *mezcal* and is correctly called *tequila de mezcal,* just as rye is a type of whiskey.

●True *tequila* is made only from *agave tequiliana,* also known as Weber's maguey, the Blue Agave or *Mezcal azul.*

- *Mezcal*, however, is made from many different types of maguey.
- Magueys are members of the agave family; they are not cacti.
- Neither *tequila* or *mezcal* is made from *pulque*. (See *Pulque*.)

Basic procedures for making both *tequila* and *mezcal* are similar; the main differences are the type of maguey used. *Mezcal* stills often look like something out of the Middle Ages, especially when compared to big modern *tequila* factories.

The traditional process begins when the long spikey leaves of the maguey are trimmed off with a *coa*, leaving a huge pineapple-like heart, called a *piña*. The hearts are roasted in enormous pits, then shredded in mule powered grinders in hand-made pottery and copper stills. Good traditional *mezcal* is not made with sugar, but where it is available, sugar is usually added to boost the alcohol content of the mash. Big-time distillers now use giant autoclaves and other machinery to process the *piñas*.

A type of fat grub that lives in maguey plants, called *gusano de maguey*, is traditionally added to each bottle of *mezcal*. These unappetizing worms are also considered a treat when fried. I've never been able to develop a taste for them, though I've tried.

Mezcal is made both legally and illegally just about wherever maguey plants can be found. The best I've tasted came from the mountains of Durango. But the most well known and widely marketed *mezcal* is from Oaxaca.

Mezcal is usually less potent than *tequila* (38 percent or 76 proof is common), but moonshine *mezcal* may be very strong, depending on the whim of the bootlegger. Most moonshine *mezcal* is unaged and clear. Commercial *mezcals*, on the other hand, are usually gold and aged, though thay rarely brag for how long.

Tequila that has been aged is also gold in color and will be called *añejo* or *reposado* (aged or rested). *Tequila joven* is young *tequila*.

Because of the demand some unscrupulous types make phoney *tequila* by adding *tequila* to alcohol and other short-cut processes. To protect consumers the Mexican government has declared that only the states of Jalisco, Nayarit and Tamaulipas can produce the proper blue agave and only *tequilas* made from agaves grown in those states can carry the letters DGN to signify that it is *legítimo* (legitimate).

The most well known brands of tequila are *Jose Cuervo* and *Sauza*. They are both moderately priced. There are so many other brands, many regional, that *tequila* drinkers should by no means restrict themselves to one label. My favorite, *Herradura* (look for a big blue horeshoe), is the only mass produced *tequila* made by traditional methods. It is sold in good liquor stores and supermarkets and is not expensive. Other good but inexpensive brands are *Viuda de Romero* (Romeo's widow), *Los Ruiz* and *Orendain*.

Specially aged and bottled *tequilas* are much more expensive than an average bottle of the same brand. If the label says *conmemorative, de reserva, especial* or other claim to better flavor, check the price carefully before buying. In my opinion the extra cost is often for the fancy packaging—a heavy glass decanter, wooden box, ribbons, etc., rather than a superior *tequila*.

In the towns of Tequila and Oaxaca, centers for *tequila* and *mezcal* respectively, factory outlets offer good discounts on bulk purchases. Customers are invited to sample various types and to admire an assortment of possible containers for their liquor, everything from a plain 5 gallon jug to a personally embossed wooden cask with a spigot. Be careful. Dishonest dealers may pull a switch, filling your container with something cheaper than what you tasted and ordered. If you are interested in the best, visit some of the smaller outlying distilleries. Most produce such limited quantities that they don't have to bother with merchandising and sell direct to regular customers.

Mezcal de Oaxaca has an uneven distribution in the rest of the country. The most common brands are *Gusano Rojo* and *Gusano de Oro* (Red Worm and Gold Worm). Both are good. The tiny bag attached to the neck of the bottle is filled with worm salt, supposedly a mixture of dried and ground maguey worms, chili and salt. It's tasty stuff.

PULQUE

Pulque is the fermented sap of the maguey plant. It tends to have a slimey texture and a nut-like flavor. *Pulque* is mildly alcoholic, about like beer, and is loaded with vitamins and minerals.

Pulque was a sacred Aztec drink, governed by the god Two Rabbit. Two Rabbit had four hundred rabbit sons, and a *pulque* high was graded in rabbits, with total drunkenness apparently reaching four hundred rabbits. I've swallowed a lot of *pulque* but it is so mild that I rarely get beyond fifty rabbits myself.

In some areas poor people literally live on *pulque*. It is so nourishing in fact, that the Mexican government has tried in vain for years to find a method of bottling it without ruining the flavor.

Although the government encourages *pulque* drinking, the soft drink and beer industries are making serious inroads and the number of *pulquerías* is steadily diminishing.

Pulquerías are renown for their quaint atmosphere and clubbiness. Because it is customary to slop a bit of *pulque* on the sawdust floor (a drink for Two Rabbit), the atmosphere is sometimes all but unbreathable. The club spirit makes women totally unwelcome, and strangers run a close second. Beer and soft drinks may be served, but rarely anything stronger.

Pulquerías usually have humorous and often ironic names: 'The Effects of the Battle,' 'The White Nectar of Black Dreams,' 'Leave If You Can,' 'The Last Station' (across from a cemetery), 'Blood of the Maguey,' 'The Great Wound,' 'Here I'll Remain,' 'Memories of the Future' and so on.

A good respectable *pulquería* will serve only pure *pulque* (*pulque dulce* is young and sweet, *pulque fuerte* is older, slightly stronger and may be sour or acid), but because of shortages some places adulterate it with water. It is best to ask a knowledgeable person for a recommendation.

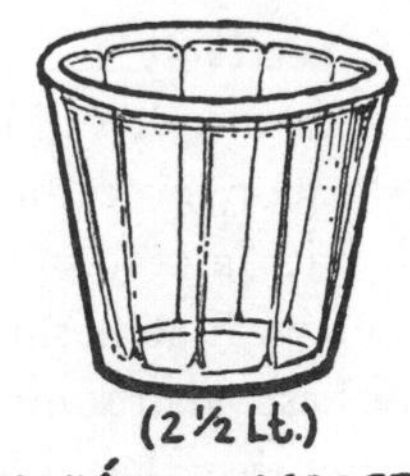

(2½ Lt.)
CAMIÓN o MACETA

"Wherever pulque can be obtained, it should be used in preference to any other drink. It is thoroughly wholesome, and has a tendency to decrease the bilious habit that in many persons is induced by an altitude of a mile above the sea level. It should be drunk...from a sense of duty."

The Mexican Guide by Thomas A. Janvier, Scribner's 1897

(1 Lt.)
CATRINA

Better *pulquerías* offer customers a variety of mugs to choose from, depending on the degree of thirst. Those shown are either of glass or decorated gourds (*jícaras*). Many places have given up the battle against breakage and serve *pulque* in cheap pottery mugs, named according to their capacities.

Detente caminante,
¡Un tornillo y adelante!

Stop walker,
A screw (a liter) and onward!

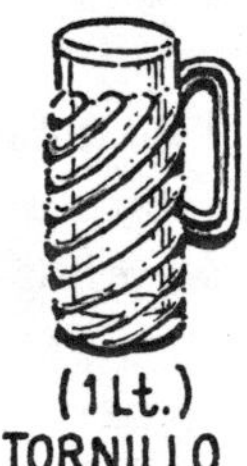

(1 Lt.)
TORNILLO

The process of making *pulque* is very simple but loaded with superstition and custom. When a maguey plant is several years old it prepares to sprout. A tall pole-like flower emerges from the center of the maguey (familiar to Americans as the Century plant). Before this sprout can develop, however, the center of the plant is 'crastrated.' A deep depression is gouged from the heart and begins to fill with sap, called *agua miel* (honey water). The *agua miel* is very tasty itself.

The *agua miel* is drawn off (a good plant will give up to a gallon a day) by siphoning with a long gourd (*acocote*; look for them in the market, they make interesting souvenirs). The man who does this is called a *tlachiquero*.

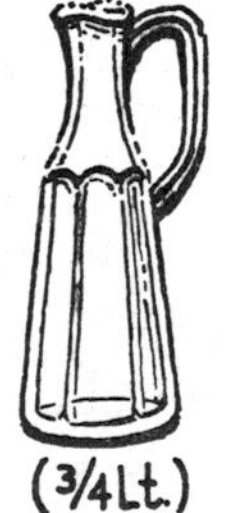

(¾ Lt.)
JARRA o TORREÓN

The *agua miel* is collected in vats or huge pottery urns in the fermenting house. This place, the *tinacal*, is still semi-sacred, an interesting holdover from Aztec beliefs. Women are not allowed

(½ Lt.)
TRIPA

(½ Lt.)
VIOLA

(¼ Lt.)
TORNILLO CHICO

(¼ Lt.)
VASO

(¼ Lt.)
OLLA

inside and men must remove their hats. Strangers are also discouraged or prohibited, depending on who is in charge. I lived next to a *tinacal* for several months and was never able to enter, though I was refused quite gracefully and eventually understood that it was not personal.

(1½ Lt.)
REYNA

A starter is usually added to the *agua miel* to speed up fermentation, though it has enough natural yeast and bacteria to do it alone. Good sweet *pulque* is produced within three days to a week, depending on the conditions. It is immediately shipped out to *pulquerías* and preferred customers. *Pulque* does not last long. It is at its best when drunk the same day it is pronounced ready.

(1 Lt.)
CACARIZA

Although most people prefer *pulque* straight, it is also taken with chili sauces (*pico de gallo,* rooster's beak) or mixed with fruit juices and pulps. I've tried it with lime (including the peel), banana, guava, pineapple and even celery, and thought all were delicious.

Pulque is very cheap, but it's not that easy for a tourist to find. The heavy demand makes people jealous of their *pulque.* The best way to get good pure stuff is through a Mexican friend, not from a *pulquería* or market vendor (almost always adulterated with dubious water).

(½ Lt.)
CACARICITA

HARD LIQUORS

Brandy is considered a status drink, though domestic Mexican brandies are not expensive. There's nothing Mexicans love better than to sit around in a *cantina* with a full bottle of brandy, inviting friends and even strangers to join in. Bottles of brandy sprout up at any good party or *fiesta*, and big seafood bashes in restaurants are incomplete without at least one. (See *Restaurants.*)

(⅘ Lt.)
CHIVATO o CABRÓN

(⅓ Lt.)
CHIVO

(1 Lt.)
JICARA

(½ Lt.)
JICARA

(¼ Lt.)
JICARA

(⅕ Lt.)
PRUEBA o PROBADITA

Common brands are *Presidente, Viejo Vergel, San Marcos, Cordon Real, Madero* and *Byass. Presidente* is probably the most popular and is made by *Pedro Domencq. Don Pedro Reserva Especial* is their best brandy.

The most popular brand of gin and vodka is *Oso Negro. Kimberly* is slightly cheaper. Imported brands are expensive.

Rum is made by several companies, the better known are *Bacardí, Ron Rico, Canaima, Potosi, Bonampak* and *Castillo.* There are many varieties of rum, from mellow aged to raw stuff that tastes like bad moonshine. *Bacardí Palmas*, for example, is a clear rum that is cheap and rough. *Bacardí Añejo*, dark and aged, is much smoother and more expensive.

Castillo is considered one of the best, but for average drinking I recommend *Ron Rico*; it's good and inexpensive.

There are a bewildering variety of liqueurs available. The most well know, *Kahlua*, is made from coffee. *Controy* (Cointreau, also called *licor de naranjas*) is made from oranges and used in *margaritas* and *coco locos.* Almond liqueurs are very popular. *Tequila almendrado* is an interesting taste experience. *Sangrita* is a non-alcoholic tomato juice and chili concoction (plus other spices) taken as a chaser with *tequila* or used in cocktails.

● Alcohol content in Mexican booze is given in percentages. GL 38° (Gay Lussac), for example, 38 percent alcohol is the equivalent of 72 proof. Beer labels also say *bebida de moderación*—a moderate beverage.

Aguardiente ('firewater,' which it definitely is) is very common and comes in many regional forms. It is sometimes called 'brandy,' though the first sip immediately confirms that it has never been near a grape. *Aguardiente* is almost always made from sugarcane and is unaged. It is known variously as *habanero, charanda, refino, trago* (literally 'a drink or swallow'), *aguar, comiteco, anís* (when flavored with anise), *bacanora, caña* and others. The potency of *aguardiente* varies from about 75 proof on up.

Alcohol (also called *alcol*) is dirt cheap in Mexico. It forms the basis for a variety of drinks, most of them just devices to camouflage the taste. Alcohol is sold in drugstores, hardware stores, liquor stores and small *tiendas* (under the counter). It's best to buy it from a large store or reliable source, someone who isn't afraid to drink what they sell, as adulteration is not unknown. Alcohol is made from sugarcane and is quite strong, usually about 190 proof. It burns well and can be used in stoves.

Alcohol rebajado is the world's most basic cocktail: cheap alcohol and water. Wretched stuff, believe me. *Alcohol compuesto* is half a step higher: with citrus peels and other fruit. When dumped into a soda it's called *teporocha* and those who are hooked on this are called *teporochos.* A tough way to go.

Alcohol is the poor people's drink. On Market day in most towns you'll see ragged drunks staggering down the street clutching a soft drink bottle half filled with clear 'popskull.'

Sophisticated drinkers prefer their alcohol in fruit juice *ponches*, as a substitute for gin or vodka. It is also served in a cocktail made by mixing one part honey, one part lime juice and two parts of alcohol.

Canela or *canelita* (cinnamon) is a common hot drink of water, cinnamon and brown sugar or honey mixed with alcohol. *Cantinas* prepare *canela* for early risers unable to face their hangovers.

HOME BREWS

Many people either can't afford factory produced spirits or just prefer their own traditional drinks. These are often regional and will be completely unknown outside a specific area; some are basic fermented drinks similar to 'beers' and 'jungle juices' made world wide. Like most homebrews they tend to be an acquired taste.

Tepache is found in many parts of the country. A basic *tepache* recipe calls for pineapple, brown sugar and water. Variations include the addition or substitution of cooked whole barley, sugarcane (pulp or juice), squash (preferably *chilacayote*), honey, other fruits, *pulque* and god-knows-what. It is drunk while still 'young,' which in some cases is only one or two days old and all but premature. It tends to be hard on the novice drinker's stomach.

Tepache picado is with the addition of a basic uncooked hot sauce. Tastes better than it sounds. *Tepache* may also be served adulterated with cheap alcohol. Tastes worse than it sounds.

Tepache is traditionally served in a *jícara* (gourd bowl). Like many of these homebrews it can sometimes be found in the marketplace, especially those attended by *campesinos* and Indians.

Amaze your friends by making your own *tepache!* (See *Recipes*.)

Chicha is the liquor produced by fermenting corn in sweetened water, but it may also be of fruit. *Chicha* made from sugarcane is similar to *tepache*. The raw cane is squeezed by animal or human power in a crude wooden press called a *trapiche*.

Tesguine or *tecuín* is made by fermenting a sprouted corn, corn stalks or wheat.

Tuba is fermented sap from the coconut palm.

Balche is made by the Mayans from a combination of sugarcane juice and the dried bark of the Lonchocarpus tree (*palo de huarapo*). Other bark, such as pine, can be used if you're short on Lonchocarpus. This drink is said to taste fairly awful, but I look foward to trying it.

Sotol is made from maguey flowers and is a sacred drink of the Huichol Indians.

Colonche is a fermented brew of cactus fruits (*tunas*).

No hay sabados sin sol,
Ni domingos sin borrachos.

There are no Saturdays without sun,
Nor Sundays without drunks.

CANTINAS

Few, if any, guidebooks recommend that tourists visit a typical Mexican *cantina.* These places, or so we are told, are only for the 'adventurous' or the person interested in a glimpse of the 'seamier side' of Mexican life. This attitude is unrealistic, comparable to warning visitors to the U.S. that the neighborhood tavern is a dangerous, evil hangout.

Don't be intimidated by your first glance into a crowded *cantina.* Mexican men, particularly farmers, ranchers and other hard working types, tend to look quite tough. With few exceptions, they are just the opposite and will treat the timid gringo with friendly consideration.

The majority of *cantinas* are honest, friendly, enjoyable places where friends and strangers gather in a spirit of masculine brotherhood. Consider this picture:

The *cantinero* (bartender), a paternal ex-bullfighter, singer or truck driver, serves one and all with democratic cheerfulness, dispensing both drinks and wise advice.

The customers, usually simple working folk, lift glasses of *tequila* ("a fiery potent liquor") and loudly proclaim toasts of mutual admiration.

Near the picturesque swinging doors a wandering group of *mariachis* strike up a rousing, lusty folk song.

The *cantinero's* son, an honest faced boy of about twelve, circulates among the tables, delivering plates of deliciously spicy regional snacks to the appreciative drinkers.

At a corner table a group of ranch hands are engaged in a lively bilingual political disucssion with a recently arrived tourist.

Now picture this same *cantina* through the eyes of the person who advises you not to go there:

The bartender, a tough looking character in a torn undershirt, watches impassively as the gringo approaches the crowded bar. Without a word, he pours the drinks and shoves them toward the customer, slopping booze onto his hands.

The tables near the bar are crowded with dirty, sweaty, yelling drunks who are doing their best to talk over the sound of the band. When the song has finished, there is a loud argument over who gets the privilege of paying for the noise.

A furtive boy throws down plates of indigestible snacks designed to burn the throat and sell more beer.

Someone is pissing into a malodorous five-gallon can in a dark corner. A dog snaps rabidly at a scrap of *tortilla* that falls from a limp hand. The scrap is soon followed by a drunken, inert body. No one notices.

In a corner a tourist exchanges totally incomprehensible phrases with several ex-*braceros* who ask repeatedly what the hell happened to their good jobs in California.

My own image of a *cantina* lies somewhere between these two descriptions. Depending on the place I've visited last, the image changes somewhat toward one extreme or the other.

Tourists are often confused by the difference between a typical *cantina* and a bar or club. The difference is quite simple: bars and clubs admit women but *women are not allowed in cantinas*. If the place admits women and provides restrooms for them it is not a *cantina*. *Cantinas* are exclusively male, though it is not unusual for a woman to own one and even to work in it. If it's a genuine *cantina* and women are drinking at the bar, they're either prostitutes or don't give a damn if they're mistaken for one.

In tourist areas a bar may present itself as a *cantina*, capitalizing on the recognition of the word. When in doubt, ask the bartender, "*¿Se admite mujeres?*" (Do you admit women?). In few cases, however, will there be much doubt in your mind. Just look for evidence of a women's restroom; even male tourists find it difficult to accept that a typical *cantina* will have the pisser along the wall next to the bar—*or is the wall itself*

Some *cantinas* state the message quite clearly over the door: *No se admite mujeres, menores de edad ni uniformados* (No women, minors or uniformed persons admitted).

Women may stand outside the door if they wish to drink discreetly, without enjoying a place to sit or a feeling of equality.

Minors under 15 are technically not allowed to drink. Anyone, however, with the price of a drink is usually given one. Kids can sit with the big people and drink pop in most *cantinas*. This is presumably to keep them off the streets and out of trouble.

Once you are accepted into the *macho* clubiness that prevails in most *cantinas*, you 'l find it difficult, if not impossible, to make a diplomatic exit. This is especially true ıf you have accepted an invitation to drink with someone.

This is all part of the *machismo* thinking process. The Big Spender who invites you to have a drink may be blowing his last 50 *pesos* but he will absolutely insist on buying the drinks until it's all gone. When his money is spent, you can both start on your's

Para que el vino sepa a vino,
Hay que tomarlo con un amigo.

In order that booze tastes like booze,
It has to be drunk with a friend.

The only sure way to avoid offending someone who offers you a drink is to leave. I usually thank them but say firmly, "*No, gracias. Me hace daño.*" (No, thanks. It isn't good for me.) The implication is that you can handle one or two drinks but no more.

If the guy can see that you're lying—you've just knocked off a dozen beers—he'll probably be offended. Should you feel uneasy, it would be best to leave before trouble develops. Trouble is not common, but it could happen.

One of the nicest things about *cantinas* is that trouble rarely involves gringos. The bartender or another customer will almost invariably steer irritating or belligerent drunks away from the tourists.

Should fighting erupt, it is definitely best to make a hasty exit. *Fights are uncommon*, but when they do occur, they are often nasty and violent.

Most *campesinos* are armed with *machetes*. They have a disturbing tendency to use them on each other to settle their differences. Pistols and knives are often carried and used in brawls. Fist fighting is considered more of an exercise than a means of resolving quarrels.

The police will arrive in time to arrest the survivors. A classic example of this was observed by a friend.

As he approached a neighborhood *cantina*, he saw a large man with a .45 pistol confronting a smaller unarmed man in the street. The smaller of the two was screaming obscenities at the other, accusing him of not being *macho* enough to use the gun. The curses and tension increased by the second and my friend, in anticipation of what seemed inevitable bloodshed, ducked into a nearby doorway.

Suddenly two policemen appeared. They drew their long, heavy clubs and rushed to stop the tragedy. Without a word, one of the cops stepped up behind the small, unarmed man and felled him with a powerful stroke of his billy club. With the other officer's help, the unconscious body was hauled off to justice.

The big man, smiling triumphantly, jammed his pistol into his belt and returned to his beer.

Cantinas fall into two general categories: scroungy and respectable. The first type is common in the more run down parts of town, where a person's appearance and behavior aren't very important. If you approach the swinging doors and see feet or bodies sticking out from underneath, it's probably best to move on.

The second type is about the equivalent of an American bar in the 'good old days.' It will be clean, if not immaculate, and trouble is not tolerated. Businessmen may be sitting at tables, reading *Excelsior*, playing dominoes or concluding a deal over an afternoon brandy. This type of *cantina* is a combination club and refuge, where conversation is not about the wife and kids, but bullfights, money, politics and *la casa chica* (lovenest).

The price of a beer or drink is often no less in a nice *cantina* than it would be in a regular couples bar. In the scroungiest, however, the prices may actually be even higher. The reason for this is that sleazy *cantinas* take advantage of their customers whenever they can, either by giving them credit on over priced booze or by capitalizing on their reluctance to go to higher class places where they would feel uncomfortable. Short changing in these places is also a problem, especially if the customer is obviously loaded. Tourists (and this includes Mexicans) who visit lower class *cantinas* may find, to their dismay and irritation, that the price of beer or liquor is strangely flexible.

Steve and I were once stuck for a long afternoon in the outskirts of a large city, waiting for a mechanic to perform some small miracle on our car. An almost steady procession of men entering and leaving a raucous *cantina* across the street caught our attention. It didn't take much mutual persuasion to agree to a drink.

There was a noticeable decrease in the noise level as we walked through the swinging doors. We went directly to the bar, realizing that they'd soon adjust to the surprise. Steve quickly ordered two *tequilas*. The bartender slid the glasses to us and demanded at least four times the going rate. The other customers visibly flinched. They might have chuckled at doubling the price, but this was too much for even gringos to pay in such a dump.

We tossed off the *tequilas*. Steve motioned to the *cantinero*, his nose safely buried between the pages of a comic book.

""Two more?" he asked warily, glancing around the room. There was almost complete silence, broken only by a drunken snore from somewhere under a table.

"No, *amigo,*" Steve said loudly, "It's too *rico* for us. Give me two drinks of Mexican gasoline at Mexican prices."

The *cantina* rocked with laughter. With a grin the *cantinero* poured two of the largest *tequilas* we'd ever seen, then charged us a fraction of the previous price.

When ordering single drinks always say, *"Una copita de tequila, ron, brandy,* etc." rather than simply asking for *tequila, ron* or *brandy*. The reason you specify *una copita* (a drink) is that many people order whole bottles to drink on the premises.

Good *cantineros* will ask what brand you'd like, others will reach for the most expensive.

Cantinas serve *tequila, mezcal* and *aguardiente* (unaged alcohol from almost any source) by the *peso* measurement and the shot. You can order, if you wish, several *pesos* worth of *tequila* instead of a *copita*.

A drink is also called a *trago* or *tragito* (swallow). This same word is used by Indians as a general term for liquor. A popular slang term for a shot of booze is *balazo,* literally a bullet or bullet wound. I prefer to use this with friends. There's something unnerving about asking a strange bartender *"Dame un balazo,"* (Shoot me.).

You can also order by the amount; just point on the side of your glass to the level you'd like it filled to.

It is not uncommon for bartenders to refill liquor bottles. I once observed a *cantinero* filling five bottles of different brands from a large jug of local inexpensive *tequila*. He did this openly (I was the only customer and probably not considered likely to complain) but then had the nerve to ask me which type of *tequila* I wanted.

Drinking etiquette is not as formalized as most gringos believe. The well-known lime-salt ritual which accompanies *tequila* guzzling has as many variations as can be managed by individual drinkers. Some lick the salt off the back of their hand, others off the lime itself and others just forget both steps and drink their *tequila* right out of the jug. As any experienced drinker knows, the object is not to eat salt and limes but to drink the booze.

The lime-salt combination does have a real purpose, however. The salt, if taken first and allowed to raise saliva at the back of the throat, will protect sensitive tissues from the burning of the alcohol. The lime will also do this and when taken after the drink cleanses the mouth of the awful taste of the liquor.

A shot of *tequila* is sometimes called a *tequilazo* or *tequilito*.

Mexicans believe that a drink of straight booze relieves the tension of an overstuffed stomach. *"El desempanze"* is the belly deflater. *"Lo del estribo"* (the one of the stirrup, stirrup cup) is the equivalent of "One for the road." It is important not to call this last drink, *la ultima*. Superstition says that the ultimate drink is quite literally your last drink on earth. Mexican say *"La penultima,"* the next-to-the-last.

"Le invito a..." is a phrase that *cantina*-goers will hear often. It means "I invite you to a ..." and then either a meaningful silence or the name of whatever you are drinking. If you accept (just say *"Gracias"*) you should raise your free drink and offer *"¡Salud!"* (Health!) in return.

Another common toast, one that usually comes when the atmosphere is loose is *"¡Arriba! ¡Abajo! ¡Al centro! ¡Adentro!"* (Up! Down! To the middle! Inside!) *Salud y pesetas* is a common contraction of the Spanish classic: *Salud y pesetas y el tiempo para gozarlas* (Health and *pesetas* and the time to enjoy them!). The longer version is considered rather corny, though by the time it is proposed most people are beyond caring.

When you're drinking beer with others, it is customary to leave all of the bottles on the table as a means of settling what is owed. A table crowded with empties is considered to be cool and *macho*.

Botanas (snacks) are often served free with beer or drinks. Most of them are quite spicy.

Should you be passed over when the *botanas* are served, just ask politely, "*¿No hay botanas?*" (Aren't there any snacks?). Many *cantineros* wrongly assume that gringo customers can't handle the *chile* or won't like the taste of whatever is being served. If you request a *botana*, however, you'll have to eat it or look stupid.

This happened to Steve and me during a visit to one of our favorite *cantinas*, "*El Hígado No Existe*" (The Liver Doesn't Exist). We noticed that everyone but us was being served plates of *tacos*. A word to the bartender quickly solved that; in fact, we were honored with napkins as an apology.

One bite of our *tacos* caused us to regret our sensitive feelings. The filling was cooked blood.

Musicians may offer to play for you but always agree to the price per song before they start. They'll always barter and some raise their prices for tourists.

Don't be shocked, however, if they charge quite a bit for a song, especially if there are more than two or three in the group. When Mexicans are partying they don't quibble over a few dollars here and there; a dozen songs can cost more than an evening's drinks.

If you don't want to pay for music say politely but emphatically, "*No, gracias.*" Don't waffle around; if you nod and mutter, "Well, I don't know," they'll blast out a quick tune and expect to be paid. Avoid potential disputes by being clear.

A jukebox is about as indispensable to the atmosphere of a good *cantina* as the bullfight posters on the walls. My favorite song, one that never fails to bring appreciative nods from other customers is:

La Que Se Fue	She Who Went Away
Estoy en el rincón de una cantina, *oyendo la canción que yo pedí* *Me estan sirviendo ahorita mi tequila,* *Ya va mi pensamiento rumbo a ti.*	I'm in the corner of a *cantina,* listening to the song I requested They are just now serving my *tequila*, Now my thoughts go toward you.
Yo sé que tu recuerdo es mi desgracia *Y vengo aquí nomás a recordar* *Que amargas son las cosas que nos pasan* *Cuando hay una mujer que paga mal.*	I know that your memory is my disgrace And I come here only to remember. How bitter are the things that happen to us When there's an ungrateful woman.
¿Quien no sabe en esta vida *La traición tan conocida,* *que nos deja un mal amor?* *¿Quien no llega a la cantina,* *Exigiendo su tequila y pidiendo* *su canción*	Who in this life doesn't know The betrayal so familiar, that is left to us by a bad love? Who doesn't come to the *cantina*. Ordering his *tequila* and requesting his song?

Me estan sirviendo ya la del estribo,
Ahorita ya no sé si tengo fe
Ahorita solamente yo les pido,
Que toquen otra vez la que se fue.

Yo lo que quiero es que vuelva, que vuelva conmigo, la que se fue.

Now they're serving me one for the road,
Right now I don't know if I have faith
Right now I only ask them,
To play again She Who Went Away.

What I wish is that she return, return with me, she who went away.

SERVICES

Postal service...Packages...Telephone calls...Useful phone numbers... Banks: cashing checks...Pure water...Ice...Bathing...Spas...Laundry... Fuels: propane, white gas, kerosene, firewood...

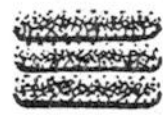

POST OFFICE

Locating the post office (*el correo*) in a large town is usually quite easy; just a matter of touring around the *plaza* and asking a few questions. Post offices in small towns are not always so obvious. They may be located in a *tienda* or dry goods store and you'll probably have to ask and search around.

Hours are determined by the government but are open to liberal adjustment by the local *administrador*. If the post office does a brisk business, it may be open during *siesta*. Package and money order services are generally offered only on weekdays and during peak hours. Hours are: 9 a.m. to 1 p.m. and 3 p.m. to 6 p.m. on weekdays and 8 a.m. to 12 noon on Saturday. (The main office in Mexico City is open until late at night and on weekends.) If the *correo* is located in a store and the owner gets sick or goes away on business, the mail will probably be unavailable for a time.

In one case, the postmistress in the village where we were living went on a drunk and was fired from her post. Unfortunately, it took more than a week to find a replacement for her. The post office was closed, of course, during that time. As a final stroke of bad luck (at least for us, since we were eagerly awaiting mail), the ex-postmistress hid what mail was on hand in an attempt to regain her job through blackmail. After a week of pleas and threats, the police finally managed to convince her to return the mail.

Postal service varies between remarkably quick and efficient to exasperatingly slow and inept. The length of time it takes for your mail to be delivered to you in Mexico or to arrive in the U.S. from Mexico is directly dependent on two factors: location of the post office in Mexico and the type of postage used. This is also true of mail sent from one place to another within the country. If you are in a large city that has direct air service to the U.S. or Mexico City, you can often receive letters from the United States within three days. If you're in a small town, however, don't expect air mail letters to arrive in less than ten days.

Use air mail if you want your letter to arrive during your lifetime. Surface mail is all but subterranean. Letters sent to Mexico from the United States should be marked Air Mail or *Correo Aereo* or just *Aereo.* Without these words Mexican postal workers won't handle it as air mail.

Rates for mail are: 1.60 *pesos* for ten grams, airmail; 1.60 *pesos* for postcards and .80 *centavos* per 20 grams for surface mail. Ten grams is about two sheets of typing paper with an envelope. The clerk will usually weigh your letters if there's any doubt.

Within Mexico airmail costs 1.60 *pesos* for 20 grams.

Stamped, air mail envelopes (*sobres aereos*) and postcards (*tarjetas aereos*) are available at the post office. Airgrams (*aereogramas*) are also available and include special handling in the purchase price.

Special handling stamps are 2 *pesos*. *Entrega inmediata* stamps are usually mistaken for special delivery or registered in the U.S. and letters with them are handled as such.

A registered (*registrado*) or certified (*certificado*) letter costs about twice as much as an airmail. Be sure to get a *recibo* (receipt).

Postal money orders (*giros*) are paid in *pesos,* even when purchased in the U.S. with dollars or other currency.

The delivery time for packages mailed to and from Mexico varies from quick to legendary. People tell of receiving packages a year after they were air mailed, but others relate how they received a crate of books sent a few weeks before. Anything less than air mail postage may be the end of your hopes that it will reach its intended destination within a reasonable length of time. Most people report that packages sent to the U.S. arrive in about three weeks. Try to send packages from larger post offices.

Packages can be sent first class (air), second and third class (books, magazines, periodicals) or fifth class. Most people use fifth class to send large packages, up to 20 kilos. The maximum weight for first class is two kilos.

Note: The declared value on a registered letter or package is not covered by insurance. You must pay an additional fee for *seguro* to cover any loss.

The Christmas Rush

Mexican postal authorities have devised the most ingenious scheme to cope with mass mailings of Xmas gifts and cards: they go on vacation and don't worry about it. During the Christmas season (December 16 to January 6), Easter Week and the last two weeks of May don't count on mail service to be anything but reluctant. During the '78 World Soccer Cup the employees in one post office refused to give service until breaks between televised games.

Because of the cost of mailing a package by air, have it weighed before telling the post office clerk that you want postage for it. When he licks the backs of a square foot of stamps and you realize that the contents aren't worth a fraction of their cost, well, too bad. Special rates for unsealed envelopes and packages are less than regular postage.

Packages are supposed to be wrapped in a box and tied with string. If the clerk thinks you should have tape, wire or convenient rope handles on the package too, you'll have to cater to his whims. Most offices will accept packages in sturdy well made baskets with lids that are securely wired or tied shut. The basket itself makes an attractive gift. Large envelopes can often be used for smaller items, especially clothing.

Shops that sell school supplies and wrapping paper often wrap packages to postal specifications. Tourist shops usually offer the same service, either free or for a small charge. Ask "*¿Puede envolver un paquete por favor?*" (Can you wrap a package, please?) In tourist areas or near the post office look for signs saying "*Se envuelve paquetes*" (Packages wrapped).

Film and magnetic recording tapes should be labelled prominently in English to avoid their being exposed to X-rays at U.S. Customs. Write: FILM! *Please do not X-ray,* and hope for the best. Sometimes they'll X-ray it anyway. Large camera shops and airport gift stores in the U.S. sell X-ray proof film bags.

Beward of sending someone at home a package of dope. Many packages are inspected by U.S. Customs and your gift may be followed by narcs.

All packages mailed out of Mexico must have a customs declaration card attached (available at the P.O.) listing the contents and their value.

Packages with a value of less than $10 U.S. can be sent duty free to the U.S. if they are a bona fide gift. Write: *Unsolicited Gift Under $10* on the outside of the package. You can send any number of these unsolicited $10 gifts, but no more than one per day to any one person in the U.S. The value of the gifts does not subtract from your duty free limit when you return.

Sending gifts to Mexico can be more of a burden than a benefit to the person receiving them. Although eyeglasses, medicines, used clothing and books are supposedly allowed in duty free, don't hold your breath. Books are rarely held for customs charges, but anything else probably will be. Toys are a favorite target for high duty. These charges are arbitrary and usually unreasonable.

Your probable address will be *Lista de Correos* (General Delivery). *Lista de Correos* is often more convenient and reliable than other methods of receiving mail (American Express, consulates, hotels, etc.) because post offices are located in every town. Using General Delivery is especially valuable when you have no firm schedule or route.

Your complete address will look like this:

Richard Smith
Lista de Correos
Oaxaca, Oaxaca (city and state)
Mexico

Tell your family and friends to print your name and address clearly, as the post office people often have trouble deciphering unfamiliar names. When the *Lista* is posted (which is should be daily but often isn't) interpret it liberally. I know that when I see *MRcarl* on the *Lista* that it's probably for me.

If the *Lista* is not posted, go to the clerk and ask "*¿Está la lista de hoy?*" ("Is today's list here?"). Should he say, "*¡Sí!*" tell him your name (better yet write it down) and he'll look through the letters.

Some post offices are quite efficient and all you have to do is note the number next to your name and the date of the *Lista*. Give both to the clerk and he'll give you your mail. He may ask for identification. Don't expect to be able to pick up mail for friends or even for relatives.

Some obliging types will give you another's mail if you show both your identification and the identification of the person who's mail you want. Other clerks may ask for a letter of authority, a *carta poder*. Forms are available at the post office for a legal *carta poder* (you must buy special stamps to affix to the letter). They will often accept a handwritten letter as well. It should say something like: *Administrador, Oficina de Correos* (name of town and state): *Favor de entregar mi correspondencia* (or *cartas*) *a* (name of person picking up mail). *Gracias.** Then your name and the date. The neater and more official it looks, the better.

*Translation: Please deliver my correspondence (letters) to (name).

All mail, including registered letters, telegrams and packages addressed to *Lista de Correos* will be posted on the daily list. Mail sent *Post Restante* will be treated as General Delivery, but not posted on the *Lista*. The addressee will have to inquire for mail. *Post Restante* is convenient for fugitives.

Mail is held for ten days when addressed to *Lista de Correos* or *Post Restante* and then returned to the sender if not claimed. Anticipate this when advising people of your address to avoid arriving somewhere after your correspondence has started the return trip.

Packages are held longer, but expect to pay a small daily storage fee.

Unless you can arrange your route and schedule very tightly, you'll eventually have to have mail forwarded from one post office to another. This can be done quite easily by filling out a small white change of address card in the post office (*Tarjeta de Cambio de Dirección*). This card can be left at the post office as a forwarding address or sent back to retrieve mail left behind or expected at a previous post office.

This is very convenient if you don't know where you are going. You can mail the change of address card to your last post office when you have decided on a destination. It should be addressed to: *Administrador, Oficina de Correos, town, state, Mexico.* Remember that the *delivery time for the card itself* will determine whether or not your mail meets you. Sending it back may take a week or more and by the time it's reached your previous post office, your mail may have been returned.

The abbreviation for U.S.A. bound mail is either EE.UU. or E.U.A., though U.S.A. is also understood.

PHONES

A home phone is considered a luxury in Mexico.

Although local calls are inexpensive, long distance is not. A sizeable tax is added to international calls, boosting their cost by about 50 percent. To avoid this make arrangements to have collect calls accepted, even if you pay for them later when you get home.

Some hotels will place calls for you and add the charges to your bill, but most restrict long distance calls to collect.

Long distance telephone branch offices are often located in restaurants, cafes and occasionally in bus depots. This is very convenient because such places are often open late at night. While you're waiting for your call, you can drink a beer and have a *torta*. Look for a sign saying *Servicio de Larga Distancia*. Many hang out a picture of a phone to aid the illiterate.

Most phone offices, main or branch, can handle a call to the U.S. or Canada with no trouble. However, the person placing the call for you may not have experience with foreign names, addresses or telephone numbers. It is important, therefore, to write out

Useful Phone Numbers

Direct dialing to the U.S. and Canada is easy and expensive, though discounts up to 34 percent are given, depending on where the call originates, day of the week and time of day. (Cheapest between 11 p.m. and 4:29 a.m.)

Key numbers are called *Ladas*. Dial the two digit number following the word *Lada,* not the word itself. Mexican area codes are 2 and 3 digit; phone numbers are variable.

Lada 91:	Station to station direct dialing within Mexico. Dial 91 + Mexican area code + Number.
Lada 92:	Person to person direct dialing within Mexico. Dial 92 + area code + Number. The operator will be standing by to assist.
Lada 95:	Station to station direct dialing to the U.S. and Canada (except Alaska and Hawaii). Dial 95 + area code + Number.
Lada 98:	Station to station via satellite with the rest of the world. Dial 98 + Country code + Area Code + Number. Country codes are given in the phone book or call the operator for help.
Lada 99:	Same as 98 but person-to-person.
02:	Long distance calls within Mexico, operator assisted (collect, person-to-person,etc.).
09:	International operator. Collect calls and calls charged to a third number. English is spoken.

In Mexico City

01:	Information within Mexico.
03:	Exact time.
06:	Police
07:	Information in Spanish, English, French or Italian on just about anything you can think of. Assistance is given in emergencies and if you're just lost or confused.

very clearly all the information needed to place the call and to attempt to help should any problems develop. If all else fails, ask to be connected with the *Operador Internacional,* who will speak English and can clear up any confusion.

There are two types of long distance calls: *A quien contesta* (station to station, literally whoever answers') and *persona a persona.*

These calls can be made collect, *por cobrar*, or paid on the spot, *pago aquí* (I'll pay here).

The procedure for placing a call is quite simple. Let's assume that you are calling home for one of the usual reasons (homesick, broke or got busted) The call will be station to station and, of course, collect.

Take a piece of paper and write:

Por cobrar (collect)
A quien contesta (station to station)
City
State
Country
Area code and number if you have them
De: your name (from...)

Should the charges be accepted, you won't have to pay anything. If you say that you'll pay and the call is not answered, you might be charged a few *pesos* for services rendered in the attempt.

Connections to the U.S. are usually made in a reasonable length of time. Sometimes the voice at the other end is very clear, other times it sounds like Donald Duck. If this happens, tell the operator at your end, "*No puedo oir*" (I can't hear). They should try to make another connection.

Credit cards are accepted at some phone offices but not at others. Ask them "*¿Acepta tarjeta de crédito?*" If they do, write the number of the credit card on the same piece of paper as the phone number and other information. You might not have to show the card itself; it depends on the attitude of the employee in the office and the credibility of your excuse if you don't have the card.

TELEGRAPH SERVICE

The telegraph office is sometimes near the post office, though often in an obscure part of town, and just might have a *Telégrafos* sign to identify it. Working hours are about the same as those of the post office, although the telegraph office is sometimes open later.

There are three types of telegrams: *urgente* (urgent), *ordinario* (ordinary, regular) and *carta nocturna* or *carta de noche* (night letter).

An *urgente* telegram will be sent immediately, an *ordinario* the same day and a *nocturna* that day or the next, arriving just a little later than the *ordinario.*

Telegrams sent from one town to another inside Mexico are very cheap

Service is good and the majority of employees in the telegrah offices seem cooperative and intelligent. Naturally, there are mistakes, especially in their spelling of English words, but the errors are usually minor.

International telegrams can be received at the *Telégrafos* office, the post office, a hotel or a private home. If you want to receive your telegram at the post office, it should be addressed just as a letter: *Lista de Correos*, etc. To receive it at the telegraph office it should be addressed with your name, *Lista de Telégrafos*, city, state and Mexico.

Money can be wired to Mexico in U.S. currency. It will be converted at the current rate of exchange and paid at the telegrah office in *pesos.* A passport or tourist card is needed for identification when you receive money by wire. This type of telegram is called a *giro.*

BANKS

Banks are very common and easy to locate. The two largest are *Banco Nacional de México* and *Banco de Comercio.* Exchange rates vary slightly from one bank and town to another, but it's always better than the rate given by hotels, shops and gas stations. To avoid paying a high fee for cashing traveller's checks, we carry large denominations and cash them only in banks. By using a Hidden Pocket (see *Personal Stuff*) and lots of caution, we've never felt too nervous with cash on hand.

Cashing Checks

It is easy to cash a traveller's check, though you must sometimes wait in one or more lines. A bank officer's initial is usually required; just go up to any employee, show your checks and you'll be directed to the proper desk or window. In some banks you'll be given a slip of paper saying *Caja* (teller) and a number. If not go to the *Cambios* or *Cheques* window. A slight charge may be made for cashing your check.

If you'll be in Mexico for more than a short vacation or are carrying large sums, I recommend opening a bank account in dollars (not *pesos*; another devaluation would be painful to you). *Banamex (Banco Nacional de México)* is probably the most convenient. Go to a large office and tell them you want a *cuenta.* The procedure is very simple. Most offices have someone around who speaks English.

Bank hours are 9 a.m. to 1:30 p.m. though they may not cash checks after one p.m. Banks are closed on weekends and holidays.

Credit cards are widely accepted in Mexico.

WATER

There are very few foreigners travelling or living in Mexico who are not constantly worrying about the purity of their drinking water.

If you believe, as most gringos do, that all water not sold in bottles is impure and a hazard to health, then the only thing to do is to buy purified bottled water, purify it yourself or stop drinking it entirely.

We have developed a sort of discipline about drinking water that has protected us from any serious ailment; at least, we have yet to suffer from dysentery, typhoid fever, cholera or any of the other dread diseases said to come from the tap. Our system is based on common sense, the necessities of travelling and a certain amount of innate fatalism. What do you do when you are invited to someone's house and handed a glass of lemonade? You know damned well that the water came from the communal faucet on the street corner. Is there a discreet way to drop a water purifying tablet in your drink without offending your host?

Reasonable Precautions

Our first precaution is to never drink water unless we have to. There are so many things, including fresh and canned fruit juices, beer, pop and mineral water, that a drink of ordinary water is usually our last choice anyway. If you buy a few bottles of mineral water for brushing your teeth, it is quite easy to go for months without touching a drop of tap water.

Our second precaution, and one that everyone can observe, is rather than spend a great deal of time and mental energy worrying about the water we're about to drink, we purify it ourselves. This can be done by boiling the water for twenty minutes (double at high altitudes) or adding either *yodo* (iodine), bleach or water purification tablets. Treated water should be allowed to stand for at least 30 minutes before drinking (see *Health*). Liquid bleach can also be used to purify water but it tastes pretty bad.

Finding Water

There are many sources or drinking water. Bottled water (*agua purificada*) is sold in large glass bottles of about five gallons capacity (a deposit is required). Your empty *garrafón* can be exchanged for a full one at the water plant or from water vendors; you only have to pay the deposit once. Water vendors have regular delivery routes, carrying the bottles in trucks, carts or specially built bicycles. If you're living in a house, you can have bottled water delivered whenever you wish.

Special metal stands that allow the heavy bottle to be tipped without dropping it or drenching your feet are sold at most water plants.

If you prefer not to carry a *garrafón* of water, the water plant or delivery trucks will fill your own containers for you.

City water systems that are connected to water purification plants are becoming common. A sign is usually posted on the outskirts of the town or village saying *Agua Potable*. Some cities, however, have potable water only in certain sections, so there's still a certain amount of doubt about the particular *pila* (faucet) you're using.

Gas stations are about the easiest and most convenient places to locate water. We always ask if the water is good before drinking it ("*¿Es buena para tomar?*" or "*¿Es pura?*"). The attendant has nothing to gain by telling you a lie. We've often been told that the water was not safe.

Hotels, motels and trailer parks will usually allow you (though often for a slight charge) to fill your containers from their taps. They always say that the water is safe. I feel that this standard answer may well be prejudiced by the fact that they don't want to scare off tourists.

Ice plants (*fabrica de hielo*), of course, have water and many of them have genuine purified water. The general practice seems to be that they won't charge for water unless it really is purified.

Wells, particularly in small towns, are common sources of water. Anyone can use the town *pozo*, but you must bring your own bucket and often your own rope, too. Be careful to avoid stirring up sediment with your *cubo* (bucket) or you'll also stir up resentment among the people waiting in line behind you. Well water should be treated with suspicion; a dirty bucket alone can contaminate a pure well.

Many people have private wells or rain water cisterns. This is particularly common in areas such as Yucatan where water is scarce or tastes strongly of minerals or salt. Good tasting water is referred to as *agua dulce* (sweet water). It always has to be paid for, though the charge is low. A private well has a better chance of being pure than the communal type as the owner takes a very personal interest in keeping it clean and salable.

Rivers, lakes, creeks, ponds and mud puddles are not safe sources of water, no matter how clean they may look. Even though the water is crystal clear, cold and burbling musically through a shady glen, don't dip your lips into it. Somewhere, far out of sight, a farmer is plowing a field that adjoins that little creek and he's using manure for fertilizer. The rain will wash some of the manure into the creek or the sun and wind will dry it out and blow it into the water. Always purify water from these sources.

Finally, if you must drink dubious water, take three seconds to chant "Pure! Pure! Pure!" It's effective but not infallible.

ICE

Many tourists make a flat rule of never using ice for drinks. We go by the same rules that we apply to water (never eat an ice cube made from a mud puddle).

Ice is sold in blocks at ice plants (*fabrica de hielo*) in most towns. For some reason, the *fabrica* is never easy to locate. One of the best ways to find it or the water plant, since they're often in the same building, is to look for a large puddle in the street or on the sidewalk. If it isn't raining, this water is a good indication that the ice plant is nearby.

A block of ice large enough to fill the average ice chest or camper ice box is one eighth of a whole block and is called an *octavo*. The price for an *octavo* will be much higher in remote areas where ice is trucked in or made in backyard factories.

Block ice can also be purchased at regular prices from the delivery trucks. It is often easier to find the truck than the factory itself. Some beer delivery trucks sell ice. When you're camped or living in one place for a while, you can arrange to have an ice truck deliver it right to your door.

Paleterías (factories for *paletas*, flavored ice on a stick) will usually sell plain ice, too. It is made in small pieces the size of a *paleta*. Don't expect the water used for ice or *paletas* to be genuinely purified, especially in small towns.

Ice cubes (*cubitos de hiielo*) are rarely sold by ice plants but they're available in many large *Pemex* gas stations and supermarkets. Ice cubes are almost always made of purified water.

An ice pick is a *picahielo.*

BATHING

Unless you are one of those lucky people who can afford to rent a hotel room just to take a bath, you'll find that keeping clean while travelling is difficult. Rivers and lakes never seem to show up at the right moment, especially when you enjoy a good wash before going to bed and not just whenever you're lucky enough to find water. One answer to this problem is to carry your own shower.

A Travelling Shower

A cheap five gallon plastic water jug with a sprinkler head can provide two to four baths per filling, if the water is used sparingly. To make the shower, just remove the cap from the container and plug it with a large cork fitted with a sprinkler head (the type used for watering flowers). This isn't going to be the kind of shower you loll around in, but it will get you clean.

Fill the jug whenever you stop at a gas station. The water will be surprisingly warm within a few hours when lashed to the roof of your car, stored in the trunk or placed in the sun.

To take a shower, have someone stand on something (the car roof) and slowly pour the water over you. Use the 'Navy Shower' technique: enough water to get wet, enough soap to get clean, and then enough water to rinse.

Public Baths

A travelling shower is a luxury many travellers, particularly hitchhikers, can't afford. Others might feel uncomfortably conspicuous bathing in downtown Culiacán. The solution for both of these dilemmas is the public bath.

Although usually located downtown and most often near the marketplace, *Baños Públicos* can also be found in some gas stations, trailer parks and dirty factory districts. For a very reasonable charge you can have a long shower or both a steam bath and shower. Steam baths are called *Baños de Vapor.* If the sign just says *Regador* or *Baños de Regador*, it's a shower bath. Soap and towels are extra; you can bring your own if you wish. The soap may be very harsh.

Couples can sometimes bathe together, but larger groups would probably cause a scandal.

If you're also looking for a room, many bath houses double as super cheap hotels. The bed and room may be extremely basic, but you're at least assured of keeping clean.

Hot Springs and Spas

Mexico has many wonderful hot springs; some in a natural state, some developed hundreds of years ago and others bright, modern and full of shrieking children. Hot springs are called *aguas termales, aguas calientes, ojo de agua* (also used for a spring or pool) or *balneario* (bathing spot, not always hot). The older spas are my favorite, with massive stone pools, private rooms and pools, shaded picnic areas and ancient people taking 'cures.' Many rent bathing suits, towels and rooms for the night.

(For locations of hot springs see *The People's Guide To Camping In Mexico.*)

LAUNDRY

When you have time, it is usually possible to find someone to wash your clothes for you. Many women are glad to earn a few extra *pesos* and they'll do a better job than you could yourself. To find someone just ask—if one woman doesn't want to she'll undoubtedly have a friend who will.

Don't let your clothes get away without first determining the price and when you'll get them back. Two days—one to wash and one to dry—should be more than enough time.

Price is almost always determined by what I call the 'Shirt Standard.' A shirt, pair of pants or towel counts as *one.* Underwear counts two for one so 24 pairs of panties is equal to a dozen shirts. Socks count four for one (48 per dozen price) and sheets go the other way, one for four (three per dozen price). The charge for a dozen (a dozen 'ones') varies but in general a 'load' costs as much as in a laundromat.

Some women will charge a flat rate for a bundle of clothes and others will ask for a 'just payment.'

Give the woman money for soap, or, if you're buying it, ask what type she prefers; powdered or bar (*jabón en polvo* or *barra*). Often they want some of each, according to the types of clothing they'll be washing.

•**Laundromats** can be found in large cities. They are usually not do-it-yourself types; you give your clothes to the attendant and come back for them in a few hours.

Most hotels offer laundry service or will direct you to a laundry or washerwoman.

A Mobile Washing Machine

This mod-con can be made from any large closed container with an opening big enough to stuff clothing through. A plastic trash can with a tight fitting lid is the most practical thing to use, but milk cans, metal ammunition boxes or any other fairly watertight and water resistant container will do.

The only other thing needed is a vehicle, preferably a car or van; carrying a load of wet clothes on the back of a motorcycle is difficult.

The basic idea is to create washing machine action by the natural bouncing of the car as you drive. If you have a van or bus with a roof rack, the 'washing machine' can be lashed above without worrying about suds and water should it leak. The trunk of a car can be used, but the machine should be packed away from anything that might be damaged if the contents are suddenly coughed up on a bad bump.

Throw a few items of clothing into the machine (avoid overloading), cover with water and add soap. Secure the container well and forget about it until you stop for the evening. The clothes should be washed reasonably well. You might like to time the rinsing with a stop at a gas station or village communal faucet.

A very crafty way of washing clothes without using your own car is to ask someone camped nearby if they would mind taking your washing machine with them when they make a side trip. They might think it strange but it beats washing by hand.

This technique also works with tightly sealed plastic bags, though the risks of a puncture are great. To heat the water just fill the bags, add the clothing and soap, and leave in the sun for an hour or two. Works with dishes, too.

While Camping

Many people ask how we get our laundry done while camping. We almost always wash our own clothes. After long hours hunched over a rock we have pared our so-called wardrobes to the very minimum. The method of washing that we use is not the way it is normally done by Mexican women. Instead of rubbing the clothes against themselves we scrub them with a heavy bristle brush, available in most stores. I've tried the other method, but just can't do it as well as with the brush.

Lay an article of wet clothing on a rock, board, mat or patch of clean dry grass. A rock works fine but it may cause minor damage to parts of the clothing that are scrubbed against bumps and sharp edges. The mat is best since it's flatter and larger than most rocks and can be moved about. Sprinkle a little powdered soap or liquid detergent on the clothing, flip a handful of water over the soap and start scrubbing. It doesn't take much soap, but it does require a lot of arm work. This method is tedious but practical. It will encourage you to have fewer clothes and will also keep your fingernails clean.

FUELS

Natural Gas

All types of bottled gas, regardless of company or brand names, are called *gas.*

Bottled gas stations are located on the outskirts of almost every town and most of them are open from morning to night, seven days a week. These stations are quite obvious; they have tanks painted with bright letters and huge signs proclaiming *Gas, L.P.,* etc.

Standard type refillable gas bottles purchased in the U.S. can be filled in Mexico. But because the weight systems are different, it's advisable to convert the capacity of your tank to kilograms before having it filled. Divide the capacity in pounds by 2.2 (pounds per kilogram) and paint this figure in prominent numbers on the tank. (For example: *Capacidad 7 kilos.*)

Some attendants are able to figure out the capacity themselves but others just guess. If you're filling a small tank, even a minor error can result in a blown valve. This once happened to us and we had to replace the valve ourselves since we couldn't prove that it was the attendant's fault.

Gas is available in remote areas of the country but many small towns do not offer refilling service. However, you can pay a deposit on another tank, called a *tambor,* (usually a big one), use it while you're in the area and then turn it in when you move on. Don't fail to get a receipt (*recibo*) for the deposit or you'll possibly be stuck with the tank.

Bottled gas can be delivered to your house or even to your campsite if you make arrangements with the nearest dealer.

White Gas

White gas (*gasolina blanca*) is never easy to locate and when you do, it's expensive. The best consistent source of *gasolina blanca* is found in the authorized government outlets of the *Pemex* company, called *Expendio de Pemex. Expendios* are little hole-in-the-wall stores found in obscure parts of town. They are usually closed and when they are open they are usually out of white gas.

Drugstores sometimes stock white gas. They will measure it out, almost drop by drop, into your container. Tailor shops are reputedly good sources; they are said to use white gas as a cleaning fluid. This is what we've often been told but we have yet to find a tailor who uses white gas or will part with it if they do. Other occasional sources are hardware stores, *tlapalerías* (paint stores), general stores and tire vulcanizing shops. These are very occasional sources.

Gas stations do not carry white gas and, in the absence of anything better, you might be tempted to buy regular gasoline, diesel fuel or kerosene as a substitute. *Do not use anything but white gasoline in your stove or lamp unless the manufacturer's instructions specifically say that it will burn other fuels.* **Note:** *Extra,* the new unleaded gasoline sold from the silver pump in gas stations, can be used in place of white gas. (See *Driving: Gas Stations.*) It burns yellow and smelly and is hard on generators, but it does work.

Kerosene, Mantles

Kerosene (*petroleo*) is also available in the *Expendio de Pemex.* In some areas of the country this is the only legal source of the stuff. Kerosene is very cheap.

Petroleo can usually be purchased in small stores or from government pumps near the market. In areas where the sale of *petroleo* is tightly controlled by the government (for some reason), you must buy it at authorized *Expendios* or under the counter. Kerosene bootlegging might sound rather silly, but it is quite a large operation. When you want some and can't find it, you'll really appreciate the little old lady who has a drum of *petroleo* in her back room. By asking discreetly, "*¿No hay petroleo?*" (Isn't there any kerosene?) you should eventually locate a source.

Expendios also sell wicks for kerosene lamps (*mechas*) and sometimes they have mantles for gas lamps. Mantles are called *camisas* (shirts) or *mechas.* They are inexpensive, so when you find them, buy several extras to give to people who couldn't locate their own.

Charcoal, Firewood

One of the most common cooking fuels is *carbón. Carbón* is charcoal, unpressed and still in the shape of twigs and branches. It makes an excellent fuel. *Carbón* is sold in and around the market, in small stores or by individuals who make it themselves and pack it into town. When used for barbecueing, *carbón* should not be ignited with gasoline, oil or *petroleo* as they will taint the food with obnoxious fumes and soot.

Charcoal briquets are sold in bags in some large supermarkets. *Carbón* is cheaper and better, though it tends to spark a lot.

Firewood (*leña*) is sold throughout the country. The price varies considerably with the time of year and availability. A burro load is called a *carga.*

The same stores that sell *carbón* often sell firewood, either by the piece *(por pedazo)*, the handful (*por mano*, two or three sticks) or by the *carga.*

In areas where considerable quantities of wood are used during the winter for fireplaces, *leña* is also sold by the *tonelada* (ton). Never pay in advance or accept firewood before it has been unloaded and you've had a chance to appraise the quality and quantity. Wet hardwoods such as *mesquite* must be dried for months before they are suitable for burning. Vendors love to unload a ton of green wood, complete with fresh leaves, on unsuspecting gringos.

Always bargain; the price varies, depending on who is selling, who is buying and what type of wood you want.

Ocote (pitch pine) is sold in the market in small bundles. It is excellent for starting fires and can even be used as a substitute for candles.

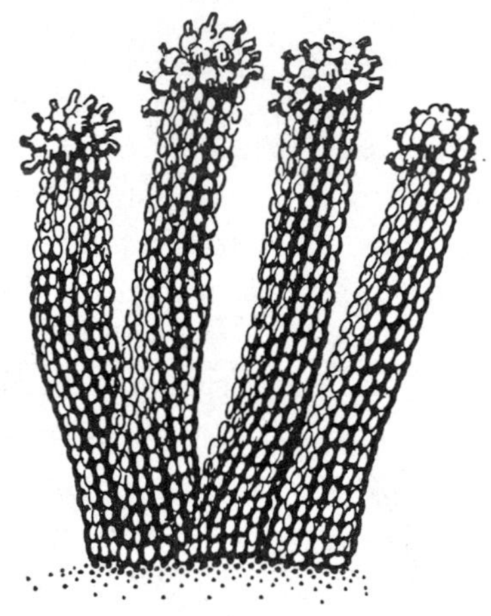

Candelabra

CAR REPAIRS

Finding a reliable garage...Selecting a mechanic...What to watch out for...Body work...Upholstery...Especially for VW's...

Not many people are qualified or equipped to repair every possible break-down themselves while travelling. Whether you need a routine oil change for your new Ford or a complete overhaul for your aging VW, you'll want to select a mechanic and a repair shop with care.

Our experience with breakdowns is extensive. We've had problems with several types of vehicles from a pickup truck to a VW van, and have formed a definite opinion about Mexican mechanics.

In general they are good, probably better than the average mechanic in the U.S. Sloppy work, cheating on parts and padding bills—common problems the world over—also occur in Mexico. However, there are precautions that can be easily taken to avoid such things. (As some consolation, if you do get ripped off, it will cost less than in the U.S.)

A Typical Repair Shop

Selecting a reliable garage isn't easy anywhere. In Mexico your troubles are compounded by the strange language and customs. One of the most difficult things to get used to is that the best garage may look like a hobo hut in the middle of a junk yard. Appearances don't count as far as the average mechanic is concerned. You'll have to learn to accept the absence of fancy hydraulic jacks, power tools and crisp coveralls.

A typical Mexican garage is incredibly filthy, littered with junk and parts, dark, smelly and filled with ragged kids casually smoking cigarettes as they wash strange metal objects in cans of gasoline.

In the middle of all this, reposes a brand new Detroit automobile, its engine strewn across several square feet of oily tarpaulin. A nervous, retired couple from Sun City are anxiously biting their fingernails as a 12 year old boy prepares to ride away with their crankshaft lashed to a rickety bicycle. He may be gone for days.

Whenever the most minor part is needed, another grease stained boy emerges from the dark shop and pedals furiously off to some mysterious supply point. Even tools must be sent for.

The *maestro* (head mechanic, 'master') notices that his clients are nervous, so he orders three of the youngest boys to wash the car. It's a minor service that will cost them nothing, but diverts their attention for an hour or so.

The elderly couple moan quietly as the boys swarm over the recently waxed car, wiping grease and dirt on the shiny new paint. One of the boys makes a particular effort to grease the windshield.

Before they can decide what to do about this 'wash job,' speeding bicycles converge on the garage. Parts wrapped in newspaper appear from beneath tattered shirts. The *maestro* produces an old pair of vise-grip pliers and attacks the dismantled engine. Gasoline is slopped carelessly and in great quantities over dirty parts. Oil is poured from dubious cans without labels.

Within a few frantic hours, the couple is on the road again, puzzling over the illegible bill and the sentimental farewells of the *maestro* and his staff.

Finding A Mechanic

The best way to find a reliable *mecánico* (mechanic) is to ask someone. Try to find a gringo who lives in the area to help you out. If this fails, ask anyone driving a vehicle similar to yours. Very few Mexicans do their own repair work and most have a favorite garage. Often they will take you there or find someone to guide you. If this fails to produce results or if your Spanish isn't up to it, you'll have to go looking yourself.

A backyard garage that is working on a vehicle similar to yours is an obvious choice. Before settling for that, however, I would look for a large truck garage. Most good Mexican mechanics learn their trade on heavy equipment such as trucks, buses and tractors. A *maestro* truck mechanic has many years of experience and is more apt to be able to apply good mechanical sense to his jobs than a person whose experience is limited to occasional old Fords and Chevys. Big truck garages can also afford to hire the best men and supply the best tools.

Mexican mechanics are usually much more skilled in the repair of water cooled engines than air cooled. It hasn't been many years since the air cooled engine, mainly the VW, became common in Mexico. The number of really good air cooled engine mechanics is probably as low as it is in the U.S.

During your search for a garage, you might happen upon the authorized dealer or agency for your car. The clean shiny showroom, organized parts department and official coveralls would seem to indicate an efficient and reliable shop. This is usually not the case. Some of the larger authorized garages are actually *worse* than an average backyard mechanic.

When a mechanic accumulates enough experience at the agency and a few spare *pesos*, he immediately begins thinking of his own garage. His wages at an agency are very low. With a few basic tools and room to park a car, he can open his own business. The result is that the agency may have just one qualified mechanic. Should he be off duty or busy with another job, your problem will be referred to someone with less experience.

In addition, everything costs more at the agency, from labor to parts, and usually takes longer to complete than in the independent shop. Backyard mechanics rarely charge overtime and they'll work long, hard hours to finish the job. If parts must be ordered from far away, the *maestro* will often send someone by bus to get them

We once decided to have a brake job done on our VW van in the U.S. before leaving for Mexico. An appointment had to be made seven days in advance. The van was in the garage for three more days. The bill was staggering.

Two years later the same job was done in a garage in Mexico. It took five hours and cost a fraction of what we'd paid at home.

In The Garage

There are certain precautions and procedures that should be observed when taking your car to any garage.

•Always ask for an estimate before the job is started. "*¿Más o menos, cuánto va a costar?*" (More or less, how much will it cost?) When there's a lot of work to be done, you might want a written *presupuesto* (estimate).

If the shop is small and the work to be done is extensive, you may be asked to pay for the parts in advance. This is common and acceptable since most small time garages operate on almost no overhead.

•Should parts be required, specify, if you wish, that only new parts be used. Most mechanics (quite unlike those in the U.S.) will use a reconditioned or used part before buying a new one.

We were once given a bill for a tune up that amounted to less than the cost of the plugs. Steve naturally asked how they had managed that one. The *maestro* proudly said that in order to save us money he had replaced our old plugs with "good used ones." We checked and found that four used plugs of three different brands had been installed.

Always ask for a *recibo* (receipt) for parts purchased in advance or used in the job. Don't be gruff about it or overly defensive; this, too, is standard procedure.

•Once the work begins, *stay with the car.* You don't have to sit in it while it's on the grease rack, but just be around, in obvious attendance. Because labor charges and wages are so low, the assistant mechanics tend to take things easy. If the car owner or a representative is present, the *maestro* will feel more obligation to do the job himself rather than delegate it to a young apprentice.

Let the *maestro* know that you're in a hurry and he'll probably let other jobs slide—those with the owner absent—until he's finished with yours.

Should you have to leave your car unsupervised, remove anything valuable or tempting. The *maestro* will ask for the key in case the car has to be moved.

•An almost unavoidable problem is that mechanics will attempt any job, whether they have the necessary tools and qualifications to do it properly or not. Don't hesitate to lend a hand or offer advice if you feel that it's needed.

•When the job has been completed, give the car a thorough going over before starting up and driving away. Check the oil, gas cap and gas gauge. It is common for mechanics to siphon whatever gasoline they need for washing parts out of your tank and it might be low. This is standard practice.

Kids are often given such minor jobs as putting in the oil. If the last truck he worked on held 15 liters, he might just assume that your car does too.

Take the car for a test drive. This is expected and the *maestro* will probably want to go along to see that you are satisfied and aren't going to leave without paying.

•Before paying, ask for a *recibo* and don't hesitate to question any vague or unusual entries.

The vaguest entry of all is usually the number of man-hours worked. This is rarely unfair, in fact, many *maestros* don't bother to charge for labor other than their own or that of top assistants.

If your car craps out after you've paid for a repair job, don't hesitate to return to the shop and complain. Do it calmly. We've rarely had any but the most apologetic and gracious treatment when asking that a job be made good.

Body Work and Upholstery

Body work, painting and upholstery are all relatively inexpensive. Before handing your car over for extensive cosmetic work, it's best to get estimates from two or more shops. The range in prices can be considerable.

If you intend to have your car painted in Mexico, it is best to buy both the primer and paint in the U.S. Be there when it is applied to make sure that your paint, rather than a substitute, is used. We once had our van painted blue after ordering that it be done brown. When we pointed out to the *maestro* that it wasn't quite the color we'd asked for, he just shrugged and said, "I got a better price on blue." As we were about to pull out of the shop I happened to look at the right side of the van. "There's no paint over here!" I yelled. The *maestro*, as imperturbable as a Zen Master, laughed and said, "It was parked so close to the wall I must have forgotten."

Foam rubber for seat cushions and other padding is very expensive in Mexico. If you expect to have such upholstery work done, bring foam with you.

•Note: automotive tools are very expensive in Mexico and most mechanics would give their eye teeth for a good set. Many gringos have found that trading tools for repair jobs saves them money and at the same time does the *mecánico* a big favor.

Especially for VW's

There are a great number of tourists driving VW's in Mexico. It seems that a depressing number of them experience serious problems as a result of improper servicing and maintenance. Wherever VW owners congregate (usually the garage), you hear stories of sucked valves, blown seals and other assorted mechanical horrors.

These tales of woe are told by the owners of aging and brand-new VW's alike. The reason for this is that the most routine type of maintenance—tune ups, oil changes and adjustments—are the jobs most often done in Mexico and most often botched by inexperienced mechanics.

The person who has limited experience working on a VW and a small number of tools is usually better off than the person who dutifully takes their car to the garage for routine work.

•Always check the oil after an oil change. If the level is much higher than it should be, drain the excess before starting the engine. Don't allow a mechanic (or anyone) to adjust the timing by ear. This may be OK on a water-cooled engine, but it is definitely not proper on a VW. The engine might sound great while it's idling in the garage, but at higher speeds will quickly overheat and may blow. This mistake alone has ruined many engines.

•Valve adjustment is critical. We know of several cases where engines, most of them new, were ruined because of improperly adjusted valves. Some of the jobs were done in large VW agencies.

•If worse comes to worst and your engine must be rebuilt while in Mexico, avoid the agency unless you're not concerned about money. Although labor costs for a rebuild are low, parts are not. By buying your parts at an auto supply store rather than at the agency, you'll save up to fifty percent. With the vocabulary lists in the back of this book and a copy of *How To Keep Your Volkswagen Alive* (see *Recommended Reading*) you should be able to rebuild your engine for less than it would cost in the U.S. If you can't handle the job on your own, find a mechanic who will help out.

HEALTH

What's the trouble?...Reasonable precautions...Take it easy... Got sick anyway...Doctor or Curandera?...Getting help...Medicinal plants...Pharmacies...Doctors, hospitals, dentists, optometrists... First Aid kit...Prevention and Cures...Secrets of the Mayas revealed!.

Many gringos get sick while travelling in Mexico. Many Mexicans get sick while travelling in the United States. Most people, in fact, get sick while travelling in distant places, even when those places are inside their own country.

Why? The current theory is that the bacteria living inside a person's body are adapted to their host's location. When you move far away from home, your bacteria can't handle it. They don't travel well. The body must then adapt to a new type of bacteria. During the adaptation process, which unfortunately seems to span most of the average vacation time, the traveller might not feel as healthy as usual.

But this is just part of it. In addition, there are such factors as rapid changes in climate, altitude and daily living routine. Throw in, on top of all this, the physical and mental strain from travel preparations, living in a strange place and driving or flying long distances and it's a wonder that the traveller can survive at all.

Of course, more tangible health hazards than rapid changes in your daily routine exist in Mexico. These fall into three general categories: food, beverages (especially water) and Acts of Nature (sunburn, bug bites, lightning bolts, etc.).

Food and beverages cause most of the problems. It's easier to come out of the sun when you begin to feel crisp than it is to run a quick microbe check on a dripping *taco.*

Most cases of diarrhea suffered in Mexico by both Mexicans and tourists who have adjusted to their location are the result of poverty and ignorance. The old man on the corner selling his wife's homemade *tamales* isn't dirty because he wants to be. He can't get pure water to mix with the *tamal* dough because he can't afford to live anywhere but half a mile from an infected community well.

He tries to keep his hands clean, but the long hard trip for wash water is too much for him. He'd also like to put the chickens in a real pen instead of on the kitchen roof, but he can't afford the materials or take the risk of having them eaten by wandering packs of dogs.

The tourist must try to imagine the conditions under which food may be handled and prepared. No matter how delicious the aroma, if the vendor's hands, dishes or utensils are dirty, the food will not be clean. Improper handling (which includes pouring a beer into a glass that has been rinsed in bad water) causes many more health problems than actual contamination of the food as it is grown or processed.

A very poor Mexican family once invited me to eat dinner with them. I accepted, knowing quite well that they had no real concept of sanitation. Water was scarce and the entire family was very dirty. To my surprise, and perhaps in honor of having a guest present, they used a whole bucket of water to wash with. The sad thing, however, was that they washed only their faces and then *after dinner* rather than before.

Always attempt to reduce the chances of infection. I say *reduce* because for the most part it is impossible to completely eliminate the opportunities to eat or drink something that is contaminated.

My invitation to dinner was also an invitation to a good case of diarrhea. I knew this when I accepted, but felt that the possibility of becoming ill meant less to me than offending friends who couldn't help being a health hazard.

This is one of the risks involved in leaving home. If the risk is too much for you, you'll have to restrict the range of your travelling and experiences.

You should not, however, carry a 'come what may' attitude to extremes. If I were offered a dirty mug filled with raw milk, I would politely but firmly refuse it. (See *The Shopping List: Dairy Products*.)

REASONABLE PRECAUTIONS

Good travellers are always aware of their bodies. "Shall I have just one more of those *tacos* and another beer?", "Should I stay out on the beach until noon or go in now?", "I wonder if I can make it all the way out to the ruins and back by tomorrow?" In each of these situations a decision is required, one that may well mean the difference between a good night's sleep and indigestion, a tan or a burn and a relaxed day versus a marathon. Since most trips are of a fairly short duration, these decisions have added importance. Yes, you can drop in at the local *farmacia* and buy a fistful of anti-acid tablets or jar of sunburn ointment, but why make it necessary? Why bear the obvious discomfort? It's much smarter, both for your health and pleasure, to know when to stop and what to avoid.

Prevention, not a list of medicines and remedies, is the best solution to health problems. The following list of common traveller's ailments is covered in much more detail in Prevention and Cure. I recommend that you look them over *before* you're in need of the Cure, not after.

•Nervous strain and tension: Your trip should relax you, not wear you to a frazzle. Do whatever is necessary to enjoy yourself, including just laying on your back staring at the sky for days at a time.

•Over-exertion: "Twenty archaeological sites, 12 museums, 6 *folklorico* performances and...oh yeah...two leg cramps, a backache, scorched nose and 14 blisters." Take naps and frequent unscheduled stops. Don't be afraid to turn in while others are forcing themselves to carry on.

Older people, including those on supervised tours, should avoid pushing themselves too hard, especially in the heat and at high altitudes. The desire to keep up with everyone else should not take precedence over your own comfort.

•Altitude changes: It takes me a full week to adjust from living near sea-level to a change of 7,000 feet (the elevation of Mexico City and much of the central plateau). Going the other way, from high to low, takes less time but still must be considered. Go very easy on exercise, alcohol, drugs of all types and life in general until you've adjusted.

•Sunburn: An extra 30 minutes of sun can cause weeks of discomfort.

•Barefeet: Except for beaches, barefeet are not worth the hazards of broken glass, rusty metal, infections from animal and human feces (very common) and hookworm. Do as the Mexicans, at least wear sandals.

•Alcohol: Some people get over-exuberant and spend their vacation peering into bottles and cocktail glasses. When combined with driving, ruin-hopping, shopping and deep sea fishing, too much drinking can leave you completely exhausted.

•Food and drink: Avoid both over-eating and eating too little. A vacation is no time for strict dieting or fasting. The purpose of eating and drinking carefully isn't just to keep ourselves well fed and content, it's also to avoid diarrhea or worse (hepatitis and dysentery).

Our attitude is, "Well, we do our best" but when the situation says, "Eat that or go without," the decision will be strongly affected by hunger, not good sense.

1) Avoid greasy foods. If you're a marginal vegetarian you'll probably find, as I have, that not eating meat in Mexico cuts down dramatically on stomach problems. If those dripping *tacos* are dripping grease rather than sauce, pass them by.

2) Avoid water. My solution to the 'What if it's not purified?' dilemma is beer, mineral water, sodas, fruit juices and wine. Yes, you can brush your teeth in Coca Cola. Purified water is widely available. You can also purify it yourself. (See *Services: Water* and *Ice*.)

3) Eat things that can be peeled. But if the peeling is removed with a dirty knife, you might be in trouble anyway.

4) Avoid uncooked vegetables in street food. This is very difficult, since Mexico is filled with tempting food stalls. When in doubt, soak it with lime juice, a natural purifier.

5) Cook all raw dairy products or avoid them entirely. (See *The Shopping List: Dairy Products*.)

At first glance, these precautions might sound as if they will prohibit just about everything you enjoy eating. This should not be true—as long as you use discretion when breaking the 'rules.'

With a minimum of effort, the person who does their own cooking can make all foods safe to eat. Cooking is one of the surest methods of killing microbes in food. For fresh raw fruits and vegetables there is another, even easier way: *yodo.*

Yodo isn't the name of a witch doctor, but the word for iodine. *Yodo* is sold in drugstores; ask for *yodo para lavar verduras* (iodine for washing vegetables). A few drops of *yodo* in a pan of water (two drops per quart of water is about right) will sterilize your fresh foods without leaving any aftertaste. If a pan is not available, you can use a plastic bag.

Soak the food for a few minutes. If possible, rinse it in *pure* water after the *yodo* bath, then wipe dry. Water purifying tablets, *Hidro-clonazone* (Mexican brand name) can also be used, but they take time to dissolve.

If neither *yodo* or purifying tablets are available you can use ordinary liquid bleach, about 2-3 drops per quart. Just be sure it's plain bleach and not a chemical cleanser.

Always carry two containers of *yodo* or pills. When one is used up or misplaced, you'll have the other and won't feel tempted to overlook the sterilizing of the food 'just this once.'

When the use of *yodo* has become a habit, you should notice a marked decrease in trips to the toilet.

GOT SICK ANYWAY...

What happens when your careful precautions let you down, as they sometimes do? It's time to decide what, *if anything*, needs to be done. Most people over-react to temporary discomfort or illness and travellers are certainly no exception. "I've got a headache, dear, please run down to the drugstore and get me some morphine." Even a conservative person reaches almost automatically for the ever present aspirin bottle.

First, and most important, when you realize that you're sick, *don't panic.* I once met a young guy who gave up plans to travel in Mexico for several months just because of a case of diarrhea. He couldn't speak Spanish and was afraid to go to a doctor by himself.

This might sound extreme if you're reading this at home, but when you're alone in a foreign country, sick and unable to communicate, it's an entirely different situation.

Curandera or Doctor? *Farmacia* or First Aid?

There are very few common traveller's ailments that require outside medical attention. The tendency to rush to a doctor or pill bottle should be avoided until other, more reasonable methods, have been given a good try. Some problems, such as diarrhea, can actually be prolonged or aggravated by standard medical treatment (see *Prevention and Cure*).

Assuming that you haven't fallen off the balcony of your hotel room and broken your neck, the problem probably stems from failure to observe one or more of the precautions already described. Can it be alleviated or cured by simple rest? If so, go right to bed. If not, it's time to decide between a visit to your first-aid kit, a doctor, a pharmacy or a *curandera* (healer).

There is a Mexican saying that goes, "When a rich man is ill he goes to a doctor; when he's desperate he goes to a *curandera.* When a poor man is ill he goes to a *curandera* and when he's desperate to a doctor."

Curanderas (healers), *brujas* (witches) and *espiritualistas* (spiritualists) probably outnumber licensed doctors and nurses in Mexico. This doesn't mean, however, that at the first sign of illness you'll be consulting someone in a bat-filled cave. Most Mexicans, especially country people, use their basic knowledge of medicinal plants and home remedies as confidently as gringos take Alka Seltzer for indigestion. Medicinal plants and natural remedies* are available everywhere, from the marketplace to sidewalk vendors to even the pharmacy.

To understand and appreciate the relationship between the average Mexican and natural medicine you must first accept that it is a *real* system. In some cases, such as the use of plants or substances that are proven sources of therapeutic agents, it is easy to see their value. *Epazote* (wormseed) is a powerful preventative and cure for intestinal parasites. The Mexican plant, *cabeza de negro,* was found to contain the hormone progesterone, which led to the development of birth control pills. *Toloache* (known in the U.S. as locoweed) contains scopolamine, a common ingredient in sleeping pills. The list is extensive and grows as large pharmaceutical firms continue exploration and research.

Unfortunately, sceptics invariably point to examples of bizarre practices and humorous superstitions as a means of discounting all natural healing. We have friends in Mexico who sincerely believe that eating watermelon while angry will cause a heart attack (I tried it and got a stomach ache). These same people have a wide knowledge of useful medicinal plants and are adept at healing massage. The contrast seems incongruous. The reason for this is that their system makes little distinction, if any, between superstition and 'reality.' The wise person will take the best and leave the remainder for entertaining anecdotes. (See *Custom and Superstition.*)

Our approach to health care is to take manufactured medicines only as a last resort. This doesn't mean waiting until you're on Death's doorstep, but giving other alternatives a good try before escalating the treatment. This same attitude also applies to natural healing; start with simple and easy treatments before resorting to anything powerful.

*For lack of a more accurate and comprehensive term I will use the word "natural" to cover home remedies, folk beliefs and practices not normally used in a doctor's office.

GETTING HELP

Anyone venturing far off the beaten path is advised to buy—and read in advance—a good first aid manual. The best I've seen was developed by a group called the Hesperian Foundation. It is called *Where There Is No Doctor*. The book was originally written in Spanish and is available in that language as well as in English. (See *Recommended Reading*.)

A first aid kit, especially for those travelling in remote areas, is well worth having. Keep it reasonable, some people lug around enough splints, bandages and emergency medicines to make a genuine para-medic jealous. The first aid kit described at the beginning of *Prevention and Cure* should be quite adequate for the average trip. It is very inexpensive, compact and easily replenished. The principle behind the kit is prevention, not just first aid.

Curanderas and Medicinal Plants

How do you locate a healer or a witch? The best way, much easier than chanting over hexagrams scratched into the floor of your hotel room, is to ask someone, "*¿Hay una persona que sabe curar?*" (Is there someone who knows how to cure?). It helps to explain or

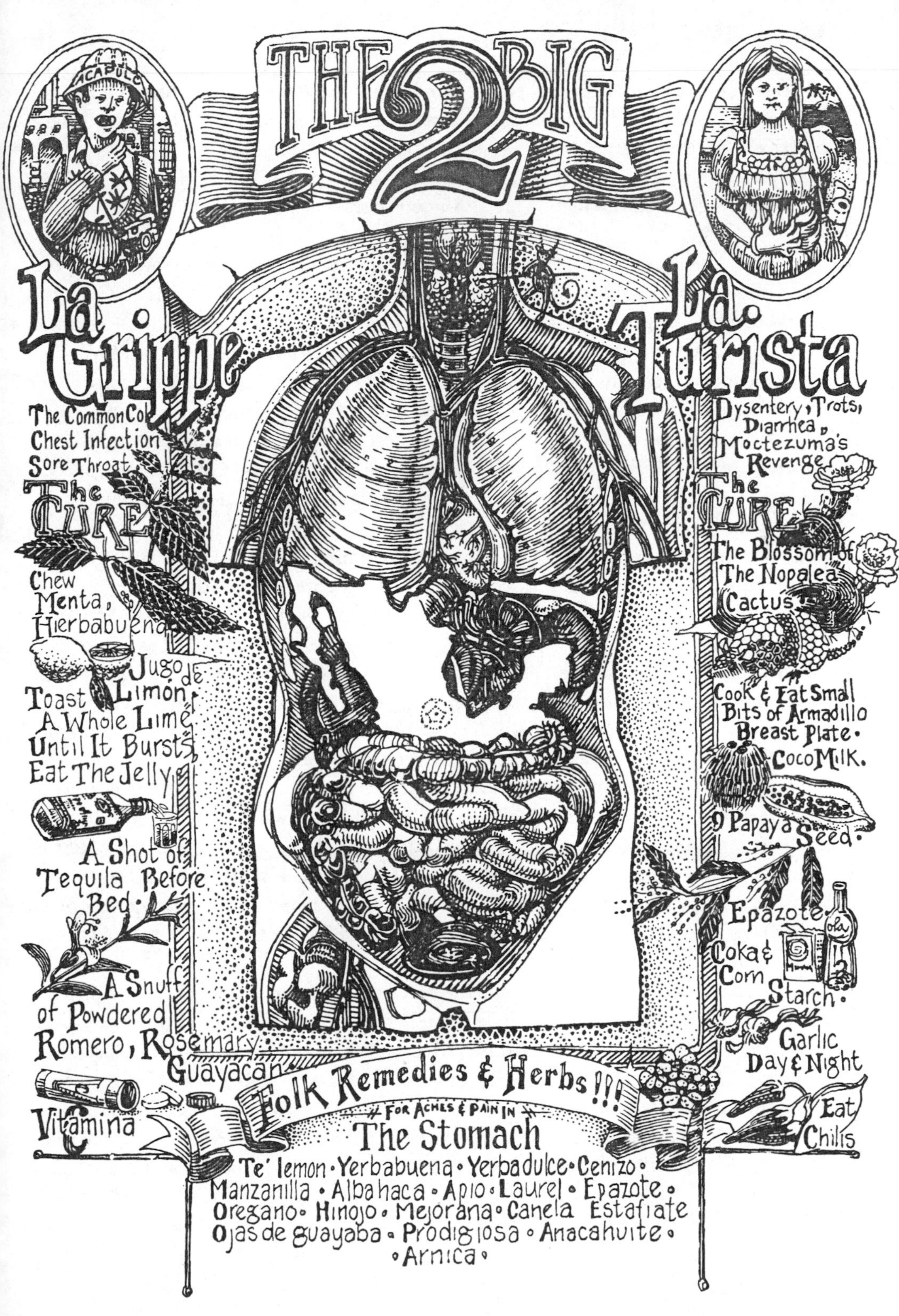

THE BIG 2
ACAPULCO
La Grippe
The Common Col
Chest Infection
Sore Throat
The CURE
Chew Menta, Hierbabuena
Jugo de Limon
Toast A Whole Lime Until It Bursts, Eat The Jelly
A Shot of Tequila Before Bed.
A Snuff of Powdered Romero, Rosemary
Guayacan
Vitamina C
La Turista
Dysentery, Trots, Diarrhea, Moctezuma's Revenge
The CURE
The Blossom of The Nopalea Cactus
Cook & Eat Small Bits of Armadillo Breast Plate.
CocoMilk.
9 Papaya Seed.
Epazote.
Coka & Corn Starch.
Garlic Day & Night
Eat Chilis
Folk Remedies & Herbs!!!
For Aches & Pain in
The Stomach
Te' lemon. Yerbabuena. Yerbadulce. Cenizo.
Manzanilla. Albahaca. Apio. Laurel. Epazote.
Oregano. Hinojo. Mejorana. Canela Estafiate
Ojas de guayaba. Prodigiosa. Anacahuite.
Arnica.

indicate your problem; many people are very leery of those who practice black magic and may suspect you of evil intentions. *Curanderas* rarely hang out a shingle, though their practice is entirely reputable.

Ask at a pharmacy, neighborhood *tienda* or an herb stall in the market. Health food shops and vegetarian restaurants are also good sources of information.

One of the most familiar and interesting sidewalk attractions in Mexico is the travelling herb salesman. Neatly wrapped parcels labelled 'Blood,' 'Kidneys,' 'Nervousness,' 'Sexual Weakness,' make up just a small part of these natural pharmacies. Among the display, usually lined up against the wall of a building, you may see more esoteric items: dead hummingbirds (a powerful love amulet), sand dollars and deer antlers (good luck), crudely printed prayers with pictures of a particular saint (*oraciones*, used to invoke luck, health, wealth, etc.), lodestones (*piedra imán*, for luck), assorted seeds (used individually or in mixtures as charms), insects, chameleons, special candles, sea shells, dried snake meat, and other things, less easily identified but essential to the practice of withcraft.

Other vendors specialize in one remedy for common ailments: intestinal parasites (displaying disgusting jars of pickled worms), lack of appetite (greatly feared), venereal disease, kidney disorders (attritubed to many ailments) and the common cold. Some sell ready mixed packages of herbs, others hawk what can only be described as 'snake oil.' What they all have in common is an incredible ability to maintain a loud and insistent spiel, warning of the dangers of whatever they're selling the cure to. Most rely on vast lung power, but others have portable loudspeakers and can warn passersby a block away of some dire ailment stalking them at that very moment.

I particularly enjoy browsing through the books that are also offered. These are very cheap editions, some reprints of old treatises on magic and witchcraft. The graphics are usually worth the price. The text itself is difficult to check in advance as few have the pages separated; the customer must do that later, with a sharp knife or razor. My favorite, a book on witchcraft by Doctor Papus (which includes some easily memorized chants) has the warning "Do Not Open This Book For Simple Curiosity!" printed over a paper seal. Who could resist?

Almost every marketplace has at least one herb stall and larger markets will have several. Many herbs and plants are displayed, usually unlabelled, and others are kept under the counter. It used to be possible, for example, to buy peyote in some places, but now that it is illegal, the vendors rarely admit that they have it. Because of strong beliefs in witchcraft and black magic, some vendors are very leery of discussing their wares with foreigners. If your interest goes beyond some simple stomach remedy, you may have to find an intermediary or a more relaxed vendor to get the information and ingredients you want.

A much easier source of information on herbal medicine is from a regular store-front distributor. These shops are found in larger cities. Travelling sidewalk vendors often operate out of a central store and these people are easy to talk to, to say the least.

When buying herbs and plants, ask how they are prepared and the dosage. The most common method is in teas, but it is important to know the proper amounts, as some can be dangerous. *Epazote*, for example, is not recommended in large doses for pregnant women.

Farmacias

A Mexican pharmacy is not at all like a typical drugstore in the U.S. Almost any type of medicine is dispensed without a *receta* (prescription), though a prescription may be legally required. (See *Tourists and The Law.*)

Although many *farmacias* are owned and operated by licensed physicians, most of the diagnoses are made on the spot by pharmacists and their assistants. This is a very convenient system, but it has its disadvantages. Doctors sometimes make mistakes and it can be assumed that a pharmacist isn't infallible either. Unless your problem is obvious—a bad case of diarrhea, upset stomach, headache or a wound—the pharmacist is usually not adequately trained to give the most reliable opinion. If you prefer to see a doctor the pharmacist will refer you to one.

Pills can be purchased one at a time and liquid medicines by the dose or measure. In addition to medicines taken orally, the *farmacia* offers *inyecciones* (injections). You pay for the medicine, the throwaway syringe and a small application fee (not a piece of paper but a charge for sticking in the needle). If you prefer to do it yourself, they'll sell you everything needed. Many pharmacies do analyses (*análisis*) of blood, urine and feces.

Drug companies operate for profit. The more pills and medicines people take the more profit is made. In Mexico (and the Third World in general) pill-pushing is not closely regulated. Medicines that should require administration under a doctor's supervision are often sold over the counter, without even a prescription. In many areas, especially where people are uneducated, antibiotics are taken for almost every complaint. A neighbor says, "My little Juanita took just two of those *pastillas* and got better." Then, when Pablo sprains his ankle or gets a gut ache from eating green mangos, his mother will also go to the *farmacia* for a few pills.

Inyecciones (injections) are becoming symbols for effective treatment. Whether it's a big blast of vitamin B for hangovers or tetracycline for the sniffles, few pharmacists turn down the opportunity to make more money by advising a lighter treatment.

When having a prescription filled be sure that you get exactly what the doctor ordered. If they don't have it go to another pharmacy or return to the doctor and ask for advice. Substitutions should be made by the doctor, not you or the pharmacist.

I was once given a package of pills that the man behind the counter assured me were "identical" to what the doctor had prescribed. For some reason I felt suspicious and opened the box. Inside were six of the largest pills I'd ever seen, so large, in fact, that I'd have to cut them into pieces to get them down.

"How can I possibly take these?" I asked.

The pharmacist shrugged and said, "With a large glass of water." A few seconds later he suddenly laughed and said, "Those are vaginal suppositories. I made a mistake." He replaced the pills with some of more reasonable size. Still laughing, he said, "Very odd. I did the same thing last week. For a dog."

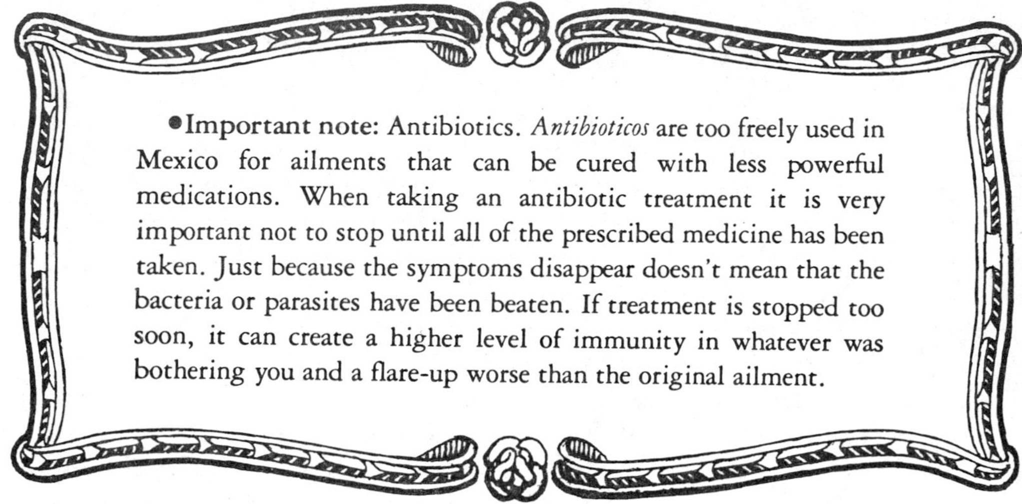

•Important note: Antibiotics. *Antibioticos* are too freely used in Mexico for ailments that can be cured with less powerful medications. When taking an antibiotic treatment it is very important not to stop until all of the prescribed medicine has been taken. Just because the symptoms disappear doesn't mean that the bacteria or parasites have been beaten. If treatment is stopped too soon, it can create a higher level of immunity in whatever was bothering you and a flare-up worse than the original ailment.

Prices for drugs are government controlled. The maximum price is marked on the package (*Precio máximo al público $...*). Some drugstores charge less than the maximum price.

Boticas look just like a pharmacy, but they deal mainly in aspirin, cosmetics and love potions. They are *farmacias de segunda clase* (second class) while an actual pharmacy is *primera clase* (first class).

After regular closing hours every town will have at least one pharmacy that is open all night. This is called *la farmacia de la guardia* or *de la vigilancia* (on guard, on duty). If the doors are closed, knock; there'll be someone dozing inside. For the address of the *guardia* go to a cop, police station or cab driver and ask.

Doctors and Hospitals

It is quite easy to find a doctor in Mexico, just inquire at any pharmacy or stop someone on the street. "*¿Dónde hay un doctor, por favor?*" (Where is there a doctor, please?)

The U.S. and British (and I assume the Canadian, also) embassies have lists of approved' English speaking doctors. The majority of Mexican doctors, approved or not, speak at least enough English to figure out your problem. Many have studied in the U.S. and Europe.

Mexican doctors make house calls and most have an open door policy on office visits. Look for a sign over the door and a waiting room filled with uncomfortable plastic chairs. Go in and sit down; if the doctor doesn't have a receptionist (many don't) he or she will be out eventually.

The average fee for consultation is a fraction of what is charged in the U.S.

Hospitals are quite plentiful, though the majority of those in smaller cities are government operated and tend to be understaffed and poorly equipped. These hospitals are commonly called *"El Seguro Social"* (The Social Security). This is from the full name, *Instituto Mexicano de Seguro Social, IMSS*. The *IMSS* is known by cynics as *Importe Madre Su Salud*, a very rude wisecrack that loosely translates as "Your health is of no damned importance."

In the largest cities all types of hospitals and clinics can be found and their health care is excellent.

Dentists

A *dentista* (also called *sacamuellas*, toothpuller) is as easy to find as a doctor. Once again, just ask at any pharmacy. Dental work is very inexpensive. Dentists often oblige tourists by doing their work immediately and without appointment. Many people plan their vacations around major dental repair. I prefer to wait until tears of pain blur my vision before resigning myself to the chair.

The best dentists tend to set up shop in the largest cities. Their equipment and techniques are the most modern and appointments are often necessary.

Optometrists and Eyeglasses

Optometristas are found in all the larger cities. In smaller towns you may find an *oculista,* a person trained to fit people for eyeglasses. Examinations are usually free and most optometrists also sell frames, lenses, contact lenses and sunglasses. Lenses are quite inexpensive but frames are not.

My experience with Mexican oculists has been very good, though I recommend one who gives a thorough sit-down examination rather than a quick at-the-counter exam.

The quickest service is by optometrists who have lens grinding facilities right at hand. In some shops you can have an examination, fitting and walk out two hours later, a *cuatro ojos* (four eyes).

Tell them that you want your lenses *blanco* (clear) or you will very likely get tinted ones. Mexicans have a fetish about sunglasses and wear them even at night.

PREVENTION AND CURE

First Aid Kit

The following is a basic first aid and prevention kit. If you have special health problems or are visiting a very remote area, it should be expanded. When travelling in the back country I carry a larger supply of limes, garlic and *yodo*. The quantities given are suggestions; if you're easily wiped out by the heat, for example, carry more salt tablets or exert yourself less.

When the first aid kit must be used ask yourself, "What went wrong and how can I avoid it next time?" An increase in your awareness should lead to a decrease in health problems.

Vitamin C	*Vitamina C*
3 limes	*Limones*
1 head of garlic	*Ajo (una cabeza)*
*goldenseal	
1 ounce of Yodo or water purifying pills	*Yodo*
1 ounce of chia seeds	*Semillas de chia*
2 ounces of paregoric	*Paregorico*
several cloves, or clove oil	*Clavos de olor, aceite de clavo*
té de perro	*Té de perro*
mint	*Menta, yerba buena*
camomile	*Manzanilla*
calcium	*calcio*
cornstarch	*Maizena*
4 aspirins	*Aspirinas*
adhesive tape	*cinta adhesiva*
Band-aids	*Vendas*
gauze	*Gasa*
12 salt tablets	*Pastillas de sal*
tweezers	*Pinzas*
needle	*Aguja*
soap	*Jabón*
book or mind occupier	
massage	

*Goldenseal is the only item not easily found in Mexico.

Discussion

•Vitamin C: *Vitamina C*. Effervescent tablets come in handy light metal tubes. They are made by Roche and are called *comprimidos efervescentes vitamina C*.

•Limes: *Limones.* Limes are an excellent source of vitamin C and a natural disinfectant. Mexicans have a great respect for the medicinal value of lime juice; one book lists 172 ailments cured by taking *jugo* or *zumo de limón* (lime juice).

Squeezing the juice over food greatly reduces or even eliminates the chances of unpleasant bacteria surviving to reach your stomach. Once you become accustomed to this you'll find that the juice also enhances flavors.

Lime juice can be used (carefully) to clean wounds, on insect bites, to remove rust from metal and to polish tarnished fishing lures.

Carry a few limes in your pocket or purse and use the juice liberally. When served food in a restaurant or street stall ask "*¿No hay limón?*" (Isn't there lime?) if it is not offered.

•Garlic: *Ajo.* Entire books have been written on the medicinal value and uses of garlic. While in Mexico we eat raw garlic every day. If you can't stand to chew it like candy, as Lorena does, you can swallow small cloves whole or chop them up and slosh them down with beer. This is an excellent protection against intestinal parasites. (Garlic tablets are also sold in health food stores in the U.S. and Mexico.)

Lorena and I rarely suffer stomach troubles while travelling, even when in areas where sanitation is very poor. We attribute this not to luck (at least not entirely), but to lots of garlic and lime juice.

Garlic can also be used to disinfect wounds and to soothe insect bites.

•Goldenseal: Hydrastis canadensis. Available in some parts of Mexico, but it's much easier and more reliable to bring a supply from a health food store at home. This root, usually taken in powder form, tastes awful but is a powerful medicine, used for everything from infections to colds. Lorena wouldn't be without it. It goes down much easier if used in capsules. (Buy capsules and fill them yourself; it's much cheaper.)

•Cornstarch: *Maizena.* Works great for sweat related rashes.

•Book or mind occupier: Restlessness seems to aggravate people who aren't feeling well and often makes them continue moving when they should be resting. Keep a good book in reserve, a game or something to occupy your hands or mind with. Lorena knits; I read or daydream. If nothing else, turn to the vocabulary section of this book and study Spanish. By resting now you'll go a lot farther later.

•Massage: Travelling often brings out aches and pains, either from long hours in a bus seat or too much body surfing. Whether it's sore muscles or muscular tension caused by a stomach ache, massage will make you feel much better and make resting more effective. If there isn't someone around to massage you do it yourself. Massaging your own feet, hands, arms, neck and legs can do wonders, especially before and after a hot bath. *Aceite de ajonjolí* (sesame oil) is sold everywhere in Mexico for cooking. It makes a good massage oil, especially when scented with herbs. Coconut oil, *aceite de coco*, also works well but is greasier. Ask for it in the *farmacia.*

1. Altitude Discomfort
2. Birth Control
3. Bites and Stings
4. Burns
5. Colds, Coughs, Sore Throats
6. Cramps, Aches and Pains
7. Cuts: see Infections
8. Diarrhea, Dysentery and Food Poisoning
9. Drowning
10. Eyestrain
11. Fever
12. *Gripe*: see Colds
13. Hangover
14. Heat Prostration and Sunstroke
15. Hepatitis
16. Infections
17. Insomnia: see Nervousness
18. Intestinal Parasites (Worms)
19. Nausea
20. Nervousness, Tension
21. Poisoning
22. Rashes
23. Shock, Physical and Cultural
24. Sprains
25. Sunburn
26. Sunstroke: see Heat Prostration
27. Toothache
28. Wounds

Altitude Discomfort

Common symptoms are headache, slight nausea, poor appetite, mental confusion, shortness of breath (while sleeping, too) and fatigue. The best cure is to take it easy on everything, from sightseeing to booze. Get lots of rest and don't charge up pyramids like an Olympic contender.

Birth Control

Birth control pills (*pastillas contraceptivas*) are common—they were invented in Mexico—and dispensed without a prescription. Brand names are different than those in the U.S.; you might prefer to bring a supply from home.

Condoms (*contraceptivas*) are sold in *farmacias*. They are not of the best quality; one brand is ominously known as *Buena Suerte* (Good Luck!). Foam spermicides (*espuma contraceptiva*) are also common. Diaphragms are available in Mexico City; if you use one, consider taking an extra. If it is lost or damaged you will have to see a doctor to order another one or resort to *Buena Suerte*.

Contraceptive injections effective for one and three months are available. The side effects are said to be similar to birth control pills and may cause sterility. Consult a doctor.

Bites and Stings

Ants, Bees, Wasps, Hornets: Slice a lime in half and press it against the sting. Some people recommend heating the lime and sprinkling it with salt. Mud packs are useful but try to get clean mud, not from an animal wallow. Baking soda mixed with just enough water to form a paste can be daubed over the sting and will quickly reduce pain. When tromping through the jungle, it is wise to carry a supply of baking soda in a 35 mm. film can. Most anything containing ammonia will give quick relief. I have used Windex and it really helps. A strong (10 percent) solution of household ammonia in water is very effective.

Aloe vera gel will relieve itching.

If a stinger is left behind, usually the case with honey bees, it should be carefully removed by scraping, not pulling.

Rub crushed garlic on the sting.

Crush the head of a match, mix with saliva and apply to the sting.

Fusalar is an ointment (*pomada*) for relieving itching of insect bites. It is sold in *farmacias*.

Chiggers: To reduce itching and to smother the chiggers, apply a mixture of 25 percent camphor and 5 percent phenol in mineral oil.

Horse Flies: Horse flies love to bite when your skin is wet or damp; by staying dry you'll attract fewer of them. Treat as an insect bite.

Jellyfish: Urine helps neutralize the poison. Treat as a bee sting. If you are stung while swimming, *don't panic*. To avoid becoming entangled in more stinging tentacles, move as slowly as possible until you're sure that you're not swimming right into the jellyfish. Many broken drifting tentacles retain their stinging abilities. You might run into one of these rather than an entire jellyfish.

Mosquitos: Garlic is a fairly effective mosquito repellant, though this concoction also repells people. Mix a handful of crushed garlic in half a cup of oil (sesame, cooking or coconut). Let this stand for a week to 10 days and strain. Use on your skin or clothing as required. If it's too strong dilute it with more oil. Add a few drops of pennyroyal oil for additional protection against no-seeums.

Parsley rubbed on the skin is said to be effective against mosquitoes. Smudge fires, especially of coconut husks, help reduce their numbers.

Repellents of any type are much longer lasting if applied to clothing. Have a shirt, pair of pants and socks that you use only when needed for protection against bugs. Don't wash them until they're really ripe; most repellents will be effective for weeks. We keep our bug clothing in a plastic bag when not in use. Mexican repellents are expensive and only one, 6-12, (*Seis-Doce*) is very effective.

A mosquito netting is the most effective protection against these pests. A *pabellón* can be purchased ready-made in some tropical areas or you can buy *manta de cielo* (sometimes called *mosquitero*) and either sew it up yourself or take it to a tailor shop.

If you're bitten by a mosquito, don't scratch; this often leads to infection. To relieve itching rub the bite with lime juice, crushed garlic, parsley or the gel from an aloe vera plant (see *Sunburn*). A mixture of equal parts of camphor and chloral hydrate also relieves itching.

No-seeums bites will go away in about ten minutes, if you don't scratch them. When the itch becomes too much to bear apply finger pressure for a few seconds and it should be relieved.

Bug-In-Your-Ear: Pour a small amount of oil (not motor oil) into your ear. I once used cheap rum with excellent and dramatic results.

Scorpions: The effects of an *alacrán* sting have been greatly exaggerated. Scorpion bites are rarely fatal, though they are very painful. Unless you have a serious heart or respiratory problem or weigh less than about thirty pounds (children under 3 years), don't worry!

Anti-alacrán (anti-scorpion) serum is sold in drugstores in areas where scorpions abound (mainly the states of Durango, Nayarit, Colima and Jalisco). This serum should not be used casually. More fatalities are attributed to *anti-alacrán* than to scorpions themselves. The serum can cause a severe reaction and a reaction test must be made before administering the serum. If you must have it around, ask a doctor for advice.

What if you've been stung? First, and most important, lie down and relax. The discomfort will only be aggravated by over-excitement and exertion. Take a massive dose of vitamin C (suck a bag of limes) and apply lime juice, crushed garlic and/or battery acid to the sting. Pack it with ice if you have it. Cooling the bitten area slows the action of the venom.

A favorite Mexican home remedy is to drink the juice of 10 limes, eat 6 cloves of garlic and then cut the scorpion in half and tape or tie the fleshy side of the head to the wound. The assumption is that the scorpion has some natural anti-venom in its body. *Quién sabe?*

Aspirin can be taken for pain but no opiates (such as Darvon or codeine). Don't eat anything, especially dairy products, smoke or drink alcohol for at least 24 hours. Fruit juices are OK. If the bite doesn't hurt after a few hours a light meal can probably be taken without ill effects.

The severity of a scorpion sting varies from very minor to quite painful. If it really hurts and you can't trust the remedies given or feel that you're seriously ill, go to a *farmacia*, hospital or Red Cross station.

•To avoid scorpions always check your bed before climbing in and shake your shoes and clothing in the morning. They prefer brush, rotten wood, rocks, piles of anything (especially if slightly damp), hollows and cracks.

Stingrays: *Rayas* are common in shallow water. Contrary to popular belief the stinger (actually a barbed shaft) is not poisonous, though it does produce a nasty, easily infected wound. To avoid being hit, shuffle your feet along the bottom rather than taking regular steps. When you bump into a ray, it will swim harmlessly away. If you step on its back, however, the tail arches over and the stinger is planted in your foot or ankle.

Treat as a puncture wound (see *Wounds*). A common folk cure is to gather a bunch of leaves from a low running, green, thick leaved plant found at the edge of the beach (known in some areas as *yerba de raya*), boil them for 20 minutes and wash the wound in the liquid.

Another remedy, one that sounds suspiciously like drowning the pain, is to be rubbed over the entire body with rags soaked in hot water, then wrap up in warm blankets and chug-a-lug a liter of *tequila*.

Ticks: In some areas you just can't avoid ticks (*garrapatas, guinas*). I've seen my clothing and body covered with thousands of the things after a short stroll through the jungle. Many ticks are almost impossible to see until they're gorged with blood. Should you walk into a bush that is infested with ticks, find a long switch and beat them off your clothing. The most effective method is to stretch your shirt or pants tightly and then whip the cloth with the switch. This will remove most of them, but you'll undoubtedly have some burrowing into your skin.

Ticks can be removed from your skin (look *everywhere*, from your ass to inside your ears) by tugging gently on the bodies. Unfortunately, this often leaves the head imbedded in the skin. To avoid this, coat the body of the tick with oil, fingernail polish or some other substance that will suffocate them and allow complete removal. Touching a hot match or cigarette to the tick will shrivel the body and may make it difficult to remove.

Snakebites: Mexico has an amazing variety of snakes, some of them amazingly poisonous. Fortunately very few tourists will ever see a poisonous snake, much less have the misfortune to be bitten by one. Treatment for *vibora* bites tends to be radical. If antitoxins are available they should be administered within 3 hours.

It is vital to keep in mind that most bites from poisonous snakes are not fatal, though they'll undoubtedly hurt like hell. Remain calm and keep still. Have someone get you to a doctor but don't go into a panic, it will only increase the speed that the venom travels through the body—*if there is any venom*. Non-poisonous snakes also bite, so your problem may be nothing more than a simple puncture wound (see *Wounds*).

Take massive doses of vitamin C and garlic.

You may also be suffering from shock, as a result of the fright of being bitten. (See *Shock*.)

Burns

Burns should be cleaned gently with warm water and soap. Cover the burn with a sterile, fine-meshed, absorbent gauze to keep it clean. Vitamin E oil or cream can be applied to the gauze. Any light oil would probably help, but never use butter or any other salted grease.

Cold water greatly relieves the pain of a burn. The gel from the aloe vera plant (*sabila*, very common in Mexico) is also very effective for pain and promotes healing.

Wet tea bags (black tea) are said to give relief when used as a poultice. Grated or mashed raw potatoes or onions also work quite well.

We carry vitamin E capsules and use them both internally and externally for burns. Just cut or bite the end off a capsule and squeeze the oil onto the burn.

Maintain treatment until the burn does not hurt, taking care to keep it clean until it has healed.

If the burn is serious, drink lots of fluids (see *Diarrhea* for a special cocktail).

Colds, Coughs, Sore Throat

Gripe is the Mexican word for anything from mild colds to severe flu. It responds very poorly to any treatment and most Mexicans resign themselves to a few days of popping aspirin.

Lorena has a standard treatment she employs at the first sign of *gripe* and it has an amazing rate of success. Take 2,000 units of vitamin C, 4 capsules (00, double ought) of goldenseal powder and 2 capsules (00) of cayenne powder. Follow this up with half dosages of each three times a day, 1 hour before meals.

If you don't have 00 capsules (*capsulas*, sold in pharmacies) a tea can be brewed. Tastes awful but it works. Add cinnamon and honey for flavoring.

Mexicans drink lots of tea for *gripe:* sage (*salvia*), cinnamon (*canela*) and bay leaves (*laurel*), either one at a time or all together. Mint (*yerba buena* and *menta*) and camomile (*manzanilla*) are also used.

My own preference is a hot tea of lime juice, honey and *tequila*. It promotes resting, which is one of the most effective cures.

Coughs (*tos*) can be relieved by drinking the juice of several limes added to a bit of hot water and two spoonsful of honey.

Mexicans use a tea of bougainvillaea (*garambullo, bugambilia*) for coughs and it seems effective. Boil several blossoms for 2 minutes, add honey and lime juice and drink. Good for sore throats, too.

Sore throats can be relieved by teas used for coughs, by gargling with warm salt water or by giving up and buying lozenges in the drugstore. They are sold individually or in packages.

A classic Mexican sore throat remedy, one so widely used that it must be effective, is to apply a poultice of hot tomato pulp or paste to the soles of the feet and throat.

Garlic, chewed slowly so the juice runs down the throat, will help clear up infections.

Cramps, Aches and Pains

Stomach cramps (*calambres*) often accompany severe cases of diarrhea and indigestion. These and other cramps—the bus seat backaches and menstrual cramps—can be relieved by taking calcium. We carry a supply of tablets and supplement them whenever possible by natural sources (sesame seeds, greens, milk and sprouts). *Calcio* is sold in drugstores or you can just dissolve an eggshell overnight in lime juice. Add to water and drink.

Calcium raises the body's tolerance to pain and should probably be taken for any injury.

Cuts: See *Infections and Wounds.*

Diarrhea, Dysentery and Food Poisoning

'Traveller's diarrhea' as the medical community now calls this ailment, is almost impossible to avoid. If you stay in Mexico long enough, you'll probably experience another case when you return home. Consider it a natural side effect of travel, like a hangover after a night on the town.

Because doctors now recognize that traveller's diarrhea is inevitable, even 'natural,' they have begun to change their approach to treatment. Strangely enough, the change has been toward remedies that sound suspiciously like those used by natural healers.

First, do not take anything that will stop bowel movement. The body needs to flush out, not plug up. This eliminates the use of Lomotil, Entero-Vioformo, Kaopectate and other classic diarrhea medicines. Using them will only prolong the problem and may even aggravate it, by forcing the body to delay healing.

The greatest danger with diarrhea is dehydration, especially in children. The following drink is recommended by the U.S. Center for Disease Control. It can be used as an aid to prevention, as well as for relief from diarrhea.

Put eight ounces of fruit juice in a glass and add half a teaspoon of honey (or sugar) and a pinch of salt. In another glass mix eight ounces of water (can use mineral or carbonated) and one quarter teaspoon of baking soda. Drink them down, alternating sips from one glass to the other. An adult should take several doses a day and a child at least four.

Avoid coffee, black tea, alcohol, chilies, black pepper, raw fruit, anything greasy, spicy or extremely hot or cold. Rest and relax; it will go away.

A normal case of diarrhea is often more severe than a person expects: cramps, nausea, vomiting, chills and fever as high as 103°F. It lasts from one to three days and may end suddenly, leaving you weak but happy. Don't resort to anitbiotics of 'liquid cork' until you've given yourself enough time for normal recovery.

Disentería is used in Mexico to describe both dysentery and diarrhea. This leads many gringos to erroneously believe that they're suffering from a case of amoebic dysentery when in fact, it's either traveller's diarrhea or food poisoning.

Food poisoning, either mild or severe, is not uncommon in Mexico. The symptoms are similar to diarrhea, but usually come on much faster and are more severe. Food poisoning also tends to end quickly, a common variety lasts only about twelve hours.

Use the same treatment for food poisoning as for diarrhea. You'll probably have no choice but to rest. Don't assume, just because the symptoms are severe, that you've got a case of dysentery. Dysentery should be diagnosed by a doctor, not by some sympathetic traveller in the next room. The treatment should be done under a doctor's supervision.

For all internal ailments drink plenty of liquids. The Mexican classic is dog tea, *té de perro*. It really works. Add a handful of the herb to one liter of boiling water. Let it stand (not boiling) for up to 30 minutes. Drink a glass whenever you're thirsty. It's good with lime juice. *Té de manzanilla* is also popular and if you can get them, *tuna de cardón* (cardon cactus fruits). Eat four a day until you've recovered. Coconut milk is good, though eating too much of the oily meat will increase the problem.

Papaya contains digestive enzymes that soothe the stomach. Many Mexicans eat 3 papaya seeds a day to prevent dysentery and 9 a day for 9 days to cure it. One teaspoon of chia seeds in a large glass of water, juice or soft drink will soothe your stomach and plug you up. We also use goldenseal (one or two 00 capsules, 3 times daily).

What if you're in a situation that makes immediate relief necessary? When I'm travelling by public transportation I carry a few ounces of *paregorico* or Lomotil tablets. Both contain opium and will stop uncontrollable diarrhea. Paregoric has no other ingredients but Lomotil is adulterated with belladonna. This produces a slight nausea, the drug company's sneaky way of preventing Lomotil addiction. The only advantage of Lomotil over paregoric is the size of the tablets: tiny and easily carried in your pocket.

Opium makes you very sleepy, a desirable state to be in when you've got diarrhea.

If symptoms persist beyond four days see a doctor. When antibiotics are used follow them up with yogurt. This helps to restore beneficial forms of bacteria to your system.

Drowning

The procedures for resuscitation should be learned from a manual on first-aid. What many books fail to mention, however, is that in order to be effective, the resuscitation must not be delayed by such procedures as loosening the victim's clothing or making a nice place to rest. Get your hands on the person as quickly as you can and go to work, even if you have to do it in neck deep water. The other things can be done later or when help arrives; the critical factor is getting air into the victim's lungs *as quickly as possible*.

Eyestrain

Drink lots of carrot juice and buy a pair of sunglasses.

Soaking a handkerchief or cloth in *té de manzanilla* and then pressing it gently against the eyes is said to give relief.

Fever

A *fiebre* can be expected with cases of diarrhea and sometimes with *gripe.* If the body temperature goes above 102°F (see *Appendices* for conversion to Centigrade), take aspirin and uncover. Fevers above 104°F can be cooled by bathing the person with wet cloths and placing damp cloths on the chest and forehead.

Fever caused by sunstroke can go very high. It should be checked with a rectal thermometer.

If the rectal temperature is over 106 degrees, the victim should be immersed in an ice water bath or wrapped in a soaking wet blanket. The skin should be massaged vigorously until the body temperature falls. The rectal temperature should be checked every ten minutes and the person removed from the ice water before it falls below 102°F.

If you're travelling alone and come down with a bad fever, ask someone to keep an eye on you. I've always found people to be very sympathetic; hotel employees will be glad to bring you tea and drinks.

A Mexican fever remedy common in desert areas is to toast a leaf of aloe vera, then slice it open, coat with cooking oil and sprinkle with a few petals of *rosa de castillo* (optional). Place against the soles of the feet, wrap and leave overnight.

The aloe gel can also be rubbed over the entire body.

Teas of lime juice, hibiscus (*jamaica*, very common), borage (*boraja*), parsley and alfalfa are also used.

Gripe: See Colds.

Hangover

The standard Mexican remedy is to continue drinking (see *Booze*). When this isn't possible they eat *menudo*, an intestine stew that is supposedly high in B vitamins. An easier way to take vitamin B is in brewer's yeast or by injection. Any *farmacia* will give you a massive dose of vitamin B. I've seen people return from the edge of the grave after a quick pick-me-up like this. Many of them, in fact, feel so much better that they decide to celebrate with another drink.

Dog tea (*té de perro*) also helps, as does a hair of the dog.

Heat Prostration and Sunstroke

Although both heat prostration and sunstroke (also called heatstroke) are caused by excessive physical exertion in heat and prolonged exposure to the sun, the symptoms and treatments are distinctly different for each.

Heat prostration can be avoided by taking it easy when it's hot (usually not difficult to do); by wearing light, loose, well ventilated clothing (heavier clothing is advisable in deserts) and by increasing the intake of fluids. Salt should be taken four or more times daily, especially in hot dry areas.

The symptoms of heat prostration are in many ways almost opposite to those of sunstroke. The skin is ashen, cold and damp; sweating may be heavy; pulse less than 100 and no significant increase in the body temperature. Other symptoms are dizziness, weakness, vertigo, headache, dim or blurred vision, irritability and mild muscular cramps.

The treatment is very simple: The victim should lie in a reclining position (feet *higher* than the head) in a cool shaded place with clothing loosened. Cool water may be taken.

Sunstroke can be much more serious than heat prostration. The measures taken to avoid it are similar to those used for heat prostration.

The attack may be sudden or preceded by complaints of weakness, headache, vertigo and nausea. A reduction or even cessation of sweating may occur several hours before the attack. The victim is flushed and the skin is hot and dry. Cramps or twitching may occur and the victim appears anxious and listless. The pupils are contracted early but dilate (open) later. The pulse may be 160 or more, respiration rate 20 to 30 per minute and body temperature 105 to 106 degrees (see *Fever*). Have the victim lie down with the feet *lower* than the head. *It's time to find a doctor.*

Because sunstroke is serious and the symptoms obvious, don't wait around until the situation becomes critical—rush to a doctor or to a place where adequate measures (ice, fast transportation, etc.) can be taken if necessary.

Hepatitis

This is a fairly common disease, caused by a viral inflammation of the liver. The most obvious symptom is jaundice: the skin and whites of your eyes turn yellowish. Other symptoms are loss of appetite, fatigue, aches and pains, brownish urine and nausea.

Hepatitis is highly communicable. It can be spread by sexual contact, by saliva and by food and drink. Many people recommend taking an injection of gamma globulin for protection from hepatitis. If someone you have contact with gets hepatitis, the gamma globulin should be taken as soon as possible to reduce your chance of infection. *Gamma globulina* is available in any pharmacy.

The danger of passing along the infection ends when the signs of jaundice have passed.

The only treatment is a good diet (lots of fresh fruits and vegetables), B vitamins (brewer's yeast) and plenty of rest. Don't push yourself too soon or you'll have a relapse. Hospitalization is required only in severe cases. If you're living with a hepatitis patient make every effort to keep separate eating utensils (boil those used by the sick person or use paper plates and cups) and, if possible, use a separate bathroom.

Avoid alcohol and cigarettes.

Infections

The most minor cut or scrape can lead to serious trouble if ignored. This is particularly true while camped on the beach or in the jungle, where even the casual scratching of mosquito bites often leads to open sores and infections. Puncture wounds are especially prone to infection as bacteria may literally be injected into the flesh and there's usually no great flow of blood to rinse them out again.

The following suggestions should be used both for the prevention and healing of infections:

Wash the wound with soap and water. If it is deep or too painful to scrub, flush it well with soapy water and then hydrogen peroxide. The foaming action of the peroxide will help to remove foreign particles. If possible soak the wound in a bucket of warm water. Add a teaspoon of soap. Hot compresses used for 20 minutes, four times daily, will improve circulation in the wounded area.

Washing the wound with lime juice (it stings!) or alcohol helps prevent infection. The use of lime juice on wounds and infections speeds up healing by killing weak tissue. Reapply if the area around the wound begins to redden.

Garlic helps prevent infections. Cover the wound and surrounding skin with some type of oil, then apply crushed garlic (a couple of cloves on a small wound). If the garlic causes burning, remove, wash and reapply, using more oil. Cover the garlic with a bandage. The wound should be cleaned two or three times a day and a fresh garlic poultice applied. Goldenseal powder can also be sprinkled on infections.

Persistent infections, usually seen as itching sores, are common in tropical areas. These are often called staph infections when in fact most are impetigo. The common practice of using antibiotic salves is seldom as effective as careful and continual washing with soap and water. Clean the sores thoroughly at least 3 times a day and keep them dry. Lime juice is also effective, applied several times a day until it no longer stings.

Blood poisoning can develop very quickly. A friend developed a noticeable red line along one arm 30 hours after poking a large cactus spine into his thumb.

A red line leading from a wound should not be ignored. Blood poisoning is quickly controlled with penicillin. Take 250 milligrams four times a day for five days. (Stop taking it if you experience any allergic reaction.) If the red line is gone before you've finished the penicillin tablets, continue to take them until they're finished. If you fail to complete the treatment, the infection can reappear.

Minor urinary infections, typified by a sensation of having to urinate but can't or burning sensation, can often be relieved by drinking large quantities of *té de jamaica* (hibiscus), herbal teas or plain water. Avoid coffee, booze, and black tea.

Vaginal infections are common for women who are unable to bathe regularly, usually the case when camping or travelling in remote areas.

If symptoms are mild (burning sensation, itching) a douche one to three times daily should be sufficient. Add one to two tablespoons of vinegar or lime juice to a liter of purified water. Do not use antibiotics unless you are unable to stop the infection with other treatments. If antibiotics are used be sure to complete the full treatment to avoid a recurrence.

If you must resort to antibiotics and are having intercourse, your partner should follow the same treatment.

Yeast infections (itching, burning and sometimes a whitish discharge) should be treated with a yogurt douche or the lime or vinegar mixture. Boric acid, in capsules, is also effective. Insert one capsule high in the vagina each morning and evening.

•*Warning:* Antibiotics actually cause yeast infections and should not be used in an attempt to treat them.

Insomnia: See *Nervousness and Tension.*

Intestinal Parasites

I have a real aversion to intestinal worms, a common problem in Latin American countries. To avoid them, as I have so far, eat lots of garlic, lime juice and drink *epazote* tea. (Pregnant women should not drink *epazote* tea.) Purify your food and water as best as you can.

Papaya seeds are also effective: take 3 a day to prevent worms and 9 a day for 9 days to eliminate them. Other common preventatives are to eat *pepitas* (squash seeds) in generous quantities and thin skinned avocados—skin and pulp, but not the seed.

Nausea

A cup of *té de perro* (dog tea) or *té de manzanilla* (camomile) will relieve that queasy feeling in your stomach after a trip through the meat stalls in the market. Add cinnamon if you have it. Soda crackers also help and if that doesn't do it, Alka Seltzer is widely available.

Nervousness, Tension

Tranquilizers such as Valium and Librium may be sold without a prescription, though a prescription is legally required. A better alternative, however, is to eat a *zapote blanco* or *zapote negro* (also *zapote borracho*). This tasty fruit is a natural tranquilizer. A tea from *zapote* leaves is also said to be calming. Teas made from mint, rue *(ruda),* valerian (*valeriana*), orange leaves, linden (*flor de tila*), lemon plant (*té de limón*) and camomile are also effective as tranquilizers. Sidewalk herb vendors will sell ready mixed packages of teas for *Nervios* and *Insomnio.* I've used them and they work.

Calcium and B vitamins (brewer's yeast) are also effective. Calcium is good for insomnia. (Natural sources are milk, greens, sprouts and sesame seeds.)

Poisoning

Induce vomiting by sticking your finger down the victim's throat or give warm water mixed with a little soap, mustard or salt.

When they've finished vomiting give milk, beaten eggs, honey and flour mixed with water or a tablespoon of powdered charcoal.

Don't induce vomiting if gasoline, kerosene, acids or corrosive substances were swallowed. Vomiting will force irritating fumes or liquid into the lungs and increase the chance of pneumonia. If pneumonia does develop (usually within a day or two), it will be indicated by a high fever. Go to a doctor right away.

Rashes

Rashes caused by sweating frequently bother travellers unaccustomed to constant warm, humid air. These rashes are aggravated by long periods of riding buses, tight clothing and not bathing. Although talcum powder (*talco*) is sold in pharmacies and *boticas*, cornstarch (*Maizena*) is even more common and much cheaper. Buy a small box and transfer the contents to something leakproof. Dust it on the rash every few hours.

Aloe vera gel soothes and promotes healing of raw rashes.

Shock

There are two types of shock: physical and mental. When you step out to flag down a city bus in Guadalajara and it runs you over, you'll soon be suffering the first variety. Although the symptoms of *physical shock* are complex, the traumatic circumstances which lead to it are usually quite obvious.

The victim should lie down or sit, head hanging between the knees. In cases of severe shock with faint rapid pulse, fast breathing, dry tongue and sweating, have the victim lie down. Elevate the feet about 12 inches. Cover, but don't allow overheating. Small amounts of liquids can be given in mild cases, but none are allowed when the shock is severe.

Mental shock, commonly known amongst travellers as 'cultural shock' is not something to laugh off lightly. It is the result of a fast and almost total change in environment, the situation most people experience when they enter Mexico. The symptoms may be complicated by genuine physical strain or minor ailments such as diarrhea, sunburn or hangover. The usual signs of cultural shock are: vague feelings of paranoia and weirdness, irritability, loss of appetite, crying jabs, sudden compulsive wishes to go to Yosemite National Park instead of Puebla and a sense of isolation from what is happening around you.

The treatment must be initiated quickly. In mild cases, a companion should read the victim selected articles from American magazines or newspapers, particulary *Time, Newsweek* and *Reader's Digest*. Evoke memories of Safeway and MacDonald's while guiding the victim through a clean, airy market place. Daydream aloud about Caribbean beaches while speculating on summer temperatures or winter snow depths at home.

Severe cases should be isolated, preferably in a section of the country that vaguely resembles home. Beaches can cure even terminal shock, but beware of setbacks caused by trips to town.

Persons travelling alone should immediately seek the company of other well-seasoned travellers, but should not indulge in the mutual exchange of 'horror stories.' Visits to traumatically American hotels, restaurants and trailer parks are very effective for some, but in other cases may lead to disastrous and perhaps irreversible addiction.

Letters from home almost invariably lead to rapid recuperation and for this reason it may be necessary for concerned friends to fabricate gloomy correspondence with appropriate news items ("All of your friends have left for Mexico," "...and then the water pipes froze and burst...," etc.).

Peanut butter, canned food, *Bimbo* bread, potato chips and candy bars should be employed only in severe or persistent cases and under the supervision of a well-adjusted friend.

Sprains

Keep the sprain (or break) as still as possible. Wrap it well to give firm support. For the first 24 hours after the injury soak the sprain in cold water to reduce swelling and pain. Afterwards, soak it in hot water several times a day.

Sunburn

Your first wonderful day on the beach may be the last you'll spend outdoors for weeks. Your initial exposure to bright midday sunlight should not be over 30 minutes, even if your skin is naturally dark. People with red or blond hair should take even less sun. When sand, water or snow is around, the exposure time should be shortened even more. Clouds are not sun filters and many people suffer very serious burns on an overcast day.

When you're in doubt about how much sun you've taken and how much more you can stand—get into the shade. Put on light clothing, but if it's loosely woven you will probably get a sunburn right through the material. Remember: burning retards tanning.

Because it seems inevitable that we find ourselves in situations where the sun can't be avoided—an unexpected invitation to take a boat ride, for example—we always carry a small tube of sun screen ointment. This stuff blocks the sun almost entirely. If you can't find it anywhere else, go to a ski shop or backpacking supply shop. Mountaineers use it lavishly, including on their eyelids and lips.

To test your skin for burning press one or two fingers firmly over the exposed area and hold down for several seconds. Now quickly release the pressure. A pale spot will mark the finger impression. If the spot is still distinct after you've slowly said, "I've got a sunburn," you're right, you do. Use this test all over your body, some parts burn much faster than others.

PABA (para amino benzoic acid) is a vitamin B ointment that is an excellent tanning cream and skin conditioner. It relieves sunburn pain, too.

Suntan lotion, sesame oil or coconut oil may prevent some burning, but are usually washed off by swimming or sweating. One of the best lasting and effective anti-burn preparations is red petrolatum.

Serious sunburns may be accompanied by heat prostration or sunstroke. Until the worst reaction is over, it is necessary to stay completely out of the sun—not too difficult as a few feeble rays will be like the touch of a blow-torch.

If you've been burned use liberal amounts of aloe vera gel. It has an amazing ability to both relieve pain and prevent blistering. Compresses of grated or crushed raw potatoes or onions are very effective. Fresh or canned milk also helps, but it must be applied frequently. Vinegar can also be used.

Peeling of the skin can lead to infection. If blisters appear, *leave them alone*. Without the protection of skin and natural fluids, the sensitive skin underneath will dry and crack, hurting like hell.

Sunstroke: See Heat Prostration.

Toothache

A few drops of clove oil (*aceite de clavo*) on a piece of cotton or tissue (or just oil alone) can be placed on the aching tooth. Whole cloves also work; put a couple as close as possible to the ache and hold there until the area is numb. An aspirin can also be used, though it is most effective if the ache is caused by a cavity. A swallow of *paregorico* will kill the pain and cause drowsiness.

Mexicans often use a prune or raisin, split open and held against the aching area.

Wounds

Abrasions become easily infected by bacteria ground into the skin. Clean the injured area thoroughly with soap and purified water or half a lime, remove all ground-in particles and cover with a bandage.

Cuts should be cleaned well with soap and water (or lime juice or alcohol and ether, if available) and bandaged. Bleeding can almost always be stopped by applying pressure directly over the wound (lean on it, even if it takes an hour!) and by elevating the wounded part as high as possible.

Tourniquets should not be used unless other measures fail. Try to locate and tie off any severed blood vessels as soon as the tourniquet has slowed the bleeding. The tourniquet can then be released. (It must be released every 30 minutes no matter what and circulation allowed to continue for one minute, if possible).

Puncture wounds should be cleaned as thoroughly as possible and, if necessary, *enlarged* (time to bite the bullet). Although you might prefer to delay the operation until it appears essential (such as the appearance of pus and swelling), a puncture would can infect rapidly if not properly cleaned (see *Infections*).

The usual early morning vocal battle between the village dogs and roosters had just erupted as I sagged wearily into my dew moistened hammock.

"Lorena! Steve!" I called weakly. "Wake up! I'm dying." The only response from the hammocks slung nearby was a low, "Hmmmmm?"

"I said, I'm dying, goddamit! The least you could do is wake up and look!" Lorena's head poked from beneath a blanket.

"Still got diarrhea?" she asked sleepily.

"Have I got it?" I moaned. "Hell, yes! I've been sitting in the bushes all night!"

I was about to launch into a detailed description of my ailments when a familiar voice called, "*¡Ola! ¡Carlitos!*" It was Nacho, an old friend who fed us during our visits in exchange for odd jobs around his tiny restaurant. I had agreed the night before to help him prepare *cochinita pibil* (baked pig). The first step, unfortunately, was to dig a deep pit in the loose sand. I looked over at him, standing patiently with a shovel in one hand and a cup of coffee for me in the other, and gave an involuntary groan.

" *Carlitos?*" he said anxiously. "What is it? Are you sick?"

"I will soon be over there, Nacho." I waved feebly at the cemetery behind his restaurant, twisting my face into an appropriate grimace of agony.

He laughed uproariously, called to Steve and Lorena, "I told you that one day Carlos would never be able to leave this beautiful place." As they chuckled over this bit of humor, I suddenly clutched my stomach and rushed into the nearby bushes.

A few minutes later, white-faced and shaking, I slipped tenderly back into the hammock. Nacho looked at me with genuine concern and said, "You look *terrible*, I'm going to get *la abuela* to help you."

"What was that?" Lorena asked, sitting upright and turning toward me with an eager look on her face. "What did Nacho say?"

"He's going to get the grandmother," I said. "At least, someone seems concerned about what happens to me."

I knew that Lorena's sudden interest came from the aura of mystery that surrounded Nacho's aged mother, a person we had seen off and on during our many visits, but only as a dark wrinkled face in the tiny kitchen behind the restaurant. It was said that she had not left the immediate area in over seven years. Because Nacho delighted in nighttime tales of strange Mayan lore, we more than suspected the grandmother of *brujería* (witchcraft). Lorena had been waiting for an opportunity such as this to break into the old woman's isolation.

Nacho soon returned, followed not only by his mother but also by the rest of the family, from his wife and children to various nieces and in-laws. Ribald comments over my condition came by the dozen.

"*¡Oye, Carlos!* How many times last night?"

"*¡Caray!* You made a new path into the woods!"

"That's what you get for drinking Tonio's rum!"

The grandmother shushed them impatiently and stared deeply into my eyes. Nacho whispered into her ear, "Shall we give him the *chiles*?" She shook her old head slowly and uttered the first words we'd heard her say in a surprisingly strong, clear voice. "No, this is bad. He needs *El Alacrán*!"

"The Scorpion?" I thought. "For God's sake, isn't this carrying things a little too far? Who is this lady anyway? What does she know?"

As I started to object, Nacho laid his hand soothingly on my shoulder and said, "Don't worry, *amigo*. It's a dead scorpion and dry as dust!"

I laughed nervously, but was interrupted by grandmother's abrupt command, "You have to eat it!"

The children chattered with excitement, "Carlos is going to eat *el alacrán*!"

Nacho broke up the entire group by adding, "With *chile* sauce."

"Quiet!" grandmother ordered sharply, motioning one of the young girls to her side. I watched anxiously as she slipped the girl a coin and muttered something in her ear.

"What was that?" I asked, amazed at the speed with which the girl had dashed off toward the village.

"*¿Mama?*" Nacho said, "What is it?"

She shrugged her shoulders casually and said, "It's nothing, just *el polvito*."

I looked sullenly at Lorena and Steve. "Now, that's it!" I said quietly in English. "She just sent off for the 'little powder' and I'm not up for that one."

Lorena fairly danced with glee; this was *the real thing*, an authenic Mayan secret remedy!

While the family followed grandma respectfully back to their morning chores, I continued my protests. "Look, you guys. I honestly don't think this is going to help me out any. That scorpion sounds bad enough but I really don't like the idea of taking 'little powders.' May it's something dangerous."

"Oh, Carl," Lorena exclaimed, "think of what a great chance this is! This may be a whole new thing for the book, a really natural cure for diarrhea!"

"I think I'd rather stick with *Lomotil*," I muttered, "and try grannie's potions on somebody else."

Steve interrupted to say, "Well, you're too late now. You'll have to take their cure so you don't hurt anyone's feelings. Besides, it's a hell of a long ways to the nearest drugstore."

Before I could protest further, Nacho called, "Come here, *Carlitos*. It's almost ready."

I trudged slowly through the sand to the single large table that comprised the restaurant's furniture. Granny was carefully grinding a large brown scorpion in her stone *molcajete.* The ground scorpion was then mixed with a white powder, presumably *el polvito.*

"Which do you want?" Nacho asked, opening the lid of the beer cooler.

"What?" I said.

"Which do you want?" he repeated. "We've got *Coca, Sidral,* grape or orange."

"Why?" I stammered, by now completely confused.

"For the cure, *Carlitos,*" he explained patiently. "You have to drink it with a bottle of pop."

I looked at Lorena; her faith in Mayan remedies had just dropped several degrees. Steve was smirking over a bottle of warm beer, enjoying the scene intensely.

"Grape," I croaked, my throat suddenly dry and chalky.

With great ceremony Nacho wiped the bottle clean and popped of the top with his teeth. Grandmother drank off the top few inches with a faint grin and then sifted the mixture of powders into the purplish liquid. Foam immediately formed and she thrust the bottle at me quickly, ordering, "Drink it fast! All of it!"

I choked down bubbly sweet mouthfuls as fast as possible, feeling the gritty scorpion stick between my teeth. As the last gulp disappeared, a loud roar of approval came from the crowd around me.

"You're cured!" Nacho laughed, slapping me on the shoulder, "and only we know what it was that did it!"

I was about to ask what that meant when a sudden cramp sent me scurrying back to the bushes. Happy shouts followed:

"Not again! There he goes!"

"Give him another scorpion!"

"Watch where you step.!"

Several hours later Nacho approached the hammock. "How goes it, *Carlitos?*" he asked.

"Bad, *Nacho,*" I answered. "That cure didn't do it."

"Yes," he said sadly, "we didn't think it would."

"What do you mean?" I asked intently. "Why not?"

"They were out of the powder we wanted, so grandmother gave you sugar instead. She thought it might help. Too bad, though," he mused. "The other stuff is really strong."

"What *other stuff?*" I asked.

"Oh, *Carlitos,* you know," Nacho said casually, "Alka-Seltzer."

TOURISTS AND THE LAW

Your rights as a tourist...Interesting legal facts...The Cops...Auto accidents...Expired Tourist cards and Car papers...Buying houses and land...Bank trusts...The Heartbreak of Marijuana...Scoring...Busts... Behind bars...Unexpected guests..

When the time came to write this chapter, I dutifully assembled and reviewed all of my notes, newspaper articles, personal experiences and unsolicited stories from friends and acquaintances. Together they would have made a great crime magazine, a compilation of almost every accident and woe to befall the person adventurous enough to leave their front yard. I was then faced with a difficult decision: leave the chapter out (and it represented a lot of work), water it down ("Prison offers ample opportunities for language study") or just hope that readers would take it calmly instead of freaking out and heading for Yellowstone. The answer came in the words of a friend: "A minute of paranoia is worth a year's detention."

When you're in trouble, whether it's in Seattle or Sinaloa, you're in *trouble.* Anything you can do to help yourself is valuable. Don't let this chapter scare you; it represents the very low odds that things will go wrong instead of right and that you'll need some advice.

To insure that my information was as accurate as possible, I decided, against my natural inclinations, to verify it with the police. My first interview was with a Mexican traffic cop in the process of arresting us for running a hidden stop sign.

"Is it legal to drink and drive?" I asked. The cop paused over the ticket book for several seconds, then said, "I drink vodka. It's relaxing." He noted our license number then added, "But if you're passing a cop and going fast—very fast—put the bottle between your legs rather than letting him see you drink."

I then arranged for a series of interviews with a judge and district attorney. To almost each of my questions the answer was the same: "It depends." In frustration, since I knew that it did indeed 'depend,' but couldn't offer just that explanation in a book, I said, "OK. Tell me what *really happens* instead of what is supposed to happen."

"Will my name be mentioned?" they asked in anxious unison.

"No." I said, and from there the interviews went quite smoothly. Not too surprisingly, their information confirmed or supported my own material in almost every detail. The following questions and answers, therefore, most accurately represent an interview between myself and friends, backed up by 'expert' opinion.

What Are My Rights As A Tourist?

As a *turista* you have almost all the rights of a Mexican citizen, with these exceptions: tourists cannot own land (though they can hold it in trust; see *Land*), cannot work without special permission and cannot vote.

Some facts about the Mexican legal system and laws (based largely on the Napoleonic Code) of interest to tourists are:

- Laws vary from state to state, but are generally modeled on the code of the *Distrito Federal* (Federal District, equivalent to Washington, D.C.).
- Judges decide all cases, not juries.
- Men and women are legally equal before the law.
- A person can be held for up to 72 hours without being charged.
- Any offense that involves drinking, drugs or minors is usually considered more severe than if it did not. If, for example, you kidnap a child and crash your care while drunk and stoned, you're in deep trouble.
- Nudity is illegal and punishable by a fine and short jail term.
- Abortion is illegal, though commonly done. There is a pro-abortion movement that is gaining strength.
- Homosexuality is not illegal. Sex acts between adults and minors, however, are illegal. Between consenting adults and/or animals, anything goes (in private).
- Prostitution is legal in almost all states.
- Pornography is illegal and common.
- All babies born in Mexico, regardless of the nationality of their parents, are entitled to Mexican citizenship (the birth must be registered).

Do Tourists Need To Worry About The Cops?

Millions of people visit Mexico each year and very few of them get thrown into jail or involved in legal difficulties of any type. The best story you can hope for will be a typical, "...so I slipped the big guy five bucks and they let us go."

Tourists who find themselves being hassled for such minor things as traffic violations, drunkenness or disputes with taxi drivers should *remain calm*. Don't shout, "By Gawd,

A Field Guide To Mexican Cops

Preventivos: Preventives, the equivalent of a regular beat cop in the U.S. Brown uniforms.

Tránsito: Traffic cops, mounted or on foot. Dark blue pants, sky blue shirt. May be armed.

Caminos: Properly known as *caminos federales* (federal highways). This is the highway patrol. Grey pants and a light brown shirt. Armed.

Judicial federal: The not very popular *federales*, also known as *jefes* (chiefs). When not in camouflage they dress like well-to-do West Texans. Armed and arrogant.

Servicio Secreto: The SS, Secret Service. Civilian clothes and very heavily tinted sunglasses. Armed.

Judicial: The judicials are general purpose cops. A friend says that they always drive Dodge Darts with two tailpipes and a CB antenna. Armed.

Comisionados: The modern day *rurales*, a rag-tag militia formed by the *ejidos* (rural cooperatives). They have no police powers.

Guaruras: Bodyguards, armed and can be considered dangerous. No self-respecting politician, *latifundo* (big landowner) or *rico* (rich man) would be without at least one. They are popularly known as *nacos* (scum, thugs).

Mordelón: A derogatory term for a cop, implying that they are 'big biters,' i.e., takers of bribes.

Note: If a town can't afford standard uniforms, the *preventivos* and *tránsitos* may be dressed differently than described above.

I'm an American citizen and you can't do this...blah...blah...!" or you'll find yourself facing strong resentment. In almost every case the police will prefer to settle the matter quietly, on the spot, rather than have you drag in tourist bureau officials or lawyers. Be reasonable; if you're in the right but are expected to pay a small 'consideration,' do it and forget about it.

•Weirdos: it's only natural that the freakier you look, the more you'll be looked at. Cops, being basically snoopy, may decide you look more like a potential arrest than the straight tourists he sees. When he decides to approach, what happens next almost always depends on you. A calm, friendly reaction will usually put you back into the tourist category rather than dope-crazed hippie.

Try your best to understand where that cop's head is at. If he can read at all, he probably laboriously scans the "*¡Alarma!*" once a month, enjoying lurid accounts of axe murders, rapes and hippies caught with tons of dope. So when you tell him you're bathing nude because, "We are all children under the sun," he thinks you're either doped, insane or covering up something even worse, something so awful he can't figure it out.

I'd say, "A dog stole my swimming suit," and apologize.

Mexican authorities are very up-tight about large gatherings of freaks. When dope and nudity become involved, some type of police reaction is automatic. Stories of mass roundups by the army and police are true. You may be jailed, fined, deported or all three. In one case a group of nude sun worshippers was set to work on the local school. They spent several days at hard labor before being shipped home.

What If I Have An Auto Accident?

First, and most important, if you have insurance show the policy to the police. This is your 'Get Out Of Jail Free' card. Without it you will very likely be held until all claims have been settled. Your insurance agent should take care of everything. In cases where liability is not easily determined or damages difficult to assess, you will be asked to remain in the area. The tourist is almost always assumed to be at fault. If you have insurance this won't present a problem.

•Fatal accidents, especially those presumed to be caused by drinking or drugs, can lead to criminal charges. What happens depends to a great extent on the report of the investigating officer. If he believes your story, you'll probably get off; if he doesn't, you'll usually be charged with 'accidental homicide.' The sentence is 3 days to 5 years, depending on the state. Tourists are often released on bond (substantial) and allowed to flee the country.

•Single car accidents: Cops are adept at turning the most minor incident—such as running off the road—into a case of negligent or reckless driving. You might be fined for 'damage to the roadbed' or the replacement of a tree, piece of curbing or fence. Whenever possible leave the scene before trouble arrives.

•Leaving the scene: This is a particularly sensitive point with tourists. The thought of 'hit-and-run' leaves most of us jelly-kneed. My advice, and that given to me by law officials, is to get away from the scene of an accident as fast and unobtrusively as possible. The other person involved is probably doing the same thing.

Unless serious injury is involved, leaving the scene is not illegal, though if you're caught you may be denied bond.

Mexican cops are infamous for working all the angles. You may not think that a fender-bender accident is worth their time or trouble, but it will be, especially if you have money.

As a tourist, you are vulnerable to bullying by the police and other persons involved in an accident. Unless you remain calm and are able to communicate the facts in a convincing manner, the cops probably won't even bother to talk to you. While the other person is filling the officer's ear with tales and his pocket with *pesos*, your position is rapidly worsening. If you're insured, this will be a minor hassle; if you're not, it will get complicated.

•Good Samaritans: The decision of what to do should you see an accident is a tough one. Very few Mexicans would advise you to stop or offer aid. Although you can be held responsible for not stopping, the fact that almost no one will must mean something. I believe that the reason for this is the attitude of the police and their tendency to make money out of other's misfortune, even if they have to squeeze the innocent to do it. I know of several cases where tourists helped injured people without hassles, but none of them waited around for an investigation. Give first aid or take the injured to a hospital door—then leave.

It is illegal to move corpses or unconscious bodies.

•Livestock: If you nail one of those cows, burros or chickens that haunt Mexican highways, don't even bother to look back. You'll notice that Mexican trucks all have large 'cow catchers' welded over the grill. The only time you're liable for hitting livestock is when speeding or otherwise violating the law. The only way they can accuse you is if you stop.

•Stolen cars: Contact your insurance agent and go immediately to the nearest police station to file a complaint. Get a certified copy of the complaint; you'll need it to leave the country if the car is not recovered. If the car is involved in an accident or crime you are not liable, but you'll need an insurance agent or lawyer to help you recover it.

Paper Problems

Your tourist card and car papers may be checked anywhere in the country by local and federal police, immigration officials or the army. Checks are common where campers congregate. Expired or lost papers could lead to trouble if the police have any desire to make things tough for you.

Passengers on buses and trains that approach the border between Mexico and the U.S. are frequently checked. You'll also be checked at the airport if you leave Mexico by plane. When driving out of the country, you may be stopped at a checkpoint about 20 miles before the border. Be prepared to pay if things aren't in order. Discrepancies can generally be cleared up for a reasonable sum.

When you reach the border, you are supposed to surrender both your tourist card and car papers *voluntarily.* Many people don't bother. Cars and pedestrians pass through by the hundreds during peak traffic hours. Unless you're stopped intentionally, the Mexican officials have no way of knowing that you're not just over for the day.

If your papers are not in order, park near the border exit point and check things out on foot. A major crossing point (Nuevo Laredo, Tijuana, etc.) is the easiest to slip through.

When crossing into Guatemala and Belize from Mexico, you have no way to avoid being checked by the Mexicans. Most of them, fortunately enough, are quite reasonable, i.e., if the price is right.

•Tourist cards: If you've lost your tourist card go to the nearest *Oficina de Turismo* (government tourist office). They will almost always know the most effective way to straighten things out. You can also go directly to a *Migración* (Immigration) or *Governación* office, found in Mexico City, state capitals, seaports and ports of entry. In case of theft a written report from the nearest police department will often speed things up.

Expired cards are more of a problem. Although tourist cards can be extended, it is a complicated and time consuming procedure. Once again, go to a *Turismo* office and explain your predicament. If you make no attempt to have it extended, you are liable for a fine, based on the length of time since the card expired. I know of many cases where people were able to make an 'arrangement' with Immigration officials at the border, as they were leaving Mexico, but this is uncertain and therefore risky.

•Car papers: Ask the *Turismo* people or find an office of *Hacienda* or *Registro Federal de Automóviles.* If your car is unable to leave the country when you do, it can be impounded until your return, shipped to the border and then towed into the U.S. or just signed over to the Mexican government. The latter option is usually done in cases of total destruction.

•Lawyers: When in doubt or really confused about what to do, consider seeking out a lawyer (*licenciado* or *notario*). Explain your problem and ask for a *presupuesto* (an estimate, preferably in writing) of charges. Lawyers have the advantage of knowing the ropes and how to untangle the more frustrating knots. They are especially useful for arranging deals of a slightly dubious legality.

•Illegal papers: Some enterprising people sell new tourist cards and car papers. The charge is usually quite reasonable, but locating them is not easy. Ask a resident foreigner. Most of these deals are done in the largest cities and border towns.

Can A Tourist Or A Foreigner Own Land?

A tourist cannot own land in Mexico, but any foreigner who meets certain immigration requirements can own land outside of the Prohibited Zone (within 50 kilometers of any coast and 100 kilometers of borders). Because immigration is a major undertaking, the government has made it possible for tourists to acquire land trusts.

Under the *Law to Promote Mexican Investment and Regulate Foreign Investment*, tourists can acquire land both in and outside the Prohibited Zone. The trust lasts for 30 years and is an agreement between the seller, the bank and the beneficiary (the buyer). The tourist can use the land, improve it, rent it and transfer or sell the rights to it. It can also be passed on in a will.

There are some restrictions, but the most important involves *ejido* land (cooperatives established by the government). Members of *ejidos* do not own their land and may not sell it, though they often make deals with tourists. These arrangements are not legal and provide no protection. In spite of this, foreigners often rent or lease *ejido* property and build houses. This type of deal is only as good as the trust between the two parties. In most cases it works out quite well. When in doubt, minimize the risk by keeping your investment low.

Tourists are frequently overwhelmed by Mexico and suddenly decide to buy a house, condominium or land. The price seems good, the people and climate agreeable and the style of living attractive, if not irresistible. Many of these impulses, however, are regretted later. *Don't rush into anything.* If you think you'd like to buy a place, try living there first. Rent a house and wait a minimum of six months before making a final decision. You might well find that the easy life is dull, or that familiar faces and surroundings are too important to do without.

For advice on buying land and real estate trusts write to:

Banco Nacional de Mexico, S.A.
Trust Department, Head Office
Isabel Católica No. 44
Mexico 1, D.C.

or

Banco de Comercio, S.A.
Venustiano Carianza 44
Mexico, D.F.

I Am Hopelessly Addicted To Marijuana. What's Up In Mexico?

In December of 1974, penalties for possession of the Devil Weed *for personal use and immediate consumption* were reduced to six months to three years in jail and a fine. This marked the beginning of a trend toward lighter penalties for simple possession. The latest development, in 1977, came when the Attorney General of Mexico ordered state law officials to reconsider all cases involving less than 100 grams of pot. Several hundred people were subsequently released. The 'word' is that no one will be prosecuted for simple possession of 100 grams or less. This doesn't mean, however, that you won't be busted—you'll just have to hope that you aren't prosecuted. (Note: seeds are weight too; get rid of them.)

It is not illegal to be a drug addict in Mexico and to possess small amounts to satisfy your weird cravings. If you have drugs, however, you must prove that you're hooked or the possession becomes a crime. According to an article in the newspaper, *Excelsior*, under Article 195 of the Penal Code, a *toxicómano* (addict) can possess up to 40 grams of marijuana. This amount is considered sufficient to keep the addict stoned for 24 hours. (The newspaper notes that this is equal to at least 20 or 30 joints and should bomb out at least 10 people.)

The article cites the case of a sailor caught with almost a pound of weed. He pleaded that he needed that much to satisfy his habit on a long voyage. He was acquitted.

How does this law affect tourists? First of all, it is necessary to be legally certified as a marijuana addict. This is presumably done after you've been caught. This might be a rather drastic measure in cases of minor possession as the tourist would almost certainly be deported as an undesirable alien.

Because this law is obscure and contradicts current medical opinion about the effects of marijuana, my advice—and that of law officials I spoke to—is, "don't count on it." Since the cops and other officials have little or no knowledge of the law, there's not much chance they'll recognize your claim to being a legal addict. You can always try, however, to have your lawyer find a doctor willing to certify you as a *toxicómano*—who knows?

•Scoring: It is unfortunately true that undercover cops set up busts in order to extort money or goodies from their victims. This is most commonly done in places where *jipis* congregate. The best way to avoid this hazard is to score only from someone you really trust. Anyone who approaches with the "Pssst, hey, you wanna buy some...?" should be considered unreliable.

•Searches: Although most of the pressure is on the big time growers and dealers, the cops (especially the local variety) still search tourists. Searches can come *anywhere* in Mexico, but the favorite areas are beaches and the northern highways. (The entire state of Sinaloa, Mexico's opium center, is very hot.)

If you like to camp, odds are that one day you'll have a visit by the Army or *federales*. No place is too remote for them. Be polite; the President of Mexico recently ordered the Army to make special efforts to insure the safety of tourists. The visit may be made to reassure you rather than a search. (For more, see *The People's Guide To Camping In Mexico*.)

Never leave dope laying around. Always keep it well hidden and preferably outside of your car. You may lose the car and everything in it otherwise. When a search does come, it will be unexpected and fast. We've greeted the cops from small planes, boats, jeeps, passenger bus and even horseback (Mexico still has a Cavalry.) They'll come at any hour of the day or night, either with great commotion or on their hands and knees in the bushes. Anything to get the job done.

In areas where the cops are looking for giant stashes, the search might be fast (especially if you aren't too hippie-like) but most of the time they'll go over everything, from Tampax to tire tubes. If you speak Spanish, you'll be questioned about smoking and probably given a lecture about how the search is part of some Operation with U.S. support, etc., etc. Keep a straight face and a serious tone to your voice; there's nothing better than a wise ass or flippant attitude to throw them into high gear.

Act as if everything you own is made of fragile china. These searches are supposed to be conducted with respect for your belongings. One *federal* made his men dust off everything after looking at it.

The army likes to pull 'John Wayne' searches. Lorena and I were alone one day in our camp on a very remote Pacific beach, enjoying an atmosphere of total relaxation. While she drowsed in a hammock, I beachcombed and swam. After hours of this, I wandered back through the bushes toward camp, ready for a quiet drink in the shady coconut grove. I was about to cross a narrow clearing when I noticed movements in the bushes in front of me. To my amazement, five soldiers in full combat regalia, including twigs and leaves on their helmets, were crawling through the weeds toward Lorena, submachine guns 'at the ready.'

After surveying this unlikely scene, I walked up behind one of them and said, "*¡Buenas tardes!*" Their reaction was so embarrassed that they made their dope search as brief as possible, even though one whispered to me that they'd come 40 miles by bus to "get us."

The motive for the army's search wasn't to bust us with a lid—or even a *kilo*—but to determine if we were big dealers. Our preference for really isolated areas tends to lead us to others who enjoy isolation, mainly large scale dope growers. They, in turn, attract a lot of heavy police activity. (Another factor against us was our VW van, commonly associated throughout Mexico with American dealers.)

The army often works in conjunction with the *federales*. You can spot a soldier by his uniform but a *federal* is most easily identified by his gun—often a light submachine gun, sawed-off shotgun or a flashy pistol. *Federales* rarely wear uniforms and may even look like *campesinos* (country people). *Federales* love to drive American cars and trucks—with American plates—that they've confiscated from unfortunate smugglers. We've seen them in everything from new Ford trucks with campers to old beat up station wagons with New York plates. Some of them like to pose as Mexican-Americans on vacation.

An undercover agent will invariably tip his hand by mentioning dope. No respectable Mexican would bring the subject up until he knew you were a friend. *Federales*, on the other hand, are impatient and not at all subtle. They like to talk about hashish, almost unavailable in Mexico. A *federal* will smoke dope with you, eat your food, drink your booze, take you to town to meet his brother and then either turn you over to another agent or take you in himself.

When we're staying in one place for any length of time, I like to find a good trustworthy local person—a fisherman, farmer or store owner—and carefully sound them out for indications that the *federales* are around. Few Mexicans like the cops and they'll often warn you when the heat is nearby.

Poor Mexicans are generally tolerant of dope smoking and may be growing some themselves as a cash crop. For this reason and others, they are also harassed by the cops and army. One of the saddest results of efforts to eradicate marijuana is that the *campesino* who is forced by poverty to grow dope is also the easiest person to catch.

Cops rarely search a person's clothing or body unless they are extremely suspicious or have already found something incriminating. Women will usually be searched only if the bust is a big one.

Unless you're blatantly dealing dope or blabbing about it to your neighbors, you'll be left alone while living in a house. Discreet smokers should have little to worry about.

•You're Busted!: If you are busted, *don't panic;* as with snake bites the outcome will depend largely on what you do in that first crucial hour.

If the amount of grass is small (a lid to even a kilo or so), you can probably get out of it with a fast bribe. The so-called 'new breed' of *federal* supposedly will not accept gratuities. If they know, however, that simple possession will not be prosecuted, they'll very likely take what they can get and turn you loose. This can be money or possessions (radios are good, as are cameras, tools and camping gear). You always offer the bribe to the person in charge. Don't claim to be the illegitimate nephew of the president of Mexico unless you can follow it up.

A good friend was arrested by the army on suspicion of being a dealer. When they got him to the door of his cell, he claimed to be a U.S. Senator. To prove it, he produced several impressive letters, decorated with seals and stamps, written in Spanish and introducing him "to whom it may concern." The officer in charge became sufficiently concerned that he decided to throw my friend an apology party, complete with sliced watermelon and cold drinks.

The usual outcome of dope busts, including some involving large amounts of grass, is a short period in jail and deportation. Since the cops know this when they get you in, their natural tendency is to make the deal as profitable as possible for themselves.

The amount you pay depends, of course, on how worried you are and what you can afford. Successful bribes can range anywhere from a few dollars to thousands. In some cases, the cops will give you a bargain deal: a bribe plus first chance to buy your dope back. Don't do it; even though it's probably an 'honest' deal, you're setting yourself up.

If one person in a group is caught, the others

will also be arrested or at least hassled. By immediately taking the blame, you can take the heat off your friends and probably keep the overall expense of the bust much lower. Since a car can be confiscated if dope is found in it, it's wise to have someone other than the owner take the blame.

The thought of going to jail alone might disturb you, but you're better off having a friend outside who can arrange your release.

You might bluff your way out of an arrest, especially if the amount of dope is very small (a roach) or you're just being taken in on suspicion. Hysterics, fainting and vomiting—especially if done by women—can wreck a cop's determination.

Scream, rant, cry, beat your head against a wall, anything to convince them you're not about to go for something you're not guilty of. If the cops feel that they don't have you in a bad spot, the 'indignant tourist' ploy can upset them completely. This is the only time such tactics are warranted.

Before you resort to theatrics, however, try a play for sympathy. A friend was released by the *federales* when he told them that the shame of having her son exposed as an addict would break his mother's heart. They tore off a chunk of his kilo, gave it to him with a warning to be more discreet in the future and sent him on his way.

•Behind bars: If you've been arrested by the city cops, you'll have to come before a judge within three days. The army can hold you for 24 hours; then they must turn you over to the *federales* who can hold you (god forbid) almost indefinitely.

When you're innocent and can prove it, you shouldn't be in a municipal jail for more than three days. If you're innocent but suspected of something fairly bad, they'll keep you around even longer. Pre-trial procedures can take several months. In cases of minor possession, you'll probably be deported fairly quickly.

Since each situation is different, it's difficult to say in advance what a person should do if you find yourself in jail and the 'wheels of justice' apparently not moving. I would sit around for a while, especially if the charge wasn't grave, and see what developed. There are many cases where the cops just let people go because it wasn't worth hassling them. And there are cases where people have waited around for a good long time.

Although you can accept the services of a court appointed legal advisor (not necessarily a qualified lawyer by any means), it is best not to; he's their stooge. Contact the American Embassy in Mexico City or the nearest tourist bureau office. About the only thing they'll be willing to do is give you the name of a lawyer to hire.

On relatively minor charges, the lawyer should be able to take care of everything for not too much money. Serious charges, such as possession of gross amounts of dope or dealing, can cost thousands of dollars and take months to negotiate. Many cases are finally settled by allowing the accused out on bond with the assumption that they will leave Mexico at top speed and never return.

•Penalties: Drug laws are federal and it is important to note that they do not apply these penalties to anyone under 18 years of age. Minors may be held by the authorities for a time, but they'll probably be deported quickly.

These penalties are for both marijuana and *estupefacientes* (stupifiers, everything from mushrooms to heroin). The line between possession, dealing and smuggling is determined by the judge.

2 to 9 years for possession and cultivation.

3 to 12 years for transporting and dealing.

4 to 12 years for causing addiction in a minor.

6 to 15 years for smuggling across a border.

6 to 15 years for owners of any place used to manufacture, deal or use drugs.

Fines also go along with jail terms.

The sun had just disappeared behind the mountains in front of us when Lorena spotted a clearing in the thick jungle. With several taps on the brake pedal, Steve signaled our friends, Bonnie and Hayden, that we'd found a camping place. Steve eased the van gently across a shallow ditch separating the highway from several starkly empty acres of dirt and gravel.

After parking side by side at the edge of a deep hole, we climbed wearily out of our vans to survey the place we'd selected.

"Well?" Steve asked. "What about it?"

Bonnie looked dubious; while in Alaska she had heard enough of his glowing accounts of Mexico to know that this wasn't one of those so-called 'paradise' spots. She and Hayden had driven thousands of miles on the strength of those stories and now that they'd joined us, here we were, spending our first night together in a gravel pit.

"Not bad, Steve," Bonnie said, surveying the desolation with hands on hips. "Not bad at all."

"This jungle is really something in the daylight," Steve said. "The country north of here is full of some pretty rough characters. A lot of interesting Indians, too," he ended lamely, looking at me for some sort of supporting anecdote to keep the conversation going.

"I'm sure it is," she said, "but right now we'd better settle for something to eat."

As I wandered away to look for firewood, I heard her ask Steve, "Which of us takes the first watch?"

Several minutes later, I was hunched over a pile of twigs in the bottom of the excavation next to our vans, trying to coax a fire out of the damp jungle wood. As the flames crept higher, casting an eerie light in the deep hole, I vaguely heard the sound of voices above me. Assuming that it was the others discussing dinner, I continued to build up the fire. After I noisily broke a large branch over my knee, a loud gruff voice barked in Spanish, "Don't move!"

I jerked up. There in the firelight stood a stocky man dressed in baggy cotton trousers, tattered denim shirt and decaying *huaraches*. "Don't move!" he repeated, tightening his grip on the submachine gun leveled at my chest.

As my knees sagged with fear, I instinctively raised my hands high over my head. Behind him other dim figures suddenly came into focus. Steve, standing off to one side of the camp, was trying to finish taking a leak while staring around the black O's of a double barrel shotgun. Several roughly dressed characters carrying a frightening assortment of weapons, from *machetes* to pistols, were arranging the rest of our group alongside Hayden's van.

With a vicious grin the man guarding me snarled, "Come here!" He raised the gun as if to fire and I all but leaped into his arms. With the barrel lightly touching the back of my shirt, he escorted me into the center of camp.

The others were standing silently, waiting, it seemed, for something appropriately awful to happen. The tension eased slightly when Steve appeared, closely followed by a shotgun.

"He finally finished!" the man yelled to his companions. "Lucky we gave him time to get it out before we came in!" Everyone laughed but us. The big man ended his laugh suddenly.

"What's wrong, *amigos*, you unhappy?" There was a menacing tone to his voice that clearly said, "You've got a reason to be."

He watched us for a few seconds, then after judging that we were sufficiently frightened, he barked officially, "*¡Capitán de policía federal!*"

Bonnie and Hayden looked puzzled as Steve, Lorena and I gave audible sighs of relief. The *federales* weren't fun but bandits with automatic weapons could be positively depressing.

"Just what the hell is going on?" Bonnie snapped.

I realized then that neither of them had understood what had been said. Hayden looked at her significantly, telepathing, "Please shut up, Bonnie, and I'll take you to France!"

"Is this some kind of a holdup?" she continued, walking boldly over to Steve and the big *federal*. The *capitán* looked at Steve knowingly, then ordered, "Tell her. You can figure out what we're here for."

"Look, Bonnie," Steve said. "These guys are federal police, probably looking for dope, and the best thing to do is let us handle it and not piss them off. Act scared!" She looked at Lorena and me—we were certainly acting scared—then conceded by returning quietly to Hayden's side.

"Hokay?" the fat *federal* asked slowly. He looked at his men. "Let's get started!" he ordered, motioning them toward our vans. With a jerk of his head he indicated that Steve and I should stand off to one side of the camp.

"You espeak Spanish?" he asked with exaggerated care. We both answered, "*Sí*," and the captain immediately launched into a long lecture, interrupted by frequent questions directed at one or the other of us. As we denied being drug addicts and affirmed our loyal support for Operation Cooperation, he stepped up the intensity of his questioning.

"Did we understand that he was merely doing his duty?"

"*¡Sí!*" we chorused.

"Did we appreciate the danger of dope?"

"Oh, *sí!*"

"Did we want our families corrupted by crime?"

"Of course not!"

I looked over his shoulder. One of the lesser *federales* was trying to open my typewriter case. I caught the tail end of the last question as a finger poked my shoulder emphatically.

"*Sí*," I muttered in exasperation, catching only the words "drug smuggler."

"What?" he gasped in horror, jumping back as if I'd plunged a syringe into his arm. "What did you say?"

Steve was staring at me in disbelief. "Oh, brother," I thought. "What have I done now?" The stunned *federal* was raising the shotgun in a menacing manner. "I'm confused!" I yelled. "Ask me again, *please!*" He gave me a quick sly look but said, "I asked if you were a drug smuggler and you said you were."

I chuckled nervously. "I thought you said, 'No, you are not a drug smuggler, are you?" The *federal* pondered this for a moment and I hastened to add, "My Spanish is bad, I just want to say, 'No, I am not a smuggler'."

He relaxed visibly and the shotgun once again hung at his side. My inappropriate answer had so disrupted his drug lecture that we stood there without further comment, watching the search continue in the corners and crannies of our vans.

Lorena was having a hell of a time explaining her large collection of herbal teas, all in unmarked plastic bags. Bonnie and Hayden watched with growing irritation as several pairs of hands fumbled through their neatly packed suitcases and cabinets. Bonnie examined and criticized the appearance and lineage of each *federal* in fluent French, while Hayden attempted to keep their things from falling into total disarray.

A shout of triumph burst from the inside of our van. A short wiry man leaped out holding a small flat can and rushed to where we stood. The *capitán* took the can distrustfully, twisting off the lid as if it might hold some powerful poison. He sniffed it daintily, then turned to us and said, "This is hashish. Where's the rest?"

"No," Steve said, his voice quavering slightly. "It's tobacoo. Snuff. You put it in your mouth." And before the *federales* could ponder this absurd statement, Steve reached over, dipped a large hit and packed it professionally under his lower lip.

"Spit that out!" the captain roared. "That stuff's illegal!" Steve's rather idiotic grin confirmed the *federal's* worst suspicions. "You Americans don't have any brains!" he snorted, motioning the other agents to stand behind us in case we tried to escape.

At this I yelled desperately to Lorena, "Get the magazine!" Within seconds she was standing next to the captain, thumbing through an issue of Esquire to a full page advertisement for Copenhagen snuff. He looked at it impassively for a few minutes, trying to translate the English by sheer will power, then waved the magazine in Steve's face with a fatherly, "you should have told me" grin. At the same time, he yelled at the men searching to give it up. We were clean!

The mood changed immediately from one of armed suspicion to friendly curiosity.

"What were we doing?" the *capitán* asked. "Didn't we know that this was a major pickup point for opium from the northern mountains?" "Didn't we know that they were there specifically for the purpose of ambushing some gringos who were on their way in VW vans to get the dope?" "How could we be so stupid?"

"We don't know anything about dope, that's why," I ventured to say.

He looked at me wisely for a second.

"You mean to say you don't even smoke *marijuana?*"

"Oh, no!" we chorused, for even Bonnie and Hayden knew that word of Spanish. "Oh, no! Wouldn't think of it! Gosh, no!"

The *capitán* shook his head in disbelief. "Well, if you don't," and he paused significantly, "you certainly ought to!"

"Look at you," he said, opening his arms as if to embrace us, cars and all, "You people can't tell me you don't know how to live. Travel, eat good, drink..." He stopped as if at a loss for words, then continued, "Hell! *Mota* is all you need!"

We smiled nervously as he motioned his men back to the jungle. When his face was just a faint warm glow in the fading firelight, the captain turned and yelled back, "Meet me at *Playa*...tomorrow. I'll give you some of the damned stuff!" With that and a hearty laugh, he slipped into the darkness.

Psilocybin

NOTES

SPEAKING SPANISH

It's worth the effort...Getting by...Greetings and Salutations...Formalities and Titles...Handsignals...Gringo...Nicknames...How to write a letter...Slang: watch your mouth!...Mexican media: books, newspapers, magazines, comics, radio, t.v., movies...

If communication were nothing more than learning the language, things would be greatly simplified; we could all unearth high school Spanish texts and start parroting phrases. The fact that this doesn't work is demonstrated by the number of people who go to Mexico right out of a formal Spanish course and find themselves faced with that frustrating stare that says so eloquently, "What the hell are you trying to tell me?"

The problem of studied efforts to communicate is well illustrated by the experience of some friends. When they went to Mexico, the woman had a degree in Spanish from a large university and her boyfriend knew several obscenities and no grammar—good whorehouse Spanish. Within two weeks she felt her nerves straining every time she was forced to speak Spanish, caught between the rigid grammatical training of school and the sloppy everyday speech of the people. He was right in there, waving arms, laughing, gesticulating over this and that, throwing in an occasional inappropriate obscenity and generally making himself understood and liked.

Before you toss your Spanish book out the window, remember that personality and attitude can communicate general ideas and moods quite well, but vocabulary, and to a lesser extent grammar, are necessary for explicit information. You can laugh and stand on your head, but if you want a prophylactic, you'll prefer to know the word rather than having to rely on sign language and demonstrations.

Fear of looking stupid chokes up many people. It is very unsettling for adults to be unable to communicate on what they feel is an intelligent and dignified level. No wonder the college graduate feels defensive when forced to say, "Want eat!" in order to find a restaurant. Swallow your pride and start talking; it's the only way you'll overcome the problem. I have never felt that remaining silent was preferable to a fumbling but honest attempt to communicate.

A friend told us that he'd spent several months in Mexico without bothering to learn more than a few words of Spanish. "For example," he said, "all I ever said in gas stations was '*cielo*' and they filled the tank right up." It wasn't until he told us this story that anyone had bothered to inform him that *cielo* means heaven and *lleno* full.

When your efforts to speak Spanish draw a blank, the most common reaction you'll get will be a polite, "*¿Mande?*" or a more blunt, "*¿Qué?*" (What?). At first, you might feel that some people are deliberately misunderstanding you because it seems that "*¿Qué?*" is heard far too often. If you listen to English conversation, however, you'll notice that "What?", "Huh?" and "What did you say?" are also used far too often and often without reason.

Should this happen, either try another word or phrase or repeat your first statement slowly, clearly and in a normal tone of voice. Don't fall back on English words, especially English words shouted at the top of your lungs. Do you think that a Spanish word would be more understandable to you at full volume, repeated several times in quick succession? It is not polite or reasonable to get mad just because you can't make yourself understood.

Although a broad vocabulary that includes everyday words will be your most valuable asset to communication, don't stop there. An amazing and disturbing number of tourists and foreign residents never make the effort to learn grammar and forms of speech that would make them fluent in Spanish. By improving your knowledge of the language, you'll also improve your understanding of the people and their customs. (See *Appendices: Schools*.)

The Mexicans, surprisingly enough, are perhaps the greatest obstacle to overcome when learning Spanish. They are so helpful and understanding that they seem able to anticipate whatever word or phrase you've so diligently practiced and you often don't get a chance to say it. Imagine the scene as a middle-aged couple approaches their first test.

"Now, Leonard," the wife asks, "are you sure you've got it down?"

"Yes, dear," Leonard sighs, wiping sweaty palms on his trouser legs. "I've gone over it at least a hundred times." Leonard sighs again. There seems no way to avoid this confrontation; it's either speak Spanish or run out of gas.

"Well, once more just to be sure," his wife insists, opening the insurance company phrase book they picked up at the border. "Go ahead, Leonard, you've got to practice."

"*Buenas tardes,*" Leonard begins, brows knit with superhuman effort. "*Llene el tanque de gasolina. Vea el aceite. ¿Cuánto es? ¡Gracias!*"

"Perfect!" his wife says, closing the book as they enter the gas station.

The attendant approaches the car briskly, not noticing Leonard's white-knuckle grip on the steering wheel. Leonard turns to the smiling face, his tongue suddenly blocking his throat as he croaks hesitantly, "*¿Llene...?*" Without a moment's hesitation, the attendant nods and is gone.

Leonard looks at his wife for help; the pump is in operation, the hood of the car up and air hisses into a rear tire. Wordlessly the attendant returns and indicates the level of oil on the dipstick. Leonard smiles weakly, but before he can ask, a small slip of paper is under his nose: 174 *pesos*.

As they're pulling back onto the highway, Leonard stretches his legs and says happily, "Now, that wasn't so bad, was it?"

This type of experience is very common; many tourists are amazed at just how easy it is to get by on the most rudimentary knowledge of the language, especially if they never leave the tourist circuit. When the first feelings of anxiety have passed, you'll find yourself feeling more self-confident and less likely to avoid personal contact with the people around you.

Keep in mind that some people can't understand what you say even when you know without a doubt that it was correct. Anyone who hasn't heard their own language spoken by a foreigner may find it difficult to follow what has been said. Others are hard of hearing or just dumb.

In many cases, particularly in remote areas of Mexico, the average person might not speak much Spanish. Indian languages are very common and you'll find yourself in the rather odd position of speaking better Spanish than the Mexicans. Sign language is important in this type of situation.

While wandering through an isolated village on the west coast of Mexico, we were approached by an old man who asked if we would sell him clothing.

"We're tourists," we answered, having often been mistaken for travelling vendors in areas where strangers were rare.

"Ah!" the old man exclaimed. "Then you must be Americans! I knew an American here several years ago. He came here to talk with us, to learn our customs."

"Was he an anthropologist?" I asked politely.

"*¿Quién sabe? Señor,*" the old man chuckled. "He said that he wanted to learn all about us, bur first he would go to the hills," and he motioned with a wrinkled hand toward a distant range of forbidding mountains, "to learn the language."

"What happened then?" Steve asked. From the seriousness with which the old man had looked toward the mountains, we felt certain that the American had encountered something unexpected.

"He came back here after six months and tried to talk to us. He tried for a long time, but he finally left."

"Why?" I asked. "Was there trouble?"

The old man looked at us with a toothless grin, then chuckled. "No, of course not. He left because none of us here are Indians. We couldn't understand a word of what he said. Only the people over there," and he waved again toward the mountains, "could talk to him."

GREETINGS AND SALUTATIONS

By American standards, Mexicans can be almost tediously polite. Friends who haven't seen each other for five minutes exchange several greetings, countergreetings, handshakes and assorted pleasantries.

The tourist often wonders if his Mexican acquaintance isn't putting him on with the apparent intensity of his feeling at each casual meeting. "*¡Qué milagro!*" (What a miracle!) the Mexican cries, though they had met just as usual in their regular *cantina*. With a warm handshake he inquires after his friend's family and health, though he'd done exactly the same for day after day.

Although these pleasantries may seem superficial or unnecessary, their importance cannot be discounted. To a Mexican these formalities all add up to an American "Hi!" and their absence is as noticeable as a cold silent stare.

Effusive greetings between strangers are common and there's hardly any Mexican so impassive that he won't instinctively respond to a polite expression.

Don't worry about such common errors as saying, "Good afternoon" instead of "Good morning" (*Buenas tardes* vs. *Buenos días*). No one expects you to speak Spanish perfectly, but they do expect to hear something, even if it's incorrect. A mistake is much better than a nervous or impolite silence.

The word *adiós* is a handy greeting to learn as it covers many situations. Though *adiós* does mean "goodbye," it is also used extensively to mean "hello." Because it does not convey any sense of time, as does, "Good day" or "Good afternoon," *adiós* is always correct when used as a greeting, *as long as you're passing someone and not greeting them with the intention of stopping to talk with them.* If you intend to stop, you should use one of the regular greetings such as *Buenos días.*

If you're greeting someone and don't know the time of day, you can just say *Buenas* and leave off the last word of the expression.

The following expressions are commonly used as greetings:

¡Ola!	*Hi!*
¡Ola amigo!	*Hi, friend!*
¿Cómo está?	*How are you?* The usual response is *Muy bien, gracias* (Very well, thanks). Other responses: *Regular* or *Así, así* (So-so).
¿Qué tal?	Same as *¿Cómo está?*
¿Cómo le va?	*How goes it?* Response: *Muy bien, gracias.*
¿Qué hay de nuevo?	*What's new?* Response: *No mucho* (not much) or *Nada* (nothing).
¡Qué milagro!	*What a miracle!* Which is meant as, "What a miracle to see you!"

The following words and polite expressions can cover a variety of situations, from meeting someone to stepping on their toes. Anyone interested in speaking with Mexicans should learn them as quickly as possible and use them liberally.

Sí	*Yes.*
No	*No.*
O.K.	Becoming quite common in many parts of Mexico.
Por favor	*Please.*
Gracias	*Thanks.* Response: *A usted* (You, too) or *Igualmente* (Equally).
Está bien, Bien, Bueno	*Very well, O.K., good, etc.*
Muy bien	*Very well.* To indicate approval. Someone offers you an item for sale and you accept by saying *Muy bien.*
Dispénseme	*Excuse me.*
Perdón	*Pardon.*
Perdóneme	*Pardon me.*
Con permiso	*With permission.*
Andele	*Go ahead.*
¡Cómo no!	*Why not? Sure.*
Lo siento	*I'm sorry.*
No le hace	*Don't let it bother you.*
No importa	*It's nothing. Not important.*
Al contrario	*On the contrary.*
Pase adelante	*Come in.*
Pase	*Go ahead. Pass.* Response: *Gracias.*
Quiero presentarle a (name)	*I want to introduce you to...*(name).
Mucho gusto	*Pleased.* A response to being introduced to someone.
¡Nos vemos!	*We'll see you! Be seeing you!*
¡Qué le vaya bien!	*May you go well!* This is a very common way to say goodbye to someone who you may not see for a while or if they're about to drive at night. The response is *Gracias.*
Está en su casa	*You're in your house.* An expression that many people unfamiliar with Mexicans take too literally. *Make yourself at home* is a more practical translation.
¿Qué? ¿Mande?	*What? Mande* is more polite than *Qué*, which may be used as *Huh?*
¡Salud!	*Gesunheit!* Response: *Gracias.* Also used as a drinking toast, *Health!*

HAND SIGNALS

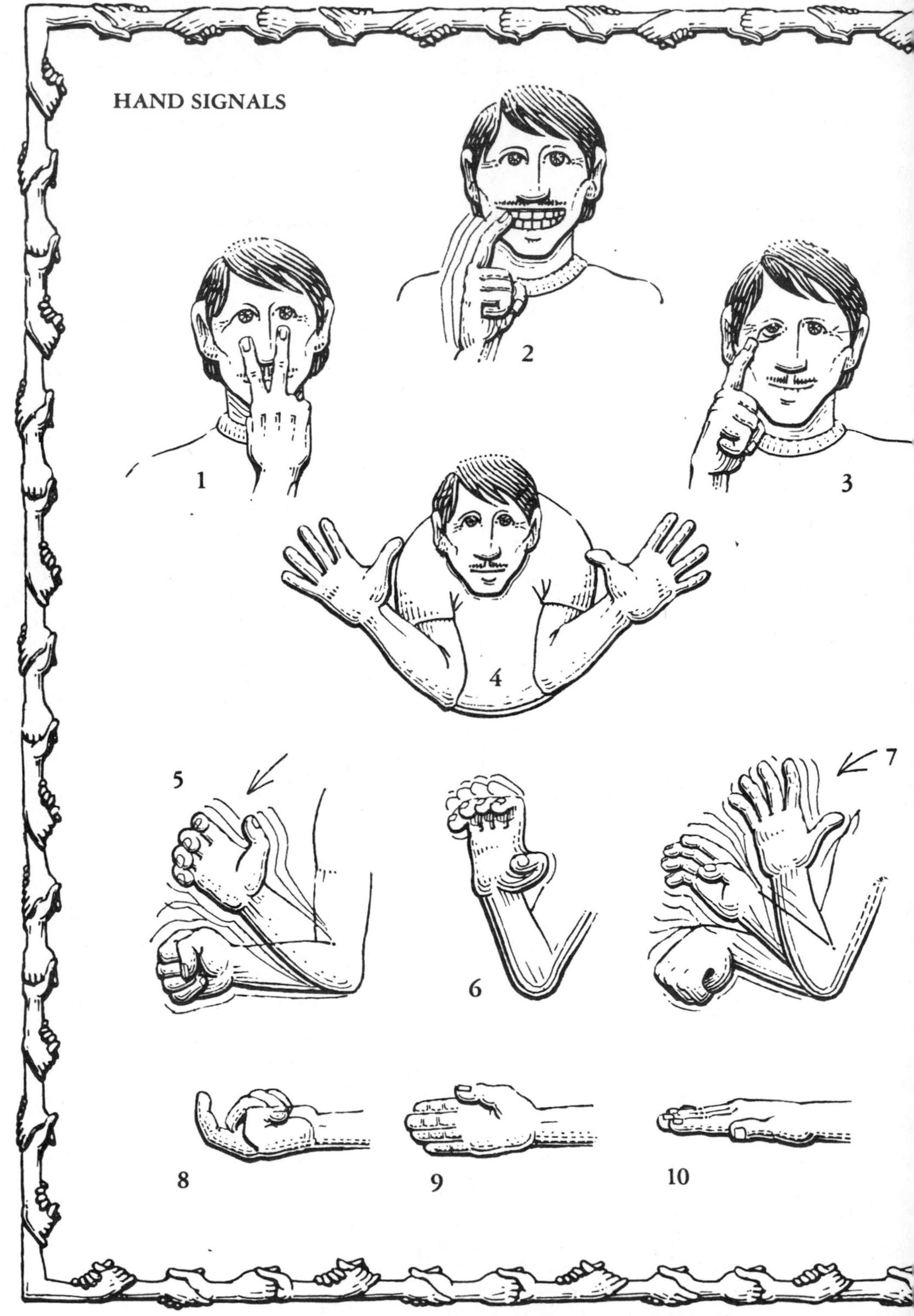

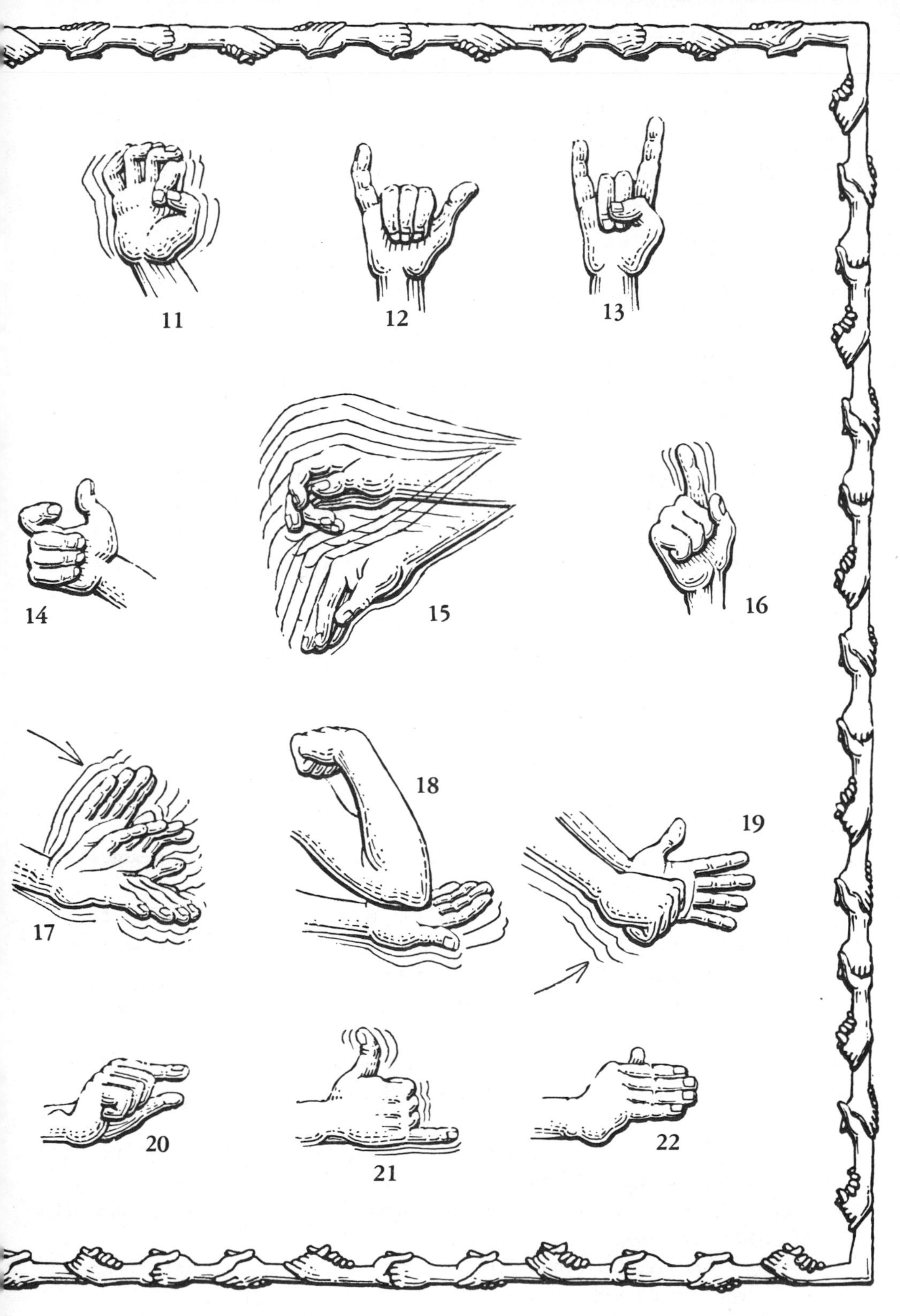
11
12
13
14
15
16
17
18
19
20
21
22

HAND SIGNALS

If a picture is worth a thousand words, most of the hand signals and gestures so loved by Mexicans would rate as novellas. Although some are not used in polite company, many others are seen everywhere. Anyone who spends time in the country usually begins to use these signals, too.

1. ***Pintar un violín*** (to paint a violin). Favored by loud mouthed school kids. It is an insult and a taunt, like "Up yours!"
2. ***Colmillo*** (eyetooth). Shrewd, crafty. Used to signal someone about a third party.
3. ***¡Ojo!*** (Eye!). The meaning depends on the situation. In reference to another person, "Watch out for him," "Be careful," or "He's sharp!"
4. ***Quién sabe?*** (Who knows?). The classic "I take no responsibility for anything past, present or future." Accompanied by meaningless grunts, moans, eyebrow twisting and general facial contortions.
5. ***¡Orale! ¡Simón!*** (Right on!). You suggest buying a bottle of brandy and a couple of kilos of *carnitas* and your friends enthusiastically make this sort of whistle-pulling affirmation.
6. ***Las uñas*** (fingernails). Thief or theft. A warning signal if someone nearby is a rip-off artist. "Where's your bicycle?" might bring "*uñas*" if it was stolen.
7. Same as *uñas*.
8. To indicate the height of people. (It can be insulting to use the wrong gesture.)
9. Height of animals.
10. Height of inanimate objects, things.
11. ***Mocoso*** (snotty). Another schoolyard taunt.

12-13. ***Cuernos*** (horns). Means both "screw you" and cuckold.

14. ***Lana*** (wool, money). Typical situations: "Have you got the *lana?*", "You'll need a lot of *lana.*", "Expensive!"
15. ***¡Ijole!*** (Wow!). The fingers flick downward and should make a noticeable *pop!* If you do it wrong, it hurts like hell.
16. ***No, Ni modos*** (no, no way). Can mean, "No, that's not right," "Cool it," "I've had about enough" or "Lay off, I'm losing my patience." A baleful stare and a wagging forefinger will discourage pesky shoeshine boys faster than anything else.
17. ***Adelante*** (ahead). "Move forward" or "Come here" looks to gringos as "Go back." Very common and very confusing.
18. ***Codo*** (elbow). Cheapskate. Saying that a person is "from Monterrey" is equivalent to "very Scotch" (stingy). When done very emphatically it means "Up yours!"
19. Sock it to 'em! Right on!
20. ***Momentito, ahoritita*** (a moment). Be right back, not much, little bit, etc. Used extensively instead of a verbal promise that can't be fulfilled.
21. ***El infle*** (drinking). "Let's have one," "Down the hatch" or, when speaking of a third person, "A boozer."
22. ***No, gracias*** (No, thank you). Very commonly used to take the sting out of a refusal of food, drink, smoke and so on.

FORMALITIES AND TITLES

Students of Spanish are often confused by the use of *tú* and *usted* (you-familiar and you-formal). When greeting a stranger do you say, "*¿Cómo estas?*" or "*¿Cómo está usted?*" When in doubt use the formal construction. The familiar form is used between family members, friends and by very casual Mexicans when speaking with strangers of their own age or social class.

When I took high school Spanish the teacher told us that "the use of the familiar form has taken over in Mexico. Don't worry about learning the formal." This just isn't true; the use of *tú* at the wrong time can be both impolite and offensive, since it implies a lack of respect in some cases. (A younger person addressing someone older, when speaking with someone of authority or high position, etc.)

The Mexican love of pomp and ceremony always makes it more advisable to lean toward formality, both in words and actions, rather than the studied and deliberate casualness affected by so many gringos.

Titles are frequently used by Mexicans. Some of the most common are *maestro, licenciado, don, doña, profesor, doctor, ingeniero* and *arquitecto.*

A *maestro* loosely translates as a 'master' or accomplished tradesperson, technician, skilled laborer or anyone else who is good at something. The woman who runs the *farmacia* can be a *maestra* at pill-pushing and on-the-spot diagnoses while the old man next door, hammering together sandals, is a *maestro* at his humble trade. The term is also used between friends as a form of respect and affection.

Licenciado-a (lawyer) is shorted to *lic* between friends.

Ingeniero-a and *arquitecto* (*arqui* between friends) are used for engineers and architects.

Profesor-a (shortened to *profe* for men) is used both for teachers and persons who are well educated or appear to be. It is used sarcastically for people who put on airs of superior knowledge.

Doctor-a is sometimes shortened to *doc.*

Don and *doña* are terms of respect. The word is used before the person's first name or entire name but not their last name. Pedro Gomez, for example, would be *Don* Pedro or *Don* Pedro Gomez, not *Don* Gomez. Traditional Mexicans use *Don* and *Doña* extensively.

When addressing women use *señorita* if they are not married and *señora* if they are (or were). The word *seño* is often used when in doubt about a woman's marital status.

Joven (young person) is commonly used. When applied to a person who is obviously not young, such as a bartender or waitress, the word is rather offensive, similar to the use of "boy" in English.

Señor is used for men but *cabellero* is very formal and rarely heard.

Fulano-a is used both as John or Jane Doe (*Fulano-a de Tal*) and so-and-so or "that person." "*Ese fulano*" is the equivalent of saying "that guy."

Who Is A Mexican?

The word *mestizo-a* is commonly applied to anyone of mixed Spanish and Indian blood. Upper class Mexicans, however, prefer to call themselves by the far grander term, *gente de razón*, people of reason or right. On the opposite end of the scale are the *gente indigena*, the Indians (also called *indios*). Indians can be sensitive about being called *indios;* it is better to call them *mexicanos* or by their tribal name. *Mestizos* also refer to themselves as *cristianos.* This is usually intended to mean, "I am not an Indian."

A *pocho-a* is a person of Mexican descent who returns to Mexico and puts on airs. It is a derogative term.

Who Is a Gringo?

A word game that some people like to play involves identification of nationalities. Are we, citizens of the United States of America, *gringos, norte americanos, americanos* or *yanquis?* Actually, we are all of them, but I've yet to find one word that will satisfy a *latinoamericano* when bound and determined to pin me down about it. And speaking of Latin Americans—it has been agreed by Spanish speaking people that the term "Latin American" is inaccurate and illogical. From now on they prefer the term *hispano americanos*, Hispanic Americans.

The potential trouble lies in the fact that everyone in North America is both an American and North American. I find arguments over these fine distinctions to be very tiring. When someone insists that I can't refer to myself as an American, the only words left are *gringo* and *yanqui* and although neither of them offends me, I realize that they are sometimes thought of in a derogatory sense.

My solution is to insist that the Mexican who refuses to allow me to call myself an American also stop using Mexican to refer to himself. If this doesn't get the point across, it's best to find more reasonable people to talk with.

Gringo isn't the opposite of greaser and many people, particularly the Indians, will call you *gringo* without the slightest intent of insult. (A Mexican dictionary gives this definition of *gringo:* "Foreigner, especially the English, Greek, unintelligible language. In Mexico and Central America, 'Northamerican;' in Argentina and Uruguay, 'Italian'.") The word *güero* (blond, paleface) is also popular and you'll hear it often, particularly in the market place.

A TYPICAL POLITE LETTER

While travelling we often meet people who we would like to drop a line to when we return home. The problem is what to say and how to say it, especially if your Spanish is weak. It's amazing what can be communicated with sign language, facial expressions and other signals, none of which are available when faced with a blank sheet of paper.

The following typical letter can be used, either by itself or in parts, to at least say to a Mexican friend: "Here I am. How are you? We haven't forgotten." Don't worry about the seemingly excessively formal tone; that's just the way Mexicans talk in their letters. If you have more to say, forget grammar and spell it out as clearly as possible. Everyone knows how to read between the lines.

Most large greeting card companies offer foreign language cards for all occasions. Sending one of these to friends and acquaintances you've made during your travels will make a great hit.

Addresses: Print the person's full name and if you don't have the exact address write *Domicilio Conocido* (house or address known) with whatever part of the address you do have. Many people, particularly in the country, will receive mail with just their name, that of their village or *municipio* (county) and *domicilio conocido.* Someone will deliver the letter or advise them it is at the post office.

Queridos Amigos:

Nuestros estimados y apreciables amigos: por medio de la presente les saludamos y les decimos lo siguiente: Hemos estado pensando mucho en Ustedes y es posible que podamos visitarles tan pronto como sea posible.

Realmente deseamos que llegue el momento de saludarlos personalmente otra vez y platicar ampliamente con Ustedes. Es por demás desearles que estén bien de salud, puesto que estén bien.

Nosotros estamos bien, gracias a Dios.

Muchos saludos a toda la familia y unos grandes abrazos.

Sus Amigos,

Dear Friends,

Our esteemed and appreciable friends: by means of this (correspondence: letter or card) we greet you and say to you the following: We have been thinking of you a great deal and it is possible that we can visit you as soon as is possible.

We really hope that the moment arrives to greet you personally again and to talk extensively with you. It is needless to hope that you are in good health since you know that it is our greatest wish that you are well.

We are well, thanks to God.

Many regards to all the family and some great *abrazos* (hugs).

Your Friends,

SLANG

The use of slang and body Spanish is as essential to a Mexican as a toothy smile and firm handshake are to an ambitious politician. There seem to be several ways to say everything. The good old U.S.-of-A. becomes *el otro lado* (the other side), *el norte, los united* or *Gringolandia.* Children are *escuincles* (after the Aztec word for dog), beers are *las buenas* (good ones), cars are *naves* (ships), money is *lana* (wool) and life is just *a todas emes* (at full m's—mothers, good!). Mexican slang can be simple and logical as in *jaula* (cage) for the jail, slightly more complicated with *lucas* replacing *loco* (crazy) and downright obscure as *¡Calmantes montes, pajaros cantantes y alicantes pintos!* (Calm down man, singing birds and spotted snakes!), an involved way of saying "Be cool."

There are three types of Mexican slang: *caló*, almost another language used in Mexico City and the underworld; regular everyday words and expressions, from innocent to obscene heard around the country, and hip or *de la onda* (of the wave, vibe), preferred by younger people. The three overlap, but for the average tourist the last two types are the most often heard.

An effort to speak the common language, without the stilted and archaic sound of a textbook, may lead you to dangerous areas of speech—namely obscenities.

A Mexican friend who spoke beautiful textbook English asked me to teach him some appropriate obscenities. I wrote down a few, explained their general meaning and use and then forget about it.

Some time later, we were sitting in his room, talking and drinking beer, when he suddenly began lacing his sentences heavily with profanity. He seemed to be particulary fond of ending simple statements with the most improbable words. "I'm going to take a trip next month, shit." His poor timing and improper emphasis on the profane words had me rolling on the floor and quickly ended his attempt to Americanize his English.

Nothing is worse than a really foul obscenity dropped into a conversation at the wrong time or with the wrong person. The only way I know to avoid this is to forget about learning them or keep profanities out of your conversations until you have good control.

The best way to relax the sound of your Spanish is to use innocuous—but safe—phrases that you'll hear wherever you go. "*¿De veras?*" (Really?) will do quite well instead of the more exciting, "*¡Hijo de la Gran Puta!*" (Son of the Great Whore!). The use of obscenities is especially risky in situations where it would be better to say nothing at all.

A friend who spoke only one word of Spanish was deported from Mexico as the result of a conversation with a cop about his long hair. Our friend couldn't understand what was happening so he got mad and repeatedly used his one Spanish word—a gross obscenity. Instead of dropping the matter, the cop arrested him.

The Mexican sense of humor is strongly based on the double meaning. These double-meanings may be quite obvious or subtle to the point of complete mystification.

Because of their frequent use, either as obvious jokes or traps for the unwary, you should learn to avoid certain words and expressions. Don't panic—in ordinary conversation there are only a few words that you'll want to use with care.

In the market you'll probably want to buy eggs. You spot a likely stall, tended by a respectable looking young man, and you ask, "*¿Tiene huevos?*" (Do you have eggs?). Immediately everyone in the area begins to laugh and shout to each other, enjoying a joke that is obviously at your expense. You fight down anger (or panic) and look beseechingly at the fellow, hoping for a little compassion.

He answers calmly, "Yes, I do. Two big ones." If this doesn't bring down the house, your flustered exit will.

The use of the word *huevo* should by now be of obvious double meaning. You've just asked the guy if he "has balls" and he's proudly confirmed that he does. The safe words for egg are *blanquillo* (little white one) or *yema* (yolk).

Grammatical constructions also lead to trouble. When you asked, "*¿Tiene huevos?*" you said, "Do you have eggs?" This seems legitimate enough but it implies that the question is personal. You might well have avoided embarrassment by changing your question to, "*¿Hay huevos?*" The translation of this is, "Are there eggs?"

Other words to avoid with *tiene* are *leche* (milk) and *chile* (chili pepper). I had the misfortune to ask a young woman tending a store, obviously about to give birth, if she had milk. The reaction of the other customers and the look on the girl's face took a year off my conversational ability in Spanish and made me acutely aware from that moment on of just *exactly* what I was saying.

To ask a woman if she has milk isn't likely to lead to trouble of the sort involved with asking a man if he "has chili" (*¿Tiene chile?*). The *chile* is always synonymous with penis and the jokes surrounding it are innumerable.

When I suspect that something I've said may be impolite or grossly incorrect, I either ask someone immediately for an explanation or note down the word or phrase to ask a friend later.

•Note: In the following discussion on slang, words which may or may not be judged obscene are included not to spice up your vocabulary but to make you more aware of multiple uses and meanings. A word that is a profanity in Mexico may be quite ordinary in another Spanish speaking country. It is important to know when to open your mouth and when not to; slang and obscenities can be powerful communicators.

After buying Arturo, our male parrot, we were delighted to hear him clearly speaking Spanish. Because he had been trained by a sweet old lady who sold flowers in the market in Guatemala City we didn't suspect the propriety of his vocabulary until later.

We noticed that Arturo would talk more if we talked back to him, using the words he did. His favorite expression, "*¡Qué verga!*" always brought a good response so we were especially fond of prompting him with "*¡Qué vergas!*" of our own.

Then one day I asked a friend, the owner of a small *cantina*, what "*¡Qué verga!*" meant. He blushed, stammered, and because Lorena was in the room, refused to answer. I finally persuaded him to write the meaning on a slip of paper for, even though Lorena did not at that time understand much Spanish, he couldn't bring himself to say it in front of her. "What a prick!" was the translation. When we realized where and how often we'd repeated that phrase...

•*Chingar:* This is the Big One, the word that gringos mistakenly translate only as "to fuck" but which in fact can mean everything from that to merely "messed up" or "Get moving!". The meaning depends on who says it, in what mood, for what purpose and to whom it is directed. As Octavio Paz said: "The word *chingar* with all its multiple meanings, defines a great part of our life and classifies our relations with the rest of our friends and fellow citizens."

Some typical uses of *chingar* are:

¡Chinga tu madre!: This is the worst insult of all, fighting words to be sure. Rape your mother! just doesn't convey the feeling of the Spanish but gives the idea.

¡Vete a la chingada!: Go to the fucked! Used as we would say "Go to Hell!" A *chingada* or *chingadera* is also a screw-up of any type. *Tiznada* is sometimes substituted.

Chingón is usually used as a compliment. "*¡El es muy chingón!*" means "He's really something!"

•*Pinche:* One of my favorite words, usually used with obscenities. It means "worthless" or "damned."

•*Cabrón:* A male goat or cuckold. Calling someone who is not a good friend a *cabrón* can be detrimental to your health.

•*Buey:* An ox, cuckold or generally cloddish person.

•*Pendejo:* A pubic hair. Used extensively to describe any fink, square, creep, idiot, wet-blanket, knothead, lout, party pooper, asshole or jerk.

NICKNAMES

Apodos are freely used by Mexicans. The most common are contractions of proper names (Tonio from Antonio, Maria from Maria de la Luz). No opportunity, however, is missed to create a name from a person's physical characteristics, employment, personality or misfortune. Gringos are sometimes offended by nicknames they hear used for others or even themselves. *Gordo* (Fatty) will inevitably be used for the overweight, *Negro* (black) for dark complexions and *Chato* if the nose is not sharp and long, in which case they'd probably use Nostrils. Between younger people nicknames are almost required. (For a sampling of common nicknames see *Appendices: Vocabulary*.)

THE MEXICAN MEDIA

One of the best ways to learn Spanish while increasing your understanding of Mexicans is through their communications media. Many travellers tend to isolate themselves from Spanish language publications, movies, radio and television because of a lack of confidence that they'll find anything interesting or comprehensible.

Since avoiding the media, especially radio, is about as easy as avoiding food, it's best to make an effort to become familiar with it. Written material is especially helpful. Listening to Spanish on the radio or combined with pictures in movies and television can greatly increase your overall comprehension and 'feel' for the language. (See *Recommended Reading*.)

•**Books:** Books translated from English are usually easier to read than books originally written in Spanish or other foreign languages. There are fewer idiomatic expressions and the sentence structure tends to be simpler. Good books from all over the world can be found in Spanish. If you're interested in books by Mexican authors, ask for advice in a bookstore; the employees are usually eager to help out.

You'll find that straightforward writing, especially adventures, historical novels, biographies, etc., is much easier to read and maintain interest in than philosophical or 'far out' works.

Read short books to build up your confidence and don't be embarrassed to read such things as children's books or school texts; after all, they are designed for beginners and may be just what you need. The more books you can plow through, the more you'll tend to continue trying. There's nothing more frustrating that trying to read a book far beyond your abilities.

A good dictionary is important for both reading and conversation. Try to find one with Latin American words. Too often a dictionary will be aimed at students of 'pure' Spanish and will ignore common words and phrases used in Mexico. If you speak any Spanish at all, you'll find an all Spanish dictionary very useful and not at all difficult to use. They are widely available in cheap paperback editions in Mexico.

In towns were gringos congregate you may find lending libraries of English books. For a few *pesos*, you can have access to a great deal of reading material. Large cities will have bookstores that handle English, French and German books. In Mexico City you can find a selection of international newspapers and magazines, both in large bookstores and fancy hotels.

•**Newspapers:** Mexican papers are difficult to read; the style and vocabulary are unlike spoken Spanish. The information contained is often biased (not too surprising) but the patient reader can extract a basic idea of what's going on.

Most newspapers carry just enough real news to get by and fill the remaining pages with social news, sports, comics and lurid accounts of murder and violence. A notable exception is *Excélsior*, often called "The New York Times of Mexico." This paper's fine reputation was tarnished in 1976 when President Echeverria staged an editorial purge but *Excélsior* is said to be making a comeback.

Scandal type newspapers (especially *¡Alarma!*) don't even bother to hide behind a front page of world news but specialize entirely in sex, violence and stomach turning photographs. They are especially fond of articles about hippies and dope. These papers are morbidly fascinating and I read them with disgust.

An English language newspaper, *The News*, is published daily in Mexico City. It is sold wherever gringos congregate. The American and Canadian Embassies advertise in *The News* for people whose friends and relatives are urgently trying to contact them.

•**Magazines:** Both *Time* and *Newsweek* are available in English in many towns. The Spanish edition of *Reader's Digest*, called *Selecciones*, is one of the most popular magazines in Mexico. It is good practice for Spanish students. (See *Recommended Reading* for more.) Many universities publish small literary magazines on an irregular basis. These are difficult to read if you're not fluent.

Most literate Mexicans read 'pulp' material, especially comic books, crime magazines and newspapers. Since the average magazine is difficult to read, travellers will find comic books more interesting and understandable.

Comic books are a national passion. They are printed in a variety of sizes, down to mini-comics the size of a pack of cigarettes. Comic books range in content from adult sex types to Donald Duck and Sir Lancelot. Satirical comics are on a higher intellectual level, but may be difficult to understand. The best of these, *Los Agachados*, attempts to educate people on everything from personal hygiene to politics. Another adult comic, *Hermelinda Linda*, is grossly hilarious, full of slang and slightly off-color jokes.

For those who prefer the Super Hero, *Kaliman* is a household word. The same heroes found on newsstands in the U.S. are also available, from Batman to Buck Rogers. You can enrich your vocabulary with words like "Intergalactic travel" or, for aficionados of the classic comic, "Raise the drawbridge, knave!"

Comics are great to have for Mexican guests, both adults and children. I like to pass them around a small group of kids and have each one read a page. They think it's fun to show off their reading abilities and it gives me a good opportunity to hear the words read aloud. Comics are handy when you feel vaguely like reading but don't want to get too involved. Those translated from English are amazingly easy to read.

•**Radio:** I'm quite sure that radio ranks as the top Mexican media, to the point of being a national mania. In areas where even the best radios are hardly usable because of poor reception, you'll see people listening to their cheap transistor sets, receiving nothing more than an occasional song or word through the static.

Radios are status symbols; the poorest *campesino* will usually have one, even though he might not be able to keep it supplied with batteries for more than a few months out of the year. When you're looking for a way to break the ice among guests, just flip the switch on your radio and stand back.

The radio cult can't be appreciated fully until you've heard the type of broadcasting inflicted upon the eager audience. The most maudlin soap operas are followed by millions of avid listeners and the music—often old American songs—is barely tolerable in any language or at any volume. (We've found that prolonged exposure to Mexican music can, somehow, be habit forming. I especially love the song, *Life is Worth Nothing in Guanajuato.*)

Popular disc jockeys read off lists of dedications before each song that sound like census rolls for entire towns. When a news program interrupts this continuous bedlam, it is accompanied by a series of electronic sounds simulating urgency and importance that more often than not obscures the rapid-fire delivery of the newscaster and makes comprehension next to impossible.

There are, fortunately, some exceptions to this type of programming, usually from very large AM and FM stations in Mexico City, Guadalajara, Oaxaca, Puebla and other major cities. At night you should be able to tune in a few American stations from Texas on even a small transistor radio. Their programming runs heavily toward Salvation and call-in talk shows.

•**Television:** The most popular T.V. shows are imported from the U.S. and dubbed in Spanish. Sports events, especially boxing and soccer, are shown almost daily.

Television offers the opportunity of hearing Spanish while watching related action. It is a very effective method for learning the language, though it might strike you odd to hear, as I did one night, "*¡Vámonos muchachos, hay pieles rojos!*" (Let's go boys, redskins!) coming from the mouth of Daniel Boone.

Cablevision, showing live programs from the U.S. via satellite and others by videotape, is available in better hotels in Mexico City.

•**Movies:** Mexicans are movie goers. Small town *cines* charge very little for admission and even first run flicks in Mexico City and other large cities are quite reasonable. Many excellent movies from all around the world are shown at universities and in theatres in Mexico City's "Pink Zone" (luxury zone).

The best movies, especially in Mexico City, may be sold out in advance. Buy your ticket as soon as possible for the performance you want. *Boletrónico* machines (automatic ticket sellers) are widespread in the Capital. Tickets (for all sorts of events, including movies) cost an additional 10 percent and must be purchased at least one day in advance of the event or performance. These machines can save you a great deal of waiting in lines.

The average Mexican movie is bad to awful, but there are exceptions. Cantinflas, the Mexican equivalent of Charlie Chaplin, is very famous. Serious Mexican movies tend to be difficult to understand without translation.

Prices for the *balcón* (balcony) are cheaper than those for the *luneta* (ground floor). If the difference in price means nothing to you the seats in the *luneta* are usually within range of the sound system. This is very important in theatres that are full of kids, though if they're there in the first place, the movie probably isn't worth listening to.

Children under 15 cannot legally attend any movie considered 'adult' (almost all of them), but in most cases the rule isn't enforced, especially if an older person is along.

If you're near a small town that has no theatre and suddenly everyone's talking about going to the movies, you're in for a real treat: travelling movies. These 'theatres' (actually a portable screen) are erected in the open air by hilarious people (usually *hungaros*, gypsies) who roam the countryside in old trucks, showing their ancient movies to enthusiastic crowds of *campesinos*. This is the ultimate movie experience; don't miss it.

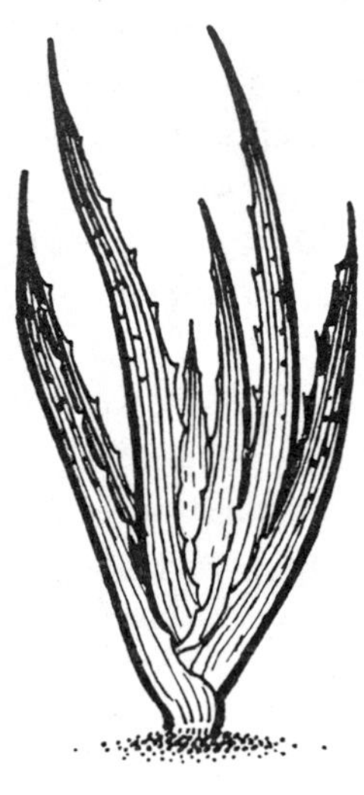

Aloe vera

CUSTOM AND SUPERSTITION

Strange encounters...Go easy on the 'natives'...Customs you'll want to observe...Dress, mealtime, parties, invitations, compadrazgo, others... Superstitions: from hot and cold to the Bogeyman...

I was sitting in a tiny store in the highlands of southern Mexico sipping a drink of the horrible local liquor, waiting for the afternoon rain to pass. Suddenly a weird, wailing cry sounded outside. Before I could get up from my bench, a boisterous crowd poured through the doorway, pushing, shoving and falling over each other.

Fifteen or twenty bodies were packed into the tiny room and it took me a second to notice that each was dressed in the most hideous costumes and masks I'd ever seen. Many of the men were dressed as women but their faces, bound with strips of inner tube, tape, foil and dirty cloth, were not human.

Although I'd seen a good many Indian *fiesta* costumes, none could compare with these. I felt an involuntary shudder of revulsion as they pressed me tightly against the wall.

With hoarse, drunken, animal grunts and moans (later I learned that by custom no intelligible word could be spoken) the group made it clearly known to the wary woman behind the counter that they wanted liquor. Mud covered hands grabbed the bottles and their contents were drained in what seemed like suicidal chug-a-lugs. When the last had been finished off, a new chorus of noise began. I had finally been noticed.

With the hair prickling on the back of my neck, I sensed that something unusual was about to happen and edged toward a corner. Suddenly a grotesque bird-like face was inches from my nose, a slender hardwood staff raised menacingly over my head. The nightmare bird grunted and rapped me sharply across the shoulder with the staff. With this, the entire group moved in, kicking, prodding, jabbing and generally bouncing me around the room.

Realizing that I was slightly outnumbered, I threw my arms over my head and retreated as best I could into a corner. I'd noticed almost immediately that although I was getting a fairly good pounding, no one made any real effort to hurt me.

Suddenly the beating stopped. I looked up apprehensively and the bird figure, apparently the leader, broke the tension by saying in clear Spanish, "Buy us a drink!"

I nodded to the grinning proprietress and resigned myself to blowing a month's *cantina* lounging in one round. To my surprise, however, she served only a small amount and there was no objection from my assailants. After drinking the liquor, they rushed for the door, grunting and brawling into the muddy street outside.

I paid my bill quickly and took the opposite direction home. A few weeks later a dignified elderly man approached me in the same store. He identified himself as the bird figure, explained the ritual significance of what they had been doing (it was an Indian dance group) and thanked me for my 'cooperation.' Although I insisted that it had been my pleasure, he offered me the use of a house, rent-free, for as long as I and my friends cared to use it. He knew he could trust me, he said, because I had acceded to his request for a drink even though the dancers could have gone ahead and drained every bottle at my expense.

"What if I had said no?" I asked.

"Oh, well," the man said with a grin. "We'd have worked you over a little longer to change your mind."

Travelling is a learning process that takes place in a real rather than an artificial environment. Mexico is not a butterfly pinned to a piece of cork, passive and subject to the curious collector's whims, nor is it a giant amusement park constructed and controlled for the tourist's benefit. By learning to treat a country (or a town, group, etc.) as a living thing, you will soon perceive its reaction to you and what you do. Specific customs can be studied in advance, but if you are a sensitive traveller you will never need a guidebook or anthropology text to tell you how the people feel about what you are doing.

Cultural shock is a popular term used to describe what happens when tourists have their minds completely blown by a foreign country and culture (see *Health*). What most tourists fail to realize is that cultural shock works both ways. Imagine, for example, the effect on a quiet farming village when two carloads of tourists unexpectedly drop in.

The automobiles, late, semiluxury models, stop in front of the tiny adobe municipal building. All eyes in the *plaza* watch curiously as five elderly couples climb out of the cars and into the hot sun. They are members of a large tour group and each wears an identification badge. The men are wearing Bermuda shorts with socks, print shirts and straw hats with translucent plastic visors. The women are wearing tight pants, new *serapes* and floppy straw hats with *Recuerdo de Mexico* emblazoned across them in brightly colored yarn. They are all very pale in complexion and peer myopically at everything in sight.

The men on the iron benches in the *plaza* are by now watching in open amazement. The tourists are having a heated conversation; one of the women keeps pointing toward an old man dozing on a bench, waving her camera and looking excited and upset. Finally she goes over to him and says quite vocally, "*¿CUANTO?*"

The old man jerks up with surprise and is again abruptly asked, "*¿CUANTO?*" He shakes his head slowly, then begins to wag his forefinger back and forth to indicate that he doesn't understand.

"What'sa matter, Phyllis," another woman calls out loudly. "Won't he let you take his picture?"

"I asked him how much he wants, but he won't answer me," Phyllis complains, ignoring the bewildered looks the old man is casting about.

"Well, just give him some money and take it anyway," her friend advises. By now a crowd is gathering and the tourists feel distinctly uneasy.

Phyllis steps back and nervously snaps the picture. Hurriedly, she rummages through her purse and hands the old man an American nickel. He accepts the coin disdainfully, then walks away to discuss the strange happening with friends.

As Phyllis rejoins the group near the cars, one of them says, "Let's get out of here; this place gives me the creeps. What are all these people staring at, anyway?"

As the cars bounce slowly out of the village, Arnold, known in the group as a real wit, says wisely, "Probably never seen a camera before."

"A cada quien su vida."
(To each their own life.)
Mexican proverb

"To each his own; it's all unknown."
Bob Dylan

Should tourists unwittingly violate some local custom, it is unlikely that the irate populace will stone them to death to appease angered gods. Establishing rapport with people is very difficult, however, if respect and appreciation for the beliefs of others is not shown. The natural gap in understanding that lies between two cultures can be bridged by an awareness that differences are not good or bad, right or wrong; they're just different.

•Customs of dress are probably the most often violated by tourists. The offenders include all groups from super straight to ultrahip.

The best way to avoid looking out of place or of offending anyone is to look as much like everyone else as you can. You don't have to conform too strictly to avoid attention, just be reasonable.

Incongruous clothing is commonly worn by tourists, even those who normally take great care with their appearance. The popular image of a red-faced American wearing a gaudy flowered shirt, a grossly large *sombrero* and painful new sandals on sunburned feet is embarrassingly accurate. What many people fail to realize, however, is that a long blonde haired hippie chick, barefoot, wearing patched jeans, a man's Oaxaca wedding shirt, a *Huichol* belt and strings of beads is even more ridiculous looking to the Mexican eye (especially the Indians).

Since women generally attract more attention then men, it is not surprising that their clothing and the way they wear it is particularly subject to inspection and comment.

In most cases the attention will be stares, smiles, frowns, shaking heads, wagging fingers and occasional whistles, leers and lewd comments. In extreme cases, such as an overexposure of bare skin, the cops may tell a woman to wear something more 'decent.'

Although the popular styles for women (mini and maxi, hot pants, bikinis, sandals, etc.) are seen in larger cities and tourist areas, they are uncommon elsewhere in the country. Among middle and lower class people, it is considered poor taste to go barefoot except at the beach. Mexicans have a high regard for shoes (and polish), even though they may be the mere vestiges of a pair of cheap plastic loafers.

Indians are especially sensitive to clothing and styles, probably because much of what they wear is handmade and has a distinctive and almost invariable appearance. The more traditional wouldn't wear western style clothing if it was given to them.

Lorena was once walking down a path wearing her favorite *huipil* (loose Indian blouse) without a skirt—since the *huipil* fell to her knees. Several women stopped her and began laughing hysterically because it seemed obvious to them that she'd forgotten to finish dressing before leaving the house.

But what particularly amused them was the fact that by the intricate design woven into the *huipil* she was a mother with children. The women knew that this wasn't true and thought it truly astounding that she would wear something with that pattern. From then on, Lorena reserved the *huipil* for areas where the design was unknown.

The best way to offend the maximum number of people, regardless of their individual opinions about clothing styles, is to go partially or fully nude in public. A man can usually wear a T-shirt and pants but a bare chest is frowned upon except at the beach. Steve once removed his shirt in a busy gas station in order to wash grease off his arms. A city cop indignantly ordered him to put it back on.

Men are often seen on crowded beaches wearing nothing but a pair of baggy, semitransparent undershorts. Though their balls may be all but hanging out in public view, they are properly attired *for the beach.*

The rules for women are much stricter and although a small boy may romp stark naked, a small girl, even though just a toddler, will cause a scandal if she appears with a bare ass. Women will occasionally bathe in secluded spots with their breasts exposed but will rarely remove their skirts. Mixed bathing with soap is not common and is considered pretty daring.

Mixed nude bathing, even in remote and *seemingly* isolated areas, is very risky and may well lead to serious trouble (see *Tourists and The Law*). I've known many cases where Mexicans tolerated open dope smoking, laughed at foolish drunken stunts and then called the cops when people swam nude.

Hippie customs and styles have almost all been accepted throughout most of Mexico. Beards are beginning to sprout on truck drivers, always a good sign that the air is clearing.

Other than clothing styles already mentioned, the only current problem is long—really long—hair on men. The average Mexican, male or female, finds it extremely difficult to accept what is considered a definite feminine characteristic on a man. Steve and I learned long ago that though it might not be reasonable or logical, whacking a few inches off of our hair made us feel distinctly more at ease.

•Food and Drink: Customs and rituals for eating and drinking are most commonly seen in humble restaurants and private homes. The more purely Mexican the surroundings, the more traditional the customs.

In tiny restaurants or eating stalls, several people will be seated at one or two tables. When you wish to sit down ask, "*¿Con permiso?*" (May I?) and one or all of the diners will say something affirmative, usually "*Andele.*" (Go ahead). This is strictly a formality, but it breaks the silence.

"*¡Buen provecho!*" (Good appetite!) is used as a greeting or blessing to those already eating and as a means of excusing yourself when you've finished. The response is "*Gracias.*" (You can also say, " *Con permiso?*" when leaving.)

The exchange of greetings and their responses may become confusing. In some areas people say, "*Gracias,*" when they leave the table. Whatever is said, answer it with something; "*Gracias*" or "*áandele,*" etc.

In a traditional household five regular meals are served, the first, *desayuno*, early in the morning (coffee and sweet breads), then early lunch (*almuerzo*), a big late lunch (*comida*, the main meal), a light meal (*merienda*, like a tea) and then *cena,* a late supper. Still hungry?

It is customary to wash your hands before eating.

Men and/or guests are always served first and many times guests will eat in front of everyone else. Disconcerting, but you almost get used to it.

Food is served, usually course by course, to the table. When one plate is clean it is quickly replaced by another dish.

This custom works both ways; if you're the host, you'll have to serve your guests everything, including second helpings without being asked, or they'll sit there for hours without eating. In the average household eating with the fingers is quite acceptable (unless it is soup). Overeating is encouraged.

When booze is being served, the same serving custom applies. The host will take it upon himself to propose toast after toast and to refill your glass constantly. Nondrinkers will find it difficult to refuse, though a token wetting of the lips is usually sufficient. Bottles of liquor are rarely left partially full, consequently a party rarely ends before the booze and participants are completely exhausted.

If a meal is given at a *fiesta*, it usually won't be served until almost midnight or even later.

It would be unusual for a blessing or grace to be said before a meal.

If a fork falls to the floor it means another guest is coming.

When inviting people to dinner, drinks or any type of social gathering, it is best to name each person you expect to attend. For example, you might wish to invite a family to dinner, but when the time comes only the husband shows up.

•Hot and cold are classifications given to foods, beverages, home remedies and even some activities. The use of hot and cold does not necessarily refer in these cases to temperature, but to a property or condition, much like the Oriental concept of yin and yang.

It is important to maintain the proper balance of hot and cold to avoid *pasmo*, an illness caused by too much of one or the other. *Pasmo* can cause cramps to heart failure; those who believe in it take it quite seriously.

Some typical hot and cold situations: I was standing in front of an open fire after bathing. A Mexican friend literally dragged me away, saying the combination of a 'cold' bath (though the water was hot) with a 'hot' fire would cause leprosy.

On another occasion we went on a short, very dry hike with a friend. When we returned to his store I asked for a cold beer. He refused, apologizing profusely, before explaining that a cold drink would either kill me or severely damage my innards. This particular combination is one that seems to make obvious sense. Once you accept one of these beliefs it should be easier to appreciate the more bizarre.

Don't be surprised if guests politely refuse or neglect a cold drink that you have served them. Beer and soda pop are usually taken *al tiempo* (at room temperature).

Water, and all things that live in it are 'cold,' but ice is hot.

Too many 'cold' fruits cause dysentery.

'Hot' foods are generally safer and more nourishing than 'cold.'

When a Mexican friend offered Lorena a recipe for lima bean soup she said, "Whatever you do, don't forget to add cumin seeds. Lima beans are 'cold' and without the 'hot' cumin it will give a woman a stomach ache."

•Private *fiestas* and *pachangas* (blow-outs) are rarely bring-your-own-bottle or potluck. Although both these customs are being adopted by middle and upper class Mexicans, at the most common type of party the hosts provide everything. Traditional Mexicans might even be insulted if a guest were to bring food or refreshments. *Machismo* says that when you invite someone to your house you make damned sure they'll be well taken care of.

In obviously poor households, however, a discreetly offered gift will almost always be accepted, especially if you say, *"Es nuestra costumbre,"* (It is our custom). If you're going to someone's house to eat and want to take something, keep it simple: flowers or a plant, a small bottle of *tequila* or a papaya or pineapple.

If the party is a birthday, saint's day or wedding a gift is probably in order. What to take? For men a bottle of brandy, for women a plant or knickknack and for children a toy. Records also make good gifts, but books are rarely given unless you're certain the person likes to read. (Most Mexicans don't. See *Speaking Spanish: Media*.)

At some parties the host or hostess is expected to give gifts to the guests. This is called *el remojo*. A *remojo* party usually celebrates a new house, car or other major acquisition.

•*Día de santo* (Saint's day) is a sort of second birthday, honoring the saint after which a baby is named. A man called Antonio, for example, would celebrate his *día de santo* on San Antonio's Day, whether or not it is his actual birthday. (See *Appendices* for *Saint's Days*.) The *barrio* of San Antonio would hold a *fiesta* on the same day and the village of that name would too.

"*¡Hoy es mi santo!*" (Today is my saint!) is the prelude to an invitation to a *pachanga* (blow-out). A birthday may go by almost unnoticed, but a saint's day must be celebrated.

•Time, invitations and obligations: The old cliché that Mexicans are always late or don't show up is one that I find difficult to argue with. Having tried and failed to understand why has led me to plain acceptance. I even go so far as to imitate them, deliberately making engagements that I do not attend. As a general rule Mexicans agree to everything but comply with what suits them.

The practice of being 'blunt,' 'honest' or 'out front,' so revered by Americans, is considered somewhat rude in Mexico. My *compadre* Nacho explained it one day when I asked why he had accepted an invitation to a party that he absolutely dreaded attending. "In order to avoid telling them 'no,' I told them 'yes'." When I pointed out that he shouldn't force himself to go, he just laughed and said, "I'm not going, of course, but it would be worse to refuse than to not show up."

•*¡Salud!* is used both as a drinking toast and as a sneeze blessing. When you sneeze and hear, "*¡Salud!*" the proper response is, "*Gracias.*" Many people believe that a sneeze means someone is thinking ill of you.

•Handshakes are very important. Friends who have met daily all of their lives will shake hands when meeting *and when taking their leave.* Men shake hands with women, children with adults, girls with boys, etc. Handshakes, even between men, are usually very gentle. Knuckle crushing is not polite. It is traditional among many Indians to just lightly touch or kiss each other's hands.

The *abrazo*, a form of greeting similar to a hug, is practiced between Mexican men, but rarely used with foreigners.

•*Siestas* are taken between two and four in the afternoon. The *comida* is usually eaten between two and three p.m. and the hour until four p.m. used to recover from over-eating. Shops close, the streets empty and life generally winds down in preparation for a long evening. Those who think the custom of *siestas* is a vice of the lazy, don't realize that most Mexicans don't go to bed until almost midnight. Night life rarely picks up until late evening and spending the entire night *en vela* (in candle, awake) is common.

•Admiring another person's possessions often leads to embarrassing scenes. It is customary to give away the object admired and no refusal, however sincere or well-intentioned, will be accepted without some offense.

Although Lorena was quite aware of this custom she recently made the mistake of admiring a friend's wedding ring. To her horror, the woman immediately took off the ring and gave it to her. Lorena tried to refuse, but the woman wouldn't hear of it, and she eventually had to accept the gift.

•The *paseo* (stroll or promenade) is a much publicized Mexican custom. A description of a typical evening's *paseo* is essential to hack travel articles: "Sharp eyed chaperones dressed in black hover behind dark eyed flashing beauties..." The reality is somewhat different, with dark eyed beauties often exchanging off-color insults with their male counterparts, slouching around the *plaza* in shiny pointed shoes, gnawing sullenly on giant wads of *Chicles*. The lively atmosphere may be enhanced by an occasional nip of *tequila*, giving one young man the courage to call out "Oh, my little dear, you have a body just like a dove!" The target of this *piropo* (flirtatious remark) responds with a rude hand signal. "A big butt and skinny legs!" the young man adds, joining his friends in sarcastic laughter.

The *paseo* occurs almost every night of the week, with full participation on Sunday evening. This is the night to dress up, for the *catrín* (dude) to put on his best *cacles* (shoes) and do a little "panthering" among the ladies. A set of keys dangles casually from the hand or pants pocket, as though an automobile were parked somewhere nearby instead of a rattletrap bicycle. The men and boys circle the *plaza* in one direction, the unattached ladies in knots of two to four and couples in the opposite. This provides a good view of the opposition and many opportunities for brief eye contacts, wisecracks and suggestive body movements.

Those who have budding relationships usually attach themselves to another couple as a sort of buffer against looking too serious. If things work out they'll be seen later, pressed into the frustrating semi-privacy of a shadowy doorway.

•*Compadrazgo* is a very important system of relationships between people who may otherwise have no formal connection. It is easiest to compare with the godparent relationship in other societies, though two people may become *compadres* without involving children. Anything of importance can lead to new *compadres:* marriage, births, buying a new house, a business deal, a close friendship and so on. We have a friend who acquired a *compadre* when he managed to save up the money for a new pick-up truck.

Compadres are supposed to support each other in times of need (though they often don't). This tightens the social structure, especially in poorer communities. *Compadres* are often on quite different social and economic levels, however. This is another type of bridge, usually based on mutual respect. A businessman, for example, who accepts an employee's invitation to be his *compadre* upon the birth of a child, is now more than just an employer, he's a shirttail relative.

You'll often hear people refer to each other as *compadre* (also *compa'*) and *comadre* or *comadre* Maria, *compadre* Pancho, etc. Once the relationship is entered into this title replaces the person's name or is added to it. Dropping *compadre-madre* is impolite.

Compadre and *comadre* are frequently used among younger people who are actually not *compadres*, but just good friends.

•Many merchants are very superstitious about the first sale of each day. It is bad luck to have a customer walk away without buying something. For this reason, the crafty, cynical barterer will tumble out of bed at the crack of dawn to test other's willpower. Lorena once bought a shawl for what was obviously less than wholesale. The vendor took the money with a weary smile, then muttered a quick blessing (another custom for the first money taken in) over the bills and stuck them away.

•*Colas* (tails, queues, waiting lines) are contrary to the Mexican sense of right and order. *"Señora, ¡hay cola!"* (Lady, there's a line!) is wasted breath in most cases. Use your energy instead to elbow and bluff your way to the front. About the only place that a line is observed is at the *tortillería* (*tortilla* factory). Ladies with biceps made hard and knotty by hours of heavy kitchen work make short work of crowders and bargers.

Gringos are often timid about shoving ahead and may be embarrassed to be served before others who were there first. Don't be; you can bet that one day you'll spend half an hour trying to buy a stamp as aggressive Mexicans make short work of you.

Because of out-of-control population growth, Mexico City is often called *la ciudad de colas* (the city of lines).

•Mexican women do not shave their legs. This isn't necessarily a sign of liberation but a holdover from times when hairy legs meant European, rather than Indian blood. Class conscious Mexicans look down upon the Indians, though they often collect their artifacts and craft works.

•*Un tesoro de la Revolución* (a treasure from the Revolution) is as common in a Mexican family's patio as a relative on the Mayflower is in New England. Because of looting, banditry and kidnap-for-ransom during the 1910 Revolution, people hid their money and valuables. The central patio of a typical large home was the logical spot, close at hand and safe from prying eyes and fingers. Many of these caches were recovered, but many others were not. Those that remain *enterrado* (buried) are guarded by ghosts.

•Business cards are vitally important to the image of anyone who has a *negocio* (business), line of b.s. or just a hope and a prayer for profit. Taxi drivers have them, as well as travelling salesmen, prostitutes, students (in early anticipation of the degree claimed), bartenders, bureaucrats, teachers and anyone else with pretensions to a title or position. *Tarjetas* are very cheap and can be quickly printed up just around the corner. "John Doe, Dealer in Rare Earths" or "Jane Doe, Specialized Consultant" can be a nice change from "bulldozer operator" and "housewife."

Identification cards with photos are also highly valued. It seems that some organizations exist solely to provide their members with these. An evening in a *cantina* invariably requires a mutual show-and-brag i.d. card session.

•Church etiquette: Although the Catholic church no longer requires women to cover their heads when inside a church, many still do. The more traditional people, particularly in small towns and in the country, still observe meatless Fridays as well. Men take their hats off in church and devout Mexican men remove them when passing a church. A very brief prayer is given when passing a church or shrine.

•*Ocho días*, eight days, make up a week in Mexico *Ocho días en adelante,* eight days from now, is what we would call "a week from today." The time is also given on the 24 hour basis: *1900 horas* means 7 p.m.(1200 noon plus 5 hours). Midnight is 2400 *horas* and one minute past midnight is 0001.

•April Fool's Day comes on December 28 in Mexico and is called *Día de Los Inocentes* (Day of The Innocents). Rather than playing such practical jokes as "You just won the lottery!" Mexicans go to elaborate ruses to borrow things. "Nice looking pen you've got there. May I look at it?" You hand it over, your favorite ballpoint that you bought at the '62 Seattle World's Fair, but instead of it being returned you hear:

Inocente Palomita
Que te dejas engañar,
En este día de los inocentes
Con tú (pluma) me he de quedar.

Which means:

Innocent little Dove
You've allowed yourself to be tricked,
On this day of the innocents
Your (pen) I'm entitled to keep.

If this bit of humor causes the person who was fooled to scream and rant, the item borrowed can be returned without a loss of face, since you were "entitled" to keep it but don't have to. I lost my pen to a waiter in a small restaurant this way, but retaliated later by admiring his wife's gold earring. In spite of the fact that there were many 'innocents' around, they didn't expect a gringo to know the rhyme. The look of dismay on the waiter's face as his wife calmly allowed me to borrow her earring "to show to Lorena" was worth a case of pens.

•*Bilis* (bile) might well be called the national ailment of Mexico. It is said to be caused by emotional upset: extreme anger, frustration, embarrassment, etc. The symptoms are as varied as the treatments, but generally appear as stomach troubles, headaches, lack of energy and loss of appetite. *Bilis* is considered to be psychosomatic by most gringos, including those addicted to Tums, Maalox and tranquilizers.

•*Limpias* (cleansings) are used to cure victims of the evil eye, those with bad luck, *bilis* or an improper hot/cold balance. The patient is usually brushed with a chicken egg (preferably a ranch egg rather than a white factory egg). Herbs may also be used. Some *curanderas* break the egg into a glass of water after the cleansing and diagnose the problem by observing the action of the egg yolk and white. People will travel hundreds of miles for a good *limpia*. The practice is followed by Mexicans from all levels.

Fortune telling can be done by some people in conjunction with the *limpia* ritual. The charge is usually more than for a standard cleansing.

•Salt is bad luck. To have *sal* usually leads to poverty, if not illness and death. Salt can be removed by a cleansing of a person or building. Protection is also provided by charms.

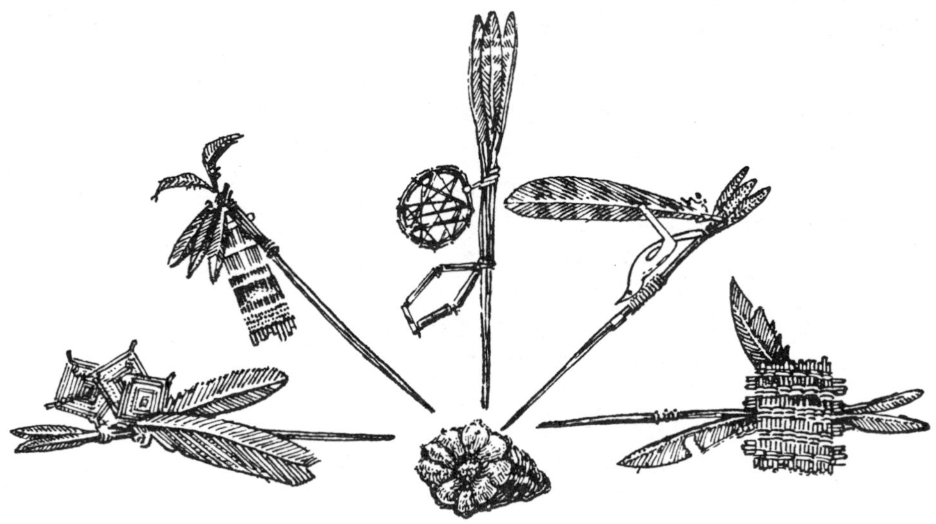

•All types of charms, amulets and prayers are commonly used for protection against illness and spiritual problems, including black magic. *Oraciones* are small printed prayers sold in herb stalls and around churches. They are used in conjunction with other charms or alone, as a chant. Each has it's special powers; ask the vendor what it's for.

Lodestones (*piedra imán*) are very powerful amulets. They are not cheap. Elaborate preparations are necessary to prepare a lodestone for use and the new owner must 'feed' metal filings to the stone.

Retablos are pictures painted by persons seeking relief from disease or aid in some venture. They are placed at the altar of a favored saint. Many *retablos* are considered to be fine examples of folk art and are bought by collectors. Never remove a *retablo* from a church or shrine!

•*Mal ojo,* the evil eye, is believed to be caused by someone who admires another person too intensely or thinks ill of them. Some people can cast *mal ojo* at will, but they are (fortunately) uncommon. An otherwise normal person can inadvertently cast the Eye on another withot being aware of it. Persistent illnesses are often caused by the evil eye. Consult a *curandera*.

•*Vientos* (winds) and *mal aires* (bad airs) are a common cause of various ailments, though usually associated with respiratory problems, toothache, cramps and paralysis. During the night and early morning you'll see people with their heads swathed in cloths or towels as a protection against bad air.

The worst aspect of a belief in winds capable of causing illness is that people avoid what we consider normal ventilation. Bus windows, even on hot days, remain firmly closed. Children go around bundled up to the ears as if for a snowstorm when their parents are behind the house, harvesting bananas. If you pick up a Mexican hitchhiker you'll probably notice that open windows will be discreetly closed or avoided.

•*Envidio* (envy) is believed by *campesinos* and Indians to be the cause of all sorts of problems, from death to poor business profits. Elaborate measures are taken against it. Not so long ago the best cure for *envidio* was considered to be eliminating the person causing the trouble.

•*Espanto* and *susto* (fright) are disorders caused by anger, shock, frustration or other emotional extremes. Indians are especially vulnerable to *espanto*. Death as a result of it is not uncommon. The cures are varied. Doctors are rarely consulted since people know by now that the medical profession either can't or won't do anything for it.

Loss of appetite is a common symptom of both *espanto* and *susto*. Even the average Mexican has a fear of loss of appetite. Overeating and being overweight are generally considered signs of good health and a strong constitution.

•The Bogeyman will be waiting for you in Mexico. He is commonly called *El Diablo* (the Devil), *El Coco* (the Head—bald) and *El Sombrerón* (also *El Sombrerudo*, the Big Hat). The *Sombrerón* has the rude habit of copulating with female horses and then braiding their tails. He is easily recognizable, look for a giant headless man wearing a huge hat and riding a flying white horse. A close friend who saw *El Sombrerón* late one night sneered when I suggested it might have been the bottle of *tequila* he'd drunk, rather than a real ghost. "The *tequila* just allowed me to see him," he answered, "If sober people could see him, they'd all be scared!"

La Llorona, The Weeper, is a woman dressed in long white robes. She drags around her floor-length hair, crying out "*¡Ay, mis hijos!*" (Ay, my children!) and giving bad little girls and boys the nightsweats.

Chanecos live in the forests and jungles. People follow their friendly laughter and then disappear. No one who has set after a *chaneco* has ever returned to describe them. (Survivors of a *chaneco* chase do exist, but they are hopelessly insane.)

Note: these are just a few examples; every area has it's own variation or embellishment on spirits and ghosts. One of the most popular in the north is the ghost of Pancho Villa. He does everything from scaring children to healing illnesses and bestowing good luck. Watch for him.

Peyote

MACHISMO

*Bragging...Death Before Dishonor!...Dealing with the macho...
Courtesy and caution...Women: the mala mujer and other fantasies...
The Macho's theme song...*

Many wise and learned things have been written about the origins and causes of the *machismo* (manliness, virility) problem in Mexico. Rather than attempting a detailed explanation, I will confine my comments to areas where *machismo* most directly and dramatically affects the traveller.

"What the hell are those guys trying to prove?" a gringo newly arrived in Mexico once asked me in a bar. He had just been through a few typical experiences involving the *macho* mentality: an insanely dangerous bus ride, an unpleasant scene with a drunk in a *cantina* and a look at the young men strutting around the *plaza*.

His question goes right to the point of *machismo, proving you are macho:* to the other driver on the highway, the passengers in your bus, the guy who dares not to drink with you, the women—especially to the women—and of course, to yourself.

This constant pressure to prove oneself can be very tiring. Tourists aren't the only people to shake their heads at a display of *machismo.* Mexicans, particularly those with some education, openly speak of the need to end the vicious circle of *machismo.* Unfortunately this is about as difficult to do as outlawing patriotism.

I had a close Mexican friend who constantly spoke of ways to eliminate *machismo.* He was a poet and political liberal, able to demolish opposing arguments in four languages, including Nahuatl. When he drank, however, he literally became everything he rejected. One night, after an attack on a *tequila* bottle, I pointed out to him that he was acting like a typical *macho.* He'd just blown the last of his salary on booze and the lottery, insulted a woman on the street and challenged a cab driver to a duel with tire irons.

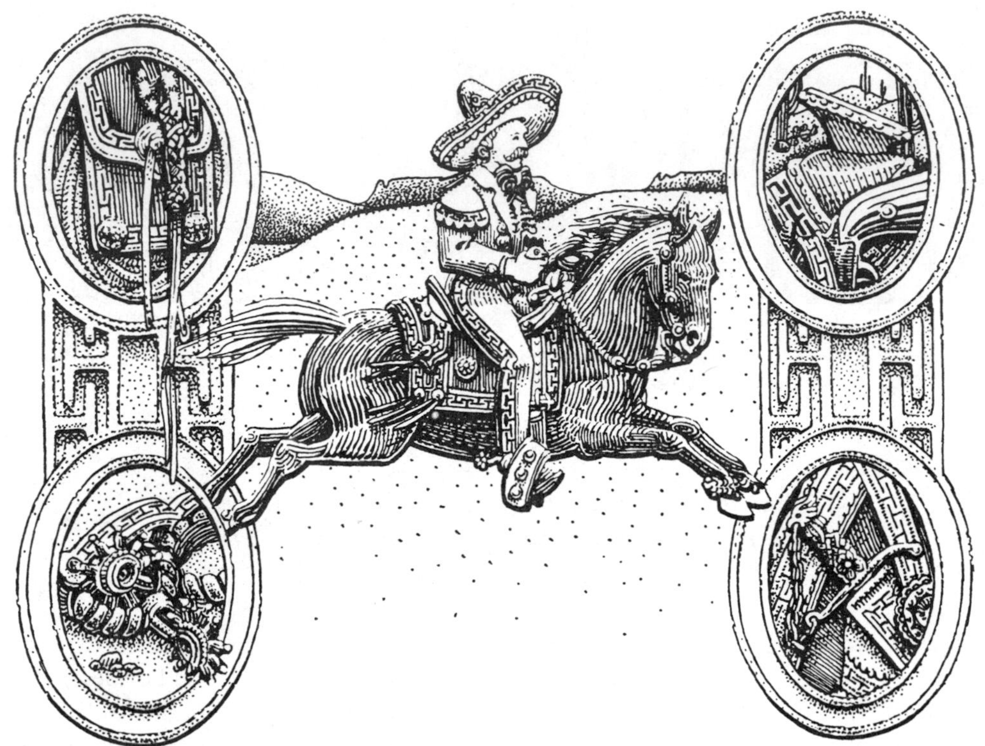

He reacted to this accusation with hysterical curses and threats, pausing only long enough to lubricate his throat with gulps of *tequila*. When he'd finally settled down he said, "Will you loan me a thousand *pesos?*"

"What for?" I countered, taken aback. A moment before he'd cursed my ancestors all the way back to the Java Man.

"You question my need for money?" he roared. "What are friends for?"

"I just wondered." I hurried to add, "I don't have much."

"Well, if you must know," he said, "I want to buy a gun. You've insulted me to the point where I have to shoot you."

I thought about this for a few seconds, realizing that he was entirely serious, if not entirely logical. "Can't you get one for less than a thousand?" I asked.

"Stop!" he howled, "Now you've gone too far! Do you think I'd shoot a friend with a cheap shitty pistol? No! I want something good!"

I refused him the loan and he threw me out, reminding me that to deny money to a friend was reason enough to end our friendship forever. And it did.

Situations such as this are not commonly encountered by tourists. A more usual form of *machismo*, one that has its humorous aspects, is bragging.

"...if the conversation is about airplanes, and no one would believe him if he says that he has one, then he will say he has a friend who has two."

Arturo Linares Suarez
Como El Mexicano No Hay Dos

Dealing with a *macho* braggart requires self control; unless you challenge a statement, neither of you has to prove that it is true. I once spent an afternoon in the countryside, listening to a man describe his magnificent fighting cocks. The top rooster in his team, called *El Capitán*, was capable of rendering feathered opponents unfit for use in soup. He had never been beaten and never would be! What a chicken!

"Can I see him?" I asked, opening a vast can of worms with that simple challenge to the rooster's existence.

I paid for my apparent doubt by having to hike ten miles under a blistering sun, only to find upon arrival at a remote *ranchito* that *El Capitán* had been 'borrowed' for the day to improve the breed on a relative's *ranchito*, even farther into the mountains. I knew then that my friend was prepared to walk the length and breadth of Mexico, leading me toward that ever receding mythical fowl.

Tourists and *Machismo*

Machismo frequently appears as what we might consider a childish and neurotic sense of pride. When someone offers you a cigarette, it doesn't matter that your polite refusal is based on the fact that you don't smoke. To the sensitive *macho*, any refusal, however rational, is still a refusal and therefore an insult.

I once asked a bartender how, in such a situation, it was humanly possible to avoid offense. He answered: "Take the cigarette and put it behind your ear. Tell the guy you will save it as a souvenir of your meeting."

Thus, you save face for the person who offered the cigarette since you symbolically join him in smoking. You soon learn the devious tricks of avoiding those conversations and situations that inevitably lead to some display of *machismo.*

- In a bar, for example, don't offer or accept anything unless you really want to become involved with the other person. This is particularly true of an offer of booze.
- On the highway *never* do anything to provoke another driver. When a truck tries to pass you on a hill, allow him to go around rather than forcing him to drop back right at the last moment. The reason for this is that he is not going to drop back, even if it kills you both.
- Irate horn honking is an invitation to do battle. ("Shave and a haircut" is very offensive in Mexico.) The true *macho* driver will never allow a question of honor to go unanswered, even when he has committed some outrageous blunder. Death before dishonor!
- Be polite and never allow yourself to be goaded into displays of anger. A *macho* always stays cool on the otside. Losing your temper automatically escalates things, whether it's horn honking or a sharp response to a suggestive look.

•Don't question idle boasting.

•When dealing with other men, a *macho* wants to hear "*Sí* and *No,*" indecisiveness is considered weak. When dealing with women the *macho* only understands "No;" everything else is taken as "Maybe."

•Don't question customs when there is no possible benefit from doing so. In the country for example, the women stay in the kitchen or sit on the edge of conversations. Accept this; you'll only embarrass everyone if you make a scene of being democratic.

"*La mujer como el vidrio, siempre está er peligro.*"
"A woman is like glass, always in da..ger."
Macho saying

•Mexican men treat female relatives and friends with great courtesy, especially in public. They are also neurotically protective of them. If an acquaintance introduces you to 'his' women, treat them like royalty. Exaggerated courtesy is the norm.

Barroom discussions of women inevitably lead to outbursts of *machismo;* I avoid them as much as possible. Any conversation that involves a *macho's* woman is potentially tricky. It's better to ask, "How is the family?" rather than, "How's your wife?"

The more rude demonstrations of *machismo* occur on the street or in casual encounters between men and women who do not know each other.

> "*...the image of the* mala mujer—*the bad woman, is almost always accompanied by the idea of aggressive activity. She is not passive like the 'self-denying mother,' the waiting sweetheart,'...she comes and goes, she looks for men and then leaves them...*"

Octavio Paz's description from *The Labyrinth of Solitude* certainly is applied to gringas as well as *mexicanas.* When a *macho* sees a woman striding down the sidewalk, hair flying and breasts jiggling, an overnight bag in one hand and a guidebook in the other, he thinks "*¡Saqué la lotería, hombre!*" (I've won the lottery, man!). The only problem, of course, is trying to figure out how to collect.

Mexican men, from lewd old businessmen to long haired pseudo intellectuals, will go to almost any lengths to lay a gringa. Any restrictions they might operate under with Mexican women are lifted in their relationships with foreigners.

The techniques range from loud, gross comments in public to intense, soul-searching conversations designed to disprove any taint of chauvinism in their character. If you just happen to be her escort, you'll be included in the conversations. But then, when you're on your way back from the rest-room, you will get a glimpse of the crux of the discussion: a hand on her knee, an intense whispering in her ear...

Single women must exert great self-control and common sense when dealing with *machismo.* Any response, even negative, is taken as an opening.

Many women have told us that travelling alone didn't scare them from the standpoint of physical danger, but that it was almost a continual hassle dealing with men on the make. The effort involved in keeping their guard up soon got most of them down. Some quit travelling alone, others gave up entirely and went home.

One of the most effective solutions to the problem is to travel with a guy, even if he's just 'borrowed' for the day. This won't stop the *machos* entirely, but it definitely tones down their approaches.

Although *machismo* can be dangerous, especially on the highway or in drunken quarrels, it is most often nothing more than a minor background hassle, something the experienced traveller learns to anticipate and avoid.

Women would do well to observe how the *mexicanas* deal with men and *machismo.* Mexican women seldom leave the house alone and travel alone only when they can't find a friend, relative or neighbor to accompany them. Follow their example; sit and associate with other women whenever possible.

Mexican women avoid eye contact with strangers, especially on the street. I've often marvelled at the seemingly impenetrable cocoon that surrounds them as they march to the store for a box of rice. We call this 'practical invisibility.' If you don't direct your attention to someone, it's less likely they'll notice you.

Pay attention to where you're going. When you notice a group of men ahead of you, especially at night, cross the street or go around the block to avoid a possible confrontation.

In a country where black hair is almost universal, anything else is highly noticeable. Blonde hair has been converted by the advertising industry into a synonym for sex. 'The high class blonde' is the trademark for a well known Mexican beer. Lorena always wears a scarf in public. When she is alone and prefers to be even more inconspicuous, she wears her hair braided and up on her head. Out of sight, out of mind.

Flambouyant clothing, bare arms and legs, or breasts showing or wiggling are considered by *machos* to mean, "I'm free and easy."

Any attitude other than aloofness is taken as flirtatious. To me one of the most irritating backlashes of *machismo* is that casual encounters with Mexican women are usually cold and impersonal. The kind of easy bantering that goes on in a supermarket, for example, between customers who collide their shopping carts near the lettuce just doesn't happen in Mexico. A curt, "Excuse me," is all you can expect. Being reserved and on the alert is so ingrained that *mexicanas* will seldom drop it, even for a few seconds. A *macho* sees an innocently friendly look or remark as an opening through which to ride his Trojan horse of compliments, exaggerations, bravado and white lies.

This doesn't mean that women travellers should be unfriendly. Remaining aloof and inconspicuous should be thought of as a defense against unwanted attention, and need not cause aggressively unpleasant behavior. Relax with other women; soon you will learn which situations can be controlled and which cannot.

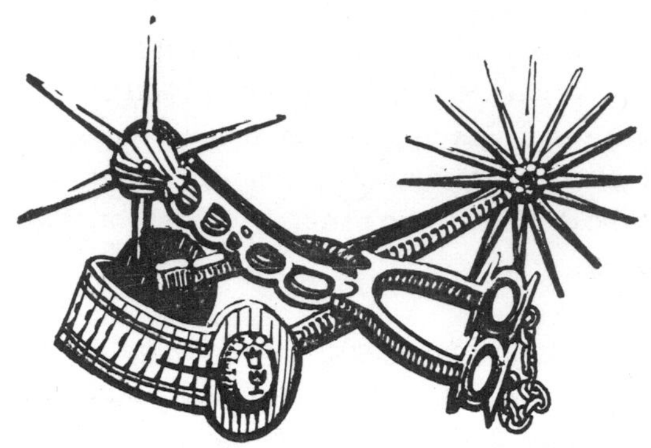

In any discussion of *machismo* it is difficult to leave the *macho* male with anything but the short end of the stick. Harsh judgments, however, will not change the situation. The following songs illustrate the dilemma in which the *macho* finds himself: the self-proclaimed king of a world without value. The first is what I call "The *Macho* Anthem." It is very popular in *cantinas*. Contrary to the aggressiveness of the lyrics it is sung in a mournful, lamenting tone. The second song, also a *cantina* classic, leaves one reaching for the *tequila* bottle with a groan of "Why bother?"

Sigo Siendo El Rey

Yo sé bien que estoy afuera,
pero el día en que yo me muera,
Sé que vas a llorar, llorar y llorar,
llorar y llorar.
Dirás que no me quisiste,
pero vas a estar muy triste,
Y así te vas a quedar.

Chorus:
Con dinero o sin dinero,
hago siempre lo que quiero
Y mi palabra es la ley;
No tengo trono ni reina,
ni nadien que me comprenda,
Pero sigo siendo el Rey.

I Continue To Be The King

I know well that I'm on the outside,
but the day in which I die,
I know that you're going to cry,
cry and cry, cry and cry.
You'll say that you didn't love me,
but you're going to be very sad,
And that's how you'll remain.

Chorus:
With money or without money,
I always do what I want,
And my word is the law.
I have no throne or queen,
nor anyone who understands me,
But I continue to be the King.

Una piedra en el camino me enseño *que mi destino,* *Era rodar y rodar, rodar y rodar,* *rodar y rodar.* *Luego me dijo un arriero,* *que no hay que llegar primero,* *Sino hay que saber llegar.*	A rock in the road showed me that my destiny, Was to roll and roll, roll and roll, roll and roll. Then a muleskinner told me, that you don't have to arrive first, But only have to know how to arrive.
Con dinero o sin dinero...chorus	With money or without money...chorus
No Vale Nada La Vida	Life Is Worth Nothing
No vale nada la vida, la vida no vale nada.	Life is worth nothing, there is no value to life.
Comienza siempre llorando y *así llorando se acaba;* *Por eso es que en este mundo, la vida no vale nada.*	It always begins with crying and so crying it ends; That is because in this world, life is worth nothing.
Bonito León, Guanajuato, *su feria con sus jugadas,* *Allí se apuesta la vida, y se respeta al que gana.* *Allí en mi León, Guanajuato,* *la vida no vale nada.*	Pretty Leon, Guanajuato, its Fair with its games, There one bets their life, and the winner is respected. There in my Leon, Guanajuato, life is worth nothing.
No vale nada la vida (chorus)...	Life is worth nothing (chorus)...
Camino de Santa Rosa, *que pasas por tanto pueblo,* *No pases por Salamanca,* *que allí me hiere el recuerdo.* *Vete rodeando veredas, no pases porque me muero.*	Road from Santa Rosa, that passes through so many towns, Don't go through Salamanca, because there memory wounds me. Go around by other paths, don't go through because I'll die.
No vale nada la vida (chorus)...	Life is worth nothing (chorus)...
El Cristo de la Montaña, del Cerro del Cubilete *Consuelo de los que sufren y adoración de las gentes.* *El Cristo de la Montaña, del Cerro del Cubilete*	The Christ of the Mountain, of the Hill of Cubilete, Consolation of those who suffer and adoration of the people. The Christ of the Mountain, of the Hill of Cubilete.
No vale nada la vida (chorus)...	Life is worth nothing (chorus)...

NOTES

¡VIVA MEXICO!

A typical fiesta...The Day of The Dead...Xmas and posadas...Carnivals and circuses...National lottery...Beggars and con artists...Whorehouses...A brief history of Mexico...What the hell is that?...The bullfight, impressions and trivia...

CELEBRATIONS AND FIESTAS

According to the Mexican Department of Tourism there are between 5,000 and 6,000 *known fiestas* celebrated each year in Mexico. Observing even a fraction of them would exhaust the most dedicated party-goer. (For a partial listing see *Appendices: Fiestas.*) Some *fiestas*, however, are nationwide; if you happen to be in Mexico when they are held you'll certainly see at least part of the action.

Almost anything can spark a fiesta. It seems that when a family isn't honoring someone's birthday, Saint Day, birth, death, promotion or return from Mexico City with a private *pachanga* they're attending a similar party at a relative's house. Neighbors celebrate their own particular patron Saint Day, as do *colonias* (neighborhoods), *pueblos* (villages), *municipios* (counties), *ejidos* (collectives), states, and even regions. When the religious calendar fails to give reason for a *fiesta* someone will promote a Strawberry Fair or a Day of the *Compadre.*

Some *fiestas* are very predictable, others come and go according to the whim of organizers and participants. If the *fiesta* in San Andres is more *vivo*, alive, than one in San Pablo on the same day, the people of San Andres will forsake their own festivities to attend the other. Weather may delay a *fiesta* or lack of money for a proper fireworks display. If the schedule says "honor San X on Thursday" his Saintedness will have to wait until Saturday or Sunday; after all, people have jobs.

The most important ingredient in a good *fiesta* is not the cost or color of the trimmings—it's the participants themselves. *Fiestas* were not designed to be observed but to be participated in. Leave your camera in your hotel room, toss the book explaining the hidden significance of everything into a corner and go out and *join in.*

Although it is late evening, crowds are just beginning to fill the small *plaza.* Children run in excited packs, gawking up at the tall *castillos* elaborate wooden and bamboo structures covered with fireworks. These will be lit much later, after the people have enjoyed snacks from the many temporary food stalls offering steaming sweet *tamales*, sizzling *tacos* and strips of charcoal broiled beef. There's cotton candy, hotcakes smeared with strawberry jam, *buñuelos*, popcorn, *churros* dusted with sugar, special sweet breads, *agua fresca*, soft drinks and plenty of washtubs filled with ice and beer. Colored lights are hanging from the fronts of buildings; crepe paper streams from lamp posts and trees.

A sudden silence falls upon the crowd, followed by a mass sigh of pleasure. A huge *globo* rises slowly over the town, its thin cloth and paper skin flickering with the flame of a kerosene pot inside. This balloon—actually a miniature blimp—rocks crazily in the breeze, then erupts into a ball of flame as the kerosene fire touches the paper. Cries of glee follow its fiery plunge onto the roof of the elementary school. Fortunately the tiles are fire proof; by early morning they'll be littered with expended rockets and flares.

The *globo* is followed by others, each raising the crowd's spirit until even the most staid citizens laugh with excitement. Firecrackers and small rockets explode at people's feet; a poorly aimed star shell showers sparks into the very center of the *plaza*, causing a moment of hilarious panic among the women operating the *kermess*, a benefit food and knickknack sale.

The interior of the church glows with the light of hundreds of devotional candles as worshippers come and go in a steady stream. In the courtyard outside dancers in wildly colorful costumes follow rhythms far older than the stone walls that tower above them. The monotonous strumming of armadillo shell guitars fades beneath the sudden blare of the town loudspeaker, announcing unintelligible self-congratulations from local *politicos* on the event of this, the greatest ever celebration of who-knows-what.

Beggars hustle between the front of the church and the *plaza*, caught in the dilemma of whether to hit up the devout or the prosperous couples who walk arm-in-arm, calling greetings to their friends. A policeman hurries by, one arm on an unruly drunk's shoulder, the other squeezing steadily on a hinged 'come-along' clamped like a nutcracker over the offendor's wrist. In the morning he will work off his fine and hangover by cleaning up the debris of the night's festivities.

A commotion near a street corner erupts into a swirl of running bodies, clouds of confetti and glitter and friendly insults. Eggshells, loaded with everything from powdered paint to metallic flakes, fly over the crowd, exploding harmlessly on the flagstones—or directly on a well chosen head. A polite young man about twelve years of age asks the tourist if he is having a good time. Before an answer can be given the boy plants a loaded eggshell directly in the center of an unsuspecting chest. What can you do but find out where they buy them and get your own?

Days of the Dead

Can you imagine holding a *fiesta* in the graveyard? On November 2, children romp around the tombs and leaning crucifixes, munching tiny sugar skulls as their parents sit near the grave of a departed loved one, eating sweet *tamales*, *pan de los muertos* (bread of the dead) and recalling fond memories of the *difuntos* (deceased).

A few older kids have set up a game on top of their grandmother's crypt; with tiny dice and nuts for markets, they play *Oca* (Goose) or one of the other traditional *Día de Los Muertos* games.

The youngest child, about four years old, arranges miniature wooden and cardboard furniture, setting the little table with pea-sized pottery dishes. These have come from the family altar, where yesterday on November 1, the souls of brothers and sisters who didn't survive their first few years, descended to play and to 'eat' the treats set out for them.

A few graves away, an older brother sips from a small bottle of *tequila*, also from the altar. Earlier in the day this same bottle cheered the souls of older family *difuntos*, along with the special breads, *tamales* and turkey *mole* they must do without for the remainder of the year.

An uncle leans against a tombstone, engrossed in the newspaper. He suddenly barks out a laugh, calling the others to listen as he reads out a bawdy, satirical poem that rudely caricaturizes the local mayor. These articles are *calaveras* (skeletons) and anyone in the public eye might find their hidden skeletons leaping from the closet to the front page on these days. Comic skeletal figures accompany the *calaveras*, portraying the *politicos* as having squandered municipal funds on the lottery.

The Days of the Dead originated in Europe in the 9th century and were introduced by Spaniards after the Conquest. This celebration blended quite nicely with already existing Aztec beliefs concerning death and departed spirits. The result is as Mexican as *mole* sauce.

About a week before the first of November vendors set up stalls and begin selling sugar skulls, coffins, tombs, skeletons and whatever else they can fashion into grisly reminders of mortality. The skulls have names: if Uncle Pancho drove his truck off a cliff last year, you'll buy a Pancho skull for the family altar and perhaps a large sugar skeleton clutching a real bottle of his favorite *tequila* and a cigarette.

Loaves of bread, representing departed souls, are also sold, as well as miniatures of almost anything one can think of to please those who have but one day a year in which to again enjoy the earthly plane. These offerings all go on the family altar. On the first of November the souls of the children descend to enjoy their treats; on the second day it's the turn of the adults. Afterwards the treats will be eaten by the family and guests.

When visiting a house during the Days of the Dead, guests bring small gifts for the altar: food, flowers (especially marigolds), candles, miniatures such as already described, and perhaps liquor. None of these offerings are eaten until the souls have had their chance to partake.

Christmas

La Navidad rates as Mexico's longest celebration: it begins on December 16 and ends on January 6. On the first night of Christmas the *posadas* begin, continuing for a total of nine consecutive nights. These are re-enactments of Joseph and Mary's search for lodging. Some *posadas* are semi-public but most are private parties. Nativity scenes are set up, many of them incredibly elaborate, incorporating miniature figures that have been in the family for hundreds of years.

Posadas are also the time for *piñatas*, decorated figures built of papier mache around a large pottery bowl stuffed with candy, money and small goodies. The children are blindfolded and take turns swinging a club at the *piñata*. Someone controls the *piñata* by means of a rope, jerking it up and down to increase the crowd's excitement as the child careens wildly around the room, flailing the air. When someone connects solidly, the *piñata* bursts, spraying its load onto the floor and prompting a mad scramble among the kids.

Some families offer fruit and candy to groups of people wandering the streets, admiring Nativity scenes and enjoying the evening's various festivities. The children, and even adults of the house, toss treats from the roof to those below. Sometimes they get carried away: my brother was peering in a window at an elaborate Nativity scene and had an entire washtub of oranges dumped on his head. Firecrackers often add to the confusion.

Christmas day is a religious holiday. January 6th is the day for giving gifts, called *Día de Los Reyes* (Day of the Kings).

CARNIVALS, FAIRS AND CIRCUSES

I won't even bother attempting to describe a Mexican carnival or fair; the only person who could do it justice would be a ten year old in from the hills for his first glimpse of the big city. To really appreciate the experience, especially when the outward trappings are not lavish, forget that you've seen Barnum & Bailey, Disneyland and the Rose Parade. Pretend, if only for a few minutes, that this is *it:* that mind-blowing trip to town you've waited for all of your life.

Then, after you're well into this new identity, you'll feel yourself being swept up by people around you, noticing the things they appreciate, not what tourists are told is especially colorful or quaint. Get drunk, buy a greasy *quesadilla* near the merry-go-round, shoot off a firecracker, throw confetti in people's faces—just don't stand on the sidelines with your camera and expect to understand what's happening.

After you've worked yourself into a real state, try visiting the sideshow, if there is one. Such rare treats as the Snake Woman so convince the *campesinos* that barkers continually reasure them that it's a fake.

Circuses, like fairs and carnivals, are not produced for a sophisticated audience. Consequently, they are very real and enjoyable. The elephants seem ready to fall in your lap rather than parading precisely around a distant arena, just one small act in a carefully executed program. If you've watched aerial acts in a big circus in the U.S. without really expecting anyone to fall, you'll appreciate the tension of the Mexican audience as a performer twists and twirls under the well patched 'Big Top.'

Small tent shows, called *carpas*, are also great fun. Many are operated by gypsies (*hungaros*).

NATIONAL LOTTERY

Almost every town has its lottery ticket sellers and most tourists ignore them, thinking they're cheats and con artists. This is far from the truth. The *lotería* (national lottery) is a major institution and its importance can be gauged by the fact that it is second only to the Social Security tax for federal revenues from a single source. Since 65 percent of that money goes back to the public as prizes, you might reconsider buying a ticket before you brush off that little old man lurking next to your elbow.

Prizes range from a few *pesos* to millions, though only a lucky few hit it big. The price of a ticket capable of winning the entire first prize may cost hundreds or even thousands of *pesos* itself. Tickets are broken down into parts, consisting of 20 fractions of a whole ticket. You have to buy all the fractions to win all of the prize. Each of the fractions has the number of the whole ticket and holders of the fractions divide the prize. You can buy from one-twentieth to twenty-twentieths (a whole) of a ticket.

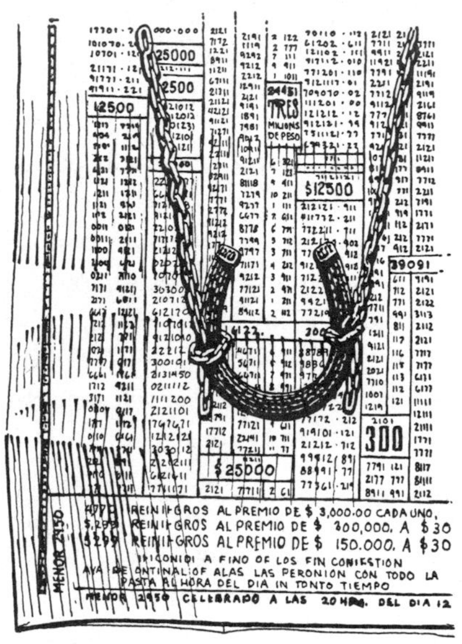

Sorteos, drawings, are held three times a week. The results are published in newspapers and posted in large sheets on the front of official lottery offices. If you win, you must pay a federal tax.

Since you can buy a lottery ticket for the price of a beer, I recommend that every tourist buy at least one; it may extend your vacation for a long time.

A new sports lottery, called *Pronósticos Deportivos Para La Asistencia Publica* (Sports Forecasts for the Public Welfare), PN for short, has recently been started. This is actually a soccer pool; tickets have to be marked with your guess at either win, lose or draw for each team and game. The ticket is then converted into a computer punched card and you are given a *talón* (ticket-stub). Drawings are held once a week. Until the success of this lottery is assured it is unlikely that tickets will be available outside of the largest cities as they require special processing equipment.

BEGGARS AND CON ARTISTS

Beggars tend to freak people out. It is a popular myth that every ragged beggar goes home at night to a well-fed family and empties bulging pockets into a wall safe or the trunk of a Mercedes. This is a good justification for not giving them anything and allows you to 'see through' the dirt and rags that have obviously been carefully applied to achieve the desired effect on the gullible tourist.

Because a few enterprising cripples and misshapen freaks have turned their problems into a means of support, people assume that every outstretched hand is a rip-off. Don't believe it. Most of the beggars you'll see are in bad shape and they need a handout to eat or to get a place to sleep, not for tires for the family car.

The most transparently phony beggars are small children trying to make a few *pesos* for a Coke and the movie.

Mexicans accept beggars as unfortunate facts of life. Store owners rarely turn down an outstretched hand, though they may give only a tiny sum. Beggars may be shooed from a restaurant or food shop but seldom leave without something to eat. Poor people, as well as the obviously affluent, will take pity on a *mendigo* (beggar); having very little themselves they can easily appreciate having nothing.

I always look upon whatever I give away as partial payment on a long-term karmic insurance policy. But if you absolutely don't want to give, don't; it is considered unlucky to offer something unless the sentiment behind the gift is genuine.

If you are approached by a beggar while you're eating or marketing and you dislike the idea of giving money, give something to eat. Often your suspicions about authenticity will disappear when the food is wolfed down hungrily.

A drunken beggar really upsets most people, but they ignore the fact that his poverty led to his begging and his begging to drinking. If you were dirt poor and had to face the prospect of having to beg to support your family, a few shots of *mezcal* would surely make things a bit more bearable.

If you are the type of person who feels guilty about not giving but really can't afford it, get a pocketful of small change. A dollar will go a long way.

Beggars usually bless you after you've donated (or curse you if you haven't) and they may go so far as to kiss your hand, the money or food. This can be embarrassing if you like to be inconspicuous, but it's just another one of those customs that you'll eventually get used to.

In tourist areas, particularly beach towns, you may run into a form of begging that is actually a con game. It often runs like this: the beggar, a child or an adult, has a 'stroke' or 'attack' near a group of tourists. The unsuspecting fish run to the victim's aid. Often it appears to be an epileptic fit and they naturally do all they can.

At the point of calling an ambulance or a doctor, the poor victim pulls together long enough to feebly extract a prescription from a pocket. A few croaking sounds and a final collapse impress the crowd with the severity of the illness.

At this point, the gringos may be approached by another person who has just 'happened along' and who helpfully translates the prescription and explains the situation. The situation is this: the victim has something wrong (epilepsy, heart trouble, etc.), has a prescription but no money and is asking for help.

The first time this trick happened to me the kid had the misfortune to pull his collapse on a hill of stinging ants. He rolled his eyeballs, did a few very convincing convulsions and then lapsed into what a 'passerby' described as a coma. The coma ended when the ants got in his ears.

If you are approached by people begging for money to buy medicine, take them to a drugstore if you can and get the druggist's help. Socialized medicine has helped a lot of people, but there are still many who, for one reason or another, are not eligible or able to get free medical aid. People often hike in from isolated villages for medicine for others who are unable to move and, with a druggist's advice and a small amount of money, you could very well save someone's life.

Unfortunately the unfilled prescription has been turned into a hustle by some people. I was approached by a woman asking for money for medicine and during her spiel I realized that I recognized her—and her routine, from the year before. "That's an old *receta*," I said. "I know you!" She snatched back the prescription and yelled indignantly, "It's not old! I've only had this one for three months!"

Finally, should you give a guy a few cents—or even a few dollars—and later see him emerge from a chauffeur driven Rolls, lighting a Cuban *puro* with a lottery ticket as he ducks into the Ambassador Hotel to meet his mistress for dinner, don't be bitter; "*¡Dios se lo pague!*", God will repay you!

WHOREHOUSES

Prostitution is an accepted and legal institution in most of Mexico. In the few states that have outlawed it, prostitution flourishes under cover and inflated prices.

Although women are not legally allowed in the average *cantina*, you'll sometimes see *putas* (prostitutes) in them. For this reason, a 'respectable' woman will not enter such a *cantina*, even if the bartender turns his head. Most prostitutes, however, are found in established houses located in groups on the outskirts of town.

Whorehouses invariably double as nightclubs with bands and dance floors. Because the majority are operated legally, whorehouses are considered just another place to meet friends and drink. There is rarely a furtive or secretive atmosphere.

The easiest way to locate *la zona* (the zone) is to ask a cab driver to take you there. Leave your car parked in a safer area, especially if you plan to get drunk. (See *Recommended Reading* for a whorehouse guide book.)

A typical whorehouse is usually a rather hilarious place. (Those that cater to tourists, especially along the border, are designed for foreign tastes and can't be considered typical.) Although the women in a border town bordello might be slightly overdone, they can't begin to approach the degree of high camp achieved by their sisters farther south.

Unless you're really horny, a visit to a small town whorehouse, one that caters to *campesinos* and local businessmen, is funny and surrealistic rather than erotic.

Christmas decorations are very popular and used lavishly in many houses to create that special mood designed to turn a nervous *campesino* into a snorting stud. The sensual glow of the red, blue and green bulbs gives just enough light to make the women clustered in a shadowy corner of the room appear tantalizing, muted and desirable.

Like colorful jungle birds they signal their potential mates with splashy purple, red, violet and crimson plumages. The real knockout women almost overwhelm the senses with hair piled high in massive 'beehives' and bleached a shocking white.

Just to rub it in they will occasionally wobble to the bar on elevating high heels, then bend over to whisper confidentially into the bartender's ear. This contortion raises the ballet type mini skirt, flashing an enormously broad and bare ass into the room.

Particularly aggressive women may approach the men themselves, but they usually wait for arrangements to be made through the bartender or pimp.

The main activities of the evening are drinking, shouting, bragging, dancing, singing and eating. Since a tiny whorehouse beer costs five times what it's worth, most of the profits of the house are made during preparations for the climactic act. The final splurge takes about as long as a trip to the urinal.

A visit to a whorehouse is expensive if you do anything more than sip a beer and watch the 'action.' The *macho* types seem to take particular pleasure in dropping hundreds of *pesos* in a few hours of intense drinking. Getting laid is incidental and, for many, a duty performed only to maintain and fulfill the *macho* image.

Although most women will haggle over prices, some whorehouses have them posted prominently over the bar. The bill of fare may range from, "Girl, one hour and room," to "Girl, all night, room, bottle of rum and six cokes."

In general, the price for getting laid isn't much more than that for a round of drinks. Prices are subject to increase on weekends and holidays.

During the holidays, many enterprising people build temporary *cantina*-whorehouses on the beach. The atmosphere is quite pleasant though the accommodations may be improvised and uncomfortable.

MEXICO: A Brief History

Mexican history is fascinating but very confusing. Did the Aztecs take over from the Toltecs or did Madero assassinate Carranza or Obregón or either one? To simplify telling the bad guys from the good guys just note which historical figures have city streets, dams and schools named after them—and which don't (Cortés and Porfirio Díaz among others).

1200 - 500 BC: The rise and decline of the Olmecs.

300 - 900 AD: The rise and fall of the Mayans.

1000 AD: Fall of the Toltecs.

1325: Founding of Tenochtitlán (Mexico City) by the Aztecs.

1440-1469: Reign of Emperor Moctezuma I, accompanied by much human sacrifice.

1519: Cortés lands near Veracruz and is mistaken for the returned god Quetzalcoatl. Moctezuma II tries to buy him off but the Spaniards join his enemies and attack.

1521: Cortés captures the Emperor, lays siege to Tenochtitlán and Moctezuma II is killed. Cuauhtémoc takes over, surrenders, and is killed. The pillage and Conquest begin. (Semi-official holiday observed on August 13.)

1521-1650: The *Conquistadores* replace human sacrifice with Christianity, the Inquisition, smallpox and slavery. Five percent survive and are put to work in the newly discovered silver mines.

1650-1800: Consolidation of Spanish control, including expansion into California, Texas and the Southwest. Jesuit order expelled. Spain gradually loses power in Europe.

16 Sept., 1810: Father Hidalgo utters *El Grito,** the cry for Independence. The 'Father of Mexico' calls for an end to slavery and *pulque* taxes and is killed a year later. Father Morelos continues the fight. (National holiday.)

1815: Morelos is captured and killed. (30 September, his birthday, is an unofficial holiday.)

1821: Mexico wins Independence, but General Iturbe declares himself Emperor, for which he is killed in 1824.

1824: Guadalupe Victoria becomes the first elected president but his term is followed by years of revolt, civil war and rapidly changing governments.

1836-48: Texas revolts, the U.S. declares war and takes half of Mexico at one gulp. Texans won't be trusted in Mexico for many years. The Caste War of Yucatan

*Some Mexicans have their own *'Grito.'* "*¡Viva México, hijos de la chingada!*"

erupts, but on the eve of victory the Mayans withdraw from a siege of Merida to plant their corn crops.

1857: A constitution is proclaimed. (National holiday on February 5.)

1859: Benito Juarez, a full blooded Zapotec Indian from Oaxaca, becomes president. The 'Abraham Lincoln' of Mexico initiates widespread liberal reforms. European forces invade the country to collect unpaid bills. (Juarez's birthday, March 21, is a national holiday.)

1862: May 5th: the French are defeated at Puebla but still manage to take over the Capital. Juarez escapes north, to the border (national holiday).

1864: Maximilian, brother of the Emperor of Austria, is declared Emperor of Mexico by the French. Juarez attacks.

1867: Mexico's last Emperor is captured and killed.

1867-1910: General Porfirio Díaz (*Don* Porfirio) controls the presidency for 35 years, creating a corrupt dictatorship. Mexico's resources are sold to the highest foreign bidder. Opposition is violently suppressed. Massive land grabs from the peasantry, forced labor camps, wage slavery and wholesale murder prepare the country for revolt.

1910-11: Pay close attention; this is where the real confusion begins.

Madero revolts in the North and is joined by Pancho Villa. Zapata rises in the South. Díaz is exiled. Madero becomes president but Zapata distrusts him and continues to lead peasant uprisings against the rich. (20 November is a national holiday honoring the Revolution.)

1913: Madero is executed by Huerta in a move supported by the U.S. Ambassador (quickly recalled to Washington for his sins). Carranza rises against Huerta, as do Villa and Obregón (who all distrust each other).

1914-15: Obregón ousts the dictator Huerta. Carranza occupies Mexico City but is forced out by Zapata and Villa, who then decide to go home instead of taking over. Obregón reoccupies the Capital and then attacks Pancho Villa and defeats him. Zapata grabs the Capital while Obregón is occupied with Villa but goes home to the state of Morelos once again and is there attacked by Obregón. (Have you got that?)

1917: Another Constitution. Carranza is elected president and assassinated, to be replaced by the hard-to-beat Obregón.

1919: Zapata is betrayed and murdered (presumbly on Obregón's orders).

1920: Pancho Villa gives up but is allowed freedom and later murdered (Obregón again?).

1925-30: The Cristero War between Church-led peasants and the central government erupts. Obregón's sins catch up: he is assassinated.

1930-37: Things finally begin to settle down.

1938: President Cárdenas shocks the world by daring to nationalize the foreign dominated oil industry. This occasion is now almost a religious holiday, especially since the discovery of vast new oil fields. The Mexican equivalent of the Boston Tea Party.

1946-52: Miguel Alemán is president and begins programs to increase national productivity.

1968: Hundreds of demonstrating students are massacred in Mexico City by the Army and professional goon squads on the eve of the Olympic Games.

1970-76: President Echeverria cripples the economy. The *peso* is devalued amid rumors of a military take-over.

1976-82: Portillo is elected president and institutes economic reforms. Mexico is discovered to have a great reserve of oil and gas. The U.S. Administration suddenly develops a craving for *tortillas* and new *amigos.*

2000: Mexico City, fulfilling it's predicted population of 35-40,000,000 souls, sinks beneath their weight and disappears into the ooze of Lake Texcoco, solving the smog and traffic problems.

WHAT THE HELL IS *THAT?*

In your travels to foreign lands you will encounter many strange and exotic customs. One of the most difficult to figure out is the Mexican bureaucracy's love of initials. A radio news broadcast might go: "JLP met with PRI and DF officials at UNAM to discuss PCM activities..." The confusion is mutual; Mexicans translate PPM as *Partido del Pueblo Mexicano* (Mexican People's Party), or *Partido Proletario Mexicano* or *Partido Popular Mexicano.*

E.U.M. — *Estados Unidos Mexicanos.* The United States of Mexico, the Republic's official name.

L.E.A. — Luis Echeverria Alvarez: Former president of Mexico (1970-76). His initials are being covered over on the sides of hills, fences and barns by those of his successor.

J.L.P. — Jose Luis Portillo: President of Mexico, 1976-1982.

LIC. — *Licenciado,* lawyer

PRI — *Partido Revolucionario Institutional:* The Institutional Revolutionary Party is the ruling political party and by far the largest in Mexico.

PAN — *Partido Acción Nacional:* National Action Party. The minority political party; said to be controlled by right-wing conservatives.

PMT — *Partido Mexicano de Trabajadores.* The Mexican Worker's Party.

PCM — *Partido Comunista Mexicano*

PARM — *Partido Auténtico Revolucionario Mexicano.* The Authentic Mexican Revolution Party.

PDM — *Partido Demócrata Mexicana*

PPS — *Partido Popular Socialista*

PPM	*Partido Popular Mexicano*
PSR	*Partido Socialista Revolucionario*
PRT	*Partido Revolucionario de Trabajadores* (Workers)
PST	*Partido Socialista de Trabajadores*
POAM	*Partido Obrero Agrario Mexicano.* Agrarian Worker's Party.
UGOCM	*Union General de Obreros y Campesinos Mexicanos*
CCI	*Centro Campesino Independente*
CTM	*Confederación de Trabajadores Mexicanos*
CROM	*Confederación Regional Obrero Mexicano*
CNOP	*Confederación Nacional de Organizaciones Populares: PRI* labor union.
CNC	*Confederación Nacional Campesina: PRI* union of *campesinos* (country people).
CROC	*Confederación Revolucionaria de Obreros y Campesinos: PRI* labor union syndicate.
CNEP	*Comisión Nacional de Erradicar Paludismo:* The National Commission to Eradicate Malaria. This abbreviation and a number painted on a house or building indicates that it has been checked and perhaps sprayed by a *paludismo* team. Malaria is almost nonexistent as a result of this program.
CDIA	*Centro de Investigaciones Agrarias.* Center for Agrarian Investigation, whatever that means.
INI	*Instituto Nacional Indigenista.* The Indigenous office, equivalent to the Bureau of Indian Affairs.
INAH	*Instituto Nacional de Antropología e Historia*
UNAM	*Universidad Nacional Autónoma de México.* The University of Mexico in Mexico City.
C.I.A.	The abbreviation for 'company' and not the organization that first came to your mind.
CFE	*Comisión Federal de Electricidad:* Federal Commission of Electricity.
D.F.	*Distrito Federal:* Federal District and comparable to Washington, D.C.
DDT	*Departamento de Tránsito:* Department of Transit or the pesticide.
DGN	A federal liquor standard. If your *tequila* bottle doesn't have this, it's not *legítimo.*

GL	*Gay Lussac:* GL 40° means 40 percent alcohol (80 proof).
M.N.	*Moneda Nacional.* National Currency, i.e., the Mexican Peso. Mexico uses this sign, $, for *pesos* or *M.N.*
ISSSTE	A federal social service agency. The name is so long I couldn't find anyone who remembered what it meant. It is popularly known as , *"Inútil Solicitar Sus Servicios Tardan Eternidades."* (Useless to Ask; Your Services Delayed Eternities.)
IMSS	*Instituto Mexicano de Seguro Social:* Mexican Institute of Social Security.
IMSSA	A manufacturer of truck bodies.
S.A.	*Sociedad Anónima:* Equivalent to 'incorporated' and used by companies that sell shares of stock.
S.A. de C.V.	*Sociedad Anónima de Capital Variable:* Same as *S.A.* but applies to very large companies.
SAG	*Secretaría de Agricultura y Ganado:* Secretary of Agriculture and Livestock (federal agency).
SEP	*Secretaría de Educación Publica*
SOP	*Secretaría de Obras Publicas:* Secretary of Public Works (federal agency).
SPF	*Servicio Público Federal:* A costly federal trucking license that allows the owner to operate throughout the country.
SRH	*Secretaría de Recursos Hidráulicos:* Secretary of Water Resources (federal agency).
Caseta Fiscal	Tax collection stations for commercial trucks. Many of these *casetas* serve only to line the pockets of local bigwigs.
Caseta Forestal	Inspection stations for forest products, all tightly controlled and taxed.
Censada	Census: A *Censada* sticker is placed on the door of each house that has been checked by the census taker.
Teepees	Large cement teepees seen in the countryside are government *(CONASUPO)* commodity warehouses. Yes, they do look rather odd.

THE BULLFIGHT

What is bullfighting? To the Spanish, who invented it, it's the *Fiesta Brava* (the Brave Celebration); to the Mexicans it's *Seda, Sangre y Sol* (Silk, Blood and Sun) and to most gringos it's a cruel, ritualized slaughter of innocent cattle.

Bullfighting, also known as the *corrida de toros* (running of the bulls), *lidia de toros* (fighting of bulls) and *sombra y sol* (shade and sun) is definitely not a sport. Some call it a spectacle while others see it as a play, filled with symbolism and hidden meaning. Siquieros, one of Mexico's most popular muralists, contemptuously referred to bullfighting as "the dance of the butchers."

Whatever you call it, one thing is certain: until you've seen a bullfight you can't begin to appreciate it. This, anyway, was what I kept telling myself as I shifted uncomfortably on the hard concrete bench, shielding my eyes from the glare of the late afternoon sun. In the ring below the young *matador* nervously maneuvered toward another attempt at a kill. The bull watched him warily, it's dusty black shoulders quivering with exhaustion and scarlet rivulets of blood. This would be the sixth *estocada* (sword thrust); less than two minutes remained for the *matador* to make hs kill or be ordered from the ring.

"Use it on yourself you *pinche*...!" a voice raged from behind us.

"We'll give the bull *your* ear!" Another frustrated *aficionado* cried, attempting to add injury to insult by hurling an expensive cowboy boot at the flustered *matador.*

"Put it up your...!"

The *matador* suddenly tensed, raising the bloody curved blade with his right arm, sighting along its length for *la cruz*, the crucial entry spot above and between the beast's heaving shoulders. The bull tossed its head stubbornly, whipping long streamers of red flecked saliva through the air. Then with a final agonized bellow, the bull's knees buckled, collapsing the huge body into the dust. The bull was dead, killed by a steady loss of blood rather than a sword thrust. The final moment of truth would have required a quick transfusion.

"*¡Cuidado compadre!*" Nacho said, ducking his head as a barrage of seat cushions, hats, shoes, and scathing insults were hurled upon the hapless bullfighter. He walked quickly toward the exit, his colorful *traje de luces* (suit of lights) the only bright spot in his miserable existence.

A large paper cup struck the humiliated *torero* (without making a kill no one would honor him with the title *matador*, killer) in the leg, soaking his immaculate white knee high stocking.

"They're throwing beer!" I laughed, amazed at the crowd's ferocious assault. A volley of cups arched through the air, causing the bullfighter to run for shelter.

"That is not beer, *compadre*," Nacho said, his face darkening with embarrassment. I looked high into the stands behind us; yes, I could see men fumbling with their pants, bending furtively over paper cups.

"A very poor fight," Nacho sighed, grimacing slightly as a half filled bottle of *José Cuervo* sailed over our heads and shattered in the aisle. Fifty feet to our right the air filled with hats. "What are they doing?" I asked, amazed to see a veritable tower of *sombreros* piled one on top of another. The majority were cheap woven straw of the type worn by *campesinos* (country people), but mixed in were others, obviously expensive.

"It is nothing!" Nacho answered. "The seats are of cement and cannot burn." As if on signal the huge mound of headgear erupted in a column of bright flame. The crowd renewed its attack with missles and expletives.

"Come, *compadre*," Nacho said. "It will only get worse." He rose to his feet and headed for the nearest exit, shoulders slumped with disappointment. By 'worse' I knew he meant the bullfights, not the crowd. It has been another washout.

A Typical Bullfight

The *corrida de toros* is not actually considered to be a fight. Rather, it is a demonstration of supreme control by the *matador* over himself, to dominate his natural fear; control over the bull, both to escape its deadly horns and to lead it through traditional cape passes; and control over the crowd. A good bullfighter works the audience with the skill of a nighttime talk show host. Some of the most popular fighters woo crowds (and through them, the judges) with flamboyant maneuvers. Kneeling before the bull, for example, with the *matador's* back to the wall, is a favorite. What most fans do not realize, however, is that the bull has no desire to collide with the wall and tends to avoid it.

The *corrida* is divided into three parts, called *tercios*. Following the preliminary formalities and the colorful parade of participants in the ring, the first bull is released.

The bull bursts from the holding pen at top speed. A few handfuls of dirt thrown on his back before he enters the ring enhance the effect of brute power as dust streams behind the animal. Cape men attract the bull's attention and work it around the ring. They take refuge behind stout barriers whenever the bull approaches, keeping the animal in motion and allowing the *matador* time to study its movements.

A trumpet sounds, beginning the first *tercio*, called *puyazos* (stabs). Two *picadores* enter on heavily padded horses. Their long lances will be used to weaken the bull's shoulder muscles, causing the head to sag downward. This helps to expose *la cruz*, the entry point for the killing sword thrust that will end the fight.

The less experienced *picador* goes first, thrusting his lance into the thick mass of shoulder muscle. The heavy metal point, the *puya*, is 8.5 centimeters long (3 1/3 inches) with a guard to prevent deeper penetration.

After the first thrust the senior *picador* moves in, giving the bull a second and perhaps a third stab. If too many *puyazos* are given, the bull will be seriously weakened and may even die. The crowd invariably screams disapproval if more than one or two stabs are ordered by the judge. In rare cases a ferocious bull may be stabbed more than three times.

The *matador* watches the bull's behavior during the first *tercio*, assessing its strength. If he is inspired he will do cape passes, called *tercio de quites*, between each attack by the *picadores*.

When the horsemen retire from the ring, the trumpet signals the second *tercio*, called *banderillas*. Men on foot, and sometimes the *matador* himself, stab brightly decorated darts, about two and a half feet long, into the bull's shoulders. Three pairs of *banderillas* are placed, alternating from one side of the shoulders to the other. This supposedly replaces the image of a horse and rider as the enemy with that of a man on foot, and makes the bull aware of danger from all sides. This *tercio* is not considered dangerous, though it calls for some fancy footwork to avoid the animal's horns as the darts are placed. Following the fight, the *banderillas* are sold to fans or given to special friends and guests of the *matador*.

The last *tercio* is what most spectators are there for: capework by the *matador* and the 'moment of truth,' the final fatal *estocada* (sword thrust).

The trumpet call sounding the third *tercio* also begins a 16 minute countdown. The bull must be killed within that time. *Aficionados* (fans) will be watching closely; good fighting is a thing of subtleties, not foolhardy displays of bravery or theatrical posturing. The *matador's* performance is judged according to four traditional criteria.

Aguantar (restraint, control) is the first—the positioning of the bull by the *matador* rather than vice versa. The bull will select a *querencia* (favorite spot) to defend, but the *matador* wants things his way. If a lady friend is in the stands he will probably use the cape to position the bull directly in front of her. Most fighters place the bull in good view of the judge and more expensive seats.

The *matador* is also judged by posture, called *parar*. Ideally he will stand fully erect, feet close together, not allowing the bull to force him to move as he works it with the cape.

Mandar (command) is control of the bull through movements of the cape and *matador's* body. The bull becomes an enormous and very angry puppet, drawn to the *matador* but not allowed to intimidate him. A fighter who commands the bull's passes is said to *torear* (from *toro*, bull). If the bull takes charge, forcing the *matador* to follow him around in order to demonstrate his cape work, it's called *dar pases* (giving passes). The crowd derisively chants "*¡Toro! ¡Toro!*" to tell the judge and *matador* that the bull is running the show.

El temple or *templar*, style and timing, is fourth. It is based on such things as the distance between the bull and the cape during a pass, the distance between the cape and fighter (holding it at arm's length isn't good) and the distance between the bull and the man. If the *torero* holds excellent posture (*parar)* but is run over and trampled by the bull, he has—or had—lousy *templar*.

The *faena* is the killing of the bull. When the *matador* feels that the bull (and the crowd) are ready, he exchanges the large cape for a smaller killing cape, called a *muleta*

Removing his hat, he approaches the judge for permission to kill The bull is dedicated, sometimes to the crowd (by holding his hat up to them). The crowd receives the honor with cheers but will expect a good kill.

Once again, the *matador* positions the bull. Before it can charge he raises the sword, sights and meets its rush with a quick cape pass and thrust.

A good *estocada* (sword thrust) will kill the bull almost instantly. The gore involved, however, may detract from 'the moment of truth' if you're squeamish about gallons of hot blood. A poor thrust can be very dangerous; deflected swords have punctured more than one unfortunate *matador.*

When the bull drops, an assistant uses a short dagger to give a *coup de grâce.* If it's still alive and standing another attempt is made by the *matador.* Twelve minutes after the beginning of the *tercio* the trumpet gives first warning, *el primer aviso.* Two minutes later, with the *matador* worried, the crowd angry and the bull suffering multiple stab wounds, the second warning sounds. At 16 minutes the *matador* is ordered from the ring, disgraced. The bull is lured back to the corrals by tame cattle and then slaughtered. The crowd loses what little remains of its self control.

A good *corrida* ends with the awarding of one or more parts of the bull to the *matador.* One ear is good, two are great and the addition of the tail is fantastic—the crowd will be on its feet and screaming.

One fight quickly follows another and six bulls will be killed by three *matadores* in a typical *corrida.*

Tickets

There are two basic types of tickets: *sol* (sunny side of the ring) and *sombra* (shady side). The *sombra* seats cost substantially more; unless you're sensitive to heat and sunlight they aren't worth the extra money. I prefer the *sol* seats for another reason: that's where the average over-excitable fan sits and where the insults and crowd reactions are most colorful. With a hat and sunglasses you should be comfortable. (The tradition of *sombra y sol* is imported from Spain, where the afternoon sun is much hotter than in Mexico.)

The seats closest to the ring are called *barreras.* In small rings the sunny side is General Admission, first come, first seated. In larger rings there are various sub-categories. The more you pay, the closer to the action you get.

Ticket scalping is popular for all Mexican sporting events (and even movies). If you don't get to the ring in time you may be approached by a *revendedor* (scalper). The mark-ups are considerable, but a real *aficionado* will pay the price.

Seasons and Fights

The main season, called the *temporada formal* or *temporada grande* is in wintertime. The off-season is summertime and is called the *temporada chica.* Fights (*corridas*) are held on Sunday afternoons, usually at four o'clock. Fights from Mexico City are often televised.

Novilladas, novice fights, are held in summertime and run the risk of being rained out. The *novillero*, novice fighter, fights *novillos*, young bulls of at least 335 kilos (837 pounds). The full *matador* fights bulls of at least 435 kilos (957 pounds) though bulls as heavy as 800 kilos (1760 pounds!) have been used.

A *novillero* becomes a full *matador* at a fight called the *alternativa*. The novice (who in spite of the term has much experience) is sponsored by a known *matador*. A bullfighter's prestige is very important; if the *alternativa* is bungled the novice is disgraced and his sponsor publicly embarrassed.

Alternativas can be held in any bull ring, but Mexico City's has much more class than one in the 'provinces.' If the event is held outside the Capital it must be reconfirmed there (or in Madrid) in another fight, called a confirmation (*confirmación de alternativa*).

A *corrida mixta* is the only time both full *matadores* and *novilleros* fight on the same program. The *matadores* go first.

The Bulls

The average Mexican fighting *toro* weighs almost half a ton. They are lighter than Spanish bulls and considered inferior to them, though six Mexican bulls from the Mimiahuapam Ranch were sent to Madrid in 1971 and supposedly fought well.

There are about 150 *ganaderias* (cattle ranches) that raise *ganado bravo* (brave, fierce cattle). About 50,000 bulls, cows and calves live on almost 500,000 acres of land. They are carefully isolated from humans and constantly culled to eliminate weaknesses in the breed.

Bulls must be delivered to the *plaza de toros* four days before the fight (Thursday if the *corrida* is Sunday). During this time they are weighed, graded and generally checked for defects or illness.

The worst calamity to befall a *ganaderia* is to have its bulls called *mansos* (meek). Although great care is taken to produce mean, aggressive bulls, there's no guarantee that one won't turn chicken in the ring. If the bull doesn't display the proper degree of ferocity, the judge orders it back to the corral for immediate slaughter. A *manso* is replaced by one of two alternates. If both alternates are used and a third bull comes out *manso*, instead of getting *puyazos* (stabs) it receives four pairs of black *banderillas*. These have points twice as large as normal. The fight goes on, but the *ganaderia* is in disgrace and its bulls are banned for one years.

Six bulls are killed in the average *corrida*. The carcasses are usually dressed and butchered on the spot (in big cities they are sold to meat packers) and the meat is sold to the public. It ends up in the stewpots of the poor and the snack plates of local *cantinas*. Any leftover blood is also sold and eaten, usually in soup or sausages. In past times the *matador* received the carcass as payment for the fight.

Bullrings

There are three classes of *plaza de toros:* third class, seating less than 4,000 persons; second class, 4,000 to less than 10,000 and first class, 10,000 and above. The *Plaza México*, largest in the world, seats (crams) 50,000 people and is twice as large as any in Spain.

In small towns, temporary bullrings of poles, sticks and planks will be literally lashed together during special *fiestas* and fairs. The fights in these improvised rings have all the excitement and uncertainty of small town rodeos in the U.S. No one quite knows what is going to happen—or to whom.

Bullfight Suggestions

•Don't worry about understanding the details of the fight until you've appreciated it as an experience. You don't have to know the names of all the players and the diameter of a baseball to enjoy the World Series.

•Watch three or four fights before taking photos. This will give you time to become familiar with the rituals and to plan your shots.

•Buy tickets in advance if you can or go at least an hour or two early. Take binoculars if you have them, especially if the bull ring is large.

•Take something to sit on, a hat and sunglasses.

•Carry enough small change to buy whatever beer or sodas you'll want. Vendors work very fast and don't like to make change or forget to return it.

•Don't carry knives. At many bullrings male fans are given a quick search for weapons. The smallest pen knife may be confiscated; getting it back would be difficult to impossible.

•If you don't like the fight—leave. Exclamations of disgust are an insult to those who see it differently.

•Watch for pickpockets, especially in big bullrings. Try to leave handbags in your hotel or car (out of sight). Keep a firm grip on everything else, particularly during hectic crowd scenes at the end of the fights.

•Each fight is different. If one is a flop, don't lose interest; the next might make the morning papers.

"*¡Olé!*" The crowd roared, thousands of *aficionados* leaping to their feet. The third bull of the afternoon dropped into the blood soaked dust, killed by a perfect *estocada*. Nacho mopped perspiration from his brow with a huge yellow bandana as he joined in cheering the *matador*. To my right an obviously well-off young rancher sailed his Stetson into the ring; his wife matched his enthusiasm by throwing down her leather purse. The *matador* took a long drink from the wineskin he'd caught in mid-air, then reached down to throw back the hat and bag, which quickly passed from hand-to-hand to their owners.

"¡Nos tocó la suerte, compadre!" Nacho grinned, draining his cup of *Corona*. Luck had indeed touched us—"and it's about time," I thought to myself, one more lousy Sunday at the bullfights and I'd take up ping pong. After many *corridas* with Nacho and his friends, I'd picked up plenty of trivia, but felt nothing more than a sense of boredom and distaste for the actual fighting.

"Today you shall see the difference," Nacho had assured me, adding an onimous *"¡Ojal!"* (God willing!). From the first charge of the first bull I'd sensed a strong current of anticipation in the crowd. The *matador* must have felt it too. He worked the bull through an especially daring series of passes before the kill, whipping the fans into a frenzy. The judge awarded him one ear, seconded by the cheers of the spectators.

"Vamos a ver, vamos a ver," Nacho muttered as the second bull burst from the pens. His hopeful "We'll see," was reflected by others seated around us. Each successful fight dramatically increased their excitement and enjoyment. But each new encounter was like a fresh hand of poker; *¡ojalá!* that it be good.

The second *matador*, a young man noted for theatrics, dropped to his knees in the center of the ring, facing the bull's head-on charge with outstretched arms. The crowd cheered its approval.

*"Villamelones"** Nacho spat disgustedly, though his eyes sparkled with pleasure. The huge animal thundered past the *matador*, tossing its head wildly from side to side. The rest of the fight, as if in appeasement to traditionalists like Nacho, followed a more classic pattern. With each cape pass the crowd's fervor increased; a storm of *¡olés!* erupted at the kill, once again almost perfectly executed.

The third bull was small. The placard announcing its weight brought indignant shouts of *"Becero"* (calf) from the stands. With two excellent fights under their belts the fans were now prepared to go wild with happiness—or mad with frustration.

Nacho signalled a passing beer vendor. The young man popped the caps from two bottles, pouring the cold brew into paper cups. He stowed the empty bottles in his bucket, safely away from anyone who might use them to bean an unpopular *matador*.

"¡Para emocionarnos!" Nacho laughed (To excite ourselves!), downing half the beer in one thirsty gulp.

In spite of its small size, the third bull had extraordinary stamina. The fight was fast and intense, the *matador* handling the animal with dangerously close *natural* passes. Now, as the team of horses was hitched to the corpse, the crowd began chanting, *"¡Vuelta! ¡Vuel...ta! ¡Vuel...ta!,"* demanding that this bull be dragged around the ring to honor its courage. The horsemen received the order from the judge and the crowd went wild. When the body had completed its circuit and the *matador* had displayed the two ears he'd been awarded, the *plaza* settled down in anticipation of the next bull.

**Villamelón* is a derogatory term for a fan who applauds a move that is not as dangerous or as well executed as it may appear. Gringos who follow the fights are notorious *villamelones*.

"Each *matador* fights two bulls," Nacho explained, "and usually keeps the best for his second fight." The fourth fight was conducted in almost total silence, broken only by perfected chorused "*¡Olés!*" as the *matador* worked the bull directly below us, favoring the cheaper seats with a magnificent performance. As he approached the judge for permission to kill, the tension in the hot afternoon air was almost unbearable.

The *matador* raised his hat to the crowd, dedicating the bull to them. The entire *plaza* exploded with cheers.

"*¡'ora sí!*" Nacho said excitedly (This is it!). The bull was worked into position and once again the *sol* (sun) seats were given the best view. Then, at the moment the sword was raised for the final killing pass, the *matador* suddenly turned his back on the bull, raising his hat once again to the fans. I heard Nacho suck in a great breath as we were given this unusual and dangerous second dedication. A few moments later the bull lay dead at the *matador's* feet.

My ears rang with shouts and cries as hysterical fans leaped from their seats and poured over the guard rails, vaulting barricades and jumping into the bullring. A veritable blizzard of cushions, hats, shoes and clothing showered upon the proud *matador*. A brass band struck up a tune, barely audible beneath the cries of adulation. I took a swig from a passing brandy bottle, then another from a wineskin. I climbed onto the concrete bench to join Nacho. His hat sailed away to honor the fighter and the bull. "Throw it, *compadre!*" He urged, tapping the brim of my own *sombrero*. And there it went, curving into the lengthening shadow that crept across the bloody arena. "*¡Olé!*" we cried, "*¡Olé!*"

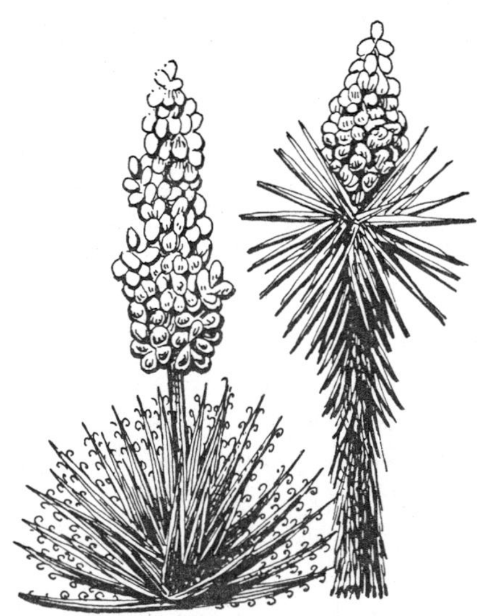

Broadleaf yucca

BUYING THINGS

Self-control or spending spree?...Bartering...Importing schemes...Sandals...Indian clothing...Blankets and sarapes...Pottery...Artifacts... Hammocks: buying and hanging...Parrot fever...

Mexico offers the traveller limitless opportunities to part with money for various art and craft items. Even the stingiest tourists find their hands twitching toward wallets and purses, rationalizing, "Well, hell! It's only ten *pesos*!" This is the type of logic that leads to overloaded luggage and unbalanced budgets.

Shopping and Bartering

Successful shopping isn't just a matter of hard bartering. In many cases, particularly with small crafts, the price is so low to begin with that it's almost no consideration.

Look around before buying, even if it's just a fast stroll through several shops or one large market. How many times have I bought the Deal Of A Lifetime and then found one even nicer at the next stall? Mexican vendors appreciate the diligent shopper and you may well find them bringing out better and better things to tempt you.

Although most items will be cheapest in the town or shop where they're made, the best overall selection is most often found in large markets and shops. For the person who doesn't care to visit each village in an area, the few extra *pesos* spent in a shop are not that important. Some dealers have exclusive rights to a particular person's product and these are often the best quality things to be found. Many Indian artisans will peddle their work from shop to shop and though you might strike a bargain with them on occasion, they'll usually ignore your offers.

Note: *Fonart,* a chain of government shops, offers a wide variety of typical arts and crafts at set prices. Their prices are a bit steep but the selection and quality are quite good.

Always buy the best quality you can afford, particularly if the price difference between it and something inferior is not great. When you see something really incredible, don't let it get away just because the seller holds out for an extra *peso* or two. When you go home empty-handed, that small sum will haunt you.

Bartering for expensive art and craft items can be a long process. To become adept, you'll just have to practice. Many shy or impatient people say, "But this is Art! How can you be so crude as to haggle over it?" The answer to this is that haggling over the price, whether it's for a potato or a fine carving, is considered proper and is expected; that's why the price will come down if you work at it. I've yet to see a vendor or artisan take a loss because some skillful gringo out-bartered him.

By not bartering you will corrupt the elaborate pricing system (which is based on the assumption that everyone with any sense will haggle) and lose the opportunity to participate in a friendly communication with the other person. (See *Markets and Stores: Bartering*.)

Imports: Fortune or Fantasy?

Within the last few years, a tremendous number of shops in the U.S. have begun handling Mexican imports. As a result, many enterprising people have gone to Mexico with the bright idea of making money by buying arts and crafts to resell at home. Most of them fail miserably and find themselves the reluctant owners of 17 *sarapes,* 34 shirts and hundreds of pounds of pottery.

Our own experience and that of many friends has been that the only items which can be easily and consistently sold in the U.S. are those that can go for less than $20 (and preferably, less than $15) and still give a three to five hundred percent profit. Unless you have a definite order or an excellent outlet, any expensive item, whether it's an incredible work of art or not, will be difficult to unload. It's easy enough to sell a 5-cent pottery cup for a dollar, but a $100 weaving, even though worth hundreds more, won't sell easily.

The average shop—and the average person—prefers things that aren't too far out. Shirts, simple skirts, blouses, sandals, small pottery items, wooden carvings and utensils, jewelry and inexpensive musical instruments will usually sell for a good profit and with reasonable ease. When buying on speculation, *never buy anything you can't afford and wouldn't like to keep.*

U.S. import regulations can complicate your scheme to buy and re-sell a hundred tortoise shell ashtrays or two bales of hand-woven pot holders. Before spending the money write to U.S. Customs, P.O. Box 7118, Washington, D.C. 20044. Ask for copies of these booklets: *U.S. Import Requirements, Customs Rulings On Imports* and *Marking of Country of Origin.* For $2.50 they'll send you a 100 page book, *Exporting to the United States.* For other publications relating to importing, write to the same address and ask for a catalog. It could save you a great deal of money and red tape.

SHOPPING

The following discussion and suggestions cover only the most obvious and irresistable things you'll find to spend your money on. For more detailed information check your local library; many fine (and usually expensive) books have been written on all aspects of Mexican arts and crafts. By jotting down the names of specific villages, markets and artisans you can save a great deal of guesswork about where to go and what to buy. (See *Appendices: Market Days,* and *Recommended Reading.*)

Sandals

Almost every tourist will purchase at least one pair of *huaraches* (sandals). A good pair, with well-nailed or sewn tire tread soles and strong leather straps will last for years. *Huaraches* vary in price, depending on the intricacy of the work involved and the type of leather and sole used.

•"Hey, pick me up a pair of sandals, would you?" is a request that all too often results in someone returning home with the wrong sized sandal for a friend. Don't rely on guesswork; take an outline drawing of both feet or measure them from heel to toe and convert this to centimeters. (See *Appendices: Conversion Tables.*)

•A non-adjustable sandal should fit snugly when new. Will you be wearing socks with your sandals? If so, wear them when you try a pair of *huaraches* on. Sandals made of leather stretch with use. The thinner the leather, the more it will stretch.

•Break in new sandals by soaking them in fresh water. (Salt rots leather.) Now wear them until they dry. Continue this process (it can take up to two weeks if the leather is thick) until the sandals have shaped themselves to your feet.

•Sandals with extra thick tire tread soles are heavy and not very flexible. I much prefer a pair with average or slightly thin soles. *Ule de orilla* (sidewall rubber) is more flexible but wears faster than *ule de centro* (center, treaded rubber).

•Check the fastenings carefully. Some straps are wired to the sole and will chafe through faster than a looped or sewn-on strap. Cheap buckles never last long and may cut through the straps. The longest lasting sandals are either a basket weave, semi-shoe type or have two or three wide leather straps. The latter type is open and cool.

•Sandal makers will copy your sandals for a reasonable price. Tire tread soles can also be put on your shoes or boots but beware, it will make them much heavier and less flexible.

Indian Clothing

The greatest problem when shopping for Indian clothing and fabrics (*ropa típica* or *indígena*) is deciding which things you can possibly do without. Comparison shopping is *important* as price and quality may vary greatly from one vendor or weaver to another.

Small shops often handle old things and these are likely to be the best examples (and the best buys) of clothing, belts, bags and ceremonial or decorative weavings.

Markups on fabric goods are usually quite steep, but unless you're in the area where an article is made, vendors may stand firm on a high price. *Oaxaca* shirts are sold to tourists in other parts of the country for as much as in the U.S.

Almost all colored fabrics are *firme* (color fast), but they should be washed with care and in cold water (at least at first). Shrinkage is a problem; most large shirts will be reduced to the equivalent of 'small' after washing.

Buttons rarely last long on most shirts so you might prefer a pullover style instead. Don't be surprised if the seams aren't very strong; it's expected that the customer (or his wife) will go over them carefully with a needle and thread.

Blankets and *Sarapes*

Unless your blanket or *sarape* will be used strictly for decoration or a rug, don't buy one that feels scratchy. Many weavers use coarse, uncleaned wool, often mixed with stiff *burro* hair. These blankets won't get softer with use but actually scratchier, especially after they pick up a few burrs and twigs in your travels.

The finest blankets and *sarapes* and the best selections are found right where the weaving is done, often a small factory. Roaming blanket vendors are crafty and adept barterers; many tourists pay two or three times the actual value of a blanket.

Price is determined by wool content, weight, pattern and coloring. A brightly colored, mixed wool and cotton blanket may cost one fourth the price of an all wool, vegetable dyed one about the same weight. A thick narrow blanket will cost as much as a thin wide one.

The price range in *sarapes* is great. It takes diligent shopping to find a really good one; the market seems glutted with those made for tourists.

Artifacts

Freshly baked *ídolos* (idols) are a big business in Mexico and Guatemala. Now that the United States has finally prohibited the importation of genuine artifacts, copies and reproductions are increasing in quality and price. Some, in fact, are made from genuine pre-Columbian molds. The clay may not have baked a thousand years ago, but the design is authentic. Many of these fine reproductions cost as much as the real thing did in the days of unrestricted artifact trading.

Genuine artifacts of small size or very common design are sometimes sold in shops. The Mexican government cracks down only when the object is of significant historical or monetary value. When in doubt, ask someone. The penalty for possession of unauthorized artifacts is stiff. When in doubt ask for an export permit from the seller.

Antiques are legally sold to tourists and may be imported into the U.S.

Pottery

Alfarería (pottery) is almost everywhere in Mexico. The variety is so great, in fact, that the average shopper could fill a semi truck if given the opportunity. If you like pottery, prepare to be dazzled.

The following excerpt* from *A Potter's Mexico* is included to clarify the problem of possible lead poisoning when using pottery for food and beverages. Your only other consideration when buying a piece of pottery should be how to put it in your suitcase without breaking the straps.

*Reproduced courtesy of the University of New Mexico Press, Albuquerque, New Mexico. Thanks.

"1. Acid foods and drinks should not be stored in glazed vessels.
2. The daily use of glazed pitchers and drinking vessels for acid drinks such as orange juice, lemon or limeade, or tomato juice should be avoided.
3. Glazed cooking pots should not be used to prepare such acid foods as tomatoes, or such fruits as limes, lemons, oranges or plums.
4. The Mexican *cazuela*, or stewpot, though an ideal shape for tossed salads, should not be used with dressings containing vinegar or lemon or lime juice; certainly, not on a regular basis.
5. Under no circumstances should *green-colored* glazed pottery be used for any drinks or moist foods. Copper, the green colorant, dramatically increases the lead release from lead glazes.

In all probability, the occasional use of Mexican glazed pottery, even for the most acid of foods and drinks, would pose no problem for the average user, though in a few rare instances it might."

From *A Potter's Mexico* by Irwin and Emily Whitaker.

Hammocks

The buying and selling of *hamacas* is a tricky business; a normally honest craft vendor may suddenly become sly and tricky when offering a tourist a hammock. The reason, perhaps, is that hammocks themselves are complicated, with many subtle variations in construction, materials, quality and comfort. I've met innumerable tourists who swore their hammock was "the biggest and the best" when in fact it was average or less. To avoid getting something other than what you want, study the following suggestions very carefully before shopping.

•The best hammocks come from Yucatan; Merida, the capital, has the widest selection. There are many shops offering a bewildering variety of hammocks, from cheap twine ones to fabulously comfortable (and expensive) linen models. (Good hammocks are also made in the state of Oaxaca, but they don't compare to those from Yucatan.)

•The largest hammocks, called *matrimonial* (marriage size) can hold two people with no crowding at all. Most tourists are so amazed at the size of an authentic single hammock that they are easily convinced it is a *matrimonial*. What's the difference? A genuine *matrimonial* will be about 16 feet long (at least one third of this the woven section) weigh 4-1/2 to 5-1/2 pounds, stretch out to 10-16 feet *in width* without pulling too hard. It should have 100 or more pairs of strings at each end (these string pairs are called *brazos*).

•A medium sized hammock, ideal for sleeping one adult or two kids, should weigh 2-1/2 to 3-1/2 pounds, with slightly smaller measurements and string count than the marriage size. ***Warning:*** A medium hammock is often sold as a *matrimonial.*

•The best hammocks are pure cotton. Nylon end strings are becoming common but they are inferior to natural fibers. The thinner the thread, the better. Thin thread is longer fibered, wears better and is more comfortable than thick threads. Cotton resists stretching, is more color fast (*firme*) and just plain feels better than synthetics.

•The edges are very important. There should be 10 to 16 strings along the edge, well secured to the body of the hammock. This is critical for maintaining the shape and to prevent uncomfortable sagging.

•Check the weave. The tighter it is the more resilient and comfortable the hammock will be. A good hammock will be double or triple woven and the holes between the thread will be small. When one person is in a *matrimonial* the weave looks almost solid, like cloth. A *matrimonial* is said to require 5 miles of thread, a medium 3 miles. Measure it. The fewer splices the better.

•Check the end loops. They should be thick and tightly wrapped.

•A *ciguana* hammock has a beeswax coating on the threads. These feel silky and are especially resistant to dampness and mildew.

•Hammocks can be ordered custom made. Ask for the best quality string and construction. Specify the dimensions; I once ordered a hammock and got one that was well made but much too small. Mayan Indians tend to be shorter than gringos and their hammocks are sized accordingly.

•Hammocks should be washed in cold water, by hand. Store them in a mouse and moth proof container; my first Yucatecan hammock lasted 11 years before being eaten by vicious rodents, those rotten little...

Hanging a Hammock

The procedure for properly hanging a hammock is simple but even a simple mistake will destroy the entire purpose—to have a comfortable bed.

The method used to attach the ropes to the ends of the hammock is important. Special S-shaped iron hooks are available, but if you don't have them use a short piece of wood (see drawing). The ropes can be tied directly to the hammock ends, but the knots soon become too tight to untie and may chafe through the end of the hammock after long use.

The hammock should be tied so that it hangs symmetrically; that is, both ends should be the same distance from the ground and tied with equal lengths of rope. The middle of the hammock should be lower than the ends but not so low that your chin touches your knees when you lie in it. The worst mistake is to hang a hammock too low. It takes only a few scrapes against the ground to weaken or break the strings, even on a new hammock.

Once the hammock is hanging properly, you shouldn't pile in and lie any old way you want. There is a proper position for the body. Lie at a 30 to 45 degree angle to the long axis of the hammock. This prevents the hammock from sagging and stretching and gives your body the type of support needed for comfortable sleeping. Don't let your friends violate this rule, either, or you'll soon find that your hammock will stretch and won't be as comfortable as it should be.

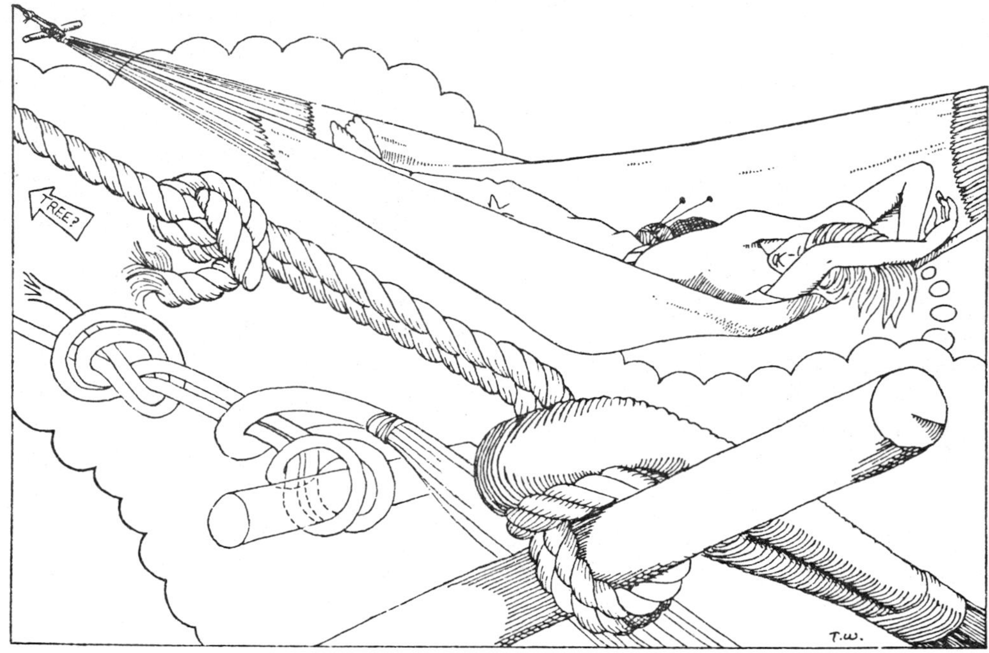

Sleeping in a hammock, particularly outdoors, is wonderful. Lie with a blanket underneath you, especially if there's a breeze. Mosquitoes enjoy a rear attack, but a blanket will stop them.

Getting into the hammock and keeping covered up with a blanket at the same time can be a real trick. First of all put a blanket cape-like over your back, allowing enough length so that your feet will be covered when you get in. Clutching another blanket to your chest like a parachute, back slowly into the hammock until it's safe to fall backwards. If you haven't opened the hammock far enough you will do a neat back flip—to the great delight of anyone nearby. Once inside, form the blankets into a cocoon. If another person is getting in, the procedure is the same except that the second person just drops in next to the first without being wrapped in a blanket.

Before doubling or coupling in a hammock, check it to insure that the ropes and whatever it's tied to will take the strain. If you're in a crude *palapa* (at least one built from my instructions) this is especially important. The posts, if not properly placed, will be pulled together by your weight and could knock you silly.

Will There Be Any Hammocks In Heaven?

I sure hope so. And if, as Steve predicts, I pass down to decidedly hotter areas, I'll want one there, too. For a portable bed, couch and lazing area, a good hammock can't be beat.

A number of friends and readers have asked us for information and assistance on buying hammocks. To make things easier on everyone, we are buying a large number of hammocks at one time. The idea is that we'll all get a hammock that we know is good and at a *fair* price. The hammocks are made in the Yucatan and are the best we can find. I haven't measured each to verify that it has four and a half miles of thread, but I'm sure you'll be satisfied. For more details, please write to me c/o John Muir Publications, Dept. H, Box 613, Santa Fe, New Mexico 87501.

Parrots

"Hey! Far out! You've got a bird!"

—"Yeah."

"That's really far out. Is it a parrot?"

—"Yeah."

"Far out! What's its name?"

—"Farout."

"Far out?"

—"Yeah."

"Where'd you get it?"

—"Guatemala."

"Really? I've always wanted a parrot. Are they much of a hassle?"

—"Yeah."

"Far out. I notice that...well...uh, you have a lot of parrot stuff on your shoulder. Can you housebreak them or anything?"

—"No."

"Gee, that's too bad. Does he talk?"

—"Yeah."

"A lot?"

—"Yeah."

"Wow! Far out! Hey, do you mind if my friends see him?"

—"No."

"Far out!"

"Far out!"

"Far out!"

"Hey! You've got two of them!"

—"Yeah."

"Any trouble getting them back into the states?"

—"Yeah."

"What do you have to do?"

—"Here, read this letter I just got."

"Dear Mr. Franz:

This is in response to your letter requesting information concerning the importation of personally-owned pet birds...

Because of outbreaks of exotic Newcastle disease, the U.S. Department of Agriculture has placed a ban, effective August 24, 1972, upon importation of all avian species with certain exceptions. One of the exceptions is the importation of not more than two personally-owned pet birds. The requirements for such importations are as follows:

I. That such birds,
   (1) are not known to be affected with or exposed to any communicable disease of poultry;
   (2) are properly caged when presented for entry;
   (3) are entered at designated ports of entry;
   (4) are found upon veterinary inspection at the port of entry to be free of signs of poultry diseases.

II. The owner will,
   (1) furnish a notarized declaration under oath or affirmation stating that the bird(s) have been in his possession for a minimum of 90 days preceeding importation and that such birds have not been in contact with poultry or other birds, including association with other avian species at exhibitions or in aviaries, (this declaration can be made at the port of entry);
   (2) execute a form (available from the Federal inspector at the port of entry) stating that the birds will be maintained in confinement in his personal possession separate and apart from all poultry and other birds for a minimum period of 30 days following importation at a place approved by the Deputy Administrator, Veterinary Services, APHIS, USDA (the designated place will usually be the home of the owner),
      a. the birds will be made available for health inspection by a Department inspector upon request until released;
      b. the owner will notify immediately the appropriate Federal officials in the state of destination if any signs of disease are noted or if the bird(s) die during the period of confinement."

The regulations for importing birds change quite frequently. For the latest information, write to:

UNITED STATES DEPARTMENT OF AGRICULTURE
Animal and Plant Health Inspection Service
Veterinary Services
Federal Center Building
Hyattsville, Maryland 20782

"...if you like pottery, prepare to be dazzled."

BAJA CALIFORNIA

A different feeling...Driving: conditions and precautions...The new Transpeninsular Highway...Money...Shopping...Food...Public transportation...Hitching...Camping, Fishing, Diving...

Several years ago I met a turtle fisherman from southern Baja who was vacationing with relatives in mainland Mexico. After a few shots of *tequila* he began ranting about the attractions of life in Baja, describing it as a veritable paradise on earth. At that time the Peninsula was still divided into a southern territory and a northern state. Like the territory of Quintana Roo, the Baja was considered one of Mexico's last frontiers.

"What makes it so different?" I asked, surprised to hear him claim that he found the mainland of Mexico to be like another country.

"Different?" he said, "Well, I'll tell you." He lifted his glass for a long drink, then slapped it back down on the bar, empty. "We've got about 2,000 kilometers of desert and mountains between us and southern California and another few hundred kilometers of *mar abierta* (open sea) between us and Mexico. We're an island!"

Baja California's isolation is now ending, due largely to the opening in 1973 of the Transpeninsular Highway and regular passenger jet and ferry service between La Paz and points in both the U.S. and mainland Mexico. But in spite of increased accessibility and tourism, Baja still remains distinctly different. Hundreds of years of isolation created a way of life that can't be erased with a two-lane highway.

Driving

Baja can be an easy drive or it can be a killer; it all depends on how well you're prepared and what you want to subject yourself and your vehicle to. When the Transpeninsular Highway was completed but not yet officially opened, Lorena and I drove its entire length, about 1,050 miles, in a 20 year old station wagon, badly overloaded and suffering from terminal fatigue. We never got stuck, never ran out of gas and never had to perform any miracles of mechanical improvisation. It was just a long drive. A few years before that, however, we almost left a VW van to bleach its bones in a deep sand trap, right in the middle of what was supposedly a road. It took a large group of dune buggy maniacs to rescue us. They shrugged off our experience as just another typical Baja driving incident.

So what can you expect? If you're driving anything—car, truck, motor home or motorcycle—that isn't designed or modified for very tough off-road travel, you won't have any trouble in Baja as long as you *stay on the highway and paved arterials.* When you're off the pavement, you're in the realm of the Baja 1000 road race: no road signs, no road maintenance and sometimes, no road at all. It's sand pits, sharp rocks, unbelievably steep grades, washouts, slides, teeth cracking ruts, blow-outs, breakdowns and uncertain supplies of gas, water, food and beer. In other words, it's a four-wheel-drive Disneyland, the mecca of untold thousands of drivers eager to pit their vehicles and themselves against something more exciting than a logging road or the local gravel pit.

Anyone contemplating more than a few miles on one of Baja's typical back roads should consult one of the books designed just for that purpose (see *Recommended Reading*). Getting well into the boondocks can be an exciting adventure, but the hazards are very real. More than one motorist has lost it all, from their supposedly tough truck to their lives, by not making adequate preparations and observing the necessary precautions.

Shortly after the opening of the Transpeninsular Highway, Mexican newspapers reported a number of fatal and near fatal accidents along its length. Most of the victims were American motorists and many of the accidents were single vehicle. The main cause of these accidents, according to Mexican authorities, was reckless driving on a highway not intended for high speeds. A large sign soon appeared near the beginning of the highway advising, in English, that the Transpeninsular Highway is intended to aid the economic development of Baja and is not for speeding.

When you've driven this highway you'll understand what this means: the road is narrow two-lane, with poorly banked curves and few, if any, shoulders. Cattle wander across it without restriction and at night livestock and wild animals are constant hazards. In the clear desert air the glare from oncoming headlights is intense and because of the narrow passing room and abrupt shoulders, close calls are inevitable.

Drive cautiously and don't drive at night. There are too many drivers from southern California, determined to relive the thrills of the Baja 1000, with a few cases of beer on the back seat and three days off work.

Whenever it rains in Baja you can expect a very quick accumulation of run-off to cross the highway. There are many *vados* (dips), most marked with depth sticks. Check these carefully if water is running and when in doubt about driving through, don't. The water drops as quickly as it rises and a few minutes can make the difference between flooding your car or a safe crossing. These *vados* are also very hazardous to vehicles travelling at high speeds; they'll put you into orbit like a downhill ski jump.

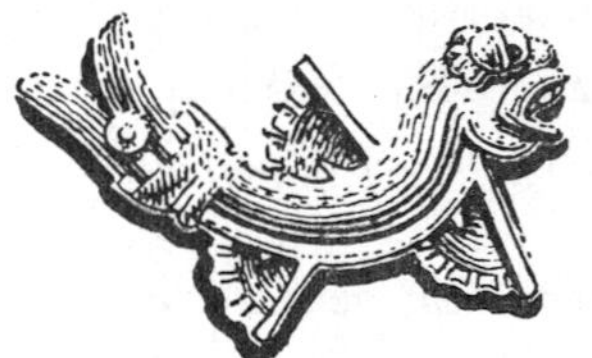
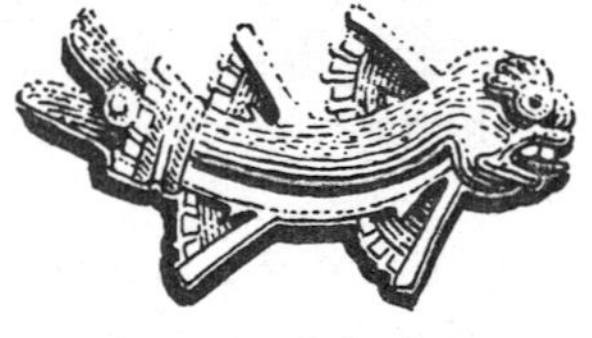

Gasoline is available along the main highway and unless you go into the back country, the days of strapping several five gallon cans to the bumpers are long past. A gas can is always a good idea, however, if only to help out the person who forgot theirs.

A jug of water should always be carried, both for the radiator and for drinking. Driving in the summertime is very hot; many people recommend driving only in the morning and evening.

Car repairs can be a problem, especially if you need parts. Parts and repairs are available in La Paz but in smaller towns you'll have to rely mostly on the mechanic's ingenuity and luck. When in doubt, carry spares. If you're driving a vehicle that can't be repaired in Baja without special tools or parts, it's best to make some arrangement with a friend to ship you whatever is needed in case of a serious breakdown.

There is regular Green Angel service along the main highway and other tourists are particularly helpful. The tradition of mutual aid continues to be a part of travel in Baja.

Money

Exchange your money at a bank; few business establishments, especially those regularly dealing with tourists, will give a good exchange rate. Because banks are few and far between I always carry more cash than I normally would. When you get away from the main road or towns, small change will be difficult to find so break large bills at the bank or in stores. (See comments on concealing money and valuable papers in *Personal Stuff*.)

Shopping

Food is more expensive in Baja than on the mainland. Much of the fresh food is imported from the mainland and canned and dry goods often come from California. Local fruits and vegetables are available in season, but the supply is far below the demand. The wonderful marketplaces of Mexico are not found on the Peninsula, though La Paz does have a small one. Bartering is almost unknown.

Grocery stores are found in small towns and many now have a *CONASUPO* outlet (see *Markets and Stores: CONASUPO*), though it may be inside a moveable trailer and not a permanent building. The concept of travelling stores is not new to Baja; many of the isolated *ranchos* and villages still rely on a pick-up truck (or boat) that follows a regular route. These people also sell to tourists, especially in popular camping areas. They offer everything from cabbages to canned beer and may also double as mail carriers and buyers for homemade cheese (a specialty in some parts), home-grown produce and fresh and dried fish.

La Paz is the commercial center of the lower peninsula and if you need something, whether it's a souvenir (almost all are from the mainland) or a fishing lure, your best chance to find it will be there. Even then, however, you may be out of luck; it is basically a small town, in spite of tourism.

Buses, Hitching, Planes and Ferries

Regular first class bus service is available along the entire length of the Transpeninsular Highway, though only a few buses run each way. The trip from Tijuana to La Paz takes just under 24 hours. It is a fast, easy ride and quite cheap.

Off the main road, bus service is irregular to non-existent; most small towns and villages rely on cabs and cooperative sharing of expenses for a private vehicle to get back and forth.

Hitching isn't difficult on the main roads, but back roads are another story entirely. I met a European hitchhiker who claimed to have spent three days travelling a hundred mile stretch of deserted desert road, including walking almost half of it. This sounds reasonable, especially when you consider that on some roads, the passing of a vehicle is so unusual that it almost rates a commemorative celebration.

Don't count on getting a ride out if someone has offered to give you one *in.* We met another optimistic hitcher who got to the end of the line, took one long look and decided to go somewhere else. There was just one problem: he was at the end of the road and there was no traffic. Fortunately the rancher who had given him a lift had extra chores that needed doing; a week later, the rancher drove out and was able to take the hitchhiker with him.

The hazards of hitching in arid and hot regions can't be stressed enough. Baja is not the place to get stranded or lost in. Be careful. (See *Hitching.*)

For many years private planes were the most practical means of transportation in Baja and they still serve a great many areas. Ranchers use them to fly in equipment or to visit the dentist and tourists like to drop out of the sky for a quick weekend of sport fishing and *margarita* guzzling.

Regularly scheduled flights to La Paz from many points in the U.S. and Mexico are available. Check with a travel agent to see if bargain fares are being offered. A travel agent should also be able to tell you about flights to other towns. Many resorts in Baja offer package deals in conjunction with smaller airlines.

Ferry service between Baja and mainland Mexico is quite good. They carry everything from walk-on passengers to semi-trucks and passenger buses. (See *Public Transportation: Ferries*.)

Camping, Fishing and Diving

It is difficult to write about camping in Baja, especially fishing and diving. I get an almost uncontrollable urge to trade this typewriter for a spinning rod and a sack of lures. The hell with any more writing! If nothing else I'll just find a nice deserted beach, sit in the sand for a few weeks and watch the pelicans and man o'war birds enjoying one of the greatest seafood smorgasbords on earth.

Baja offers everything from mountain trout fishing and hiking in the north to fantastic deep-sea fishing and beach lounging in the south. In between there's shell collecting, exploring, rock climbing, whale watching and hot spring stewing, not to mention bird watching, boating, some surfing, hunting and general goofing off all around. Too much, in fact, to cover in this small space. Right now I'll have to content myself with a few brief remarks; more can be found in *The People's Guide To Camping In Mexico.*

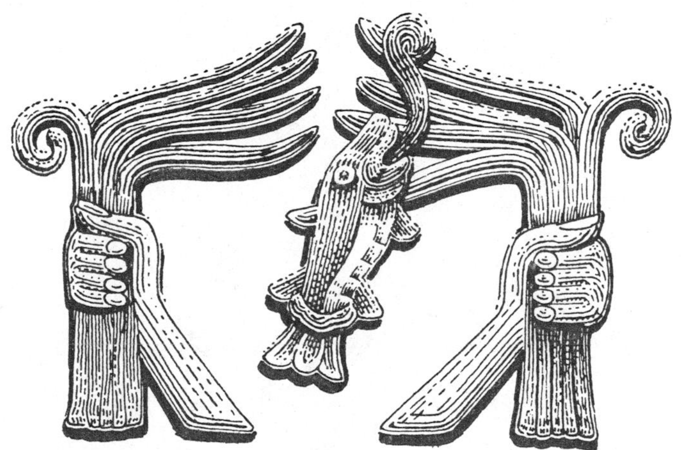

The abundance and variety of life in the Sea of Cortez has long been the object of slack-jawed awe by anyone who has fished or gone diving there. It is certainly no exaggeration; once you've stood on a beach, watching schools of gamefish beating the water to a froth just a few feet in front of you, the attraction of Baja becomes a compulsion. This profusion of life, however, has its limits. For example, the *totuava*, a gigantic type of seabass that formerly delighted anglers, is now virtually fished out.

Baja seems to inspire waste in a certain type of person, whether it's a commercial fisherman who keeps only the best of the catch and throws the rest to the sharks or a gringo who can't resist just one more hour of fishing, though half of the fish hooked may be injured or die. "I threw 'em back" doesn't mean much if they go straight to the bottom for the crabs to feed on.

Baja is vulnerable to the depredations of the tourist; clams are already disappearing in many popular camping beaches. Unless self-restraint is practised, the problem of over-fishing will never be solved in time.

Red Tape

A tourist card is not required for those visiting the border zone, but anyone travelling south must have one. The immigration check point is just south of Ensenada. Pick up your tourist card beforehand; though they can issue you one there, they'll do it reluctantly.

Permits for your car and other vehicles are not required unless you intend to cross over to the mainland. These permits are issued at the border or in La Paz. Ask for directions; it's a small town and the government office is easy to locate. For more details see the main text: *Red Tape* and *Public Transportation: Ferries.*

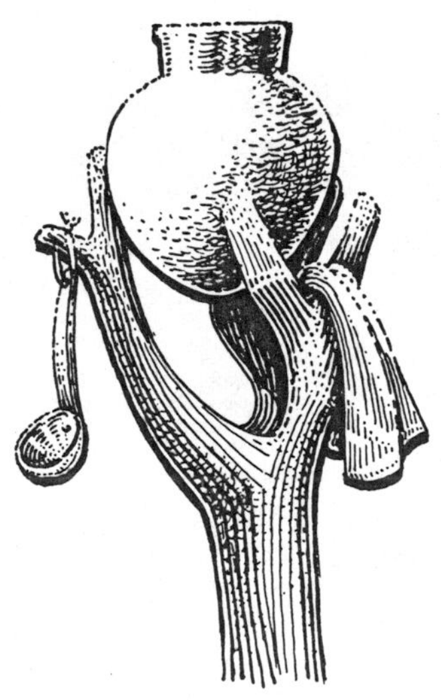

GUATEMALA

It's not another Mexico...Red Tape...Money, Measurements, Maps ...Driving and roads...Gas, car repairs...Buses, trains, hitching. Camping...Houses, hotels...Restaurants...Shopping...Booze...Services...Customs...Arts and crafts...Back to Mexico...

Many travellers mistakenly assume that Guatemala is just a smaller version of Mexico. This is not the case; Guatemala is very different, not only from its northern neighbor* but from the rest of Central America as well. There's no doubt that a large Indian population contributes greatly to the distinct change in *ambiente* (mood, atmosphere) that one feels after crossing the border. These people, many of whom preserve traditional costumes, customs and Indian languages, make Guatemala one of the most interesting areas easily accessible to tourists in the western hemisphere. For those who find the *alegría* (gaiety) of Mexico to be a little too frantic or the *machismo* wearing on the nerves, Guatemala will be a welcome relief. (Just don't look out the bus windows on those mountain curves.)

The best preparations you can make for travelling in Guatemala are mental. Because it is such a small country, it is possible to miss much by travelling more than a few miles or hours a day. Distances become almost irrelevant, especially in the highlands where two villages separated by a small mountain may have different languages and customs Paved highways and fast buses make it possible to start your day in a chilly mist shrouded Mayan village and end it under a palm tree at the beach.

Tourist Cards, Cars, Pets, Red Tape

There are two major entry points into Guatemala from Mexico for those travelling by land: Tapachula, near the Pacific coast and Ciudad Cuauhtémoc, south of Comitán in

*There is a popular saying in Guatemala about those who travel to Mexico: "*Salimos de Guatemala y entramos a Guatepeor.*" This translates as "We left Guate-bad (*mala*) and we entered Guate-worse (*peor*).

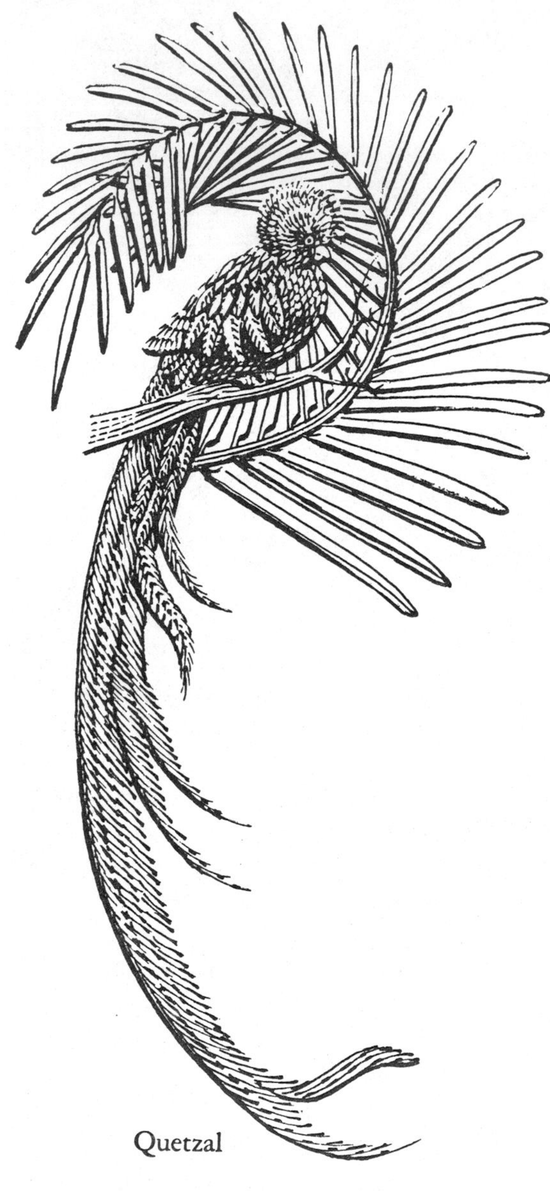
Quetzal

the highlands. We prefer the latter route; it is cooler and passes through one of the most interesting areas of Mexico. On the other side of the border, in Guatemala, you find yourself right in the middle of mountains and Indians.

Tourist cards are available at the border but it is more convenient to get them in advance at the consulate in Mexico City or Tapachula (or ask a travel agent elsewhere). A tourist card costs one dollar and is valid for up to six months. Visas are also available at consulate offices, free of charge, but are seldom used by tourists. You'll need a passport, birth certificate or other proof of citizenship.

•Smallpox vaccination certificates are no longer required.

•You will probably be asked to show proof of solvency, i.e., money, before being allowed into the country. Most travellers report that $200 does the trick, which is quite reasonable.

•Hassles at the border over beards, long hair or money seem to vary with the disposition and mood of the official on duty. We have never been treated discourteously by Guatemalan border officials but we do know people who have been.

From time to time the government apparently decides to give those tourists a bad time who don't look quite straight enough. And to look straight in Guatemala is to look like something out of *Boy's Life* in 1957.

Be as neat, clean, calm, polite and solvent as possible when crossing and you should make it with a minimum of trouble.

•Car papers are issued for 90 days, no matter for how long your tourist card or visa may be valid.

Before the end of 90 days, you must go to the National Palace in Guatemala City to have the car papers renewed or else take the car out of the country. Should you not do this, you are liable for the duty on the value of the vehicle, usually a considerable sum.

Renewing the car papers takes about three days. It is a complicated procedure but often done by tourists. Your best bet is to find someone who has done it recently and ask for detailed instructions on where to go and whom to see. We've had to do it differently every time.

•Pets can be admitted into Guatemala with the same papers you used to get them into Mexico.

•Car insurance can be purchased in Mexico City, Oaxaca, at the Tapachula border crossing or inside Guatemala.

•Baggage searches are common going into Guatemala and may be extensive. Usually you'll be asked to carry a few large items—suitcases, duffel bags, guitar cases, etc.—into the customs house for a perfunctory inspection. Do this willingly, but don't take anything out of your car that you aren't specifically told to remove. The officials don't enjoy the inspections much more than you so there's no need to encourage them.

WARNING: Don't smuggle firearms; should you be caught, you'll be in serious trouble.

It's possible that the health inspector will confiscate certain kinds of food. (Lorena lost her entire collection of herb teas.)

•After the baggage search, someone will swab your car's wheels with disinfectant. This is required to remove all Mexican bacteria and pests. Do not laugh; you pay a small fee for the service.

Following the sterilization, someone will attach a metal ring seal to your inside rear view mirror and a tourist sticker to the windshield. Leave both intact; they will be inspected if you are stopped at checkpoints inside the country.

It is advisable to have a few loose dollars on hand to facilitate your crossing.

•Guatemala has now discovered the 'exit tax'; be prepared to pay for the privilege of leaving the country. Your car pays extra, too.

Money, Measurements and Standards, Maps

The currency of Guatemala is based on the *quetzal*, conveniently worth one dollar U.S. The *quetzal* is broken up into pennies, nickles, dimes, quarters and half-*quetzals*. All but the half-*quetzal* are coins. The *quetzal* and half-*quetzal* are bills.

Money is usually called *pisto* and pennies (*centavos*) are called *leng* (Indian words).

You can exchange dollars and *pesos* into *quetzales* or vice versa at the border. Note: fluctuations in exchange rates make it advisable to have your *pesos* exchanged to *quetzales* at a bank. We always carry several American dollar bills; most border officials will take them in place of *quetzales*. To avoid unfair and expensive exchange rates when returning to Mexico (they'll beat you too, on *quetzales*) keep enough *pesos* in reserve to last until you find a bank.

Traveller's checks usually have to be cashed at a bank, supermarket, hotel or large *tienda.* Gas stations sometimes accept small checks, but don't count on it.

You'll notice men with machine guns in every bank. If they're wearing plain clothes, it's probably a holdup but if they are in battle dress, they are guards. Robbing banks is the guerrilla's major fund-raising activity.

Don't act suspicious and obey their orders (guerrillas' or guards') should they tell you to do something. Everyone in the bank is made to stand in line and anyone crowding will receive a quick reprimand from the guards.

Weights are measured in pounds (*libras*) but distances are measured in both miles and kilometers. Liquids are usually, but not always, based on the liter. Altitudes are in feet.

Maps are rarely available in gas stations and when they are the price isn't a bargain. Detailed maps are available in Guatemala City and from the *Instituto Geográfico Nacional, Avenida Las Americas, 5-76, Zona 13.* For some reason certain maps are available only by mail. (See *Appendices: Maps.*)

Driving and Roads

Major roads are paved and relatively good. Other than the Pan American, highways are narrow with frequent sharp curves and steep grades.

Unpaved side roads can be a real nightmare, especially in mountainous areas. Narrow dirt roads may be almost impossible to climb, even in the dry months. Slides and washouts are common during the rainy season.

Drunks are a real problem on Guatemalan highways. Not drunken drivers but drunken pedestrians staggering into the middle of the road. They are common in the mornings as well as at night.

Military checkpoints are not uncommon on major roads leading in and out of Guatemala City, especially during election times and periods of guerrilla activity. Most are within a few miles of the city itself. There are also checkpoints, some permanent and others temporary, on side roads, particularly in the areas east of the Pan American Highway.

Never run through or ignore a checkpoint. We know of one case where a soldier fired his rifle into the rear of a VW van because the driver casually ignored a signal to stop.

The standard procedure when stopped by soldiers or police is to hand over your driver's license immediately. This will usually satisfy their curiosity.

Sometimes, however, they will inspect the contents of your vehicle, supposedly to see whether you might be smuggling arms to the guerrillas. Soldiers are particularly suspicious of army surplus camping gear and have even been known to confiscate Official Boy Scout equipment as 'war materials.'

These stops and searches can be irritating but it behooves you to keep calm.

Gas Stations, Servicing and Repairs

American gas stations and automotive products are widely distributed. Gasoline costs about a dollar a gallon. It's wise to carry extra gas when travelling on side roads.

Agencies for most common American and foreign cars are found in the major cities. Small backyard garages are not as common as in Mexico, probably because most cars are relatively new and their owners affluent.

Public Transportation, Hitching

Guatemalan bus service is not as extensive or as cheap as it is in Mexico. Many of the roads are too steep for anything but humans, 4-wheel drive vehicles and pack animals to negotiate. The person interested in truly out-of-the-way places may have to walk instead of riding the bus. Fares are high enough to keep the poor on foot.

Train service is very slow. There is one stretch serviced by a 15-hour train trip with more than 50 stops that can be covered in just over four hours by bus. The train, however, is much more interesting and picturesque than a fast ride on a retired Greyhound.

Hitchhiking can be difficult because of the small amount of traffic. The best way is to ask another tourist for a ride.

Camping

We've never had any problems while camping in Guatemala. There are many beautiful sites high in the mountains, some near streams, and firewood is usually abundant.

Most of the people are so shy of strangers that you'll rarely have them visiting your camp.

There are alarmists who claim that camping off the main road is an open invitation to a guerrilla raid, kidnapping and other adventures. We've frequently camped in what was supposedly the center of guerrilla country without ever being attacked.

For more see *The People's Guide To Camping In Mexico*. It includes camping and backpacking in Guatemala.

House Renting

Anyone who intends to spend more than a few weeks in Guatemala should certainly consider renting a house.

Rents vary widely, from fancy vacation homes with all the mod-cons to Indian style houses of adobe or wood. A basic house or hut, complete with fleas, shouldn't cost more than $20 a month, if that.

Hotels

Experience in basic hotel accommodations in Mexico will prepare you well for Guatemalan rooms. The cheap rooms are very cheap and basic. The best rooms are not unreasonable and quite comfortable.

Restaurants

A typical Guatemalan restaurant is rather disappointing. Inexpensive meals are easily available and nourishing, but generally uninspired and monotonous. Giant *tamales*, requiring several bottles of beer to flush them down, are popular.

Most cheap restaurant fare can be divided into two categories: cheap and supercheap. The difference is in the size of the portions. A favorite meal (for the cooks) is a bowl of watery stew, *tortillas*, gritty sweetened coffee, rice and meat with sauce. As Steve said despondently, "You either get red meat with grey sauce or grey meat with red sauce."

Breakfast consists of a watery mush, *tortillas* or bread, beans, eggs and more sweetened gritty coffee. Unsweetened coffee is served only in better restaurants and is very good.

Salvation lies in larger cities and tourist towns prosperous enough to attract skilled cooks. Guatemala City, for example, has many fine and inexpensive places to eat. The best, in my opinion, both for quality and economy, are Chinese restaurants. The City has an international community and the variety of foods they offer makes up for the bland diet of the 'provinces.' Walk into a full-scale German bakery and see how long you mourn those dry *tamales*.

Street food hardly exists in Guatemala, which rates as a national tragedy when compared to the goodies available in Mexico. Fortunately fresh foods are excellent, generally inexpensive and widely available.

Food Shopping

Almost all markets are 'Indian markets' and extremely interesting. The main activity takes place about nine a.m. and may be all but finished by noon. Prices for fresh foods are low (especially those in season) and bartering is expected for even the smallest purchase.

It is advisable to carry your money in the smallest change possible. Few vendors have change or wish to part with it. You will often be given your change in merchandise.

Torn or defaced bills or disfigured coins are rarely accepted. If you accept them yourself, you'll probably have to go to a bank to get rid of them.

Tiendas are almost as common as in Mexico. In towns without a daily market, the *tienda* is the source of everything, from eggs to booze, sewing needles to firewood.

Supermarkets are found only in the largest cities. The reason why many people say food is expensive in Guatemala is that prices in supermarkets for packaged food are truly astronomical in comparison to fresh things in the market.

A red flag outside a doorway means "Fresh Meat." Regular daily meat markets are also found in and around the market or at other strategic points. Meat is relatively inexpensive.

Seafood is available in Guatemala City and in very large markets in other towns. Excellent fresh-water fish is sold in many markets, but it tends to be more expensive than meat.

Dairy products are hard to find outside of the larger towns, especially anything pasteurized or packaged. Some *tiendas* sell bottled milk very early in the morning. The stock usually doesn't last long. Powdered milk is sold in *tiendas.*

Booze and *Cantinas*

Guatemalan booze, including wine, beer and distilled liquors, is pretty bad. And it isn't, with the exception of the wine, very cheap. Whatever the label or the bottle may lead you to believe, the so-called wine is probably manufactured from oranges or cashews. Check the fine print to be sure. This wine is more palatable if mixed with 7-Up or mineral water.

The most common hard liquor is *aguardiente. Aguardiente* is basically just unaged cane alcohol, but the people who make it in Guatemala add something else for flavor. They might have been better off to leave it alone.

Guatemalan rum and scotch don't cost much in comparison to U.S. prices, but after tasting them you'll see why. Alcoholic beverages are sold in *tiendas, cantinas* and supermarkets.

If you're a drinker, I recommend bringing a supply with you from Mexico.

There is an entirely different drinking scene in Guatemala than in Mexico. The difference is especially noticeable in small *cantinas.* It usually goes like this: A man, obviously Indian, walks into the *cantina* (a tiny room with one table and no chairs) and taps his coins on the counter to attract the owner.

The owner walks in and a few unintelligible words are exchanged. An *octavo* of *aguardiente* (one-eighth of a liter) is purchased. The owner twists the top off and hands the bottle to the customer who tips it up and chugs the entire contents in three gulps. Without a word, except perhaps a strangled *adiós*, he lays the bottle carefully on its side and walks out.

Very few bars can legally dispense liquor by the drink, hence the small bottles. This is the result of a Spanish colonial law to curb drinking by the Indians.

Although 'social' drinking does go on in the larger bars, most of it is done as I've described.

Ritual drinking is very common among the Indians. Basically, it involves anyone who is an official of any type within the Indian community getting totally smashed in order to carry out his duties properly. The degree to which they carry out this ritual duty is incredible and sometimes frightening.

Guatemalan *fiestas*, renowned for their color and excitement, are also scenes of incredible mass drunkenness among the participants; men, women and a few of us tourists included.

Water, Ice and Fuels

Water is readily available. Use the same precautions as in Mexico about drinking it. Bottled purified water is not common.

Ice is very hard to find outside of the largest cities and it's best just to forget it.

Bottled gas can also be a problem. Our small four pound tank could only be filled in one place in Guatemala City. The easiest thing to do if you're staying in one spot for a while is to put a deposit on a large returnable tank.

Firewood and *carbón* are available in the market.

Post Office, Telegraph, Phones

These are all very similar to Mexico. Use *Lista de Correos* for General Delivery.

Phone connections may require several hours of waiting. The *telégrafos* is often located in the post office.

Health

Drugstores, as in Mexico, dispense almost anything without a prescription.

For serious medical problems, I would ask someone (a resident gringo, Guatemalan friend, etc.) for advice on doctors and hospitals.

Customs, Traditions and Hassles

The average Guatemalan *ladino* (non-Indian or *mestizo*) is a conservative person. The average traditional Indian is an *extremely* conservative person. The average Guatemalan cop is so conservative that he might do something as irrational as arresting someone for playing a musical instrument in public. What does this mean for the average liberal gringo who comes to Guatemala, puts on local dress (and some men literally wear Indian women's dresses as shirts) and proceeds to 'go native'? It means, at least on the part of the Guatemalans, dismay, disbelief, and sometimes open disgust. (See *Customs and Superstitions.*)

Sensitive tourists should be aware that in a traditional society some things just aren't done: nudity, drugs, public craziness, wild or improperly worn clothing and just general gringo fun are not appreciated by the locals. Save it for your return home; it will make everyone happier in the long run and avoid problems.

As anywhere where there is trouble, the best thing to have if busted is 1) money, 2) connections or 3) a lawyer.

People who are discreet in whatever they do, respectful towards local laws and customs and able to keep cool should have no problems.

Buying Things

For the traveller who has steadfastly resisted the temptations of Mexico's craft markets, Guatemala often comes as the final, crushing straw. Intricately hand loomed textiles, embroidered clothing, carved masks, musical instruments and other irresistible bric-a-brac are offered at what seems bargain prices. My motto is "Keep your eyes straight ahead and barter like hell." As soon as you've succumbed to one thing another catches your attention.

Although buying direct from artisans or wandering Indian vendors is both entertaining and enlightening (as a smiling ten-year-old asks five times an item's value and makes you feel lucky to pay it), the average tourist would do well to visit shops. As in Mexico, many store owners either buy direct from Indian artisans or employ buyers who scour the countryside for the best bargains and finest work. Unless you're a competent and determined barterer and an excellent judge of comparative quality, you'll find shops hard to beat.

Note: Guatemala has finally wised up and an export permit is required for pre-Columbian artifacts. Fine copies are sold but to avoid possible confusion with the real thing, ask for a detailed receipt, describing the article and giving the name and address of the seller.

Re-entering Mexico

A new Mexican tourist card will be issued to you after leaving Guatemala (and paying the exit tax). It is much more convenient, however, to apply for a tourist card inside Guatemala, at a Mexican consulate. This cuts down on the chances of being given the run-around if you don't have much money after blowing it all on crafts.

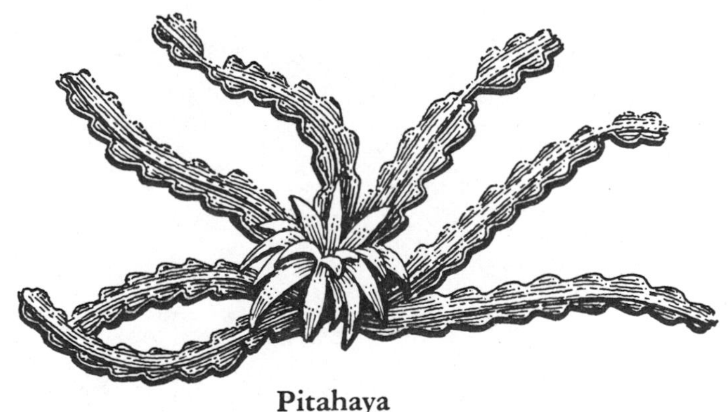

Pitahaya

NOTES

BELIZE

It's different and exciting...Red tape: grin and bear it...Money...Driving, buses...Food, booze, hotels...Camping...Rip-offs...Back to Mexico and Guatemala...

Belize (formerly British Honduras) is a very small country sandwiched between Guatemala and the Mexican territory of Quintana Roo. Formerly a colony, it is now a British Protectorate, with national defense and foreign policy controlled by England. This situation is unlikely to change until Guatemala drops its claim that Belize is actually a Guatemalan possession. (Tourists, however, should avoid using the name British Honduras as it offends many Belizeans who are sensitive about independence.)

Belize is a sort of poor relation to other Central American countries, though its standard of living is reasonably high. The government likes to call it "The emerging new nation." Cynics question what Belize is emerging from and where it can possibly go. Aldous Huxley's oft-quoted remark that "If the world had any ends, British Honduras would surely be one of them," should, in my opinion, either be ignored by the traveller or taken as a challenge to go there.

Belize is a unique country, one that appeals to a certain type of person and draws a blank with others. We happen to be among those who love it.

Belize's proximity to predominantly Spanish speaking countries in no way means that its culture is similar to that of its neighbors.

The population of Belize is comprised of blacks, Mayan and Caribe Indians and a strange assortment of caucasians, including Mennonites, soldiers of fortune and European farmers.

Although English and Spanish are both commonly spoken, there are many who prefer Maya, Caribe or the local dialect of English that sounds as though it comes from the

West Indies. Casual conversation, especially among black citizens of Belize, is heavily laced with "Hey, mon!" type expressions. The headline on a Black Power newspaper, *Amandala*, proclaimed, "Di New Barge Sink!" when a large barge went to the bottom of the harbor in Belize City.

After Mexico or Guatemala the strange British colonial atmosphere of Belize seems rather surrealistic. Everything about the country, from the tin roofed houses on stilts to the inevitable red beans and rice for lunch and dinner, make the visitor feel that Belize really ought to be somewhere other than in Latin America. But where?

Red Tape

One of the problems of visiting Belize is not only getting into the country but being allowed to stay there long enough to see anything.

Border officials are notorious for being unfriendly, uncooperative, unreasonable and just plain nasty to tourists. Their attitude is at least democratic: Belizean officials give almost everyone a hard time, no matter how straight they look or how much money they have. (Those arriving by air are seldom hassled.)

> You're probably saying to yourself right now: "Ends of the earth? Unfriendly border officials? Why even bother?" The answer to that is the people of Belize. Although I dislike statements such as "the natives are friendly and courteous" the fact is that the average Belizean makes up for the surly attitude of at least four border officials. Once you're inside the country, you'll probably wonder if it wasn't all a mistake and feel guilty about thinking ill of anyone. A few other good reasons to grin and bear it at the border: Belize has the second longest barrier reef in the world, a fishing and diving Nirvana, not to mention many Mayan ruins, old pirate hang-outs, jungles, rivers, cheap rum and, for those so inclined, smoking herbs of great potency.

Tourists entering from Guatemala can expect delays and hassles to vary with the current political climate between the two countries.

Visas will be issued at the border. We have been told that people who go to the trouble of getting visas in advance are given a harder time by border officials. This sounds stupid but not surprising.

A passport, birth certificate or other good identification should be sufficient. You will almost certainly be asked to show money. The official may go so far as to record the number of every traveller's check in your possession.

The average tourist is given seven to thirty days to stay in the country. If this isn't enough time, go to the tourist office in Belize City and ask for an extension. This is supposedly the easiest and fastest way to extend your visit, much better than a futile argument at the border.

Tourists arriving by bus or hitching are usually subjected to even more harrassment than those with their own car. You might be told, for example, that $100 is not enough money to cross Belize. The trip takes just one day.

Taking a pet into Belize is really a hassle. Even if you have gone to the trouble and expense of securing the necessary health papers and shots for your pet, you'll probably have trouble. This is especially true for dogs. There seems to be a perpetual anti-rabies campaign going on in Belize. In some areas, dogs are killed on sight.

Don't be surprised if you have to leave your pet at the border and go into Belize in search of a health official to authorize the pet's entry. Once inside Belize with your dog, don't let it out of your sight and preferably not out of your car.

Border officials will usually search baggage and cars. They go to the extreme of looking for 'seditious' literature. A friend had a copy of *Soul on Ice* confiscated.

Money

The Belizean dollar fluctuates with the English pound sterling. It is based on the decimal system with pennies, nickles, dimes, etc.

Driving, Roads, Gas Stations, Public Transportation

It is possible to drive across Belize in one day but it's a real grind. Because almost all roads are narrow, bumpy and pocked with holes, driving is both exhausting and hazardous. Side roads are even worse than the main highway, although the absence of broken pavement is sometimes a blessing.

Road conditions keep speeds fairly low, but passing, either from behind or head-on, should always be done with extreme caution.

Gas stations are located in most towns.

Bus service is infrequent, erratic and uncomfortable. Travellers on foot must walk or take a cab from the border station adjoining Guatemala to the bus stop a few miles inside Belize.

Food, Booze, Hotels

The standard fare in a restaurant is beans and rice. Sometimes it is beans, rice and meat. Meals are fairly good, at least until you become bored with them, and inexpensive.

Good fresh food is not easy to locate. The majority of city people seem to live on canned food. Even the meat in the beans and rice is usually from a can. Most foodstuffs are imported from various parts of the British Commonwealth.

If you are going to shop in the market place in Belize City, get there early or the selection will be poor.

Booze is also imported and usually expensive, though cheap locally made rum is available.

Hotels are inexpensive but not very comfortable. Because of the heat, it is wise to use a hammock.

Camping

Camping places on the main road are not exactly choice. Heat, swamps and insects can make camping something of an ordeal if you are not tough or properly prepared.

Farmers are very nice about allowing people to camp on their land. It is best, however, to ask for permission rather than assuming you have it.

Rip-Offs

Anyone who has heard much about Belize has probably heard about the incredible danger of rip-offs there. This is largely exaggeration.

Belize City itself is a bad place to leave a car unguarded on the street. Elsewhere, however, extra precautions are usually not necessary.

As you'll soon discover yourself after visiting Belize City, it is not at all typical of the rest of the country. Although the city can be a rough place, it doesn't have to be if you keep cool, watch your things and act friendly.

Re-entry into: Mexico, Guatemala

Mexican officials in Chetumal, the entry point to Mexico from Belize, do not like to issue a tourist card for more than 30 days. They can require you to return to Belize if you want a longer tourist card.

Tourist cards for a longer time can be arranged by a little 'dollar diplomacy,' but it's best to do the paper work in advance while still in Belize.

Tourist cards are available at the Mexican Consulate in the city of Belize. Go during the week and as soon as possible. Their hours tend to be vague.

Not too many people enter Guatemala from Belize. This is mainly due to the fact that not many people know that the road is open from there to the Pan American Highway inside Guatemala. The Guatemalan officials at the Belize border are reasonable people.

ENTERING MEXICO: RED TAPE

Tourist cards...Student visas...Car permits...Trailers, Cycles, Boats...CB radios...Insurance...Pets...Hunting and fishing licenses... Travellers checks...Official documents...Mexican Customs inspections... Border hassles...Bribes...

Tourist Cards

There is just one thing that really makes going to Mexico different from crossing the border between neighboring U.S. states: a tourist card.

A tourist card is your permission from the Mexican government to visit Mexico. It is available free of charge at the border, at Mexican consulates, at Mexican Government Tourism Department Delegation offices (in large U.S. cities), at travel agencies or from the airline office if you are flying.

American and Canadian citizens will be issued a tourist card upon presentation of proof of citizenship: birth certificate, voter's registration card, passport, discharge papers or a notarized affidavit of citizenship. Naturalized citizens must have a passport or naturalization papers.

The parents' written notarized consent is required if a minor (under 18) is going to Mexico alone or with another person, even if that person is the other parent. For example, a father must have the mother's consent to take any children under 18 into Mexico. This rule is not always enforced but it *may be.*

Children under 15 may be included on their parent's tourist card. Although this eliminates some paperwork, the child will not be allowed to leave without the parent or the parent without the child.

Validation of the tourist card is very important. This is done in Mexico, either at the border or at the airport when you land. The length of your stay is determined at this point. Always ask for more time than you think you'll need. Most tourists are given the maximum of 180 days, but some say, "Oh, just give me a 30 day card. I'll only be here a few weeks." Then, when they've found their dream spot and would like to spend an extra month, their short tourist cards force them to return.

Tourist cards are stamped with a date that indicates the date by which the card *must be used.* This period is 90 days from the day of issue.The length of time you may remain in Mexico is written or typed in the space preceded by the words in Spanish, English and French: *Authorized To Remain In Mexico* ---- (number of days) *Days From Date of Entry.*

Extending your tourist card is possible but very difficult and can be done only in cases of real emergency. To stay longer than 180 days you'll have to leave the country, if only for a few hours, and re-enter all over again. This is commonly done. (If your card is lost or expired, see *Tourists and The Law.*)

●There are no mandatory vaccinations or shots needed for travelling in Mexico.

Student Visas

A renewable, one year Non Immigrant Student Visa is available for those who intend to study in Mexico without leaving the country for more than 180 days a year. The requirements include proof of solvency, a good conduct letter from your local police,

extra photos, etc. Not even school and immigration officials advise going through the red tape if you can get by using a regular tourist card. Contact the nearest Mexican Consulate for further details and requirements (see *Appendices*).

Car Permits

If you are taking a motor vehicle you will be given a combination tourist card and car permit. This form will be issued at the point where you cross the border or at a checkpoint about 15 to 20 miles inside the country. At the same time you will probably have tourist stickers affixed to the front and rear windows of the car. (Baja drivers won't need this permit. See *Baja California.*)

The car permit cannot be extended.

If the car belongs to you, the title or registration are sufficient for proof of ownership. If it isn't yours, you must have a notarized affidavit from the legal owner or lien holder authorizing you to take the car into Mexico.

You will also need a valid driver's license and current license plates.

Extra equipment such as spare tires, radio, air conditioner, heater, small trailers and outboard motors will usually be noted on the car papers. They become *part of the car* and will have to leave Mexico with you and the car.

To leave the country without the car the owner will have to either: (1) Leave the car in custody with Customs at the airport in Mexico City, (2) with the *Registro Federal de Automóviles* in Mexico City or (3) with the *Oficina Federal de Hacienda* (offices in towns of any size). These offices will charge a small storage fee. The car cannot be left at any of these offices—or in Mexico—beyond the expiration date of the car papers (see *Tourists and The Law*).

If several people are going as a group in one car, it should be firmly decided and arranged legally who is going to be responsible for the vehicle and accessories. I've seen several cases where groups split up causing problems for the car owner. In one instance, the owner of the car went one way and the owner of an outboard and his motor went another. When the car owner tried to leave Mexico, he had to pay duty on the missing outboard.

A tip to the car paper official should fix any irregularities, including such legitimate discrepancies as an expired driver's license, seven radios or no registration.

When travelling with friends who don't look very respectable, the owner of the car should approach the car paper desk alone. When practical, friends should pool whatever money they have in case the owner is asked to produce any. (At this point they will already have their tourist cards and should be sitting in the car looking humble.)

Trailers, Cycles and Boats

The regulations for trailers and motorcycles are the same as those for cars.

Technically a tourist cannot import more than one self-propelled vehicle into Mexico. In reality, many people enter with extra cars and cycles. To minimize hassles be prepared to pay off.

Boats over six feet long must be bonded at three percent of their value. This regulation is also flexible. If you don't have a title for your boat or motor a notarized affidavit will do.

CB Radios

CB'ers will be happy to know that the ban on their radios has now been lifted. Three channels have been assigned: 11 (emergencies), 13 (caravans) and 14 (for general gossiping). Permission from the government is required to use other channels.

Car Insurance

The minute you cross the border your U.S. car insurance becomes useless.*

Being involved in an accident in Mexico is different from the same sort of thing in the U.S. and the Uninsured Motorist (a dreaded term anywhere) is particularly vulnerable to legal action.

When an accident occurs all parties involved may be detained for investigation and their vehicles impounded. After the claims have been settled everyone gets to go home. Everyone, that is, but the uninsured motorist who doesn't have enough cash to pay all the expense of the accident. An insurance policy is considered a guarantee that damages will be paid and it can be your ticket out of jail, even though you are at fault. When you don't have an insurance agent to intercede for you, you'll have to deal with the police on your own. If you don't speak Spanish, the situation could become very complicated. Should the other party decide to try a fast one and shift part or all of the blame onto you, all the righteous indignation you can summon up won't help. (See *Tourist and the Law.*)

By now you should be ready for a policy and I recommend that you get one. There are a bewildering number of very obvious insurance agencies on both sides of the border and they'll whip out a policy in just a few minutes. Some of these companies, such as Sears and Sanborn's are handled by Americans, if that makes you feel any safer.

Should you buy insurance for a longer period of time than you actually spend in Mexico, you can apply for a refund. Some companies (Sanborn's for one) offer rebates if you visit Central America while your Mexican policy is in effect. Once again, you leave your coverage behind when you cross a border.

Insurance rates are government controlled and minimum charges cannot legally vary between companies. The rates, based on a sliding scale, decrease significantly for longer policies. When you buy insurance, the agent will certainly try to sell you maximum

*There are exceptions. Some policies will repay you for collision damage in Mexico. Photos of the accident scene would be useful. Check with your agent or read the fine print of your policy. One of the greatest advantages of a Mexican policy is having the services of a Mexican claims agent.

coverage. If you're not too worried about body work, meteorites, medical expenses or unreasonable Acts of God, just get liability. If you can't afford to buy insurance for the entire trip, it's a good idea to buy a few days worth; enough to get you to your intended destination. When you move on or head home, you can again buy a few more days of insurance. Large towns have agents who sell policies by the day or month.

Theft insurance usually covers only total loss of the car. Since most thefts involve the contents or parts of the car, read the policy carefully before buying.

Check several companies and ask if they offer little side goodies such as maps and books. Sanborn's will give you a guidebook called *Sanborn's Travelog* that has very detailed road information and good city maps. The restaurants and hotels recommended are aimed at the affluent.

If you belong to AAA they will write your Mexican insurance and give you maps and a guide book with good road information, though some of it is out-of-date.

Pets

To take a dog or cat into Mexico, you must have a veterinarian's certificate stating that the animal is in good health and has been innoculated against rabies within the past six months. This certificate must ve visaed (stamped) by a Mexican consul for a fee. Have this done at the consulate nearest your home; each may certify pets only within a certain area.

Check with your veterinarian, the Mexican consul or a state or federal animal health official for regulations about pets of other types. You may find that you can take your pet into Mexico with no trouble but when you come back to the U.S., the poor thing will be considered 'undesirable' by U.S. customs officials. (See *Buying Things*.)

A good friend of ours who travels with a chicken solved this problem by having her feathered companion smuggled across the border in a paper sack by a Mexican child. If you're travelling with a pig, this wouldn't be easy.

I honestly cannot think of enough positive reasons for taking a pet on a long trip to justify doing so. My comments on pets and travelling will therefore tend to be negative. If you have a pet and are quite attached to it, I'm sure that no amount of negative advice will deter you from taking it with you. (We used to travel with two boisterous parrots.) Let my comments then at least serve as warnings to help you avoid unexpected difficulties.

Pets in general do not enjoy the same exalted status in Mexico as they do in the U.S. This is particularly true of dogs. Dogs are considered by most Mexicans to be on the borderline between pests and severe inconveniences. Someone has estimated the canine population of Mexico City to be around 1,000,000. The fact that the majority of these dogs aren't owned or supported by any particular person or family and just run free is a good clue to the reason for their low esteem.

The threat of rabies causes both civil authorities and private individuals to carry out methodical programs of extermination among the dog population. Many tourist's pets have been inadvertently poisoned.

What does this anti-dog attitude mean for Killer, your cuddly 150 pound German Shepherd? It means you'd better keep him close to you and under control. If he races into the market, knocking over food and people, you may spend hours settling damages and cooling tempers. At best, you'll rescue the beast and face a torrent of angry abuse.

Pets are not allowed in hotels or motels, almost without exception. It doesn't matter if you've tranquilized, muzzled and wrapped it in a log chain, your dog will have to find accommodations elsewhere. Pets aren't allowed on first class buses and must travel in the baggage car on trains.

Before committing yourself to caring for a pet on a long trip, consider not only how you'll feel if it becomes a problem, but how your pet will feel. The animal may never forgive you for being dragged along on a leash, teased by kids, kept prisoner in a hot car for hours on end and otherwise made to feel like less than a member of the family.

Hunting Licenses

A hunting license now costs a staggering $150 (dollars!). There is an additional fee, per state, of about $25, plus more red tape. The paperwork involved in taking guns to Mexico is considerable. Two firearms are allowed, but no handguns or military weapons of any type. I won't even bother to list the detailed requirements. If you are serious about hunting in Mexico write to Wildlife Advisory Services, P.O. Box 76132, Los Angeles, CA 90076 or call them at 213-385-9311. They'll explain the regulations, seasons, bag limits and help you do the paper work.

Illegally importing a gun is extremely stupid. The illegal possession of a firearm is like a reserved ticket for a prison cell. Even those Mexicans who use their guns for subsistence hunting are being harassed by the authorities as laws concerning firearms become increasingly strict.

Fishing Licenses

The fee for a fishing permit is quite reasonable and I recommend that you get one. Although enforcement is lax you are open to fines and/or losing your gear (including boats) if they crack down. Popular bass fishing lakes are fairly well patrolled; some wardens will sell you a license if you don't already have one.

Children under 12 do not need a license. Lost licenses cannot be replaced, you must buy another.

Fishing (includes spearing) licenses are available at *Oficina de Pesca* in Mexico (at port cities) or by mail from the Mexican Department of Fisheries, 233 "A" Street, Suite 709, San Diego, CA 92101 (phone 714-233-6956) or *Oficina de Pesca*, 395 W. 6th Street, Suite 3, San Pedro, CA 90731 (phone 213-832-5628). Some tackle stores and travel agents also sell licenses.

Boats taken to Mexico and used for fishing also require a license. The necessary information will be included with your application for a fishing permit when you write the above offices.

Traveller's Checks

When you get to Mexico you'll want to convert some of your dollars to *pesos*, the national currency. This can be done at any bank and at most large business establishments in tourist areas. (See *Services: Banks* and *Appendices: Money*.)

Money not needed for immediate operating expenses should be converted into traveller's checks before leaving home. (This can also be done in Mexican banks, most of which handle American traveller check companies.)

Although these companies would lead you to believe that their checks are as easy to use as real money, the truth is that they are not. Because of counterfeits, frauds, thefts and general lack of confidence, many Mexicans balk at cashing traveller's checks. To minimize such difficulties buy only the most well known brands of checks (American Express and Bank of America) and in small denominations. Many merchants refuse checks larger than $20; $50 or larger must usually be cashed in a bank.

Canadians should purchase American traveller's checks or U.S. dollars to avoid cashing and exchange problems.

Once you get off the beaten track (and you don't have to go very far) cashing traveller's checks is very difficult unless you go to a bank.

As soon as you buy your checks, record the numbers on the page provided at the end of this book. If this seems like a bother, which it is, just consider: when lost or stolen, the checks are no better than cash if you can't reclaim them.

After cashing a check strike its number off your list. If you have to reclaim a lost check you'll want to know exactly which one it was. Reclaiming a check in Mexico can be difficult or even impossible if you: 1) don't know the exact number or have the carbon copy recording the purchse or 2) are trying to reclaim a check from a company that is not well-known. (Even with the check number this second hang-up may prevent a refund before you return home.)

Your tourist card is usually required for identification when cashing a check. The official look of a passport, however, will often sway a hesitant gas station attendant or store owner in your favor.

Sign the check clearly. Mexicans prefer a signature that has a final flourish but don't overdo it.

Banks and businesses familiar with traveller's checks charge very little to cash them. At other places you may have to pay what seems to you an unfair rake-off. There's nothing you can do about it except try somewhere else.

Official Documents

After you've been issued your tourist card, car papers, pet papers, gun permit, insurance policy, etc., put them all in a safe place where they won't get lost, dirty or damaged. When driving we keep our various paper valuables in a plastic 'diplomatic pouch.' When we encounter a routine immigration checkpoint within Mexico, our tourist cards and car papers are immediately at hand. And they aren't dirty, folded, torn, chewed or otherwise defiled in such a way that would arouse the wrath of officialdom.

A Hidden Pocket makes a convenient and secure place to carry both money and documents, especially for those travelling by public transportation or on foot. (See *Personal Stuff.*)

If you want to avoid potential bureaucratic problems, tourist cards and other government issued documents shouldn't look like pages from a well-thumbed sex novel. An irate immigration official once told Steve that his dirty fingerprints on his tourist card were "an insult to the Republic." The only thing that could take his outraged eyes from the card was a bank note, also well-thumbed.

Mexican Customs Inspections

Tourists are subjected to very brief and perfunctory baggage inspections by Mexican customs officials at the point where the car papers are issued (buses stop there, too) or at the airport where they land.

Should you have anything you wish to conceal or just not want to be bothered, a tip will usually do the trick. The inspector might shine a flashlight into the trunk and ask, "What's in that box?", but rarely go deeper.

If anyone is sleeping inside the car, the inspector will often very courteously restrict the search to the front or to the trunk.

Border Hassles

If you do not look like the average tourist (and you long-haired, bearded, beaded and braless people have already guessed that there was a catch somewhere), you may not get average treatment when entering Mexico. Instead of "Stamp! Stamp! Sign here please, Next?" you might hear, "Where's your money? How much? Go back!" This is what is very commonly known as the border hassle.

Mexican border officials have a straightforward attitude: people without money are hippies and therefore less desirable as tourists. The degree of their desirability is determined by how little money they have and how much they look like a Mexican's idea of a hippie. People with money are not hippies, even though they may affect hippie styles.

Once you accept the logic that is used to determine who is hassled and who isn't, you can avoid exposing yourself to close official scrutiny. The best methods for this are deceit and camouflage.

Before crossing the border we always adjust our clothing style to fit our budget. If we're well-off we just drive on without even combing our hair, but if we're broke we stop ahead of time and put on our 'thousand dollar suits.' We bought our suits for three dollars each from an old lady selling used clothing on the side of the highway. A last minute pressing costs about 75 cents and makes us look as crisp as a page out of a Sears' catalog.

I liberally wet down my hair or get a slight trim with the scissors. Lorena fixes her long hair into a tight bun at the back of her head. She wears a knee-length skirt, a thin baggy sweater and carries a shiny black purse. We look like small town school teachers or college students from the early Sixties. The border officials love it.

You must not only look the part of the respectable tourist; you must play it as well. Be friendly but nervous, polite, ingratiating, curious, and slightly stunned if asked to show a large amount of money. Have a good story ready to cover all flaws in your act. "I'm a wounded war veteran and I get a pension every month, but I don't have that much on me," "My father sends me money whenever I need it," etc.

You will be asked your profession for entry on the tourist card. Don't blow it by saying "unemployed," but don't overdo things by claiming to be an astronaut, movie star or nuclear physicist. Teachers and businessmen are good occupations if you're not really young and technical trades such as mechanic, secretary, electrician and plumber are always reasonable choices.

Be ready to explain why you're on a six month vacation.* Never claim to be entering Mexico for business reasons (prohibited for tourists) or for school. This requires a student visa.

When asked your ultimate destination give a large city, preferably not too far south. Don't say, "Oh, I'm going to Huatla to take mushrooms!" A letter of invitation from friends already in Mexico, offering to put you up during your stay, can be very effective.

Be confident but never condescending toward officials. A sneering, arrogant or contemptuous attitude will foul up even the most affluent tourist or at least make the crossing long and tedious.

When crossing the border with a friend, don't bother claiming to be married if you aren't; they don't care.

*Border hassles are usually encounteed only by those requesting a long stay on little money.

Should the border official make a friendly overture, respond in a positive manner. If he says, "Oh, you'll like Mexico City," don't answer with "I've been there. The smog almost killed me!" Pretend, if necessary, not to know a damned thing about Mexico.

If all your acting and ploys fail to get the desired results, there are other courses of action: try a different border official or a different border crossing or wait until the shift changes and go through your routine again. If the first guy was totally inflexible because of your long hair, do something about it—comb it, cut it off, get a wig or a hat.

Many people have tried for hours on end at one border crossing and then gotten through because an official sympathized with their plight or talked to them so long that they became friends.

Because the Mexican government would like to encourage tourism, they allow travel agencies and airlines to go through the red tape of getting the customer's tourist card. The people who work in these offices aren't concerned in the least with what you look like or how much money you have; you're just another client. For the price of a bus or train ticket, air fare or just a travel agent's service charge (without buying a ticket at all) you can often get a 180-day tourist card in advance. (There must be a Mexican Consulate, however, in the city in which you're buying your ticket.)

Your tourist card will still have to be validated, but the possibilities of a hassle are greatly reduced by just having it in your hot little hand. With a bus or train ticket to a point inside Mexico, you can prove that you are not bumming completely. People flying into Mexico rarely encounter hassles, no matter how strung-out they may look.

If you personally go to the Mexican Consulate for your tourist card, it's best to go to an office in a very large city. They've seen more freaks and they're getting used to them. We always get our tourist cards at a consulate rather than the border. The staffs are generally younger, better educated and less likely to hassle you for no good reason.

Bribes

When someone tells me that they followed my advice on border crossings to the letter but only got a 30-day tourist card, I immediately ask, "Did you pay anyone off?" The usual response is, "Pay 'em off? You mean *bribe* somebody? *Bribe a government official?* Are you kidding?"

Even though many Mexicans claim that the *mordida* (the 'bite') no longer exists or that it is unnecessary, we have found it to be alive and working quite well in all parts of the country. I have given 'considerations' to everyone from post office workers who couldn't seem to remember my name to border officials who didn't like my looks.

The *mordida* is easy, relatively inexpensive, convenient and even has certain procedural rules to keep it 'honest.' To say that circumventing the law is immoral is to assume that the law itself is moral and right. A Mexican border official once told me that he had to show a large amount of money before being allowed into the U.S. "Is it not fair," he asked, "that I should enforce our laws on you in the same manner?"

"Yes," I replied, "but it's not reasonable. Here's a few dollars."

"How long a tourist card would you like?" he asked, reaching for his typewriter.

You don't bribe someone by stuffing a wad of bills in his pocket and saying, "Here ya go baby, a little something for the wife and kids!" There are more subtle and respectable techniques used to feel out the other person on their attitude and price. The easiest of these for the inexperienced person to adopt is the, "Gee whiz, I sure wish you'd tell me what to do" angle. Other effective openers to the pay-off are: "Isn't there *any way* this can be worked out?", "Will there be an extra charge?" and the national favorite, "Is there no other way of arranging the matter?" (See *Appendices: Vocabulary: Red Tape*).

Unless the response is unmistakenly negative, you can proceed immediately to the next step—the money. The handing over of the *mordida* is done discreetly and without embarrassment on the part of either person. None of this, "Pssst! Meet me in urinal four at eight o'clock!" Instead you reach casually into your wallet (or your pocket if you're really prepared), extract a dollar or two and hand them over. If it isn't enough, the official will shake his head. You pull out another dollar and another and when the right amount has been reached, business will proceed as usual. Border officials generally take only minor amounts and manage to restrain themselves from bilking people. Being offensive, however, will really up the ante.

Handle the situation with the proper attitude; just assume that every bribe is a legal and required fee. Don't act like a naughty child or a criminal or the person being bribed will react defensively and probably raise the price. When you both pretend (I really believe it in most cases) that a small consideration is legitimate, the transaction will be fast and friendly.

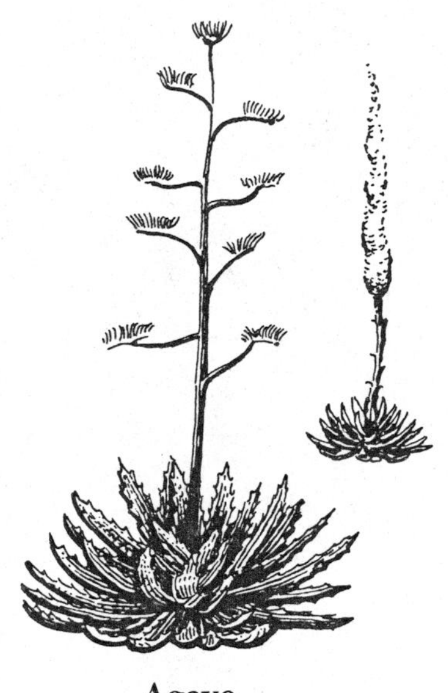

Agave

BACK TO THE U.S.A.

Lots of questions and answers...Searches...Declaring your purchases... Restrictions...Duty free...Don't smuggle!...GSP...Endangered species... A typical border crossing...

Your return to the U.S. may well be the most traumatic incident of your trip. After turning over your tourist card and car papers to Mexican border officials, you must then turn yourself over to American Customs agents. Don't even bother to offer them a few dollars to overlook the baggage inspection; their price, if they have one, is beyond reason.

The inspection that you and your belongings are given can vary anywhere from a glance into your suitcase to a down to the skin search. Although most people are given quick courteous treatment, you just can't anticipate anything. Customs officials are well aware that not all crooks and smugglers look like characters from Zap Comix.

Freaks are almost invariably given a closer and more thorough examination, but this too is unpredictable. One hairy character may get a heavy dope search, complete with sniffing dogs and laboratory analysis of pipe scrapings, while another, equally strung-out person, is only quizzed briefly about the value of souvenirs. Be prepared for the worst; hopefully, you won't get it.

When you enter the inspection area, an agent will give you a quick once-over. You'll be asked where you've been and for how long. Since they have no way of checking your answer, make it innocent. This may help keep the search and questions to a minimum. Don't say, "I've been gone a year and been just about everywhere."

You will be asked where you were born and if you've ever been arrested. Give straight answers; they can check you out very quickly on their 1984 computer and a lie always increases their interest and suspicion in you. Remember, *it's their scene* and you've got to keep cool. Never volunteer anything—these people are cops—make them ask. The best attitude is one of calm resignation. Arguing, being stubborn or acting too eager to please will attract attention.

The actual inspection, even at it's worst, shouldn't take more than ten minutes to an hour if you're on foot and not carrying much. During this time, the agent may ask such loaded questions as, "Ever see anyone smoking that mary-g-wanna down there?" Give "yes" and "no" answers and you'll avoid Dick Tracy traps.

Car searches can last quite a long time. Most travellers in heavily loaded cars and vans report searches, including questioning, of one to two hours.

Everything must usually be unloaded, probed, prodded, squeezed, sniffed, pinched, tapped, hefted, tasted and in some cases, taken inside for laboratory analysis. During all this, they'll be watching your reactions. If you're clean, it will be nerve-wracking. "Did I really get rid of those roaches I had in the I Ching?" For those who aren't clean, it can be a hair-raising ordeal. "Oh, God! He's sniffing the air coming out of the tire valve. Five keys!"

Few inspections go to the point of taking the car apart (mechanics are available to do this, if necessary), but a detailed look into nooks and crannies, from trunk to chassis, is common. Panels will be thumped, the air cleaner removed and possibly the cardboard liners of trunks and dashboards taken out. Three or four agents can cover an incredible amount of territory in a few short minutes. Specially trained dope-sniffing dogs can do it even quicker.

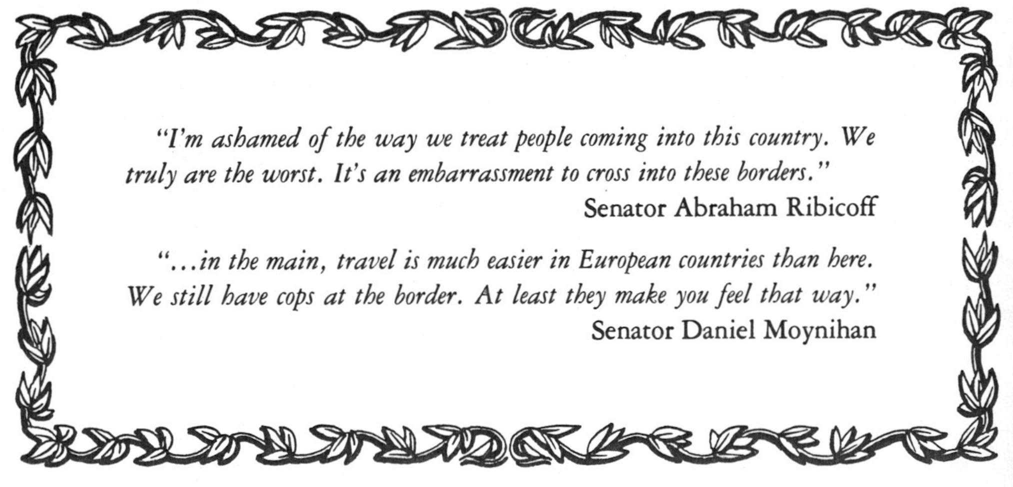

"I'm ashamed of the way we treat people coming into this country. We truly are the worst. It's an embarrassment to cross into these borders."
Senator Abraham Ribicoff

"...in the main, travel is much easier in European countries than here. We still have cops at the border. At least they make you feel that way."
Senator Daniel Moynihan

You'll be asked if you have anything to declare. Be safe, declare *everything,* even if you're not sure you still have it with you. Any excuse, however trivial, to raise you to a higher level of suspicion will be jumped on eagerly. They don't get advanced in the Customs service for being nice.

Small amounts of medicines, when accompanied by a U.S. prescription or a good excuse are usually allowed to pass. Switchblade knives must be destroyed by you with an

agent watching. Border states allow tourists to bring in a quart of liquor and they won't quibble if it's actually a liter; at least, as long as you declare it as such. Any violation, intentional or not, can result in an administrative fine—on the spot—or heavy legal action in serious cases.

Few agents will go to the trouble of actually figuring the value of your souvenirs. Many things are difficult to appraise. Although Customs agents are very experienced at judging retail value, they'll usually take your word for it as long as you don't have a lot of identical items. The duty free limit is $100, including anything you've purchased in Mexico and have been using.*

The list of what you can or cannot bring into the U.S. is long and complicated. In general, don't bring meat, plants or anything dangerous, narcotic or obscene. Citrus fruits won't get through, but you can get by with peanuts, garlic, papayas and most foods not grown in the U.S. There is no limit on cigarettes but a limit of 100 on cigars.

Your dog will need a rabies vaccination certificate (see *Pets*), but your cat, if in good health, probably won't.

Warning: Many unfortunate people, mainly freaks, don't expect hassles at the border. When the agent digs diligently into their bag of dirty underwear and finds the joint they were going to enjoy that evening, they suddenly wish they'd been more paranoid. Although you may spend many hot hours at the side of the highway cleaning out your car and then simply be waved through U.S. Customs, what if you aren't? Smuggling penalties are *harsh*.

*Legislation has been proposed to increase the duty free limit to $250 per person. It is expected to pass and Customs inspectors may allow for this even before the new exemption becomes law.

Leave it to the professionals; when you get safely home, you can work for a month at honest labor, buy a key of good Mexican grass from your local dealer and plan your next trip to Mexico.

As you travel, you'll undoubtedly hear the following questions from other tourists: "Can I get this across?", "What do I need to throw away?", "Do you think I ought to risk buying this?", etc. The only way to be sure is to write for the current U.S. Customs pamphlets. They'll send them quickly and it will end worrying and wondering. General questions (pets, liquor, $100 exemption, etc.) are answered in *Customs Hints for Returning U.S. Residents.* This costs 35 cents from the Superintendent of Documents, U.S. Government Printing Office, Washington, D.C. 20402.

So You Want to Import a Pet, which includes information on cats, dogs, monkeys and parrots, is available from the Commissioner of Customs, Washington, D.C. 20226. (Also, see *Buying Things: Parrots.*)

Questions about plants should be addressed to the Import and Permit Section, Plant Quarantine Division, 209 River Street, Hoboken, NJ 07030.

District Director of Customs offices are located in most major U.S. cities and they can also provide answers to specific questions.

GSP

The General System of Preferences is a bureaucratic way of saying they've lifted the duty on certain items imported from Mexico and other countries. If you are buying a lot of one thing, or would like to, write for the booklet detailing what is currently allowed in duty-free.

Endangered Species

Anything made from feathers, hides, shells, hair or skins may well be prohibited under the Endangered Species Act. Don't believe what they tell you in the shop; it's the inspector and regulations at the border that count. Once again, write for details or don't buy anything made from unfortunate birds and beasts—the best choice, anyway.

"Where you folks coming from?" the customs agent asked, leaning down to give the inside of the van a quick once-over. His eyes widened.

"Mexico." Steve whispered, his hands gripping the steering wheel, eyes frozen on the inspection area ahead.

"What was that?" the agent said, bending closer.

"Mexico." Steve repeated. His eyes were glassy, his breathing fast and shallow, complexion pasty beneath a heavy tan. The agent's attention moved from Steve's face to his hands, clenching and unclenching on the wheel.

"Are you all U.S. citizens?" he continued, glancing back at Lorena and then turning to me. His cheek twitched slightly as he noted my beard, my hair, my sandals. I felt like screaming, "Look at my J.C. Penney sport shirt and slacks! Can't you tell that I'm straight? This guy next to me is just naturally nervous; he's not a smuggler!"

"U.S. citizens?" Steve said, running his tongue over dry lips. Sweat beaded his forehead; it had been his idea to cross the border in late afternoon, in the heat of the day. "Day shift will be too hot and tired to tear us apart," he'd said, "and the evening shift won't be in high gear until later." I looked at the customs man. In spite of Steve's planning the officer looked as though they'd just lifted him off a coat hanger. The creases in his uniform were sharp enough to cut bread. Sweat began to pour down my chest.

"Yeah, we're U.S. citizens." Steve finally answered. He sounded about as convincing as if he'd claimed we were Russian ballerinas.

"How long have you been out of the United States?" the agent asked. The quickening excitement in his voice had been barely controlled: these weirdos were right out of a Customs Service training manual. He'd bet his badge against a six pack of Lone Star that there was enough of *something*, somewhere inside this van, to get everyone on duty promoted on the spot. It would just be a matter of rooting it out.

"Ah...well...a long time," Steve stammered, giving a sickly grin and shrugging his shoulders helplessly. The agent didn't bother to press for a more definite answer; without taking his eyes from us he backed into the booth and reached for the phone.

"Now you've really blown it!" I hissed. "I told you to let me drive through! He probably thinks we're the Mexican Connection!" Steve waved his hands in front of his face; this was all too much for him, nothing was going according to The Plan. I stared out my window, grimly remembering all of our preparations, the long hours spent packing, cleaning and sorting. It had all gone to waste in a few moments, a few fumbled answers to simple questions. They'd tear us down to the frame and then chop up the pieces.

"Would you folks mind pulling up over there?" The agent's voice dripped with false sincerity as he pointed to a long metal table in the inspection area. Flourescent lights cast an unforgiving glare on the shiny metal surface, banishing afternoon shadows. Behind the table stood a group of men and women in Customs uniforms. The staff had turned out to welcome us back.

"Yeah, sure," Steve croaked, lifting his foot off the clutch. He maneuvered the van alongside the waiting inspectors and stopped. He contorted his upper lip, chewing nervously on his moustache.

"Mind shutting it off?" a grey haired man asked. Steve fumbled for the key. There was a long silence.

"Would you please step out now?" he added, giving the others significant looks. Steve opened his door and edged out cautiously. The older man smiled graciously; all he lacked was a long pointer: "Now this, ladies and gentlemen, is your classic counter-culture smuggler. Please note the slight tremble at the knees and the furtive eye movements."

The agent waited for a few more moments and then said, "Now would you mind opening the doors of your vehicle so we can proceed?" One of the younger agents chuckled, but caught a quick look from the older man and turned it into a discreet cough. "Please take everything out," he added, a note of anticipation in his voice.

"*Everything?*" Steve asked, looking up hopelessly at the long roof rack, piled high with baskets, boxes and unidentifiable lumps and bundles.

"Everything!" the agent repeated, "Laid out on that table."

"Is this haaashish?" The agent drawled wearily, reaching into the hand carved wooden chest. He gingerly removed a cylindrical bundle of heavy dark lumps wrapped in dried corn husks. After two hours, dreams of sudden promotion and banner headlines, (*Trio Nabbed In World Record Haul of Zonko Root!*), had turned into a sweltering snipe hunt. The high good humor of the first hour, with many wisecracks about the incredible amount of junk we'd collected on our travels, was rapidly changing to a grim determination to find something, *anything* to justify the blitzkrieg search they'd dropped on us.

"No," I sighed. "That's not hashish. It's incense. Homemade *copal* incense from Chiapas." He gave me a doubtful look and managed a controlled, "We'll just check that out in the lab." While he awaited the results of the analysis, he pointed to the top of the van and said, "Get that box down, please."

I looked up. A vague premonition stirred in the back of my mind. Wasn't that box actually...?

"Hey, Steve!' I called. "They want to look at your box. You know, *the little one?*" Steve had been leaning against a tall steel stanchion, desperately trying to look casual. Whenever one of Lorena's plastic bags of herbs was sent off to the lab his knees buckled and his breathing became ragged.

At my mention of the box he took a few quick steps toward us and then stopped dead in his tracks, a look of complete panic twisting his face. He moved hesitantly to the van and began climbing slowly to the top, like a condemned man ascending a scaffold to perform the ultimate rope trick. As he handed the box down to me I caught the desperate message pulsing from his eyes: Think fast, smart ass, this was your idea!

I cradled the box in my arms and carried it to the table. The agent was busily burrowing through a huge pile of Mexican Indian clothing. "You folks have got enough stuff here to open your own store." He laughed, turning toward us with a weary smile. He looked at the box. The smile faded. "What in the...?" He stopped, eyes bulging slightly. His hand moved cautiously to the lid.

"Hahahaha! Well," I choked, "you see, it's a, it's a sort of a, you know...a...a coffin." Other inspectors, sensing the kill, quickly gathered around us, abandoning a detailed search of our dirty laundry, moldy tent and coffee cans filled with broken seashells.

"A coffin?" The question was a blend of outrage and disgust. "You mean that's a *baby coffin!*" he yelled, struggling to regain his composure. There were low growls from the assembled agents. How could I explain that it was actually a nicely crafted pine box that we'd bought from a Guatemalan carpenter? That with a bit of wood stain, varnish and some brass hinges we'd converted it into an ideal container for our odds and ends. It was a coffin only in name. It was a simple matter of *perspective.*

"Open!" he barked, sucking a great breath of air in anticipation of some unprecedented horror. His wife had been right, he should have gone into the Postal Service!

I twisted the little brass latch and raised the lid.

"Oh, Lord...!"

"You've gotta be...!"

"Unbelievable...!"

We stood in guilty silence, cries of outrage ringing ominously in our ears. Steve turned to face south, toward Mexico and freedom. I knew what he was thinking: Run! Now! While their attention was on the coffin...leap the pipe barricades...fast and low, crouching to avoid the .357 magnums...into that alley...shave his head...change identity...

The officer reached hesitantly into the coffin and began removing the little pink arms, torsos, legs and heads. His hands shook noticeably as he lined the grisly plastic parts along the edge of the inspection table. A miniature morgue.

"It's...it's kind of a long story!" I blurted, pulling my eyes away from the gruesome display. "You see we were camped on the Caribbean and every morning I went beach-combing..." They didn't seem to be listening; one of the older inspectors, a man who looked like my grandfather, was shaking his head from side to side. "I've seen it all now," his expression said; "It's time to retire!"

"...and I started noticing, you see, these, uh, pieces of doll babies all along the beach. An arm here, a head there. You know, litter. Doll baby litter. It seemed kind of, well, *hilarious.*"

No one laughed.

"So then I started picking them up. Cleaning the beach, you might say." I hurried on, "And we had the coffin already, got it in Guatemala for a good price. Couldn't pass it up, actually. Seemed, well, *natural* to put the baby parts in it..."

At the word "natural" one of the women inspectors shuddered and steadied herself against the table. Others began drifting away, picking distractedly at the array of junk that had yet to be searched.

"I mean...don't you think it's...?" The agent raised his hand, cutting me off. I looked over at Steve and Lorena; they were staring at the corrugated metal roof.

A strategy conference convened. We stood nervously next to the van, trying to ignore the occasional hard stare from the assembled inspectors. I had the feeling we were still a long way away from an All American hamburger and cold beer. At least it was cooling off; the sun had gone down almost an hour before.

I quietly scooped up the pitiful remains of the doll babies and dumped them into the coffin, carefully closing the lid. Out of sight and out of mind, I hoped.

"Oh, boy, get ready," Steve muttered, watching as the meeting broke up, one officer going to the phone, another hurrying into the main building. They looked grim and determined. We had beaten the first wave, now they would call in the reserves.

The big black Labrador crouched in the back of the van, head tilted upward, his chest rising and falling as he howled mournfully. The handler turned to the chief inspector with a puzzled look. "I've never seen him do this before," he said, shaking his head in wonderment. The handler ordered the dog from the van, looking at us suspiciously.

"Whatever it is, it's weird!" he said, quickly leading the dog away. The agent glanced at his watch and then over at us. He'd thought of calling in sick, but had decided to come to work in spite of a nasty chest cold. Nights weren't so bad lately unless you got stuck with a bunch like this...

"He probably smelled the coyote," I offered. "We picked up this guy named Ramón, a rancher from around Monterrey. His pick-up had broken down and he had his pet coyote with him. Cute little thing, completely tame. He slept back there on the floor for a whole day."

The customs agent smiled knowingly. A clever story but not quite clever enough! He called to another man and ordered up a battery of powerful flood lights, a hydraulic jack, floor crawlers, stethoscopes, probes, hammers and whisk brooms.

"Or it could even have been the pig," Lorena added helpfully. "It took days just to clean up all of the..." Her voice trailed off; if he didn't believe the story of the coyote how would he handle a pregnant five hundred pound brood sow? "It was near Tepic," she continued. "Our landlord said he'd knock something off the rent if we'd take this pig to Guadalajara. His brother has a..."

The chief inspector turned his back on her, ending any further explanations.

"It's clean," an agent said half an hour later, pushing himself from beneath the van. No hidden compartments or clever modifications to hide illicit goods. Steve wiped sweat from his brow; he could take the same van through the border time after time and still worry that they'd manage to find something incriminating.

Another man was inside, tapping at the panelling with a tiny mallet. He worked as methodically and intently as a master safecracker, but found nothing. A third inspector scrutinized the screwheads attaching the panelling to the interior for scratches or other evidence that we had taken down the thin wood and stuffed the empty spaces with forbidden powders or herbs. Still others removed the headlights, hubcaps, heater ducts and heavy cardboard liners beneath the dashboard.

I was tempted to tell them that Steve's paranoia had driven us to check and clean those same spaces the day before. We had spent hours in the middle of the desert, sweating under a blazing sun, dusting, sweeping and washing every corner and crevice in the van. Two miles before the border crossing Steve had suddenly stopped, demanding that we swear an oath that we weren't smuggling anything. Lorena and I had answered with laughter, but Steve had insisted we pledge to be clean and innocent.

"A minute of paranoia is worth a year's detention!" he repeated, time after time, until I was ready to swear to anything just to get moving again.

Another conference was called, the inspectors moving carefully out of earshot. An argument seemed to have developed between those who had given up hope and those still thirsting for the kill. Fate intervened in the form of a brand new white Cadillac. The driver, a huge red-faced man wearing an improbably large cowboy hat, was having trouble understanding what was being asked of him.

"Open the trunk? What for? Some kind of trouble here?" He glared at us from around a thick cigar, as though we had brought this upon him. I looked at the various Customs people. Perhaps it was true; they all wore the expression of hungry frustrated sharks.

The man's wife, a small silver haired woman, peered suspiciously through the tinted windows, looking at the inspectors as if they were bandits. One of them was standing behind the car, waiting for the trunk to be opened. The rear bumper seemed unusually low to the ground.

"Why don't you folks just pack your things up and go along your way?" the chief inspector said, his interest already focusing on the Cadillac. We sighed with relief; we'd be lucky to find a tavern open at this hour, but if we hurried...

"Don't forget your coffin!" one of them snarled.

"Well, that about does it!" Steve said, trying a final knot around the seabag and checking the lashings on the outboard motor. We squeezed into the front of the van, exhausted but triumphant: they hadn't found it! We still had it!

"ONE BOTTLE! ARE YOU SERIOUS?"

Steve had just put the van in gear. The man with the cowboy hat was waving his arms wildly, his face dark with anger. There were enough bottles of liquor on the inspection table to stock a large *cantina.*

"Check that out," Steve giggled, motioning toward the Cadillac. An inspector was helping the wife remove several large boxes from the rear seat. The sharks had found their prey.

We pulled by them slowly, chuckling with relief and amusement. The man in the cowboy hat glared malevolently, then suddenly leveled his smoking cigar at us like a pistol. "What in the hell do you call *that*?" he yelled.

Steve's head jerked forward. It was a classic trick, to turn attention to another when caught red-handed. I held my breath as Steve flicked on the headlights. If they were bright enough they might not...

"Hold it right there!" an inspector shouted, moving quickly in front of us. Steve stepped on the brake, then slumped over the wheel, nervously probing his teeth with a long thumbnail. I could imaging what he was thinking: 'almost' only counts in horseshoes. They had us.

We got out of the van, joining the group of agent staring silently at the front bumper.

"OK, what is it?" the chief inspector asked, shining the beam of his flashlight onto the black fuzzy ball.

"It's a..." Steve hesitated. "It's a duck," he confessed, "The *Pato de Paz.*"

"The Peace Duck?" someone sputtered.

I groaned. After the incident of the coffin I would have thought they'd take a duck in stride.

"Well, you see..." he hesitated again; these people just didn't seem to have a sense of the bizarre humor that is so dear to Mexicans. But maybe, once they heard the story..."Carl had this terrific attack of diarrhea last year in Baja and..."

"You mean to say that this duck is from Baja California?" a stern voice interrupted, "and that you have had it in your possesion for *more than a year?*"

"Well, yeah," Steve continued, "but like I said, Carl had this attack and wandered off into the bushes and found the duck. In a bush. It was dead, you see, but it had got hung up in this bush. Perfectly dried out. Preserved, just like a mummy."

Heads nodded. Mummy, doll baby parts. Coffin. Oh, yes.

Steve hurried on with the story. "You see it occurred to us that it would be neat to wire him to the front bumper, like a hood ornament or a mascot. Mexicans loved it. Every time we stopped it drew a crowd. Nobody has ever tried to steal it. We don't even have to take it in at night."

Heads nodded again. Yes, they could certainly understand why we didn't have to take it in at night. Steve began to elaborate on the tale, but the words weren't coming out quite right. He choked, stammered and then suddenly buckled forward. He jammed a fist into his mouth as great bellows of laughter reverberated off the metal ceiling overhead. Several hours of tense waiting had taken their toll on our sanities; Lorena and I joined him, tears streaming down our faces. The Customs agent grew more and more impassive.

As our fits passed one of the inspectors stepped forward and between tightly clenched jaws said: "Under the Endangered Species Act...of... 1973...I hereby...confiscate...... *this duck!*"

His self control suddenly slipped. Before we could protest he reached down, grabbed the Peace Duck and jerked it toward him.

Steve looked sadly at the empty bumper. The duck had seen a good many miles, from northern Baja to El Salvador and back, through deserts, jungles, mountains and cities, spreading peace and good will to millions. Well, hundreds at least. He reached down and gently pried the skinny little legs from the piece of twisted coathanger. After carefully brushing the brittle black feet against his shirt to clean off the dust and road grime, Steve handed them solemnly to the seething customs man. "Don't forget his feet; they're endangered, too."

As we climbed back into the van the inspectors were walking slowly back toward the Cadillac. Their shoulders were slumped, their pace weary. It had been such a long day.

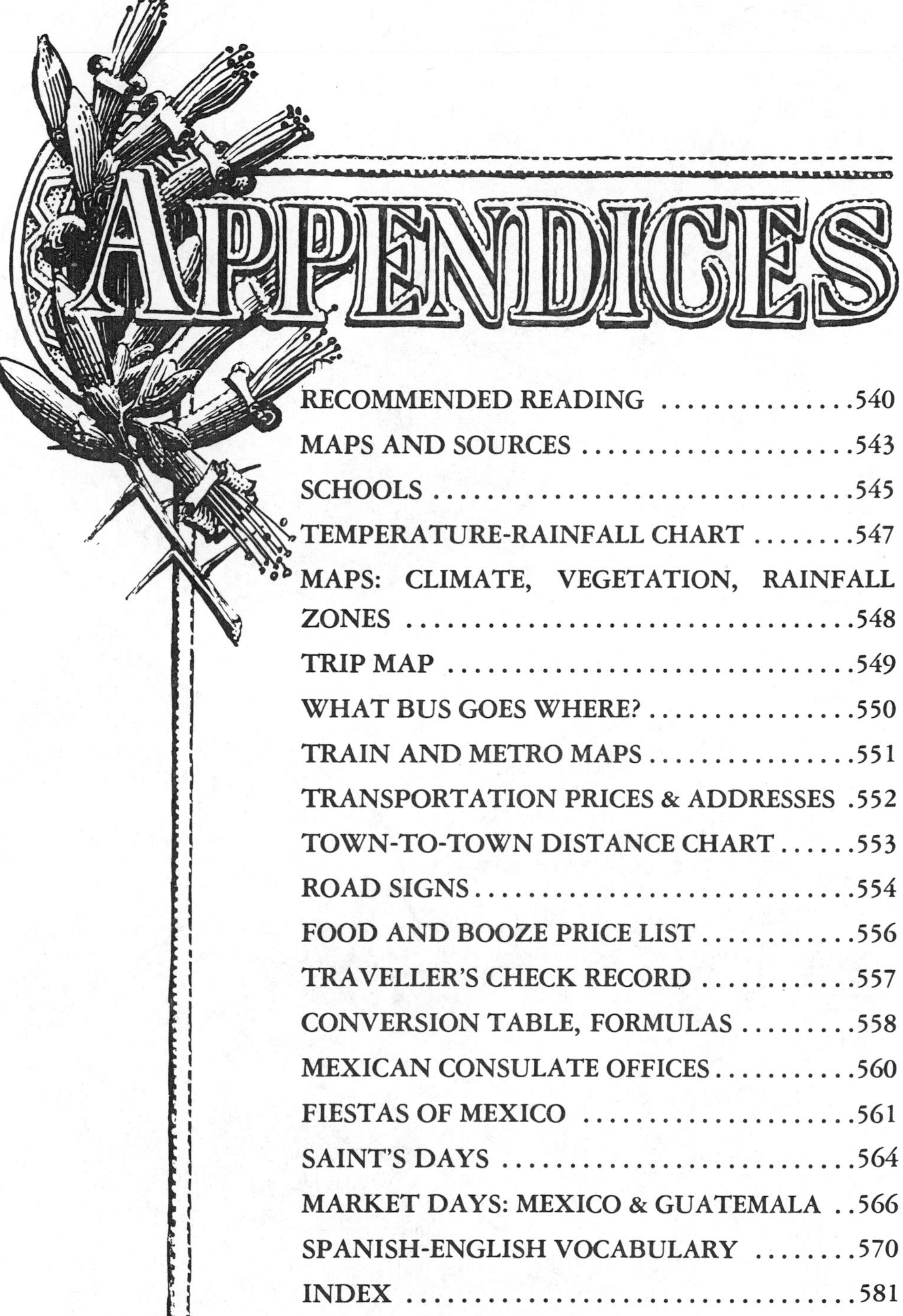
APPENDICES

A Sierra Madre Occidental; B Vizcaino Desert; C Magdalena Plain; D Bolson de Mapimi; E Sierra Madre Oriental; F Volcano Zone; G Sierra Madre Del Sur; H Sierra Madre de Chiapas; I Sierra Norte de Chiapas; J Yucatan Peninsula K Bolson de Mayran;

RECOMMENDED READING

Mexico: Places and Pleasures by Kate Simon. World Publishing, Times Mirror, NY. In spite of what my mother says, there are other guidebooks worth reading and even buying. This is my favorite.

The Baja Book II by Tom Miller and Elmar Baxter. Baja Trail Publications, Huntington Beach, CA. $8.95. They also publish ***Mexico West***, an informal newsletter and ***The World of the California Gray Whale*** (by Tom Miller, $4.). All nicely done.

Offbeat Baja by Jim Hunter. Chronicle Books, 870 Market St., San Francisco 94102. $4.95. I'll take this the next time we drive to Baja.

Land of Clear Light by Michael Jenkinson. E.P. Dutton. $13.95. Covers the U.S. Southwest, Sierra Madre and Baja Peninsula of Mexico. Well written, with many excellent photos and lots of solid information.

Where There Is No Doctor by David Werner. The Hesperian Foundation, Box 1692, Palo Alto, CA 94302. $5.00 plus shipping. A fantastic book: readable, practical advice designed to keep you healthy with a minimum of treatment. Used extensively in the Third World. A non-profit publication, sold cheaper in poor countries.

Good Food From Mexico by Ruth Mulvey and Luisa Alvarez. Collier Books.

A Potter's Mexico by Irwin and Emily Whitaker, University of New Mexico Press, Albuquerque. $17.50. I'm not a potter and I read this cover-to-cover. Invaluable information for anyone wanting to buy the best pottery, including the names of specific artisans.

A Shopper's Guide To Mexico by James Norman. Doubleday. Outdated but still quite useful.

A Layman's Guide To Mexican Law by Alberto Mayagoitia. University of New Mexico Press, Albuquerque, NM. $3.95. Written by a Mexican lawyer with 20 years experience. Anyone considering setting up housekeeping or business in Mexico should read it.

Zona Roja: A Guide To Prostitution Along The Mexican-American Border by Raul Mocho, Mission Publications, P.O. Box 426, Union City, CA 94587. $4.95. "Be informed, not fooled!" he says. Why not? This book isn't a joke. Clearly written with good maps and level-headed advice.

Mexico In Transition by Philip Russell. Colorado River Press, Box 8004, Austin, TX 78712. $5.95. An engrossing survey of Mexican history, society, politics, economy and relationships with *Gringolandia.* Illustrated by Rius, a man with a very sharp pen. (They've also done ***Cuba In Transition.***)

The Spanish Game by Luisa M.A. de Jaubert and Fernando Diez de Urdanivia. Editores Asociados, S.A., Angel Urraza 1322, Mexico 12, D.F. A book for gringo students of Spanish written by Mexicans—an indispensable aid. It's also interesting and entertaining. Costs about $2.00.

2 Rabbit, 7 Wind: Nahuatl Poems by Toni de Gerez. The Viking Press, NY. Poems from ancient Mexico retold from Nahuatl texts. My favorite is the reaction of the conquered to the Conquest: "...we cannot agree/that our gods are wrong/is it not enough that we/have already lost/that our way of life has/been taken away?/is that not enough?/this is all we can say/this is our answer/to your words o lords/do with us/as you please."

Many Mexicos by Lesly Byrd Simpson. University of California Press, Berkeley. A highly readable and very enjoyable history of Mexico.

A History Of Mexico by Henry Bamford Parkes. Houghton Mifflin Co., Boston, More scholastic in tone than *Many Mexicos* but still good.

The Rise and Fall of Maya Civilization by J. Eric S. Thompson. University of Oklahoma Press, 1954. Extremely interesting.

The Bernal Diaz Chronicles. Translated and edited by Albert Idell, Dolphin Books, Doubleday Co., Inc. Bernal Diaz accompanied Cortés and recorded what they saw in great detail and with a high degree of accuracy.

Incidents of Travel In Yucatán and Chiapas by John Lloyd Stephens (many editions). These books combine exploration, adventure and archaeology with wonderful drawings of many ruins.

In The Magic Land of Peyote by Fernando Benitez. Recently available in paperback. Excellent.

Castaneda's Journey: The Power and the Allegory by Richard de Mille. Capra Press, 631 State St., Santa Barbara, CA 93101. Did Carlos Castaneda write his famous Don Juan books in an L.A. motel room? A witty and unrelenting examination of that possibility. Well documented.

Secrets of the Mind-Altering Plants of Mexico by Richard Heffern. Pyramid Books, NY. Covers everything from medicinal plants to ritual hallucinogens. Fascinating and well-researched.

Amistad. Apdo 555, Mexico 1, D.F. The magazine of the American Society of Mexico. Monthly. Rather straight and dry, but some good articles on Mexico. Aimed at the business and diplomatic community.

Mexico Desconocido by Harry Moller. Editorial Harry Moller, S.A., Aguascalientes No. 31, colonia Roma, Mexico 7, D.F. This is a monthly travel magazine, in Spanish, that explores little-known areas of Mexico. Easy to read, though the prose is a bit thick. Good photos. A book by the same name, covering many interesting areas of the country, is about to be reissued. Write *Señor* Moller (in English if you wish) for details.

Nueva Picardía Mexicana by A. Jiménez. Editores Mexicanos Unidos, S.A. Samples of Mexico's ribald sense of humor, past and present. A sort of off-color Mad Magazine.

Mexico Geográfico. Insurgentes Sur 300-801, Mexico 7, D.F. Monthly magazine, $30 a year airmail to the U.S. Easy and interesting reading in Spanish. An obvious copy of the National Geographic Magazine.

Guatemala Guide by Paul Glassman, Passport Press, Box 596, Moscow, Vermont 05662. $6.95 (add 75 cents for postage). I'll carry this on my next trip to Guatemala; my highest recommendation.

The Guatemala News. 10 Calle 6-72, Zone 9, Guatemala City. A weeky paper with interesting articles on the country and people.

Along The Gringo Trail: A Budget Travel Guide To Latin America by Jack Epstein. And/Or Press, Berkeley, $6.95. Covers Mexico to the West Indies. Good but understandably sketchy in places considering the broad area covered.

A Traveler's Guide To El Dorado and the Inca Empire by Lynn Meisch. Headlands Press, $8.95. Covers Columbia, Ecuador, Peru and Bolivia, *in detail.* If you're headed farther south—or just interested—you'll need this book. Excellent advice on buying things, especially fine textiles.

How To Keep Your Volkswagen Alive by John Muir. $9.00, John Muir Publications, Box 613, Santa Fe, NM 87501. If you don't have this book in your VW, get one; you'll certainly need it, if only to check what that mechanic is doing. Now in Spanish ($6.50). A great gift for a Spanish speaking friend or *mecánico.*

Note: When price or publisher are not mentioned it's because I either don't have the information or can't trust it not to change soon. Go to a library or large bookstore and ask to see *Books In Print.* This massive reference book has everything you need to locate a publication.

Publishers and Distributors

Tolliver's Books, 1634 S. Stearns Drive, Los Angeles, CA 90035. New, used and out-of-print books on "Life and Earth Sciences," a broad term, since they carry everything from guidebooks to scientific monographs. Tell them your interest and they'll send you a specific catalog that will drive you wild with temptation. Book lovers beware; they've got something for everyone.

The Rio Grande Press, Inc., Glorieta, NM 87535. Fine reprints of classic works on the Southwest and Mexico. These are the kind of books you won't loan out casually.

University of New Mexico Press, Albuquerque, NM 87131. Many diverse subjects, from Mexican music to pottery.

Minutiae Mexicana, S.A. de C.V., Insurgentes Centro 114-210, Mexico 4, D.F. Special mini-guides (in English) on everything from Mexican Witchcraft to Birds, Tequila and Speaking Spanish. Nicely done and authoritative.

MAPS AND SOURCES

Roadmaps are not handed out as liberally in Mexico as they are in the United States. In fact, it's easier to get a roadmap of Mexico in the U.S. Ask at gas stations near the border, tourist agencies, large hotels, insurance offices and bookstores. Maps are sometimes available from Mexican government tourist offices and consulates.

Members of AAA (American Automobile Association) will be given free Mexican road maps and driving logs upon request. Sanborn's Insurance Company also gives away free road logs. Most insurance companies offer some type of map, though they are rarely as good as the *Carta Turistica* or *Serie Patria.*

Campers, hikers and boaters will want something more detailed than a gas station map. For a discussion on sources of topo maps and sea charts see *The People's Guide To Camping In Mexico.*

•*Carta Turistica* series by *DETENAL (Dirección General de Estudios del Territorio Nacional*). A series of large maps designed for motorists and tourists. In Spanish but easily translated. Each map is a guidebook in itself, with a great deal of information on points of special interest, from waterfalls to historic sites. The best general roadmap series I've yet to see. Their only disadvantage is size: almost too large to open up in a small car's front seat.

The *Carta Turistica* series is available in larger bookstores in Mexico or from these (and presumably other) *DETENAL* offices:

San Antonio Abad No. 124, México 8, D.F.

Balderas No. 71, México, D.F. (one block from Hidalgo Metro station).

Centro Civico Comercial, 16 Septiembre 734, Guadalajara, Jalisco

16 Septiembre 734, Guadalajara, Jalisco

Cuauhtémoc 734, Monterrey, N.L.

M. de Cervantes S. 201-F, Leon, Gto.

These maps cost only 25 pesos each, a real bargain. Write to *DETENAL* (formerly *Cetenal*) offices for a catalog of their other maps, including topographical, climate and land use.

•*Serie Patria* roadmaps, by individual state. Issued by *Librería Patria, S.A., Cinco de Mayo 43, México, D.F.* These are commonly known as the *Serie Azul* or Blue Series because of the bright blue cover. The maps, in Spanish, give a brief history of the state and a chart indicating tourist facilities and attractions. Detailed roadmaps, reasonably accurate. The back of each map has good city maps for the state. Available in book-stores and not expensive

•National Geographic Society, Washington, DC 20036. Their Map of Mexico and Central America is available for a staggering $7.00. It came out in the March 1953 issue, if you have a friend or relative who hoards back copies. The very interesting Archaeological Map of Middle America, now out of print, appeared in the October 1968 issue.

•The Central Intelligence Agency produces General Reference Maps (includes roads). They come in a protective envelope. Prices are subject to change. For a complete listing write to the Superintendent of Documents, U.S. Government Printing Office, Washington, DC 20402.

Mexico: 22 by 31 inches: 041-015-00019-5 is 90 cents.

Guatemala: 25 by 16 inches: 041-015-00029-2 is 65 cents.

General and topographic maps of Guatemala are available from the Instituto Geográfico Nacional, Avenida Las Americas 5-76, Zona 13, Guatemala, C.A.

•San Diego Map Centre, 2611 University Ave., San Diego CA 92104. Phone 714-291-3830. I don't like to plug individual businesses, but the Map Centre deserves an exception. They stock both map series mentioned previously, as well as aeronautical maps, charts, satellite photographs, topographical maps and many books on Mexico, particularly Baja. They have no main catalog but will give information based on your particular needs or interest. Fair prices and personal service. Their store is a map lover's Mecca.

•Many tourist offices inside Mexico, especially those located in state capitals, will prepare their own maps. These may not be of the best quality, but they often have information on *fiestas*, spas and points of interest that don't make it into other publications—and they're free.

•If you come upon a new map or a good source of maps, please drop me a line, giving the necessary details (address, price, type of map, etc.) for the next edition.

SCHOOLS

It seems that wherever three or more educated Mexicans gather, a school is formed. Add a footloose gringo with a college diploma and you've got an international university. Although most of the schools listed are for Spanish language study, others have a broader curriculum. The easy-going life style of Mexico, combined with favorable climate and low cost-of-living, make studying easier and more rewarding. A study-vacation isn't the same as trying to make up a few badly needed credits in some underheated, over-crowded lecture hall in the north.

Foreign children often study in Mexico public schools, but due to extremely crowded classrooms they may not be admitted unless arrangements are made well in advance of a term. For those goig beyond the sixth grade, an evaluation test is required (in Spanish). Most foreigners find private schools more convenient and expensive in comparison to public schools. Note: Unless otherwise indicated I have no personal knowledge of the schools mentioned. Make careful inquiries or find someone who has studied at the school you're interested in. Some are dull and some exciting; what you get depends very much on the teachers and other students.

Student discounts

Students holding valid Mexican student I.D. cards are eligible for discounts on everything from hotel rooms to museum tickets. For details ask at the school you are attending or write to the nearest Mexican consul.

•***Instituto Fenix,*** Apdo 102-B, Cuernavaca, Morelos. Spanish and culture. Study programs in a mountain village (Chalchihuites). *Fenix* was started by friends of ours; it's among the top. The atmosphere is casual but exciting. They don't fool around—either at study or when just enjoying Mexico.

•***Ceilo,*** Apdo 109, San Cristobal Las Casas, Chiapas. Spanish and culture. Their motto, "Small is beautiful" sounds reasonable. A nice area to study in.

•***Provecto Linguistico Francisco Marroquin,*** Apdo 237, Antigua, Guatemala, C.A. A non-profit school. Spanish and Mayan.

•***Instituto Nacional de Bellas Artes.*** The National Institute of Fine Arts is controlled by the Secretary of Education. They have 38 schools, most located in state capitals. Courses are offered in everything from music and art to dancing and metal work. Tuition is reasonable. For more information write to a Mexican Consul or Tourist Bureau office. (A fine Bellas Artes school is located in San Miguel de Allende, Guanajuato.)

•***Centro Internacional*** (The Center For International Studies), San Miguel de Allende, Guanajuato. Courses in culture, literature, folk beliefs, cooking—you name it, if they get enough interest and a teacher they'll offer a course. (Non-profit.)

•***The San Miguel Writing Center*** (shares facilities with *Centro Internacional*) is a non-profit school offering workshop courses in all types of writing: fiction, non-fiction, travel, drama, short story, television, poetry and so on. The faculty are all professional writers. (Many writers are retired or vacationing in the town.) Tuition is very reasonable and some scholarships are given.

For more information on both schools write: Pila Seca 1, San Miguel de Allende, Gto., Mexico.

•***Academia Hispano Americana,*** Insurgentes 21, San Miguel de Allende, Gto. Spanish, literature, other. They are often full so write for details in advance.

•If you know of a school (any type) that would be of interest to others, please sent full details to me, c/o John Muir Publications, Box 613, Santa Fe, N.M. 87501.

These publications list hundreds of schools offering various study programs in Mexico. Write for their latest catalogs.

•CIEE (Council on International Educational Exchange). 777 United Nations Plaza, N.Y., N.Y. 10017 or 236 North Santa Cruz, No. 314, Las Gatos, CA. 95030. *The Whole World Handbook: A Student Guide to Work, Study and Travel Abroad.*

•*The New Guide to Study Abroad.* Harper & Row, Dept. 372, R. Brengel, 10 East 53rd St., N.Y., N.Y. 10022.

•*Study Abroad.* UNESCO, write: UNIPUB, P.O. Box 433, Murray Hill Station, N.Y., N.Y. 10016.

•Institute of International Education, 809 United Nations Plaza, N.Y., N.Y. 10017. Many useful publications.

ANNUAL AVERAGE TEMPERATURES AND RAINFALL

	Altitude	Jan. T*	Jan. R*	Feb. T	Feb. R	March T	March R	April T	April R	May T	May R	June T	June R	July T	July R	Aug. T	Aug. R	Sept. T	Sept. R	Oct. T	Oct. R	Nov. T	Nov. R	Dec. T	Dec. R
Acapulco, Gro.	23	78	0.4	78	0.0	79	0.0	80	0.0	83	12.	83	17.	83	8.6	83	9.8	82	14.	82	6.7	81	1.2	79	0.4
Aguascalientes, Ags.	6258	55	0.5	58	0.2	63	0.1	68	0.1	72	0.7	70	4.8	69	5.8	67	4.1	67	3.6	66	1.3	64	0.7	56	0.6
Apatzingán, Mich.	2237	78	.16	80	.28	84	.06	86	.04	90	.56	88	3.5	84	7.4	82	6.8	83	6.6	83	1.8	81	.32	78	.63
Campeche, Camp.	26	72	0.7	74	0.4	77	0.5	79	0.2	81	1.7	81	6.1	80	7.0	81	6.7	81	5.7	80	3.4	76	1.2	74	1.2
Chetumal, Q. Roo	13	73	3.0	75	.86	77	1.1	80	1.2	81	5.5	82	7.0	82	5.1	82	4.2	81	5.5	79	8.4	75	3.4	75	3.7
Chihuahua, Chih.	4690	49	0.1	52	0.2	59	0.3	65	0.3	74	0.4	79	1.0	77	3.1	75	3.7	72	3.7	65	1.4	56	0.3	49	0.8
Chilpancingo, Gro.	3800	66	0.1	67	0.2	70	0.1	72	0.2	73	2.8	70	6.0	70	7.8	69	6.6	69	6.2	70	3.4	69	0.9	67	0.8
Cd. Obregón, Son.	131	65	.27	68	.20	72	.06	77	.16	81	0.0	90	.07	93	.27	93	1.8	91	1.7	85	.57	75	1.7	67	.51
Cd. Victoria, Tamps.	1053	60	1.4	64	1.0	70	0.8	76	1.5	79	5.0	81	4.8	81	4.1	82	2.7	79	7.9	74	4.3	67	1.7	60	0.6
Colima, Col.	1657	72	0.5	72	0.3	74	0.0	77	0.0	79	0.3	79	5.7	78	7.7	78	7.2	77	7.7	78	3.1	76	0.9	73	1.3
Cordoba, Ver.	3049	61	1.8	63	1.5	67	1.5	62	2.2	73	4.3	72	13.	70	15.	70	16.	70	18.	68	9.1	65	3.7	63	2.1
Creel, Chih.	7724	41	1.9	41	.31	42	.59	50	.55	55	1.1	63	5.3	63	5.3	61	5.5	59	1.1	54	2.6	44	1.3	39	1.8
Cuernavaca, Mor.	5000	65	0.1	67	0.2	70	0.3	72	0.3	74	2.1	70	7.8	68	8.6	68	8.7	68	9.7	68	3.1	67	0.3	66	0.1
Culiacn, Sin.	216	67	0.4	69	0.4	71	0.2	74	0.0	79	0.1	83	1.2	83	5.8	82	6.8	82	4.6	80	1.6	73	0.4	67	2.1
Durango, Dgo.	6209	53	0.5	56	0.4	60	0.0	65	0.1	69	0.5	62	2.4	69	4.9	69	3.6	67	4.0	64	1.2	58	0.6	54	0.7
Fortín, Ver.	3326	61	1.9	64	1.5	67	1.6	70	2.1	72	5.0	71	14.	71	15.	70	16.	70	18.	69	8.5	64	3.5	62	2.4
Guadalajara, Jal.	5220	58	0.7	61	0.2	65	0.1	70	0.0	72	0.7	71	7.6	69	10.	68	7.9	67	7.0	65	2.1	61	0.8	59	0.8
Guanajuato, Gto.	6835	57	0.5	60	0.3	64	0.2	68	0.2	71	1.1	68	5.4	67	6.6	66	5.5	65	6.0	63	2.0	60	0.7	59	0.6
Guaymas, Son.		64	0.3	66	0.2	69	0.2	73	0.1	73	0.1	84	0.0	87	1.8	87	3.0	86	2.1	81	0.4	72	0.4	65	1.1
Hermosillo, Son.	638	60	0.1	63	0.6	68	0.2	73	0.1	79	0.1	88	0.1	90	2.8	88	3.3	87	2.5	79	1.6	70	0.2	60	1.0
Ixtapan la Sal, Mex.	6349	84	0.6	67	0.5	70	0.3	72	1.2	75	2.3	73	6.4	68	7.3	68	11.	69	9.5	67	0.6	66	0.6	66	0.3
Jalapa, Ver.	4540	58	2.1	60	2.1	63	2.1	67	2.3	68	4.7	67	12.	66	8.5	66	8.0	65	11.	64	5.1	60	2.8	52	1.9
La Paz, B.C.	59	64	.13	68	.45	71	.03	74	0.0	79	0.0	81	0.0	88	.25	88	1.6	85	2.0	80	.37	72	.54	60	1.3
León, Gto.	6180	58	0.5	61	0.2	66	0.2	70	0.1	73	0.9	71	4.3	68	6.6	68	5.5	68	5.2	66	1.5	61	0.7	60	0.5
Manzanillo, Col.		75	0.9	74	0.5	74	0.0	76	0.0	79	0.1	81	4.0	83	5.4	83	7.4	81	15.	81	5.0	79	0.7	77	2.1
Mazatlán, Sin.	3	67	0.5	67	0.4	67	0.1	70	0.0	75	0.0	79	1.1	81	6.6	81	9.6	81	10.	79	2.4	74	0.5	69	1.7
Merida, Yuc.	30	73	1.2	74	0.6	78	0.8	81	1.0	82	3.2	81	5.9	81	5.5	81	5.1	81	6.0	79	4.0	75	1.2	74	1.2
México, D.F.	7240	54	0.2	56	0.3	61	0.4	63	0.5	65	0.2	63	4.2	61	4.9	61	4.1	60	4.6	59	1.3	58	0.6	54	0.3
Monterrey, N.L.	1749	59	0.8	62	0.9	68	0.6	74	1.1	78	1.7	81	3.3	81	2.9	82	2.5	78	8.1	72	4.3	63	1.0	57	0.9
Morelia, Mich.	6234	57	0.5	60	0.3	64	0.3	67	0.3	69	1.7	67	5.2	65	6.8	64	6.4	64	6.2	63	2.3	60	0.8	58	0.2
Oaxaca, Oax.	5068	63	0.1	66	0.1	70	0.4	72	1.0	73	2.4	71	4.9	70	3.7	69	4.1	69	6.7	67	1.6	65	0.3	64	0.4
Orizaba, Ver.	4079	59	1.8	61	1.6	64	1.0	68	1.9	70	5.3	68	14.	67	15.	67	13.	67	17.	66	7.3	61	3.9	66	2.1
Pachuca, Hgo.	7999	53	0.2	55	0.5	58	0.6	61	0.7	61	1.3	60	2.8	59	2.3	59	2.1	59	3.1	56	1.9	54	0.8	55	0.2
Patzcuaro, Mich.	7180	57	0.8	56	0.5	61	0.3	64	0.2	68	1.5	68	7.9	63	9.8	63	9.5	63	8.5	61	3.1	58	1.0	55	0.9
Progreso, Yuc.	46	73	1.3	74	.67	76	.59	80	.70	79	2.1	80	2.9	80	1.8	80	1.8	80	2.1	79	2.7	76	.80	74	1.0
Puebla, Pue.	7200	54	0.2	60	0.2	62	0.5	65	0.5	66	2.9	64	6.2	63	5.4	63	5.8	62	7.4	61	2.2	58	0.8	56	0.3
Queretaro, Qro.	6160	57	0.4	60	0.1	64	0.2	68	0.5	70	1.1	69	3.7	67	4.1	67	3.4	66	4.8	63	1.3	61	0.4	59	0.5
Sn. Cristóbal L. C., Chis.	7087	54	0.3	55	0.0	57	0.4	60	1.4	60	5.1	60	10.	60	5.6	60	6.3	60	9.9	59	6.0	55	0.9	55	0.6
San Jose Purúa, Mich.	6335	57	0.7	60	0.6	63	0.3	67	0.3	70	0.2	71	6.3	70	7.1	69	6.6	68	7.0	65	2.5	64	0.8	60	2.5
San Luis Potosi, S.L.P.	6157	55	0.5	59	0.2	63	0.4	69	0.2	70	1.2	70	2.8	67	2.3	67	1.7	65	3.4	63	0.7	59	0.4	57	0.6
Tampico, Tamps.	39	65	2.1	68	0.9	71	0.5	77	0.4	80	2.0	82	7.9	82	5.8	82	5.9	81	13.	78	7.0	72	2.2	67	1.7
Tapachula, Chis.	551	77	.28	78	.24	80	1.2	81	2.9	80	12.	78	19.	78	12.	78	13.	77	18.	77	16.	77	3.4	77	.45
Taxco, Gro.	5500	66	0.0	69	0.2	72	0.4	75	0.9	76	3.0	72	10.	70	12.	70	14.	69	13.	69	3.5	68	0.2	67	0.1
Tehuacán, Pue.	5509	60	0.1	62	0.1	65	0.1	68	0.6	70	2.6	69	3.7	67	2.8	68	2.2	68	4.7	65	1.3	61	0.2	61	0.3
Tehuantepec, Oax.	328	58	1.5	66	0.2	69	0.3	72	1.4	74	3.6	72	6.5	69	4.9	71	3.2	69	8.5	68	3.6	67	1.5	66	0.6
Tepic, Nay.	3000	63	1.2	63	0.8	65	0.0	70	0.0	71	0.1	74	6.8	74	14.	74	12.	74	8.1	73	8.0	78	0.3	64	2.1
Tlaxcala, Tlax.	7500	55	0.2	57	0.1	61	0.3	63	0.7	64	2.9	63	5.0	61	5.3	61	5.9	61	5.4	60	1.9	58	0.3	5[illegible]	0.2
Toluca, Mex.	8712	49	0.4	52	0.4	55	0.4	57	1.1	59	2.0	58	5.3	56	3.6	56	5.7	56	6.0	54	1.9	52	0.8	50	0.3
Torreon, Coah.	3720	54	0.5	60	0.2	65	0.0	70	0.2	81	0.5	83	1.5	80	2.1	81	0.9	80	1.4	74	0.9	62	0.5	56	0.5
Tuxpan, Ver.		67	1.6	70	1.0	72	1.0	78	1.5	81	3.4	83	8.0	82	6.9	82	6.7	81	12.	78	8.9	72	2.1	78	1.5
Tuxtla Gutierrez, Chis.	1759	71	0.0	73	0.2	77	0.4	80	.22	81	3.0	79	9.2	78	7.0	78	6.1	77	8.0	76	3.2	73	.16	70	.25
Uruapan, Mich.	5500	61	0.6	62	0.8	68	0.3	70	0.2	72	1.3	71	11.	70	14.	69	13.	69	16.	68	7.1	64	1.5	61	1.2
Valladolid, Yuc.	72	70	2.5	73	1.0	77	1.0	80	3.0	81	4.7	80	6.0	80	5.5	80	6.3	79	7.0	77	5.7	73	1.9	72	2.2
Villahermosa, Tab.	33	72	5.5	75	3.9	77	1.8	80	1.8	83	3.5	83	8.0	82	7.6	83	7.6	82	10.	80	11.	76	5.6	73	7.1
Zacatecs, Zac.	8187	49	0.4	51	0.2	54	0.1	59	0.1	62	0.9	61	2.1	57	3.5	58	2.3	57	3.0	56	0.9	52	0.6	50	0.5

* T = Temperature in °F, R = Rainfall in inches. Altitudes are in feet.

VEGETATION ZONES

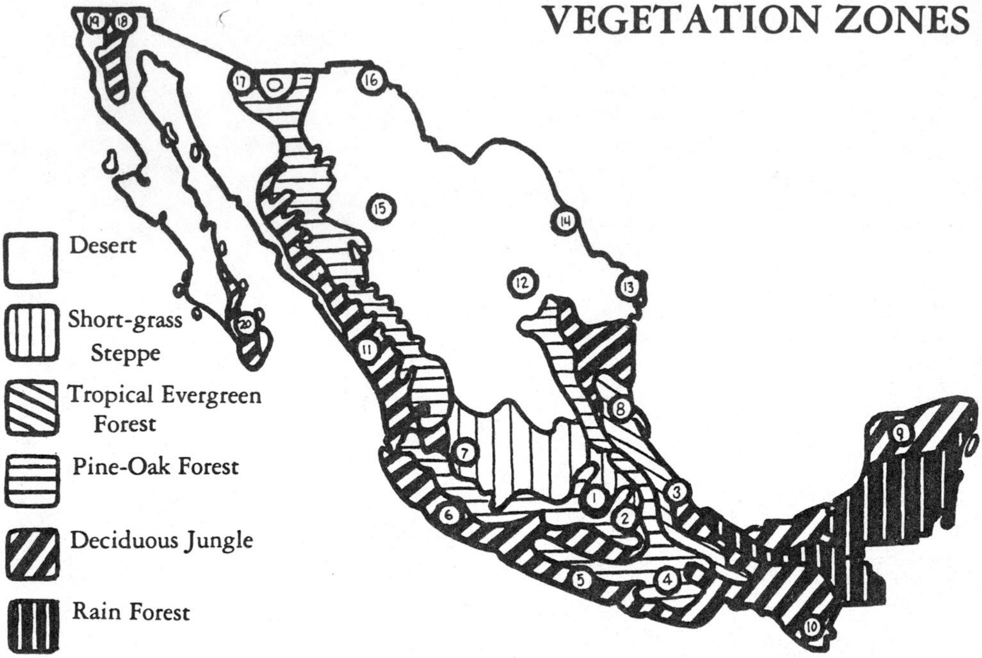
Desert
Short-grass Steppe
Tropical Evergreen Forest
Pine-Oak Forest
Deciduous Jungle
Rain Forest
19
18
17
16
15
14
13
12
11
20
9
8
7
6
5
4
3
2
1
10

*Refer to train map for city names

CLIMATE ZONES

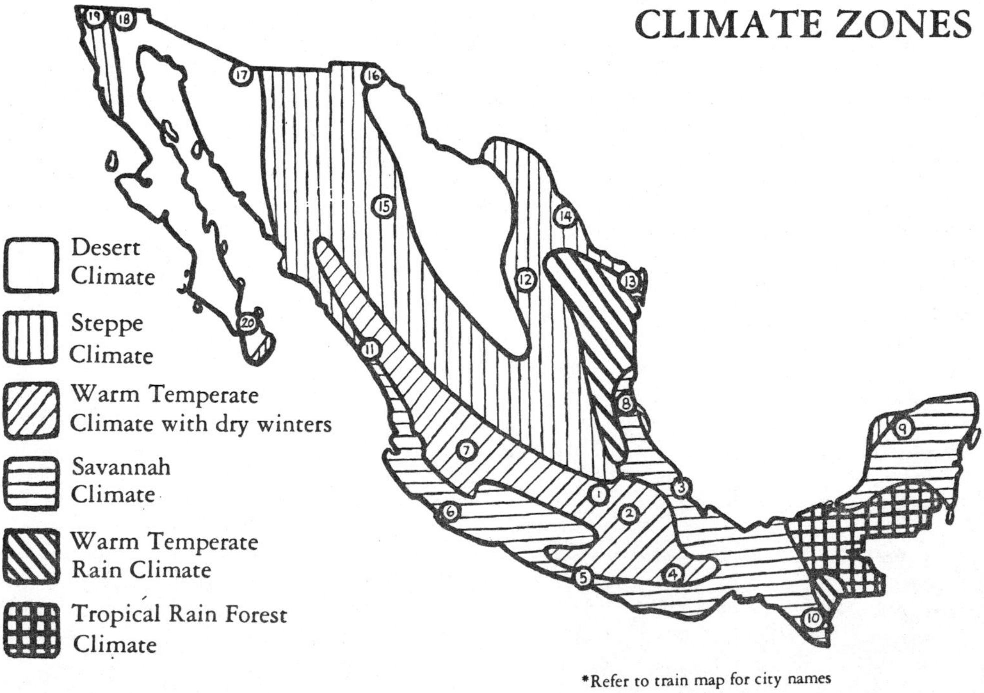
Desert Climate
Steppe Climate
Warm Temperate Climate with dry winters
Savannah Climate
Warm Temperate Rain Climate
Tropical Rain Forest Climate
19
18
17
16
15
14
13
12
11
20
9
8
7
6
5
4
3
2
1
10

*Refer to train map for city names

AVERAGE ANNUAL PRECIPITATION

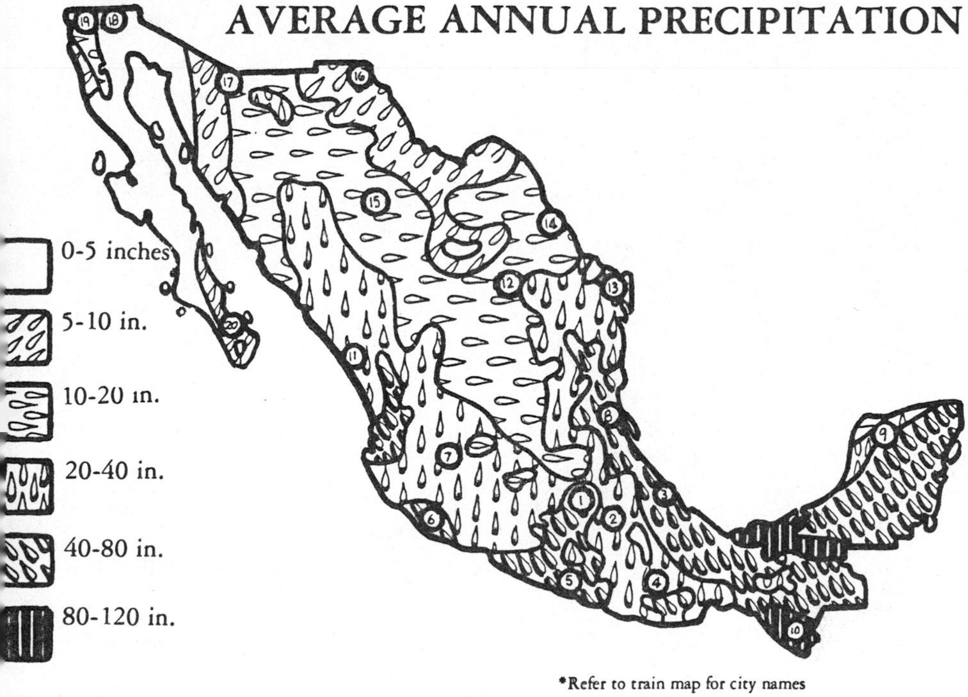

0-5 inches
5-10 in.
10-20 in.
20-40 in.
40-80 in.
80-120 in.

*Refer to train map for city names

TRIP LOG

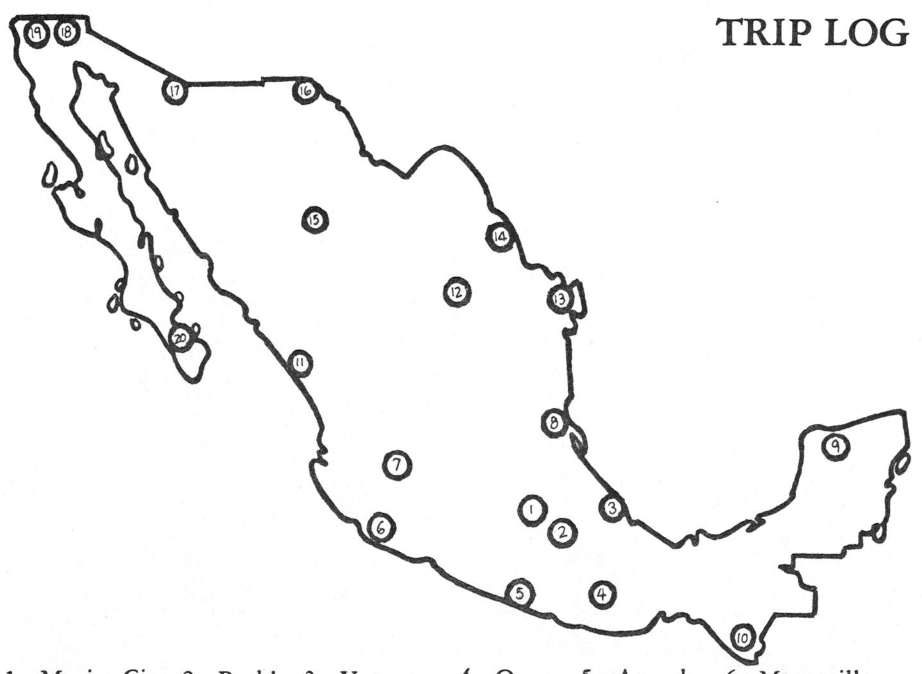

1. Mexico City 2. Puebla 3. Veracruz 4. Oaxaca 5. Acapulco 6. Manzanillo 7. Guadalajara 8. Tampico 9. Merida 10. Tapachula 11. Mazatlan 12. Monterrey 13. Matamoros 14. Nuevo Laredo 15. Chihuahua 16. Cuidad Juarez 17. Nogales 18. Mexicali 19. Tijuana 20. La Paz

WHAT BUS GOES WHERE *

Destination	Bus Lines
Acapulco, Gro.	EO FR
Acambaro, Gto.	FA AO
Aguascalientes, Ags.	FA EB OM TCH
Apatzingan, Mich.	AO ALP TEO
Barra de Navidad, Jal.	TP TNS
Cacahuamilpa, Gro.	AMZ FR
Campeche, Cam.	ADO LUMS
Cancun, Q.R.	ADO
Catemaco, Ver.	ADO AU LUMS
Celaya, Gto.	AA FA AO TEO EM OM ALP OO TNS TCH
Cd. Del Carmen, Cam.	ADO LUMS
Cd. Guzman, Jal.	ALP AO EB OM
Cd. Juarez. Chih.	EB OM TCH
Cd. Mante, Tamps.	EB OM TN
Cd. Obregon, Son.	TEO TP TNS
Cd. Valles, S.L.P.	EB TN ADO OM AMZ
Cd. Victoria, Tamps.	EB OM TN TEO OO
Coatzacoalcos, Ver.	ADO AU CC LUMS
Colima, Col.	FA AO ALP OM TEO TNS
Comitan, Chis.	CC
Cordoba, Ver.	ADO AU LUMS
Cuautla, Mor.	AMZ CC FR
Cuernavaca, Mor.	AMZ EO FR
Culiacan, Sin.	TEO TP TNS
Chetumal, Q.R.	ADO LUMS
Chihuahua, Chih.	EB OM TCH
Chilpancingo, Gro.	EO FR
Delicias, Chih.	EB OM TCH
Dolores Hidalgo, Gto.	FA TNS TEO
Durango, Dgo.	EB OM TCH TN
Ensenada, B.C.	TEO TNS
Fresnillo, Zac.	EB OM TCH
Guadalajara, Jal.	FA AO EB ALP TEO OM OO TP TNS
Guanajuato, Gto.	FA AO ALP EB TCH TNS TEO OM
Guaymas, Son.	TEO TP TNS
Hermosillo, Son.	TEO TP TNS
Iguala, Gro.	EO FR
Irapuato, Gto.	AA FA AO TEO EB ALP OO OM TCH TNS
Ixtapan De La Sal, Mex.	FR
Jalapa, Ver.	ADO AU LUMS
Jojutla, Mor.	AMZ FR
La Paz, B.C.	TEO
La Piedad, Mich.	FA ALP AO EB OO TNS TEO
Las Estacas, Mor.	AMZ FR
Lazaro Cardenas, Mich.	AO
Leon, Gto.	AA FA AO EB ALP TEO OM TCH TNS
Los Mochis, Sin.	TEO TP TNS
Matamoros, Tamps.	ADO EB TEO OM OO TN
Matehuala, S.L.P.	AA EB TN
Manzanillo, Col.	FA AO ALP TEO TP TNS
Mazatlan, Sin.	EB TEO TN TP TNS
Metztitlan, Hgo.	AMFR
Merida, Yuc.	ADO LUMS
Mexicali, B.C.	TEO TP TNS
Minatitlan, Ver.	ADO AU CC LUMS
Monclova, Coah.	AA
Monterrey, N.L.	AA EB TEO TN
Morelia, Mich.	FA AO ALP TEO EB FR TP TNS
Nautla, Ver.	ADO AU
Nogales, Son.	TEO TP TNS
Nuevo Laredo, Tamps.	EB TEO TN
Oaxaca, Oax.	ADO AU CC
Oaxtepec, Mor.	AMZ CC
Ometepec, Gro.	FR
Orizaba, Ver.	ADO AU LUMS
Pachuca, Hgo.	ADO ALF EB TN AMP
Palenque, Chis.	ADO
Parral, Chih.	EB OM TCH
Patzcuaro, Mich.	FA AO ALP TEO
Piedras Negras, Coah.	AA
Pichucalco, Chis.	CC LUMS
Pinotepa Nacional, Oax.	FR CC
Poza Rica, Ver.	ADO EB ALF OM OO
Puebla, Pue.	ADO ER AU CC LUMS
Puerto Escondido, Oax.	FR ADO CC
Puerto Vallarta, Jal.	EB TEO TP TNS
Queretaro, Qro.	AA FA AO TEO EB ALP OO TCH TNS OM
Reynosa, Tamps.	AA ADO EB ALF TEO OM OO TN
Salamanca, Gto.	AA FA AO EB TEO OM TCH TNS
Saltillo, Coah.	AA EB TN
San Luis Potosi, S.L.P.	AA FA EB TEO OM TN TCH TNS
San Miguel de Allende, Gto.	FA TNS TEO
Tampico, Tamps.	ADO EB ALF TEO OM OO TN
Taxco, Gro.	EO FR
Tapachula, Chis.	CC
Tecolutla, Ver.	ADO
Tehuacan, Pue.	ADO AU
Tehuantepec, Oax.	CC ADO AU
Tepic, Nay.	TEO EB OM TNS TP
Tijuana, B.C.	TEO TP TNS
Tlaxcala, Tlax.	ATAH
Toluca, Mex.	AO FR TMT
Torreon, Coah.	EB OM TCH TN
Tulancingo, Hgo.	ADO ALF EB OM
Tuxpan, Ver.	ADO ALF EB OM OO
Tuxtla Gutierrez, Chis.	CC LUMS
Uruapan, Mich.	FA ALP TEO AO TNS TP
Veracruz, Ver.	ADO AU LUMS
Villahermosa, Tab.	ADO CC LUMS
Zacatecas, Zac.	EB OM TCH
Zamora, Mich.	FA AO ALP TEO TNS TP
Zihuatanejo, Gro.	AO EO FR
Zitacuaro, Mich.	AO TP
Zimapan, Hgo.	AMZV

Bus Terminals in Mexico City

AA	Autobuses Anahuac, Terminal Central del Norte
FA	Autobuses Centrales de Mexico Flecha Amarilla, Terminal Central del Norte
AO	Autobuses de Occidente, Dr. Lavista 27
ADO	Autobuses de Oriente, Ruta Sureste: Buenavista 9. Ruta Noreste: Terminal Central del Norte
EB	Autobuses Estrella Blanca, Terminal Central del Norte
ER	Autobuses Mexico Puebla Estrella Roja, F.S. Teresa de Mier 266
AMZ	Autobuses Mexico Zacatepec, Terminal Central del Sur
AMP	Autobuses Mexico Pachuca Flecha Roja, S.A., Terminal Central del Norte
AMZV	Autobuses Mexico Zimapan Valles Flecha Roja, Terminal Central del Norte
AMFR	Autobuses Mezcos Flecha Roja, S.A., Terminal Central del Norte
AU	Autobuses Unidos, F.S. Teresa de Mier 350
ALF	Autotransportes La Flecha, Terminal Central del Norte
ALP	Autotransportes La Piedad Cabadas, Terminal Central del Norte
ATAH	Autotransportes Tlax ala Apizacho Huamantla, M. Doblado 88
TEO	Autobuses Tres Estrellas de Oro, Terminal Central del Norte
CC	Omnibus Cristobal Colon, Ignacio Zaragoza 38
EO	Estrella de Oro, Terminal Central del Sur
FR	Lineas Unidas del Sur Flecha Roja, Terminal Central del Sur
LUMS	Lineas Unidas Mexico Sureste, F.S. Teresa de Mier 350
OM	Omnibus de Mexico, Terminal Central del Norte
OO	Omnibus de Oriente, Terminal Central del Norte
TCH	Transp. Chihuahuenses, Terminal Central del Norte
TN	Transp. del Norte, Terminal Central del Norte
TP	Transp. del Pacifico, Terminal Central del Norte
TNS	Transp. Norte de Sonora, Terminal Central del Norte
TMT	Turismo Mex-Toluca Triangulo Flecha, A. Caso 187

*Reproduced courtesy of *Mexico Desconocido* magazine and Harry Moller. (See *Recommended Reading*.)

TRAIN MAP
1. Mexico City
2. Puebla
3. Veracruz
4. Oaxaca
5. Acapulco
6. Manzanillo
7. Guadalajara
8. Tampico
9. Merida
10. Tapachula
11. Mazatlan
12. Monterrey
13. Matamoros
14. Nuevo Laredo
15. Chihuahua
16. Cuidad Juarez
17. Nogales
18. Mexicali
19. Tijuana
20. La Paz
TACUBA
CUITLAHUAC
POPOTLA
COLEGIO MILITAR
NORMAL
SAN COSME
REVOLUCION
TLATELOLCO
GUERRERO
BELLAS ARTES
ALLENDE
HIDALGO
JUAREZ
ZOCALO
PINO SUAREZ
BALDERAS
CUAUHTEMOC
INSURGENTES
SEVILLA
CHAPULTEPEC
JUANACATLAN
TACUBAYA
OBSERVATORIO
NINOS HEROES
HOSPITAL GEN
CENTRO MEDICO
SALTO DEL AGUA
I. LA CATOLICA
MERCED
CANDELARIA
SAN LAZARO
MOCTEZUMA
BALBUENA
AEROPUERTO
GOMEZ FARIAS
ZARAGOZA
SAN ANTONIO ABAD
CHABACANO
VIADUCTO
XOLA
VILLA DE CORTES
NATIVITAS
PORTALES
ERMITA
GENERAL ANAYA
TAXQUENA
STC
METRO
METRO MAP

TRANSPORTATION PRICES

Mexico City to:	Tijuana	Cd. Juárez	N. Laredo	Veracruz	Acapulco	Oaxaca	Mérida
First Class Bus	727.0	448.0	286.6	111.0	134.0	119.0	387.2
First Class Train	481.8*	318.5	204.6	70.0	—	88.5	261.8
Tourist Airfare	2,199	1,836	1,110	454	427	513	1,194

—ALL FARES IN PESOS—
*Service available only to Mexicali, B.C., when going north.

Gas and Oil:

	Peso/Liter	Dollar/Gal.*
Extra	4.00	$.67
Nova	2.80	$.47
Diesel	.65	$.11 !

	Peso/Liter	
Pemex Sol (oil)	8.50	$.37
Faja de Oro (oil)	15.00	$.66
Havoline (oil)	18.00	$.79

calculated at 22.65 pesos per dollar

Rent-A-Car
- Volkswagen: 265 pesos per day plus 1.8 pesos each kilometer.
- Dodge Dart: 351 pesos per day plus 2.3 pesos each kilometer.
- Valiant: 387 pesos per day plus 2.2 pesos each kilometer.

Note: does not include deposit or insurance. These are only sample prices. Check carefully as prices vary from one company to the next.

Car Insurance, sample costs* (Sanborn's) Public Liability:

One person/One Accident	Per day (dollars)
25,000 - 50,000	$1.64
30,000 - 60,000	$1.94
40,000 - 80,000	$2.54
50,000 - 100,000	$3.14
100,000 - 200,000	$6.14
100,000 - 300,000	$8.14

*Daily cost does not cover fees for writing policies, tax or long-term discounts.

Baja Ferry: Cabo San Lucas - Puerto Vallarta

Passengers	Pesos
Salón	125.00
Tourist	250.00
Cabin	500.00
Special	800.00

Vehicles	Pesos
Car, length to 16.4 feet	750.00
Car, 16.4 to 21.3 feet	850.00
Car with trailer to 29.5 feet	1,500.00
Car with trailer, 29.5 to 55.7 ft	2,400.00
Motorcycles	90.00
Buses	1,000.00

Useful addresses for fares, schedules and information:
- National Railways of Mexico, Passenger Traffic Department, Buena Vista Grand Central Station, Mexico 3, D.F., Mexico
- Foreign Agent, National Railways of Mexico, P.O. Box 2200, El Paso, Texas
- Traffic Superintendent, Sonora-Baja California Railway, Box 182, Mexicali, BC, Mexico
- Agent, Chihuahua-Pacific Railway, Box 46, Chihuahua, Chih., Mexico
- Note for 1982 edition: due to a recent devaluation the value of the peso is now floating.

  The prices listed above were calculated at 22.65 pesos per dollar and should now be used only for comparison.

TOWN TO TOWN DISTANCE CHART

	ZACATECAS, ZAC.	VILLAHERMOSA, TAB.	VERACRUZ, VER.	TUXTLA GTZ. CHIS.	TUXPAN, VER.	TORREON, COAH.	TOLUCA, MEX.	TLAXCALA, TLAX.	TIJUANA, B.C.	TEPIC, NAY.	TEHUACAN, PUE.	TAPACHULA, CHIS.	TAMPICO, TAMPS.	SN. LUIS POTOSI, S.L.P.	SALTILLO, COAH.	SALINA CRUZ, OAX.	REYNOSA, TAMPS.	QUERETARO, QRO.	PTO. JUAREZ Q. ROO	PUEBLA PUE.	P. NEGRAS, COAH.	PACHUCA, HGO.	OAXACA, OAX.	NVO. LAREDO TAMPS.	NOGALES, SON.	MONTERREY N.L.	MORELIA, MICH.	MEXICO, D.F.	MEXICALI, B.C.	MERIDA, YUC.	MAZATLAN, SIN.	MATAMOROS, TAMPS.	MANZANILLO, COL.	LEON, GTO.	JALAPA, VER.	HERMOSILLO, SON.	GUANAJUATO, GTO.	GUADALAJARA, JAL.	ENSENADA, B.C.	DURANGO, DGO.	CHIHUAHUA, CHIH.	CHILPANCINGO, GRO.	CHETUMAL, Q. ROO	CULIACAN, SIN.	CUERNAVACA, MOR.	COLIMA, COL.	CD. VICTORIA, TAMPS.	CD. JUAREZ, CHIH.	CD. CUAUHTEMOC, CHIS.	CAMPECHE, CAM.	AGUASCALIENTES, AGS.
ACAPULCO, GRO.	630	788	519	823	459	869	260	326	2051	752	414	906	579	513	792	653	887	380	1383	334	1065	314	480	988	1676	845	414	255	1931	1183	934	882	738	493	443	1503	481	611	2090	810	1150	82	1142	1073	203	679	690	1383	1071	1064	547
AGUASCALIENTES, AGS.	81	850	580	974	473	320	306	388	1576	301	475	1052	354	105	311	799	503	186	1445	396	583	326	632	506	1201	364	201	317	1455	1245	459	591	377	79	506	1027	115	160	1614	261	601	490	1204	598	370	325	399	835	1134	1126	
CAMPECHE, CAM.	1183	276	573	686	779	1422	848	747	2604	1305	682	768	898	1066	1308	567	1277	940	319	729	1581	823	712	1401	2229	1258	1002	808	2484	119	1487	1272	1326	1047	639	2056	1034	1164	2643	1363	1704	982	262	1632	861	1267	1080	1937	844		
CD. CUAUHTEMOC, CHIS.	1190	569	580	158	786	1429	855	766	2611	1312	688	404	906	1073	1318	350	1284	947	1164	748	1625	830	495	1408	2236	1265	1009	815	2491	964	1494	1279	1333	1053	647	2063	1041	1171	2650	1370	1710	899	923	1012	779	1274	1087	1943			
CD. JUAREZ, CHIH.	754	1661	1392	1785	1239	517	1117	1199	1987	1022	1286	1803	1101	871	691	1610	884	977	2256	1207	964	1138	1443	887	1611	744	1036	1128	1866	2056	869	945	1161	913	1316	1438	949	945	2025	672	233	1301	2015	1009	1181	1109	922				
CD. VICTORIA, TAMPS.	411	804	514	929	301	445	474	465	1877	653	562	1011	181	294	231	809	197	421	1399	483	504	383	749	321	1502	178	480	434	1757	1199	760	192	729	416	515	1329	426	512	1916	562	689	608	1158	899	487	677					
COLIMA, COL.	362	991	722	1115	663	519	419	529	1604	306	616	1193	631	383	583	941	775	386	1587	537	856	495	774	779	1230	636	265	456	1484	1387	488	837	62	316	646	1056	290	165	1644	536	876	597	1346	627	511						
CUERNAVACA, MOR.	427	585	316	616	257	666	93	124	1848	549	211	703	376	311	590	446	684	184	1881	132	863	111	283	787	1474	643	246	53	1728	981	737	679	570	291	240	1300	278	408	1887	607	948	121	940	871							
CULIACAN, SIN.	517	1351	1081	1475	985	494	807	889	977	321	976	1553	882	634	668	1300	861	687	1946	897	941	827	1133	864	603	721	687	818	858	1746	139	922	679	614	1006	429	650	462	1017	337	775	991	1705								
CHETUMAL, Q. ROO	1261	354	651	764	857	1500	927	825	2682	1383	760	846	976	1145	1387	645	1355	1018	477	808	1659	901	791	1479	2308	1336	1080	887	2562	277	1566	1350	1405	1125	718	2134	1112	1242	2722	1441	1782	1062									
CHILPANCINGO, GRO.	548	706	437	736	377	787	178	244	1969	670	331	823	497	431	710	571	805	298	1301	252	983	232	404	906	1594	763	332	173	1849	1101	853	800	656	411	361	1421	399	529	2008	728	1068										
CHIHUAHUA, CHIH.	521	1428	1158	1552	1006	284	884	966	1753	789	1053	1630	868	638	458	1377	651	764	2023	974	731	905	1210	654	1378	511	803	895	1633	1823	636	712	928	680	1083	1205	716	711	1792	439											
DURANGO, DGO.	180	1087	818	1211	665	157	544	625	1314	350	712	1289	546	297	331	1037	524	424	1602	633	604	564	869	527	940	384	462	554	1194	1482	198	585	588	340	742	766	376	372	1353												
ENSENADA, B.C.	1534	2367	2098	2492	2002	1511	1823	1903	67	1338	1993	2569	1899	1650	1685	2317	1877	1704	2963	1914	1957	1844	2150	1880	549	1737	1703	1835	159	2763	1156	1939	1696	1631	2022	587	1667	1479													
GUADALAJARA, JAL.	198	888	619	1012	523	248	433	426	1440	141	513	1090	467	218	418	838	611	224	1484	434	691	365	671	614	1065	471	224	355	1320	1283	323	672	217	152	543	892	188														
GUANAJUATO, GTO.	196	758	489	883	393	435	214	296	1627	329	383	960	380	132	411	708	547	94	1354	305	684	235	541	606	1253	464	109	226	1507	1154	511	618	405	36	413	1079															
HERMOSILLO, SON.	946	1780	1511	1904	1415	923	1236	1318	548	751	1405	1982	1312	1063	1097	1730	1290	1116	2375	1326	1370	1257	1562	1293	173	1150	1116	1247	428	2175	569	1352	1109	1043	1435																
JALAPA, VER.	562	364	74	488	214	801	227	117	1983	684	144	572	333	446	725	370	712	319	959	115	998	183	337	836	1608	693	381	188	1863	759	866	707	705	426																	
LEON, GTO.	160	771	502	895	405	399	227	309	1591	293	396	973	371	122	401	720	537	107	1366	317	674	247	553	597	1217	454	122	238	1471	1166	475	608	368																		
MANZANILLO, COL.	414	1050	781	1174	722	644	478	588	1657	358	676	1252	690	435	635	1000	828	446	1646	597	908	554	833	831	1282	688	324	518	1537	1446	540	889																			
MATAMOROS, TAMPS.	484	996	706	1121	493	428	666	657	1900	813	754	1203	373	486	254	1001	62	613	1591	675	527	575	941	214	1525	201	672	623	1780	1391	783																				
MAZATLAN, SIN.	378	1211	942	1336	846	355	667	750	1117	182	837	1413	743	495	529	1161	729	548	1807	758	802	688	994	725	742	582	547	679	997	1607																					
MERIDA, YUC.	1302	395	692	805	898	1541	968	866	2723	1424	801	888	1017	1186	1428	686	1396	1059	200	849	1700	942	832	1520	2342	1377	1121	928	2603																						
MEXICALI, B.C.	1374	2208	1939	2332	1843	1351	1664	1746	120	1179	1833	2410	1740	1491	1525	2158	1718	1544	2804	1754	1798	1685	1991	1721	390	1578	1544	1676																							
MEXICO, D.F.	374	533	263	657	204	613	40	71	1796	497	158	735	297	258	537	482	631	131	1128	79	810	58	315	733	1421	590	193																								
MORELIA, MICH.	282	726	457	850	388	521	153	264	1664	365	351	928	420	241	520	675	656	121	1321	272	793	230	508	716	1289	573																									
MONTERREY N.L.	283	982	692	1107	479	227	579	644	1698	612	740	1190	360	332	53	988	140	459	1577	669	326	562	905	143	1324																										
NOGALES, SON.	1117	1953	1684	2078	1588	1097	1410	1492	510	924	1579	2155	1485	1237	1271	1903	1463	1290	2549	1500	1544	1430	1736	1466																											
NVO. LAREDO TAMPS.	426	1125	835	1250	622	370	722	787	1841	755	891	1332	503	475	196	1131	153	601	1720	812	469	705	1048																												
OAXACA, OAX.	689	436	329	337	458	929	355	270	2111	812	193	420	638	573	852	167	946	446	1032	253	1125	373																													
PACHUCA, HGO.	384	547	257	715	158	623	98	82	1805	506	178	793	277	267	547	541	580	140	1142	99	820																														
P. NEGRAS, COAH.	503	1305	1073	1467	802	447	799	881	1918	832	891	1544	683	552	273	1292	465	679	1901	889																															
PUEBLA PUE.	384	454	185	590	205	692	119	17	1874	576	79	672	324	337	616	420	680	210	1049																																
PTO. JUAREZ Q. ROO	1502	595	892	1006	1098	1741	1168	1066	2924	1625	1001	1088	1218	1386	1628	886	1596	1259																																	
QUERETARO, QRO.	244	664	395	788	298	483	120	202	1664	365	289	866	375	127	406	613	542																																		
REYNOSA, TAMPS.	423	1001	711	1126	498	367	662	663	1838	752	759	1208	378	415	193	1006																																			
SALINA CRUZ, OAX.	856	291	303	192	508	1096	522	438	2278	979	360	275	628	740	1019																																				
SALTILLO, COAH.	230	1032	743	1194	530	174	527	608	1646	558	695	1240	410	279																																					
SN. LUIS POTOSI, S.L.P.	117	791	521	915	368	356	247	329	1611	359	416	993	249																																						
TAMPICO, TAMPS.	427	622	333	747	119	584	363	307	1860	608	463	830																																							
TAPACHULA, CHIS.	1109	492	504	245	710	1348	774	690	2530	1237	613																																								
TEHUACAN, PUE.	532	406	136	530	284	771	198	96	1953	654																																									
TEPIC, NAY.	339	1029	760	1154	664	507	485	567	1299																																										
TIJUANA, B.C.	1494	2328	2059	2452	1963	1471	1784	1866																																											
TLAXCALA, TLAX.	455	471	191	607	188	684	111																																												
TOLUCA, MEX.	364	572	303	697	244	603																																													
TORREON, COAH.	239	1146	877	1270	704																																														
TUXPAN, VER.	485	503	213	628																																															
TUXTLA GTZ. CHIS.	1031	410	421																																																
VERACRUZ, VER.	638	297																																																	
VILLAHERMOSA, TAB.	907																																																		

All distances are in miles.

ROAD SIGNS

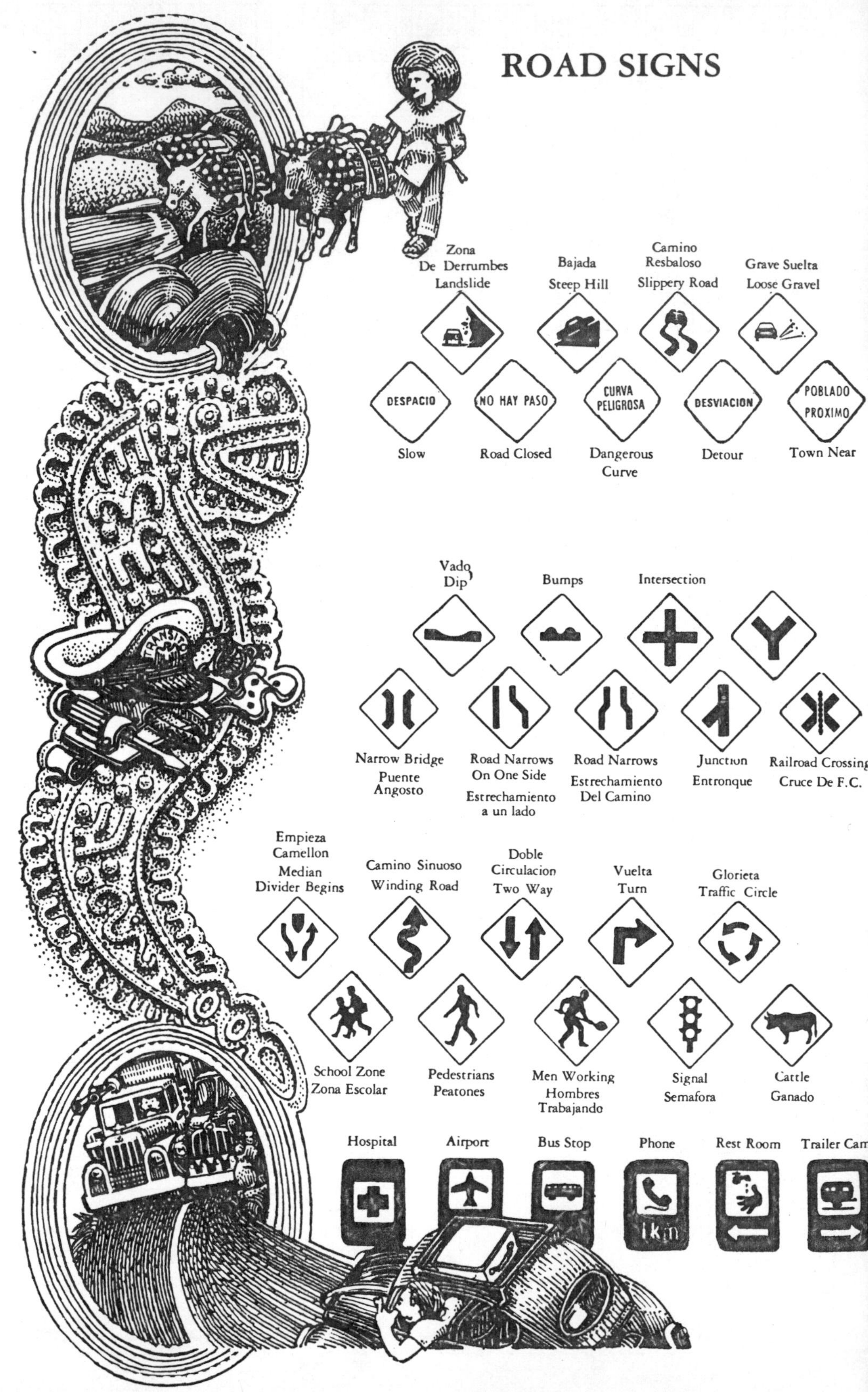
Zona De Derrumbes
Landslide
Bajada
Steep Hill
Camino Resbaloso
Slippery Road
Grave Suelta
Loose Gravel
DESPACIO
Slow
NO HAY PASO
Road Closed
CURVA PELIGROSA
Dangerous Curve
DESVIACION
Detour
POBLADO PROXIMO
Town Near
TRANSITO
Vado
Dip
Bumps
Intersection
Narrow Bridge
Puente Angosto
Road Narrows On One Side
Estrechamiento a un lado
Road Narrows
Estrechamiento Del Camino
Junction
Entronque
Railroad Crossing
Cruce De F.C.
Empieza Camellon
Median Divider Begins
Camino Sinuoso
Winding Road
Doble Circulacion
Two Way
Vuelta
Turn
Glorieta
Traffic Circle
School Zone
Zona Escolar
Pedestrians
Peatones
Men Working
Hombres Trabajando
Signal
Semafora
Cattle
Ganado
Hospital
Airport
Bus Stop
Phone
1km
Rest Room
Trailer Camp

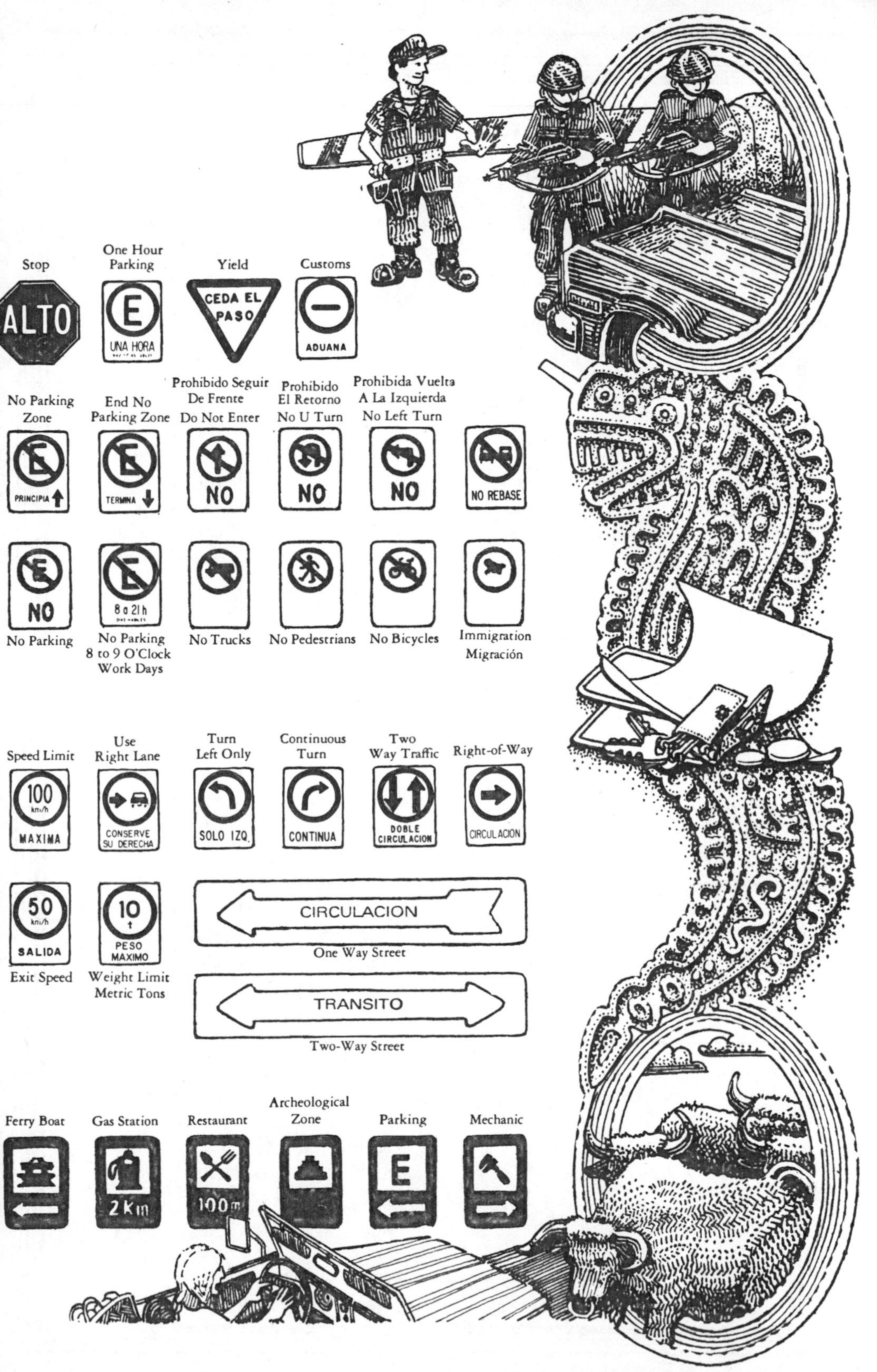
Stop
ALTO
One Hour Parking
E
UNA HORA
Yield
CEDA EL PASO
Customs
ADUANA
No Parking Zone
PRINCIPIA
End No Parking Zone
TERMINA
Prohibido Seguir De Frente
Do Not Enter
NO
Prohibido El Retorno
No U Turn
NO
Prohibida Vuelta A La Izquierda
No Left Turn
NO
NO REBASE
NO
No Parking
8 a 21 h
No Parking 8 to 9 O'Clock Work Days
No Trucks
No Pedestrians
No Bicycles
Immigration
Migración
Speed Limit
100
km/h
MAXIMA
Use Right Lane
CONSERVE SU DERECHA
Turn Left Only
SOLO IZQ.
Continuous Turn
CONTINUA
Two Way Traffic
DOBLE CIRCULACION
Right-of-Way
CIRCULACION
50
km/h
SALIDA
Exit Speed
10
t
PESO MAXIMO
Weight Limit Metric Tons
CIRCULACION
One Way Street
TRANSITO
Two-Way Street
Ferry Boat
Gas Station
2 Km
Restaurant
100 m
Archeological Zone
Parking
E
Mechanic

PRICE LIST

	UNIT	PRICE
Avocados	kilo	24-30
Bananas	kilo	4.0
Beans	kilo	8-12
Beer	6 cans	48.00
	24 bottles	93.00
Bimbo bread	small loaf	3.80
Bolillos	each	.50
Butter	100 grams	6.50
Cabbage	each	6-12
Carrots	kilo	6.0
Cornflakes	Large	17.0
Cheese, Chihuahua	kilo	70-80
Chilies, serranos	500 g	10.0
poblanos	500 g	5.0
canned *jalapeños*	330 g	5.70
Coffee, ground	454 g	48.0
instant	200 g	48.0
Crackers, salted	240 g	5.80
Cucumbers	kilo	8.00
Detergent	250 g	3.90
Eggs, white	kilo	16.00
brown	each	2.00
Flour	kilo	6.00
Garlic	kilo	10.00
Jam	500 g	20.00
Juice, cans	350 g	6.00
		Pesos

	UNIT	PRICE
Lettuce	head	5-6
Limes	kilo	10.00
Lentils	kilo	21.00
Macaroni	200 g	1.80-2.60
		Pesos
Mangos	kilo	12.00
Margarine	450 g	12.00
Mayonnaise	405 g	21.00
Meat, beef	kilo	60.00
pork	kilo	60.00
chicken	kilo	38.00
Milk	liter	6.50
Nido	340 g	24.70
Oil, *cartamo*	Liter	28.00
olive	180 ml.	30.0
Onions	kilo	5-9
Oranges, small	each	1.00
Papaya	kilo	8-10.00
Peanuts	kilo	18-30.00
Peanut butter	340 g	24.50
Pineapple	each	10-16.00
Potatoes	kilo	6-8.00
Rice	kilo	12.00
Soup	can	7.45
dried	2 cubes	2.20
Soy sauce	175 g	35.50
Squash	kilo	10.00
Sugar	kilo	2.50
Toilet paper	4 rolls	15.80
Tomatoes	kilo	9-13.00

BOOZE:

Wine:	Los Reyes, red	750 ml	42.00
	white	750 ml	42.00
Tequila:	Cuervo, white	liter	51.00
	gold	liter	68.00
	Herradura	liter	82.00
Rum:	Bacardí, Carta de Oro	liter	138.00
Brandy:	Presidente	7.50 ml	106.00

See page 552 for prices of gas, oil and public transportation.

Bank and town where purchased: ______________________

Date purchased: ______________ Amount: ______________

Issuing company (American Express, etc.): ______________

Refund offices in Mexico: ______________________,
(ask when buying) ______________, ______________

Check Number	Denomination	Where Cashed	When

Receiving Money In Mexico

•**Postal money order:** *Giros.* Takes 5-21 days, depending on where you send it from and receive it. Paid out in *pesos.*

•**Telegram:** *Giros.* Takes 2-5 days. Paid in *pesos.* (The charge can mount up for large sums.)

•**Personal checks:** Must be co-signed by an account holder at the bank or influential person. May be held for payment even then.

•**Cashier's checks, bank drafts.** May require co-signing or be held for payment, if very large or if drawn on a small bank. Use *Banco Nacional de México.* Checks can be delayed by the mail.

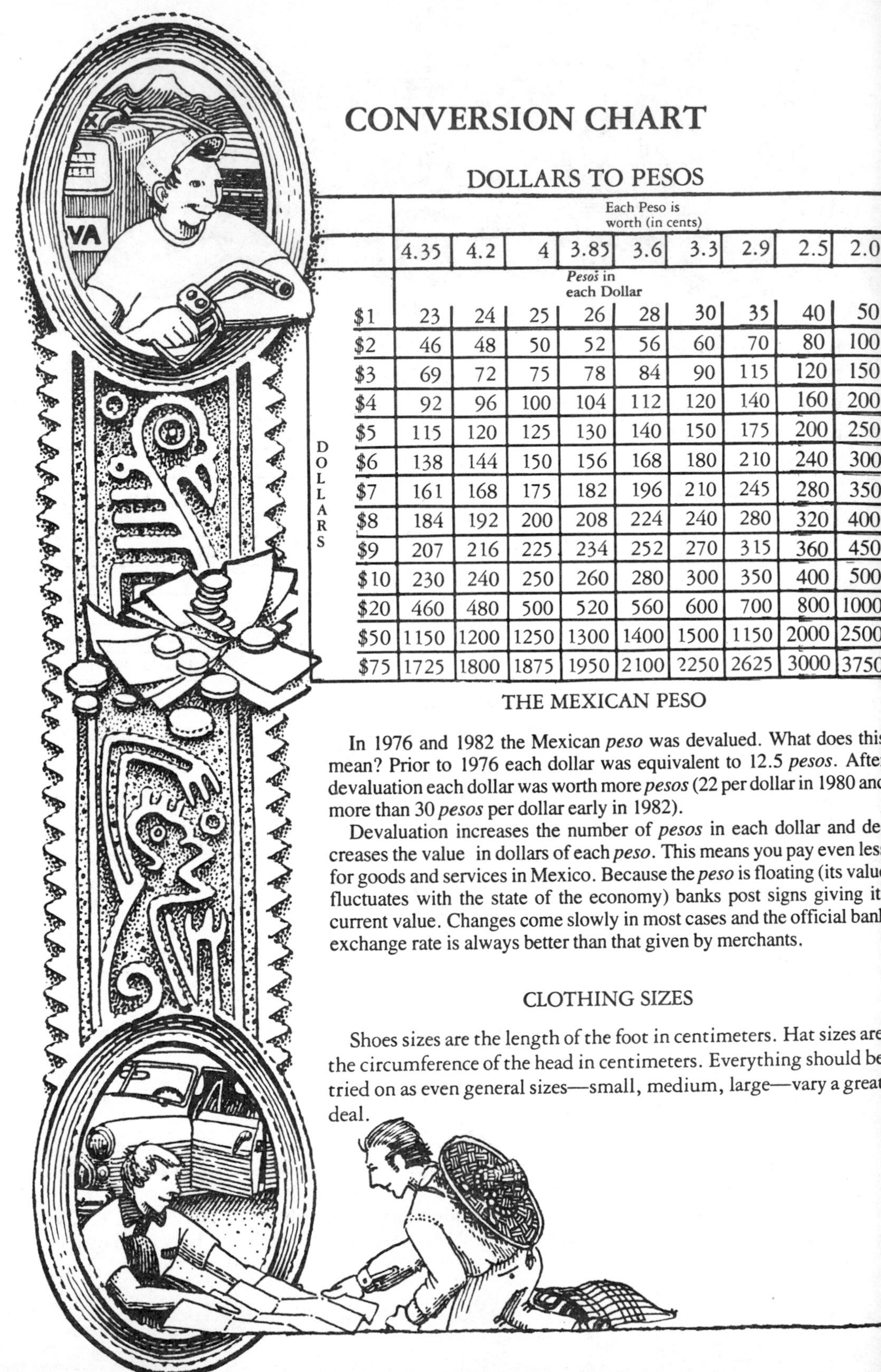

CONVERSION CHART

DOLLARS TO PESOS

	Each Peso is worth (in cents)								
	4.35	4.2	4	3.85	3.6	3.3	2.9	2.5	2.0
DOLLARS	*Pesos* in each Dollar								
$1	23	24	25	26	28	30	35	40	50
$2	46	48	50	52	56	60	70	80	100
$3	69	72	75	78	84	90	115	120	150
$4	92	96	100	104	112	120	140	160	200
$5	115	120	125	130	140	150	175	200	250
$6	138	144	150	156	168	180	210	240	300
$7	161	168	175	182	196	210	245	280	350
$8	184	192	200	208	224	240	280	320	400
$9	207	216	225	234	252	270	315	360	450
$10	230	240	250	260	280	300	350	400	500
$20	460	480	500	520	560	600	700	800	1000
$50	1150	1200	1250	1300	1400	1500	1150	2000	2500
$75	1725	1800	1875	1950	2100	2250	2625	3000	3750

THE MEXICAN PESO

In 1976 and 1982 the Mexican *peso* was devalued. What does this mean? Prior to 1976 each dollar was equivalent to 12.5 *pesos*. After devaluation each dollar was worth more *pesos* (22 per dollar in 1980 and more than 30 *pesos* per dollar early in 1982).

Devaluation increases the number of *pesos* in each dollar and decreases the value in dollars of each *peso*. This means you pay even less for goods and services in Mexico. Because the *peso* is floating (its value fluctuates with the state of the economy) banks post signs giving its current value. Changes come slowly in most cases and the official bank exchange rate is always better than that given by merchants.

CLOTHING SIZES

Shoes sizes are the length of the foot in centimeters. Hat sizes are the circumference of the head in centimeters. Everything should be tried on as even general sizes—small, medium, large—vary a great deal.

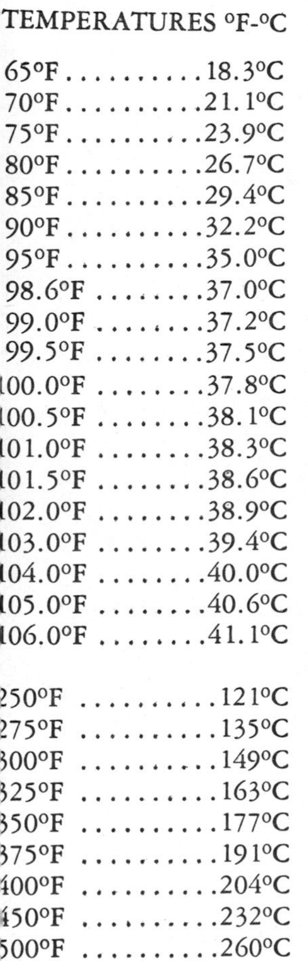

TEMPERATURES °F-°C	
65°F	18.3°C
70°F	21.1°C
75°F	23.9°C
80°F	26.7°C
85°F	29.4°C
90°F	32.2°C
95°F	35.0°C
98.6°F	37.0°C
99.0°F	37.2°C
99.5°F	37.5°C
100.0°F	37.8°C
100.5°F	38.1°C
101.0°F	38.3°C
101.5°F	38.6°C
102.0°F	38.9°C
103.0°F	39.4°C
104.0°F	40.0°C
105.0°F	40.6°C
106.0°F	41.1°C
250°F	121°C
275°F	135°C
300°F	149°C
325°F	163°C
350°F	177°C
375°F	191°C
400°F	204°C
450°F	232°C
500°F	260°C
550°F	288°C

WEIGHTS AND MEASURES	
2.2 pounds	1000 grams (1 kilo)
1 pound	454 grams
1/2 pound	227 grams
1/4 pound	113.5 grams
1 ounce	28.35 grams
1 quart	.95 liters
1 gallon	3.875 liters
5 gallons	19.4 liters
10 gallons	38.75 liters
15 gallons	58.1 liters
20 gallons	77.5 liters
25 gallons	96.9 liters
1 inch	2.54 centimeters
1 foot	30.5 centimeters
1 yard	91.5 centimeters or .915 meters
1 mile	1.61 kilometers
centimeter	.39 inches
meter	3.28 feet
kilometer	.62 miles

TO CONVERT:

- Temperature in degrees F to Centigrade: °F-32 x .55 = °C.
- Temperature in degrees C to Fahrenheit: °C + 17.8 x 1.8 = °F.
- Multiply *liters* by .26 to get *gallons*.
- Multiply *gallons* by 3.8 to get *liters*.

Albuquerque: BCA United Investor's Inc. Building, Suite E, 1020 Tijeras Ave., N.E., Albuquerque, NM 87106
Atlanta: 550 S. Omni Int'l Bldg., Atlanta, Georgia 30303
Austin: Perry Broocks Bldg., 716 Brazos Street, Austin, Texas 78701
Boston: 294 Washington St. (208), Boston, Mass. 02108
Brownsville: Pasol Bldg. 214-215, 940 E. Washington, Brownsville, Texas 78520
Calexico: Imperial Ave. & 7th St., Calexico, CA 92231
Corpus Christi: 148 Guaranty Bank Plaza Bldg., Corpus Christi, TX 78475
Chicago: 201 N. Wells St., 21st Floor, Chicago, Ill. 60606
Dallas: 4229 N. Central Expressway, Dallas, TX 75205
Del Rio: 1010 S. Main St., P.O. Box 1275, Del Rio, TX 78840
Denver: 1050 17th St., Suite 2500, Prudential Plaza Bldg, Denver, CO 80202
Detroit: 1502 Industrial Bldg., 232 West Gran River, Detroit, MI 48226
Douglas: 515 10th St., Douglas, AZ 85607
Eagle Pass: 140 Adams Street, Eagle Pass, TX 78852
El Paso: 601 North Mesa St., Continental Nat. Bank Bldg, P.O. Box 812, El Paso, TX 79901
Fort Worth: 1001 W.T. Waggoner Bldg., 810 Houston St., Fort Worth, TX 76107
Fresno: 600 United California Bank Bldg., 2030 Fresno St., Fresno, CA 93721
Houston: IC World Trade Center Bldg., 1520 Texas Ave., Houston, TX 77002
Kansas City: 400 Waltower St., Kansas City, MO 64102
Laredo: 1612 Farragut St., P.O. Box 659, Laredo, TX 78040
Los Angeles: 125 Paseo de la Plaza, Edificio Biscailuz, Los Angeles, CA 90012
Lubbock: 1st Nat'l Bank Bldg., Suite 1242, 1500 Broadway, Lubbock, TX 79401
McAllen: 1418 Beech St., P.O. Box 603, McAllen, TX 78501
Miami: Rivergate Plaza, 444 Brickell Ave. (418), Miami, FL 33131
Nogales: 135 Terrace Ave., Nogales, AZ 85621
New Orleans: 1140 International Trade Mart, 2 Canal St., New Orleans, LA 70130
New York: 8 East 41st St., New York, NY 10017
Phoenix: Saguaro Savings Bldg., D 5755, N. 19th Ave., Phoenix, AZ 85015
Philadelphia: 2333 P.S.F.S. Bldg., 12 S. 12th St., Philadelphia, PA 19107
Presidio: 730 O'Rily St., P.O. Box 938, Presidio, TX 79845
Sacramento: 809 8th St., Sacramento, CA 95814
San Antonio: 127 Navarro St., San Antonio, TX 78205
San Bernardino: 528 N. Mountain View Ave., San Bernardino, CA 92401
San Diego: 1007 5th Ave., Suite 424, San Diego, CA 92101
San Francisco: 870 Market St., Suite 516, San Francisco, CA 94102
Saint Louis: 1015 Locust St., Locust Bldg., Suite 922, St. Louis, MO 63101
San Jose: Bank of America Bldg., 12 South 1st St. (1014), San Jose, CA 95113
Seattle: 535 Securities Bld 1904 3rd Ave. & Stewart, Seattle, WA 98101
Washington: Embassy. 2829 16th St., NW, Wasington, DC 20009
Toronto, Canada: 2701 Commerce Court W., P.O. Box 255, Toronto 105, Ontario
Vancouver, Canada: Suite 1402 Royal Centre, 1055 W. Georgia St., Vancouver 5, BC
Winnipeg, Canada: 1808 Kensington Bldg., 275 Portave Ave, Winnipeg, Manitoba
Montreal, Canada: 1000 Sherbrooke W. (2110), Montreal, P.Q.
Ottawa, Canada: Embassy. 130 Albert St., Suite 206, Ottawa, Ontario KIP 5G4

MEXICAN NATIONAL TOURIST COUNCIL OFFICES:

Peachtree Center, Cain Tower—Suite 1201, Atlanta, GA 30303 • John Hancock Center—Suite 3610, Chicago, IL 60611 • Two Turtle Creek Village—Suite 1230, Dallas, TX 75219 • Gold Mall 46, Cinderella City, Englewood, CO 80110 • Pennzoil Place, South Tower—Suite 1080, Houston, TX 77002 • 9701 Wilshire Blvd, Beverly Hills, CA 90212 • 100 Biscayne Blvd—Suite 612, Miami, FL 33132 • 1 Place Ville Marie—Suite 2409, Montreal, P.Q., H3B 3M9 • One Shell Square Bldg., Concourse Level, New Orleans, LA 70130 • 405 Park Ave—Suite1002, New York, NY 10022 • 3443 N. Central Ave, Financial Center—Suite 101, Phoenix, AZ 85012 • 304 North St. Mary's Street, San Antonio, TX 78205 • 245 Westgate Plaza Mall, San Diego, CA 92101 • 219 Sutter St., San Francisco, CA 94108 • 101 Richmond Street West—Suite 1212, Toronto, Ont. M5H 2E1 • 2744 East Broadway, Tucson, AZ 85716 • 700 West Georgia St., Vancouver, B.C. V7Y 7B6 • 1156 15th St., NW—Suite 922, Washington, D.C. 20005

"Most of the Mexican fiestas are the products of boredom..."

Herbert Cerwin
These Are The Mexicans, 1947

JANUARY

1: Tapeapulco, Hgo.
1-5: Chalma, Mex. Pilgrimage, dances.
6: *Día de Los Reyes* (Day of The Kings). All Mexico. Xmas gifts given.
15: Tenango del Valle, Mex.
17: Blessing of farm animals and pets.
18: Taxco, Gro. Dances, fireworks.
20: León, Gto. Fair
Tenosique, Tab.
Guanajuato, Gto.
Chamula, Chis.

Note: *Fiesta* dates may vary from year to year. Fairs are longer and therefore you're less likely to miss one entirely.

FEBRUARY

February

1: Comitán, Chis.
2: *Candelaria.* All Mexico. Plants sold.
5: Constitution Day. Holiday.
1-8: Tzintzuntzan, Mich.
5-13: Zitacuaro, Mich. Fair.
12-20: Chalma, Mex. Pilgrimage.
24: Flag Day. Holiday.
The week before Ash Wednesday: *Carnaval!* Veracruz, Mérida, Mazatlán, Acapulco

MARCH

March

1-5: Durango, Dgo. Fair
9: San Gregorio Altapulco, D.F.
10: Almoloya de Alquisiras, Mex.
10-20: Huachinango, Pue. Flying dancers.
18: Taxco, Gro.
19: Huichapan, Hgo. Cuautla, Mor.
21: Birthday of President Benito Juárez. Holiday.
Semana Santa. Holy Week, all Mexico, just before Easter.
24: Ixtapalapa, D.F.

APRIL

April

1: Xochimilco, D.F.
5: Ticul, Yuc. Fair.
9: Santiago de Las Penas, Oax. Dances.
15-17: Fortín de las Flores, Ver. Flower festival.
16: Coyococ, Mor. Dances, fireworks.
20-26: Tuxtla, Chis. Fair.
25-5 May: Aguascalientes, Ags. Fair.
29-24 May: Puebla, Pue. Fair.

MAY

May

1: Labor Day. Holiday.
1-10: Morelia, Mor. Fair.
2: Cuernavaca, Mor.
3: Day of The Cross. All Mexico.
3-4: Ixmiquilpan, Hgo.
Santiago, Tianguistenco, Mex.
3-10: Valle del Bravo, Mex.
5: Defeat of the French at Puebla. All Mexico. Holiday.
5-12: Contreras, D.F.
6: Tepotzlán, Mor.
15: All Mexico. Animals decorated.
18-25: Juchitan, Oax.
22: Chihuahua, Chih.
31: Guanajuato, Gto.

JUNE

June

2: Ojinaga, Chih. Fair.
13-29: Uruapan, Mich.
24: Tlahuac, D.F.
San Juan del Río, Qro.
Navojoa, Son.
Tehuantepec, Oax.
29: Guadalajara, Jal.
Tehuacán, Pue.
All towns named San Pedro and San Pablo.

JULY

1-13: Huamantla, Tlax. Fair.
3: Oaxaca, Oax. During July watch for *Lunes del Cerro,* 2 weeks of Indian fiestas near Oaxaca.
4: Lagos de Moreno, Jal.
Acambaro, Gto.
8: Teotitlán del Valle, Oax.
Actopan, Hgo.
7-15: Comitán, Chis.
16: Tehuacán, Pue.
Celaya, Gto.
19: Juchitan, Oax.

July

21-23: Xico, Ver.
24: Torreon, Coah.
31: Guanajuato, Gto.

25: All Mexico
Chalco, Mex. Fair.

August

AUGUST

1-7: Saltillo, Coah. Fair.
2: Tulancingo, Hgo.
2-6: Comitán, Chis. Fair.
6: Lagos de Moreno, Jal. Fair.
8: Paracho, Mich.
15: All Mexico.
Milpa Alta, D.F. Fair

8-16: Mérida, Yuc.
19: Tlamanalco, Mex. Fair.
21: Mexico City
28: Chalma, Mex. Pilgrimage.
31: Oaxaca, Oax.

September

SEPTEMBER

3: Juchitan, Oax.
1-8: Tepotzlán, Mor.
San Bartolo Naucalpan, Mex. Fair.
8: Cholula, Pue. Fair.
10-16: Chihuahua, Chih. Fair.
14: Charro Day (Gentlemen Cowboys), all Mexico.
Queretaro, Qro.

6-15: Zacatecas, Zac. Fair.
16: Independence Day. Holiday.
San Miguel Allende, Gto. Fireworks!
Dolores Hidalgo, Gto.
29: Uruapan, Mich.
Chalma, Mex. Pilgrimage.
Tuxtla, Chis.

October

OCTOBER

3: Ocotlán, Jal. Fair.
4: Many towns.
1-7: Ciudad Delicias, Chih. Fair
2-6: Cuetzalán, Pue.
7-15: Alvarado, Ver. Regattas.

12: Columbus Day (also called *Dia de la Raza*). Holiday.
4-26: Pachuca, Hgo. Fair.
22-25: Ciudad Guzmán, Jal.

November

NOVEMBER

1: Tlaxcala, Tlax. Fair.
1-2: Days of the Dead. All Mexico. (See *¡Viva Mexico!*)

3-12: San Martín Texmelucan, Pue. Fair.
20: Anniversary of the 1910 Revolution. Holiday.

December

DECEMBER

1-8: Compostela, Nay. Fair.
8: All Mexico.
Pátzcuaro, Mich. Fair.
San Juan de Los Lagos, Jal.
Tenancingo, Mex.
5-15: Iguala, Gro. Fair.
7-15: Taxco, Gro. Silver fair.

8-14: Tuxtla, Chis. Fair.
12: Our Lady of Guadalupe, patroness Saint of Mexico. Everywhere.
16-25: Christmas season.
23: Oaxaca, Oax. The Radish Festival.
25: Christmas. Holiday.
31: New Year's Eve. Midnight supper.

SAINT'S DAYS

January		February	
2.	San Macario	1.	San Ignacio
6.	Los Santos Reyes	3.	San Blas
13.	San Gumersindo	5.	San Felipe de Jesus
15.	San Mauro	10.	San Guillermo
16.	San Marcelo	11.	N. Sra. de Lourdes
17.	San Antonio Abao	13.	San Benigno
19.	San Mario	14.	San Valentin
24.	Ntra. Sra. de la Paz	16.	San Onesimo
30.	Sta. Martino	23.	Sta. Marta
31.	Sta. Virginia	28.	San Hilario

March		April	
2.	San Frederico	2.	Sta. Ofelia
6.	Sta. Felicitas	3.	San Ricardo
7.	Sto. Tomas de A.	5.	Sta. Emilia
8.	San Juan de Dios	8.	San Alberto
14.	Sta. Matilda	12.	San Julio
17.	San Patricio	18.	San Perfecto
19.	San Jose	21.	San Anselmo
22.	San Octaviano	23.	San Jorge
28.	Sta. Dorotea	25.	San Marcos
31.	San Benjamin	30.	Sta. Catalina de S.

May

1. Sta. Berta
8. San Bonifacio
9. San Gregorio N.
10. San Antonio
15. San Isidoro
20. San Bernardino
25. Corpus Christi
26. San Felipe Neri
27. Sta. Carolina
30. San Fernando

June

3. Sta. Clotilde
7. San Roberto
9. San Feliciano
15. San Modesto
17. San Gregorio
21. San Luis Gonzaga
24. San Juan Bautista
26. San Antelmo
29. San Pedro y San Pablo
30. Sta. Lucina

July

1. San Aaron
2. San Martiniano
7. San Fermin
8. Sta. Isabel
11. San Abundio
19. Sta. Rufina
24. Sta. Cristina
27. San Celestino
28. San Victor
31. San Ignacio de Loyola

August

1. Sta. Esperanza
6. San Justo
9. San Roman
10. San Lorenzo
12. Sta. Clara
20. San Bernardo
25. San Luis Rey
27. San Armando
28. San Agustin
31. San Ramon N.

September

1. N. Sra. de los Remedios
4. Sta. Rosalia
8. San Sergio
10. San Nicholas de T.
19. San Genaro
21. San Mateo
25. Sta. Aurelia
27. San Cosme
29. San Miguel
30. San Jeromino

October

3. San Gerardo
4. San Francisco de Asis
5. San Placido
13. San Eduardo
15. Sta. Teresa de Jesus
17. Sta. Margarita
18. San Lucas
24. San Rafael Arc.
27. San Florencio
30. San Claudio

November

4. San Carlos B.
6. San Leonardo
7. San Ernesto
8. San Victorino
11. San Martin
13. San Diego
17. San Gregorio
23. San Clemente
25. Sta. Catalina
30. San Andres Ap.

December

1. Sta. Natalia
4. Sta. Barbara
7. San Ambrosio
13. Sta. Lucia
15. San Arturo
17. San Lazaro
18. San Ausencio
20. San Filogonio
21. Sto. Tomas Ap.
27. San Juan Ap.

MARKET DAYS — MEXICO

Acámbaro, Gto.	except Thurs.
Acatlán (de Osorio), Pue.	Sun., Tues.
Acatzingo, Pue.	Tues.
Acayucan, Ver.	Daily
Acaxochitlán, Hgo.	Sun. & Weds.
Acolman, Mex.	Weds.
Actopan, Hgo.	Weds.
Aguascalientes, Ags.	Daily
Agulilla, Mich.	Fri.
Alamos, Son.	Sun.
Alfajayucan, Hgo.	Sun.
Almoloya de Juárez, Mex.	Sun.
Alvarado, Ver.	Sun.
Amecameca, Mex.	Sun.
Amozoc de Mota, Pue.	Sun.
Angangueo, Mich.	Sat., Sun.
Apan, Hgo.	Sun.
Apatzingán, Mich.	Sat. & Sun.
Apizaco, Tlax.	Sun.
Arriaga, Chis.	Daily
Atlacomulco, Mex.	Sun.
Atlixco, Pue.	Tues., Sat.
Banderilla, Ver.	Sun.
Cadereyta, Que.	Sun.
Camargo, Chih.	Mon., Sat.
Capulhuac, Mex.	Tues.
Celaya, Gto.	Tues., Sat.
Chalco, Mex.	Fri.
Chetumal, Q.R.	Daily
Chiconcuac, Mex.	Sun., Tues.
Chicuautla, Hgo.	Sat.
Cholula, Pue.	Sun., Weds.
Cd. Hidalgo, Mich.	Sun.
Cd. Lopez Mateos, Mex.	Sun.
Cd. Mante, Tamps.	Sat., Sun.
Cd. Serdán, Pue.	Sun., Mon.
Concepción del Oro, Zac.	Sat. & Sun.
Cosamaloapan, Ver.	Sat. & Sun.
Cotija, Mich.	Sat. & Sun.
Cuauhtémoc, Chih.	Daily
Cuernavaca, Mor.	Sun.
Cuetzalan, Pue.	Sun.
Dolores Hidalgo, Gto.	Sun.
Ejutla, Oax.	Weds.
Etla, Oax.	Weds.
Fortín, Ver.	Sun.
Fresnillo, Zac.	Sun.

Gómez Palacio, Dgo.	Daily
Guadalajara, Jal.	Daily, Sun.
Guanajuato, Gto.	Sun.
Guasave, Sin.	Daily
Huajuapan de León, Oax.	Sun.
Huamantla, Tlax.	Sun. & Weds.
Huachinango, Pue.	Sat.
Huejotzingo, Pue.	Thurs. & Sat.
Huichapan, Hgo.	Sun.
Iguala, Gro.	Sun. & Sat.
Irapuato, Gto.	Tues., Sun.
Ixmiquilpan, Hgo.	Mon.
Ixtapan de la Sal, Mex.	Sun.
Izúcar de Matamoros, Pue.	Sun., Mon.
Jacala, Hgo.	Sun.
Jilotepec, Mex.	Fri.
Jiquilpan, Mich.	Sat.
Jocotepec. Jal.	Sun.
Juchitán, Oax.	Sun.
Juchitepec, Mex.	Weds.
La Piedad Cavadas, Mich.	Sun.
León, Gto.	Mon., Tues.
Lerma, Mex.	Sat.
Luis Moya, Zac.	Sun.
Manzanillo, Col.	Sat., Sun.
Martínez de la Torre, Ver.	Sun.
Matehuala, S.L.P.	Daily
Mérida, Yuc.	Daily
Metepec, Mex.	Mon.
Metztitlán, Hgo.	Sun.
Miahuatlán, Oax.	Mon.
Mitla, Oax.	Sun.
Morelia, Mich.	Thurs. & Sun.
Moroleón, Gto.	Sun. & Mon.
Motul, Yuc.	Mon.
Nochixtlán, Oax.	Sun.
Nuevo Casas Grandes, Chih.	Daily
Oaxaca, Oax.	Sat.
Ocotlán, Jal.	Sat. & Sun.
Ocotlán, Oax.	Fri.
Ocoyoacac, Mex.	Weds.
Ozumba de Alzate, Mex.	Tues. & Fri.
Papantla, Ver.	Sun.
Parras, Coah.	Sat. & Sun.
Pátzcuaro, Mich.	Sun., Tues. & Fri.
Perote, Ver.	Sun.
Poza Rica, Ver.	Daily
Puebla, Pue.	Thurs., Sun.
Puerto Peñasco, Son.	Daily
Puerto Vallarta, Jal.	Sun.
Queretaro, Qro.	Daily
Quiroga, Mich.	Sun.
Sabinas, Coah.	Sat. & Sun.
Sahuayo, Mich	Sun.
Salamanca, Gto.	Sun., Tues.
Saltillo, Coah.	Daily
Santiago de Anaya, Hgo.	Thurs.
Santiago Tianguistenco, Mex.	Tues.
San Bartolo Naucalpan, Mex.	Sat.
San Cristóbal de las Casas, Chis.	Daily except Sun.
San Francisco del Rincón, Gto.	Tues., Sun.
San José Purúa, Mich.	Sun.
San Juan de los Lagos, Jal.	Daily
San Juan del Río, Qro.	Sun.
San Martín Texmelucan, Pue.	Fri. & Tues.
San Miguel de Allende, Gto.	Sun. & Tues.
Sayula, Hgo.	Mon.
Silao, Gto.	Tues. & Sun.
Tabasco, Zac.	Sun.
Tamazunchale, S.L.P.	Sun.
Tasquillo, Hgo.	Sun.
Taxco, Gro.	Thurs., Sun.
Tecali, Pue.	Tues., Fri.
Tecamachalco, Pue.	Sat.
Tecozautla, Hgo.	Thurs.
Tehuacán, Pue.	Sat.
Tehuantepec, Oax.	Sun.
Temascalapa, Mex.	Thurs., Sun.
Tenancingo, Mex.	Sun. & Thurs.
Tenango, Mex.	Thurs., Sun.
Tepeaca, Pue.	Fri.
Tepeji del Rio, Hgo.	Mon.
Tepetlixpa, Mex.	Mon.
Tepotzlán, Mor.	Sun. & Weds.
Tequisquiapan, Qro.	Sun.
Tetela de Ocampo, Pue.	Sun.

Texcoco, Mex.	Sun.	Valle de Bravo, Mex.	Sun., Thurs.
Teziutlán, Pue.	Fri., Sun.	Veracruz, Ver.	Daily
Texmelucan, Oax.	Tues.	Villa del Carbón, Mex.	Sun., Thurs.
Tierra Blanca, Ver.	Daily	Villahermosa, Tab.	Daily
Tinguidín, Mich.	Sun.	Xicotepec, Pue.	Sun.
Tlacolula, Oax.	Sun.	Xochimilco, D.F.	Sat., Thurs.
Tlahuelilpa, Hgo.	Tues.	Xuchitlán, Hgo.	Mon.
Tlalnepantla, Mex.	Fri., Sun.	Zaachila, Oax.	Mon.
Tlaxcala, Tlax.	Sat.	Zacapú, Mich.	Sun.
Toluca, Mex.	Fri.	Zacatlán, Pue.	Sun., Fri.
Tonalá, Chis.	Daily	Zacualtipán, Hgo.	Sun.
Tula, Hgo.	Sun.	Zimapán, Hgo.	Sat. & Sun.
Tulancingo, Hgo.	Thurs., Mon.	Zitacuaro, Mich.	Sun.
Tuxtla Gutiérrez, Chis.	Daily		
Uruapan, Mich.	Daily		

MARKET DAYS — GUATEMALA

Town, Department (State)			
Aguacatán, Huehuetenango	Thurs., Sun.	Malacatán, San Marcos	Sun.
Antigua, Guatemala	Thurs., Sun.	Mataquescuintla, Jalapa	Wed.
Cantel, Quezaltenango	Sun.	Mazatenango, Suchitepéquez	Sat., Thurs.
Chiche, El Quiché	Sat.	Momostenango, Totonicapán	Sun.
Chichicastenango, El Quiché	Thurs., Sun.	Nahualá, Sololá	Sun.
Chimaltenango, Chimaltenango	Daily	Nebaj, El Quiché	Thurs., Sun.
Chiquimula, Chiquimula	Daily	Olintepeque, Quezaltenango	Tues.
Chiquimulilla, Santa Rosa	Daily	Palín, Escuintla	Sun., Wed.
Chuarrancho, Guatemala	Thurs., Sun.	Panajachel, Sololá	Sun.
Cobán, Alta Verapaz	Daily	Patzicia, Chimaltenango	Wed., Sat.
Comapala, Chimaltenango	Sun.	Patzún, Chimaltenango	Sun.
Cotzal, El Quiché	Sat.	Quezaltenango, Quezal.	Daily
Cuilapa, Santa Rosa	Daily	Rabinal, Baja Verapaz	Daily
El Progreso, Progreso	Daily	Retalhuleu, Retalhuleu	Daily
El Rancho, Progreso	Daily	Sacapulas, El Quiché	Thurs., Sun.
Escuintla, Escuintla	Daily	Salamá, Baja Verapaz	Daily
Flores, Petén	Daily	Salcajá, Quezaltenango	Sun.
Guatemala, Guetemala	Daily except Sunday	San Andrés Semetabaj, Sololá	Tues.
Huehuetenango, Huehuetenango	Thurs., Sun.	San Antonio las Flores, Guatemala	Tues.
Itzapa, Chilmaltenango	Fri., Sun.	San Cristóbal Verapaz, Alta Verapaz	Sun., Tues.
Jalapa, Jalapa	Daily	San Francisco el Alto, Totonicapán	Fri.
Jutiapa, Jutiapa	Thurs., Sun.	San José Nacahuil, Guatemala	Thurs.

San Juan Chamelco, Alta Verapaz	Daily
San Juan Ostuncalco, Quezaltenango	Sun.
San Juan Sacatepéquez, Guatemala	Daily
San Lucas Tolimán, Sololá	Thurs., Sun.
San Marcos, San Marcos	Tues.
San Martín Jilotepéque, Chimaltenango	Sun.
San Martín Sacatepéquez, Quezaltenango	Fri.
San Pedro Carcha, Alta Verapaz	Daily
San Pedro la Laguna, Sololá	Thurs., Sun.
San Pedro Sacatepéquez, Guatemala	Sun., Fri.
San Pedro Sacatepéquez, San Marcos	Thurs., Sun
San Raimundo, Guatemala	Thurs., Sun
Santa Cruz del Quiché, El Quiché	Thurs., Sun.
Santa Lucia Utatlán, Sololá	Thurs.
Santa Maria Chiquimula, Totonicapán	Thurs., Sun.
Santiago Atitlán, Sololá	Thurs., Sun.
Santiago Sacatepéquez, Sacatepéquez	Sun.
Sololá, Sololá	Fri.
Tactic, Alta Verapaz	Thurs., Sun.
Tamahu, Alta Verapaz	Wed., Sat.
Tecpán, Chimaltenango	Thurs.
Totonicapán, Totonicapán	Tues., Sat.
Tocuru, Alta Verapaz	Thurs., Sun.
Zacapa, Zacapa	Sun.

VOCABULARY

GETTING AROUND

Ticket window	*Caja, taquilla*	Train	*Ferrocarril, Tren*
Reservation	*Reservación*	Airplane	*Avión*
Reserved seat	*Asiento reservado*	First class	*Primera clase*
Arrivals & Departures (posted on 24 hour time system)	*Llegadas y Salidas*	Second class	*Segunda clase*
		Taxi	*Taxi, Libre, Coche*
		Taxi stand	*Sitio*
On the hour	*Cada hora*	Boat	*Lancha*
Every half hour	*Cada media hora*	Canoe	*Canoa*
Daily	*Diario*	Pack animal	*Bestia*
Passenger	*Pasajero*	Bus station	*Terminal* or *estación de autobuses*
Driver	*Chofer*		
Line or company	*Linea* or *campañiá*	Bus stop	*Parada*
To get aboard	*Subir*	Train station	*Estación de ferrocarril*
To get off	*Bajar*	Ticket	*Boleto*
Airport	*Aeropuerto*	Ride	*Aventón, Ride*
Bus	*Autobús, camión*	I'm going to...	*Me voy a...*
City bus	*Servicio urbano*	Where are you going?	*¿Dónde va?*
		Get in.	*Sube.*

I want a ticket to... — *Quiero un boleto a...*
How much is a ticket to...? — *¿Cuánto cuesta un boleto a...?*
What bus line goes to...? — *¿Qué linea tiene servicio a...?*
What is the number of the bus? — *¿Qué es el número del autobús?*
What time does the bus leave for...? — *¿A qué hora sale el camión a...?*
Where does it leave from? — *¿De dónde sale?*
Where does this bus go? — *¿Dónde va este autobús?*
How many hours is it to...? — *¿Cuántas horas a...?*
I lost my baggage. — *Se me perdió mi equipaje.*
How much time do we have here? — *¿Cuánto tiempo tenemos aquí?*
Let me off at the corner (off here). — *Quiero bajar en la esquina (aquí).*
Will you give me a ride to...? — *¿Me da un aventón a...?*
I'm travelling by thumb. — *Viajo por aventón.*
What will you charge to take me to...? — *¿Cuánto me cobra llevarme a...?*

HOTELS AND HOUSES

Hotel	*Hotel*	Hammock	*Hamaca*
Motel	*Motel*	Bathroom	*Baño*
Inn	*Posada*	Bath	*Baño*

HOTELS, etc. (cont.)

Boarding house, Guest house	*Casa de huespedes, Pensión*	Shower	*Regador, Regadera*
Room, double	*Cuarto doble*	Hot water	*Agua caliente*
Key	*Llave*	Fan	*Ventilador, abanico*
Bed	*Cama*	Air conditioned	*Aire acondicionado*
Double bed	*Cama matrimonial*	Manager	*Gerente, Dueño*
Extra bed	*Cama extra*	Dining room	*Comedor*
Blanket	*Cobija, cubierta*	Bar	*Bar*
Cot	*Catre*	Swimming pool	*Alberca, Piscina*
		Noise	*Ruido*

Do you know of a cheap hotel? — *¿Conoce usted un hotel económico?*
Do you have a room for two? — *¿Hay un cuarto para dos personas?*
Do you have a room with bath? — *¿Hay un cuarto con baño?*
with meals — *con comidas,* without meals — *sin comidas*
Is the car safe? — *¿Está seguro el coche?*
Is there a night watchman at the parking lot? — *¿Hay un velador en el estacionamiento?*
Do you have ice? — *¿Hay hielo?*
Please put in a cot for the child. — *Favor de poner un catre para el niño.*
The toilet is stopped up. — *Está tapada la taza.*

House	*Casa*	Electricity	*Electricidad*
To rent	*Alquilar, Rentar*	Room	*Cuarto*
For rent	*Se renta, Se alquila*	Bedroom	*Recámara*
To sell	*Vender*	Living room	*Sala*
For sale	*Se vende*	Kitchen	*Cocina*
By the week, month	*Por la semana, el mes*	Stove	*Estufa*
Landlord, owner	*Dueño-a*	Refrigerator	*Refrigerador*
Furnished	*Amueblada*	Maid	*Criada*

Is this house for rent? — *¿Está de renta la casa?*
Who owns this house? — *¿Quién es el dueño de esta casa?*
Where does s/he live? — *¿Dónde vive?*
How much is it per month? — *¿Cuánto es por mes?*

FOOD AND DRINK

Restaurant	*Restaurante, Comedor, Lonchería, Fonda*	Beverage	*Bebida*
		Fork	*Tenedor*
Daily special	*Comida corrida*	Spoon	*Cuchara*
Menu	*Menú*	Knife	*Cuchillo*
An order	*Un orden*	Cup	*Taza*
Meal	*Comida*	Glass	*Vaso*
Plate	*Plato*	Napkin	*Servilleta*
Snack	*Antojito, Botana*	Toothpick	*Palillo*
Dessert	*Postre*	The bill	*La cuenta*

What is there to eat? (to drink?) — *¿Qué hay de comer? (de tomar?)*
Are there...? (beans, eggs) — *¿Hay...? (frijoles, huevos)*
I want... — *Quiero...* We want... — *Queremos...*
The bill, please — *La cuenta por favor.*
We want to pay separately. — *Queremos pagar aparte.*
The meal was very good. — *La comida estuvo muy sabrosa.*

Liquor	*Licor*	Aged	*Añejo*
Drink	*Copita*	Soda water	*Agua mineral (con gas)*
Cocktail	*Coctel, Jaibol*	Ice cubes	*Cubitos de hielo*
Glass	*Vaso*	Bottle	*Botella*

FOOD, etc. (cont.)

Beer	*Cerveza*	Case	*Cartón*
Dark beer	*Cerveza oscura, negra*	Bottle opener	*Destapador*
Draft beer	*Cerveza de barril*	Bottle cap	*Ficha*
Wine	*Vino*	Ice pick	*Picahielos*
Sweet	*Dulce*	Opened	*Destapada*
Dry	*Seco*	Room temperature	*Al tiempo*

I'm really drunk. — *Estoy bien pedo.*
I have a terrible hangover. — *Estoy muy crudo.*
I'd like to buy you a beer. — *Le invito a una cheve (cerveza).*

POST OFFICE, TELEGRAPH, TELEPHONE, BANK

Post office	*Correo*	Special handling	*Entrega Inmediata*
General Delivery	*Lista de Correos*	Registered	*Registrado*
Letter	*Carta*	Certified	*Certificado*
Address	*Dirección*	Postal money order	*Giro*
Return address	*Dirección del remitente*	Package, box	*Paquete, caja*
Return to...	*Remite a...*	Wrapped	*Envuelto*
Envelope	*Sobre*	String	*Cuerda*
Stamp	*Estampilla, timbre*	Glue	*Pegamento*
Post card	*Tarjeta*	Duty, tax	*Impuesto*
Airgram	*Aereogramo*	Weight	*Peso*
Airmail	*Correo aereo*	Change of address card	*Tarjeta de cambiar dirección*
Regular mail	*Ordinario*		

Is there any mail in General Delivery for Joe Blow? — *¿Hay algo en la lista para Joe Blow?*
Weigh it, please. — *Péselo, por favor.*
Does it need more postage? — *¿Necesita más estampillas?*
Three airmail envelopes, please. — *Tres sobres aereos, por favor.*

Telegraph office	*Telégrafos*	Regular	*Ordinario*
Telegram	*Telegrama*	Night letter	*Carta nocturna, Carta de noche*
Urgent	*Urgente*		

I would like to send a telegram to... — *Quiero mandar una telegrama a...*

Telephone	*Teléfono*	Long distance	*Larga distancia*
Telephone office	*Oficina de teléfonos*	Collect	*Al cobrar*
To call	*Llamar*	Person to person	*Persona a persona*
A call	*Una llamada*	Station to station	*A quien contesta*
Number	*Número*	Credit card	*Tarjeta de crédito*
Operator	*Operador*	Hello!	*¡Ola!, ¡Bueno!*

I want to call the United States, please. The number is... — *Quiero llamar a los Estados Unidos. El número es...*

Money	*Dinero, lana*	50 centavos, 20,	*Tostón, Viente,*
Change	*Cambio, feria, suelto*	Dollar	*Dólar*
Check	*Cheque*	Bill	*Billete*
Personal check	*Cheque personal*	To cash, change	*Cambiar*
Traveler's check	*Cheque de viajero*	Bank	*Banco*
Bank draft	*Cheque del banco*	Teller's window	*Caja*
Money order	*Giro*	Signature	*Firma*
Mexican currency	*Moneda Nacional (MN)*		

Can you cash a traveler's check? — *¿Se puede cambiar un cheque de viajero?*

HEALTH

Health	*Salud*	Cough syrup	*Jarabe para tos*
Doctor	*Médico, Doctor*	Pill	*Pastilla*
Hospital	*Hospital*	Capsule	*Cápsula*
Drugstore	*Farmacia*	Aspirin	*Aspirina*
Sick	*Enfermo*	Salve, ointment	*Pomada*
Pain	*Dolor*	Bandage	*Venda*
Fever	*Fiebre*	Adhesive tape	*Cinta adhesiva*
Headache	*Dolor de cabeza*	Cotton	*Algodón*
Cold, Flu	*Gripe*	Vitamin	*Vitamina*
Stomach-ache	*Dolor de estómago*	Birth control pills	*Pastillas contraceptivas*
Diarrhea	*Diarrea*	Kotex, Tampax	Use brand name
Cough	*Tos*	Dentist	*Dentista, sacamuelas (molar puller)*
Burn	*Quemadura*		
Sunburn	*Quemadura del sol*	Toothache	*Dolor de muelas*
Cramp	*Calambre*	Shot, injection	*Inyección*
Medicine	*Medicina*	Toothbrush	*Cepillo dental*
Antibiotic	*Antibiótico*	Toothpaste	*Crema dental*

I have a headache, stomach-ache, etc. — *Me duele la cabeza, estómago, etc.*
I have a cold, flu, cough, etc. — *Tengo gripe, tos, etc.*
I need medicine for diarrhea. — *Necesito medicina para diarrea.*
Do you know a good doctor? — *¿Conoce un buen médico?*

GAS STATIONS, CAR PARTS, TERMS

Gas station	*Gasolinera*	Grease	*Grasa*
Pump	*Bomba*	To grease	*Engrasar*
Gas cap	*Tapón, tapa*	Grease job	*Lubricación, grasa*
Tank	*Tanque*	Oil change	*Cambio de aceite*
Gasoline	*Gasolina*	Oil	*Aceite*

Fill it up, please. — *Lleno, por favor.*
Check the oil and water, please. — *Vea el aceite y agua, por favor.*
I want an oil change and grease job. — *Quiero un cambio de aceite y lubricación.*
Check the oil in the transmission and differential. — *Vea el aceite en la caja y diferencial.*
Put in a liter of 30 weight oil, please. — *Eche un litro de aceite número treinta, por favor.*
Put 30 pounds of air in the tires. — *Ponga treinta libras de aire en las llantas.*
Where is the restroom? — *¿Dónde está el baño?*
Do you have a map of Mexico? — *¿Hay un mapa de la republica?*

Accelerator	*Acelerador*	Ball bearings	*Baleros*
Adjust	*Ajustar*	Ball joints	*Rótulas*
Adjusting stars (brakes)	*Ajustadores de frenos*	Battery	*Acumulador, batería*
		Battery cable	*Cable de acumulador*
A-frame	*Horguilla*	Block	*Monoblock*
Air filter	*Filtro de aire*	Body and paint shop	*Hojalatería y Pintura*
Air filter cartridge	*Cartucho del filtro de aire*		
		Boot (tire)	*Huarache*
Alternator	*Alternador*	Brakes	*Frenos*
Armature	*Rotor*	Brake drum	*Tambor*
Assemble	*Armar*	Brake fluid	*Líquido de frenos*
Auto electric shop	*Taller auto-eléctrico*	Brake line	*Mangera de frenos*
Auto parts	*Refacciones*	Brake lining	*Balata*
Auto parts store	*Refaccionería*	Brake pedal	*Pedal de frenos*
Axle	*Eje*	Brake plate	*Plato de frenos*
Brake shoe	*Zapata*	Gas tank	*Tanque de gasolina*

Brushes	*Carbones*
Bumper	*Defensa*
Bus	*Autobús, camión*
Bushing	*Bushing, buje*
Cable	*Cable*
Camshaft	*Arbol de levas*
Camshaft bearings	*Metales de árbol de levas*
Car	*Coche, automóvil, carro*
Carburetor	*Carburador*
Carburetor float	*Flotador*
Carburetor jet	*Esprea*
Choke	*Ahogador*
Clutch	*Clutch*
Clutch disc	*Disco de clutch*
Clutch pedal	*Pedal de clutch*
Coil	*Bobina*
Condenser	*Condensador*
Coil springs	*Resortes*
Crankcase	*Monoblock*
Crankshaft	*Cigüeñal*
Cylinder	*Cilindro*
Cylinder sleeve	*Camisa*
Differential	*Diferencial*
Dismantle	*Desarmar*
Distributor	*Distribuidor*
Distributor cap	*Tapa de distribuidor*
Drive	*Manejar*
Drive shaft	*Flecha cardán*
Electrical system	*Sistema eléctrica*
Fan	*Ventilador*
Fan belt	*Banda de ventilador*
Fan belt	*Banda de ventilador*
Fender	*Guardabarros*
Fields	*Campos*
Fly wheel	*Engrane volante*
Frame	*Bastidor*
Front wheel alignment	*Alineación*
Front wheel bearings	*Baleros de las ruedas adelantes*
Front wheel spindle	*Mango*
Fuel pump	*Bomba de gasolina*
Fuse	*Fusible*
Garage (repair)	*Taller mecánico, taller automotriz*
Gas cap	*Tapón de gasolina*
Gas line	*Tubo, mangera de gasolina*
Gas tank	*Tanque de gasolina*
Gasket	*Empaque, junta*
Gasket set	*Juego de empaques*
Gear	*Engrane*
Gear shift lever	*Palanca de cambios*
Generator	*Generador*
Ground	*Tierra*
Hand brake	*Freno de mano*
Head	*Cabeza*
Head gasket	*Empaque de cabeza*
Headlights	*Focos*
Horn	*Klaxón, bocina*
Hose	*Mangera*
Hose clamp	*Abrazadera*
Ignition key	*Llave de switch*
Ignition switch	*Switch*
Jack	*Gato*
Kingpin	*Perno, pivote de dirección*
Kingpin carrier	*Portamango*
Leaf springs	*Muelles*
Lever	*Palanca*
Main bearings	*Metales de bancada*
Manifold	*Múltiple*
Exhaust	*Múltiple de escape*
Intake	*Múltiple de admisión*
Master cylinder	*Cilindro maestro de frenos*
Mechanic	*Mecánico, Maestro*
Motor	*Motor, máquina*
Muffler	*Mofle*
Oil	*Aceite*
Oil filter	*Filtro de aceite*
Oil pump	*Bomba de aceite*
Panel truck	*Camioneta, panel*
Patch	*Parche*
Pickup truck	*Camioneta*
Piston	*Pistón*
Pitman arm	*Brazo Pitman*
Points	*Platinos*
Pressure plate	*Plato de presión*
Pulley	*Polea*
Push rod	*Levador, puntería*
Radiator	*Radiador*
Radiator cap	*Tapón de radiador*
Radiator hose	*Mangera de radiador*
Re-cap (tire)	*Recubierta*
Relay	*Relé*
Rings	*Anillos*
Compression ring	*Anillo de compresión*
Oil ring	*Anillo de aceite*
Rocker arm	*Balancín*
Rod	*Biela*
Rod bearing (insert)	*Metales de bielas*
Rotor	*Rotor*
Seal	*Retén*
Shaft	*Flecha*
Shock absorber	*Amortiguador*
Solenoid	*Solenoide*
Spark plug	*Bujía (Candela* in Guatemala)
Spark plug wire	*Cable de bujía*
Starter	*Marcha*
Starter ring gear	*Cremallera*

Steering gear — *Caja de dirección*
Steering wheel — *Volante*
Stop light — *Luz de stop*
Stud — *Birlo, perno prisionero*
Tail pipe — *Tubo de escape*
Thermostat — *Toma de agua, termósı*
Throw out bearing — *Cojarín*
Tie rod — *Barrilla de dirección*
Tie rod end — *Terminal de barrilla de dirección*
Tighten — *Apretar*
Timing gear — *Engrange de árbol de levas*
Tire — *Llanta*
Tire balancing — *Balanceo*
Tire gauge — *Calibrador*
Tire repair shop — *Vulcanízadora*
Tire tube — *Camara* or *Tubo*
Tire, tubeless — *Llanta sin cámara*
Tire valve — *Válvula*
Tow truck — *Grúa*
Torsion bar — *Barra de torsión*
Transmission — *Transmisión, Caja* (box)
Truck — *Camión*
Tune — *Afinar*
Tune up — *Afinación*
Turn signals — *Direccionales*
Turn signal flasher — *Destallador*
Universal joint — *Cruceta y yugo, cardán*
Upholstery shop (auto) — *Cubreasientos*
Vacuum advance — *Avance*
Valves — *Válvulas*
  exhaust — *válvula de escape*
  intake — *válvula de admisión*
Valve cover — *Tapa de pulerias*
Valve guide — *Guía de válvula*
Valve lifter — *Buso, levantaválvulas*
Valve springs — *Resorte de válvula*
Valve spring keeper — *Cazuela de válvula*
Valve stem — *Vastigo de válvula*
Van — *Camioneta*
Voltage regulator — *Regulador de voltage*
Water pump — *Bomba de agua*
Weld — *Soldar*
Wheel — *Rueda*
Wheel cylinder — *Cilindro de frenos*
Windshield — *Parabrisas*
Windshield wiper — *Limpia parabrisas* or *Limpiadores*
Windshield wiper blade — *Pluma*
Wire — *Alambre*
Wrist pin — *Perno, Pasador de émbolo*

It's bent. — *Está doblado.*
Adjust the clutch. — *Ajuste el clutch.*
Adjust the brakes. — *Ajuste los frenos.*
To bleed the brakes. — *Purgar los frenos*
To rebuild the wheel cylinders — *Cambiar las gomas*
To turn the brake drums — *Rectificar los tambores*
Adjust the valves. — *Ajuste las válvulas.*
To grind the valves — *Asentar las válvulas*
Engine overhaul — *Ajuste general*
To turn the crankshaft — *Rectificar la cigüeñal*
To charge the battery — *Cargar la acumulador*
The engine is knocking. — *Suena la máquina.*
The engine is overheating. — *El motor se calienta.*
The engine is throwing oil. — *La máquina está tirando aceite.*
The engine is burning oil. — *La máquina está quemando aceite.*
The radiator is leaking. — *Está tirando la radiador.*
I want a major tune-up. — *Quiero una afinación mayor.*
Pack the front wheel bearings. — *Engrace los baleros de las ruedas adelantes.*
The tire is punctured. — *Está ponchada la llanta.*
The tire has a slow leak. — *La llanta está bajando poco a poco.*
Put a boot in the tire. — *Vucanice la llanta.*
Put 30 pounds of air in the tires. — *Ponga treinta libras de aire en las llantas.*

TOOLS, HARDWARE & ODDS AND ENDS

Acetylene torch — *Soplete oxiacetilenico, Equipo de autógeno*
Allen wrench — *Llave de alán*
Axe — *Hacha*
Bag — *Bolsa*
Chisel — *Cincel*
Compression gauge — *Compresión metro*
Cotter pin — *Chaveta*
Crescent wrench — *Perico*
Crowbar — *Barra*

Bolt	*Tornillo*
Box end wrench	*Llave ástria*
Bucket	*Cubo*
Can opener	*Abrelatas*
Feeler gauge	*Calibrador*
File	*Lima*
Flashlight	*Foco de mano*
Flashlight batteries	*Pilas*
Funnel	*Embudo*
Gasket cement	*Shelac*
Gear puller	*Extractor de engranes*
Glue	*Pegamento* (white glue-*Resistol*, brand name; epoxy glue-*Pegamento Epoxy*)
Grease gun	*Inyector de grasa*
Grill (cooking)	*Parilla*
Hack saw	*Cegeta*
Hammer	*Martillo*
Hardware store	*Ferretería*
Hatchet	*Hacha*
Hose	*Mangera*
Iron rods	*Barras de fierro*
Jack	*Gato*
Juice squeezer	*Exprimidera*
Key	*Llave* (Woodruff key—*Cuña*)
Liquid wrench	*Afloja todo* (brand name)
Lug wrench	*Llave de cruz*
Needle (sewing)	*Aguja*
Nail	*Clavo*
Needle nose pliers	*Alicates*
Nut	*Tuerca*
Open end wrench	*Llave española*
Phillips screwdriver	*Desarmador de cruz*
Pin	*Perno*
Pipe wrench	*Llave Stillson*
Pliers	*Pinzas*

Drill and bits	*Taladro y brocas*
Emery paper	*Lija de esmeril*
Extension (socket)	*Extensión*
Pottery	*Cosas de barro*
Ratchet	*Matraca, Llave de trinquete*
Rope	*Soga*
Sandpaper	*Papel de lija*
Screw	*Tornillo*
Screwdriver	*Desarmador*
Sharpening stone	*Afiladera*
Shoelaces	*Agujetas*
Shovel	*Pala*
Scissors	*Tijeras*
Socket wrench	*Llave de dado*
Solder	*Soldadura*
Soldering iron	*Soldador*
Spark plug wrench	*Llave de bujias*
Spring	*Resorte*
String, cord, twine	*Cuerda*
Tape	*Cinta* (Plastic electrical tape—*cinta de plástico*)
Thread	*Hilo*
Timing light	*Lampara de tiempo*
Tin snips	*Tijeras de cortar lámina*
Tools	*Herramientas*
Torque wrench	*Llave de torque*
Vise	*Tornillo*
Vise grip pliers	*Pinzas de presión*
Washer	*Rondana*
Water pump pliers	*Pinzas de extensión*
Wire	*Alambre* (electrical wire-*alambre eléctrico*)
Wrench	*Llave*
Zipper	*Cierre, zípper*

RED TAPE

Tourist card	*Tarjeta de turista*
Passport	*Pasaporte*
Vaccination Certificate	*Certificado de Vacunación*
Immigration	*Migración*
Inspection	*Revisión*
Suitcase	*Maleta*
Minor	*Menor de edad*
Single	*Soltero (a)*
Divorced	*Divorciado (a)*
Profession or occupation	*Profesión* or *ocupación*

Registration	*Registración*
Insurance	*Seguros*
License plates	*Placas*
Border	*Frontera*
Customs	*Aduana*
Baggage	*Equipaje*
Age	*Edad*
Marital status	*Estado civil*
Married	*Casado (a)*
Widowed	*Viudo (a)*
Car permit	*Permiso de automóvil*
Driver's license	*Licencia de manejar*

Car owner	*Propetario de automóvil*	Boat	*Lancha*
Title	*Título (de propiedad)*	Outboard motor	*Motor de fuera borda*
Motorcycle	*Moto*	Guns	*Armas*
Pets	*Mascotas*	Hunting license	*Licencia de cazar*
Rabies vaccination	*Vacunación de rabia*	Fishing license	*Licencia de pescar*

Is there no other way of arranging this problem? — *¿No habría modo de resolver el problema de otra manera?*

FISHING & DIVING

Fishing rod	*Caña (de pescar)*	Spear shaft	*Flecha*
Line	*Cuerda*	Spearhead	*Punta*
Hook	*Anzuelo*	Swim fins	*Aletas*
Bait	*Carnada*	Diving mask	*Visor*
Sinker	*Plomo*	Snorkle	*Snorkle*
Lure	*Curricán*	Diving equipment	*Equipo de bucear*
Speargun	*Arpón, pistola*	To dive	*Bucear*
		To fish	*Pescar*

SLANG

¡Aguas!	Careful!	*fregar*	screw up
agua de riñon	beer	*frías*	beer
alivianar	help out	*forjar*	roll joints
aliviane	aid	*gandalla*	ass (person)
apañar	to arrest	*gañan*	thug
azul	cop	*gasofia*	gasoline
baboso	fool	*gerolan*	drunk
banquetazo	big meal	*gorrón*	cheapskate
bolo	drunk	*huevón*	lazy
bravo	tough	*¡Ijole!*	Oh, wow!
bruja	broke, poor	*infle*	a drink
buey	clod, fool	*jetear*	play the fool
buque	car	*la julia*	the cops
caco	thief	*lana*	money
café	marijuana	*libar*	to drink
cante	squeal	*ligar*	to score (sex)
caño	a joint	*loco*	stoned
carcacha	old car	*lorenzo*	crazy, nuts
carnal	brother	*lucas*	crazy, nuts
carrujos	smoking papers	*luz*	money
chavo-a	guy, girl	*madre*	good, great
chelas	beers	*mafufo*	stoned
cheves	beers	*mamacita*	little mama
chota	cop	*mamosota*	big mama
chupar	to drink	*mamón*	sucker
coco	head	*mango*	pretty woman
codo	cheap, stingy	*mano*	'brother'
conchudo	insensitive	*marmaja*	change, money
conectar	get with it	*mear*	to piss
cuete	drunk	*¡Mecacho!*	Wow!
dineral	lot of money	*mocoso*	snot-nosed
desmadre	screw-up, mess	*moler*	to bother, bug
esquincle	kid, brat	*mordelón*	cop
¡Entrale!	Get it on!	*mordida*	bribe, bite
fachas	Chicle sellers	*mota*	marijuana

SLANG (cont.)

muerto	broke, poor
naco	thug
nave	car
nieves	no
nones	no
nortearse	beat it, scram
onda	vibe
padre	very good
la papa	food
papear	to eat
pedo	drunk
pelarse	escape, avoid
pendejo	creep
pinche	damned, useless
pintarse	escape, avoid
pomos	wine, booze
ponchado	husky
quemacoco	convertible
quemarse	to be silly, stupid
regarla	screw up
el rol	the vibe
sabanas	rolling papers
simón	yes, right on
suave	really nice
suelto	change, money
tamarindo	traffic cop
tira	cop
toque	toke
troca	truck
yerba	marijuana
zoquete	knothead

NICKNAMES FROM PROPER NAMES

Beto	Alberto, Roberto
Bety	Beatriz
Billi	Guillermo
Chabela	Isabel
Chala	Rosalía
Charo	Rosario
Chela	Graciela
Chelo	Lucero, Cielo
Chepito	José
Chico	Francisco
Chivio	Silvia
Chole	Soledad
Chon, Chona	Concepción
Chucho	Jesús
Chuy	Jesús
Cleto	Anacleto
Concha	Concepción
Cuca	Refugia
Curro	Francisco
Fallo Fello	Rafael
Foncho	Alfonso
Güicho	Luis
Gus	Gustavo
Juancho	Juan
Lacho	Horacio
Lalo	Abelardo, Eduardo
Lencho	Lorenzo
Lety	Leticia
Licha	Alicia
Lola	Dolores
Lucha	Maria de la Luz
Lupe	Guadalupe
Lupita	Guadalupe
Luz	Maria de la Luz
Manolo	Manuel
Mari, Maruca	Maria
Mariquita	Maria
Mayté	Maria Teresa
Mela	Carmela
Melu	Manuel
Memo	Guillermo
Mima	Irma
Moy	Moisés
Mundo	Edmundo
Nacho	Ignacio
Nando	Fernando
Nardo	Leonardo
Neto	Ernesto
Nico	Nicolas
Paco	Francisco
Pancho	Francisco
Panta	Pantaleona
Pepe	José
Pita	Guadalupe
Queta	Eriqueta
Quique	Enrique
Rico, Ricky	Ricardo
Tacho	Anastasio
Tere, Teté	Teresa
Tina	Florentina
Toño, Tony	Antonio
Vicky	Victoria
Willi	Wilfrido

SLANG NICKNAMES

Bruja-o	Witch
Chaparra-o	Shorty
Chata-o	Pugnose
La Chilindrina	Naughty girl
Chino	Curly, Chinaman
Chiquis	Squirt
Chiva	Goat
Chula	Cutie
Colocho	Curly
Cuatro Lamparas	Four eyes
Dandy	Dandy
Diablo	Devil
Enano	Dwarf (also Giant)
Fede	Ugly
Flaco-a	Skinny
Gachupín	Pale
Gorda-o	Fatty
Greñas	Messy Hair
Gringo	Gringo
Guero-a	Blondie
Hijín	Sonny
Huevo	Baldy, Ballsy
Mocho	Square, Fink
Negro-a	Blackie
ero-a	Pal
Orejón	Big ears
Pachuco	Punk
Pecoso	Freckles
Pelón	Baldy
Pelos	Hairy
Perico-a	Parrot
Pinolillo	'Dennis the Menace'
Pirinola	Spinning top
Pistolón	Big Pistol
Pollo	Chicken
Prieta-o	Darky
Puas	Unshaved
Puerco-a	Pig
Rorra	Doll
Tigre	Tiger
Tuercas	Bolts
Yaqui	Yaqui

INDEX

A

B

C

D

E

F

G

H

I

J

K

S

THE PEOPLE'S GUIDE TO MEXICO

Harper's Magazine called it "The best guidebook to adventure in the whole world . . .outrageous."

I'd like to save on postage, so send me _____ copies of *The People's Guide To Mexico* (at $10.50 each). You folks at John Muir Publications will pay the postage since I'm using this coupon.

NAME ____

ADDRESS ____

_____________________________________ ZIP ____________

Send your order with a check or money order to:
John Muir Publications • P.O. Box 613-B • Santa Fe, NM 87501

Complete your set of Carl Franz's guides to Mexico — and save a buck using the order form below . . .

Please send me _____ copies of Carl's great Camping Book at $10.00 /copy.

I'd like _____ set(s) of The People's Guide To Camping in Mexico and the People's Guide to Mexico for the discount price of $19.50.

NAME ______________________________

ADDRESS ______________________________

______________________________ ZIP ____________

Send your order with a check or money order to:
John Muir Publications • P.O. Box 613-B • Santa Fe, NM 87501